Americans in a World at War

Americans in a World at War

Intimate Histories from the Crash of Pan Am's *Yankee Clipper*

Brooke L. Blower

OXFORD
UNIVERSITY PRESS

Oxford University Press is a department of the University of Oxford. It furthers the University's objective of excellence in research, scholarship, and education by publishing worldwide. Oxford is a registered trade mark of Oxford University Press in the UK and certain other countries.

Published in the United States of America by Oxford University Press
198 Madison Avenue, New York, NY 10016, United States of America.

Library of Congress Cataloging-in-Publication Data
Names: Blower, Brooke L., 1976– author.
Title: Americans in a world at war : intimate histories from the crash of
Pan Am's Yankee Clipper / Brooke L. Blower.
Other titles: Intimate histories from the crash of the Yankee Clipper
Description: New York, NY : Oxford University Press, [2023] |
Includes bibliographical references and index.
Identifiers: LCCN 2023004896 (print) | LCCN 2023004897 (ebook) |
ISBN 9780199322008 (hardback) | ISBN 9780199322022 (epub) |
ISBN 9780197676240
Subjects: LCSH: Yankee Clipper Crash, Portugal, 1943. |
Aircraft accidents—Portugal—Lisbon—History—20th century. |
World War, 1939–1945—United States—Biography. | World War, 1939–1945—Portugal. |
Yakee Clipper (Airplane) | Pan American World Airways, inc.—History. |
Transpacific flights—History—20th century. | Aircraft accident
victims—Portugal—Biography. | War and society—United States.
Classification: LCC TL553.53.P8 B56 2023 (print) | LCC TL553.53.P8
(ebook) | DDC 973.90922—dc23/eng/20230414
LC record available at https://lccn.loc.gov/2023004896
LC ebook record available at https://lccn.loc.gov/2023004897

DOI: 10.1093/oso/9780199322008.001.0001

Printed by Sheridan Books, Inc., United States of America

For Ailish,
My favorite, my only

Dead people never stop talking and sometimes the living hear.

—Marlon James, *A Brief History of Seven Killings* (2014)

CONTENTS

PREFACE

ON FEBRUARY 21, 1943, THE celebrated Pan American Airways seaplane, the *Yankee Clipper*, took off from New York's Marine Air Terminal and island-hopped its way across the Atlantic Ocean. Arriving at Lisbon the following evening, it crashed in the Tagus River, killing twenty-four of the thirty-nine passengers and crew on board. This book traces the backstories of seven people on that plane, seven worldly Americans, their personal histories, their politics, and the paths that led them toward war. Only two of them would survive the crash.

Combat soldiers made up only a small fraction of the millions of Americans, both in and out of uniform, who scattered across six continents on the eve of and during the Second World War. Long before GIs began storming beaches, and beyond the war's most famous battlefields, Americans forged extensive political and economic ties to other parts of the world. Between spring 1939 and fall 1945, Pan Am's regular transatlantic service alone transported 83,000 noncombatants back and forth across the ocean. Tens of thousands more travelled along the airline's Pacific, Latin American, and African routes. Filing down the gangplank went bankers, oil brokers, ordinance experts, physicists, farmers, photographers, purchasing agents, plastic surgeons, statisticians, civil defense planners, fact-finding politicians, radio announcers, and more. *Americans in a World at War* revives this panoramic and often surprising history—of how a diverse cast of people were drawn into global crisis, how they navigated an era of unprecedented mobility and perilous interdependence, and how their deep and sometimes contradictory international engagements would shape and in turn be strengthened, transformed, or else derailed by the US war effort. It is a story about Americans in the world before the Allies were winning.

Hindsight can teach us how and why the Allies prevailed in the Second World War. But thinking forward in time through the eyes of individuals instead dramatizes how much Americans headed into the conflict not with ultimate victory in view but still grappling with the fallout from previous battles and still consumed by the passions and partisan divides of the 1920s and 1930s. It brings to life the singular emotions, the worry and fright, as well as the contingencies and unknowns of the war's early years. It drives home how quickly the international order can collapse and how fragile the future of democracy can be.

The individuals profiled here are not stand-ins for larger groups. They are complex people who were in some ways representative but in other ways exceptional. They lived lives of contradiction and complication, like most human beings. As their biographies accumulate, intersect, and sometimes work at cross-purposes, they defy expectations, spilling out over social categories, national borders, time periods, and other schemes for order. They put flesh and bone to otherwise hard-to-grasp events of global scope and invite those who follow them to revisit even well-known history with fresh eyes. They help to better situate the early-twentieth-century United States in the stream of world history.

Americans in this era—even many of those labeled "isolationists" by their opponents—were remarkably cosmopolitan. Indeed, they were curious and worldly in ways that Americans no longer needed to be after the United States emerged as a "superpower" at the end of the war. It's just that they did not agree—about diplomacy and military strategy, the purpose of government, the place of women and people of color in their society, the role of the press, the merits of capitalism and communism, and the future of the planet's colonies. The worldviews of the *Yankee Clipper*'s passengers spanned the political spectrum. Some were progressive, others were conservative. One leaned toward socialism, another toward fascism. This is not surprising given their diverse regional, professional, and family backgrounds. Of the seven travelers profiled here, all but one of them was a child or a grandchild of immigrants, and two of them were immigrants themselves. They came from families of Irish and Spanish Catholics, Southern evangelical and mainline East Coast Protestants, old-stock German and newly arrived

Russian-speaking Jews. Among them they knew almost a dozen different languages and at formative moments had lived in Spain, France, Romania, Ukraine, Panama, Singapore, the Philippines, and the Netherlands East Indies. Wartime commitments, which for many of them began before the bombing of Pearl Harbor, would take them to India, Australia, England, Egypt, Brazil, Portugal, the Soviet Union, and the Belgian Congo, among other places. As these Americans crisscrossed the globe they found their beliefs sorely tested. Two of them would find their work the subject of angry congressional hearings. Another would be arrested on suspicion of aiding the enemy. Together, their actions do not amount to a united national crusade but rather stand as a testament to the variety, ingenuity, and sometimes folly of Americans' wartime endeavors, and to the cumulative impact of a series of separate decisions that hurtled a group of strange compatriots toward one shared tragedy that cost five of them their lives.

Not so long ago, an attempt to trace the stories gathered here would have ended after an unsuccessful flip through the phonebook. But online search engines make it possible to track everyday people like never before. Electronic databases yielded up census records and passport applications. Word-searchable newspapers unearthed other enticing clues, which in turn led to alumni records, love letters, and FBI files. The ability to find some of the *Yankee Clipper* passengers' living relatives at the stroke of a keyboard produced yet more material gathering dust in family basements and closets: century-old correspondence on parchment paper, scrapbooks encrusted with ration coupons and yellowing photographs, steamer trunks stuffed with business records and journals. In addition to writing biographies about people because they embody something we deem important in retrospect (and because they deemed themselves important enough to leave an archive), it is now possible to write about people simply to see where they can take us, places we might otherwise never think to go.

CAST OF CHARACTERS

The Pilot.
Robert Oliver Daniel Sullivan

The Shipping Agent.
Manuel Diaz Riestra

The Lawyer.
George Alfred Spiegelberg

The Writer.
Benjamin Franklin Robertson, Jr.

The Salesman.
Frank Joseph Cuhel

The Performer.
Tamara Drasin Swann

The Oil Man.
Harry George Seidel

Sources (previous page): Sullivan: Courtesy of Special Collections, University of Miami Libraries, Coral Gables, Florida. Diaz: Courtesy of Harvard College Library, Widener Library. Spiegelberg: Courtesy of Ann S. Brown. Robertson: Special Collections and Archives, Clemson University Libraries. Cuhel: Courtesy of Michael Safranek/University Archives, The University of Iowa Libraries. Drasin Swann: Photograph by James Hargis Connelly/Special Collections and University Archives, Rutgers University Libraries. Seidel: Courtesy of Geraldine Seidel.

A NOTE ON NAMES AND LANGUAGE

ONE OF THIS BOOK'S CENTRAL subjects—Tamara—preferred to be known only by her first name. To avoid calling the only woman in the group by her first name while identifying men by their last names, all the main characters and their close confidants are referred to by first names, sometimes nicknames. Perhaps this is fitting for such intimate stories. Famous figures who make cameo appearances are identified by their full or last names.

The surnames of Manuel and his business partner, Marcelino Garcia Rubiera, originally included accents in Spanish: García y Díaz. But in forming their New York company, they dropped the accents, which is followed here: Garcia & Diaz. In Spain, a person's name customarily includes three parts: a given name, a father's surname, followed by a mother's maiden name.

Japanese and Chinese surnames appear first, given names second. Chinese words are rendered in pinyin except when alternative romanizations are more recognizable (Chiang Kai-shek rather than Jiang Jieshi) and for established institutions (Peking Union Medical College).

Place-name spellings preferred by locals are employed whenever possible (Kyiv rather than Kiev, Hawai'i rather than Hawaii), but in cases where doing so would introduce historical inaccuracy, colonial terms are preserved (Léopoldville versus Kinshasa, Netherlands East Indies versus Indonesia). For famous cities with variable spellings, the version more recognizable to English-language readers is used (Calcutta not Kolkata, Guernica not Gernika, Nuremberg not Nürnberg).

Black and White are both capitalized when referring to historically constructed—and consequential—racial identities. Spurious concepts such as white supremacy and white virtue, however, remain lower case.

Quotations from Ben's notes, dispatches, and telegrams, which he often drafted in cablese, have been converted into regular English for easier reading. Translations from Russian are by April French. Interpretations of French, Spanish, and Dutch sources are by the author.

Nothing that follows has been embellished. All dialogue and details derive from letters, testimony, and other historical documents—but with care and crosschecking. Newspaper accounts often contain inaccuracies. Public records can be wrong. People omit or exaggerate, misremember, mislead, and sometimes lie.

Americans in a World at War

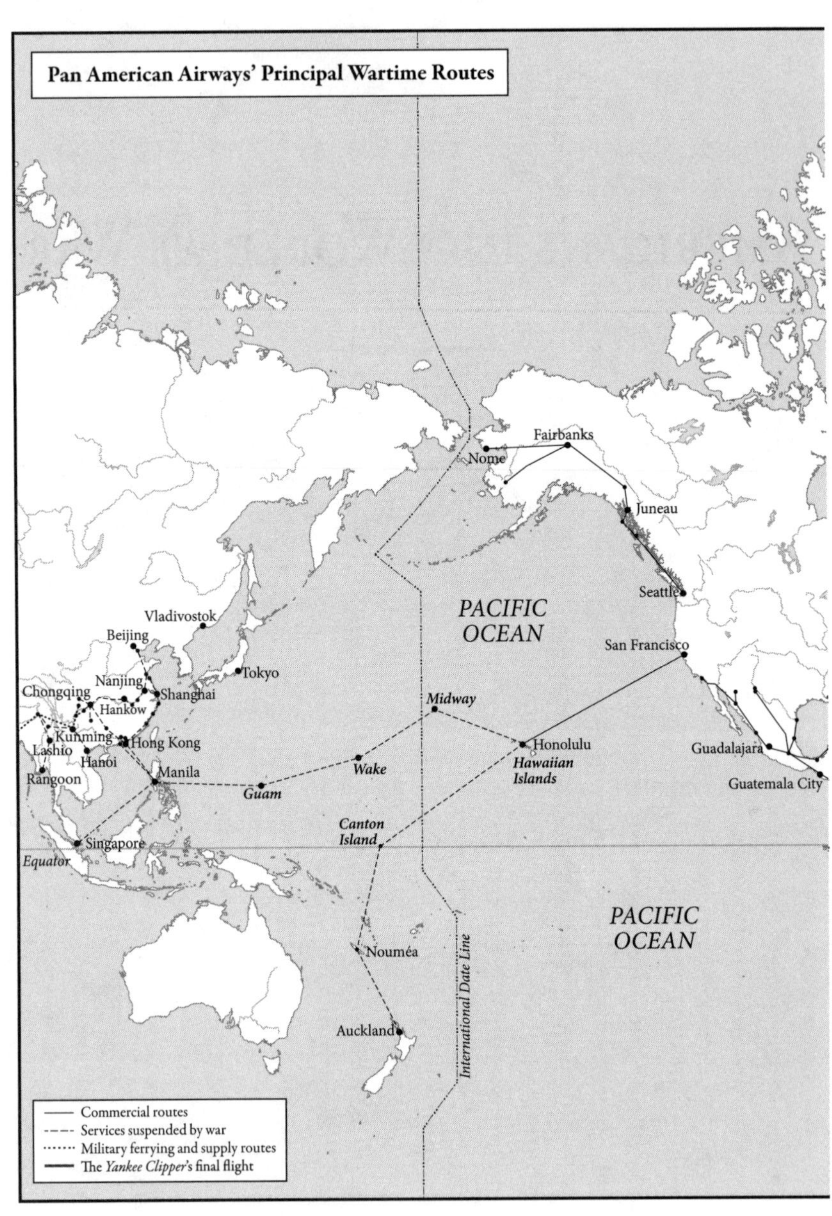

Pan American Airways' Principal Wartime Routes
Fairbanks
Nome
Juneau
Seattle
PACIFIC OCEAN
San Francisco
Vladivostok
Beijing
Tokyo
Nanjing
Chongqing
Shanghai
Hankow
Midway
Kunming
Lashio
Hanoi
Hong Kong
Honolulu
Hawaiian Islands
Guadalajara
Rangoon
Manila
Wake
Guam
Guatemala City
Canton Island
Singapore
Equator
PACIFIC OCEAN
Nouméa
International Date Line
Auckland
Commercial routes
Services suspended by war
Military ferrying and supply routes
The Yankee Clipper's final flight

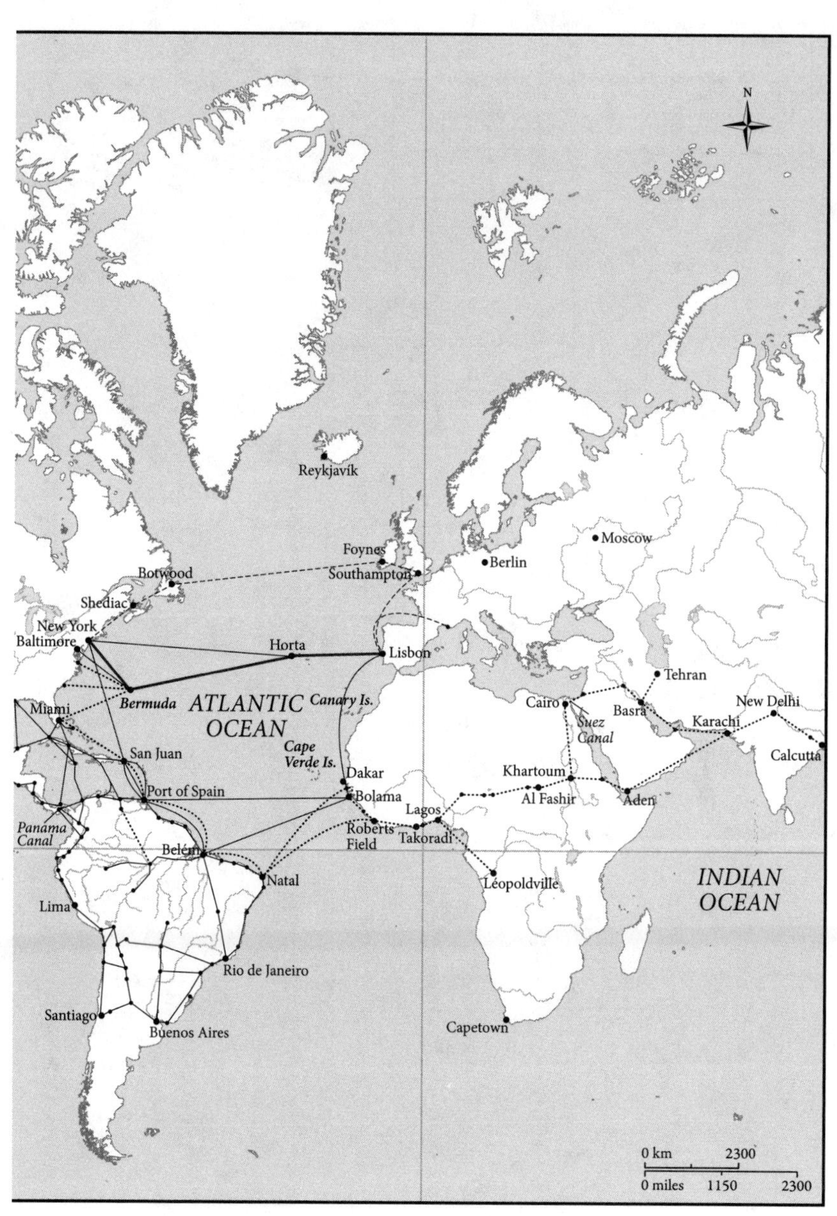
N
Reykjavík
Foynes
Southampton
Botwood
Shediac
New York
Baltimore
Horta
Lisbon
Moscow
Berlin
Tehran
Bermuda
ATLANTIC
OCEAN
Canary Is.
Cape
Verde Is.
Miami
San Juan
Port of Spain
Panama
Canal
Dakar
Bolama
Roberts
Field
Lagos
Takoradi
Cairo
Suez
Canal
Basra
Karachi
New Delhi
Calcutta
Khartoum
Al Fashir
Aden
Belém
Natal
Léopoldville
INDIAN
OCEAN
Lima
Rio de Janeiro
Santiago
Buenos Aires
Capetown
0 km
2300
0 miles
1150
2300

1. Manuel's birthplace, Gijón, Spain
2. George's brother serves on the Western Front
3. Harry fails to save Romāno-Americanā's oil fields
4. Tamara flees Velyki Sorochyntsi
5. Frank stows away on the SS *America*
6. Frank places in the Amsterdam Olympics
7. Harry's Normandy villa
8. Harry's boss strikes a deal with IG Farben at the Luena factory
9. Frank hocks Hormel hams in Palestine
10. Harry negotiates Iraqi oil production after the strike at Baba Gurgur
11. Sully lands the first transatlantic commercial passenger flight
12. Ben watches the Battle of Britain from Shakespeare Cliff
13. Manuel's *Navemar* departs Sevilla for its "hell ship" voyage
14. Ben makes his only tour of the Eastern Front
15. IG Farben's Buna plant at Auschwitz
Helsinki
Stavanger
North Sea
Baltic Sea
Edinburgh
Belfast
Copenhagen
Liverpool
Berlin
Warsaw
London
The Hague
Plymouth
Dunkirk
Meuse R.
Cologne
English Channel
Dieppe
Rhine R.
Prague
Brest
Paris
Danube R.
ATLANTIC OCEAN
Vienna
Budapest
Bay of Biscay
Alps
A Coruña
Genoa
Guernica
Nice
Vigo
Bilbao
Pyrenees
Marseille
Ebro R.
Rome
Madrid
Barcelona
Tagus R.
Lisbon
Valencia
Málaga
Sicily
Gibraltar
Algiers
Oran
Malta
Atlas Mountains
Casablanca
Mediterr
0 km 250 500
0 miles 250 500

Europe, the Middle East, and North Africa
N
Murmansk
Arkhangelsk
Urals
Volga R.
Leningrad
Kalinin
Klin
14
Moscow
Kuybyshev
Smolensk
Minsk
Voronezh
Kursk
Grodno
Prypiat R.
Stalingrad
Kharkiv
Chornobyl
4
Kyiv
Poltava
Donets R.
Don R.
Bug R.
Dnipro R.
Ekaterinoslav
Rostov
Carpathian Mountains
Caspian Sea
Iași
Odesa
Krasnodar
Grozny
Maykop
CRIMEA
Caucasus Mts.
Baku
Sevastopol
Tbilisi
3
Bucharest
Constanța
Black Sea
Alborz Mts.
Tehran
Balkan Mts.
Istanbul
Dardanelles
Tigris R.
Mosul
10
Kirkuk
Ramadi
Baghdad
Athens
Tripoli
Damascus
Haifa
9
Jerusalem
anean Sea
Alexandria
Tobruk
El Alamein
Cairo
Nile R.

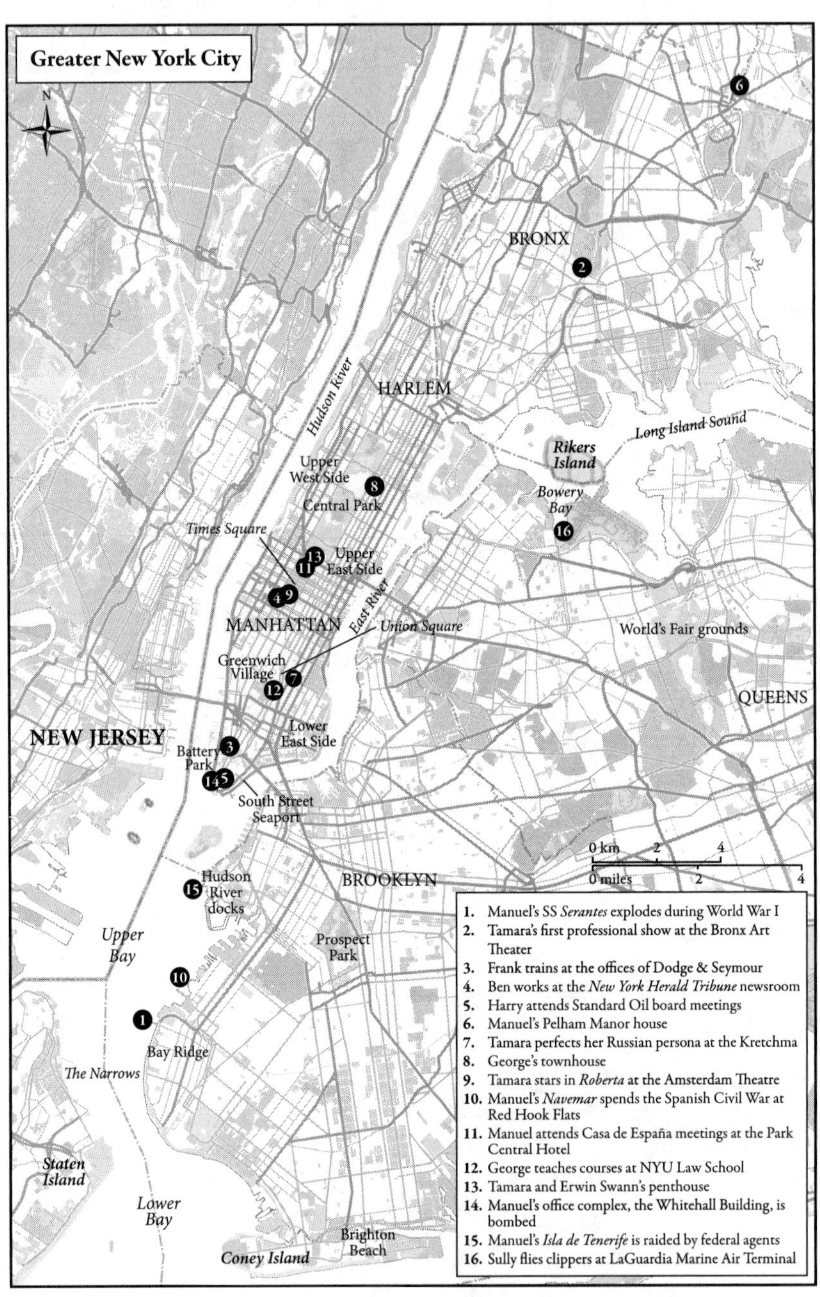

Greater New York City
N
BRONX
HARLEM
Hudson River
Long Island Sound
Rikers Island
Upper West Side
Central Park
Bowery Bay
Times Square
Upper East Side
East River
MANHATTAN
Union Square
World's Fair grounds
Greenwich Village
QUEENS
Lower East Side
NEW JERSEY
Battery Park
South Street Seaport
0 km 2 4
0 miles 2 4
Hudson River docks
BROOKLYN
Upper Bay
Prospect Park
Bay Ridge
The Narrows
Staten Island
Lower Bay
Brighton Beach
Coney Island
1. Manuel's SS *Serantes* explodes during World War I
2. Tamara's first professional show at the Bronx Art Theater
3. Frank trains at the offices of Dodge & Seymour
4. Ben works at the *New York Herald Tribune* newsroom
5. Harry attends Standard Oil board meetings
6. Manuel's Pelham Manor house
7. Tamara perfects her Russian persona at the Kretchma
8. George's townhouse
9. Tamara stars in *Roberta* at the Amsterdam Theatre
10. Manuel's *Navemar* spends the Spanish Civil War at Red Hook Flats
11. Manuel attends Casa de España meetings at the Park Central Hotel
12. George teaches courses at NYU Law School
13. Tamara and Erwin Swann's penthouse
14. Manuel's office complex, the Whitehall Building, is bombed
15. Manuel's *Isla de Tenerife* is raided by federal agents
16. Sully flies clippers at LaGuardia Marine Air Terminal

Colonial Southeast Asia
N
CHINA
Yangtze River
Shanghai
Hiroshima
Tokyo
JAPAN
Nagasaki
PACIFIC OCEAN
INDIA
BURMA
Rangoon
Hong Kong
Hainan
Luzon
PHILIPPINES
Manila
Bangkok
FRENCH INDOCHINA
Spratly Islands
Bay of Bengal
Saigon
South China Sea
Cebu
Mindanao
GUAM
MALAYA
Equator
Sumatra
Singapore
Borneo
Balikpapan
Celebes
Palembang
Java
See inset map
Bismarck Islands
Rabaul
Solomon Islands
NEW GUINEA
Gona
Buna
Tanimbar Islands
Timor
Port Moresby
Milne Bay
Kokoda Trail
Guadalcanal
NETHERLANDS EAST INDIES
Darwin
Coral Sea
Broome
INDIAN OCEAN
Townsville
AUSTRALIA
Brisbane
Fremantle
Sydney
Melbourne
1. Ben works at the US consulate in Surabaya after college
2. Harry pushes for East Indies concessions after the oil strike at Talang Akar
3. Frank relocates from Singapore to Batavia
4. Sully and the *China Clipper* crew land the first commercial transpacific flight at Naval Base Cavite
5. Frank sells diesel-burning tractors in Thailand's teak forests
0 km 500 1000
0 miles 500 1000
Musi R.
Sungai Gerong oil refinery
Borneo
Sumatra
Java Sea
N
Merak
Sunda Strait
Batavia
Indramayu
Rembang
Bandung
Semarang
INDIAN OCEAN
Surabaya
Java
Cilacap
Pacitan
Malang
Bali
0 km 200
0 miles 100 200
Frank's escape from Java
to Fremantle

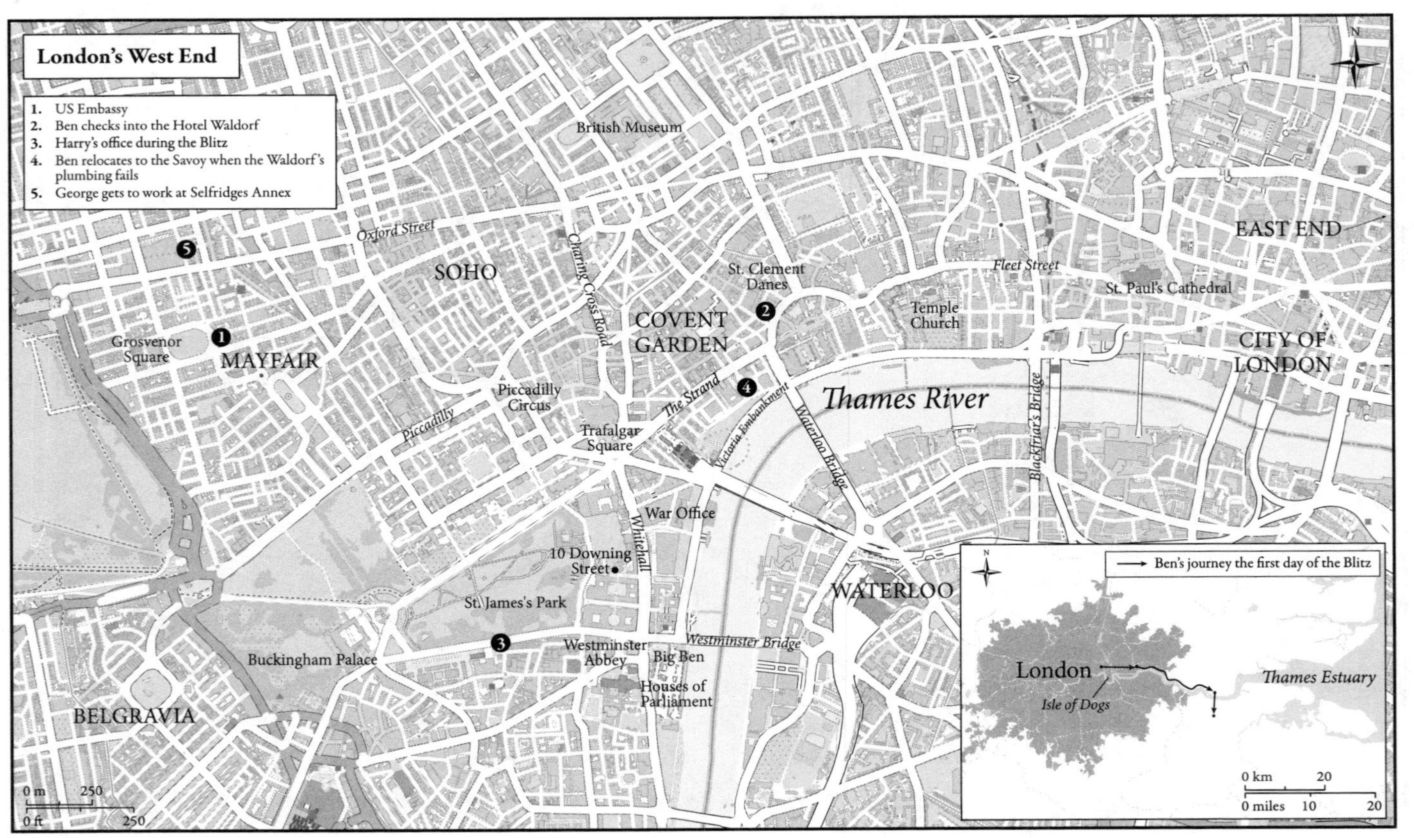
London's West End
1. US Embassy
2. Ben checks into the Hotel Waldorf
3. Harry's office during the Blitz
4. Ben relocates to the Savoy when the Waldorf's plumbing fails
5. George gets to work at Selfridges Annex
N
British Museum
Oxford Street
SOHO
Charing Cross Road
St. Clement Danes
Fleet Street
St. Paul's Cathedral
EAST END
Temple Church
CITY OF LONDON
Grosvenor Square
MAYFAIR
COVENT GARDEN
Piccadilly Circus
Piccadilly
The Strand
Victoria Embankment
Waterloo Bridge
Thames River
Blackfriar's Bridge
Trafalgar Square
War Office
Whitehall
10 Downing Street
St. James's Park
WATERLOO
Westminster Bridge
Westminster Abbey
Big Ben
Houses of Parliament
Buckingham Palace
BELGRAVIA
0 m 250
0 ft 250
Ben's journey the first day of the Blitz
London
Isle of Dogs
Thames Estuary
0 km 20
0 miles 10 20

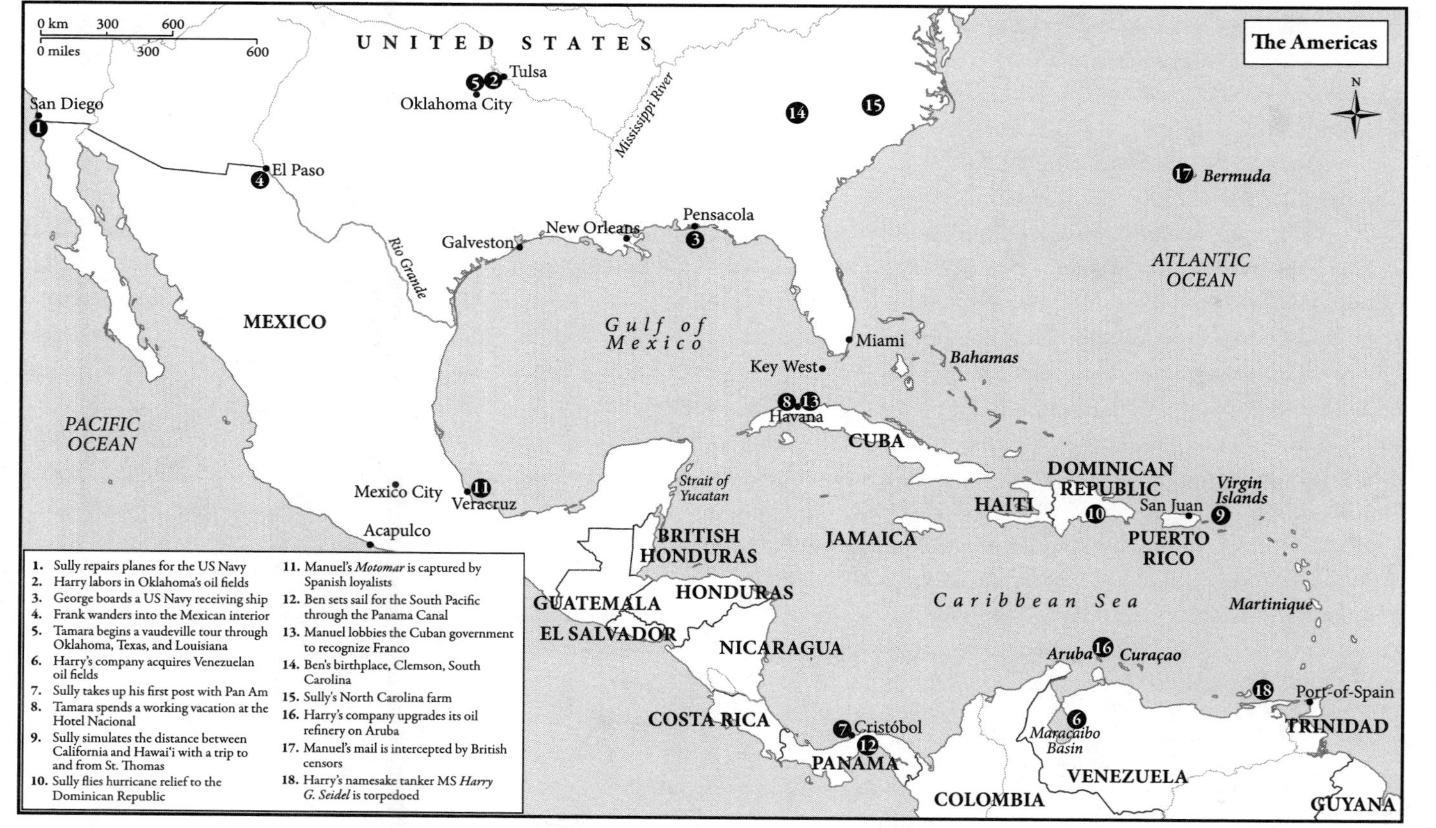
The Americas
N
0 km 300 600
0 miles 300 600
UNITED STATES
MEXICO
PACIFIC OCEAN
ATLANTIC OCEAN
Gulf of Mexico
Caribbean Sea
Strait of Yucatan
Mississippi River
Rio Grande
San Diego
El Paso
Tulsa
Oklahoma City
Galveston
New Orleans
Pensacola
Miami
Key West
Havana
Mexico City
Veracruz
Acapulco
Bermuda
Bahamas
CUBA
JAMAICA
HAITI
DOMINICAN REPUBLIC
San Juan
PUERTO RICO
Virgin Islands
Martinique
BRITISH HONDURAS
GUATEMALA
EL SALVADOR
HONDURAS
NICARAGUA
COSTA RICA
PANAMA
Cristóbol
COLOMBIA
VENEZUELA
Maracaibo Basin
Aruba
Curaçao
Port-of-Spain
TRINIDAD
GUYANA
1. Sully repairs planes for the US Navy
2. Harry labors in Oklahoma's oil fields
3. George boards a US Navy receiving ship
4. Frank wanders into the Mexican interior
5. Tamara begins a vaudeville tour through Oklahoma, Texas, and Louisiana
6. Harry's company acquires Venezuelan oil fields
7. Sully takes up his first post with Pan Am
8. Tamara spends a working vacation at the Hotel Nacional
9. Sully simulates the distance between California and Hawai'i with a trip to and from St. Thomas
10. Sully flies hurricane relief to the Dominican Republic
11. Manuel's Motomar is captured by Spanish loyalists
12. Ben sets sail for the South Pacific through the Panama Canal
13. Manuel lobbies the Cuban government to recognize Franco
14. Ben's birthplace, Clemson, South Carolina
15. Sully's North Carolina farm
16. Harry's company upgrades its oil refinery on Aruba
17. Manuel's mail is intercepted by British censors
18. Harry's namesake tanker MS Harry G. Seidel is torpedoed

Introduction

Into the Vortex

THE PLANE WAS DELAYED BY almost a week. First for maintenance—a backfiring engine, a warped exhaust valve, a sticky piston—then crew illness, then weather conditions. This was not uncommon. Regular transatlantic air service to Portugal, where passengers caught connecting flights to the British Isles, North Africa, and other danger zones, had been running for less than four years, only since the spring before Adolf Hitler's forces invaded Poland. Fingerprinted, passported, and vaccinated, travelers awaited their boarding instructions in New York apartments and hotel rooms, smoking cigarettes, listening to the radio, or reading the latest about the war.[1]

Frank Cuhel was anxious to get going. New York was driving him "batty." The Olympic athlete-turned-export salesman had spent the previous decade living it up as a bachelor in colonial Southeast Asia—until forced to flee and almost killed by the Japanese. Camped out at Greenwich Village's Hotel Lafayette, he likely pored over reports that US Marines had finally clawed their way to full control of Guadalcanal, even though costly naval and air skirmishes continued around the Solomon Islands. He would have read about North Africa, too, where he was headed after talking his way into a job with the Mutual Broadcasting System and where untested American troops had just been humbled by Field Marshal Erwin Rommel's tanks in their first face-to-face engagement with the Germans near Tunisia's Kasserine Pass. "It rather looks as though I shall be on my way in a very few days," he wrote to his sister on February 14. When he got there, he told her, she might be able to hear him on the radio every night. He would keep close to the action, and when the drive on Europe began, he would be "right up there with the first ones."[2]

At her penthouse just off Central Park West, the Broadway star Tamara Drasin Swann packed her things: a shoe box, a hat box, a suitcase piled with evening gowns, costume jewelry, hair clips, lipstick, and sheet music. By February 19, she and the other members of her USO-Camp Shows troupe knew that they would be embarking first to England and then to further combat areas to entertain Allied forces. Cultivating the persona of a mysterious Russian songstress, Tamara had been known only by her first name, and hiding her Jewish background, since 1933 when she found fame debuting the ballad "Smoke Gets in Your Eyes." But she often thought of her traumatic escape from war-torn Ukraine in 1920 and the grandmother she left behind and who was by now almost surely gone.[3]

At his Upper East Side townhouse, George Spiegelberg—a six-foot-tall, hazel-eyed major on General Dwight D. Eisenhower's London staff—was enjoying a brief reunion with his wife and small children after nearly a year's absence. The stern Republican lawyer was no fan of President Franklin D. Roosevelt and his New Deal, but he was thrilled to have the wartime overseas commission he had been dreaming about since 1918, when his brother found glory as an aviator in France while he remained stateside. Charged with procuring local supplies to feed, house, and equip US forces in Britain, he had been temporarily recalled to Washington to defend the merits of Lend-Lease against skeptics in his own party. Now set to return to his post, he also readied his belongings: woolen underwear and socks, a shaving brush, vitamin tablets, a made-in-England US Army uniform, and a standard-issue Colt. 45 automatic pistol.[4]

The city's newspapers hardly captured the horrors these and thirty-six other Americans would soon be speeding toward at more than 150 miles per hour. In Europe, the Third Reich ruled over a larger and more populated landmass than that of the United States. Relying on brute force rather than administrative savvy, Axis leaders were growing harsher in their reprisals against every hint of resistance. In France, under total occupation since November, deportations to the death camps had resumed and a new compulsory labor service had just been announced. Marseille, once a beacon of hope for refugees, strained under martial law and the whims of the SS regiment Hitler sent there to "cleanse" the Mediterranean port of its undesirables. Only days earlier, the occupiers had finished systematically ransacking and demolishing the town's entire historic district.[5]

Eastern Europe suffered even worse in the crossfire between the Wehrmacht and the Red Army. After months of gruesome house-to-house combat, and at the cost of more men than the United States would lose in the entire war, Soviet fighters had just wrested from the encircled German Sixth Army the uninhabitable wasteland that was once Stalingrad. But Einsatzgruppen and SS execution squads, armed with daily kill quotas, continued to liquidate ghettos and entire villages in Belarus and Ukraine, slowed only by the challenge of burning or burying so many bodies in winter. Beyond the places where labor camps were even bothered with, in regions that would never be seen by liberators from the West, Germans and their collaborators shot entire families over mass graves, sometimes shoving the youngest into the pits alive. The specially built Zyklon B chambers and crematoria of Birkenau would not be operational until the following month, but more than three quarters of the Holocaust's victims were already dead.[6]

At the other end of the Eurasian continent "Greater Japan" had also reached its outward limits, stretching from Burma to the borders of Siberia on mainland China, across into the US Aleutian Islands at the edge of the Bering Sea, and down to Portuguese Timor, less than five hundred miles from northwest Australia. During the previous year, the empire's soldiers, who now ruled over some 350 million people, had slaughtered or marched to their death untold millions of resisters and ethnic Chinese as they raped and pillaged their way through Shanghai, Saigon, Bangkok, Hong Kong, Manila, Singapore, and Batavia. Japanese guards also controlled the fates of some 350,000 American and European civilians and POWs confined to rapidly deteriorating camps—some of them were Frank Cuhel's friends. But few outside the region fathomed the extent to which these populations were being brutalized. Few knew about the sexual enslavement of "comfort women," or that Japanese scientists were spreading plague and other infectious diseases among unsuspecting peasants and conducting surgical experiments on human test subjects.[7]

The nightmares of that winter, the cheapening of life, extended far beyond these occupied zones. In China's Henan province, millions starved as local corruption exacerbated the pain of the previous year's harvest failure. Families were eating leaves and peanut husks and selling their children. In Bengal, poor weather and pest infestations had also destroyed the season's rice crop. With overland imports blocked by the closure of the Burma Road, and food stores throughout India alarmingly low, pleas for relief shipments had been pouring into London for weeks. Nevertheless, British officials were diverting more ships away from the colony for use in the Atlantic, a decision that would cost the lives of three million people.[8]

The stakes of the global crisis by February 1943—which some Americans were beginning to call World War II—had escalated to ghastly heights. Promoting the new objective of "unconditional surrender," which he and Winston Churchill formulated weeks before during their conference at Casablanca, Franklin Roosevelt insisted that Americans would fight "through to the finish" and "impose punishment and retribution in full." Germany's propaganda minister Joseph Goebbels thundered back over the international airwaves, promising conflict "more total and more radical than we can even imagine it today." Like a vortex, this war devoured not just battlefields and their soldiers but everything and everyone in its vicinity. The majority of its sixty million fatalities would be civilians.[9]

On February 21, Pan American Airways finally summoned passengers for Trip 9035 to LaGuardia's sleek art deco Marine Air Terminal. The comings and goings of the airline's giant clippers used to be celebrated by newsreel cameramen, who once lingered in the skylit rotunda hoping for glimpses of disembarking celebrities and statesmen, and sightseers, who paid a dime to crowd the observation deck and watch the flying boats lift off from Long Island Sound. But now ground crew, sworn to uphold the Espionage Act, closely guarded schedules and manifests. Japanese forces had overrun Pan Am's string of Pacific bases from Midway to Hong Kong, killing or capturing more than ninety of the airline's employees. It was not inconceivable that the Axis might target the company's Atlantic network, too. The clippers' wings and tails still displayed commercial registration marks, requisites for safe passage to neutral Portuguese territories. But they had an obvious utility for the Allied war effort as the world's only aircraft capable of carrying large payloads across the oceans. Indeed, the army and navy had secretly commandeered the seaplanes after the US declaration of war and periodically diverted them and their crews for military missions.[10]

Instructed to keep the timing of their flight a secret, the travelers arrived early that Sunday morning. At the check-in counter, Harry Seidel handed over a one-way ticket. The fifty-two-year-old Standard Oil of New Jersey executive, sporting brand-new 14-karat gold cufflinks, had retained much of the fashionable looks and silky brown hair that had turned heads during

Onlookers admire two B-314 clippers at LaGuardia's seaplane base before the US declaration of war. Office of War Information/PhotoQuest/Getty Images.

his youth. His firm was now caught in its worst scandal in decades due to revelations about its extensive ties to the German chemical corporation IG Farben. But Harry would not relinquish his position as one of the company's top overseas directors. Brokering high-level international oil deals had brought him an uncommon amount of wealth and social standing for the son of a smalltown bakery owner.[11]

Ben Robertson, a proud Southern Baptist and Democrat with sensitive blue eyes and a lilting South Carolina accent, showed up from his midtown hotel carrying a book by one of his favorite authors, Thomas Wolfe, and wearing a heavy silver identification bracelet announcing his new affiliation with the *New York Herald Tribune*. A seasoned newspaperman, he had reported from Roosevelt's Washington, London during the Blitz, and Moscow under threat of invasion. But witnessing British colonial rule up close in India the previous fall had sorely tested his conviction that the Allies were merely fighting the good fight. That morning's news would have angered him. Despite growing concern about the deteriorating condition of Mahatma Gandhi, eleven days into a hunger strike and demanding immediate freedom for the subcontinent, the State Department reiterated that the United States would not intervene "in a matter essentially British."[12] This war's twisted logics, its fragile alliances and sometimes unsavory bargains, would not lend themselves easily to simple morality tales, though many like Ben had tried to make them.

Other passengers filtered through the terminal's steel double doors, some with obvious purpose, others with an air of secret errands. The man looking after a padlocked pouch containing confidential documents was the State Department's James Wright. Couriers like him appeared on nearly every clipper flight. William Walton Butterworth, a Princeton-educated foreign service officer known for his literary flair, also carried a briefcase stuffed with diplomatic business. He was spearheading an economic warfare operation on the Iberian Peninsula, buying strategic supplies off the black market so they did not fall into the wrong hands. Others' true objectives remain more of a mystery. Arthur Lee was a movie distributor who claimed credit for introducing American audiences to Alfred Hitchcock's films. Theodore Lamb, according to notations on Pan Am's manifest, was engaged in some kind of work for the Office of Civilian Defense.[13]

Security agents took special note of the appearance of Manuel Diaz. A touch short, with brown eyes encircled by spectacles and dark hair that had salt and peppered with age, Manuel—Manolo to his close friends—had cofounded the most important shipping agency in the Spanish-speaking world. Vessels entrusted to his care had plied the waters between New York, Latin America, and the Iberian Peninsula since the First World War, and they had been aiding far-right activists at least since Francisco Franco's coup, which overthrew the Spanish Republic. Suspected of fascist sympathies, Manuel was arrested for smuggling oil and radio transmitters off a Brooklyn pier only days after the United States entered the war. But he escaped conviction, and his "neutral" boats still crisscrossed the Atlantic, sometimes transmitting information about Allied convoys to German submarines. At the terminal inspectors carefully combed through his leather overnight bag, finding suits, neckties, handkerchiefs, bedroom slippers, pajamas, a toiletries kit, a Red Cross button, and miscellaneous correspondence. But nothing incriminating.[14]

By contrast, airport personnel had been taught not to second guess the steady stream of US military officials who arrived at the airport in the guise of civilians. The ruse gave the airline plausible deniability, although observers in neutral overseas ports were hardly fooled by the disembarking men flashing regular passports but parading through their territories in standard-issue shoes and haircuts and with obvious "soldierly bearing," as one Irish intelligence agent put it. Today, twelve army officers booked for the flight, including George Spiegelberg, posed as "civil servants." Their names, ages, and home addresses left only the barest of clues about their former lives. Captain Joshua Edelman was the son of a Philadelphia plumber. Major Burton Mossman had grown up on a New Mexico cattle ranch. Later, when family members applied for their bonuses—or their headstones—other details, maybe true, would surface. Lieutenant Clifford Sheldon seemed to have been engaged in support operations for the US Army Air Force's accelerating bombing raids on Europe's northwest coast. Major Earle Stoy, his relatives believed, had been assigned some kind of classified mission by the Quartermaster Corps. Given the unprecedented "tooth-to-tail" ratio in the US military—only an estimated 16 percent of American uniformed personnel saw ground combat during World War II—and considering the vast array of technical, medical, administrative, logistical, and other noncombat work undertaken by army officers around the world, the possibilities were vast.[15]

Reserving a seat on the clipper took clout—distinguished professional standing, important contacts, and taken-for-granted, deep-seated racial privilege. This was, after all, a conflict being fought with a segregated military that under-enrolled Black Americans and steered the majority of those it did recruit into lowly manual labor positions, a practice that determined whose talents would be marshalled on behalf of the war effort and whose would be squandered, whose ideas would shape policies and US relations with others, and whose insights would be dismissed while they packed, loaded, unloaded, tidied, dug, and buried. The least "White" person bound for Lisbon that day was the Italian American crewmember Philip Casprini, referred to by one passenger as "the dark steward."[16]

Yet it would be a mistake to imagine that international clipper travel during the war was sporadic, rare, or reserved for only an elite few. Pan Am's founding visionary, Juan Trippe, named his fleet of seaplanes after the speedy masted merchant ships that revolutionized ocean trade and travel the previous century. Indeed, what those legendary clippers had done with wind and sails, these airborne successors did with wings and oil, shrinking time and distance, turning weeks crossing the Pacific into days, and days on the Atlantic into hours. Passenger demand exploded from the very start of the global crisis, because clipper flights made improbable itineraries suddenly possible. Built for a world not yet paved over with runways, flying boats could go anywhere within reach of a river, a lake, or a lagoon. They took Winston Churchill to Washington, DC, Roosevelt to North Africa, and Australian prime minister Robert Gordon Menzies around the world. But far less-famous figures made up most of the traffic—bureaucrats, former refugees, or the sons of plumbers and cattle ranchers who found themselves thrust by the war into unexpected, urgent endeavors: buying and selling weapons, bartering technological know-how, swapping intelligence, greasing the wheels of Allied cooperation, or, sometimes, conspiring with enemy agents. These were in-between people, surfing along far-flung networks of trade, transport, and political maneuvering, knitting the US mainland to the world's other staging zones and battlegrounds in ways that defied simplistic imaginaries like "war front" and "home front."[17]

To accommodate this growing stream of consultants, fundraisers, spies, and others clambering for seats, Pan Am doubled its scheduled service to Europe from two times per week in 1939 to four times per week by the summer of 1941. After the United States entered the war that December, bookings climbed a further 140 percent. Between then and August 1945, the airline's crews, flying along regular routes that stretched beyond 90,000 miles, would complete close to 18,500 ocean crossings. Each flight contained its own peculiar cross-section of people. Each could tell a unique story, unlocking more of the war's vast reaches. Yet on some deep level all would attest to the same history, about how an age of air power had brought an unprecedented number of people across the continents into intimate, sometimes harrowing contact—and how Americans found themselves in the midst of, and fought, all those overlapping conflicts that would bleed together and become the Second World War.[18]

In the departure lounge the *Yankee Clipper*'s passengers faced another delay while mechanics rushed to replace a defective throttle quadrant on one of the plane's engines. Tamara passed the time posing for pictures with the other members of her variety troupe: the husband-and-wife comedic dance duo Jean Lorraine and Roy Rognan; the platinum blonde singer Yvette; the puppeteer Grace Drysdale; the classically trained radio star Jane Froman; and Tamara's longtime friend from the New York nightclub circuit, the accordionist Gypsy Markoff, who claimed to be a "full-blooded Romany princess" but was really Olga Witkowska from Milwaukee.[19]

In Pan Am's lounge, Tamara (*far left*) takes photographs with her USO troupe mates: Jane Froman, Grace Drysdale, Gypsy Markoff, Yvette, and Jean Lorraine. The State Historical Society of Missouri, Columbia, MO.

They looked like a "happy bunch of artists," as Grace Drysdale put it, but in fact Jean Lorraine had "dreaded this trip more than anything"—and surely she was not alone in worrying about the perils of air travel. A month earlier, the *Dixie Clipper* had encountered only minor mechanical trouble while carrying President Roosevelt on his 17,000-mile round trip to Casablanca, but that same week another clipper disappeared north of San Francisco during a storm. Searchers found it ten days later at the bottom of a canyon. "Identifying 19 Dead in Airplane by Teeth," declared the *New York Times* headline stretched above an outsized photograph of a burned and crumpled metal heap. In time, twelve of the twenty-eight clipper flying boats built by Boeing, Sikorsky Aircraft, and the Glenn L. Martin Company would meet with violent ends.[20]

But the waiting travelers could take comfort that their plane was the newest and most advanced clipper model, one of twelve state-of-the-art B-314s, equipped with four 1600 horsepower Wright Twin Cyclone engines and Hamilton Standard hydromatic, full-feathering three-blade propellers. The world's largest commercial aircraft, and the first to run on 100-octane gasoline, it sported a two-story interior and catwalks inside its wings for inflight engine repairs. Ever since Eleanor Roosevelt christened it with a bottle filled with water from the seven seas in March 1939, the *Yankee Clipper* had enjoyed a perfect safety record. It blazed the first flight across the Atlantic with paying passengers and, traversing that stormy expanse more than 240 times, became the first aircraft to complete more than a million transatlantic miles. The *Yankee Clipper* and its sister ships now appeared everywhere as icons of American ingenuity and derring-do—in ads and movies, as toys, on cocktail napkins.[21]

At last, one bell signaled the crew to board. Captain R. O. D. Sullivan emerged from the Code Office clutching classified data and route instructions, which he would lock in a concealed safe on the flight deck. Rod, or Sully as colleagues sometimes called the stocky veteran flier with a ruddy complexion, could maneuver seaplanes more skillfully than just about anyone, soaring them over, or under, bridges and steering them through swells like speedboats before stopping on a dime. He had joined Pan Am in 1929, when it was still only a risky start-up, after spending the previous decade in Southern California, working as a navy mechanic and flight instructor as well as stunt doubling for the movie star Monte Blue and performing test hops on Charles Lindbergh's *The Spirit of St. Louis*, custom built at San Diego's Ryan factory. Helping to pioneer Pan Am's Caribbean, Pacific, and Atlantic routes during the 1930s, he quickly ascended to the company's top rank, "Master of Ocean Flying Boats." Lately Sully had been commanding secret military missions between Brazil and Africa in addition to regular commercial flights to Lisbon. With more than 14,000 flying hours under his belt, he had just become, weeks earlier, the first person in the world to fly the Atlantic one hundred times.[22]

A dozen other crisply uniformed flight officers—including two engineers, a pair of radio technicians, and a spare employee who would disembark at Bermuda— followed Sully down the pier jutting into Bowery Bay. None of these crewmembers had Sully's experience. All had joined Pan Am in the last five years, fresh from college, plucked from military training programs, or recruited from other professions. The steward Philip Casprini was a veteran of New York's hotel business. The assistant engineering officer, William Manning, had spent eight years as a Boston airport mechanic. But all had been trained in skills ranging from radio telegraphy, celestial navigation, and dead reckoning to first aid, seamanship, and maritime law. All had just passed a comprehensive physical exam, and, with two men for every station on board, they would be able to take breaks for sleep and rest during the long stretches over the ocean.[23]

Two bells finally sounded shortly before 9:30 a.m., and the passengers trailed outside after the flight officers. Against a backdrop of Bronx smokestacks, men lugging briefcases, women in head scarves and wool suits, tiptoed across the waterwing lashed to the dock and stepped into the clipper's boat-shaped hull—its once shining silver exterior now coated in camouflage paint. From the lounge, the stewards directed them left and right into seating compartments separated by arched doorways.[24]

On the upper deck, crewmembers arrayed themselves at their own workstations—a portside navigator's chart table, the radio operating post, and an engineer's desk surrounded by thermostats, pressure gauges, and other purposeful-looking levers and dials. In front of them, on the master's bridge, Sully and his copilot secured the overhead emergency hatch, tested the intercabin phones, and unlocked their controls. First Officer Herman Rush, the Philippine-born son of an army surgeon, knew something of Sully's operating style. The two had flown together several times, including on a recent classified mission to Liberia.[25]

With weather forecasts doublechecked, the altimeter adjusted, and propellers cocked into low pitch position, Sully signaled for the crew to hoist the sea anchor and cast off the mooring lines. Firing up the engines as the craft eased away from the dock, and assured that his path was clear, he opened the throttles and sped past Rikers Island. After reaching full power, it took roughly thirty seconds for a B-314 to break free from the water's surface. The motors whined as the *Yankee Clipper* climbed away from the channel . . . 2,000 feet . . . 4,000 feet . . . 6,000 feet. At about 8,000 feet Sully leveled the plane off. The engines settled into a softer drone, and a course to Bermuda was set.[26]

Lives and careers would soon be destroyed in an instant, and a great airship, symbol of a distinctive era of US foreign relations, would be reduced to scrap. But a paper trail, preserved because of the crash, gave hints at two decades' worth of personal and political choices that had brought these Americans to this place. Their stories offer a reminder of how compromising and complex this war was—as an intense episode of imperial conflict, international development, and global engagement—and a warning about how quickly the world can fall apart.

PART I

1914–1920

Ukraine, 1917. © Imperial War Museum, Q 60374.

I

Balloon Work

HIS OLDER BROTHER WAS OVER there, fighting in France. Outdoing him.

In October 1918, George Spiegelberg was learning to fly observation balloons at the Goodyear naval aviation school outside Akron, Ohio. But Frederick, the namesake son, the only one whose war experiences their father would carefully record, had already reached the rank of second lieutenant. He was flying night reconnaissance missions in the Meuse-Argonne offensive. And writing war poetry about it.[1]

George had gone to Cornell like his brother, played hockey and lacrosse like his brother, parted his hair down the center like his brother. Later, their university's alumni office would misplace some of George's records in Frederick's file. The friendly rivalry began early. Freddie was a "ray of sunshine," thought their father, "always bright, lively and good." Frederick Spiegelberg, Sr., gazed with equal fondness upon "son No. 2," who arrived in December 1897, because George was "the very double of his older brother."[2]

Now, suspended from a hydrogen-filled gasbag two thousand feet above the training field at the edge of Wingfoot Lake—on a clear afternoon with the sun at his back—George could have seen as far east as Youngstown. But he was quite a distance from his family's Manhattan townhouse, filled with his father's annotated rare books and carefully tended to by four live-in servants. He was farther still from the continent where his brother was—and where the Spiegelberg family had been vacationing in August 1914 when German troops swooped through neutral Belgium in hopes of defeating France before Russia fully mobilized.[3]

Since then, as fighting on the fields of Flanders and Picardy stalled, the Western Front had burrowed underground. Mazes of bunkers, communication tunnels, and firing ditches extended four hundred miles from the Belgian coast to the Swiss border—a subterranean civilization with street signs and wall carvings, piped for water, wired for electricity. War sprouted overhead, too, as deadlock transformed the conflict into not only a trial of attrition but also a contest of observation. Biplanes and carrier pigeons—some 100,000 of the birds had been enlisted by the British alone—crisscrossed the air above the "khaki cliffs," as George's brother called the trenches.[4] Interspersed with the busy bird's lofts were some three hundred kite balloons hugging the battle lines by 1918, their handlers tracking enemy train deliveries, calculating wind direction in case of gas attack, estimating the slope of not-so-distant ridges they aspired to one day reach. Spurred on by wartime needs for more accurate atmospheric information, meteorologists were beginning to theorize from balloon height that clashing three-dimensional air masses caused weather disturbances. "Fronts," they would call them.[5] No longer simply temporary battle lines—flanks formed by bodies—fronts had become distinct spaces with their own rules and physicality. The Western Front especially was a world apart, and it haunted the thoughts of young Americans like George.

The Spiegelberg family's intersection of loyalties made their relationship to the First World War complex. George's grandfather Solomon Jacob

George Spiegelberg as a graduating senior. Courtesy of Rare and Manuscript Collections, Cornell University.

Spiegelberg, a migrant from Hanover and early Jewish pioneer in the New Mexico territory, had established a well-reputed trading firm in Santa Fe before moving to New York, where he became a pillar of the city's German Jewish elite—the treasurer of Temple Emanu-El, a trustee of Mount Sinai Hospital. He then returned to Germany in the 1890s to live out his days. George's father, a respected New York Municipal Court judge who voted with the reformist wing of the Republican Party, was known for his equanimity, broad knowledge of current events, and efforts promoting "mental and moral improvement" among the city's poor Russian and Polish Jews. Born in New York but educated in Frankfurt and Leipzig, he returned frequently to Germany to visit his parents and siblings.[6] Indicative of the family's intense transatlantic belonging, when George's grandfather Solomon died, the Spiegelbergs buried their patriarch in New York but kept his US naturalization certificate in a Munich bank vault.[7]

George would have had good reasons, and much company, if he had opposed the United States joining the conflict that broke out in Europe in 1914. Most German Americans, who comprised some 10 percent of the total US population, chafed at the thought of going to war against friends, family, and the fatherland. Jewish Americans similarly opposed American involvement until the overthrow of the tsar, because it would have meant forming an alliance with the antisemitic Romanovs. Many other Americans simply reasoned that the violence was indeed a calamity, but that it was Europe's calamity, the consequence of a broken old world alliance system and festering imperial rivalries that had allowed the assassination of a Habsburg royal to destabilize an entire continent, a foreign power struggle that hardly warranted sending the nation's sons to the slaughter.[8]

Yet class and political affiliations, rather than ethnic allegiances, would drive George's and his brother's strong pro-Allied passions and service—as they did for many other German Jewish elites. Freddie recorded the sentiments that George seems to have shared. Britishers had "grit," he thought. Sure, they had "made mistakes" building their empire, but they were champions of "humanity" who ensured the world's free trade and always played "fair and square." German *Kultur* by contrast was "rotten," and "the Huns" only understood force. Freddie fantasized about razing German cities "with Freedom's high explosives," fitting revenge, he reasoned, for Belgium's "murdered babes and ravished women" and for the desecration of "most holy" Reims Cathedral.[9]

Such outrage at German "barbarism," and war euphoria in general, had surrounded George and his brother since 1914 when they waited with their parents in England for passage back to New York after their summer holidays. Reporting the sacking and burning of Louvain, British papers at the time detailed how the Belgian city's prized library and other monuments were reduced to ashes in a matter of days. Sailing out of Southampton past empty transports awaiting conscripts, the Spiegelbergs' ship carried over six hundred American evacuees trading tales about Germans' shocking contempt for international norms. Many Americans distrusted the British and suspected that they weren't fighting to safeguard the rights of small nations but rather to shore up their own empire. But Eastern Establishment men of law and letters like George's father saw Anglo-American culture as a protector of civilization, a defender of constitutional government and the sanctity of the rule of law.[10]

Emotions were running high when the Spiegelbergs returned to New York. European consulates were doubling as recruiting stations and propaganda dens. Street fights broke out when German butchers refused to extend credit to Polish, Russian, and Slavic customers. Among the city's reformers, expectations for what war might accomplish swelled. This was no ordinary European squabble, no run-of-the-mill, faraway battle, some said. It would be a force for progress. Many policymakers and intellectuals dreamed that mass mobilization could unify and uplift the impossibly varied inhabitants of the United States, channel their energies, and give them noble purpose. Democracy would flourish abroad, too, idealists hoped. Vanquished aristocracies would be swept away by new, self-determined states. Even victorious powers, some predicted, would have to acknowledge the contributions of their own long-subjugated minorities. It was a priceless chance to "finish the glorious work" that Americans had started with "the shot heard 'round the world," the *North American Review* celebrated. "We are for war; of course, we are," said the magazine, "and for reasons good and plenty."[11]

The seductions of combat itself also swirled around the Spiegelberg brothers. "The popular imagination fairly fattens on the thought of wars," the philosopher William James had written shortly before the conflict, recognizing the enduring temptation to regard battle as "the *strong* life," redemption from everyday pettiness and tedium. Perhaps nowhere did this allure of military engagement prove stronger than at East Coast colleges.[12]

The European conflict dogged George's undergraduate years at Cornell. He had been a freshman when reports of the sinking of the *Lusitania* crowded varsity baseball news on the school newspaper's front page. The ocean liner was torpedoed off the Irish coast, students learned, while unsuspecting passengers finished lunch. By George's sophomore year, not only outrage but also excitement mounted on campus. War! The greatest test of manhood and the noblest adventure. Many young men bristled at the thought of missing out on history in the making. Amateur diplomacy and battlefield strategizing crept into nightly dormitory talk. Tales trickled back from France about the exploits of peers already driving ambulances or flying planes, and more students itched to get "in the game." Just before graduating that spring, George's brother Freddie entered a speech contest and chose "Patriotism" for his topic. The next year, George enrolled in the Reserve Officers' Training Corps (ROTC). With the spring thaw and Germany's resumption of unrestricted submarine warfare, the military exercises spilled out of Drill Hall, one of the nation's largest armories, and onto Cornell's main quad, where cadets unfurled their pup tents and sliced their bayonets through the air with growing purpose. In April, the US declaration of war threw the end of George's junior year into disarray. The university sent him and his classmates home without final grades.[13]

By the start of George's senior year, enrollments had plummeted. Faculty were leaving for government posts. Fraternities suspended their rushing rituals, and the cafeteria introduced meatless Tuesdays. Freddie had already passed through the Plattsburg Training Camp, famous for catering to advocates of "preparedness" from elite New York families, as well as a stateside pilot program. In November he joined some of the first student aviators to cross the ocean under the auspices of the US military. "Oh truth! The path of life's not straight," Freddie rhapsodized upon his departure:

> So have I chosen the harder way
> Fraught with fire and molten lead
> And onrushing hordes clad in sickish gray,
> To withstand this shock and as others bled
> Perhaps to die; that a future shall live
> I, one human life, do gladly give.[14]

Back at Cornell, swarming with aviation recruiters, George stuck out the rest of his liberal arts program and showed himself to have "excellent character" and "considerable intellectual ability." He added German to his coursework, but, uninspired, he squeaked through with an uncharacteristic D. Finishing in May, he returned home and, though still underage for the draft, walked into a New York recruiting station. Armed with letters of recommendation, including one from the state governor Charles S. Whitman attesting that he represented "the very highest type of American young manhood," George explained that he had gone to a military prep school before Cornell, could speak French, box, ride horseback, and make minor car repairs. He wanted so much to qualify as a pilot that he would consider the navy's heavier or lighter-than-air aircraft training courses. Little more than a week later, he had been accepted into the observation balloon program.[15]

When the United States entered the war, the navy had only four less-than-functional observation balloons and precious few experienced operators, not enough aerial surveillance personnel for domestic defense, let alone overseas operations. Planners scrambled to amass equipment and establish ground schools that could funnel qualified applicants like George into the lighter-than-air naval aviation detachment at Akron. From there, trainees hoped for assignments across the Atlantic piloting dirigibles—blimps, the British dubbed them—or manning kite balloons hitched to the back of patrol ships. Those considered less fortunate would be posted instead to defense stations plotted along the coastline between Cape Cod and Key West.[16]

It took a lucid mind and a steely stomach to slip away from the ground in a skittish wicker basket, dangling from a rubberized silk bag that plunged into each pocket of air. "Every time a gust hits the balloon you imagine it is coming to pieces," confessed one trainee. Once aloft, and still swinging with the gales, cadets like George unwrapped their altimeters, compasses, and cloth-mounted maps to survey the landscape below. Balloon work demanded a knack for judging distance and direction as well as an eye for detail. Through field glasses they might have to tell a wave from a torpedo wake, friendly fire from hostile shelling, enemy troops moving into attack position from a regiment shuffling off to furlough. Balloonists also needed patience, to weather their positions for as many as twelve hours, tallying shipment arrivals, estimating convoy trajectories, making ballistic calculations. They needed a broad conception of battle, to be less enamored with frontline heroics and more attuned to the payoffs of long-range strategy and planning. Whether or not George relished balloon work, he was suited to it. During training, he passed all his subjects and received top marks in meteorology and good ratings for sobriety and obedience. His commanders consistently sized him up as "very good officer material" with "excellent military bearing."[17]

A navy scout watches for U-boats along the Atlantic coast during World War I. United States National Archives/Popperfoto via Getty Images.

Ballooning was dangerous. Dirigibles collided with other aircraft in congested training centers. Kite balloons broke loose from their cables and sailed for miles. One runaway airship drifted from an Omaha army base to the Iowa countryside, where farmers and National Guardsmen took it for a German zeppelin and ambushed its crew. Other balloons exploded when static electricity in their envelopes' folds ignited their hydrogen insides and engulfed passengers in flames.[18]

But for young men wanting to prove their mettle, balloon work was still not dangerous enough. It lacked the obvious drama of piloting airplanes. Freddie wrote from France:

> Fifty kilometers over the Hun
> With a thousand machine guns popping away,
> Certainly makes for a good night's fun
> If balloons and their cables stay out o' the way.

It was common for plane crews to belittle the skills of their lighter-than-air counterparts. "Balloonists float, they don't fly," scoffed another aviator.[19]

While George slogged through elementary flight instruction, Frederick served at several sectors of the Western Front. Although it was not always clear from his poetry, he was not a pilot but an observer, or what the French called a *bombardier*, a spotter and bomb dropper assisting the pilot in a biplane's open-air cockpit. He had been a member of the first group of Americans trained in these capacities at Cazaux and Clermont-Ferrand and then sent in May 1918 to the 125th Escadrille, a French bombardment group in the Champagne district.[20] His earlier enthusiasms continued unabated. "This is paradise, not war!" he gushed.

> Can I be anywhere 'cept here,
> Can I stand the domestic life
> And the humdrum days in the rear?

Frederick's flying duties intensified in October 1918 when he was transferred back to US military command and reported for duty to a night reconnaissance unit, the 9th Aero Squadron, the only American outfit of its kind. He and two dozen of his compatriots readied themselves to join the Meuse-Argonne offensive, what would become the largest and costliest battle in US history.[21]

The campaign was to be one last great Allied push before winter, but already fog and rain forced fliers into riskier low work. The day Frederick arrived, one of the squadron's crews went missing during a routine sortie. Still, he thrilled at the assignments that took him north of Verdun along the Meuse River and out "into the shell shot air," dodging the searchlights to "seek out dope" and "drop a few stings."[22] In moonlight at a thousand yards he could detect movement on rail lines or other kinds of out-of-the-ordinary activity that might reveal enemy intentions. But on black or overcast nights, he set out with his pilot into obscurity. Blast furnaces or the edge of forests made useful landmarks, but mist and high trees shrouded roads, water, and other potential markers. Only flares provided fleeting glimpses of the world below. Nearing their destination, observers like Frederick lit them windward of their objective as the pilot crooked their Breguet two-seater into a tight, downward spiral. All activity below halted in the artificial light. An observer had only seconds to take in the scene, and perhaps strafe or bomb the target, before searchlights locked on the plane's location. Returning to base had its own perils. Getting lost was so common that fliers dropped flares as much to figure out where they were as to sight enemy positions, and truck headlights or bucket bonfires, not proper landing lights, guided them to the runway.[23]

At the end of the Meuse-Argonne campaign, Frederick's squadron counted 259 flights, twelve crashes, five wounded, and three killed. The carnage was worth it, he told himself. The "awful toll" had been "Paid to principle." Words like "Destiny," "Freedom," and "Right"— singular and capitalized—anchored Frederick's poetry. Only hints of the "maze of mutilated nature" and men "crushed to fragments" crept into his writing, just enough gore to drive home the stakes and bring gravity to the high diction. Pushing against these stray references were far more dominant passages in which Frederick celebrated flying in France as a test of prowess and teamwork. Like many others, he stuffed war into the framework of intervarsity sports, a common strategy for young men trying to find meaning under difficult circumstances. After all, the proving grounds of the pitch, or the diamond, were the closest most of them had come to the heart-racing risks of battle. "Oh, it's a wonderful, wonderful game," one of Frederick's peers wrote home. "The only sport there is," thought another.[24]

George had in his sights two visions of war. His brother's example of individual heroism—of a lone bomber barreling down on enemy batteries in the light of a single nighttime flare—had heat and guts and melodrama. The balloonist's sunlit perspective by contrast drew the eye across a depersonalized landscape toward the distant horizon. It turned war into a logistical contest determined by stopwatch measurements, itemized supply lists, and calculated waiting.

The closest George got to the Western Front was a Pensacola receiving ship on the Gulf of Mexico. Maybe that brought him relief. Or maybe missing this war would be hard to live down, as it was for Dwight D. Eisenhower—on whose staff George would later serve with distinction. "I suppose we'll spend the rest of our lives explaining why we didn't get into this war. By God, from now on I am cutting myself a swath and will make up for this," Eisenhower vowed. Many impatient recruits in stateside camps wrote similar letters on the eve of the ceasefire. "If Germany quits cold now, it will spoil the whole war for us. After training for a year and a half for the big game—and then to be left sitting on the bench," bemoaned one trainee, who like George had an older brother already fighting in France.[25]

Freddie's poetry, and his definition of heroism, would remind George of the war he had missed long after his older brother's life was cut short. Frederick completed his tour of duty with the Army of Occupation in the

Rhineland and then returned to a job in New York selling hides and leathers. Accounts of his war days grew to include a Croix de Guerre and a stint with the famous pursuit pilots of the Lafayette Escadrille. When he married in 1920, he chose the anniversary of the Armistice for his wedding day. Five years after that, Frederick Spiegelberg, Jr., died after being thrown from an automobile. His friend lost control at the wheel and crashed into a tree while speeding on the wrong side of a New Jersey roadway, coming home from the great game that had inspired so many young men in the muddy fields of France—the Princeton-Harvard football match.[26]

The imaginations of most young Americans, like Freddie and George, had fixed on places like Château Thierry, St. Mihiel, and Verdun. But behind the Western Front's ossified earthworks lay a continent unraveling, where wars within wars brought pain and ambiguity rather than clarity— and where the violence was not confined to trenches or to the years between 1914 and 1918.[27]

2

Autumn Flies

ON JUNE 28, 1914, THE roofless sports coupe carrying Archduke Franz Ferdinand, presumed heir to the Austro-Hungarian throne, and his wife, Sophie, made a wrong turn off the Appel Quay in Sarajevo. When their driver slowed to turn around, Gavrilo Princip, a Bosnian Serb nationalist who had been stalking the royal couple for days, stepped out and shot them dead. Officials in Vienna blamed the Serbian state for the act, and, assured of backing from their German allies, declared war on their Balkan neighbors a month after the assassination. Aware that a major war might stretch Russia's already struggling regime to its limits, Nicholas II's Council of Ministers nevertheless urged a show of force against the hawkish rival powers to the west. The tsar ordered a general mobilization on July 30. Germany welcomed such a clear casus belli and announced war against Russia on August 1.[1] That's when Tamara's world fell apart.

Born in Odesa in 1907, Tamara Drasin was the eldest child of Jewish tailors. Her mother Hinda, or Eda, was a gifted singer whose mouth turned down at the corners even when she smiled. Boris, her father, was an aspiring "Russified" intellectual.[2] Later, Tamara would expunge many of these facts from her biography in order to disguise her Jewish origins.

During Tamara's earliest years, the little family likely resided not far from Odesa's central boulevards, where Jews enjoyed less segregation and more opportunity than elsewhere in Russia. Perched on a plateau above the Black Sea, the city resounded with music. Symphonies wafted out of its opera houses. Gramophones echoed folk songs through small apartments.

At sidewalk cafés, children like Tamara lapped up ice cream while listening to klezmer clarinetists riff off eclectic musical traditions, weaving together novel melodies of joy and pathos.[3] In New York's nightclubs and on Broadway, this would become Tamara's specialty, too.

In many ways, Tamara's birthplace was not so different from the New York she would come to know in the 1920s. Both cities thrived off their ports, which linked vast overland empires to foreign markets, drawing a polyglot mix of migrants to their factories, refineries, and sweatshops. Like the restless youth of American prairie towns dreaming about Manhattan, forward-thinkers throughout Russia's Pale of Settlement—where the vast majority of the empire's Jewish subjects were required to live—dreamed about Odesa. Its sidewalk bargaining and backroom dealing transcended barriers of language and religion, promising that, here, the pursuit of worldly pleasures just might win out over the old ways.[4]

But all was not well in Odesa. The garment industry's switch to mass-produced clothing displaced more and more artisans like Boris in favor of semiskilled piece workers. Many, probably including Tamara's father, channeled their frustrations into underground labor activity. At the same time, the city's all-important grain trade had not recovered from its plummet during the war with Japan in 1904–1905 and the revolutionary disturbances and violence that followed. A downtown showroom hawking state-of-the-art American binders and reapers reminded passing pedestrians of growing US competition for European buyers. Sometime before Tamara reached school age, the Drasins joined a growing exodus from the ailing port city, taking a twenty-four-hour train ride northeast to Ekaterinoslav, Boris's birthplace.[5]

Once an imperial backwater, Ekaterinoslav had grown fast and ugly into Russia's fifth-largest manufacturing center after the development of coal mines in the nearby Donets Basin in the 1880s. The train from Odesa approached the city across a high iron bridge spanning the Dnipro River, clogged with barges lugging grain, lumber, and other goods. Ekaterinoslav had little of Odesa's cosmopolitanism. Smoke from foundries and steel mills obscured the old town's gold church domes and brightly painted rooftops. A few half-presentable hotels and second-rate theaters sufficed as the requisite cultural markers for an industrial city on the make.[6]

Though only in his twenties, Tamara's father kept a successful tailor shop on one of the town's best streets. The peach-fuzz mustache and wispy goatee he sported when Tamara was a baby grew into a beard— not the long, splayed whiskers of a cantor but a look worthy of socialist *intelligenty*. Tamara remembered parties with joyous singing at their small living quarters. In 1913, a brother Eliezar ("Lasya" or, eventually, "Lee") was born. She might have led a rather unremarkable childhood, she later reflected, were it not for the outbreak of the Great War the following year. She was about seven when her father was drafted into the tsar's army and then disappeared.[7]

The conflict and its revolutionary aftermath proved a watershed for women and girls in the Russian empire. Daughters like Tamara watched their mothers take charge of families, businesses, and farms as some fifteen million men departed for military service. Ekaterinoslav residents remained far from the front lines but, like other urban populations, battled outbreaks of cholera and measles as well as food and fuel shortages. As advancing (and then retreating) Russian forces violently expelled Jews from Galicia

Tamara, likely in Ekaterinoslav, around the time of the First World War. Special Collections and University Archives, Rutgers University Libraries.

and the western Pale—regarding them as potential enemy collaborators—refugees poured into Tamara's city. By the summer of 1916, some 30,000 displaced persons, many sick or injured, taxed already overstretched housing and health facilities and sent prices for basic goods soaring. Hinda nevertheless may have found purpose running Boris's shop or contributing to Ekaterinoslav's wartime relief efforts. The city center's Jewish self-defense organization would have given a mother on her own some sense of security, and being a *soldatka* entitled her to consideration in her community, even though soldiers' wives ultimately received little support from the state.[8] War would force Hinda to make life-or-death decisions. But she may not have contemplated abandoning the family business or uprooting Tamara from school until the events of 1917.[9]

That February, women filled the frontlines of protests in Petrograd, marching against inept government policies, throwing rocks in disgust at food prices, and finally staging a demonstration on International Women's Day that brought so many into the streets that authorities lost control of the crowds. As police forces disintegrated and troops brought to restore order defected to the side of protesters, Nicholas II abdicated the throne.[10]

At first, Hinda and Tamara would have welcomed the overthrow of the Romanov dynasty, which had treated the Drasins as second-class citizens. When news of the establishment of a socialist-leaning Provisional Government in Moscow reached Ekaterinoslav in March, celebrants crowded the central avenue and toppled its monument to Catherine the Great, the city's namesake. With the prospect of no more censorship, no more Pale, no more suppression of minority languages, and, for workers, a fair shake, euphoria swept Ukrainian and Jewish communities across the south.[11]

Over the next several months, however, day-to-day difficulties dashed the high expectations, especially as the new regime failed to extricate Russia from the Great War. Then the Bolsheviks' seizure of power in November plunged Ekaterinoslav into anarchy. Revolutionaries confiscated weapons and other property from wealthy inhabitants and ousted the Provisional Government from the river port. Gun battles raged between Bolsheviks in the Governor's Palace, who claimed nominal control over the district, and rival anarchist and socialist factions holed up in the main post office and various commandeered hotels. Townspeople who ventured out crept past ransacked stores, dead horses and dogs, and fires set by hoodlums. Full civil and legal equality may have been officially granted to women, but the turmoil unleashed by the coup would leave them and their children particularly vulnerable.[12]

The standoff continued into 1918. Train and mail service to Ekaterinoslav ground to a halt. Rumors poured into the Jewish quarter about coming pogroms and steel workers' plans to kill the bourgeoisie and strangle their children. The city had "gone mad," decided one young girl trapped in the neighborhood, which nightly echoed with gunfire. Panic peaked in early March as Red Guards lost their grip on the area and news spread that German soldiers, moving into Ukraine under a peace agreement struck with Kyiv's Ukrainian nationalists, would soon besiege the town. Schools and shops were boarded up as looting spread and even children Tamara's age were mugged on the streets. People prayed in their homes instead of going to church and slept in their clothes in anticipation of hasty departures.[13]

In the coming multidimensional civil war, Tamara's family would be regarded as enemies by all sides. The Bolsheviks, who condemned even petty merchants and artisans as "bourgeois," threatened their freedom and livelihood. Ukrainian nationalists and various "White" counterrevolutionaries meanwhile singled out Jews as economic parasites, Bolshevik collaborators, or Christ killers. They threatened not only the Drasins' rights and property but also their lives. If Hinda and the children had not already left Ekaterinoslav, they probably fled now in the footsteps of the retreating Red Army, escaping some 140 miles north, either overland or by river barge, to the home of Hinda's parents in the village of Sorochyntsi.[14]

Coming here was a gamble. Not far from Myrhorod in Poltava Oblast, Velyki Sorochyntsi had not changed all that much since 1829, when Nikolai Gogol wrote about the "cacophonous din" and "clashing colours" of his hometown's market fair, where peasants traded their wares, their daughters, and stories about the devil. Residents of thatched roof cottages still marked time by the sun and the seasons. In winter, young girls' duties—cooking, cleaning, and running errands—were broken up by sleigh rides and walks home in the crisp, starry night by the light of menorah candles in the windows. Spring's gluey mud finally dried around Passover, when fragrant blooms dotted the unpaved roads.[15] Such an out-of-the-way place off the train lines just might have been passed over by the political chaos.

Food, too, promised to be more plentiful in this famed black earth region of Ukraine's "breadbasket" lands, which had at first produced bountiful wartime harvests.[16] And reuniting with relatives offered comfort. "I can remember the times when she and her sisters would sing," Lee Drasin later recalled of his mother. The haunting folk melodies helped sustain the family.

Music had long been an integral part of village life in Sorochyntisi. Songs brought by visitors, passed down from mothers to children, and sung in the ripening fields imparted knowledge and instilled courage. Under the tsar, singers had been nurtured by Jewish communities, because music opened up a path to civil rights; those who earned the status of "free artists" could live wherever they chose. Tamara, possessing a beautiful voice and a natural talent like her mother, followed Hinda around the house, soaking up ballads while sewing and finishing her chores. She practiced reciting the verse fables of Ivan Krylov, learned to play the guitar, and waited eagerly for neighbors to call at the house and provide her an audience. She was "a ham," her brother explained, who dreamed of being in the theater.[17]

But conditions in Sorochyntsi grew increasingly dire. The prolonged absence of able-bodied men and heavy grain requisitions, first from Moscow and then from German occupiers, brought hunger to the region. A wholesale collapse of the economy and the handicraft industries that had kept peasants going in between harvests led to bartering and frantic scavenging for food and bedding. People wore garments until they turned into rags and saved their shoes for snowfall. Possessing "few remaining treasures" from their former lives, the Drasins, like others, lived hand to mouth. At eleven, with wistful brown eyes and dainty features, Tamara grubbed in the fields for food and tilled potato gardens in exchange for payments of salt, sugar, or cheap calico, which had become "as precious to the family as gold."[18]

And Sorochyntsi wasn't safe. It belonged to a rural district with the lowest percentage of Jewish inhabitants of any part of the Pale, a place dominated by peasants with longstanding resentments against landlords and the Jewish middlemen who often served as their agents. It had been the site of one of Russia's largest rural uprisings in the wake of the 1905 Revolution when locals ransacked and burned the village's wealthy estates. As tensions rose once more, Jewish residents fearfully withdrew from public life and sank deeper into poverty.[19]

Then, when German occupation troops departed following the Armistice in November 1918, all hell broke loose. Competing militias of Ukrainian separatists, counterrevolutionaries, and rebels of other vague convictions or simple opportunism vied for power, sustaining their military campaigns against the Reds and each other by raiding Jewish shtetls in their path. Armed bandits trampled gardens, roughed up inhabitants, and rifled through homes for weapons and valuables. Everything mobile, from chickens to pianos, they carted away, with Ukrainian peasants often trailing behind them, confiscating the pillows, blankets, or samovars of their Jewish neighbors.[20]

Such attacks quickly escalated beyond pillaging and harassment into frenzies of mass murder, ultimately claiming anywhere from 30,000 to 200,000 lives. Investigators documented some 1,500 pogroms and similar excesses in Ukraine during the civil war. More horrors went unrecorded, particularly in small villages on the left bank of the Dnipro, like Sorochyntsi. Sieges often lasted for days, and many towns were attacked multiple times. Jewish villagers particularly feared the Cossacks. Galloping into hamlets, they bayonetted pedestrians, dragged toddlers from their hiding places and split open their heads, put whole families to death, and left their babies to starve. There was "no end to the butchery" and the "appalling orgies of torture and rape," British military officials cabled from the region. Gangs unleashed sadistic fury upon female populations, mutilating little girls and violating women to destroy their honor and self-worth. A war within a war against a gender. Those who managed to hide or play dead were left to mop up the blood trails and pick through rubble for the corpses of loved ones. "Ruined widows and orphaned children sent threatening curses against the whole world, threw themselves in measureless grief on the ground and begged God for death," mourned one witness. What "shameless cruelty of man, who desires to gain power at such a price," reflected another. Even Jews ideologically opposed to the Bolsheviks began to hope for the Red Army.[21]

Poltava Oblast, home to many virulently anti-Bolshevik peasants, lacked any sort of law and order during 1919. Hetmans, or warlords, who had broken off from Symon Petliura's Ukrainian army in neighboring Kyiv Oblast, terrorized its roads and waterways. With few firearms or even sabers left to defend the village, Tamara's community suffered such visitors on several occasions. Sometimes only neighboring peasants came to steal what they could. Other times roving outlaws arrived and plundered at will. Violence peaked in the late summer as detachments from General Anton Denikin's White Russia Volunteer Army advanced through the area, boosted by supplies from US warships in the Black Sea. A *New York Times* correspondent praised the "extraordinary dash and gallantry" of Denikin's men—some of them donning donated British uniforms—as they "simply hoorooshed" through the picturesque villages "described in Gogol's stories." Poltava's peasants "wept for joy" as they were "liberated from the Bolshevik yoke," he relayed: "No one who saw that marvelous sight could doubt what our aid means to those sufferers."[22]

These forces, celebrated by many for their anti-Bolshevism, obliterated Jewish enclaves in their path. Tamara forever shuddered to recall the day not long before her twelfth birthday when townspeople scrambled for cover: "The bandits, the bandits are coming!" The reputation of Denikin's troops for rape preceded them. In a village across the Dnipro, one confused child who had witnessed such acts related how a neighbor had been "robbed of her clothes." Villagers often took extra care to hide attractive daughters or, failing that, to disguise their beauty by dressing them in frumpy clothes, which only made girls more sensitive to the special dangers they faced. Tamara ran. With her baby brother and grandmother she hid in a haystack, spending the night under the musty straw, cowering at the sound of gunshots around her. When the troops finally tired of their plundering they torched everything in the town that would burn, including the children's hideout. But the haystack proved too wet to catch fire.[23]

It was after staring at Sorochyntsi's flaming cottages (in a place where water would have been hauled in pails), that Tamara and her mother resolved to get out of Ukraine. This was a brave decision, for it would take them into the unknown. They had little information, if any, about the fate of Tamara's father. The postal system would not function normally until 1923. Boris Drasin was merely one man among the 600,000 Jews who had served with the tsar's military between 1914 and 1917, quite possibly among the empire's 1.8 million military dead or among another 1.5 million POWs still languishing in defunct Central Powers prison camps.[24]

Nor were there any easy exit routes. War had disrupted the old migration support networks and replaced them with new visas and other bureaucratic hurdles. Concerned about capital flight, Bolshevik authorities instructed frontier *chekas* to turn travelers back if they did not produce departure permits and other permissions that most refugees could not secure.[25]

Yet at the same time, with the collapse of Germany and Austria-Hungary—and the Red Army's resolve to take the revolution deeper into Eastern Europe—it was not even clear where the borders stood. Tamara's family eyed the closest exit: north of Chornobyl across the Prypiat River and eventually on to Grodno, a city from which only recently evacuees had fled after Cossacks rampaged through the town, dismembering and executing Jewish residents hiding in their cellars. But where was Grodno? In 1918 it lay in a nascent Belarusian Republic still occupied by Germans, then in 1919 it temporarily fell under the aegis of Lithuania before being taken over by Polish forces. After the Red Army captured the city in July 1920, it served as a key battleground in the Polish-Bolshevik War. Only that October did a truce agreement put Grodno in Poland.[26]

Perhaps spurred on by a rumor about a safe route or a scrap of encouraging news in a month-old paper from Kyiv, the Drasins took their chances in 1920. Saying tearful goodbyes to the grandparents Tamara would never see again, they set out hoping to bargain their way through the ongoing mayhem.[27]

By train they got as far as Kyiv's rat-infested central station. Even this leg of the journey would have been traumatic. Freshly expelled from the United States and travelling the same route that year, the anarchist Emma Goldman marveled at the disarray of railroad service between Poltava and the Ukrainian capital. Jewish communities along the line lived "in constant terror," and refugees packed each station "to suffocation," Goldman reported. There was no ticket system at work, no timetables. Parents and their emaciated children waited weeks on the platforms, hoping for room in a cattle car attached to trains requisitioned for troop movements. Goldman cringed watching people climb onto the outsides of departing trains while soldiers tried to drive them off. More than a few of those who made it out of the station fell to their death, she averred, crushed by wheels or swept into ravines by low bridges.[28]

Tens of thousands had been killed in the pogroms. Even more starved or froze and died on the roads. As many as 10 percent of Ukraine's Jewish population perished between 1918 and 1920. "The people died like autumn flies," remembered one child survivor of early twenties Ukraine who had subsisted on ground-up acorns and grass soup: "If it would have been possible they would have eaten the lice that crowded over them, but the lice were stronger and ate the people, infecting them with typhus."[29] Tamara had witnessed a unique tragedy, yet one that foreshadowed the string of horrors soon to return here as well as spread to other corners of the globe: a civil war sparked by competition over local power and resources, fanned by religious and ethnic hatreds and then escalated and sustained by foreign intervention that imbued the struggle with geopolitical significance.

From Kyiv, the Drasins followed other fugitives creeping toward Romania or Poland. People displaced from their shtetls entered a period of suspended life that often lasted months. There was no time for proper burial rites for those who succumbed to disease or injuries along the way. Even some of the most Orthodox sacrificed the Sabbath, dietary laws, and prayer rituals to boost their odds of survival. But hazardous weather caught travelers off guard. They lost their way after dark or fell victim to bandits. Promising to help, swindlers and sex traffickers manipulated and betrayed the desperate. At the border, guards stripped people of their valuables or shot at them as they attempted river crossings in boats or on foot over frozen patches. Children found wandering on the other side recounted tales about parents who had fallen through the ice.[30]

But women had been leaving Russia illegally for generations. Indeed, three-fourths of Russia's emigrants in the decades before the Great War had slipped across the border at night or bribed their way out, among them wives who had not been allowed their own passports under Imperial Russian law. Inspired not by great men or great theories but the politics of motherhood, they defied the priorities of armies and states and set off with insufficient money or knowledge and needy children in tow.[31]

Continuing the tradition, Tamara's mother hid her boy and girl in the back of a farmer's cart. Under a stuffy cover of wheat, they lay for hours bored but terrified, bumping over potholed roads. The Drasins joined some 150,000 Jews from Ukraine who made it to Poland by September 1921.[32] They spent a year in Grodno searching for Boris before a Jewish relief agency miraculously located him, alive and well in the Bronx.[33] At thirteen, Tamara was already a veteran of war. She knew how armed conflict wasted life, made a mockery of decency, and derailed the best of plans. How would she be persuaded, two decades later, to sacrifice everything that mattered to her and enter the fray of battle once more?

3

Blood of the Earth

IN 1914 HARRY G. SEIDEL lied on his passport application. In the space where he claimed that his father was native born, the cursive letters were smaller, just a touch different than the handwriting on the rest of the form, as though he had left that part blank, to think about whether to mention that his father was German. It's not that he didn't know. On subsequent forms he would indicate that Hermann Seidel came from Dresden.[1]

But keeping things uncomplicated when petitioning the US government for approval to travel to the oil fields of East Central Europe, a politically sensitive region, on behalf of Standard Oil of New Jersey, a corporation deeply distrusted, certainly was expedient. Just as working for the Germans later helped to save his life in Bucharest. Harry was learning to play both sides. Romania during World War I was an excellent place to practice.

Two years earlier, Harry had been a senior at Brown University, where he ran with Providence's smart set, cultivated the air of a "real society swell," and placed in the yearbook's straw poll for "handsomest man in the class." Though he was extravagant—he would never be caught with a dirty collar—his friends counted him "a right good fellow." It amused them to know that "Hot-house Harry" was actually a baker's son from the declining mill town of Fitchburg, Massachusetts.[2]

Harry intended to "chase the coin around the blocks of business" after graduation, but he worried that he faced a practical workplace with only theoretical schooling. He and his close friend Ryland B. Andrews hit upon a plan. They would seek help from a fellow Brown alumnus and one of

Harry Seidel as a young man. Courtesy of Geraldine Seidel.

Ryland's fraternity brothers: John D. Rockefeller, Jr. For years, Standard Oil had been losing market share and fighting off lawsuits and muckraking exposés of its monopolistic practices. It was the most vilified corporation in the United States, ordered by the Supreme Court only eleven months earlier to break up its vast holdings. Even so Harry and Ryland approached the son of the firm's founder for an entrée into the petroleum business. Maybe, like Rockefeller senior and other industry leaders, they believed that oil was a providential gift that portended enlightenment and prosperity.[3] Likely they dreamed of pressed suits and sleek boardrooms on the upper stories of Manhattan's skyscrapers.

Over lunch Rockefeller counseled the two young men that Standard's New York headquarters was firing not hiring employees in the wake of the Supreme Court ruling. Their best chance to break into the industry, he told them, was on "the production end." Even when rolled into a single corporation, petroleum was actually many distinct businesses—discovery, extraction, transportation, storage, refining, and marketing. Producing was undoubtedly its rowdiest wing with the most disorderly participants, but it also had the most open doors. The financier could "make no promises" of help, but by mid-June the telegram Harry and Ryland hoped for arrived at Providence:

> . . . COME HERE ON ONE OCLOCK TRAIN TODAY . . . TO SEE HEAD OF WESTERN OIL PRODUCING COMPANY WHO GOES WEST TOMORROW . . .[4]

Harry and Ryland landed jobs with the former Standard subsidiary Prairie Oil and Gas Company, a leading producer and distributor in the newly discovered oil fields of Oklahoma. Eighteen miles south of Tulsa at Kiefer, a notorious dive of a boomtown spawned by the nearby Glenn Pool strike in 1905, the two Brown graduates were "thoroughly initiated to the pick and shovel," as Harry put it. Harry served as a roustabout, or general unskilled laborer, while his friend worked the pipeline, and the months "passed like weeks, and quite needless to add, have been full with many interesting incidents," he reported back to Rockefeller.[5]

Harry was underselling the experience. Swarming with prospectors when the two young men arrived in 1912, Oklahoma was a world hammered together from wooden planks. False-front stores and shotgun board-and-batten shacks accumulated out of the dust into towns with names like Bowlegs and Whizbang. Movie sets were built to last longer. Liquor flowed almost as freely as the crude despite local dry laws, and, with few jails, prisoners were sometimes chained to telephone poles or confined to box cars that only the drunkest could not escape. Bodies surfaced in creeks and other places. When drained, the storage tank behind Kiefer's Mad House Saloon alone disgorged seven skeletons.[6]

Not long before, this had been Indian Territory, some of the least-wanted land in America. After the US government drove Cherokees, Choctaws, Chickasaws, Creeks, and Seminoles from their ancestral homes east of the Mississippi and dumped them here in 1830s, the Five Civilized Tribes spent decades camping near the area's oil seepages, igniting their gas for heat and bathing in them to ease rheumatism. When chemists figured out how to distill kerosene from the crude in the 1850s, petroleum became one of several popular sources of light. Gasoline, a byproduct of the refining process, found small use for making solvents. But soon ship and factory boilers also began to take the fuel, and the advent of the automobile at the turn of the century drove demand to new heights. The year Harry landed in Oklahoma, Americans registered 902,000 motorcars, up from only 8,000 in 1900. The acres around Tulsa were no longer settler colonial frontier but prime real estate, because oil was no longer any old commodity. It was black gold.[7]

When Prairie began developing leaseholds near the Drumright pool, discovered outside Cushing earlier that March, Harry was sent there to haul supplies by horse and buggy over miles of dirt that drivers called "the road from Jericho to Jerusalem." Like others, he worked seven days a week. In the race to drain the precious liquid before someone else did, work sites operated around the clock. Sweat ran down men's legs and collected in their shoes. Exposed gears and drive chains mangled limbs. Saltwater from the holes burned open cuts. At the end of a shift, fingers that had gripped hatchets and saws for hours needed to be pried apart and bent to hold a match.[8]

As Drumright turned out to be the state's largest oil field yet, men streamed into Cushing, sharing beds, sleeping on pool tables, in theater seats and barber's chairs. The area's crude, the highest grade west of the Mississippi, could be tapped at shallow depths, and gas pressure brought oil to the surface without pumping, but impatient drillers shot their wells with nitroglycerin torpedoes just the same. Gushers sprayed backyards and nearby crops, and their runoff collected in large artificial lakes that attracted ducks to their doom. In heavy rains, the storage ponds overflowed into the local water supply. Thousands more barrels were lost each day through evaporation, seepage, and fire. Natural gas, as yet unwanted, was simply allowed to vent into the atmosphere, collecting in low-lying pockets, waiting for a cigarette or an engine spark to ignite. The oil that did make it to refineries—some 22 million barrels annually by 1914—crashed the market.[9] A clear philosophy animated the fever at Cushing: Life was short. Get it while you can. Get it before the other guy.

Yet Harry and Ryland were playing an entirely different game. Unlike the wildcatters who dug and the farmers who leased to them, praying for one-time fortune, or the pipe layers and rig builders who stayed for the unusually high daily wages, they had come to Oklahoma for knowledge and access to the industry's executive ranks. After a year in the fields, they had reached "the second rung of the ladder," Harry assessed, and intended to climb higher. So when offers arrived to work for an obscure Standard Oil subsidiary building facilities on the northern periphery of the Balkans, a region at war since 1911, the two jumped at a chance most money-minded job seekers would have judged not worth the risk. Ryland telegrammed home:

HARRY AND I HAVE ACCEPTED POSITION IN ROMANIA. . . CALL UP MRS. SEIDEL.[10]

With his friend Ryland and his newly minted passport, Harry arrived at the oil fields south of the Carpathians in March 1914.[11] Here he would discover that the search for oil was becoming so much more than a quest for profits. In Romania, it was being slowly wrapped up in matters of sovereignty, security, and survival.

For decades, Romania's crude had been distilled in small batches to lubricate cart wheels and illuminate boyars' courtyards. But following an 1895 mining law that encouraged development, foreign investment poured in, transforming the kingdom in little more than a decade into the world's fourth largest oil producer after the United States, Russia, and Mexico. Hoping to compete with Russian and Galician producers for continental markets, in 1904 Standard Oil agents formed Români-Americană, the New Jersey holding company's first foreign production enterprise. Challenges beset the subsidiary from the start. Soft sands and low gas pressure made drilling in the Prahova Valley tedious. Contracting with local workmen who spoke no English made it more so. In 1909, E. J. Sadler, a Prairie Oil and Gas engineer, took charge of Standard's wells in the Ploieşti and Moreni fields as well as its refinery at Teleajen. Wrenching results from the installations with American technology, Sadler acquired more property and recruited more employees from the United States. By the time Harry and Ryland arrived Româno-Americană was turning a respectable $2 million profit.[12]

Split up from Ryland and tasked with general office work as Sadler's assistant manager, Harry found his first six months in Romania a "discouraging period." The five hundred or so Americans working in the fields lived in special company housing with electric light, mattresses, and maid service, though American magazines, breakfast cereal, and other home comforts arrived only irregularly via the Black Sea more than 150 miles away. A gulf separated the company's largely foreign technical and managerial staff from its common Romanian laborers, who, as Ryland marveled, "all step to one side and tip their hat when an American passes." Harry confessed to Rockefeller that he "felt at sea" amid "the strange sounding language" and the "natives," who, though "improving," were still "decidedly unreliable."[13] His spirits only began to lift as he spent more time in Bucharest.

Only a half century before, Bucharest had been an unremarkable outpost on the plains, encircled by antiquated forts, serviced by ox-drawn wagons, and still in the shadow of the Ottoman Empire. But the arrival of the Orient Express in 1883 put it on the map and turned it into a capital befitting the newly independent kingdom—a rump Romania consisting of only two principalities, Moldavia and Wallachia, but with dreams of becoming a Greater Romania that might one day also encompass southern Bessarabia, Bukovina, Transylvania, and the Banat. Around the corner from Harry's Bucharest office on the Strada Stavropoleos, elites debated their nation's future among the gilt cherub wall carvings and legendary pastry of Capşa's restaurant.[14]

Visitors from the United States described the capital, with its imitation Second Empire boulevards and architecture, as a Francophile island surrounded by a Slavic sea. The "surface coating of French frivolity" little impressed the visiting American journalist John Reed, who scoffed at the overdressed elites promenading through their "get-rich city," while an hour away illiterate peasants lived in sod hovels. Reed, a socialist who would die in Moscow and be interred in the Kremlin wall, proclaimed that "never was a country so ripe for revolution" as Romania.[15]

Harry, too, was struck by the people's "lavishness with money" and "fondness for display," which led many to "live beyond their means" and tolerate "unscrupulous" practices. But while John Reed dreamed of a class reckoning, Harry looked forward to a different kind of "progress"—a future of stability and cooperation steered by responsible leaders of private enterprise. He brushed up on German—Bucharest's business language and likely learned from his parents—and French, which he had studied in college. Within a year he had also mastered conversational Romanian. He found it a "distinct pleasure" to understand these tongues and resolved to learn "foreign methods of doing business" as well. "On the whole," he rationalized, "it has been an education for which I am happier than I can express."[16] That education would soon include up-close lessons on how wars and states must be accounted for in business, on how there was no clear connection between national affiliation and corporate interest, or between armed conflict and profits.

When the Great War broke out in the summer of 1914, Romania at first remained neutral, but business instantly floundered. Banking transactions and exports ground to a halt until trade agreements could be struck with the belligerents bordering Romania on all sides. The Ottoman Empire closed the Dardanelles, cutting off one of the kingdom's primary transport routes.

Shipments backed up in storage facilities. Steel casing, nails, and other supplies usually imported from Germany became harder to get. So did field laborers as the Romanian army partially mobilized. Still Harry remained optimistic. In 1915, new wells came online and Romăno-Americană's petroleum output reached more than 1.6 million tons, 23 percent of the kingdom's total, edging ahead of even Deutsche Bank's Steaua Română and Dutch-owned Astra Română. "Undoubtedly when the terrible war is over and business conditions are again normal, the development of our company's good prospects here will enrich the work," Harry reasoned.[17]

Years later, many would assume that Harry had been negotiating oil sales to the Allies during World War I.[18] But by 1916, his company sold almost exclusively to the Austro-Hungarian Empire and Germany. "We are shipping a great deal of oil in tank barges on the Danube," Ryland told his father after spending that May in Hungary facilitating the deals. He and Harry seemed to have no qualms about doing business with the Central Powers and merely tired of the war's hindrances on trade. "This morning we received news of a big German naval victory in the North Sea," Ryland recorded with a touch of excitement. "I sincerely hope before long the nations here make peace."[19]

But the lure of war was proving hard for Romanians to resist. The question was simply which side to join. Paris-educated Liberals favored the Entente, pointing out that France and Russia had supported the kingdom in 1913 when it seized southern Dobrudja from Bulgaria during the Second Balkan War. Popular sentiment also championed the Allies, or more precisely reviled the Habsburg Empire, which ruled Transylvania and the Banat, suppressing the language, religion, and political participation of its 3.5 million Romanians. In the United States, Allied supporters decried German "barbarism." But in Bucharest they rallied instead against Austro-Hungarian "tyranny."[20]

Yet Romanians also had reason to support the Central Powers. Strong ties especially drew them to Germany, not least a secret defensive alliance signed in 1883. The Reich moreover supplied more than 40 percent of the kingdom's imports and floated practically all of its loans. German investors controlled more than a third of Romania's electricity, oil, insurance, and banking industries, and Prussian officers had trained and equipped its army. Berlin-educated Conservative politicians found much to admire in German *Kultur*. So did King Carol, a member of the Hohenzollern family and Kaiser Wilhelm II's cousin.[21]

On only one thing almost all in Bucharest agreed. They wanted to annex not only Transylvania and the Banat from Hungary but also Bukovina from

Austria, which was home to a quarter of a million Romanians, and southern Bessarabia from Russia, which held a million more. Since creating Greater Romania would require taking territory from both sides, it called for some very careful maneuvering. The Entente and Central Powers alike courted Romania aggressively, due to its key location, grain, oil, and manpower. But "do not dip your spoon into the pot that does not boil for you," cautioned one Romanian proverb. The kingdom's statesmen watched and waited.[22]

In August 1916, the pot finally seemed to boil. King Carol was dead, replaced by his nephew Ferdinand, much less enamored with German *Kultur* and married to Queen Victoria's granddaughter. Battlefield developments also made siding with the Entente increasingly attractive. The Germans were struggling to hold their ground at the Somme, and in Galicia the Russian Brusilov offensive devastated Austro-Hungarian forces. On the 27th, Romania declared war against Austria-Hungary with plans to take Transylvania. "Romanians!" King Ferdinand exclaimed as troops streamed through the Carpathians to free their "brothers beyond the mountains." War had "shaken the old foundations of Europe," he announced. It had brought about the moment "awaited for centuries by the national conscience: the day of the union of the Roumanian race."[23]

Bucharest's pedestrians "radiate from their persons the news from the front," Harry reported to John D. Rockefeller, Jr. Life had "changed so much that it almost seems as though we are in a different country." As a foreigner, Harry was required to deposit his passport with military authorities, but he was not interned like German, Turkish, Bulgarian, and Austro-Hungarian men. He felt "happy to be here and witness the development of the so-called Balkan situation which for the moment is the most interesting event in Europe."[24]

The euphoria proved short lived. Coming to the aid of their allies, the Germans declared war against Romania, sending reinforcements that halted the advance into Transylvania. At the same time, a multinational army commanded by the German Field Marshal August von Mackensen pressed north from Bulgaria, opening up an unexpected two-front war for Romania's determined but inexperienced army. The capital became a prime target. Though it had no military value, defeating "Festung Bukarest," as the Germans called it, would send a message that the Central Powers had not been demoralized by recent setbacks elsewhere. Airplanes and zeppelins began bombing the city days after Romania joined the war.[25]

Harry at first found the bombardments "extremely interesting to watch." But as the "fearful and monotonous killing" intensified—producing four hundred casualties during one September day alone—his fascination faded. The city had no air raid sirens or antiaircraft defenses. Policemen simply blew their whistles to signal the daily attacks. The top floors of hotels went vacant, and at night, residents used candles behind windows pasted over with black paper.[26]

With "almost no distractions except bombardments," time dragged on for Harry. But slowly it also revealed how much the conflict had fundamentally transformed the significance of oil. At the start of the war, both sides' armies had underestimated the importance of petroleum. As late as May 1915, Russian forces did not even bother to destroy the supplies and infrastructure of the Galician oil basin when they retreated from the area. But growing demand to fuel ships, planes, trucks, and submarines as well as looming shortages had since made the resource's signal role in victory clear. Oil had become more than a prized commodity, more than black gold. It was, as one French official put it, "the blood of the earth."[27]

With fuel in mind, von Mackensen took Constanța on October 22, inheriting that Black Sea port's enormous oil stocks intact, including the contents of Româno-Americană's storage tanks. British leaders fumed that Romanians had not destroyed the city's petroleum reserves before retreating. They eyed the Ploieşti oil fields further inland, some 200 square miles of derricks and refineries, thousands of bore holes, and years of hard labor that needed to be obliterated before the enemy got to them. With "no confidence" in Romanian authorities' promises to deny the Central Powers the rest of the kingdom's oil industry, the British Cabinet turned to Sir John Norton-Griffiths, a famed engineer who had been tunneling under German trenches at Ypres. Dispatched to Romania by way of Moscow, "Empire Jack" was ordered to destroy everything "at any and all cost."[28]

Arriving at Bucharest on November 17, Norton-Griffiths realized he faced a "stupendous task." Export traffic had slowed to a trickle since 1914, but that had not stopped Româno-Americană and other companies from continuing to tap their wells and even dig new ones. Wallachia was bloated with oil, some 700,000 sitting tons. Romanian officials, moreover, proved deeply resistant to the idea of total destruction, just as the British had suspected. Thinking ahead to peacetime, they wanted to drain the oil but preserve the tanks and pipelines, plug the wells rather than burn the derricks to the ground.[29]

The multinational composition of Romania's oil industry created further complications. Dealing with Steaua Română, owned by Deutsche Bank, was no problem. The Romanian government had already ousted its executives and expropriated its property. Winning cooperation from British firms also took little more than patriotic appeals and reminders of the urgency of denying fuel to the U-boats threatening to choke off Britain's supply lines. But the Dutch and especially Romåno-Americanā's representatives were stubborn negotiators.[30]

Tempers flared. British oil men resented that the Americans and the Dutch had made "immense profits" since 1914 selling benzene, lubricating oils, and other critical supplies to the Central Powers, while local British firms had refrained from such trade. The neutrals reasoned that they had broken no laws. The arguments dragged on for days, before vague indemnity agreements were reached, the details about which Harry and the British government would squabble fruitlessly for the next decade.[31] Then on November 23, von Mackensen's forces crossed the Danube and began racing toward Bucharest twenty-five miles to the north. Negotiation time was over.

Church bells rang incessantly as authorities ordered all weapons to be delivered to the town hall. By declaring Bucharest an open city that would not resist the invaders, they hoped to spare it a violent takeover. Still, women and children mobbed the US Legation begging for protection. "Conditions are serious and city is in a panic. People leaving by all kinds of conveyances," the Minister Charles Vopicka cabled to Washington. On foot or in luggage-loaded cars and carriages, refugees fled Wallachia for the safer Romanian province of Moldavia. By November 29 the outbound caravan included members of the diplomatic corps, the royal court, and other officials, who relocated the Romanian government to Moldavia's leading city, Iași. Ryland and other American oil employees joined the exodus, but Harry stayed behind as Standard's sole representative in the capital. Likely he flew the American flag from his window, as Vopicka recommended.[32]

Norton-Griffiths meanwhile set off with British oil men for Româno-Americanā's most productive wells at Moreni. The Romanians who greeted them there on the early morning of November 29 protested that setting the property alight "might roast a whole village and the people sleeping there." Issuing orders at gunpoint, Norton-Griffiths flooded the power station's basement with oil and ignited a few wells to see how they would burn. By nightfall, the conflagration was "quite out of control," but still his workforce pressed on the next day, filling the pump station with benzene, throwing lit straw into spillage around the tanks, and then retreating to watch the handiwork. Engulfed by flames the containers blew their tops or exploded sideways, plowing up the dirt in front of them as they hurled fifty yards distant. As fire tore through the surrounding fields, derricks collapsed on all sides, and black smoke choked the air. One 10,000-ton reservoir, the largest in Europe, burst its side joints and collapsed with an unceremonious whimper. At 2:00 p.m., the destruction party retired for lunch.[33]

From Moreni, Norton-Griffiths sprinted east toward other installations, steps ahead of the German Ninth Army converging on the area from the northwest. By December 2, the engineer had reached Româno-Americană's great refinery and machinery shops at Teleajen. Three days later, he was sledgehammering motors and igniting tanks at Ploieşti. Fleeing Bucharest, the French ambassador caught sight of the inferno in Prahova Valley. It wasn't just the earth burning, he marveled. Underground was on fire, too. Back in the capital, a sinister glow in the night sky would have revealed to Harry what had become of Standard Oil's first foray into overseas production. By noon the next day, December 6, columns of German soldiers paraded into the capital, singing:

Deutschland, Deutschland über alles . . .
Über alles in der Welt . . .[34]

On the heels of these combat troops came the officers of an occupation government—reserve men, former diplomats, bankers, and professors, many of whom had lived in Romania and spoke the language. With clinical precision they took over the city's public buildings as well as its best hotels and restaurants, wiring their new command posts together with confiscated telephone equipment. Notices plastered on city walls declared martial law and warned that aiding the enemy would be punished with death. Those stopped on the streets without proper identification papers were whisked away to unknown jails. Others faced house arrest or deportation to camps in Bulgaria and Germany.[35]

The Central Powers had conquered Festung Bukarest for the symbolism, but they also came for the supplies. Police moved door-to-door, gathering blankets, linens, clothing, and mattresses. Military supply officers confiscated typewriters, microscopes, and all manner of tools and machines. Requisition orders greeted readers when they opened their morning newspapers. The announcement of a prohibition on making or trading soap was particularly ominous. Sickness and disease were rife, and one of the first things the Germans packed up and shipped off were the local medicine stocks.[36]

Still, Harry had every intention of staying. The United States was not involved in the conflict, after all. Many of the 250,000 Americans vacationing or living in Europe when war broke out had fled back across the Atlantic, but thousands more had since arrived as relief workers and other kinds of neutral agents and volunteers. By late December Harry was able to travel to the oil fields to survey firsthand the British destruction of Româno-Americană's property. Discovering that what hadn't burned had been looted in the aftermath by former employees, he arranged for a German military guard to stand watch.[37]

Back in Bucharest, Austrian officers ensconced themselves in Româno-Americană's offices but not before Harry managed to secret away many of the company's most valuable operating records to a safe at the American Legation. Weeks later, however, the US Minister was pushed out of the city. In mid-January Vopicka sealed the Legation and departed, communications with the Romanian government in Iași ceased, and Bucharest's residents descended into isolation. Harry's parents and employers lost track of his whereabouts and wellbeing, and for the next two years, as his friend Ryland put it, he "lived in darkness."[38]

Matters of fuel and food would have preoccupied Harry that first occupation winter, which was so "bitterly cold" that it even impressed First Lieutenant Erwin Rommel, whose troops were thawing machine guns with alcohol while perfecting night infiltration tactics against holdout Romanian fighters north of Bucharest. In the capital itself, the customary firewood piles stacked against peasant cottages and then the public fences disappeared. So did the side street market stalls piled with sausages, dried eels, pumpkins, and poppy seed bread rings. As prices soared and black markets flourished, only those with savings and connections avoided destitution.[39]

That Harry not only survived this occupation but came out of it "a little bit fatter," as Ryland found him two years later, spoke volumes about his resourcefulness, negotiation skills, and cooperation with the occupiers. Not without reason, those who stayed in Bucharest instead of departing for Iași were viewed as Germanophiles, and given Harry's language skills and previous work selling to the Central Powers, he certainly would have come across this way. Due to Standard Oil's ongoing "affiliations in Germany," E. J. Sadler had not worried at all about leaving his twenty-six-year-old assistant behind. "Under no conditions," he predicted, would Harry "have any difficulty under the German regime."[40]

Moreover, with the rising geopolitical significance of oil and the destruction of Romania's fields, Harry was a necessary person. The occupiers determined to repair the 2,500 derricks and wells that had been burned or plugged and to revive the industry as quickly as possible. To do this, they brought specialists from Germany to supervise thousands of POWs and

Kaiser Wilhelm and his staff visit Romania's damaged oil fields. *New York Times,* November 25, 1917/Library of Congress.

civilian workers plucked from nearby villages in rebuilding and new exploration, ordering Harry and other managers to assist under threat of internment. By spring, debris had been fished from Româno-Americană's wells at Moreni and Băicoi, the Teleajen refinery came back online, and the fuel began to flow. All told, the Germans would reap three million barrels from the installations entrusted to Harry's care.[41]

But Harry's position grew far more precarious when the United States entered the war that April. The occupiers seized the keys to Româno-Americană's cash deposit boxes, gathered up all the records they could find, and placed the company under the direction of an official from the Deutsche Bank's subsidiary Steaua Română. Still Harry stayed, determining to smuggle updates about the company's property and assets back to directors in New York. He bristled as the new director scavenged equipment for Steaua's use, provided no receipts for reckless purchases charged to Româno-Americană's accounts, allowed its leases to expire, and ran up the electric bills. To his chagrin, he was even charged rent for the offices taken over by Austrian officers.[42]

Harry's prospects worsened further in early 1918 as the Bolsheviks pulled Russia out of the war. When word of peace negotiations reached still unoccupied Moldavia, the Russian forces helping to defend that Allied stronghold disintegrated, wreaking havoc as they went. Following the Treaty of Brest-Litovsk on March 3, Germany choked off the beleaguered region's communication channels, began liquidating Romanian companies with Allied capital, including Româno-Americană, and threatened to wipe the kingdom off the map if its negotiators did not surrender and meet the Central Powers' demands. As news arrived of stunning German gains on the Western Front, the US military mission and American Red Cross personnel evacuated Iași. Maybe to reassure himself as much as to comfort them, Harry wrote to his family that he was "well but lonesome":

> Report to the police once a month, but otherwise am not greatly restricted. Food expensive, etc. Don't know when I will leave. Always remember that I am in perfect health and thinking of you.
>
> Love and Kisses,
> Harry[43]

Shortly after he wrote this letter, but long before his parents actually received it, Harry was arrested for commercial espionage. Blocked from sending mail or telegrams, he had been using private messengers to communicate with Ryland and others outside of Wallachia. But when a Russian pilot was contracted to fly mail to Salonika, including Harry's correspondence with details about the petroleum business, the double crosser delivered the stash to German authorities instead. Harry faced "a good chance of being shot," as Ryland explained, when he appeared before Bucharest's military court were it not for Alexandru Marghiloman, Romania's leading pro-German collaborator, who intervened on Harry's behalf.[44]

Reversals in the faraway trenches also soon improved Romania's fortunes. By summer, the initiative rested with the Allies as arriving American doughboys helped to break the delicate stalemate on the Western Front. Romania shrewdly resumed war on November 10, 1918, the day before the Armistice, hoping for a share of the spoils. Already the kingdom had annexed Bessarabia in the chaos following the Bolshevik revolution. Under the peace accords it also acquired Bukovina and Transylvania. Greater Romania emerged from the conflict more than double the kingdom's prewar size and population.[45]

Nevertheless, old problems and new threats loomed at the start of 1919 as Harry stood in for E. J. Sadler as Româno-Americană's manager. At the beginning of the war, Romania's gold reserve had been sent to Russia for safekeeping. But with the Bolsheviks in charge, there was no getting it back. The value of the lei had plummeted, and a confusion of prewar currencies circulated through the cobbled-together nation, throwing its economy into disarray. Bridges, railroads, and crops were in shambles, and refugees from Poland and Ukraine poured into already congested Bessarabia and Moldavia. Inside one windowless train arriving at Iași, Minister Vopicka recorded, were women "so far gone with cold and hunger that they did not know their children were dead." Full-blown famine was only avoided by strict rationing and shipments from Herbert Hoover's American Relief Administration. Even the sheep were dying off. They had been sheared an extra time in autumn to meet wool quotas and could not endure the winter cold.[46]

Political instability also rocked the region. Militants' successes in Russia emboldened Romania's own leftwing activists, who formed a new Radical Socialist Party and launched a series of powerful demonstrations. By March 1919 Bolshevism had spread to Hungary, where Béla Kun proclaimed a Soviet Republic, until Romanian troops crossed the border in August and ousted him. The visibility of radicals and refugees drew fierce backlash from the right. Antisemitic student movements and gangs of hooligans proliferated. The shrill talk already foreshadowed the nation's later turn to fascism.[47]

The leftwing labor unrest reached into the oil fields, where only mass arrests prevented workers from taking over the wells. Harry also had to reckon with unrepaired wartime damages, unending transportation and supply woes, and unresolved indemnity agreements. Most threatening of all, with pro-German Conservative politicians discredited, the National Liberal Party dominated the government and hoped to reach their long-held goal to wrest the nation's economy, and especially the oil industry, back from foreign investors. While refugees stumbled amid states' new passport and border controls, businessmen faced growing threats of state regulation or even takeover. By 1920, the future of foreign oil companies in Romania appeared "most uncertain" as the government instituted prohibitively high duties on exports and a monopoly on domestic sales, unleashing rumors of the impending nationalization of an industry and "a commodity which is becoming so important to the entire civilized world."[48]

The atmosphere toward Americans in particular was "not sympathetic," one consular official reported. Liberals, who had long distrusted Standard Oil, renewed their intentions of thwarting the corporation's intention of "nabbing Romanian oil lands." Suspecting that government officials were intercepting Româno-Americană's correspondence with Jersey Standard representatives in Paris and New York, Harry requested to use the US Legation's diplomatic pouch.[49]

Oil was no longer one source of wealth in a commercial market. It had become the life force of states, the tipping point in wars. Anyone interested in profits might look elsewhere for lines of work less hitched to the fate of nations and therefore less likely to be caught in the crossfire of battling armies or expropriated by ambitious governments. All kinds of less complicated opportunities beckoned. Postwar Romania needed "heaps of things," one British traveler surmised while watching peasants reap corn by hand. US consular officials warned that British and French dealers stood poised to capture markets that had been monopolized by Germans before the war and urged their nation's businessmen not to "be left in the dark as to the possibilities of this country as a market for American goods."[50]

Such prospects fired the imagination of Harry's friend Ryland. "I have some big business ahead with goods from U.S.A.," he told his parents. "I want to get the sole agency in Roumania for Fords, Colgate's products, shoes, stockings, Waterman's fountain pens." Surveying the spread of radicalism from Ukraine to Hungary, Ryland wagered that "restoration of commerce is the best propaganda against Bolsheviks." Products flowing into territories under Allied control would create "a desire for order and sanity everywhere." Distancing himself from the volatile oil industry where "every obstacle is in our way," Ryland amassed capital for his own trading company. "There is a great deal of money to be made here after things get settled again and I want to be in on the start," he explained as he parted ways with Harry and Jersey Standard.[51]

Despite the oil industry's vulnerabilities, Harry stayed with his firm. In less than a decade he would sit on Jersey Standard's board of directors back in Manhattan. But Romania was not the last place he would live through sustained aerial bombardments. This war was not the last time he would collaborate with the Germans. And it was not the last time great oil facilities developed under his care would be burned to the ground by the Allies.

4

Tramp Trade

THE HATCH OF THE NO. 2 hold of the SS *Serantes* blew shortly after noon on a humid Saturday in July 1918, followed by a column of fire and smoke. Loaded with more than 10,000 barrels of Jersey Standard oil, the aging steamer lay anchored off Brooklyn's Bay Ridge awaiting customs clearance to sail for the Spanish port Bilbao. Submarine patrol boats, fixtures of the wartime harbor, rescued survivors dogpaddling between ribbons of flaming crude, while the Staten Island ferry steered off course to avoid burning barrels disgorged from the listing vessel's hatchways. The boat's cook, who had gone into the bay with his hair and beard ablaze, came out "as bald as a mountain eagle." Four members of the shovel crew were not so lucky. The Spanish stokers who had signed on to the *Serantes* in Vigo some months back had been caught in the shaft tunnel and presumed dead.[1]

"It was a pity," thought the ship's local agent Manuel Diaz Riestra. Especially to lose the oil. But the old tramp had "more than paid for herself in the last four busy years."[2]

Manuel hadn't yet founded the most important shipping agency to ply cargo traffic between New York, Latin America, and the Iberian Peninsula, but already he had been living the American dream. Or at least one version of it. In 1907, as a sixteen-year-old "student," he sailed to New York without his family and disappeared into its bustling crowds. A native of Gijón, the largest seaside city in the northern province of Asturias, the young Spaniard had left a region blessed by coal and iron-rich mountains, where emigration served less as an escape hatch for its poorest inhabitants than as a path chosen by some of its more enterprising. Information about faraway opportunities arrived at Gijón's waterfront with the coalers and fishermen taking refuge from approaching storms. Triumphant migrants returned after years abroad, building themselves grand villas and bankrolling the region's industries. The Hamburg America Line—*La Hamburguesa*—had become a household name by the time Manuel boarded its SS *Amerika*. He had reason to be hopeful. He carried more than $50 and a first-class ticket, exempting him from the invasive Ellis Island examination that awaited the ship's steerage passengers.[3]

Between the mid-nineteenth century and the start of the Great Depression, some four million Spaniards migrated to the Americas, outnumbering all the settlers who had come during all the centuries of Spanish colonial rule. Manuel relocated at the peak of this exodus, but his decision to go to New York stood out. Those who "crossed the puddle" during the early twentieth century more likely opted for Mexico, where the stable if dictatorial reign of Porfirio Díaz brought a renewed stream of arrivals, or Spain's erstwhile colony Cuba, where so-called *peninsulares* still dominated the retail trade and made up more than 10 percent of the population. Even more headed for Argentina. On the eve of World War I, Buenos Aires, the third largest Spanish city in the world after Madrid and Barcelona, boasted cutting-edge amenities and a death rate lower than that of New York or Paris.[4]

Manuel would have nevertheless counted his choice of Manhattan fortuitous. The city's small *hispano* elite proved easier to penetrate than the entrenched hierarchies of Buenos Aires. As late as 1890, New York housed fewer than 1,500 Spanish residents, scattered across lower Manhattan and Brooklyn. Artisans and merchants had been among the earliest settlers, patronizing the *bodegas* and *centros*, or mutual benefit societies, clustered along West 14th Street. After the turn of the century, the migration of all kinds of Spanish speakers quickened, bringing wealthy South American bankers and middle-class clerks as well as poorer Spanish and Cuban peasants employed in shipping, cigar rolling, and sugar refining. Female arrivals, out-numbered by men four to one, eschewed public life beyond the church or, when necessary, worked as domestics or in the needle trades. Men by contrast found plenty of camaraderie on the streets of *Nueva York*, especially in the northwest corner of Greenwich Village adjacent to the Hudson River docks, where *cantinas* and poolrooms flush with sailors served as clearinghouses for information about the local community and the Spanish-speaking world at large.[5]

Manuel furnished an early link in a successful migrant chain that drew to New York a host of other relatives and acquaintances who would become trusted business associates.[6] His own Atlantic crossing had been paid for by Marcelino Garcia, a childhood friend from Gijón six years his senior who had migrated to Mexico City before moving to New York. In exchange for passage, and maybe also room and board, Marcelino likely expected Manuel to work for him, an apprenticeship arrangement common among Spaniards in the Americas. Marcelino no doubt needed extra hands for his new Wall Street office, where he managed cargo trade for a Havana company that exported manufacturing supplies, grease, and coal while importing sugar, hides, and glue stock. This business granted him, and his soon-to-be business partner Manuel, entrée into the high-risk but potentially lucrative field of merchant shipping. Marcelino had been in the city for only five years, yet already he basked in professional and personal success. On the same boat that carried Manuel, he had arranged passage for a French maid and a Spanish governess. His American-born wife was expecting their first son.[7]

During his first years in New York, Manuel continued to list Gijón as his permanent residence, suggesting that like many *retornos* he did not plan to remain in the United States. When faced with census takers and other officials, he claimed to be an alien or a citizen depending on what seemed most expedient.[8] Spaniards of his generation, after all, had been raised to distrust the United States as a historic rival, profiting at Spain's expense ever since the 1810s takeover of Florida. Manuel had been an impressionable boy of eight during the Spanish-American War, when his nation suffered "*el Desastre*," the humiliating loss of its last New World and Pacific colonies at the hands of *los yanquis*. In the decades after 1898, Spanish intellectuals and politicians anguished over that defeat and dreamed of national regeneration. Little more than a century before, the Spanish empire had dwarfed Anglophone North America in terms of size, population, and riches. Spain's imperial project had been so much more virile, spiritual, and noble than the crassly money-driven ventures of the British and the Americans, young men like Manuel had been taught. Many harbored hope that the Motherland, *la Madre Patria,* might yet again become an influential force in the Western Hemisphere, defying Americans' presumptuous Monroe Doctrine and drawing Spanish-speaking Republics together into a powerful cultural and economic bloc, united by a renewed dedication to the heritage of *hispanismo*.[9]

Yet even after the Spanish-American War, *norteamericanos* continued to set obstacles in the way. American businessmen and politicians strong-armed governments south of the Rio Grande for economic advantages, intervened in elections, shelled harbors, and landed troops when necessary—from the province of Panama, whose secession from Colombia Theodore Roosevelt helped to engineer in 1903, to the port of Veracruz, bombarded and occupied on Woodrow Wilson's orders in 1914. Spanish newspapers criticized these actions, and tensions between the two nations grew. Meanwhile, Americans deflected attention away from their own expansionist history by propagating a myth about Spain's villainous record in the New World—a deceitful Black Legend, *la Leyenda Negra*, as the historian Julían Juderías labeled it the year the Great War began. Yankees were "the enemies of our soul, of our civilization," one Spaniard articulated a common sentiment. Migrants like Manuel—witnessing gunboat and dollar diplomacy up close, experiencing Americans' prejudices against Hispanic people and culture firsthand—understood intimately that they were living at the intersection of two long-competing empires.[10]

The outbreak of war in Europe in 1914 only intensified the antagonism. New York's newspapers speculated openly that the crisis would be American entrepreneurs' "golden opportunity" to edge out European traders and investors in Latin American markets. To solidify US political and military preeminence in the Western Hemisphere, President Wilson dispatched an army under General John Pershing into northern Mexico, fortified the newly opened Panama Canal, directed navy patrols to the shores of Honduras and Venezuela, sent occupying forces to Cuba, Nicaragua, and Hispaniola, and bought the Danish West Indies. By early 1917 resentments against the "Colossus of the North" in the Spanish-speaking republics were so fierce that Germany's foreign secretary, Arthur Zimmerman, thought that it might be possible to goad the Mexicans into invading Arizona, New Mexico, and Texas, and thereby bog Americans down in fighting far away from Europe's trenches. Revelations about Zimmerman's plot finally tipped American opinion in favor of declaring war against Germany. Manuel, a healthy twenty-six-year-old with no dependents, was swept up in that summer's compulsory draft registration drive. But he refused to serve.[11]

Men like Manuel who claimed exemption from the draft as foreigners forfeited their rights to ever seek US citizenship (he would later get it anyway). In Manhattan, superpatriots stalked the streets accosting such "slackers."[12] But Manuel would have found plenty of company with other dissenters down by the docks. Shippers complained bitterly about the British navy's cutting of German cables and searches and detentions of neutral vessels. Many longshoremen, the majority of whom had German or

Irish backgrounds, questioned Allied motives in the war, and sometimes even sympathized with the Central Powers. In New York harbor a steady stream of suspicious fires and explosions plagued ships departing for Allied ports. Later, government authorities would wonder about Manuel's activities during the Great War. Was that oil shipment on the *Serantes* destined for a clandestine U-boat refueling rendezvous or for transshipment to enemy territories, which were desperate by 1918 for every drop of fuel? Manuel's sponsor Marcelino Garcia was known to War Trade Board officials as an "intensely pro-German" Spaniard working for the city's leading Central Powers export operation G. Amsinck & Company, which had been blacklisted by the British in 1915 but continued to operate in New York under various subsidiaries.[13] At the very least, taking in the competing array of ethnic and ideological agendas at New York's waterfront would have taught Manuel that the spread of European conflicts to American shores would never be a straightforward affair. Such a raucous wartime democracy left plenty of room for maneuver.

It also opened up a window of opportunity for aspiring entrepreneurs like Manuel, eager to break into international shipping. Luxury ocean liners may have captured the imaginations of travelers, but cargo vessels were the lifeblood of the industry and the industrializing nations they served. Rising populations were fed from their cavernous holds, stuffed with grain from the North American heartland, the Rio de la Plata, and the Russian ports of the Black Sea. Local industries prospered on deliveries of Egyptian or American cotton, piles of Baltic lumber or tropical hardwoods, barrels of Mexican or East Indian oil. Maritime traffic made concrete the seemingly amorphous forces of modern capitalism, sprinkling across the globe coaling stations, repair yards, deepwater docks, and the service agencies that kept goods and people moving. It built and sustained empires. With almost half the world's tonnage at the turn of the century, Great Britain had dominated ocean trade routes, trailed by the United States, France, and Germany. Freighters set off from Southampton or Liverpool to provision settler communities as far away as Australia and New Zealand. They transported the guns and armies used to pacify the Sudanese, the Boers, and the Boxers, and they returned the precious metals, stones, and tea that muffled doubts about whether the violence had been worth it.[14]

Stripped of nearly all their captive colonial markets after 1898, Spanish shippers operated on the periphery of this global system, concentrating on European coastal trade and irregular tramping rather than scheduled service to the Americas. When migrants like Manuel headed for the New World they typically sailed under foreign flags. But World War I exploded demands for neutral shipping. Faced with requisition orders from an Admiralty in need of hospital ships and troop transports, British merchants ceded many of their distant routes. Its entire fleet swept from the sea lanes, Germany's Hamburg America Line, the largest in the world, lost all of its overseas property and would have to rebuild from scratch after the ceasefire. Greek, Scandinavian, and Spanish concerns sailed into the breach. Encouraged by the invention of war risk insurance, and freight rates soaring five to ten times what they had been before 1914, Spanish investors funded expanded lines and regular cargo services that would continue after the Armistice.[15]

Manuel gained a toehold share of this traffic, setting up an office among the other middlemen clustered around Manhattan's South Street Seaport. To earn a 5 or 6 percent commission, shipping agents like Manuel had to have wide-raging gifts of personality. They had to be ace troubleshooters who choreographed the loading and unloading of cargoes, big shots who dined with consuls, masters who tamed radical and unruly seamen, and sweet talkers who mollified customs agents and other port authorities. By 1918 Manuel counted himself the regular overseas representative for two Spanish lines engaged in modest tramp trade, trekking paprika and anchovies to the Western Hemisphere and hauling automobiles and typewriters back.[16]

The war brought welcome business for Manuel but also anguish, because the conflict tore apart his beloved homeland. Although Spain remained neutral, Spaniards disagreed bitterly about the war, exposing a set of political fault lines that would last for decades. Republicans, socialists, and liberal intellectuals saw Britain and France as guarantors of a secular and democratic Europe, and they cheered on the Entente. But most members of the clergy, monarchy, military, and economic elite championed Germany as a defender of order and traditional authority. Rightwing Spaniards despised the libertine French and the British occupiers of Gibraltar, along with the anticlerical, materialist, permissive nature of modern liberalism, or what one critic called "the principal cause of evil in the contemporary world." The Allied fight, another rightwing Spaniard put it, was nothing but a "foolish crusade for democracy."[17]

The debates in Spain soon led to bloodshed. While leading merchants, industrialists, and shippers reaped enormous profits during the conflict, the majority of Spaniards' fortunes deteriorated so dramatically that many could not afford basic staples. By 1916 and 1917, demonstrations gripped large cities. When the army declared a state of war in Madrid and machine-gunned protesters there and elsewhere, members of the ruling classes rationalized that only such drastic measures could preserve order. But unrest only increased as strikes and riots erupted in the nation's industrial centers and anarchists spread word of the Bolshevik revolution across the rural south. Peasants seized land and burned crops and estates. Women and children raided bakeries. By 1918, Spain was clearly sliding toward civil war. Spaniards like Manuel drew a firm conclusion from these events: a world ruled by the Allies would mean anarchy. Only a strong Germany stood in the way of such an appalling future.[18]

Germans encouraged this interpretation, presenting the Kaiserreich as a bulwark of the ruling order while portraying the Allies as sponsors of revolution. Dangling the possibility of territorial gains for Spain in Africa if the Central Powers won the war, the Germans were granted use of Spanish islands and ports to gather intelligence, refuel ships and submarines, and maintain a last line of communication and trade with Latin America. The conflict had transformed and enlarged the role of nonbelligerents. Far more than passive bystanders, they had become necessary players in the landscape of total war, clever subverters of international laws and norms, subtle tools to be used by those who recognized the new possibilities conveyed in the status of neutrality.[19]

German agents quickly applied these lessons in the Western Hemisphere, where the Kaiser's operatives, even before Zimmerman's scheming, had been working to provoke regional conflicts that would deflect US manpower and supplies away from the battle across the Atlantic. Spanish priests, consuls, and other elites living in the Americas proved willing collaborators in such schemes, because they believed that a German victory would enable Spain's rightful tutelage over Latin America and check the United States' growing power in the region. Spanish ship captains and other merchant seamen, many of whom had served in the Spanish-American War, spirited spies and secret correspondence past Allied inspectors, smuggled contraband in food barrels, and transmitted information about Allied ship movements.[20]

But as the odds turned against the Central Powers, rightwing Spaniards like Manuel watched events unfold in horror. Germany lost, and liberal democracy emerged triumphant. Only three democratic states had existed in Europe before the war. Afterward there were thirteen, including right next door to Spain in Portugal, where the monarchy had been overthrown in favor of an unstable republic. Orgies of Bolshevik violence and chaos meanwhile erupted in Russia, Ukraine, and Hungary. Banditry and godlessness seemed ready to take the Mexican Revolution in radical directions and showed signs of spreading to Cuba or Ecuador. All this free-wheeling tyranny of the masses, rightwing Spaniards like Manuel fervently believed, would destroy society.[21]

The war's unsettling aftermath also impacted Manuel's business. Following the Armistice, the shipping industry crashed. Too many freighters, including confiscated German vessels sold to the highest bidders, competed for reduced cargo loads. Freight rates plummeted, and ships sank into receivership. To better his odds, Manuel partnered with Marcelino Garcia. During the early 1920s, they secured a few corporate accounts, set up their first foreign office in Bilbao, and offered monthly service from New York to various Spanish ports, as well as shipments to Cuba and, eventually, other Latin American destinations. Ships provisioned by their company, Garcia & Diaz, carried electrical and automobile supplies, hardware, and dry goods to Spain and brought back olive oil, canned fish, and ores.[22]

Manuel's firm prospered after the war, thanks to growing trade between the United States and Latin America—to that expanding US influence that Spanish proponents of *hispanismo* decried so much. Aided by faster ships and newly established cable hookups, and with the might of the US Marines at their backs, Americans invested in transportation schemes in the Antilles, oil deals along the Gulf of Mexico, and mining operations in the Andes. New York City had maintained strong commercial links to Caribbean and South Atlantic ports since the early nineteenth century, due to its role as a leading financial center and the main transshipment point for cargo going up the Erie Canal or across the Atlantic. Now Americans even outpaced previously dominant British traders in the region, whose wartime retreat occurred just as the Panama Canal opened to traffic. Pioneering routes across the isthmus to New York, the Compañía Sud Americana de Vapores, a Chilean venture supported by American funders, finally cracked the British monopoly on long-haul traffic along the South American Pacific coast. This so-called Chilean Line became one of Manuel's and Marcelino's most profitable clients.[23]

By the end of the decade, Garcia & Diaz operated the largest fleet of ships, many of them German-built, plying between North and South America. Exploiting a coffee boom in Colombia, a sugar boom in Cuba, and the favor of rulers elsewhere who courted foreign investment and trade, the firm turned impressive profits even when other companies faltered. "The strides made by Garcia & Diaz in the South American trade," the *New York*

Herald Tribune admitted, had been "little short of amazing." Reporting on the firm's growing automobile exports in late 1929, Manuel gushed to the press that their business had not even been affected by the stock market crash.[24]

The political climate, too, gave Manuel cause to rejoice. The revolutionary chaos of wartime and its aftermath had been met almost everywhere with staunch reaction. In Spain, Miguel Primo de Rivera's coup d'état in September 1923 pushed back against years of leftist agitation. Primo aimed to make Spain into a great protector of civilization in a world under siege by what one Spaniard called "barbarous liberalism and its still more savage children, socialism and communism." Many breathed a sigh of relief when Primo jailed radicals and censored their newspapers. He promised to uphold traditional hierarchies, but by dissolving Spain's Cortes and Cabinet, he also intimated that more than old-fashioned monarchy and Catholic orthodoxy would be needed to vanquish the insidious forces unleashed by what another commentator called "the false Protestant Reformation, and the Satanical French Revolution." Primo's regime promoted a form of modern authoritarian salvation and national rebirth, moving beyond the mystical *hispanismo* that had appealed equally to liberals and conservatives in the wake of 1898, and toward a more strident and antidemocratic *hispanidad*, something much more exclusively the purview of the right. Manuel's partner Marcelino publicly praised this impressive leadership by Spain's new dictator.[25]

Events beyond Spain only boosted rightwing Spaniards' confidence that they stood on the cutting edge of history. In quick succession, coups aiming to stem the tide of red terror installed authoritarian regimes in Hungary (1920), Italy (1922), Bulgaria (1923), Greece (1925), Poland (1926), Portugal (1926), and Yugoslavia (1929). Militant far right groups meanwhile blossomed in Romania, France, and Germany. Faith in the efficacy of democracy wavered everywhere. In Latin America, antipathy toward the United States was growing. A Catholic revival washed over Venezuela, Colombia, and other places in the 1920s, reversing previous decades' secular trends. In Chile, elite youths flocked to reactionary grassroots movements. Six of the region's republics fell to dictatorships in 1930, and more would follow. The left's threat to private property, religion, family, sanity itself, many thought, had been blessedly thwarted.[26]

Aspiring to make Spain a leader in this new rightwing world order, Primo forged unprecedented ties to German military and intelligence agencies, offering fly-over and access rights, arms deals, and other secret collaboration circumventing Versailles Treaty prohibitions in exchange for assistance modernizing Spain's air services and armed forces. In January 1926—more than a year before Charles Lindbergh's transatlantic flight—Spanish aviators attended mass before the same altar where Christopher Columbus prayed on the eve of his historic journey and then set off on a record-breaking flight to Buenos Aires in a German-designed seaplane. Spanish emigrants in the New World greeted the aviators with rapturous glee.[27]

Primo poured resources and rhetoric into other kinds of outreach to Spanish America during the 1920s, taking census counts of overseas Spaniards, boosting diplomatic representation as well as better radio, telegraph, and shipping links across the ocean, and sponsoring a bevy of delegations, exhibitions, and cultural exchanges. Well-placed Spanish merchants in the Americas, like Manuel, were singled out as foot soldiers for advancing Spain's growing transatlantic ambitions. Said one government official: "They are continuing the work begun by the Spanish conquerors and making it possible, on some remote day in the future, for all the people of Spanish America to say 'We are Spaniards.' " In New York City a new Spanish tourist board, headed by Primo's son, and the Spanish Chamber of Commerce, of which Manuel would serve as president for seven years, took on the task of protecting Spain's image and the heritage of *la raza*.[28]

Outward appearances, however, gave little hint of these political engagements. Manuel looked a picture of the admirably industrious, upwardly mobile immigrant. A bachelor living in Brighton Beach in 1917, a decade later he had achieved uncommon wealth and social distinction. In 1919, he married Edith Gilmour, the daughter of a Scottish engineer who had relocated his family to Brooklyn from the island of Jamaica in 1898. The newlyweds set up house near Edith's childhood home in a middle-class neighborhood south of Prospect Park. By 1927, Manuel's success outgrew even this prosperous community. For more than $63,000 he purchased a French colonial manor in the affluent Westchester suburb of Pelham Manor, where he and Edith raised their two children. Keeping one of the most expensive houses on the block, they blended in with the neighborhood's executives, admen, and stay-at-home wives. They hired Black servants and kept society columnists apprised of their holiday travels. He hosted country club dinners. She entertained ladies for bridge.[29]

The Manhattan skyline viewed from Brooklyn, where Manuel's cargo ships docked. Eugene L. Armbruster/The New-York Historical Society/Getty Images.

The Great War had cracked the world open. Even far from the battlefields, it had stoked ideological divisions, upended the balance of power, rewrote the role of neutral parties, and toppled time-tested regimes. While Europe's leading nations stumbled, people in the United States seized the chance to expand their reach.

Interlude

New York to Bermuda

4 hours, 45 minutes
671 nautical miles
Partly sunny

FEBRUARY 21, 1943. LATE MORNING. Nervous first-time passengers on the *Yankee Clipper* surveyed their surroundings. The upholstered, davenport-style chairs, distributed through eight seating compartments, faced inward toward each other, not unlike in the first-class cabins on a European train. Roy Rognan, sitting with his USO dance partner and wife, Jean Lorraine, fixed a piece of tape dangling from a funny little handle labeled "emergency exit." To make it "a little more solid," he assured her. She wondered about the square porthole windows. Did they open? And where were the life preservers? Later, Jean and other survivors of this flight will suggest to investigators that travelers be told upon boarding what to do in case of an accident. Exits should light up in the dark, they will advise. It would be better if seat cushions could float.[1]

As the plane slipped away from the Eastern Seaboard, some passengers struck up fleeting friendships. Others kept to themselves. In one compartment, Harry wrote a letter to his wife, Rosamond—they had wed shortly after his return from Romania. Elsewhere, Ben Robertson chatted with the USO volunteer Yvette, who had been touring training camps in the United States and the Caribbean during the past year. It turned out that she was a Southerner, too—Elsa Harris Silver from Montgomery, Alabama. When she began to feel ill, he gave her his copy of Thomas Wolfe and told her to lie down and rest it on her stomach.[2]

The *Yankee Clipper* was not pressurized, but otherwise its interior felt roomy and comfortable, "virtually a 'Park Avenue suite on wings,'" the airline's promotional material promised. The walls had soundproofing insulation, and thermostats controlled the temperature, drawing heat from the engines. Smoking was allowed only in the central lounge. Some of the plane's finery—its carpets and decorative wall paneling—had been stripped out to save weight for wartime cargo loads, and its sterling silver and fine bone china had been swapped for lighter Lucite tableware. But art deco fixtures still lit the men's and women's dressing rooms, and the stewards' galley still stored everything needed to simulate the fine dining rituals of a luxury ocean liner from tablecloth clips and celery boats to oyster forks and an ice cream scoop.[3]

Pan Am likened flying on a clipper to more familiar experiences—train travel, ocean cruises, a stay on Park Avenue—because mechanical flight had been a reality for less than a lifetime. It was "still a miracle," as Ben put it, the crowning achievement at the end of a century of innovations in transportation. First locomotives and steamships, then automobiles, now airplanes had shrunk time and space and unlocked new kinds of life on the move.[4]

But human flight had done even more. To be no longer earthbound. To be airborne. It pledged not just to speed people to their destinations but to fundamentally alter their relationship to the planet and the other people on it. For some, a view from the sky broadened horizons. It revealed connection, interdependence. It nurtured cosmopolitan worldviews and farther-flung bonds of sympathy. But for others, looking down from above had unleashed an aloof sense of superiority, a drive for mastery over the depersonalized, invisible creatures below. It took human beings almost no time at all to reimagine this joyous invention, the airplane, as a tool of empire and a weapon of war. World War I dramatized the wondrously

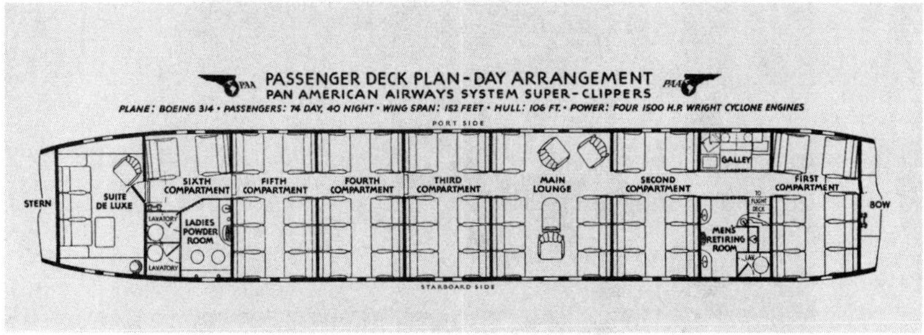

The *Yankee Clipper*'s passenger deck layout. Courtesy of Special Collections, University of Miami Libraries, Coral Gables, Florida.

destructive potential of air power, both to those dropping the bombs, like George's brother, and to those, like Harry, who found themselves under them. But this new war—in which the Allies and the Axis together would produce some 800,000 aircraft—stretched flight's potential to new limits. It threatened not just to obliterate human scale but humanity itself.[5]

An hour or two after takeoff from New York, Captain R. O. D. Sullivan, like other pilots on this route, climbed down the spiral staircase from the cockpit to have a smoke, meet his latest strange assortment of passengers, and put uneasy minds to rest. During these visits he "inspired real confidence by his cool, cheerful manner," Juan Trippe's wife, Betty, found when she flew with him in June 1939 on the first passenger flight across the Atlantic. He was, recalled another contemporary, "the picture of a jolly Irishman with a full face, a pug nose and twinkly eyes."[6]

Sully visits the passenger deck of a B-314. The Pan Am Historical Foundation.

Sully had played a role in each step of Pan Am's rapid expansion as the first successful US overseas airline. When Juan Trippe founded his company in 1927, American carriers lagged far behind their European counterparts in international air travel. Indeed, Britain's Imperial Airways, France's Air Orient, and Royal Dutch Airlines, known as KLM, were transporting mail and passengers to Karachi, Cape Town, Saigon, Batavia, and other far reaches of their nations' empires before a single US service ventured beyond the Americas. But Trippe and his associates—wealthy Wall Street backers, the army aviator Henry "Hap" Arnold, and Charles Lindbergh, who signed on as a consultant—had big ideas. After wrangling landing rights from Cuba and beginning a mail run from Key West to Havana, they set their sights on ringing the Caribbean and South American coastline with regular routes. Capitalizing on mounting concerns about the prospect of foreign airlines operating in the vicinity of the Panama Canal, Pan Am won US government backing in the form of a generous $2-per-mile subsidy from the Postal Service and State Department muscle, which, by the time Sully was hired, had extracted landing rights, tax exemptions, and other concessions from twenty nations south of the US border. With the help of a newly recruited batch of pilots and various on-the-ground agents, Trippe strangled or swallowed his competitors across the region. Posted in Panama, Sully distinguished himself maneuvering Ford Tri-motor land planes around the mist-shrouded volcanoes of Costa Rica, Honduras, and Guatemala as well as shuttling twin-engined Sikorsky S-38 amphibians back and forth to Florida.[7]

Trippe next wanted to establish transatlantic service to Europe, but because the British would not grant Pan Am landing rights in Bermuda, Newfoundland, or their other stepping-stone territories until they were ready to fly the route themselves, he seized instead on what seemed at first a pipe dream—forging a line from California to China, a distance of some 8,700 miles, more than four times the length of the world's longest existing air service flown by French mail pilots between Dakar and Natal. Nothing about the plan was safe. More than a dozen fliers had already died trying to cross the Pacific. And the shortest path, north via Alaska, Siberia, and Japan, posed weather too harsh for passenger traffic as well as the impossible task of securing landing rights from the Soviets and the Japanese.[8]

Instead Trippe decided his seaplanes would blaze straight across the ocean's expansive middle, island-hopping through US imperial domain. On the first leg from San Francisco Bay to Honolulu, Sully and the other crewmembers chosen to make the survey flights would have to learn how to make their fuel last more than eighteen hours against a headwind. From there they would need to travel over thousands more miles of trackless water to locate the pinprick islands of Midway and Wake, neither of which had suitable landing areas yet, before pressing on to Guam and the Philippines. Trippe secured assistance from the navy, which offered the use of its Pacific air stations, and from the Glenn L. Martin aircraft company, which promised to develop an oceangoing seaplane fit for the route. In March 1935 he dispatched a construction crew on a chartered steamer, loaded with windmills, generators, furniture, stoves, timber, and other cargo, to build a string of docks, radio stations, and other specialized facilities in some of the most remote parts of the world. Those who set sail from San Francisco's Pier 22 on the SS *North Haven*, along with the Chinese servants and Hawaiian powderman they recruited on O'ahu, faced a daunting task. At Midway, they were greeted only by a small staff manning the island's lonely cable station. At Wake, they found nothing but birds, thick underbrush, and an abandoned Japanese fishing hut.[9]

The subsequent test flights that year, undertaken by Pan Am's senior pilot Ed Musick and Sully, second in command, fired imaginations across the Pacific. Well-wishers cheered from rooftops, bridges, and shorelines as the flying boats came and went on surveys that ventured, step by step, farther across the ocean. The largest crowds yet turned out along San Francisco Bay on November 22, when the crew gathered for their inaugural flight to Manila in the first Martin M-130, christened the *China Clipper*. Radio announcers readied their coast-to-coast broadcasts for send-off speeches, while an old-fashioned stagecoach trundled up next to the airship to deliver a cargo of historic mail. Sully and the others climbed aboard in matching navy-blue suits and ship captain's hats and set sail against a din of boat whistles, sirens, and smaller planes droning overhead.[10]

Postal payloads alone, however, would not make these ocean crossings profitable. As Pan Am's regular transpacific service opened in 1936—and as negotiations nudged Trippe closer to landing rights for a transatlantic network—the airline also needed a dependable stream of paying passengers, customers who had overcome their fears of crashing. Pan Am's public relations department went to work burnishing the image of the company's top aviators not as adventuring daredevils but sober professionals carrying out commonplace operations. Sully's subsequent statements to the press sounded preapproved, canned, as though the airline had issued comments on his behalf or instructed him what to say. Likely he made the same kind of comments while strolling through the *Yankee Clipper*'s first-floor cabin and greeting his guests.[11]

"It's no stunt," he had insisted before.

"Nothing out of the way . . ."

"It's faster than surface ships, and just as safe."

"Nothing to get excited about," he said.

"A routine matter . . ."

"Old stuff this."[12]

Not long after the lunch buffet the plane neared its target: a remote, coral-pink archipelago, shaped like a fishhook and less than 25 miles in length. Bermuda had long served as a winter refuge for Royal Navy squadrons, but recently it had blossomed into a veritable "Pearl Harbor of the Atlantic." A patchwork of troop barracks, seaplane hangars, fueling depots, and anchorages overtook the colony's oceanfront gardens. Cobblestoned lanes, once left to bicyclists and horse-drawn carriages, overflowed with American defense personnel, British sailors, and Canadian airmen on convoy escort duty.[13]

As the clipper began its descent and the islands came into view, the stewards passed through the cabin, handing out landing papers and blacking out the windows. The War Department required such security curtains whenever commercial planes flew near military installations. Sully brought the flying boat down on a large ocean inlet and taxied to the seaplane base on Darrell's Island. Little stood there besides a control tower, pier, gas line, and some mooring equipment shared by Pan Am and the Royal Air Force (RAF). Guards directed passengers to a small white shack for customs clearance, while inspectors swarmed over the craft and its contents.[14]

Bermuda's contraband control officers had their rummaging down to a science. They combed through a vessel's nooks and crannies and mined its cargo holds—in this case containing not only Frank's typewriter, Grace Drysdale's puppets, and Gypsy Markoff's accordion, but also express shipments of military gear, engine manuals, airplane parts, Bell telephone equipment, and more than 1,400 copies of *Time* magazine. Meanwhile hundreds of censors took charge of mail bags bound for Europe, sorting letters by language and genre, running tests for secret ink, and photostatting suspicious pieces before sending them on their way. Americans had at first protested these impositions, but three years earlier, after Bermuda's examiners began forwarding hundreds of useful tips to US intelligence agents each day—including intercepts of Manuel's correspondence with officials in Madrid—a form of clandestine cooperation prevailed. Pan Am followed an "elaborate scheme" to slip the island's security guards advance notice about the arrival of "questionable" persons or property to expedite the search process. This day, Sully received clearance for takeoff in under two hours. Topped up with gasoline, including four and a half hours' worth of reserve fuel, and with George, Tamara, Harry, Manuel, Frank, Ben, and the other passengers back in their seats, the clipper lifted off from Bermuda's waters just after 5:00 p.m. local time and hooked left into the wind.[15]

PART II

1920–1939

Barcelona, 1939. Photo by Winifred Bates, © Imperial War Museum, HU 33149.

5

Free Lunches

HE WOULD CARRY A BURGUNDY and gold-embossed passport, muddied with indigo ink, the stamps and scribbled notes of an international generation of bureaucrats, in English, French, Dutch, Thai, and Arabic. He would charm Syrian officials with cognac, bribe an Iranian border guard with an alarm clock, and have a roadside altercation with his chauffeur along the mountainous route to Tehran. He would see the inside of the quarantine station at Ramadi and the police headquarters of Hong Kong. He would carouse with RAF pilots in Jerusalem's King David Hotel and join a torch-lit procession to Bethlehem, singing hymns on a starry Christmas Eve. He would drink ice cream sodas in Karachi, grow a handlebar mustache in Thailand, be licensed to drive in Singapore, and spot a wild tiger in the Sumatran dawn.[1] An export agent tasked with selling American products in the Near and Far East, he would remake himself into a radio correspondent upon the outbreak of the Pacific War in 1941. But in 1923, he was still in Cedar Rapids, an orphan at eighteen, who had never left the Midwest or known the taste of beer.[2]

Frank Joseph Cuhel was born in 1904 to Czech-speaking immigrants from Moravia. He spent his childhood on the Iowa farm of his maternal grandparents, the Halvas, along with his widowed mother and three sisters.[3] The Halva homestead honored the seasons: fresh-baked poppyseed *koláče* rolls in winter; dandelions and sunburns in the spring; summers of crawdad fishing and homegrown sweet corn. The start of school was always "something to be endured." Yet Frank loved those days after the first frost, when cobwebs flitted through wind gusts but the sun still warmed his bones. Even

Frank Cuhel as a boy in Iowa. Courtesy of Michael Safranek/University Archives, The University of Iowa Libraries.

the "country style discipline" he periodically earned from his grandfather for skipping chores failed to douse Frank's spirits. Later—after he won second place in the 400-meter hurdles at the 1928 Amsterdam Olympic Games—he reckoned that he had learned to run so fast and jump so high by fleeing those beatings.[4]

Midwesterners like Frank may have grown up far from the oceans beckoning overseas adventures, but they were worldly in their own ways. Grain prices and railroad rates kept distant developments front and center in dinner table conversations. Commercial opportunities knocked in the colonies of Asia. Missionaries and YMCA directors returned from years abroad with notions about God-given duties in faraway lands. And newcomers from Poland, Germany, Scandinavia, and elsewhere poured into the heartland, sometimes bypassing the Midwest's largest cities for its smaller towns. Czech-speakers like Frank's kin formed a quarter of the

Cedar Rapids population, spreading out from Little Bohemia into other neighborhoods.[5]

To many, Cedar Rapids exuded youthful enterprise. Bisected by busy railroad tracks and clean-swept streets, surrounded by towering grain elevators, the place was "hustling in its progressiveness," said the local Chamber of Commerce. But others bemoaned it as "the American wasteland," as the journalist William Shirer put it, a place run by "standpat" conservatives who couldn't see past biblical doctrine and the grand old Republican Party, philistines who lionized athletes but not artists, and boosters who worshipped nothing but profits. "Get the hell out of Cedar Rapids as quickly as possible," the fellow native son and writer Carl Van Vechten had warned Shirer. Frank, who graduated from the same high school as Van Vechten and Shirer, shared the wanderlust of his hometown's critics but not their politics. Religion wouldn't stick with Frank past his childhood, but he would champion American business across the continents and vote Republican even in Franklin Delano Roosevelt's landslide 1932 election.[6] And small-town Midwestern sports, more than anything else, offered Frank a compelling way to understand the world as he came of age, one that would guide him through a life of international trade, empire, and war.

Just before Frank entered high school, the Halva farm faltered, so it was sold. The three generations moved to town, where Grandpa Halva took a job as an ironworker, and Frank's mother "worked out some." Frank "coasted along" without any particular goals besides taking on odd jobs to earn date money. With no father to buy him trousers, he was still wearing knee-length knickers at the start of 1921 when his antics got him expelled from school. He consoled himself by playing checkers and obsessing over girls. "I get a dandy from Betty," he confessed to his diary. Two weeks later it was: "Oh Boy, Rosalie." In the spring he hitchhiked to Minnesota to visit his uncle Godfrey, who bought him his first pair of long pants. But the charms of "bumming around" soon wore off. Grandpa Halva made him repaint the house. Things grew complicated with Betty and Rosalie. By summer's end, Frank was "more than ready" to go back to school.[7]

Religion began to organize Frank, as it did so many other young Americans. During his expulsion, he had lingered at the Cedar Rapids YMCA and sometimes taught Sunday school at St. Paul's Methodist Episcopal Church. The visiting gospel crusader George Wood Anderson inspired him by preaching about the need to read the Bible instead of dime novel "trash" and to become truly converted. "Dr. Anderson says that our young folks can catch the enthusiastic Christian spirit only by thinking Christian thoughts and by putting them into action in our Church Sabbath School and daily life," Frank wrote in his Sunday school newsletter. The church drew Frank with its message but even more, it lured him with its athletic facilities. He spent hours playing basketball in St. Paul's state-of-the-art gymnasium, and, when he returned to high school, its head coach, William Novak, encouraged him to pursue football and track. Washington High had no athletic field or gym, so Novak raced Frank and his other charges through Cedar Rapids' tree-lined streets, leading them to championships in track and field, football, basketball, tennis, and wrestling.[8]

By the 1920s, the United States had become such a sporting nation that it was easy to forget that, not long before, many Americans had doubted the value or even morality of athletics. Nineteenth-century medical experts had cautioned against the dangers of bodily overexertion. Ministers preached that celebrations of the flesh came at the expense of the soul. Games were for idlers. But turn-of-the-century political and religious leaders began to reconsider the merits of physical prowess and competition amid concerns that American men and boys were losing their "fighting edge"—that they were being feminized by women's influence in the church and at home, atrophied by office work, and out-bred and out-brawned by immigrants of supposedly inferior races. Shoring up White American manhood required rededication to "the life of strenuous endeavor," as Theodore Roosevelt famously put it. Building muscle, many theologians soon concurred, also built character. The body was not the adversary of the soul but its temple. Reformers prophesied that physical recreation would solve all kinds of social ills. It would corral youth away from dance halls, divert military cadets from drinking, and distract workers from political protest. What couldn't sports do! During Frank's adolescence, playgrounds, courts, and fields blossomed in city parks, near factories, at YMCAs, and in schools.[9]

Sports seemed so natural by Frank's high school years that it was easy to miss their ideological dimensions and the fact that they were only one of many kinds of organized physical activity. Instead of playing basketball at St. Paul's, Frank might have gravitated to Sokol Hall's well-appointed gym a few blocks away. Like American sports, Sokol organizations, which originated in Bohemia, aimed to build moral men and good citizens, but through tournaments known as Slets that centered on mass calisthenics, drills, and marches—performances of conformity and equality. American athletics by contrast had been hardwired with capitalist logic. Promising competition on a field of "fair play," they rewarded initiative and risk taking with personal glory. Track and field, said one coach, was a system of "survival of the fittest."[10] Athletics taught Americans to pick themselves up and dust themselves off when they failed, to work hard to best their opponents, not to question the rules of the game.

In 1923, Frank turned eighteen, and his mother and grandmother both died. Grandpa Halva "got lonesome for the old country" and went home to Moravia, leaving the Cuhel children to fend for themselves.[11] But Iowa produced no shortage of orphans who nevertheless made good, among them the baseball player-turned-preacher Billy Sunday and the engineer-turned-humanitarian Herbert Hoover. Frank kept running.

In large part due to Frank's performances, Washington High's track team took the title two years in a row at the University of Chicago's prestigious Stagg meet. By the end of his high school career, he stood as Iowa's first three-time state track meet winner and held the national interscholastic records in the 120-yard high and the 220-yard low hurdles. Area newspapers hailed him as a wonder. His medals and trophies decorated the shop window of Cedar Rapids' downtown cigar store. After winning three races at one national contest, fans hoisted him onto a table and declared him "America's foremost high school track man who would help Uncle Sam to win the Olympic Games."[12] After graduation, he headed east to try out for the team that would compete at Paris in the summer of 1924.

The Olympics did not feature his favorite event, the 220-yard low hurdles, but he qualified for the 110-meter high hurdle finals. At Harvard Stadium he dug a hole in his lane next to the other runners and crouched for the starting pistol, knowing that the match's top performers would sail for France in a matter of days. Frank's chances of being on that boat ended shortly thereafter when he clipped the first barrier and was disqualified. Determined to make Paris anyway, he signed up to work his way across the Atlantic on an oil tanker. Like so many other curious and carefree young Americans, eager to exploit the new century's travel possibilities, Frank had no need for fancy accommodations or first-class tickets. When he had to, he would ride the rails and stow away. A friend bid him farewell: "Don't forget to knock off some French poolong for me."[13]

Frank spent two weeks heaving rope and standing watch on the Atlantic Refining Company's SS *H.C. Folger*. With his new white sailor pants and budding beard, he thought he looked "awfully 'tough.'" He practiced shipboard lingo and learned words from the cook that he had "never heard before." He acquired a coffee drinking habit to stay awake on the graveyard shift. At dawn one morning, he watched a school of porpoises leap and play in the ship's wake. The first mate promised to let him steer on the open sea.[14]

Yet the food was terrible, and seasickness soon set in. Frank cleaned railings, polished brass, and coated rusty pipes with graphite. "But my biggest job is keeping out of sight so I don't have to work," he snickered to his diary. He received a "fine bawling out" for falling asleep on night watch and got caught sneaking off to his berth instead of washing windows on the bridge. The captain was "sore" at him. The crew laughed at his misfortunes. He inquired about a job in the galley, figuring that might be easier. The cook told him that he would not have Frank in his kitchen if he were "the last man on the boat." On July 4, he spotted an ocean liner bound for the United States and "sort of wished to be on it."[15]

But when the Cornish coast finally appeared on the horizon Frank felt like Columbus. Losing little time in England, he narrowly made the boat train to France, before slipping into first class with a third-class ticket and promptly drifting off to asleep. In Paris, he "fell in" with one of the American team's coaches who directed him to the Olympic Village on the city's outskirts. There, he recounted, "I met many of the boys and they set me right so I guess I'll stay with the team for a while." Sleeping on the champion sprinter Jackson Scholz's floor, sneaking into the athletes' dining hall for meals, and borrowing contestants' badges to get into Colombes stadium, Frank finagled complimentary front-row access to the best-attended Olympic Games yet.[16]

The Olympic Games had been revived in 1896 in hopes that sports could divert conflicts between nations into friendly rivalries. Proponents likened athletes to missionaries or ambassadors who would forge fraternities across borders. Expectations for the Games' peacekeeping possibilities—the notion that sports offered a "language common to all nations," as Frank's Paris roommate put it, and that skirmishes on the playing field could supplant violence on the battlefield—rode high in 1924, little over five years after the Great War Armistice. Nearly two decades later, even amidst another devastating world conflict, Frank would still cling to the notion that sports could foster "international understanding and goodwill."[17]

Yet utopian goals for modern sports sat uncomfortably alongside their obvious imperial roots. Americans mused openly about the potential of sports not only to strengthen their own nation's capitalist democracy but also to spread those values to other parts of the globe. Far from universal, competitive athletics had been at first the purview of White Christian men, invented and standardized in Great Britain and the United States and then quite consciously exported—cricket, rugby, and polo to British colonies, baseball to the US territories of the Caribbean and Pacific. A large part of the world's people "did not know how to play," insisted one proponent of competitive games. They had to be taught. Sports would be a means of social and political reconstruction in war-torn Europe, an agent of civilization in the vast reaches of the Far East, a rubric for ranking the world's people and judging their abilities, all according to the measures set by the sons of Empire. In the early twenties, the YMCA's foreign department dispatched seventy-five physical education directors to posts in twenty-five countries.[18]

Sports had also become an undeniable part of nation building and war making, even if fields, stadiums, and velodromes were not yet being used as detention centers and concentration camps. The US military incorporated them into basic training programs for millions of recruits during World War I, convinced that they would instill not only practical skills like grenade throwing and hand-to-hand combat but also other "soldierly values" such as focus under pressure and esprit de corps. Sports instilled a "brave and simple faith and binds man to man in links as true as steel," celebrated Douglas MacArthur, who, believing they had directly contributed to the recent Allied victory, made them obligatory for all West Point cadets during his tenure as the academy's superintendent between 1919 and 1922.[19] Frank, who would know and admire MacArthur, first as the head of his Olympic team in 1928 and again as the supreme commander of the Southwest Pacific Area in 1942, absorbed these same hopes for athletics, even if at first unknowingly.

Later, observing the island fronts where GIs battled doggedly against the Japanese, Frank's thoughts would crystalize. A "generation of manhood," he would write, discovered "the rudiments of organization" on the vacant lots of grade schools, where "the sore-heads and bad losers" had been "worked over by the lads who didn't like that sort of attitude." Young American men then further "sharpened their minds and ambitions" and "learned principles of conduct" on the football fields, running tracks, and basketball courts of high school and college. This upbringing had made them "physically fit" and "mentally equipped" not only for victory in the Pacific War, Frank imagined, but also for effective postwar leadership across the globe.[20]

Because athletic prowess seemed to say so much about nations' prestige, the occasion of the 1924 Paris Games inflamed as much as it transcended international tensions. The Soviets declined to participate in the capitalist ritual, and the Germans had not been invited. Arguments erupted during rugby, boxing, and fencing matches. Resentments ran particularly high against Americans, who won too much. "Animosity and bitter jealousy" marred the occasion, said the International Olympic Committee founder Pierre de Coubertin. He counted his final turn as the event's organizer a wasted opportunity.[21]

If Frank sensed these dynamics, he did not record them in his diary. When not watching track and field events, he loafed, napped, and gambled. Sometimes he ventured into the city center, determined to "do Paris up right." He walked for hours, gawking at "the queerest customs." He flirted with American girls on the way to the top of the Eiffel Tower, ate tarts until he was almost sick, and drank his first glass of wine, even though he did not like the taste. Getting lost one day, he grew "mad enough to sock the next Frenchman" until finally finding someone who "could speak American." Another day, he purchased gifts for friends and family and then squeezed his way onto the overcrowded bus back to the Olympic Village, sitting "on a fellow's lap," his arms piled with parcels.[22]

When the American track and field team embarked on a three-day tour of the Great War battlefields, Frank crashed that, too. Their chartered bus lumbered to Château-Thierry, where, the athletes were told, Americans had prevailed even though outnumbered three to one. At Verdun, where guides said some 300,000 French dead were never identified, Frank struggled to "imagine such a thing taking place." He photographed houses in ruins, disabled tanks atop regrown grass, and seas of white crosses. Later, while reporting on the use of field guns to dislodge Japanese forces on New Guinea, he would remember vividly these obliterated French forests, the way that acres of treetops had been shot off with unnerving evenness "as though a gigantic hedge clipper had been used." On the way to Reims Cathedral, he gave all his francs to a disabled veteran. But the field trip's horrors did not stop him from also appreciating its amenities. The French beds were "knock outs," and the food better still. The night he returned to Paris, he tucked into a delicious chicken dinner and then dreamed of a German air raid.[23]

The trip had gone so splendidly that Frank wagered he could hitch a free ride home on the Olympic team's ocean liner, the SS *America*. Trailing the athletes and looking as "Olympicish" as possible got him all the way to Cherbourg, but there port officials were crosschecking passports and ship manifests. "GOODNIGHT," Frank thought. He had no money, having lost his few remaining dollars in a game of blackjack on the train from Paris. But he was once again saved, in that way that young White boys so often expected. The head of the team, Colonel Robert Means Thompson, stepped in and arranged for Frank and a few other stragglers to work their way across in steerage.[24]

Frank didn't think he "belonged with any 3rd class immigrants," so he strutted on board as though he "had the best stateroom on the boat" and slept on the floor of a friend's cabin until a crew member shooed him down below to the waiters' dorm. For crowding up their room with his excessive baggage Frank's bunkmates dubbed him "the Prince of stowaways." Relegated to kitchen duty, he shelled peas and peeled potatoes, which proved not so bad, especially when he overslept the 6:00 a.m. shift start. He passed the days by "sneaking up to see the boys" and by "devouring about half" of the galley's food supply. If only, Frank thought, he could "be hungry all the time." But the easy days on the open ocean ended when the SS *America* neared New York Harbor, and the ship's officers ordered Frank into the brig.[25]

"Wow!"

Frank passed a long night in an airless cell. When the Statue of Liberty appeared out the windows the next morning, he took a picture of it through the bars. Port authorities recorded Frank as a stowaway but seemed satisfied to simply send him on his way. That left only one more hurdle to clear. He had stolen a formidable number of souvenirs during his travels: a half dozen ashtrays, two cheeses, an Olympic flag, and that most egregious form of 1920s contraband, liquor. At the docks, Frank waited for his moment, and then sprinted through the line of customs agents and disappeared into lower Manhattan. He spent the night in a YMCA dorm before train-hopping his way back to the Midwest. He was "pinched" and hauled to the police station only once for pulling "a side door Pullman."[26]

Back home, friends and mentors urged Frank to go to college in the East, where he "would see some real things." His athletic skills amounted to a "chance of a lifetime," his high school coach told him; the idea of staying in "little old Iowa" was "all bunk."[27] But Frank remained unsure. Indirection was an obstacle he had yet to overcome. Sticking close to home, he enrolled at the University of Iowa, not thirty miles south of Cedar Rapids.

He earned terrible grades during his freshman year. He ran up debts at his dining and lodging halls, violated the terms of his scholarship, got caught trying to con his way out of mandatory ROTC training, and went "to the dogs" over women.[28] "Use your head, kid," his older sister Ermengarde chided him. Frank's sisters mended and laundered the endless stream of ragged clothes he sent home. They advanced him money and baked him birthday cakes (he would forget to thank them). "You are the most thoughtless, selfish creature that exists," Ermengarde scolded when Frank failed to repay one of her many loans. "I suppose now that you have reached the mature age of 21 you have put aside all of your childish habits and realized that at last you are a MAN," she teased him another time, without any real expectations.[29]

Where Frank did inspire was on the racetrack. He was a bit short for a hurdler, with long arms, brown eyes, and a face like a baboon that earned him the nickname Bab. He developed an athlete's superstitious habits. When the team traveled, he always claimed his Pullman car's upper six bunk. Rumors told that he slept in a tracksuit, combed his hair with a cleat, and never walked but ran everywhere—that his dates had to roller skate to keep up with him. At meets he gave his legs pep talks. "Legs, hot diggety, we gotta be in there today." He sailed over the sticks and cinders. In between events he refused to towel off. "Feel like going," he explained, "when I'm slimy and dirty." Frank spent summers off from classes "looking around" and competing in yet more track meets. In 1925, he raced in San Francisco and El Paso, wandered into the Mexican interior, and then made his way to North Dakota with the harvest gangs. The next year, he drove with friends to the National Amateur Athletic Union tournament at Philadelphia before working his way to South America on a United Fruit Company steamer. By the end of his senior year, Frank had been the anchorman for the Hawkeyes' crack one-mile relay team, winner of three Western conference championships in the 220-yard low hurdles, and captain of the track squad. In 1928, he finished college, won the Midwestern Olympic tryouts in the 400-meter high hurdles, and sailed for the Amsterdam Games.[30]

"We are about to meet the enemy," MacArthur, as President of the American Olympic Committee, told Frank and the rest of the team as their boat pulled out of New York Harbor. He insisted that his charges "win" at Amsterdam. Others matched his intensity. The 288 Olympians on the SS *Roosevelt*, bragged one journalist, were setting off to "beat the world." The United States had reigned supreme at every modern Games, and this year's team just might be, he predicted, "the greatest of all."[31]

In Amsterdam, animosities surfaced just as they had four years earlier in Paris. The French team boycotted the opening ceremonies, because they had been blocked from practicing in the stadium the day before. With MacArthur's tacit approval, the athlete carrying the US flag refused to lower it before the royal stand as customary, creating a minor scandal. "I rode them hard," remembered the future general. "I stormed and pleaded and cajoled. I told them we represented the greatest nation in the world, that we had not come 3,000 miles just to lose gracefully." In the following days Americans squabbled with Canadians about judging decisions in boxing, lacrosse, and the rowing regatta. Audiences gleefully rooted for "anybody who can trim an American."

Women, allowed to participate in track and field for the first time, faced their own form of hostility. "They called us 'muscle-molls,'" one runner explained.[32]

Pundits predicted that in Frank's event the gold would go to his teammate, the 1924 Olympics champion and world record holder Morgan Taylor. Frank won his own heat, placed just behind Taylor in the semifinals, and then drew pole position for the championship, putting him only thirty yards from the starting gun. But he was slow off his haunches when it fired, and the other runners kept a furious pace in the first furlong. Rounding into the backstretch, Frank began to make up lost ground. He edged past Taylor into second place. But Britain's Lord David Burghley, running with flawless stride, beat him to the finish line.[33]

Overall Americans took home more medals than anyone else at Amsterdam, setting seventeen new Olympic records. "Nothing has been more characteristic of the genius of the American people than is their genius for athletics," MacArthur concluded. Preoccupied with self-congratulation, many failed to notice signs of others' ascent. Germany, no longer banned from participating, outscored the United States in group competitions, and Japan, for the first time, took two gold medals. India and the Philippines, though colonies, fielded their own teams and placed in three events, raising all kinds of anti-imperialist possibilities. The Americans and the British had determined the rules, but in time they might be beaten at their own games.[34]

Frank hardly knew what to do once he had his Olympic medal. He toyed with the idea of cruising down the Rhine or trying to pursue law at Oxford. He thought about returning home but even more about a job offer he had received from the New York export house Dodge & Seymour. Founded in 1916 by Henry Trowbridge Seymour and the brothers Villard Atherton and Henry T. Dodge to funnel volume trade from the United States to India, Malaya, Burma, and other parts of Asia, the firm made its first large commissions selling Fords in British colonies and to Allied regiments stationed in the Middle East during the Great War. Touting the wonders of American service and marketing methods, the company soon handled a range of products dispersed to nearly thirty overseas branch offices—in Calcutta, Karachi, Rangoon, Singapore, Hong Kong, Osaka, and elsewhere. An opportunity to apprentice in Manhattan for foreign trade work in the Far East seemed to Frank "interesting to say the least." He wrote friends about possible openings back in Cedar Rapids, but they had not stumbled upon any great opportunities, even for themselves. Some were employed by their fathers. Others made a living with some insurance company or were selling real estate. He confessed to his sister: "I fear Iowa will not see me for some time but of course I'll be back—some day."[35]

Except for a few short visits, Frank never went back. He spent the next two years in New York, mastering the ins and outs of the hardware business, the properties of paint varnishes, and the overseas markets for cold cream and Ex-Lax. After hours, he topped off his "education" at Manhattan's speakeasies. In 1930, he relocated to the Philippines to take over Dodge & Seymour's Manila office. He would live in Southeast Asia for more than a decade, chased out only by invading Japanese forces. When the Allies were losing everywhere, when Westerners' precious colonies in the East were gone and they faced their greatest peril, Frank drew strength from a vivid memory of his youth back in Iowa, during a tough meet against Illinois, when the university relay team had gathered around coach George Bresnahan, and he told them: "Grit your teeth, put on a little more steam and you'll throw the hatchet right in his face."[36]

6

Unfinished People

IN REFUGEE-CLOGGED WARSAW, TAMARA'S MOTHER, Hinda, waited months for a US visa for herself and her two children, even after Tamara's father, Boris, pledged to pay for their passage to New York. The Emergency Immigration Act of 1921 had placed unprecedented restrictions on admission to the United States for "unassimilable" newcomers, not least Eastern European Jews. A last-minute exemption in the hastily adopted bill, which allowed resident aliens to sponsor close relatives, ultimately enabled the Drasins' entry.[1] But Hinda, carrying only the bare minimum of cash, faced extra scrutiny from border agents, who regarded unaccompanied women as especially likely to become public charges or prostitutes. Tamara and her mother had managed to keep themselves and Lasya alive in a war zone, but when they arrived at New York in June 1922, it was the assurance of Boris waiting with four furnished rooms that convinced immigration inspectors to allow them to land. The clean-shaven husband and father who came to collect them dressed in American clothes was barely recognizable.[2]

Somehow, Boris had made it out of Russia in 1916, even before the tsar's army collapsed. He had rented a room in a Bronx building that housed many Eastern European garment workers and found a job making high-end women's wear for the up-and-coming designer Hattie Carnegie. A self-described "radical" and "strong adherer to trade unionism," he immediately became, in his own words, an "active and faithfull member" of the International Ladies' Garment Workers' Union (ILGWU).[3] He sank himself into the city's socialist culture right as it reached a peak of influence.

The years Boris spent apart from his family had been astonishing, glorious, and awful all at once for New York's Russian Jewish socialists. Tamara's father did not need to travel to the Lower East Side—historic hub of the city's radical Jewish "Russian colony"—to soak up the heady political climate or to cross paths with spellbinding leaders such as Leon Trotsky. That revolutionary exile lived with his family only blocks from Boris in an apartment furnished on the installment plan. Fast developing a reputation for Jewish activism, their neighborhood buzzed with the prophesies of stoop sitters, rallies on behalf of striking subway conductors, and picket lines by angry housewives. Years later, Trotsky still remembered the Bronx women who overturned vendors' carts and accosted shoppers who violated their boycott against inflated food prices in February 1917.[4]

Emotions bubbled over into the streets the following month, too, when word arrived of Nicholas II's abdication. "A New Light Rises over Russia," Boris's ecstatic neighbors read in the popular daily *Forverts*. The US declaration of war weeks later somewhat dampened socialists' spirits, but mobilization also brought prosperity and leverage to the city's workers. The membership of Boris's union soared as the ILGWU won better wages and conditions in its shops, fast becoming one of the nation's most important labor organizations. Socialist candidates also drew more than four times their party's usual share of votes in that November's elections, and formidable strikes—some five hundred in New York City alone—followed after the Armistice, buoyed by news of leftwing insurrections in Europe. Enormous possibilities suddenly appeared on the horizon, even what Boris called "the great goal, the emancipation of the working class the world over."[5]

But leftist agitation also stoked tremendous backlash, which bore down disproportionately on the city's Russian Jewish immigrants. During the wartime "slacker raids" in September 1918, authorities arrested more than a thousand men suspected of draft dodging in a single evening in the Bronx, pulling them off street cars, nabbing them at subway exits, or plucking them from their theater seats. Shades of old Russia. Radical, Jewish, and unregistered for the draft, Tamara's father was all those things that stoked the ire of furloughed soldiers and other red-hunting vigilantes. The aftermath of World War I—when reactionaries continued to disrupt garment workers' meetings and harass socialists, and Attorney General A. Mitchell Palmer's raids targeted thousands of Russian activists for arrest and deportation—was a time when men like Boris cast glances over their shoulders.[6]

All the while, gut-wrenching information trickled across the Atlantic about violent chaos near Ekaterinoslav, where he had left his family. The unprecedented pogroms in Eastern Europe—and mounting antisemitism in New York—forced newcomers like Boris, who preferred to imagine themselves as "Russian," to contemplate the ways in which they were also "Jewish." In Odesa and Ekaterinoslav, acculturated city dwellers like Tamara's father regarded Yiddish as inferior to the more learned Russian; but in the halls of the ILGWU and the butcher shops of the Bronx it became a language of humor and necessity. In Ukraine, Jewish tradition had seemed to socialists as archaic as the tsar's policies, as oppressive to the individual as the capitalist system; yet the vibrancy of New York's leftist politics showed how it might become a source of strength.[7] Boris's union joined a broad-based Jewish campaign to transport relief to sufferers in Poland and the former Pale. Still, there was no sign of Hinda and the children when reports of Ukraine's famine began appearing in the local newspapers. By early 1922, the *New York Times* estimated, one million residents in his wife's childhood Poltava Oblast were starving. "People were eating bark, roots, hides, dogs, cats and even human flesh," the paper relayed.[8] The Drasins had much to tell each other.

How overwhelming it must have been for Tamara to be reunited with her father in New York. Was she excited or intimidated by the curious alphabet, the disarming smiles of strangers, the mysteries of subway turnstiles? Other newcomers disembarking from her part of the world marveled at the amusements of Times Square, as brassy as those back in Odesa, and at the poverty-stricken neighborhoods nearby—"even filthier than Minsk," the writer Vladimir Mayakovsky gasped. Alongside startling class inequality, the metropolis tolerated a growing complex of unspoken racial codes, some of which the Drasins would have found bewildering, others all too familiar. "A person who calls himself American is a white who considers even a Jew black and does not shake hands with Negroes," Mayakovsky noted. Even the great Russian poet Alexander Pushkin, he ventured, given his dark, kinky hair, "would not be admitted into a single 'decent' hotel or living room in New York." Prejudice against Jews, like the echoes of Jim Crow that dashed the hopes of Black migrants pouring in from the South, reverberated across the postwar landscape. Exclusion from certain clubs, jobs, schools, and neighborhoods, the subtle snubs of waiters and doormen, impinged more and more on the city's 1.5 million Jewish inhabitants.[9]

By the end of the 1920s, more than a third of those residents would live in the Bronx, where Boris shepherded his family to an apartment just south of Crotona Park. Since the subway's arrival in 1905, developers had crammed the area's vacant lots with multi-story brick buildings—five facades into every three standard land parcels—but the borough's residences were still a step up from the old dumbbell tenements of the Lower East Side. When the Drasins came to climb the four floors to their cold-water walkup, signs of Bronx summer would have already been in evidence: mattresses flopped onto fire escapes, the ice man delivering his strange frozen blocks.[10]

Immigrant children typically acculturated to American life with greater ease than their parents, pushed along by public schooling and their peers who mercilessly mocked "greenhorn" mistakes. But teenagers like Tamara struggled more than their younger siblings. They had arrived with an immature knowledge of their mother tongue, yet often proved too old to shed their native patterns of expression. Tamara found herself suspended between languages, grasping for ways to articulate her feelings. In English she phrased her thoughts awkwardly and spoke with an accent. Her writing in Russian, too, leaned on a limited vocabulary, which she supplemented with Yiddish phrases and English verb constructions. Adolescent newcomers like her remained "unfinished people," one Bronx contemporary surmised: "It took a very adventurous temperament to move ahead."[11]

Tamara, determined not to fall behind, finished elementary school in a single year, only slightly older than her fellow students. And an even more compelling education awaited her outside the classroom. School happened on street corners and tarred rooftops, where friends traded theories about love and sex. It happened at the movies, where girls learned how to walk and smoke and kiss. And it happened while listening to the radio. Even before she could sing in English, Tamara imitated the warble of Tin Pan Alley songstresses.[12]

The Drasins settled into the rhythms of working-class New York. They socialized with the neighbors and quarreled with the landlord. They embraced the fast-growing tradition of a camping holiday in the Catskills' "Borscht Belt." Like other aspiring couples, Hinda managed the home and Boris assumed the mantle of provider, winning election to the post of Secretary for the ILGWU's Local 38, a group of eight hundred couturier and theatrical costume tailors scattered across some seventy high-end workshops in Manhattan, Brooklyn, and the Bronx. The position earned him $50–$60 per week.[13]

But by the mid-1920s, the garment industry—and Tamara's family's prospects—faltered. Employers conspired to roll back shop floor gains won during the war, and the decade's simplified, loose-fitting dress styles allowed managers to lay off more highly paid finishers, whose skills were no longer needed to sew tucks or pleats and buttonholes on even haute couture gowns. In 1924, Boris mounted a strike to shore up the position of custom

Tamara and her mother on a Bronx rooftop. Special Collections and University Archives, Rutgers University Libraries.

dressmakers, but Irish, American, and German seamstresses, working for elite houses such as Bergdorf Goodman and Bendel's, proved impervious to the arguments of the ILGWU's Jewish and Italian organizers. They accepted lower-paying nonunion jobs for the cachet of working on Paris designs. Factionalism meanwhile tore the union apart. Women revolted against the group's male leadership. Radicals inspired by the Bolsheviks scorned the caution of run-of-the-mill unionists and formed disruptive cells. At mid-decade, far-left candidates swept the ILGWU's elections, ousting Boris from his post. Even though he regained his position in 1927, the union had almost been destroyed by Communists who plundered its treasury and allowed racketeers to worm their way into its locals during a long and disastrous strike campaign. To keep the organization going, loyal officers like Boris waived their salaries and lived off the generosity of family and neighbors.[14] Still in high school, Tamara had to think carefully about her future.

She might have prepared to become a teacher—by 1930, 44 percent of the city's new public school instructors were Jewish—or she could have looked for a position as a bookkeeper, a stenographer, a typewriter, or a shop girl. Immigrant daughters could secure such "pink collar" jobs if they did not look too exotic or sound too foreign, and office work offered steadier if not always higher wages than the clothing trades where her father worked. But the typical workplace offered women only a dead end. Employers viewed their presence as temporary, their aptitude as inferior. Clerical staff and department store saleswomen, like seamstresses, could expect little recognition or advances beyond the sexual variety.[15]

The best option, at least as far as most of Tamara's peers saw it, was to find a husband. Getting married brought autonomy from parents, agency in the community, relief from punching a clock, and the possibility of upward social mobility. Yet Tamara—like other proponents of women's rights who were beginning style themselves as "feminists"—harbored reservations about marriage. Running a household entailed its own sorts of drudgery but without the paycheck and career that could be a source of pride. To marry and save herself from wage labor (for few husbands would countenance their wives working if they could avoid it) would also mean abandoning her parents and brother, who grew to depend on her earnings.[16]

Tamara saw life on the stage as a way to pursue her talents without letting her family down. Maybe she could sing herself into existence and become "a person among people," as the writer Anzia Yezierska famously captured the yearnings of Jewish immigrant girls in 1920s New York. At parties, Tamara regaled neighbors with her music and made friends with drama types, who asked her to join a local theater group. "I became very excited about it," she admitted. Peering out at a patch of New York skyline through a small apartment window, she marveled at how sweet life could be.[17]

The seed for this ambition had been planted back in Ukraine. During Tamara's childhood, popular theater had thrived in the Pale, invigorated largely by scripts and headliners smuggled in from New York's renowned Yiddish playhouses. As government censorship eased and traditional Jewish disapprobation of acting faded in the early twentieth century, itinerant troupes trafficked in melodramas about migration and modern love, or light, singable operettas peppered with free-spirited waifs and Yankee slang. Sensing the emancipatory potential of the stage, young people snuck into beer gardens or fairgrounds to glimpse these touring shows and then staged their own imitation productions in stables or grain stores festooned with streamers. As aspiring performers, girls discovered they could speak up. Where they lived, what their parents did, how they worshipped finally seemed to matter less than who they could pretend to be.[18]

By the time Tamara settled in New York, transatlantic influence was running fast in the other direction. A series of landmark visits by Russian and Eastern European performers in the early 1920s introduced Manhattan audiences to cutting-edge continental techniques. Lower East Side and Greenwich Village crowds delighted in the stylized antics of Nikita Balieff's Chauve-Souris cabaret theater and the gloomy modernist productions of the Vilna Troupe. Dance enthusiasts swooned at the grace of prima ballerina Anna Pavlova. And, perhaps most profoundly, actors thrilled at Konstantin Stanislavski's revolutionary approach to dramatic performance, as modeled by the Moscow Art Theatre during its 1922–1923 US tour. Gone were the glued-on beards, the rubbing of eyes, gnashing of teeth, and other histrionics. In place of the star system, Stanislavski promoted ensemble work, immersing seasoned players and apprentices alike in intense rehearsal periods, during which participants learned to tap reservoirs of personal emotion in order to bring forth unprecedented sincerity on the stage. A new naturalism and psychological depth to performance promised to reveal higher meaning to scripts, forge authentic connections with audiences, and elevate acting to the status of a master craft.[19]

Performers inspired by these imports congregated near Tamara's apartment at the Bronx Art Theatre. Under the rumbling 180th Street El station, they experimented with novel forms of working-class entertainment, mixing comedy and poetry, English and Yiddish, crowd-pleasing farce and sharp social commentary. In that tiny, cheerful playhouse, Tamara made her professional debut, strumming guitar and singing songs from her childhood in a two-act revue spiced with titillating burlesque. The production's backers hoped to capitalize on the moment's Russian vogue when the show moved to Broadway in March 1927 as *The New Yorkers*. Though not yet graduated from high school, Tamara went with it.[20]

"The exotic numbers sung shyly by Tamara Drasin have an elemental rhythmic appeal," decided Brooks Atkinson, one of Manhattan's most influential critics, on opening night. But he was otherwise unimpressed with the revue. Cringing at the chorus girls' Bronx accents (stretching sure into shew-er), and a mess of awkward scene shifting and uncertain curtain work, Atkinson declared that "although amiable and willing," the novice cast was "scarcely up to the responsibility of entertaining cash customers."[21] The show folded in no time.

Tamara must have known that no feelings would be spared in show business—on amateur nights in the Bronx, giant hooks yanked unpopular performers from the stage to the savage delight of audiences—but she was determined to get another chance. She camped out in Manhattan waiting rooms, angled to catch the eye of casting agents, and tried to talk her way into managers' offices. Chorines in Florenz Ziegfeld's *Follies* or Earl Carroll's *Vanities* earned about $100 per week, so she auditioned for the chorus line. But she was "turned down flat."[22]

Amazed by the fierce scrutiny and competition endured by young women like Tamara, the entertainer Jimmy Durante speculated that if the average businessman "was as ambitious and willing to work hard as these girls, he'd be a success in no time at all." The singers and dancers who flocked to the booking houses near Times Square dreamed of economic independence and other opportunities. But on Broadway's stages and dance floors, women still had "a harder time than any of the men," and the prettiest "had the toughest climb," according to one revue promoter. A beautiful actress struggled to be recognized as smart and serious. If she did well, she battled assumptions that she had slept her way to the top. Rehearsal instructors yelled abuse at her or made passes at her in the theater wings. Talent scouts or "pickers" pored over her body, judging the size of her thighs and the shape of her breasts. The only way for a woman to make it was to be "discovered" by male producers, critics, and other string pullers.[23] In search of freedom, Tamara had stepped out of one patriarchal realm and into another.

By the 1920s, show business, hawking promises of more and better, stood out as one of capitalism's greatest triumphs. And vaudeville, where Tamara finally scored a role, was the belly of the beast. Bookers assembled performers into travelling bills like so many other standardized products for national distribution, and yet cleverly exempt from interstate antitrust laws. Vaudeville moreover remained uniquely impervious to effective labor organization. After a successful Actors' Equity strike in 1919, other entertainers enjoyed better contracts. But vaudeville managers' "Combine" used blacklisting and other ruthless tactics against strikers. The industry's moguls colluded to keep salaries down, taking advantage of the fact that stage hopefuls sold themselves in a buyers' market. Approximately 20,000 vaudevillians vied for 5,000–6,000 weekly engagements in the early twenties, and underemployment only worsened over the course of the decade. "No performer was safe and no contract was designed to protect him," said one promoter for Loew's bargain circuit. Even talents who were "better than good" sometimes went hungry. Meanwhile theater owners' profits soared. When Tamara went to work for the Keith-Albee circuit, its heir, Edward F. Albee, stood among the nation's wealthiest impresarios, worth an estimated $25 million.[24]

But as a Bronx girl plucked from the multitudes and chosen to tour with an outfit known as Eddie Pardo's *All Collegiate Show*, she was supposed to feel grateful. After all, vaudeville had offered a path from the Yiddish theater scene to wider acclaim for performers such as Belle Baker and Sophie Tucker, and a player who earned $75 per week netted three times the annual income of a factory worker. Tamara trusted that it would be a "great, great experience." In August 1928, she bounded off to Connecticut for rehearsals, laboring with the rest of the young cast to master a "jam-up" sequence of snappy songs and situations, opening with a tightrope routine and finishing with a "frolic" by the full cast. "They say that our lighting and costumes are all very beautiful. I should like to see myself and the others on stage," Tamara wrote to her family in Russian: "Say hello to whoever asks about me."[25]

When the show set off for engagements in Oklahoma, Texas, and Louisiana, Tamara resolved to "enjoy every day and take the most good out of everything." She stayed up late giggling with the other girls. She thought the clear sky and the open plains were good for the soul. "What's the matter with you big boy?" she teased her brother for not writing to her. She urged him to work hard so that one day he could go out and "see this beautiful country." "Be good," she instructed, "Love, Tamara."[26]

But the grinding schedule and unfamiliar landscape soon dampened her spirits. "You know the crowd isn't from our 'bunch' at all. I feel as though I wasn't quite in my own boots," Tamara confessed. Little more than a decade before, during vaudeville's golden age, entertainers on the "big time" circuit had performed stand-alone shows twice a day. But this was the "big small time," where female players made as little as $25 per week, pouring their hearts out three or four times a day to impatient spectators packed into 35¢ bargain seats. The customers now came mostly for the feature films that had become a staple of "combination bills." With only short breaks between shows, dancers and singers lived backstage, scarfing down food in dilapidated dressing rooms and dashing off letters to their families in between acts. They worked a "frightful amount," Tamara admitted, covering two cities per week by catching overnight trains after finales, only to begin rehearsals and debut performances the next morning. The cast received a rare day off in Tulsa, but Eddie's girls (not the boys) were expected to spend it promoting the show by raising funds for Red Cross hurricane relief. "Today we did not work. Praise God!" Tamara exclaimed when she finally received a break.[27]

By Texas, she was "exhausted as hell" and had deposited only $80 in the bank. No one received wages for rehearsal weeks, and when paychecks did arrive, at least 10 percent had been skimmed off for agents and the circuit's mandatory in-house booking office. Other expenses ate into what was left: railroad tickets, hotel stays, publicity material, props, and freight charges. Vaudevillians paid their own way. At each stop, performers tipped the stage crews and the baggage men who hauled their trunks to and from the theater. Managers could fine them at will—if their train was late, if they swore on stage, or if they otherwise displeased the house. "I cannot save a lot of money," Tamara admitted after many weeks on the road. It was colder down south than she anticipated, but she stopped herself from buying a good jacket.[28]

The trip also brought to the surface tensions with her parents. Viewing the struggle for success as a collective enterprise, Jewish immigrant parents commonly expected daughters to turn over all but a fraction of their wages, to work to put their brothers through school, and even to delay marriage if necessary. If parents could afford a daughter to break away, they expected her to present suitors for their approval and, even within secular households, to marry within the faith. The Drasins seemed to share these expectations. While Tamara toured, they demanded information about everything from her health to how she spent her money. In missives scribbled on hotel stationery, she tried to convince them that she took her responsibilities seriously. She related her weight—"so clearly I am eating enough"—and reassured them that she was putting every penny possible in the bank: "Don't forget that just a few things cost me a lot of money. I am not wasting money in vain."[29]

Even more, Tamara's parents fretted about men. Tamara was seeing "Harry," but others also vied for her affections. "There is nothing to worry about," she declared when her parents panicked that a doctor had asked her to run away with him to London. She dismissed her latest suitor as a little boy and a fool. "No girl can up and leave her work and fly to the end of the earth for no reason," she professed: "He's simply crazy." Her parents' lack of confidence disappointed her. "I was surprised that you are worrying, for I have not yet lost my mind, which you already know," she reminded them.[30]

Yet even as she sought to reassure Boris and Hinda, Tamara's own frustrations about the family's fortunes mounted. To stretch their shrinking income, the Drasins cut corners on their wardrobes, a difficult concession to make in the house of a tailor. "Buy Lasya a coat. I will send you the amount that it costs," Tamara instructed with growing authority. Repeatedly she complained that her mother did not have proper clothes. "I have had enough" of mama looking like "some kind of *shmendrik*," she groaned. The heavy obligations of an eldest daughter could breed resentment and exhaustion. "I don't know what will happen with us—if only we could grab onto something solid—there's no money, and there's still no money—I am already sick to death of this situation," she rambled in another letter. "Who does Papa think he is? Will he live by the union his whole life? Or does it all hang on me?"[31]

The outburst devastated Boris, who remained "offended" for weeks. Relocating to the United States and subsequent economic hardships had dramatically reworked the balance of power in their household. In Ukraine a prosperous artisan who kept his family in modest comfort could pay a *shadchen* to find a suitable son-in-law and provide a dowry, all of which reinforced his right to dictate the life choices of his daughter. In New York, where young people scoffed at the use of matchmakers and where daughters often brought in 40 percent of the household income, a father's place in the family hierarchy grew more precarious.[32]

Moreover, as Boris knew, the ILGWU was floundering. Two million dollars in debt, run from a shabby headquarters lacking even a telephone, the union clung to a mere fraction of the members it had boasted a decade before, and many of those were defaulting on their dues. Ready-to-wear, high-turnover fashions were putting more and more custom dressmakers out of work. Sweatshops paying piecework rates had reappeared across the city, and large manufacturers were fleeing the state for places with lax labor laws.[33]

Boris won for his members a 40-hour week plus time-and-a-half pay for Saturday work from the Couturiers' Association. In a last ditch effort he hoped to launch another campaign to unionize some five thousand other "terribly exploited girls," who made as little as $18 per week, hunching over their kitchen tables on Sundays to finish gowns that would sell for thousands of dollars. The drive would eventually enlist the support of society matrons, stage stars, and the New York governor's wife, Eleanor Roosevelt. By September 1930 it would culminate in mass picket demonstrations on Fifth Avenue and a general walkout. The strikers would scuffle with scabs and take beatings from the police—"Tammany Cossacks," leftists would call them—actions that would galvanize the ILGWU. But it would fail to make headway with the Couturiers' Association, which that November would decide it could make do without Boris and his striking tailors.[34] The following month, the Bank of the United States would collapse, wiping out the savings of 400,000 of its mostly Jewish and garment trade depositors.[35] A few months after that, Boris would relinquish his union post.

But as Eddie Pardo's tour neared its end, before all this happened, Tamara's thoughts lay elsewhere. The cast itched to reunite with their families before ringing in the new year of 1929. "But we are afraid to even think about that," Tamara explained, because their itinerary remained at the mercy of the syndicate's orders. "The people in New York have promised that they will let us know next week. Even Eddie doesn't know what will happen." Rumors threatened that they would be sent to California or the Midwest instead of returning to New York.[36]

The situation was even more dire. Vaudeville had finally lost its long battle with the movies. The previous season only three hundred of the circuit's two thousand acts had received regular routes. Others cobbled together four-week bookings at slashed salaries and endured weeks or months of layoffs. While Tamara was on tour, the Keith-Albee-Orpheum Corporation's chief stockholder, Joseph Kennedy, had dissolved the company's vaudeville production department and engineered a merger with RCA to reorient the business toward film. By the following fall, RKO Pictures would rank among the five biggest motion picture studios, and vaudevillians would find themselves out of work. Those who could migrated to musical comedy, nightclubs, chorus lines, or the radio, taking the genre's jokes and gags with them. Others wound up in soup kitchens and breadlines.[37] Tamara drifted into New York's unemployment pool at the dawn of the Great Depression.

7

The Silk-Stocking Revolt

GEORGE SPIEGELBERG CALLED THE AFFLUENT stockbroker to the stand. During the early 1920s, James Leopold had been arrested for reckless driving in New Jersey, for speeding on Staten Island, and for speeding in the Bronx. Nevertheless, when it came time to renew his license, he made a sworn statement that he had no previous motor vehicle violations. George asked him why he had done that.

"I thought the question meant something serious—an accident," the defendant explained. He appeared nervous, erratic.

"You didn't think speeding was serious?" George pressed.

"I do now—when I've learned my lesson. I never thought anything was serious before this accident."

In 1925 James Leopold had killed George's older brother, Frederick Spiegelberg, Jr., veteran airman of the Meuse-Argonne. James and Frederick had gone to New Jersey to watch the Princeton–Harvard football game. James later admitted to having "some drinks." Following the Princeton victory, they piled into James's car, the two men in the front, Frederick's wife and her sister in the back. James sped northeast on the Freehold-Manalapan Road. A light rain slicked the pavement as he swerved left to overtake a knot of traffic. Frederick's wife pleaded with him to slow down, but he accelerated to forty-five—or maybe it was fifty-five—miles per hour before the car skidded into a roadside ditch and smashed into a tree.[1]

James didn't think about Frederick at first. The women were injured. But then he turned back. "It was the worst walk I ever took in my life; one of the worst things I have ever gone through," he admitted. Some distance behind the vehicle lay Frederick's lifeless body. Police arrested James on site, but Frederick's family refused to press charges. The Spiegelbergs had known the driver since he was a little boy. George believed that his brother would still be alive if James had "exercised more care," but he harbored "no ill feeling" toward their childhood friend. He took comfort that James's license had been suspended.[2]

But when the Motor Vehicle Bureau reinstated James Leopold's right to drive less than a year later, George was furious. He wrote a letter to the Motor Vehicle commissioner Charles A. Harnett—a longtime ally of Tammany Hall, the city's Democratic machine—demanding to know how many times a Manhattan stockbroker had to be convicted before being removed from the road. Commissioner Harnett didn't appreciate George's insinuation of favoritism and called for a full airing of the facts.[3]

George had stood in his brother's shadow during the Great War, but after leaving the navy's observation balloon program in 1918 and earning a Harvard law degree he walked in the footsteps of his father, the prominent municipal court judge Frederick Spiegelberg, Sr. His elite German Jewish upbringing had primed him for a life of hard work, public service, and political engagement. It molded him into the kind of person who wrote letters to politicians and editors and expected his input to be taken seriously. And it made him, like his father, a Republican who distrusted Tammany Democrats. Poised to make partner at the Manhattan law firm Mack & Taylor, the twenty-eight-year-old approached the hearing at Commissioner Harnett's office with the intensity of a criminal prosecutor.[4]

Over several days, George solicited testimony from a parade of witnesses and fended off every move by James's counsel. This was not a case of double jeopardy, George argued, nor were James's prior traffic violations inadmissible just because they occurred before New York began issuing statewide drivers' licenses. The matter was simple, George contended. James had shown "complete disregard of life and property in violation of the law," and it was "unsafe to the people of this State to allow a man of his obviously neurotic temperament to ever again drive a motor vehicle on the highways." In the end, Commissioner Harnett agreed. He revoked James's license and the registrations for his two cars. Harnett liked to think that his office gave the same treatment to stockbrokers as to "the fellow on the curb." A poor man could not afford a chauffeur to drive him around if he lost his license, the commissioner reasoned, so a rich man shouldn't have that option either.[5]

George devoted his life to jurisprudence because he wanted to live in a society governed by the laws of the open courtroom, not the whims of bureaucrats and their backroom deals. He believed in the "fair interchange of ideas by fair minded men" and had no patience for "unsound argument" or fools. He subscribed to Alexis de Tocqueville's characterization of lawyers, with their orderly habits and respect for formalities, as the closest thing the American Republic had to an aristocracy and its best defense against what the French political philosopher had called the "unreflective passions of democracy." George would become a leading advocate for "character" examinations and other means to shore up the exclusivity of his profession. As he saw it, when left in intelligent hands, "the genius of the common law" mediated between competing interests without fear or favor. It conferred restitution on the wronged and caught up with the wicked. Later, when Motor Vehicle commissioner Harnett himself failed to live up to his promise to be fair to the fellow on the curb, the law would catch up with him, too. In 1938, he would be indicted for extortion and bribery.[6]

Like many elite lawyers, George's aspirations extended beyond courtroom advocacy into the world of governance. He entered the political fray at the start of a transformative era of partisan realignments. The nation's two major political parties had long counted among their ranks both conservative and progressive members, but slowly they were becoming standard-bearers for opposing ideological orthodoxies. Under the leadership of Franklin Delano Roosevelt and other New York reformers, the Democratic Party would emerge as a driving force for economic regulation and social welfare. George's own Republican Party, spurred on by the convictions of Herbert Hoover especially, would in turn array itself against the expansion of the federal government. George would join the resistance to Roosevelt's leadership, serving on his district's Republican committee and running for Congress in 1934 as an opponent of the New Deal—until world events, particularly the growing power of the Nazis, began to overtake his domestic political priorities.

Republicans enjoyed phenomenal success on the national level during the 1920s, controlling both chambers of Congress and sending three consecutive presidents to Washington, but in George's own city they were in trouble. Advocates of strong central government, including many progressives, once steered the Grand Old Party's direction, but Warren G. Harding and Calvin Coolidge sidelined them, stocking their cabinets instead with fiscal conservatives and entrepreneurs. This ascendant corporate tax-cutting, regulation-busting, budget-balancing "business of the American people is business" brand of Republicanism did little to woo New York's laborers or the urban poor, to sway newly enfranchised mothers concerned about school conditions and safer milk supplies, or to earn Black Americans' continued loyalty to the party of Lincoln. Manhattan had routinely sent dozens of Republicans to the state legislature at the start of the decade, but by 1926 their numbers dwindled to a handful.[7]

Voters broke instead for the innovative coalition assembled by the state's Democratic governor, Alfred E. Smith, a cigar-chomping Catholic son of the Lower East Side, who melded the neighborhood gladhanding style of Tammany with an openness to policy expertise. Smith launched a flurry of administrative reforms and social welfare programs, streamlining Albany's budget process, strengthening the state's workers' compensation program, and pumping resources into health facilities, schools, and other services. When Smith ran for president against the former Secretary of Commerce Herbert Hoover in 1928, his ability to draw backing from both elite Protestant progressives and the urban Catholic and Jewish masses would not be enough to win him national office, but it foreshadowed the mix of support that would propel his successor at the New York governor's mansion, Franklin Delano Roosevelt, to the White House four years later.[8]

Still, like many New York elites, George could not see how the Democrats' New York Tammany wing—the hurly-burliest of machines built on political favors—would ever offer anything but a corruption of how American governance ought to work. Its populism undercut the leadership of responsible professionals. Its profligate ways and increasingly experimental legislation imperiled free enterprise and individual liberties. Yet to George's chagrin, the New York Republican Committee's longstanding chairman, Samuel S. Koenig, had proven open to compromises with the city's Democrats, even imitating the patronage structures and transactional compromises of Tammany Hall itself. George, his law partner Walter Mack, and other prominent lawyers determined to oust the powerful "Koenig machine" in favor of Republican leadership that would stand pat against the Tammany Democrats out of "political principle." During their party's 1926 primaries, George and three other Koenig opponents caught "the regular organization members napping" and won seats on the 15th District's Republican County Committee by surprise write-in campaign. The Hungarian-born Koenig would not go quietly, dismissing his challengers as "blue bloods" who simply couldn't "reconcile themselves to being led by an East Side boy." But now on the inside, George and the others bided their time.[9]

An opportunity finally emerged when scandal engulfed the Democratic mayor, Jimmy Walker, and his Tammany-backed regime in the early 1930s. As the Great Depression washed over New York and budget shortfalls inched the city toward insolvency, calls for a state investigation into municipal corruption mounted, sentiments which Governor Roosevelt, increasingly eager to distance himself from machine politics, could not afford to ignore. He authorized the retired judge Samuel Seabury to inspect the inexplicably large bank balances of some court magistrates, a probe that quickly metastasized. Investigators dredged up evidence of ever more graft, stretching from the police department's vice squad and the corner bail bondsman to the city's permit and zoning boards, the backrooms of Tammany's own clubhouses, and, eventually, the mayor's office itself. Overwhelmed by the sensational public hearings and headlines, Walker resigned in September 1932. Amid the shake-up, George's faction finally ousted Koenig from his post and nominated the Republican Fiorello La Guardia to run for mayor on a platform promising an end to government by bosses, brokers, and other "fixers." Four years earlier, La Guardia had lost the mayoral race to Walker by a half million votes. This time—appearing as a Republican-Fusion Party candidate so leftist voters could back him without actually voting for the GOP—he and several other Republican candidates sailed into office.[10]

But just as fortunes swung in Republicans' favor in New York City, disaster struck the party at the national level. In 1928, Herbert Hoover had captured the presidency, thanks to a wave of prosperity (and significant anti-Catholic bigotry against Smith), but in 1932 his stay-the-course insistence on austerity, even in the face of unprecedented economic catastrophe, lost big to Roosevelt's New Deal plans for unemployment insurance, old age pensions, better regulations for the safety of the citizen, and higher wages and shorter hours for the dignity of labor. The Washington takeover by Roosevelt Democrats with an ambitious progressive agenda dismayed Hoover. He could not envision how their proposed programs and agencies could be anything but bloated, inefficient, and grasping. Giving regulatory powers to executive officials, he warned anyone who would listen, would unleash "bureaucratic tyranny." It would stifle innovation and lead to the "regimentation of men." It spelled doom for the liberal ideal of ensuring that man was "master of the state, not the servant." Building a social welfare apparatus in turn would obliterate personal responsibility and transform a nation of self-supporters into a population of "sycophants eating at the public trough." Whether it portended the nationalization of Tammany's improvidence and corruption or marked the road to communist dictatorship—both eventualities Hoover feared—the New Deal would, he was sure, "destroy the very foundations of our American system." The former president and his supporters girded themselves for a rearguard battle against Roosevelt and aimed to remake the Republican Party into a base for their operations.[11]

Bucking the prevailing political headwinds, New York's "Hoover men" resolved to resist not only the ascendent Democrats but also their own party's progressives, who had already "trailed off on the Roosevelt bandwagon" or who contemplated making peace with the New Deal. If the GOP was "doomed to remain in the minority for the time being," they reasoned, it should at least "form a 'decent minority,' without affiliation with the opposing party." In search of like-minded candidates for the 1934 midterms, they tapped George to run for the House of Representatives from the 17th Congressional District. His vocal support of the La Guardia administration also won him an endorsement from the Fusion Party.[12]

The 17th was New York's "silk stocking" district, a prong-shaped swathe of territory running from the high-rent properties of Lexington and Park Avenues east of Central Park, down to 14th Street between 4th and 8th Avenues, and north again through the Upper East Side. Since 1932 its had been represented by the Democrat Theodore A. Peyser, an insurance agent and ally of Senator Robert Wagner who had won the seat on an anti-Prohibition, pro–New Deal platform. But it was as likely a Republican-Fusion territory as could be found in Manhattan.[13]

"The New Deal is attempting the impossible," George proclaimed, accepting the nomination. He swore to be "fair to labor," and he did not oppose old age pensions, unemployment insurance, or "workable legislation for emergency relief," so long as they were set up to be "economically practicable." But he worried about inflation and out of control government spending. "These billions that are being used to prime the pump will have to be paid by the taxpayers," he predicted. George argued that Roosevelt's agenda not only endangered private enterprise but also threatened to transfer powers rightly vested in the judiciary to regulation boards, a recipe for tyranny by "political bureaucracy." It portended, he said, the "Tammanyizing of the Federal Government." Parroting Hoover even further, he declared that "Government must be the servant of the people—not their master."[14]

George earned the endorsement of the "Hooverite" Republicans Ogden L. Mills and Ruth Baker Pratt, who had held the 17th District Congressional seat before Peyser. George's close friend Frederick Warburg, son of the banker and philanthropist Felix Warburg, volunteered as campaign treasurer and set out to raise fifteen thousand dollars, reasoning that men like George were needed in Congress "if we are not to be regimented out of existence." The advertising executive Bruce Barton—the bestselling author of *The Man Nobody Knows*, which sought to convert businessmen to Christianity by portraying Jesus Christ as a master of salesmanship—agreed to chair his campaign committee and offer "some ideas as to the *tone* which a Republican candidate might adopt this fall."[15]

Brochure advertising George's congressional campaign. Courtesy of Ann S. Brown.

George hit the campaign trail as "A Practical Liberal with A Workable Program." He met with women's clubs and youth groups. "Sound government. Sound money. Sound business," cheered his campaign brochure, to "protect the American investor, safeguard the dollar and help the small business man." Behind the scenes, Bruce Barton worked his press contacts. The 17th district's incumbent was "a gentleman who can read and write but who, so far as I know, has very few other qualifications to be a legislator. We hope to turn him out and put Mr. Spiegelberg in," the advertiser explained to Helen Rogers Reid at the reliably Republican *New York Herald Tribune*. George, he promised her, would "be against no sound progressive measure but he will stand like a rock against the nuts." In his own speeches George blasted one of Roosevelt's least-popular policies, the National Industrial Recovery Act, for encouraging monopolies and limiting production "by government decree." Closer to home, he set out to tar his opponent as a Tammany loyalist. Peyser had discharged his secretary after she refused to donate part of her salary to a "kickback racket," George alleged. Peyser shot back that George knew full well that the matter had been investigated and dismissed by a federal grand jury. It would be settled in the voting booth. On November 6, record crowds showed up to their polling places.[16]

The opposition party typically made gains in midterm elections. Not so in 1934. Already a minority in both chambers, Republicans shed a further thirteen seats in the House and ten seats in the Senate. "Not since the disappearance of the Federalist and Whig parties," the *New York Times* proclaimed, "has a major political group received such a blow in this country as those bearing the label 'Republican' suffered in yesterday's elections." George lost his own race 42 percent to 54 percent.[17]

Armed with a fresh mandate, Roosevelt launched an even more ambitious round of initiatives during the second half of his term, which included the union-empowering National Labor Relations Act, the Social Security Act, and the Works Progress Administration (WPA). Seeking reelection in 1936, the president recounted for the crowds at Madison Square Garden the past four years' accomplishments. Unlike his Republican predecessors' "hear-nothing, see-nothing, do-nothing Government," he thundered, his administration had "rolled up its sleeves." He touted the New Deal's work on behalf of the underdog laborer and the cash-strapped shopper, the struggling student and homeowner, the beleaguered borrower and commuter, the blind, the crippled, the aged, and the unemployed. He talked of securing savings, electrifying homes, conserving water, controlling floods, reseeding the forests, and restoring the farms. Yet the agents of "organized money," he warned, were striving to undo these gains for the everyday citizen. "They are unanimous in their hate for me—and I welcome their hatred," he explained, because the recovery Americans were fighting for encompassed more than just economic recovery. It included a restoration of "justice and love and humility, not for ourselves as individuals alone, but for our Nation." Three days later Roosevelt trounced his Republican challenger Alf Landon in a landslide.[18]

After losing his bid for Congress, George continued "striving to make the scales of our blind goddess balance" in the courtrooms of New York. He prospered in his private practice, solidifying his reputation as an "ardent, thorough-going lawyer," and took a part-time appointment as an associate professor of law at New York University. Following a discreetly ended first marriage to the reporter and future award-winning historian Dorothy Borg, he married Helen Pisek, a Vassar graduate thirteen years his junior. The couple purchased an elegant, five-story brownstone on the Upper East Side. George demanded a household of tidy order and fastidious routines. A Japanese servant prepared the family's formal dinners. A live-in nurse helped to instill impeccable manners in the Spiegelbergs' two small children, Frederick and Ann.[19]

George also continued to recite the homilies of Herbert Hoover. Property rights came before personal rights as enshrined in the Constitution, he lectured one Brooklyn audience: "Unless property rights are protected there can be no such thing as personal liberty." He still regarded Roosevelt as a threat to this tradition, not least when the president unveiled his controversial plan to "pack" the Supreme Court. He could nevertheless take comfort that by 1938 his own party seemed poised at last for a rebound. Roosevelt's popularity was stumbling amid renewed recession and as more and more voters grew uneasy with the widening scope of New Deal reforms. In that year's midterms, the Republicans gained ground in Congress for the first time that decade.[20] Even in New York, birthplace of the Democrats' transformative new coalition, GOP prospects brightened. Tammany continued to hemorrhage support. Mayor La Guardia had coasted to an unprecedented second term for a Fusion candidate, and Republicans recovered control of the state senate.[21]

Yet all the while, disturbing developments were brewing overseas, events that would test the limits of George's partisan loyalties.

Germany's conservatives thought they could control Adolf Hitler when they supported his ascension to Chancellor in January 1933, but with power, manipulation, and outright brutality the Führer and his henchmen quickly undermined the frail democratic institutions of the Weimar Republic, disappeared their political opponents into torture cellars and concentration camps, and transformed the Reich into a one-party dictatorship hell-bent on purifying the German population and overturning the international order. National Socialists aimed to destroy all those values George held most dear. They disparaged the rule of law and twisted it to their own extra-legal ends. They perverted the cause of justice by carrying out arbitrary arrests, indefinite confinements without trial, and state-sanctioned theft and murder. They demeaned intellectual pursuits, running professors out of the academy and heaping books onto bonfires. And they obliterated personal liberty, demanding blind devotion from the ranks of the highest government office down to every last women's club and men's choir. Antisemitism was rising in many places during the 1930s, but the Nazis, as they steadily stripped German Jews of jobs, property, and citizenship, presented a special, existential peril.[22]

George must have been keenly aware of how fortuitous it was that his father had stayed to raise his family in New York when his grandfather returned to Germany. George did not identify as particularly faithful to Judaism—when asked about his religion in 1937, he said he had "none"—and his wife, Helen, was Presbyterian. Yet that would not have mattered in the Third Reich, where Jewishness was regarded as an inherited race, not a religious affiliation. Had George come of age in Germany, he would never have received his university post, and he would have been hounded out of the legal profession. Nazi civil service laws made it easy to dismiss Jewish employees, and gangs of Brownshirts dragged Jewish lawyers and judges from courtrooms, warning them never to return. Those few who continued to practice soon found Stars of David painted on their chamber doors. The Nuremberg laws, which forbade sex or marriage between Jews and Aryans, would have prohibited George from making a life with a woman like Helen.[23]

In 1938, the same year George's party fared so well in the US midterms, the prospects for German Jews took a particularly dark turn. With his rearmament plans well under way, Hitler was growing less concerned about international opinion and ready to embark on a series of territorial conquests to enlarge the *lebensraum* of the Third Reich. The Anschluss in March triggered swift arrests and graphic assaults on the sidewalks of Vienna and other annexed Austrian towns. These scenes, in turn, inspired an escalation of antisemitic attacks across Germany, culminating in November's state-sanctioned night of orgiastic violence that would be called *Kristallnacht*. As reprisal for the assassination of a Nazi official in Paris by a Jewish refugee, vandals burned every synagogue in sight from Düsseldorf to Dresden. Mobs dug up gravestones in Jewish cemeteries and raided Jewish shops and homes. They singled out propertied men for special abuse, dragging them into the streets in their nightshirts, hosing them down, spitting on them, bludgeoning them, and making them dance, before bystanding authorities carted them off to the camps. Those left behind endured a battery of new restrictions.[24]

If George had lived in Germany, by the end of that year he would have been barred from all libraries, theaters, and parks and forced to deposit his assets and valuables in a special blocked account. *His* driver's license and car registrations, without cause or so much as a hearing and notwithstanding his own scrupulous respect for the law, would have been summarily revoked. Levied with steep taxes and fines and excluded from nearly all remaining forms of gainful employment, men like him who did not find a way to emigrate were conscripted into compulsory street sweeping, garbage collection, and road work.[25] Nazism posed a form of madness far more extreme than Kaiser Wilhelm's militarism, which the Spiegelberg boys had so enthusiastically volunteered to combat in 1917. George would soon be willing to risk his life to defeat it.

This was not, however, a sentiment shared by many leading figures in his own party. The increasingly unbending Herbert Hoover insisted that nations, like people, ought to be self-reliant and ruggedly independent. He saw no pressing need for the United States to embroil itself in Europe's internal squabbles. Others dismissed the idea of the Nazis as a first order threat, even as the Wehrmacht steamrollered Czechoslovakia and Poland. Republican newspaper editors and members of Congress frequently spent more energy denouncing the Soviets and doubting the motives of the British than worrying about the Nazis. Nursing a blinding hatred for Roosevelt, many of them could not imagine following the president into a war that, they believed, would only serve as a pretext for his own self-aggrandizement, maybe even an excuse to suspend elections and assume dictatorial powers. Roosevelt's refusal to rule out seeking a taboo-shattering third term fed their fears.[26]

In January 1940, with renewed determination to seize the White House, New York's GOP stalwarts gathered at the Waldorf-Astoria Hotel for the

15th Assembly District Republican Club's annual gala. George watched the spectacle from the expensive box seats alongside other notables, including his former campaign chairman Bruce Barton and the presidential hopeful Thomas E. Dewey. For entertainment, the group had hired Minnie the elephant from Frank Buck's Jungleland on Long Island. Brushed with face powder, blue eye shadow, and a quick coat of red nail polish, and topped with a wide-brimmed hat, Minnie followed her handlers from the service entrance to the hotel's ballroom floor, where they proclaimed her that year's "Republican Glamour Girl." Minnie shimmied and tapped her foot to answer questions, predicting Republican victory at the polls.[27]

But the festivities disguised growing divisions between the party's many anti-interventionists—Bruce Barton and Herbert Hoover among them—and a small number of East Coast elites contemplating collaboration across the aisle in the interest of principle and national security. One month after the gala, the leaders of the previous war's Plattsburg movement, which had recruited George's brother, reconvened at New York City's Harvard Club to once again talk "preparedness": rearmament, universal military training, and aid to the Allies to ensure that war in Europe did not jeopardize the "safety and free institutions" of the United States. Their ranks included many Republican lawyers and judges. After France fell that June, more members of the GOP defected from the party line. George's preferred newspaper, the anti-Roosevelt *New York Herald Tribune*, came out in favor of intervention. Two high-profile Republicans—Henry Stimson and Frank Knox—joined the president's cabinet.[28]

Members of their own party, however, denounced them and stood firm against cooperation with Roosevelt. In September, even as the Luftwaffe's bombing campaign against London underscored the reach of modern war, the passage of the nation's first peacetime draft still faced considerable Republican opposition. Political loyalties die hard. That November, when nearly 90 percent of Jewish New Yorkers pulled the lever to reelect the president, George instead cast his vote for Roosevelt's less interventionist opponent, Wendell Willkie. But that would be the last time he supported a Republican for the White House so long as war raged in Europe.[29]

8

Twelve Mile River

"PRESS?" A GUARD ASKED. "PRESS," replied Ben Robertson without producing a pass as he strolled through the iron gates of the White House in February 1935. This kind of accessibility, Ben thought, offered a grand testament to Thomas Jefferson's ideal that all men were created equal.[1]

He joined other reporters in a cramped West Wing office full of chipped and cigarette-burned furniture. When a door opened at 4:00 p.m., he surged forward with the wave of notebooks into the Oval Office. While the newsmen jostled for position close to Franklin D. Roosevelt's desk, Ben stood back to admire the president's collection of model ships. He looked for them whenever he attended these biweekly press conferences. His favorite was a replica of the *Lightning*, the fastest of the legendary clippers of the 1850s, built for the Australian gold trade, a symbol of the "growing power of America," he thought, and the urge to strike out beyond the nation's shores. "Nothing finer for a man's inspiration," Ben concluded.[2]

He turned his attention back to the president's desk. Behind its incredible clutter—glass and metal knick-knacks, a pink candy box, a copy of Charles Beard's latest history—sat Roosevelt, smoking and beaming as the reporters filed in. "Well, boys, I don't think there is any news today except that I see Steve has a new suit," quipped the Democratic leader. There was that "famous personal touch." Ben approved.[3]

A year earlier Ben had taken a job with the District of Columbia's largest news bureau, the Associated Press, in order to gain a front-row seat to the unprecedented political developments transforming the nation and its capital. During those long years of Republican control Washington had not been the kind of place a journalist and Southern Democrat like Ben would have wanted to be. But Roosevelt's inauguration injected new purpose into the city. The number of accredited reporters clambering into its press galleries doubled. At the AP office on Pennsylvania Avenue where Ben worked, staffers swelled to sixty-eight.[4]

Covering the president and his cabinet members made Ben certain that his own sympathies rested with the startling innovations of the New Deal. Watching the forces of reaction and big business rally against every new initiative to protect the poor—seeing "the lobbyists at work, day after day, the same mugs appearing before committee after committee, unreasonable, opposing with all their great power, every single progressive measure"—had convinced Ben that the Republicans stood only for "property rights." The Democrats by contrast stood for "human rights." So did he.[5]

Those who worked with Ben said he had a "rare spark of human understanding." Shy but fiercely observant, he could find meaning in the lack of a wedding ring on Secretary of Labor Frances Perkins's finger or in a Congressman's untucked shirt. The broadcaster Edward R. Murrow called Ben the "least hard-boiled newspaperman" he ever knew. Female reporters singled him out for treating women with respect and camaraderie at a time when so many others discounted their abilities.[6] Maybe it was because he had no interest in courtship or marriage. "I don't care if I don't ever go to another dance but you know the reason," he confided to one close female friend. During trips to the Pacific and in New York he gravitated to the cruising grounds and company of sailors. At home in the South, confirmed bachelors of discretion still avoided the open censure of polite society.[7]

But beneath Ben's still surface lay passionate concerns. He fretted about the declining quality of the South's soils and the hardships of its small farmers. He wrote with empathy about the plight of New York's homeless men and Kentucky's coal miners. He was "very much the defender of the poor and oppressed," explained a fellow reporter, Helen Kirkpatrick.[8] Ben would lobby politicians on behalf of the welfare of the Catawba Indians and argue that the people of Guam deserved citizenship and representation in Washington just like "any other 21,000 Americans."[9] After at first opposing American intervention in Europe's conflicts, he would become an early, consequential voice calling for war against Hitler. Ben was not afraid to admit that he had gone astray and seek forgiveness. Growing up in the Southern

Baptist church made him wide awake to the ecstasies of revelation and repentance.[10] London's Blitz would cure him of his pacifist predispositions. Bearing witness to freedom betrayed in New Delhi would sweep away any remaining thoughts about the grandeur of empire and transform him into a champion of India's independence.

Yet never would Ben abandon his sureness that "the facts in the South were the facts" and that living with dignity in South Carolina required the strict rules of Jim Crow segregation. About other matters, Ben believed that sometimes society needed radical change. Even revolution, he said, "had its place." But with regards to the "race question," he insisted that "suddenness was not the way." Normally so interested in knowing people, so alert to the telling detail, Ben never pushed his portraits of Black Americans beyond self-comforting caricature. Easily tricked "darkies," freedpeople who wistfully remembered the kindnesses of their former masters, and "simple and friendly" Black servants flitted through his writings. Ben believed in the paternalistic duty to promote "the welfare of the tenants and of the colored people about us." He condemned lynching, of course, and like other White Southerners who fancied themselves liberals or moderates, he thought the rhetoric of the region's loudest race-baiters sometimes went too far. But in the end he cast his allegiance with his Confederate elders who had ridden with the Ku Klux Klan and helped to draft the state constitution that disenfranchised South Carolina's Black majority. "We never had the slightest intention of being dominated by former slaves," he explained. "We would give the black man equal protection under the law but not the right to vote." Like his forefathers, Ben didn't take kindly to outsiders meddling in his region's affairs—carpetbaggers, his people had called such intruders after the Civil War. Before the 1930s had ended—after sensing the growing potential for such interference by the interracial Democratic coalition building strength in the North—he would back away from the New Deal and, like his college classmate Strom Thurmond, emerge as an early proponent of White Southern defection to the Republican Party.[11]

One of Ben's favorite childhood lessons had come from his Great Aunt Narcissa, who took him high up a cliff to see the spot where the wide, clear Keowee River, flowing swiftly out of a forest of pine and poplar trees, met Twelve Mile River, a narrow creek, clouded red with clay. Great Aunt Narcissa wanted Ben to observe "how quickly the water of a little muddy stream could foul all the clean pure water of a big one." It was, she told him, "a wonderful example of sin." It was also a compelling metaphor for the myth of embattled white virtue and the stain of anti-Black racism on Ben's life and times.[12]

Born at the foot of the Blue Ridge Mountains in 1903, Benjamin Franklin Robertson, Jr., grew up in the same backwoods as his ancestors had for nearly two hundred years. His were upcountry people of Scots Irish stock, "hickory-nut homespun Southerners," he put it, who had come down over the first western trail to carve an empire out of the wilderness, "a divorceless, Bible-reading murdersome lot of folks" who lived on lands won by conquest from the Cherokee and the King of England. His Grandma Bowen told Ben never to forget that their family was "older than the Union in Carolina."[13]

Especially after his mother died, Ben hung on the words of his maternal grandparents, William Bowen, a gaunt and erect farmer with a beard as sandy as Robert E. Lee's who hated the banks and liquor, and Rebecca, his short, round, wavy-haired wife, who loved to dress up and listen to good preaching. At their hilltop farm—Ben liked to call it a farm, not a plantation—he found plenty of time to dream while wandering the cotton patches. This secure world, Ben's elders explained to him, had been hard won.[14]

Their stories tumbled out at nightfall on the Bowens' wide piazza against the chorus of crickets, first about the Civil War—about Great Uncle Joe, who had been killed at Fredericksburg, about how Great Uncle Bob took a bullet to the hip at Missionary Ridge. Grandpa Bowen volunteered only two days after rebels fired on Fort Sumner and fought all the way to Appomattox. He and others recounted their military campaigns in such loving detail that Ben sometimes felt as though he had taken part in the fighting himself. He did not imagine that embracing the Confederacy made him disloyal to the United States. He invested in a notion widely shared by many of his generation, that slavery had been "un-economical" and was dying off naturally in the middle of the nineteenth century, making the war between the states a needless one provoked by fanatical Northern abolitionists sticking their noses in other people's business and cavalier elites down in Charleston selfishly "bidding for glory"—not by Ben's well-meaning uplands people, who merely wanted "time to abolish our slavery." This was nothing more than a comforting myth. The South's slaveholding economy had been soaring to new heights during the 1850s, and its leaders thrilled at the prospects of further expanding its influence. The number of people held in bondage by Ben's own great-grandfather Reese Bowen increased by more than a half in the single decade before South Carolina became the first state to secede in 1860, reaching seventeen in all, including a "mulatto" infant.[15]

Nevertheless, on and on went the tales. About victories snatched in the Shenandoah Valley. Fearless defenders at Petersburg. The courageous gamble of Pickett's charge. Always they hurled Ben toward the same mournful conclusion: "We had lost, we had lost." The Yankees invaded South Carolina. They flooded the rice fields, destroyed the granaries, and set fire to Columbia. Great Aunt Narcissa declared that she hoped General William Tecumseh Sherman "burned forever in the hottest stove in hell."[16]

And that "was only the start of our disaster," Ben's family warned. After the war, Republican radicals in Congress aspired to strip authority from former Confederates, dissolve their rebel state legislatures, and, by extending the right to vote and hold office to freedmen, establish interracial democracy in the South. The enormous upheavals of Reconstruction, carried out by armed forces and other agents from the North, stoked outrage across the region but almost nowhere more so than in South Carolina, where formerly enslaved Black men suddenly made up 60 percent of the electorate. After "the North forced the Negro vote on us with the bayonet," Ben had been taught, "the worst elements" took control, inaugurating an era of rampant crime and corruption. Rumors of extortion, robbery, assault—unspeakable depredations supposedly visited upon good folk by scurrilous Northerners and freedpeople ill-prepared for self-government—grew only more exaggerated over time. But Ben had little reason to doubt them. During his youth, Confederate retellings of the past received the imprimatur of the nation's leading historians, and White Southerners wielded this history like a weapon, fortifying parks and town squares with statues of Confederates and commandeering schools, roads, and holidays in their honor. When Ben was twelve, silver screens far and wide lit up with D. W. Griffith's wildly popular feature-length film *The Birth of a Nation*, a tribute to the so-called Lost Cause set in Ben's South Carolina hills.[17]

Ben understood why his elders "had taken the law into their own hands." They had to "protect the white minority." During the last three decades of the nineteenth century, Klansmen and vigilantes known as Red Shirts—Ben's family members belonged to both—took to the upcountry roads. They intimidated, threatened, and murdered those who crossed them or tied wooden rods around their necks and threw them in the rivers to drown. One Black girl, who grew up in Ben's own Pickens County, could not forget the mob that hung her neighbor from a persimmon tree and would not let anyone take his body down. So he stayed there "till he fell to pieces."[18] Because even this terror did not stop freedmen from coming to the polls, White South

Carolinians eliminated precincts in heavily Republican areas after federal troops withdrew from the region in 1877. They concocted voting procedures impossible to navigate without the help of election managers and rigged the ballots. Finally, a new state constitution, which Grandpa Bowen helped to draft in 1895, implemented a poll tax and other requirements that removed Black voters from the state's rolls with surgical precision. South Carolina's former Confederates had doctored one of the nation's most fully realized white supremacist political regimes.[19] To Ben's kinfolks, it was Redemption.

This history, and the system of Jim Crow segregation that emerged from it, permeated every aspect of Ben's upbringing. He intuited from an early age that his region's strict codes of racial conduct—choreographing the use of front doors and back doors, the right-of-way on streets, the rules of browsing and buying in clothing shops—were essential for South Carolinians, Black and White, to plant their crops, pray, and otherwise lead respectable lives. "We knew what had happened to make it so," he reasoned. Like drawing room decorum, Jim Crow etiquette promised to take the danger out of mixed company. It made safe his casual childhood friendships across the color line and his cozy, philosophical kitchen talk with his family's Black servants.[20] Such intimacies took on enormous importance for White Southern liberals like Ben who did not want to imagine themselves as party to anything but a well-intentioned, benevolent system doing its best to address the most challenging of circumstances.

A yawning gap in fact separated the childhoods of South Carolina's Black and White children. Ben's upbringing shared many surface similarities with that of Benjamin E. Mays, future mentor to Martin Luther King, Jr., who grew up in a neighboring county. Born only years apart, both "Bennies" enjoyed ploughing the furrows and shouting in church, but otherwise they came of age in alien worlds. Whereas Ben Robertson's elders helped him trace his lineage back before the Revolutionary War and taught him that those who forgot the deeds of their ancestors could "achieve nothing worthy," slaveholders' dehumanizing recordkeeping had assured that Benjamin Mays would never be able to trace his ancestry. While Ben Robertson "lived like a wild bird" growing up, Benjamin Mays learned early that an "ever-present menace of white violence" loomed just above the polite chatter with bosses, shopkeepers, and landlords—if he didn't cede a sidewalk fast enough, if eye contact lingered too long, if the wrong words were said. During the boys' youth, their state hosted a lynching roughly once every four months. "The curse of heaven is on South Carolina," pronounced the nation's leading Black newspaper, the *Chicago Defender*, as droves of Black refugees fled its jurisdiction.[21]

School portraits for the contemporaries Ben Robertson and Benjamin Mays. Special Collections and Archives, Clemson University Libraries/The Edmund S. Muskie Archives and Special Collections Library, Bates College.

Besides heading north in search of a safer life, a menial job, and an hourly wage, Benjamin Mays had few options in front of him. Black students received only 12 percent of South Carolina's education funds, and only one state college allowed them to attend. Ben Robertson faced no such limits. He lay in bed at night, listening to the rumble of trains pierce the country quiet, beckoning him to travel the world and seize its seemingly endless possibilities.[22]

First, he enrolled at nearby Clemson College, founded by the Red Shirts leader "Pitchfork" Benjamin Tillman, a revered figure in Ben's household. At that White, boys-only school many of Ben's peers would signal their ascension to manhood by developing prowess on the sports field and with the "fairer sex." Strom Thurmond, for example, earned a reputation as an athlete and a "ladies' man of the 'first water.'" Ben, nicknamed "Millie," stood out instead as a "gossip fiend," a member of the Glee Club, and chairman of the Decoration Committee, with a "peculiar" habit of "prowling around" the rooms of underclassmen. "Fresh Meat is Ben's hobby, and Oh! How he can pull," teased his senior yearbook entry. Sexual experimentation among adolescent boys, in locker room showers or behind dormitory doors, if not too flagrant, still passed with little more than eyebrow raises so long as it didn't breach the color line. But as adults, men of Ben's generation who continued to enjoy the company of men would have to be much more careful. Sodomy had always been a criminalized sin in South Carolina, and the state constitution, which Grandpa Bowen helped draft, denied voting rights to those convicted of it. In the coming years those who succumbed to it regularly would be permanently set apart as pathological deviants, "inverts," "homosexuals."[23]

At Clemson Ben developed, among his other interests, a love of writing. So after graduation, he departed for the University of Missouri, which had just established the nation's first (also Whites-only) school of journalism. That program's founder, Walter Williams, taught Ben that "knowledge is power" and that, as "trustees for the public," those who joined this exciting new profession would have to be insatiably curious, accurate, and honest. Unlike the partisanship that had characterized so much newspaper content in the past, the new century's best reporting, Williams lectured, had to be "unswayed by the appeal of privilege or the clamor of the mob."[24] Once Ben had gotten what he could from the classroom, he emptied his savings for a ticket to Honolulu, where the *Star-Bulletin* was looking for a financial reporter. Two years in Hawai'i led to another reporting job in Australia, followed by six months working as a clerk in the US consulate on Java. Ben admired what "Dutch colonial genius" had accomplished in the East Indies. He pored over maps, dreaming about where he might go next.[25]

When he finally grew anxious to get back to the United States, he parlayed his travel writings into a job with the *New York Herald Tribune*. Though Republican in slant, the *Trib* was revered as a newspaperman's newspaper, boasting well-written, in-depth coverage, and one of New York's highest circulations. Dean Williams had instilled in Ben the importance of professionalism and objectivity, but the *Herald Tribune*'s city news editor, Stanley Walker, gave him license to write with voice and feeling. "Get the details down to the last drop," Walker implored his roster of young reporters before sending them out into the streets. Ben struck a wide beat from Chinatown to the Brooklyn docks. He investigated the legality of the one-piece bathing suit on the beaches of Coney Island and profiled the gorilla at the Bronx Zoo. He interviewed ship captains, pilots, pigeon fanciers, hostile cowboys, blind actors, and unhappy clowns.[26] He discovered that he could trade on his South Carolina manners. He flattered and charmed to get what he wanted "without a flicker of regret." White Southerners were supposed to have a special way with "Negroes," so when the *Trib*'s managers had second thoughts about hiring the veteran Black journalist Lester A. Walton, they gave his assignments to Ben instead. Depression was washing over the city, but Ben's boss promised him a raise. Ben figured that if he ever ran out of money he could walk home like Grandfather Robertson said he had done in 1865, after leaving a New York POW camp.[27]

Ben knew what he would be giving up when he left New York for the Associated Press in Washington—a byline, latitude to pursue human interest stories, or the freedom to write with any flourish. The AP's managers, ever mindful of wire costs and the different leanings of the more than 1,300 papers they served, demanded terse copy, free from any kind of "tittle tattle." But the chance to witness the return of Democratic influence to the nation's capital, at long last, proved impossible to resist. Ben gathered up more than he could say over the telegraph during his reporting, and what he couldn't put into print he poured into his private journals.[28]

Ben believed that by bursting "the industrial bubble," the Great Depression had thrown into question the leadership of Northern capitalists and would vindicate the values of his own region. Only one Southerner—Woodrow Wilson—had reached the White House since the Civil War. But Roosevelt, with his Southern running mate and cabinet members, seemed, at least at first, like the next best thing. Moreover, the Democratic landslide in 1932 catapulted legislators from the former Confederate states into important Congressional committee positions. Thanks to the powers of seniority and the Senate filibuster, no law passed without their express approval. They would bend the New Deal to their will. Grandpa Bowen had predicted as much before his death. "The country will swing to us again," he had assured his grandson.[29]

Yet Ben did not simply yearn to turn back the clock like his region's Agrarian intellectuals. He welcomed promises from Washington to improve lives and regretted that foes of the New Deal lurked at every turn. Attending hearings on the Hill, he watched the usual suspects scuttle forward to derail plans for public hydroelectric power, rural electrification, and other farsighted initiatives. Always the coal lobbyists, the National Association of Manufacturers, and other capitalist cronies hawked the same story. Increased taxation would ruin the country, they said. Industry would be driven into bankruptcy, they said. "Always they confuse themselves with the national prosperity," Ben seethed. They talked in general terms but meant merely to protect their own interests. Most of all, Ben hated those ultraconservative reactionaries, those Tories, at the Chamber of Commerce. Dispatched to cover the group's annual convention, he stood agape at the opulence of their Washington headquarters. No one here was his brother's keeper, he surmised. You knew it by the fortune-favors-the-brave slogans carved on the ceilings and the group's chosen heroes pictured in banners on the reception room walls. Sir Francis Drake, a "pirate," Ben gasped. Hernando Cortés, "the plunderer." Ben frowned: "What of those other virtues required of a civilized state—what of love and hope and charity. Nothing. What of the rights of the weak? Nothing." The Pilgrims and the Puritans, he was sure, did not intend for the nation to become "a memorial to the profit motive." Ben determined that never again should a big businessman be elected president, and he took comfort that Roosevelt "held that the people were more important than all of a nation's wealth."[30]

Still, these self-appointed captains of industry had allies in government. Ben eyed them from the press balconies of the Capitol building. "I wouldn't trust Bertrand H. Snell around the corner," he decided about the arch–New Deal opponent from New York. Or the clothing manufacturer-turned-Pennsylvania representative Robert "I object" Rich, who walked around with a copy of the federal deficit in his pocket, warning fellow House members that future generations would not know the freedom of their fathers. Ben wondered how much freedom there was in Rich's woolen mills.[31]

But the biggest, hollering menace to progress, Ben quickly learned, could be found at the Supreme Court. It incensed him to watch the bench's conservative justices void regulation of the coal industry, strike down a New York minimum wage law for women and children, and find against the Agricultural Adjustment Act, the National Industry Recovery Act, and other reforms. Only in this "mausoleum," Ben decided, could otherwise unconscionable arguments favoring the rights of the rich and the exploitation of the common man hide behind a strict interpretation of due process. Ben believed that the constitution was "broad enough, like the Bible, to have read into it whatever the changing times impel." But those without heart wanted to freeze it just as winter froze the Potomac. In his spare time, Ben amused himself by working on obituaries for the Court's so-called Four Horsemen—James Clark McReynolds, Pierce Butler, George Sutherland, and that "rock-ribbed reactionary" Willis Van Devanter. These "fossils" weren't dead yet. He just prayed they would be soon.[32]

Long walks helped to recharge Ben's civic faith. He liked to wander inside the Capitol's corridors, admiring the eagles and plaster stars while imagining the founding fathers tracing the same steps. From there, he strolled to the fountain in Union Station Plaza to catch sight of Columbus presiding in marble over the bounty of his new world. On the hike back to the Mall he gazed up at the Washington Monument piercing the heavens. To Ben the district's statues and stone edifices kept alive the memory of brave men "who stood for the people's battles," Northerners and Southerners alike. "There is freedom in this city," he decided.[33]

Yet Ben made no note of how the freedoms and pleasures Washington afforded to someone like him had come at the explicit deprivation of others. Racial segregation, long practiced informally in some of the capital's restaurants, theaters, and hotels, had crept into nearly every corner of the city since the 1910s, when Woodrow Wilson extended it to all government offices. Proponents of the policy portrayed it as a progressive reform that would promote harmonious workplaces and public order as well as cleanse the city of "race friction." This kind of "efficiency" also suited Wilson's Republican successors after World War I, since by then their party had traded its historic antiracist commitments for pro-business policymaking and imperial venturing. To those who believed in unbridgeable difference, having racialized elevators and lunchrooms seemed natural and advisable, like having gendered bathrooms.[34]

By the time Ben moved to Washington, New Deal programs and the expansion of the federal government had pumped some life and confidence back into the city's White businesses, but Black Americans shared little of this bounty despite having been hit hardest by the downturn. They were hired only for the lowliest kinds of labor and received only a fraction of normal pay. Overcrowding intensified as poor Southern migrants poured into the city's apartments and government offices gobbled up more of the city's blocks. In Washington's notorious alley dwellings—converted stables and shacks tucked behind the row houses just blocks from the White House—many lacked even plumbing or heat. Racial covenants pushed others out of more desirable housing as well as the city's best schools. Black residents made up about a quarter of the capital's population but two-thirds of its relief cases. It was a cliché that Washington was a symbol of American democracy, a beacon for world freedom. But it had become just as commonplace to call it out as one of the nation's most unequal cities.[35]

Ben wanted not to see any of this. The privilege of whiteness carried him through his day in ways he did not know or cared not to recognize. The easy access to the Oval Office that he celebrated depended on approval from the White House Correspondents Association, which welcomed even fascist propagandists to Roosevelt's press conferences but not Black journalists, who were barred until 1944 and who likewise "had as little chance of interviewing

Children play baseball in the back alleys of Washington, DC. © CORBIS/ Corbis via Getty Images.

a cabinet officer as of getting an interview with God," as Enoch Waters of the *Chicago Defender* put it. At the Capitol building, where Ben spent so much of his time, he sat in press galleries where no Black American had been admitted since Frederick Douglass. At the Senate restaurant, where he sometimes took his lunch, he enjoyed fine service reserved for his race since 1917. And in the evenings when he straggled home to Georgetown, he went to housing rented for only a half or a third of what Black tenants paid.[36]

The evil genius of Jim Crow was physical and economic, steering health and wealth, the best pay and property, to White people. But it was also psychological, forcing all to perform racial superiority and inferiority in every word and gesture. It warped minds. Maybe especially the minds of Whites, who read the hat doffs, bows, scrapes, and smiles of Black Americans as proof of a natural order, rather than the coerced charade that it was. Not on his walks, not during press conferences, not over dinners with White Southern friends—occasions for particularly unguarded talk—was Ben tested to consider and explain the easy peace he had made with segregation.[37] It would take a Nazi agent to level that challenge.

"What do you think of the black people being here?" Germany's Washington correspondent Kurt Sell queried Ben during intermission. Ben often spent his evenings at the theater, but this night in March 1936 was especially notable. The cast of George Gershwin's hotly anticipated jazz opera *Porgy and Bess* refused to perform unless the National Theater opened its Whites-only seating to Black patrons.[38] Sell's question was meant to provoke.

Ben had been "bitter" about the passage of the Nuremberg laws four months earlier and he was no fan of Hitler, but he enjoyed a casual friendship with DC's resident German reporter. The two often crossed paths at the State Department and other Washington headquarters. With the sudden remilitarization of the Rhineland that month, tensions were growing between their governments, but Ben did not really expect the situation to develop into war—at least "not this year"—and comradeship among reporters often transcended nation and politics in this way. Sell threw lavish parties for the city's correspondents, where over barrels of imported Munich beer they rubbed shoulders with American politicians and employees of the German Embassy. Ben didn't know that Sell was feeding off-the-record information to Nazi officials.[39]

Many German leaders were still hopeful of maintaining cordial ties with the United States. Indeed, they viewed their own unapologetically racist regime as an endeavor that echoed the society Americans had built for themselves. The Nuremberg laws had been inspired in no small part by American statutes that banned interracial sex and marriage, prohibited those deemed racially inferior from immigrating or naturalizing, and otherwise consigned people of color to second-class citizenship. White Southerners, National Socialists imagined, ought to have been especially sympathetic to Hitler's cause, having also experienced humiliating defeat and perceived unfair punishment after a needless war, and because they, too, knew the threat a supposedly intractable, unassimilable minority population posed to the integrity of the body politic.[40]

Black newspapers and civil rights activists never lost a chance to call attention to the parallels between the Third Reich and the former Confederate states, which the writer James Weldon Johnson branded the "Fascist South." But White Southerners roundly denied the comparison. So, when Sell asked Ben what he thought of Black audience members attending *Porgy and Bess*, defending Jim Crow would have meant admitting that he harbored a racist vision that paralleled that of the Nazis. Ben refused the bait. Many of his friends, he explained, liked to keep the races separate but equal and believed that "equality had nothing to do with fraternity." But, Ben told Sell, he believed that it had "everything to do with it." He was "very glad" to see Black attendees at the theater that night.[41] The German press correspondent wrested out of him what seems to have been the strongest statement he would ever make in favor of racial equality.

Indeed, during the next two years, Ben's enthusiasm for Roosevelt's Washington and the equalizing spirit of the New Deal would fade. That fall, after getting all he could from his AP job, he left it for the independence of freelance work and to contemplate new adventures. A certain restlessness stirred in him "like a rising wind" whenever he lingered long enough in one place. His most faithful pen pal—another lifelong bachelor, the sea captain Thomas W. Sheridan—recounted how he had "spent a month in Furious, Foggy, Frenzied Frisco" to satisfy certain secret "business." The two reminisced about their own "nocturnal visits" together in New York, and Ben decided that he, too, would sign on to the crew of some ship bound for the South Pacific. His previous vagabond travels, after all, not only spurred writing ideas, but also afforded a liberating kind of anonymity—to revel in the "lusty" poetry of Walt Whitman on a Java mountaintop, away from the judging eyes of kin and neighbors, to follow sailors down the alleys off Honolulu's King Street and into the darkness of a theater. Whatever furtive desires these excursions stoked, they could be tucked away in private fantasies or commemorated in coded text after he returned to South Carolina, as he always did. Sexuality, more than skin color, could be hidden. By 1938 Ben had settled in back into his father's home to write a first novel. Imagining a couple in their marital bed, he wrote from the bride's point of view as her gaze lingered over the body of her "strong young husband"—over "his eyes . . . his lips . . . his belly . . . his thighs."[42]

Spending time in South Carolina in the late thirties also put Ben up close to White Southerners' growing concerns about their own flagging influence over the direction of the Democratic Party. Delegates at the 1936 national convention had eliminated the two-thirds nomination rule in favor of a simple majority, making Southern blessing no longer essential for aspiring presidential candidates. That November, Roosevelt's nationwide support proved so strong that, for the first time ever, a Democrat would have won the election without any electoral votes from below the Mason-Dixon line. Other trouble was brewing as Black Americans in the North streamed into the party ranks. Only 25 percent of them had voted for Al Smith in 1928, but in 1936, Roosevelt won 75 percent over to the Democrats. The prospect that New Dealers were actively courting—and might soon even cater to—Black voters, combined with the growing power and ambition of civil rights groups and labor unions dedicated to interracial organizing, threw the future of Jim Crow into sudden doubt. Roosevelt himself had always taken care to placate conservative Southern Democrats but by 1938, he, too, seemed emboldened to challenge them. Declaring the South the nation's "No. 1 Economic Problem," he urged its "rehabilitation" and took aim at the region's most reactionary politicians by endorsing their more liberal challengers in that year's primaries. The moment proved radicalizing for White Southerners. A small minority moved left and began to imagine, even advocate for, a world without white supremacy. But far greater numbers, including moderates like Ben, rededicated themselves to it. To them, rehabilitation sounded suspiciously like Reconstruction. Warnings about the return of Yankee carpetbaggers splashed across the pages of Southern newspapers.[43]

Ben closely followed that summer's raucous Democratic primary campaigns—the only ones that mattered in one-party South Carolina. He hailed the wit and wisdom of old-fashioned barnstormers who countered hecklers with parables and bible quotes, spinning folk tales out of the hot summer air. Almost no one had mastered this art better than the short-tempered, tobacco-spitting, pain-in-Roosevelt's-side Ellison DuRant Smith. "Cotton Ed" Smith, a thirty-year fixture in the US Senate, was in a fight for his political life against the state's governor, Olin D. Johnston, who vowed to work with the president to ensure South Carolina received its share of the bounties of the New Deal. More than any other contest that summer, the Senate race dramatized the crossroads at which White Southerners found themselves: accept more federal aid to reform and revive the region's still floundering economy but risk upsetting its racial status quo, or dig in against further intrusion from Washington and safeguard white supremacy.[44]

Johnston took to the campaign trail with assurances that he posed no threat to South Carolina's racist regime. He opposed the antilynching bill circulating through Congress, and he had just signed a state law ensuring that the 8,000 Black hopefuls who had managed to register to vote in that year's elections would be struck from the rolls before November.[45]

But Smith climbed on the stump with apocalyptic prophesies. A vote for his opponent, he insisted, was a vote for the downfall of civilization. He had seen the future that would be conjured by further cooperation with Roosevelt.

"Ed tell us about Philydephy." A cry from the audience would prompt the signature climax of Smith's stump speech.

Cotton Ed recounted how he had stormed out of the 1936 Democratic National Convention in Philadelphia in protest of its integrated proceedings. "When I came out on the floor of that great hall, bless God, it looked like a checkerboard—a spot of white here, and a spot of black there," he continued:

> I had no sooner than taken my seat when a newspaper man came down the aisle and squatted down by me and said, "Senator, did you know a n—— is going to come out up yonder in a minute and offer the invocation?"
>
> I told him, I said, "Now don't be joking me, I'm upset enough the way it is." But, then, Bless God, out on the platform walked a slew-footed, blue-gummed, kinky-headed Senegambian!
>
> And he started praying and I started walking. And as I pushed through those great doors and walked across that vast rotunda, it seemed to me that Old John Calhoun leaned down from his mansion in the sky and whispered, "You did right, Ed."

Between relief and recovery on the one hand and white supremacy on the other, Cotton Ed would choose the latter every time. Crowds ate it up.[46]

When it was time for Ben's county to select its delegates, he and his neighbors went to the courthouse to sing and pray and thank God for their "free American heritage." The chairmen reminded them that they represented the nation's "purest Anglo-Saxon strain" before urging understanding for those who could not "write a pretty hand." With this wink and nod, poor and illiterate White registrants were helped through a process intimidating and arcane by design. Then old Cousin Charlie Martin closed the gathering with a "rip-roaring speech" about how he had seen the horrors of Reconstruction with his own eyes. "Eternal vigilance must always be the watchword for the Democratic Party," he intoned. "Boys, you got to keep your fences horse-high, bull-strong, and pig-tight." Ben celebrated the scene as "American democracy at its source."[47]

Amid high turn-out, Smith pummeled Johnston by more than ten points, a result the *Atlanta Constitution* judged as proof of "the right of free Democrats to cast their ballots uninfluenced by federal interference." Ben rationalized Cotton Ed's enduring appeal: "We see ourselves who belong to the younger generations smiling and saying to ourselves 'He's a tragic figure; he's the last of the old order; but we'll vote for him once more just because he's been there so long.'" Governor Johnston, by contrast, Ben judged not "of Senatorial caliber."[48]

After 1938, Ben took to giving public lectures in defense of "the common man's South." "We had rather be Economic Problem No. 1 than live like men in the Bronx," he told one audience, "we don't give a hoot really about what New York calls success." It was time, he warned members of the United Daughters of the Confederacy, for the region "to fight for its own rights." Doing this, Ben now believed, required rethinking White Southerners' partisan affiliations. "There is nothing damn Yankee about me—my folks have voted for every Democrat since Jefferson," he assured listeners at one gathering in Atlanta, but "the Democratic Party has grown so strong in the North that the Southern branch can no longer bargain with it. . . . Why should not the Republican Party be the coming party of the South?" Ben left unsaid the racist motives behind his pleas to "rise above devotion to the Democratic party," but his audiences grasped them immediately. "The New Deal is thoroughly committed to having the Negroes vote everywhere," one listener explained Ben's reasons for urging defection. "It is quite possible, as Mr. Robertson suggests," wrote another, "that 'bargaining' would bring the Republican party closer to Southern interest."[49]

It would, though the process would take another generation—and the forces unleashed by another shattering war. Mobilization for the fight against the Axis would transform the American South. Government orders would pump life into the region's industries, including South Carolina's cotton mills. Infrastructure projects would upgrade its ports and roads. Troops would pour into an expanding network of military bases from Texas to Virginia, and once again Black Southerners would depart Dixie in droves for higher-paying factory work elsewhere. This Great Migration built formidable Black voting blocs in northern and western cities. Their dogged grassroots pressure, little by little, would wrest commitments from Democratic leaders to oppose discriminatory employment practices, segregation, and disenfranchisement. In a stunning turn-around, the party of slavery and Jim Crow would take up the banner of civil rights. And in time, just as Ben predicted, Republican officials would prove receptive to the grievances of those who recoiled from the Democrats' new priorities. No longer the party of Lincoln, the GOP would traffic in racially coded arguments for states' rights.[50]

For Black Americans, including Benjamin Mays, who had just become president of Morehouse College where King would soon enroll, the early 1940s buzzed with sudden possibility. The battle against racism abroad, many hoped, might inspire a long-overdue reckoning with inequalities at home. Membership in civil rights groups soared. Black students, workers, and soldiers staged sit-ins and picket lines, refused to give up bus seats, and threatened a march on Washington if Roosevelt did not ban discrimination in the nation's defense industries. Yet across the country fierce White resistance met this growing militancy. Confrontations escalated into riots and other violent altercations. The arrival of arms-bearing Black troops to training camps in the South sparked special dread among the region's leaders, who insisted on naming the new bases after their Confederate heroes. As Ben set off to report on the fighting spirit in London and Moscow—and to find in those besieged cities echoes of his own ancestors' courage—Klansmen returned to his beloved upcountry roads. Black and White South Carolinians would both fight the Nazis. But they would not be fighting the same war.[51]

9

Woman and Bird

IN JANUARY 1931, TAMARA WAS singing at the Club Abbey on West 54th Street, described by *Variety* as "Broadway's most profitably operated all night mob hangout." She was lucky to have the job. The economic crisis already counted among its victims those who municipal caseworkers labeled the "new poor": able-bodied men from the flagging building trades, waiters whose full-service restaurants had been displaced by cafeterias and automats, and increasingly desperate garment workers, including Tamara's father.[1]

Entertainers, too, filled the ranks of the city's half million unemployed. Ticket sales and investment for Broadway productions had declined so sharply since the crash that half of the district's theaters had gone dark. Musicians' gigs dried up, as radio and the recording industry undercut demands for live music and talkies did away with piano or orchestra accompaniment at movie theaters. Variety troupes laid off from vaudeville circuits scrambled for picture-house work, juggling and hoofing as opening acts for the silver screen. Better-off actors and band leaders threw benefit concerts to keep their colleagues from destitution.[2]

Bankrolled by the mobster Owen "Owney" Madden, the Abbey kept Tamara and a dozen or so other entertainers in rent. Attached to the Hotel Harding, and therefore exempt from the city's 3:00 a.m. curfew, the Abbey's spicy floorshow went late.[3] Venues like this seemed to be places where women could flout convention, dance, and drink as they could not do in old-fashioned saloons. But under the surface, nightclubs—where bootleggers and racketeers held court in silk shirts and three-piece suits while laundering their illicit profits—proved "as glamorous as a thumb in the eye," as the producer Billy Rose put it. Hostesses, coat checkers, and other female employees faced unwanted attention and abuse from customers and coworkers alike. "Don't let anyone tell you that the night club is an easy spot for a girl," cautioned the entertainer Jimmy Durante. "Every man on the loose figures she is there to be made." Corrupt policemen, protecting their criminal associates, posed a danger, too. The NYPD framed hundreds of young women during the early 1930s. Unable to bribe or fight their way out of conflicts, showgirls found themselves at risk when trouble broke out, as it did at the Abbey on January 24th.[4]

Tamara would have been just finishing her shift around dawn. Some eighty stragglers milled around the dance floor or picked over orders of ham and eggs when Charles "Chink" Sherman, an associate of the recently murdered underworld banker Arnold Rothstein, entered the club and spotted the Bronx beer runner Dutch Schultz holding court at a corner table. Sherman nursed a grudge against Schultz, who was elbowing his way into the area's extortion and gambling enterprises.[5] Someone pulled a gun, sending customers and entertainers scurrying for the exits. More than a dozen bullets ricocheted around the room, shattering china, grazing the walls, and piercing the light globe above the night clerk's head in the abutting hotel. Schultz and his muscleman Martin Krompier (a.k.a. Marty the Wolf, a.k.a. The Crumpet) smashed a table over Sherman's body and gave him "the works." Police inspectors hauled Tamara, the Abbey's cigarette girl, Mavis King, and other employees down to the station for a reported thirty hours of the "third degree," but the investigation went nowhere. A wounded Schultz went "on the lam," and even the off-duty detective who had been sitting with him before the shooting lied about being there that morning.[6] The club closed, the mobsters reinvested elsewhere, and the showgirls lost their jobs.

As Tamara navigated the wreckage of the Great Depression, she would chase three largely incompatible goals: economic survival, respect and independence on feminist grounds, and participation in the social democratic politics of the left—a near given in her Jewish immigrant community. Puzzling over who she would be—on stage and off—Tamara engaged in a series of flirtations, both personal and political, that took her from the socialism of her father's garment worker union organizing to the gangster capitalism of New York's nightlife, to the Popular Front movement of a newfound lover, the playwright Clifford Odets. When none gave her all that she wanted, she refashioned herself into a Russian émigré. Forsaking both her working-class affiliations and her Ukrainian Jewish past, this new persona nagged at her conscience but catapulted her into stardom.

After the shooting at the Abbey, Tamara scrambled for any kind of work. She hustled for fifteen-minute spots on local radio stations, gradually earning callbacks and guest appearances with Rudy Vallée's orchestra. She donned "Russian gypsy clothes" and sang in the kitschy theme bars of lower Manhattan. She won a bit part in the Roxy Theatre's "Fads and Fancies," joined an opening act for the film *Second Hand Wife*, and sang "sad, Russian moujik wails" in Billy Rose's bawdy Broadway revue *Crazy Quilt*. "Tamara sings beautifully and looks even better," ran a typical review.[7]

Her steadiest work she found at the Kretchma. The inexpensive table d'hôte restaurant on East 14th Street catered to Russian émigrés as well as American "seekers of the Bohemian," as the *New Yorker* put it. Some six thousand rightwing Russian Whites had settled in the city in the wake of the Bolshevik Revolution: aristocrats who mourned the tsar; military officers who had battled the Reds; conservative students and bourgeois professionals, who may have made peace with the Provisional Government but never with the Communists. In Ukraine, Whites had treated Jews as mortal enemies. In Manhattan they shared a shopping district between Second Avenue and Tompkins Square.[8] Working alongside balalaika musicians, borscht-serving waitresses in embroidered blouses, and Caucasian dagger throwers, Tamara became a sensation at the Kretchma. She entranced customers with folk songs warbled in "one of those take-me-home voices," comforting exiles homesick for the old order.[9]

Had Tamara been too young in Ukraine to understand the links between antisemitism and White politics? Or did she decide that these refugees, like her, had been victims of circumstance? Did she play the role of Russian émigré songstress purely for economic opportunity, or did she tell herself that she was shrewdly manipulating stereotypes? One thing was for sure. Tamara could not wait to be "through with singing in night clubs." She wanted more serious work. An "ideal arrangement," she imagined, would be to split her time between the legitimate stage and the radio.[10]

Her first chance at dramatic acting came in early 1933, when she scored a role in *They All Come to Moscow*, a satire about Americans in the Soviet Union, staged by a small offshoot of the Theatre Guild, the city's leading art company. Critics praised Tamara's performance as "quietly effective," but the play flopped. It bore "no resemblance whatsoever to an entertainment," panned one reviewer.[11] It did, however, pull Tamara into the orbit of New York's leftist actors, including members of the Group Theatre, on the cusp of acclaim as some of the decade's most innovative and socially relevant repertory performers. Tamara began seeing the experimental company's aspiring playwright Clifford Odets, who had played her husband in *They All Come to Moscow*.

Their affair marked a turning point in her life. Clifford was also a child of Jewish immigrants who had spent much of his youth in the Bronx. He, too, had performed in vaudeville and the cafés of Greenwich Village. He knew about the Dnipro, the river of Tamara's childhood, and was inspired by Russian novelists, Dostoyevsky especially. He was attractive, broody. She mesmerized him with her "coolness and violin string quality."[12]

The relationship continued into the summer even when Clifford left New York City and she remained behind seeking work. "I'm unhappy," he told her while visiting his parents in Philadelphia. He lay awake fantasizing about her "small body" stretched out across his sheets. He wanted to fill her ears with his voice: "you I love—Russian Jewess, Tartar Chink, woman and bird as one!"[13]

She was "careful" writing back to him. She said she was "suspended in midair about a job" and had been pounding the pavement looking for engagements. She felt disadvantaged compared to those who did not have to strain to comprehend American talk. She spent part of each day in study, practicing folk songs on her guitar and learning standards. She took elocution lessons and analyzed the way people spoke. She taught herself Spanish lyrics from Cuban sheet music and pored over Black jazz and spirituals, which she adored. At night, she fell into bed, asleep in her tailored pajamas as soon as her head hit the pillow. But often she found herself wide awake two hours later, turning over some tune in her mind. Grabbing her guitar, she picked away at the chords in the dark. She refused to be held back, she vowed to Clifford, because life gushed from her in great amounts.[14]

To impress her with his worldliness, he sniffed at the "provinciality" of middle-class Philadelphians. (Slowly, he was shaping their lives into the play that would become his masterpiece, *Awake and Sing!*). Respectable homeowners were as "uncultured as bedbugs," he told Tamara. "They all want to go to Moscow," he derided their faddish political ideals. "Christ, am I sorry for this lot." Yet he betrayed his own romance about radicalism. "A good clean wind is needed and two or three generations of a new life. Revolution! Flaring and burning in the streets, rot, decay, then new growth. Let the new fresh grass grow up. No men and women, only children," he wrote. Tamara talked often, with great pain in her eyes observers said, about her experiences in Ukraine. Had Clifford forgotten that she had actually seen what flaring and burning in the streets did for children? "Listen Darling, write," he demanded. "You've got no right not to write. What's the big idea? I'll choke you with my useless hands and leave red marks on your throat."[15]

She called him a fanatic, but he continued to lavish her with letters. "Oh you shy lover!" he wrote undeterred when she returned quick telegrams. "Darling, let me scatter my fingers on your mouth and arms to love you," he rhapsodized. "Hey girl. I sing your brave little body, proud in the neck and shoulders and the slimness of the ankles. I shout your heart!"[16]

She conceded that she might visit him at the Adirondack resort Green Mansions near Lake George, where Group Theatre members would entertain for their summer keep. But, she explained, there were just so many things she wanted in life. Clifford intimated that he was going places, and that—"as things are now"—she did not "have much chance" of reaching her own career goals. "Why don't you settle something in your own heart. Make a good clean swing and know what your life will be from now on," he suggested.[17]

It was true. In less than two years he would achieve enormous success—as the "lyric poet of American Jewry" who captured everyday immigrant struggles in *Awake and Sing!* and the darling of the radical left who dabbled in Communist Party membership and delivered the electrifying strike drama *Waiting for Lefty*. In five years, Clifford would grace the cover of *Time* magazine. "There is nothing I want so much as you, Tamara Lotus," he assured her. "This is the first time I've ever been in love, truly, in love with someone outside myself." He went to her in the city on the way to upstate New York. "We were together and talked ourselves clean," he recorded in his diary. "I say we are in love, I say we are for each other. She says so too, but has an edge of doubt in her mind concerning herself, me."[18]

In many ways, the atmosphere at Green Mansions would have appealed to Tamara. The Group Theatre dramatists inhaled the clean air, stuffed themselves with fresh food, and sunned on the banks of the lake. They lived communally and rehearsed intently. They studied pacing and prop work, talked Lenin and Stanislavski, and dreamed of a form of theater that could reinvigorate a bankrupt society.[19] Like Tamara, who had begun to lend her time to benefit concerts for humanitarian causes, they believed that entertainment had social functions. Art and revolution had nourished each other in Russia; so too they should in the United States. Group performance modeled the power of collective action and helped to envision a better world without poverty, prejudice, or war. Tamara, no less than other New York stage folk, would be swept up in this so-called Popular Front ethos of the 1930s.[20]

But as the eldest daughter of struggling parents, she could not afford to cavort on a summer camp stage for room and board and neighboring farmers' bootlegged applejack. Tamara paid most of the Drasins' bills. Her father, Boris, sold life insurance for a while and took work where he got it, but he had not had reliable employment since leaving his union post. By the end of that year, he would be writing the ILGWU's president David Dubinsky: "I am in need of a job—badly in need and am appealing to you." He hoped that the new agencies being set up by President Roosevelt would create openings for someone like him.[21]

So Tamara trudged the dulled streets near Broadway, past decomposing parked cars and shoals of aimless, unemployed men who once had families and homes. After auditions, she returned to more of Clifford's letters. "Darling, I want you unoppressed, free and glad. New York is no place for a little tired girl. I hear her say she has to work. But forever?" He wagered that bodily pleasure could pull her away. "I know the feeling of your thighs under my hand—the give of the flesh. The tentative exploring game of your lips." Here, in striking form, Clifford's missives documented the lure of passion and partnership that ambitious women often had to resist, tempting as they might be, to seek a career.[22]

She continued to write Clifford about how hard she was working and put off her visit. In July she toiled alongside Paul Tisen's Gypsy Orchestra and the tango dancers Rosita and Ramon in a Loew's theater variety show accompanying the James Cagney film *Picture Snatcher*. When Ramon offered her a gig singing Russian and Spanish songs at the out-of-town El Patio nightclub, Tamara added a Long Island Railroad commute to her schedule. Her long nights ended with more work in preparation for the next day: manicuring eyebrows, curling lashes, and applying restorative pastes and oils to her skin. Female performers, who had to look immaculate on and off stage, coped with a range of costs and labors about which their male colleagues knew little. Tamara did not mind. "Nothing that is worth getting is easily achieved," she told herself.[23]

Her attention to details paid off. While out to lunch one day, she caught the eye of the producer Max Gordon, who invited her to try out for his forthcoming Broadway production, *Gowns by Roberta*, a fashion show thinly disguised as a musical comedy about a down-home American footballer who inherits his aunt's exclusive Paris dress shop. Tamara won the part of the shop's manager, Stephanie, a Russian princess who, wrapped in royal robes, sings a rousing version of the tsarist anthem at the culmination of the second act. Tamara convinced herself to view playing the part of a Russian White as a musical challenge rather than a betrayal of her real loyalties. Besides, the show had other qualities that would have appealed to her. Tamara's character served as a moral center for the other cast members' cavorting, and Stephanie's pursuit of romance across national lines dramatized how love could conquer difference and serve as a form of diplomacy that trumped transactional politics. In one scene opposite the newcomer Bob Hope, she would debut Jerome Kern and Otto Harbach's lovely lament, "Smoke Gets in Your Eyes."[24]

Later that year, the production, retooled as simply *Roberta,* would become the longest running musical of the 1933–34 season.[25] Tamara's singing would consistently stop the show. Promotions would splash her face all over the newspapers, reporters would hail her as a "new legend," and Marshall Field's department store would sell replicas of her stage jewelry. F. Scott Fitzgerald would reference "Smoke Gets in Your Eyes" in his stories, and young people would dance to the tune as far away as Nazi Germany. Backstage at the Amsterdam Theatre, while slipping into her costume before curtain call, Tamara would gush, "It's grand to be so busy, and I really hope I never do catch up with myself."[26]

But as she struggled that summer—before *Roberta*'s opening—Clifford's letters pushed back against her efforts. "I know you enjoy working (and need to), but a slow tearing down goes with all this work, a sort of melting away of an inside thing," Tamara read in early July. "Personally I don't see why I won't have lots of money some day with which to buy you many many nice things and what you want. It's the old story, Darling, that behind many men's success is a woman." The next day, he wrote again. "I want to be with you like hell," he purred. "Girl, what do you want of me? Girl, what can I give you?"[27] She had told him many times, but he refused to listen.

Instead, Clifford luxuriated in his own sexual suffering, missing her "more than sun on a naked body." He spoke about Tamara to anyone who would listen. His fellow Group Theatre member Stella Adler told him that most men "fall" for Tamara. Her brother, Luther Adler, who had also "wanted her badly," agreed. She was "a nice girl," he warned, "but mad for a career." To regain confidence, Clifford seduced a married woman whose husband had yet to arrive at camp. He did it, he told himself, because she reminded him of Tamara. "I kissed her and made an exploring game with my hands," he confided to his diary. After coaxing her back to her room, they undressed quietly while her child slept in the next bed. "There was a danger of conception," she reminded him, and her husband always "used something." But Clifford refused: "I was in her now, quietly, strong, hard. . . . Don't move! No, she wouldn't and didn't." At their next encounter, he ignored her. "It's that way. Take this and move on," he wrote contemptuously. "I am sick of that thing, of how a woman may so easily stuff her marital relations behind her. . . . I feel as if all women are in a conspiracy against men. I'm for the men against all women. I'm for her husband, for instance, much more than I am for her." Meanwhile he wrote to Tamara: "I can't believe you exist . . . I think we will be very happy here together . . . to think of you working and tense in the city. . . . You write you can't relax or sleep. I want to teach you how." By August, Tamara relented and joined him in the mountains.[28]

Though Clifford continued to promise her "a good life," she must have suspected that both he and the Group Theatre offered an uncomfortable bargain. For all the talk of breaking new ground at the edge of Lake George, conventional gender roles persisted. "But, of course, the Group was really a man's theatre," remembered Stella Adler, one of the company's most talented and experienced members. They put on "plays for men," she explained, because "they understood men." Any actress who stayed, she asserted, was "ruined, absolutely neglected." "Well, all of us felt that we did not get the kind of fair shake the men did," Phoebe Brand corroborated with less sharpness. At a time when the struggle against capitalism took precedence over other forms of oppression, feminism held the taint of bourgeois liberalism for many activists on the left. Patterns of male privilege, even in circles promising sexual liberation, proved difficult to eradicate.[29]

When Tamara broke off their affair, Clifford vowed to her that he would "replace the lost thing with a new incentive." He informed her: "Just as one would want to sleep with a loved woman, the same way one should be about life and art."[30] It didn't occurr to him that this was precisely what Tamara had been fighting for the right to have herself.

Later she would look back on this moment in 1933 as an impasse, when uncharacteristically she did not know what to do. She swore she would have gone back to Russia that summer if she could have. But her citizenship, like that of other refugees, had been revoked for leaving without Soviet permission.[31] She had been so hopeful when she came to New York, but neither the dazzle of Manhattan's nightlife nor the leftist fervor of her father and Clifford Odets had offered her true range of motion. By keeping her independence from tight-knit factions like the Group Theatre, Tamara would spare herself many of the heartaches suffered by other female radicals who gave themselves fully to causes dominated by men. But it would not be easy to pursue feminist dreams while also remaining committed to the proletarian collectivism of the Popular Front.

This was it, she told herself. If success did not come now it would be "forever lost." There were "more ways of being discouraged than there are pages in a mail-order catalogue," she reasoned, and she was nearing twenty-five, a ripe old age for a woman in show business. The most senior member of the city's chorus girl union was twenty-six.[32] To get what she wanted she would have to be two years younger. And she would be all Russian. Not American. Not Jewish.

After leaving Clifford, Tamara embraced full-time the persona she had crafted at the Kretchma. Subsequently, no trace of her Jewish background appeared in the ballooning press coverage of her career. Known simply as "Tamara," she hesitated to reveal her last name to reporters. "I call myself Tamara because I like it," she declared when pressed.[33] She revealed that her mother sewed some of her clothes—but not that her father did as well, nor that he had been an ILGWU activist. She buried other aspects of her past that observant readers would have understood as "Jewish": her birthplace, Odesa, the walkup in the Bronx, vaudeville. She admitted to speaking English, Russian, Ukrainian, German, and some French, but made no mention of Yiddish. Going beyond simple omission, she retold her early history with Russifying details that skillfully pointed away from her Jewish roots. She stated that she was born in the same village as Gogol. Her parents, she said, had named her after the Caucasian princess in Lermontov's poem "Demon." Tamara made subtle not grand changes. She never claimed royal lineage—a pastime among the era's social climbers and a likely sign of an invented background—but rather characterized her father as a well-to-do merchant with no title, a clarification only a Christian, or maybe a Rothschild, would need to make. Her refugee story betrayed nothing but a typical White émigré saga. Her family had escaped "during the revolution," she put it. Though she spoke many times about marauding "bandits," she never revealed them as pogromists. *Roberta*'s playbill, which pictured Tamara draped in fur and jewels and crowned by a tiara, noted only that her family's property had been confiscated during the unrest.[34]

In certain ways, Tamara's efforts to hide her Jewish heritage were not altogether remarkable. Many children of immigrants chose to distance themselves from their parents, to be "thoroughly made over," as the writer Mary

Tamara as the Russian princess Stephanie in *Roberta*. Photo by Vandamm Studio © The New York Public Library for the Performing Arts/Museum of the City of New York, F2013.41.6375.

Antin had put it, to change how they talked and dressed, or at the very least to cordon off their inherited faith and traditions from their public presentation of self. By the 1930s, only a minority of young Jewish New Yorkers regularly spoke Yiddish or attended synagogue. And Tamara was far from the only upwardly mobile Jewish American with an altered name.[35]

Pressures to assimilate only grew stronger as antisemitism soared in New York, inspiring everything from "Christians only" hiring practices at Manhattan offices to Jew-baiting street gangs who prowled the streets of

Yorkville and the South Bronx. By passing as a "comely Muscovite," Tamara had no trouble gaining access to the Stork Club and other exclusive venues that discouraged, or even outright barred, Jewish clientele. She escaped, too, the stereotypes that painted Jewish women as loud, immodest, or garish, and which read their bodies and faces in unflattering, predetermined ways. Observers did not focus on the shape of her nose and mouth but saw "beautiful teeth," "high cheekbones," and "tragic wisdom" in her eyes. Her face was described not as biblical but as "saintly," her body not as oriental but "agile." Admirers heard not broken English but a "pleasing accent." There was a "keen suggestion of Latin enthusiasm in her voice," insisted one reporter. "But she is 'all Russian.' "[36]

In the early twentieth century, making oneself over was a dangerous but exciting proposition and, for an entertainer like Tamara, a natural extension of the practice of acting on stage. Her decision to no longer be Jewish may have been instrumental, playful, or sincere—perhaps she simply felt more "Russian"—or some combination of all three. And yet, in certain ways, Tamara chose a highly unusual path. Jewish girls who grew up under similar conditions may not have worshipped as their parents did, but nearly all of them valued their heritage. It served as a lifeline to a tangible past while they navigated a tumultuous era and puzzled over questions about belonging, desire, and duty. Though passing as Gentile promised a way out from under Old World hierarchies and New World prejudices alike, most women ultimately rejected it as a shameful betrayal. Jewish belonging came with patriarchal pressures, decided Mary Antin, but it also gave a person a distinctive voice. Even the rebellious novelist Anzia Yezierska had felt a tremendous threat of loss as she contemplated moving away from her family's customs. "When you deny your parents, you deny the ground under your feet, the sky over your head," she wrote; you doomed yourself to "wandering between worlds." Especially in light of Hitler's rise to power—which spurred many Jewish women to acknowledge and embrace Judaism as never before—Tamara's decision to pass took on even greater significance.[37]

Tamara, moreover, did not have to hide her Jewishness in order to be a successful performer. Positive role models for her may have once been rare, but by the 1930s a number of female stars, such as the torch singer Libby Holman and the modern dancer Tamiris, appealed to broad audiences without hiding their backgrounds. Or, like Theda Bara, she might have concocted some story about Arab, French, or otherwise mysterious origins. The sophisticated-but-not-easily-placed European temptress had become a staple character in American entertainment, propelling the careers of Greta

Garbo, Hedy Lamarr, and others. Among all the possible exotic guises women crafted on stage and on screen, the Russian émigré—a White who stood on the side of the tsar and the Cossacks—carried particularly reactionary and antisemitic connotations.[38]

Her decision to pass also contrasted sharply with her parents' growing Jewish allegiances. In 1934, Boris became one of the head organizers for a project to build a Jewish socialist commune near Hightstown, New Jersey, where needleworkers relocated from the city would pool their resources to operate a women's wear factory and then devote themselves to ennobling farm work during the garment industry's slack seasons. Boris had dabbled in cooperative enterprise back in Ukraine, possibly by participating in one of Odesa's revolutionary producer artels, and he believed deeply in the concept. Jersey Homesteads, as the town came to be called, drew federal subsidies from New Dealers who relished the idea of revitalizing rural areas and easing urban congestion with one stroke. In early July 1936, Tamara's parents and brother, along with six other pioneer households, moved into a muddy construction site full of promise.[39]

In time a hundred or so Russian and Eastern European families trickled into this "Zionist and anti-capitalist, pro-Marx and pro-Roosevelt" community, as the writer George Weller characterized it. But quickly the homesteaders ran into building delays, creeping costs, and government red tape. During the short four years of the cooperative experiment, rightwing reporters descended regularly on the "crackpot Utopia" with notebooks and cameras, decrying the waste of taxpayer money and raising the specter of foreign radicalism growing wild in the Garden State. As one of the project's leading spokesmen, Boris insisted that no other "ism" but "common sense-ism" motivated their endeavor. Nevertheless, he became a prime target for critics, a "Russian-born little Stalin," scowled one hostile journalist. Tamara's family and their neighbors took refuge in the commune's close-knit camaraderie. The town observed the Sabbath, and Yiddish flourished at picnics and sing-alongs, even among those who had not used it much before. The Drasins grew a vegetable garden, acquired a car, and shopped at the settlement's kosher grocery store. By 1938, Boris was having conversations with the American Jewish Congress leader Rabbi Stephen Wise and others about the possibility of settling refugees from Nazi Germany at Hightstown.[40]

In a rare candid moment, Tamara confessed profound ambivalence about the way she presented herself. "Sometimes I sit and brood until I start to cry. And then I look at myself in the mirror and say: 'You are a fake, Tamara.'" But her strategy had cleared a path to those things she wanted most—creative control, financial independence, and egalitarian relationships with friends, colleagues, and lovers. These were common feminist yearnings in largely unsympathetic times, when the struggles of male breadwinners took precedence. Tamara maneuvered through New York's political landscapes by sidestepping the Americanization conundrum that had troubled intellectuals such as Mary Antin and Anzia Yezierska. Instead of dwelling on the possibilities and pitfalls of assimilation, she traded one exoticism for another. This allowed her to maintain a sense of rootedness, tradition, and distinctiveness, but without inherited expectations from her community. She embraced her status as a foreigner and played with ethnicity as a construct, all the while evading the stereotypes that dogged Jewish Americans, New York's largest immigrant group. For her fans she pulled off a paradoxical feat. She appeared "wholesomely exotic."[41]

After the national tour that followed *Roberta*'s smash season on Broadway, Tamara received top billing on radio programs and headlined at the Palace, "her sultry loveliness working full blast." She endorsed dependable consumer products and socked money away for retirement. She plucked her eyebrows and cut her hair to star in her first feature length film, *Sweet Surrender* (1935).[42] At summer stock theaters on Cape Cod she relished devoting time to serious drama. She bantered with costars, earned universal praise from women as well as men, and refused to gossip. "All I remember are dinner dates and lyrics to songs," she claimed when pressed by a snooping reporter. Having "seen and suffered," said one supporter, Tamara brought an admirable "knowledge of the world and of humanity" to her craft.[43]

All this success enabled rather than diminished Tamara's commitment to Popular Front politics. She leveraged the celebrity she gained playing White émigré roles to support an array of leftist causes, singing at benefits for the poor and unemployed and fundraising for health care facilities, the Wayside Day Nursery for working mothers, and Chinese war orphans. She donned a Mexican flower girl costume at a Greenwich Village fundraiser for loyalist refugees from the Spanish Civil War, and rallied to the defense of the Federal Theatre Project when conservatives set out to abolish the New Deal program that had put so many artists and actors back to work. She helped celebrate the one-year anniversary of the far left, antifascist Cabaret TAC's opening, and, at an Apollo Theater benefit for the Harlem Boys' Center, she joined Count Basie, Abbott and Costello, Molly Picon, Noble Sissle, and Billie Holiday on stage for an inspiring night of integrated entertainment that lasted until 5:30 in the morning.[44] At the same time, she continued to support her parents, pay her brother's tuition, and send money to other family friends. Quietly, she propped up Jersey Homesteads' kosher grocery cooperative when it went bankrupt.[45]

And she fell in love—with Erwin D. Swann, a creative advertising executive at Lord & Thomas, the agency that broke ground by selling Lucky Strike cigarettes to women. Erwin was far from the most handsome of Tamara's lovers, but he was a rare man who admired her success instead of feeling threatened by it. He understood that her "right to a career" was "equal to his and under no circumstances interferes." She confided to her family that he brought her "so much joy."[46]

Like Tamara, Erwin was not entirely who he said he was. He left no trace in official records before 1940 and gave conflicting accounts about his education, claiming at various times to have attended five different colleges. He, too, seemed to be hiding Jewish origins. Assuming a new identity was indeed easier to do in advertising than other professions, since the field required no clear credentials or certification.[47]

After they married, Tamara and Erwin rented a 58th Street penthouse overlooking Central Park, which they filled with worn books and fresh-cut roses. Theirs was a small, heretically bourgeois, but nourishing collective. Erwin, who got "a kick" out of having a star for a wife, reassured her, encouraged her. "She isn't a phony. She's a real person. I call her 'Joe' . . . after an old prizefighter named Joe Tamara," he explained, "and she calls me 'Joe' too. It's simpler." They were, confirmed one visitor, "easy-going, utterly happy."[48]

During the 1938–1939 theater season, Tamara was starring in her latest Broadway hit, *Leave It to Me!* Set in Moscow, the musical comedy's plot centered on Alonzo P. Goodhue, a Topeka bathtub manufacturer and Democratic Party donor whose wife's scheming had landed him an unwanted ambassadorship to the Soviet Union. Pining for Kansas, he engages in a series of outrageous stunts, including kicking the German ambassador in the belly in hopes of getting recalled. But these acts only further endear him to his hosts. It takes a proposal for world peace to finally get himself removed from his post. Cole Porter's music for the show featured a rousing riff on the "Internationale" and, for Tamara, the enchanting ballad, "Get Out of Town."[49]

The production somehow managed to delight mainstream audiences, theater critics, and the far-left press alike. The *New Masses* praised it for taking barbs at Benito Mussolini, Hitler, and the Japanese ambassador while portraying Joseph Stalin as "a pleasant, enthusiastic gentleman" who briefly swing dances at a Red Square demonstration. "They show very clearly that their sympathies are with the Soviets and democracy," agreed the *Daily Worker*, which also complimented Tamara for "looking attractive enough to start a stage door riot, and singing nicely as well."[50]

After nearly 300 performances, though, Tamara was ready for a break. "I want a rest," she declared, to "rest my throat and rest my soul." While *Leave It to Me!* took its summer hiatus, she sailed for Europe, vowing not even to sing in the bathtub during her journey.[51] She hoped to travel as far as Russia and Ukraine, but Stalin's bureaucrats denied her an entrance visa. After hunting for new sheet music and the latest Paris fashions, she returned to New York on August 15, 1939. Eight days later the Soviets signed a pact with the Nazis, clearing the path for both to pursue new territorial conquests in Eastern Europe. Overnight *Leave It to Me!*'s lighthearted treatment of the Communist regime felt out of step with the darkening turn in world affairs. Show runners scrambled to update the musical before its September reopening. Dancing Stalin would have to be cut. And another war was about to destroy so much more.[52]

10

Tea-Time

FRESH FROM HIS APPRENTICESHIP AT Dodge & Seymour's New York headquarters, the former Olympic athlete Frank Cuhel moved to the Philippines in 1930 to "cut his eye teeth in export trade."[1] Spending the next decade in that US colony—and in Singapore and the Netherlands East Indies—put him up close to debates about imperialism, the place of Americans and Europeans in Southeast Asia, and the geopolitics of trade and human movement. By 1941, all these issues would converge to form the Pacific War. He would find himself unexpectedly thrust into the role of radio correspondent, one of the last to broadcast reports out of Java as it succumbed to Japanese invasion, before narrowly escaping capture himself.

But at first life was grand.

Frank took a room at the American Army and Navy Club in Manila, a sprawling complex at the height of its glamour, sporting a ballroom, barber shop, bar, and, on the upper floors, seventy furnished rooms for "reputable" male residents. Bougainvillea flowers bloomed at the edges of the club's back lawn, next to the tennis and squash courts and the swimming pool overlooking Manila Bay, where Frank liked to take early morning dips. Filipino servants stood by to open doors, pour drinks, clip nails, and swat flies. "As soon as you jump out of your clothes," Frank marveled, a *lavandero* was there to whisk them off for laundering. It was a paradise for young American bachelors in white mess jackets, where pesos went further than dollars, where liquor flowed freely outside the bounds of mainland Prohibition laws, and where late-night bull sessions on the world's problems hinged on grandiloquent statements like "take Russia for instance." No one would have believed that in a matter of years, the club's dance floor would be stacked with evacuation supplies and the upstairs bedrooms crammed with bomb victims.[2]

Taking charge of the Dodge & Seymour office, Frank put in full days amid its display cases and sample trunks. He racked up an early victory selling meters to the Manila Yellow Taxicab Company and offloaded a large order of Pond's Cold Cream at the Farmacia Central. To fill his weekends, he bought a copper-bottomed sailboat, made on the island of Corregidor, where he also occasionally reported for reserve officer training. Frank and the other volunteers rehearsed maneuvers around invasion points that the Japanese would later use, though with little sense of urgency. Military fortifications on "The Rock," Americans told themselves, ranked "second to none in the world."[3]

American exporters had first come to the Philippines three decades earlier on the heels of the military, serving as sutlers for troops as they wrestled the territory from Spain in 1898, crushed the Filipino independence movement, and fashioned a US colony. But the future of the island chain remained deeply uncertain, even after 1902, the declared end to hostilities that had claimed the lives of more than two hundred thousand people. American businessmen invested only tentatively in the archipelago as debates raged in the United States about the wisdom of following Europeans into the business of formal overseas colonialism.[4]

A few Americans argued that subjugating the Philippines constituted a betrayal of the nation's core democratic principles. "We have been treacherous," Mark Twain seethed about the broken promises made to Filipino forces who had helped to defeat the Spanish, "we have stamped out a just and intelligent and well-ordered republic . . . we have robbed a trusting friend." He jibed that "there must be two Americas," one that "sets the captive free," and another that "kills him to get his land."[5]

Others also opposed keeping the Philippines, but for entirely different reasons. Many White Americans loathed the thought of sweeping millions deemed racially inferior into the national fold, even on the unequal terms of subjects rather than citizens. The archipelago, they complained, was too far away, too foreign, and too much inhabited by "barbarous Asiatics" and—nearly as bad—"descendants of Spaniards." Proposals were floated for auctioning off the islands to the highest bidders, remitting them to Spain, or simply abandoning them to their own devices.[6]

Against these various objections, proponents of empire had strained to make their case. "The Philippines are ours forever," thundered Senator Albert J. Beveridge. This "garden and Gibraltar of the Pacific" gave Americans a base in the East, and it was "the last land left in all the oceans," so they had better keep it. Commerce in the Pacific was the key to world power. Wars would be fought over it, Beveridge was sure. Withdrawal would encourage one of the region's other powers—Britain, or worse, Japan—to seize the islands for themselves. Even if they did not, chaos would reign, because the Filipinos were "not of a self-governing race." Beveridge and other imperialists did not question their right to rule over Filipinos any more than they questioned the right of parents to preside over their progeny. "We must never forget that in dealing with the Filipinos we deal with children," Beveridge cautioned, and worse yet, ones "schooled in Spanish methods." The matter was not simply practical; it was also providential. Administering government "among savage and senile peoples" was "the divine mission of America," Beveridge implored, "and it holds for us all the profit, all the glory, all the happiness possible to man."[7]

Americans kept the Philippines. US counterinsurgency forces stamped out uprisings. Mainland firms came to string up telegraph lines and lay down roads. Congress scooted the territory under the nation's tariff umbrella. Demand for tropical commodities back in the States soared. Soon Americans were buying up nearly all the colony's sugar and coconut oil exports and most of its tobacco and hemp. Members of the growing American business community in Manila, which was staunchly Republican, shuddered at the election of President Woodrow Wilson, a Democrat, in 1912. The "Filipinization" policies of his governor general, Francis Burton Harrison, along with the Philippine Autonomy Act of 1916, gestured at the territory's future independence. But confidence rebounded when Republicans returned to power in the 1920s.[8]

By the time Frank arrived to sell cold creams and taxi meters, 63 percent of the archipelago's imports were coming from the United States, up from only 9 percent in 1899. The same brand-name goods stocked at American dime stores piled up in Manila's shop windows. Few dwelled on the risks of such economic intimacy—of being subject to the whims of the mainland's boom and bust cycles—until after the stock market crash.[9]

Instead, Americans congratulated themselves for having transformed a Spanish imperial backwater into the "Pearl of the Orient." Manila's cityscape, they thought, showcased the wonders of their own can-do attitude. The moat surrounding the old quarter Intramuros had been reborn as a golf course and athletic grounds, the Spanish mint transformed into headquarters for a public school system, and the Luneta waterfront, once the site of political executions, now used as a spot for Constabulary band concerts three times a week.[10] Under American rule, Filipinos' standard of life surpassed "that of any other person in the Orient," claimed Henry Stimson, who, as governor general in the late 1920s, attracted unprecedented investment to the islands. "Wisely or unwisely," Frank agreed, the US government had been "playing the part of Santa Claus" in the Philippines for two generations.[11]

As the Great Depression seeped into the local economy, however, Frank felt less and less generous. He managed to sustain normal accounts during the first two quarters of 1930, but by June sales slowed with the rainy season. As export profits dwindled, buyers and lenders grew more cautious. Frank held on with decent sales in auto parts, Canada Dry ginger ale, Schwinn bicycles, and Benjamin air rifles. But sitting at his desk, next to the adding machine, he worried and wanted more. When he found a Midwestern firm willing to ship a large consignment of lime a few cents under market price, he leaped at the deal, even though plenty of the sugar-refining product was produced locally. "If we can get a big enough slice I think we can put the lime producers here out of business," he told his sister. "It is a little bit heartless to go after them in that manner, as it means knocking a lot of men out of work, but business unfortunately is a rather cold-blooded proposition all over the world, and if you do not get somebody else, they will get you."[12]

The dog-eat-dog atmosphere worsened as the slump hit new lows on the eve of President Franklin D. Roosevelt's inauguration in early 1933. The mainland's emergency banking holiday that March disrupted local financial transactions, and Frank expected "the bottom to drop out about May." Firms were cutting down staff. The local rubber trade people were "cutting each other's throats." Down-and-out friends back in the States were writing to Frank in search of jobs. Then news arrived that Dodge & Seymour could not afford to grant him the home leave he was due. Frank fired back that the New York office needed to force suppliers and shipping agencies "to sharpen up their pencils and get down to some fighting figures." To lower his own overhead, he let his Filipino assistant go.[13]

Hard times also renewed calls back on the mainland for Philippine independence—out of Americans' self-interest rather than any widespread crisis of conscience about the wrongs of empire. Labor unions decried Filipino workers' access to US borders. Dairy lobbyists obsessed over the threat of coconut-oil carrying margarine. Beet sugar producers schemed against duty-free cane. Others objected to draining government coffers to prop up the colony's schools, public works, and defenses. Concluding that

Frank poses with one of his buyers in the Philippines. Courtesy of Michael Safranek/University Archives, The University of Iowa Libraries.

the islands presented a security liability, military strategists drew up defense plans that amounted to little more than glorified evacuation policies. Quietly they admitted that if the Japanese wanted to, they could take the archipelago in a week.[14] The notion was not overly fanciful. Japan had been studiously seizing overseas territory for decades—Formosa in 1895, southern Sakhalin (the spoils of an upset victory over Russia) in 1905, Korea in 1910, Germany's possessions in China and the Pacific during World War I, and most recently Manchuria in 1931.

But Frank worried more about all the independence talk "hovering over the islands," damaging business prospects that were already "bad enough." When Roosevelt's appointee for governor general, Frank Murphy, disembarked at Manila, the American Chamber of Commerce threw the Democrat a welcome luncheon, but not a very warm one. Longtime community leader Samuel Gaches opened the Whites-only gathering with a "stirring" defense of US control of the islands that had, Frank noticed, everyone "sitting on the edge of their seats." Already "in a hole" when he got up to speak, Governor Murphy tried to assuage the audience by touting his successes working with businessmen as mayor of Detroit, which was, Frank griped, about as compelling "as a song and dance in Chinese." Like other Manila Americans, Frank had voted for Herbert Hoover.[15]

But in 1934, the Tydings-McDuffie Act settled the debate. The Philippines would move rapidly toward commonwealth status, followed in ten years by full independence. Butter makers and Asian freedom fighters rejoiced. And the development cast the colonial status quo across the entire region into doubt. If Americans withdrew from the islands, one popular prediction went, "the Japanese will be in there by tea-time." The move, warned one British official, would "set the whole East ablaze."[16]

The Philippines had been a much-needed safe haven for American exporters, Frank reasoned, a place where they had been shielded from European competition and colonial preference schemes as well as the "tremendous tariffs that have been levied against American products all over the world." Predicting that US interests in the archipelago were "finished," Frank pondered going home. But Americans' expansionist projects in the part of the world soon to be known as "Southeast Asia" did not begin or end in Manila. By 1935 US trade with the region surpassed that with China and rivaled that with Japan. When Dodge & Seymour offered Frank a post at their Singapore office, he jumped at the chance.[17]

Americans had been a notable presence in the ports of East Asia and the South Pacific since the founding of the United States. In the nineteenth century, businessmen took up residence in the settlements for foreigners in Canton and Macao. After the 1840s, a series of treaties strong-armed extraterritorial privileges for such Americans and other Westerners even in places that had escaped formal colonization such as Japan and China. Diplomats, missionaries, and others from the United States relocated to self-governing international quarters from Yokohama to Shanghai, reassured by the lingering proximity of US military detachments and gunboat patrols. By the turn of the twentieth century, as international rivalries mounted over access and influence in the Far East—over naval bases, railroad concessions, and other resources that promised not only profits but also prestige—consuls encouraged American businesses to post more on-the-ground agents in the region. Buyers, shippers, oil men, ad men, insurance agents, repair technicians, and distributors arrived in growing numbers, spurred on by expanded transportation and communication networks—first telegraph and steamship lines, then telephone and commercial aviation services as well.[18] Later, most American accounts of the origins of the Pacific War would forget about these overseas communities, narrating the coming conflict instead from the perspective of militants in Tokyo and moralists in Washington.[19]

By the time Frank settled in Singapore in 1935, that island colony at the tip of the Malay Peninsula had become a glittering and modern metropolis of startling inequalities, lorded over by a British minority with pageantry, bribery, threats, and implacable complacency. Claimed by its rulers to be a "bigger and better Gibraltar"—impossible to invade by sea and laughable that any army would march on it by land—it was the kind of place, explained the reporter John Gunther, where, with only the suggestion of battleships thousands of miles away, a single officer could "boss 10,000 people with a swagger stick and a dinner jacket." If Americans ever awoke to racial and imperial injustice in Asia, that epiphany was likely to happen in Singapore.[20]

But most Americans quickly grew accustomed to colonial privilege. They had been primed for it by their nation's own racial segregation, discriminatory immigration laws, and imperial conquests. White skin conferred automatic standing in Singapore no matter what colonists' social status had been back in the States—instant deference from rickshaw pullers, top salaries at the firm, easy credit at the bank. Forming the second largest group of Westerners in the city by the 1930s, Americans expected Whites-only balcony seats at the theater and gratefully made use of the General Hospital's "European" ward. They internalized the local codes of contact—sometimes working closely with Chinese confidants at the office but never drinking with them at the Raffles Hotel, perhaps sleeping with Malay women but never walking with them down the street.[21]

Frank, like so many of his peers, had few qualms about British imperial traditions. He joined Singapore's polo club as its only American member. Traces of British spelling crept into his writing, hints of an English accent drifted into his speech. When he made a visit to Iowa in 1937, he showed up wearing Burberry and carrying a cane. Like other colonists he worked to look a certain way, smell a certain way, and shave a certain way. "The American Man must 'dress' to maintain his morale in the tropics," he reasoned.[22]

Following the custom of spending a number of years at their posts before securing the consent of their firms to marry, Frank and half a dozen other bachelors set up house in a sprawling villa dubbed the American Mess. Called Bab in college, he was given the nickname Frankie now, signaling his acceptance into a tightknit brotherhood that included the likes of handsome, pink-cheeked Tommy Thompson of Ford, Johnnie Walker of Coca-Cola, Ed O'Connor of MGM, Standard Oil's Bill "Buy and Sell" Merkel, and the pharmaceutical dealer from Detroit Rus "Fats" Muckle. The Mess combined the servant count of an aristocratic manor with the unmistakable air of a fraternity house. The housemates threw raucous parties, hosted visiting senators, and went "berserk at the sight of attractive femmes" disembarking from cruise ships. When toothbrushes, cuff links, and bow ties went missing, they "sacked" their servants for the petty robberies. When it turned out that wild monkeys had been the actual culprits, they laughed. It was less funny when the animals trampled Johnnie Walker's mint garden, grown from seedlings transported from Bombay to supply cocktail garnishes.[23]

Frank soon settled in at Dodge & Seymour's Singapore office, in operation since 1924. Before World War I, few American companies had sought business in Malaya, but in the decade after the Armistice US exports to the region increased more than five-fold. Bucking the Depression's headwinds, all kinds of American goods, from canned food to boilers, continued to arrive. Advertisements in the local papers sang the praises of the inventories lugged across thousands of miles of ocean by Dodge & Seymour: alarm clocks for "heavy sleepers," three-minute oat flakes for "careful mothers," Mum deodorant for "busy women," and Marbelite shaving stick cases for "men everywhere."[24]

Frank also traveled extensively in search of new markets, crisscrossing Asia as well as the region some had begun to call the "Middle East," gaining knowledge that would later prove useful for conveying the significance of those places to American radio listeners. His job was explorers' work or, as Frank put it, "cruising along the frontiers of civilization in search of that elusive enchantress known as 'American Export Trade.'" He trekked Champion spark plugs, Parker pens, and Eveready flashlights into remote jungles. He offloaded seventy thousand Dr. West toothbrushes on a single tropical island. He scanned the horizon for places with "a boom town atmosphere," where new wealth extracted from the earth translated into orders for refrigerators, where people proved eager to avail themselves of the twentieth century's "wonderful advances." He thrilled to see Tehran become "motor minded" under the modernizing leadership of Reza Shah. He found the Jezreel Valley, once little more than donkeys and sand dunes, now irrigated and plowed by the latest American farm implements, a "most inspiring sight." He prided himself on having replaced lumber-hauling elephants in Thailand's teak forests with Cleveland Tractor Company diesel burners—and for being "the guy who introduced Hormel's Ham to Palestine and Scott Tissue to Persia." Frank's bosses trusted him to staff branch offices from Jerusalem to Bangkok. To curry their favor, he recounted his adventures in letters covering "all phases of life in each country, the hotels, standards, customs, laws." They passed the colorful missives around the New York office. Globe-trotting capitalists like Frank relished the idea that the places they touched would never be the same.[25]

Of course, some developments troubled him. After watching refugees from Nazi Germany overrun the port facilities of Jaffa, pack tent encampments in Tel Aviv, and be turned away by the boatloads at Singapore, he began to read up on Hitler's regime. "The plight of the poor Jews is certainly a dismal one," he concluded. Obstacles to business also stood in his way. International exchange carried special risks. Information, credit, and goods had to be translated and transported across complicated terrains and incommensurate markets. Disputes and cultural misunderstandings had to be smoothed out across languages. Most inhabitants of Asia and the Middle East, moreover, could not afford such luxury items as fountain pens or clocks. Those who could were reluctant to abandon trusted brands and longstanding arrangements with European suppliers. It took "backbreaking missionary work," as Frank put it, to win converts in British, French, and Dutch territories.[26]

One of Frank's biggest challenges was simply dealing with his "old fashioned" bosses back in New York. They sent him export catalogs full of slogans like "Hotcha" and "Whiz Bang" and other "hokum" that were utterly tone deaf to the mentalities of buyers abroad. Worse, they refused to sell goods on consignment or otherwise release them without upfront payment, and they were squeamish about taking on new accounts. Buying and selling products involved a leap of faith (as Frank well knew from the time he was hauled before the Singapore criminal court for importing gramophone needles that turned out to be counterfeit). So, even more than money, trust was the currency of long-distance trade. Frank's workdays revolved around the problem of establishing and maintaining it. He filled his correspondence to the home office with talk not about profitability but about potential clients' character. "We have great confidence in Mr. Parker," read one typical letter, "otherwise we should not have recommended entering into this deal at all." He assured his bosses that he always thoroughly investigated "all the angles" to confirm that business contacts were "the right kind."[27]

Frank judged character by observing whether a man carried himself well and took part in the right rituals: if he golfed, what he drank, whether he could follow "high-powered puns" and put up with "leg pulling." Being someone who was easy "to get next to" required saying things like "make it snappy" and "how the hell are ya?" It meant telling truth "straight from the shoulder" and taking jabs at the New Deal. It also meant talking an awful lot about women and not getting uncomfortable if the "chaps" did not keep their discussions "up around the chest." When such banter startled one newcomer to the East, Frank noted that he was "quite a bit shy, but he will learn—he will have to."[28]

Having character also meant associating with the right characters. Frank's circle included Charlie Fossum, Dinty Gunn, Mac McSorley, and his old Manila roommate Bill Hart, the Fuller Paint Company technician whose marriage, Frank imagined, came much to the relief of husbands along the China coast. Frank was also friends with "Tiny" Worden, the six-foot-three-inch all-American tackle now Texas Oil employee stationed in Saigon, who sent Frank two feet of an elephant he jokingly claimed to have run over with his bicycle. Frank, too, liked to gift golf clubs and other luxuries to friends and clients, tributes intended to seal relationships. They in turn threw him business when they could. In Depression-era Southeast Asia—a region laced with tariffs and quotas, with Buy British campaigns, Chinese boycotts of Japanese goods, and other nationalist consumer causes—trade had become deeply tribal.[29]

By the mid-thirties none of these growing rivalries irked Frank more than what he labeled the "Menace of Japanese Competition." Americans' enactment of anti-Japanese immigration policies and other laws in recent decades had deeply offended the Japanese, and tensions continued to mount as the United States and Japan jockeyed for greater influence in Asia and world power status more generally. Both nations had penetrated markets ceded by Europeans during World War I and emerged from the conflict as creditors, and both had supported streams of citizens moving to overseas business enclaves, anchored by consulates, banks, and chambers of commerce. But while American firms faltered in the 1930s, Japanese agents had leapt into the breach, flooding markets from India to the Philippines with their exports, winning over colonial subjects with cheap textiles and other goods. Western governments pushed back with new trade and travel restrictions. Animosities and resentments festered. Deeper narratives were at stake in the rise or fall of economic fortunes. The sight of British, Dutch, French, and American offices boarded up in the ports and capitals of their colonies, of destitute Westerners begging a meal, punctured the illusion of the colonizers' infallibility. In Asia, the Great Depression was understood as a "white man's economic collapse," and one that seriously weakened arguments in favor of the current imperial regimes.[30]

Against this "decline of Western prestige," as the longtime American resident of China Edgar Snow put it, Japan's political and military leaders grew ever bolder. A sense of mission to forge a new order in the East, embodied by the young Emperor Hirohito who had been enthroned in 1926, intensified longstanding Japanese desires for territory and control of strategic resources beyond the home islands. Japan's self-preservation, many thought, demanded more places to settle its people, more raw materials to mine for its factories, and more markets in which to sell its goods. "Real peace," argued one Japanese intellectual, could only be had with the destruction of Western tariff barriers, "the emancipation of raw materials," and long-denied "freedom of immigration." To drive home White imperialists' hypocrisy, in 1932 the Emperor's spokesmen declared a Monroe Doctrine for Asia. Japanese leadership would uplift the entire region and purify it of Western influence. "Asiatics, awake! . . . Overthrow white domination!" blared leaflets dropped over Chinese cities by Japanese planes. "A fundamental shift in the racial fronts is taking place," warned Snow. Nations like these, he cautioned, would not be "stopped by mere frowns of disapproval."[31]

To weather the growing competition in the region, Frank recommended a range of schemes to diversify his company's business. He pitched buying a pineapple plant, to "get another finger in the Malaya pie," or developing an insurance line. Not a single American company in Singapore—Goodyear, Eveready, Palmolive, Standard Oil's local subsidiary—was satisfied with their marketing set up, Frank reported to New York. If Dodge & Seymour started an advertising agency and "operated it on an aggressive American basis," they could get this business given the "natural affinity" between compatriots. He proposed opening a branch office in the East Indies, assuring his bosses that he knew how to finagle the liability so they wouldn't get "nailed to the cross" by Dutch taxes. He had already spotted a rental in Batavia. But each idea was shot down in turn by his skeptical superiors. "You fellows in the field during the past seven years haven't fully realized just what all corporations have been up against because you have always received your pay regularly and whether the company made any money or not," Seymour admonished him. Things were getting "tougher and tougher all over the world." War might erupt any moment in Europe. And there was the "battle against the New Deal" at home. The moment, Seymour lectured, demanded "care and caution." Frank pushed back, telling his bosses that they didn't understand, being so far away in New York, and eventually they agreed to a modest budget for an office in Batavia.[32] The posting would be Frank's last as a businessman in Southeast Asia.

The Netherlands East Indies, a three-thousand-mile-wide island chain wedged between the Indian and Pacific Oceans, had been a prize Dutch colony for more than a century, a fertile, oil-rich region sixty times the size of and with seven times as many people as the Netherlands itself, a money maker for the metropole. Despite its extractive resources, however, the islands depended on imports such as rice from mainland Asia, textiles from Japan, and machinery from Europe and, increasingly, the United States. American trade with the East Indies soared during and after World War I, soon surpassing even Dutch economic ties to the colony. By the 1920s, Americans bought roughly half of the archipelago's rubber, nearly all its tea and quinine, and 80 percent or more of its palm oil, cigar wrappers, and raw coffee. These materials slipped almost unnoticed into tires, soaps, and other consumer goods. Most Americans reflected little on the supply stream until it was lost.[33]

Though fewer than those who went to the Philippines and China, Americans came to the East Indies in record numbers after World War I. Tourists filed off ocean liners. Botanists and anthropologists hiked through rain forests. Missionaries moved to Borneo, and artists and writers congregated on Bali. General Motors, Goodyear, and other US corporations sent employees to the islands to manage their deepening investments. "Shorty" Elliot from Oklahoma presided over American employees at the Palembang concession Standard Oil had wrestled from the Dutch in 1927. By the late thirties, the $257 million installation encompassed storage tanks, a refining plant, and some 520 wells, producing 44,000 barrels a day. "All this is protected by British Singapore," *Life* gushed about the magnificent complex.[34]

Many Americans heaped compliments on the Dutch as "wise" colonial rulers—certainly more enlightened than British and French civil servants in Asia and perhaps only surpassed, they ventured, by US officials' own stewardship of the Philippines.[35] The image was one that Netherlands officials had cultivated since the turn-of-the-century unveiling of a new *Ethische Politiek*, or Ethical Policy, which promised to leave behind the unsavory legacies of the Dutch East India Company's plunder of the Spice Islands in favor of a new era of reform. Colonial managers irrigated fruitful lands to make them even more bountiful, propelling the island chain to the forefront of the world economy. They stamped out disease with sanitation and inoculation programs. They taught villagers to fight insect plagues, prevent root rot, and play sports. They built scientific institutes, wildlife preserves, and sparkling canals. Even Imamura Hitoshi, the commander of Japan's 16th Army, after swimming ashore during the invasion of Java in 1942, would stop to admire the Dutch-built roads.[36]

Taking the Dutch at their word, White Americans rarely dug below these showy aspects of colonial rule to try to understand the archapelago's complex politics. They noted the islands' land policies, which favored Indonesians, but said little about their race-based salary scales. The pictorial road signs that Americans found charming were necessary, because Dutch officials declined to spread education and literacy too widely. Some 90 percent of the population still could not read. The daily recitals of superiority and inferiority enacted in dining rooms and parlors, the rote repetition of clichés about the "natives," whose requests to be called Indonesians went unheeded—all the pretenses and convenient fictions of empire, growing ever more threadbare, most Americans, like most Europeans, preferred to ignore. White visitors and residents instead saw what they wanted to see: an unusually safe and orderly place, populated by complacent people, "happy and contented in their bamboo huts," in the words of one US consul, who would not be ready for independence, he estimated, for fifty to seventy-five years.[37]

In fact, political movements were flowering across the East Indies and Southeast Asia more broadly. The Chinese Revolution of 1911, and subsequent battles between Nationalists, Communists, and other factions as well as with the Japanese, had politicized the region's large overseas Chinese population. Independence movements in India and the Philippines meanwhile galvanized activists in other colonies, not least in the East Indies, where Asia's first Communist Party had been founded in 1920 and which was now also home to a number of anti-imperialist, pan-Islamic, and radical labor groups. Indonesians "opened their hearts" when Whites were out of earshot, discovered the Filipino writer and future president of the United Nations General Assembly Carlos Romulo. They voiced anger, eagerness to gamble on change, confessions of admiration for the way Tokyo defied the Western powers. "Everywhere I went I heard talk in favor of Japan," he explained.[38]

Dutch security forces crushed any signs of such indigenous organizing with brutal force. When insurgencies rocked Java and Sumatra in 1926 and 1927, they arrested some thirteen thousand Communists and other activists and sent a tenth of them to Boven-Digoel, a prison camp built in the remote Papua interior to house opponents of the regime. By the time Frank moved to Java, staunch conservatives had gained control of the government, rolling back some of the more liberal policies of previous decades and jailing or exiling prominent anticolonialists, including the future Indonesia leaders Sukarno and Mohammad Hatta. Even as war drew closer, Dutch officials continued to balk at Indonesians' requests for a full parliament, squandering any potential for a broad-based alliance to resist a foreign invasion. Repressive policies in the colony led Hatta and others to conclude that freedom would only be gained by bloody upheaval.[39]

Ignoring these tensions as much as possible, most Americans found Java, the East Indies's central island, a "delightful revelation." Its tiered rice paddies scaled up the sides of steaming volcanoes "like stairways for giants," thought one visitor. Home to more people than all the states from Maine to Florida, the island's *kampungs*, or villages, were networked by roads overflowing with bicyclists, peddlers balancing harvests on their heads, and buffalo-drawn carts whose lackadaisical drivers drove Frank crazy. He wondered what a Kansas City truck driver would make of these scenic but chaotic byways.[40]

White inhabitants lived well in Batavia's exclusive suburbs, taking tea in their pajamas and afternoon naps to beat the heat. Frank enjoyed dining on the terrace of the luxury Hotel des Indes, carousing at the nightclub Ye Olde Chat Noir, and picnicking with friends on the beach at Merak. He never imagined that Japanese troops would pick that same palm tree shaded stretch of sand to launch an invasion.[41]

Many Westerners on Java—who had watched with unease as the Japanese withdrew from the League of Nations in 1933, signed the Anti-Comintern Pact in 1936, strayed from their Washington Naval Treaty agreements, and poured funding into their military's budget—had taken perverse comfort from the eruption of full-blown war between China and Japan in 1937. Bogged down on the mainland, the Japanese would be "too busy to bother us," cheered the East Indies (it turns out last) governor general. But as the Emperor's soldiers gobbled up Shanghai, Nanjing, Canton, and other Chinese cities, and when, by early 1939, they occupied Hainan and the Spratly Islands in the South China Sea, doubts nagged at Dutch officials who knew that if Japanese forces turned their attentions further south, their domain would be a logical target. Rumors told of Japan's fishermen and pearlers charting the waters off the archipelago's outer islands, of its agents building football fields in Malaya for use as airfields, establishing a secret settlement on a remote island near New Guinea, or angling to buy Portuguese Timor.[42]

The growing suggestion that Japanese forces might try to drive White colonizers out of Asia gave hope to many Indonesian anticolonial nationalists. But most Westerners dismissed the notion as ridiculous. They fundamentally underestimated the abilities and ambitions of Japanese leaders. Policymakers back in Washington believed that they could restrain Japan with economic pressure—first with a "moral embargo," discouraging American businesses from selling the Japanese key materials, then by allowing a thirty-year commercial treaty between the two nations to lapse, and eventually with obligatory export controls on airplanes, munitions, machine parts, and aviation gasoline. The strategy proved as effective as throwing water on a grease fire, pushing the Japanese closer and closer to a spectacular decision: if the United States cut off all fuel sales, as seemed increasingly possible, Japan would have to wrest a new source of supply from the Dutch, by diplomatic means if possible, by military ones if not.[43]

In the meantime, Frank remained preoccupied with his new Batavia office, which had not performed as hoped. Eager to cast American businessmen as "interlopers" and poach as many of their clients as possible, "short sighted and selfish" Dutch importers were establishing their own agencies in New York. Motorcar companies, moreover, had begun drafting contracts with clauses that required buyers to purchase parts from manufacturers rather than third parties, leaving Dodge & Seymour able to sell only garage equipment and special supplies that the principals did not produce themselves. Worse still, as communication and travel networks became more reliable and as market connections forged by pioneers like Frank became comfortable and routine, customers were learning to buy all kinds of brands direct, bypassing middlemen altogether. By virtue of their own success, trade intermediaries like Frank threatened to make themselves obsolete.[44]

Disappointed with his company's continued lack of daring, Frank began talking to the directors of another trading house based in Semarang, a day's drive east of Batavia. Their operation was "high calibred." They listened to his ideas. An import-export firm at heart, they nevertheless had branched out into production, finance, insurance, and shipping. The firm presided over sugar and tapioca factories in the East Indies, a distillery in China, and branch offices in Bangkok, Calcutta, Karachi, and elsewhere. "This organization is exactly what I have been urging on D&S for several years," Frank boasted to his sister. Gradually he scaled back his responsibilities to the New York office and began working for this other company—the Oei Tiong Ham Concern, the largest Chinese firm in Southeast Asia.[45]

Tracing its roots to Oei Tjie Sien, a Fujianese immigrant who began his business by peddling cheap imported porcelain, silks, tea, and herbs door to door on Java in the 1860s, the family firm made a killing in sugar speculation during World War I. By the time Frank joined the company as one of its only non-Chinese executives, the conglomerate was directed by the founder's grandson, Oei Tjong Hauw, who Frank admired as "a very intelligent and likeable chap," willing to take risks and embrace modern commercial methods while others wavered.[46] As the general manager for the Kian Gwan Import Division on Java, which handled some ten million guilders worth of business annually, Frank took charge of an operation far larger than anything he had directed for Dodge & Seymour. Working with "a very smart Chinese" at his elbow, he had "absolute freedom" to purchase from anywhere, not just the United States. The hectic pace was exciting. But the move baffled his New York bosses. It was so hard to get "competent help" in the East, Seymour warned Frank. One had to be "hardboiled" to direct Asian employees, and he predicted for Frank a "rude awakening" when "American business methods come in juxtaposition with the placidity of the Orient." To save face for the fact that their man was working on such equal terms with Chinese traders, Dodge and Seymour told clients back in the States that they had "lent" Frank to Kian Gwan "to organize their business along American lines." Frank paid this no mind. "There is practically no limit to the size of the company I shall be permitted to build," he exclaimed to his sister.[47]

Businessmen like Frank did not want the disruptions war would bring. Trade was supposed to create new affinities, connections that would lead to understanding and interdependence. But businessmen wanted things that often led to war nevertheless. They wanted control over resources, a lock on customers, a leg up on competitors. They trafficked in strategic materials and ethnic trust networks that made war more likely and more possible. Where things went and in what quantities, who would or wouldn't sell to whom, spoke volumes about the power and plans of nations on the make. So, when Frank's German contacts started to refuse to fill his orders in 1939, he took it as an ominous sign. The invasion of Poland that September came to him as little surprise.[48]

II

Stolen Soil

HE TRIED TO MAKE PEACE with them. Or at least he made it look like he had come to terms with Spain's Second Republic, which succeeded General Miguel Primo de Rivera's dictatorship in 1931, and with the administration of Franklin D. Roosevelt, which came to power two years later. Manual Diaz's shipping agency after all would thrive off the policies of both left-leaning governments. At least for a while.

Even in hard times, New York harbor commanded 85 percent of US foreign passenger traffic and 54 percent by value of its foreign maritime commerce. Whistling towboats, car floats, ferries, barges, and the vessels of some ninety steamship lines zipped in and out of Manhattan's cruise terminals and dumped mounds of freight onto Brooklyn's skids and slips. On the borough's wharves, commodities were unpacked, sorted, and whisked away by an army of escalator trailers, lift trucks, crane hoists, chisel prongs, and newsprint scoops.[1]

Boats were cheap, so in 1932 Manuel and his partner, Marcelino Garcia, bought two secondhand cargo ships, the *Motomar* and the *Navemar*, and founded their own South America Line. Shortly thereafter, Roosevelt's Good Neighbor policy led to lowered tariffs and new trade treaties as well as a sharp uptick in tourist travel to Latin America. The repeal of Prohibition meanwhile revived the transatlantic wine trade. The Second Republic increased subsidies and support for Spain's shipping lines and granted Garcia & Diaz the blue chip Compañía Trasatlántica account, which had just modernized its fleet. Manuel handled the affairs of the so-called Spanish Line's luxurious flagships, the *Marqués de Comillas* and the *Magallanes*, which covered a triangular route between Spain, Cuba, and New York. Newspaper ads featuring a lithe flamenco dancer beckoned travelers to Garcia & Diaz's romantic cruises. The firm soon doubled its sailing schedules and procured its own terminal at Pier 42 on the Hudson River.[2]

Manuel's fortunes earned him and his wife, Edith, a place among New York's Spanish-speaking elite. They hobnobbed with diplomats in the ballroom of Sherry's and the suites of the Waldorf-Astoria. Their luncheons and costume parties graced the society columns. As president of New York's Spanish Chamber of Commerce, Manuel led toasts. At a reception for Claude Bowers, Roosevelt's ambassador to Spain, he praised his homeland's fledgling republic for embarking, he said, on its very own "new deal." But he did not really mean it. Like many businessmen, he opposed progressive labor legislation. He and Marcelino soon joined dozens of other agents in organizing an association to head off new shipping codes stipulated by the National Industrial Recovery Administration. More consequentially, they would collaborate with the fascist-inspired Falange Party—founded by the late dictator Primo de Rivera's son, José Antonio—and assist General Francisco Franco's Nationalist coup in hopes of toppling the Spanish Republic.[3]

Falangists and other rightwing Spaniards advocated radical action to stave off the world's growing leftist threats as well as to revive their nation's status as a leading maritime power. Such transatlantic ambitions thrilled men like Manuel. "Spain will seek its glory and its riches across the seas," promised the Falange's founding manifesto. Reactionary Spanish papers heaped scorn on those who stood in the way of Spain's rightful dominion over the Hispanic Americas, which, they believed, were bound to *la Madre Patria* by tradition, language, and religion. They deplored the "Monroeism" of US politicians. They decried the supposedly predatory influence of Wall Street "plutocrats" and "international Jewry." One Falangist sheet beseeched readers never to forget who had "annihilated us as a world power"—the United States. Spanish nationalists across the Western Hemisphere "talked morosely, mystically, but *seriously*, of the glorious day when the Spanish Empire would again come into its own," discovered one investigative journalist.[4]

Manuel and his partner could hardly be considered unusual for their rightwing allegiances. New York in the 1930s had no shortage of fascist sympathizers. Its large Italian population harbored enormous numbers of Mussolini supporters. Forty percent of the German American Bund's members resided in New York, especially in Manuel's one-time borough

Manuel returns from a trip to Spain on his ship, the *Motomar*, with his daughter (*left*), wife (*third from left*), and son (*third from right*). *Brooklyn Times Union*, September 18, 1934.

Brooklyn, and an estimated twelve thousand of the city's out-of-work Irish longshoremen, off-duty cops, and sundry Nazi enthusiasts answered the antisemitic radio priest Father Charles Coughlin's call to form the paramilitary Christian Front in 1938.[5] But what did make Manuel and Marcelino exceptional was their ability, as international shipping agents, to throw up legal roadblocks against their enemies, to pressure diplomats and leaders located along vital trade routes, and to open up or choke off information and supply networks. The contest over ships during the Spanish Civil War—the lessons it delivered about how global slipstreams directed or diverted the men and materiel that would determine the fate of countless others—helped to prepare Manuel for future battles on the Atlantic.

Civil War came early to Asturias, the province Manuel had come from and one of the most polarized regions of Spain. In 1934 a miners' strike snowballed into full-blown insurrection. Radicals raged against industrialists and landowners. They murdered priests, burned churches and convents, and occupied several towns, including Manuel's birthplace, Gijón. General Franco repressed the movement using the same merciless tactics he used to subjugate the colonized people of Spanish Morocco, winning him gratitude and a following among the upper classes. The inept leftist government, many Spaniards concluded, had given too much license to anticlericalists, communists, anarchists, strikers, socialists, and separatists—troublemakers all. Thus when a rightwing coalition of *Nacionales*—"true Spaniards"—rose up in July 1936 to take back the country, patriots like Manuel saw it as a heroic attempt to save their nation.[6]

Manuel reeled from the highs and lows of the early days of the insurrection and lived "from hour to hour pending news from Spain." He rejoiced in the remarkable spirit of "our troops" but agonized over setbacks at Madrid, where Republican loyalists held out. Cut off from his firm's Barcelona office, he had no idea how "our people" fared in that "bad place," surely doomed, he despaired, "for we know what element is dominating there." In early August, Manuel's first ship to arrive from Spain since the start of the uprising docked at New York. Visibly shaken tourists hurried off the bullet-riddled *Magallanes* with tales of their narrow escape from crossfire in the harbor of A Coruña. Slowly, through letters and telegrams, he learned about unfortunate friends back home, suffering "a thousand hardships" at the hands of the "reds." He prayed, "may God will" that they find refuge in some embassy or across the border. The fate of Gijón remained uncertain as leftist miners besieged nearby towns and, though outnumbered, beat back Franco's forces. One rebel insurgent wrote to Manuel that he would be "astonished to see so much destruction" on the Asturian front. The Nationalists would not take Gijón, the final Republican holdout in the north, until the following October. But they would savor their reprisals when they did, dumping two thousand bodies into a single mass grave.[7]

The effects of the civil war famously rippled outward from Spain, mobilizing foreign volunteers and relief workers, inspiring artists, and emboldening Italy's and Germany's dictators, who tested their latest weapons on the peninsula's rugged terrain, while rattling the confidence and credibility of liberal governments, not least those of France, Britain, and the United States, which lacked the spirit to come to the Republic's aid. Wherever Spanish émigrés could be found, their factions waged surrogate wars in local newspapers, and police forces struggled to keep the peace between rival street demonstrators. In Mexico, the conflict exacerbated debates about land reform and the role of the church and the military. In

Cuba, it provoked questions about the prominent position of Spaniards in the economy. In the United States, as in Europe, the war lent itself to emerging narratives about the great struggle between democracy and dictatorship as well as intensifying tensions between Jews, many of whom favored the Republic, and Catholics, who flocked to the other side.[8]

The vital role played by ships, their agents, and crews ensured that the war's effects bled out from Spain's borders in other, less remembered ways. Like most modern civil wars, this one depended on overseas financing and provisioning. From across the Portuguese border, supplies, troops, and funding from exiled businessmen poured into the Nationalist cause. German planes and Italian battleships brought further reinforcements, turning what otherwise would have been a failed coup into a protracted conflict. Meanwhile the Republic found far fewer wealthy backers and often lost out against Nationalists competing for arms purchases on Europe's open market. What money could be raised by exhausting the state's coffers and selling off gold and silver reserves surreptitiously to foreign takers, including the United States government, still could not solve the problem of securing enough imports. The Spanish navy remained far more loyal to the Republic than the army in the war's early stages, but it struggled to maintain maritime supply lines under the Nationalists' ever tightening blockade. Foreign ships cut a wide berth around the Iberian Peninsula to avoid its minefields and submarines. The handful of British and French blockade runners willing to defy their governments' noninterventionist policies to bring weapons or humanitarian aid ran great risks to sneak past rebel bombers and vigilant patrol boats in the Bay of Biscay. The Republic scraped by on paltry rations, second-hand goods hauled over the Pyrenees, and Soviet charity flown in for an unspoken price.[9]

Resenting their disadvantages, the Republic's leaders lashed out at the capitalists who had propped up the "Military Fascist uprising" and began issuing decrees commandeering the property of hostile enterprises. Loyalist sympathizers argued that ship owners and agents stood among the worst such offenders—from Juan March, the Mediterranean tobacco smuggler turned shipping mogul who almost singlehandedly bankrolled Franco's bid for power, to a host of lesser-known merchants "working in collusion" with rebel fundraisers and overseas gunrunners. Getting word of government intentions to confiscate the vessels of rebel-friendly shipping lines, Spanish Republican crews stationed on ships throughout the Atlantic mutinied against pro-Franco officers and took control of their vessels. From New York, Manuel watched as the war swallowed the Spanish Line boats he had tended, one by one. In September 1936, the crew of the *Manuel Arnús* revolted against its rightwing captain and steered the ship to Havana, where it was interned under Cuban naval guard. That same month, barely recovered from its escape from A Coruña, the *Magallanes* detoured to Mexico under government orders to load an arms shipment before running the rebel blockade. The *Marqués de Comillas,* taken by loyalists, would be captured and lost and recaptured by rebels in the first year of the war. Each time the ship changed hands, its raiders summarily executed the old crew.[10]

A ship was like a patch of Spanish soil, adrift, reenacting the war in microcosm on the high seas until it collided with the laws and politics of other nations. Manuel and his partner in particular saw to it that the United States and other neutral nations would not be able to cordon off the war zone neatly with an embargo. Refusing any shipments to ports held by the loyalists, Garcia & Diaz routed transports through Lisbon instead, unloading Chilean nitrates and other freight at least once a month in the Nationalists' main provisioning base. The two shipping agents quickly topped the Spanish Republic's list of overseas enemies. Rather than recognizing their duty to transport vital supplies for a democratically elected government under siege, loyalist officials raged, they prolonged the war "by aiding in the criminal work of the Fascists with a cleverly disguised and stubbornly maintained attitude." As retaliation, the Republic stripped Manuel of his signatory powers as New York's Spanish Chamber of Commerce president and expropriated his and Marcelino's South American Line ships, the *Motomar* and *Navemar.* "In Valencia they have honored us, not only with the decrees of confiscation of the two ships," Manuel scowled to a Franco ally in Spain, but also with others taking "all that my partner and I possess 'for services given to the Fascist cause.'" Undeterred, the agents prepared to mount their own personal war from New York City. Installing a miniature ship flying the Nationalist flag at the entry to their offices, they wrote letters to the State Department in hopes of obtaining permits to export arms and munitions themselves.[11]

The Republic first targeted the *Navemar* in October 1936, notifying its crew of a planned government takeover when they called at Rosario, Argentina, but allowing them to proceed to New York to first discharge an American-owned cargo. Upon arrival at the Brooklyn docks, the boat's Nationalist officers went ashore to plot with Manuel and Marcelino, who wanted to defy the order. In their absence, leftist sailors took command of the vessel in the name of the Republic. Manuel and Marcelino arranged for US marshals to come to the docks to read a court order through an interpreter, declaring the ship theirs. The unimpressed mutineers gathered on its decks and swore they would "resist by force." Despite protests from the furious agents, port authorities declined to take the craft with violence. Manuel and Marcelino filed a motion accusing the renegade crew of being in contempt of court, and while the loyalist seamen came ashore to answer the charges, the agents' partisans snuck off and occupied the *Navemar*. Although the "Valencia bandits" had done them "as much harm as they could," Manuel gloated, he and his partner had thwarted their "scheme" with a "judicial expedient." Protests by the Spanish Republic's ambassador aroused no one at the State Department, so, with no other options, the loyalists returned to the courts. The ship collected barnacles under federal guard for the duration of the civil war while the case wound its way through a series of rulings and reversals all the way up to the Supreme Court, which sent it back to start over at the district level. American judges tried to contain the dispute's explosive implications by pondering bloodless questions about jurisdiction and business procedure. But the *Navemar*, now a seemingly permanent harbor monument, offered Staten Island commuters a daily reminder of how easily somebody else's war could come cruising into the Upper Bay.[12]

While the *Navemar* descended into legal purgatory, loyalists turned their sights on the *Motomar*. En route from Buenos Aires to New York with a cargo of linseed, the ship received orders from Republic agents to divert to Mexico. Catching wind of the captain's intentions to obey, Manuel and his partner bullied him with radiograms, insisting the ship resume course but to no avail. The vessel had been "stolen from us on the high seas," Manuel wailed, and then, docked in Veracruz, it was guarded by Mexican soldiers who imprisoned its two Nationalist officers. Again, Manuel and Marcelino tried to pry the *Motomar* loose with legal maneuvering, but their efforts went nowhere in the only country, besides the Soviet Union, openly selling arms to the Republic. The *Motomar* lingered in Veracruz for months while its crew loaded the vessel with guns, garbanzo beans, and other supplies. Manuel pestered a local Spanish customs house broker for information: "I regret bothering you about this matter, but you will understand how important it is for all of us."[13]

At last some good news arrived from Spain in early 1937. Manuel rejoiced when Nationalists and Italian troops besieged Málaga in February, killing thousands, including women and children as they fled the city. The Falangist son of the *Navemar*'s captain unfortunately had died in the brutal takeover, one of the most infamous chapters in the war, but otherwise Manuel counted it a "great moral and material triumph for General Franco." In the north, too, he predicted Basque separatists were "*muy listos*"—finished. He expected them to surrender Bilbao to prevent its destruction. "May God will that I am not mistaken," he declared.[14]

But thoughts of his lost ships still consumed him. When Nationalists captured the *Marqués de Comillas* that same season, arming it for Mediterranean patrols and unceremoniously disposing of its loyalist crew, Manuel thought it "*magnifico*." He hoped that when the *Motomar* finally sailed from Veracruz they would catch it, too, and hang its captain and first engineer from the mast. But the *Motomar* stayed put, and another loyalist ship, the *Mar Cantábrico*, appeared off the coast of Mexico after racing out of New York harbor with a cache of hastily loaded munitions, only hours before Congress broadened the recently enacted Neutrality Act's prohibition on arms sales to warring nations so that it also applied to the "civil strife" in Spain. In coded cablegrams, Manuel's contact in Veracruz reported everything he could about the vessel, and when the *Mar Cantábrico* sailed, Manuel alerted the liaison "who is to warn our government in Spain." Nationalist patrols were therefore ready for the ship, which they ambushed in the Bay of Biscay, confiscating its cargo and shooting the loyalists on board. "It is a pity," Manuel reflected, that Franco's rebels did not extend the war into the Western Hemisphere by posting a "speedy armed ship in the strait of Yucatan."[15]

Waging legal battles to recover ships in at least four countries—the United States, Mexico, Great Britain, and Cuba—Manuel tormented the Republic's diplomats as well as the officials of other nations caught in the crossfire.[16] In Mexico, the local Spanish Republican chargé d'affaires, struggling to get the *Motomar* across the Atlantic and "obviously working under considerable strain," begged US officials to help defend the vessel against the efforts of Marcelino and Manuel, who "will do anything they can to embarrass the Spanish government." But the State Department was in "no blinking mood with regard to neutrality questions." Believing that the *Motomar*'s cargo included supplies exported from the United States under false pretenses, its agents instead scurried to track down loyalists' transshipment networks in Latin America with the help of local informants and Pan American Airways employees.[17]

Manuel's persistence caused no less fallout in Havana, to which he traveled several times during a year and a half of litigation regarding the *Manuel Arnús*. While there, he lobbied Fulgencio Batista's government to recognize Franco. That failed but, by March 1938, Manuel had at least received permission from the courts to take possession of the *Manuel Arnús*. Defying the court ruling, however, local Spanish Republicans in collusion with Mexican diplomats plotted the ship's escape by negotiating with sympathetic Cuban officials and bribing Havana's navy patrols. At last minute the vessel slipped out of the city's harbor under the command of a Mexican naval officer flown in for the purpose. The island's rightwing press erupted with protests, prompting resignations in the Cuban cabinet and spreading rumors that Mexico planned to convert the ship into a tanker to carry oil to Japan. The boat in fact met an even more ignominious end in Veracruz after it broke free of its moorings and drifted onto a sandbank. There the *Manuel Arnús* would lay stranded until 1942, when the Mexican government lobbied the United States to buy it for use as target practice.[18]

Back in New York, Manuel and his associates turned their attention to founding the Casa de España, a social club for Spanish merchants but one with unvarnished political objectives. As Marcelino's first act as the Casa's president (Manuel was treasurer), he sent a cable to Franco, "to greet you," he said, who "save our country and defend the fundamental principles of civilization. As true patriots we are unconditionally at your orders for whatever you desire." Falange officials traveled to New York to school the Casa's members in the objectives of the Falange Exterior, the party's overseas branch, akin to the German American Bund. In Spain, the group had been dominated by roughnecks and rogue intellectuals, but in the Americas it also attracted upper-class émigrés like Manuel, who brought to the movement substantial resources, connections, and a patina of respectability.[19] Buoyed by Franco's assurances that, under his rule, "Spaniards who live abroad will no longer be abandoned like outcasts," members of the Casa gathered in the dining room of the Park Central Hotel in their Sunday best. Marcelino presided, toasting the illustrious Caudillo for leading the "glorious movement for the new Spain." Informants who infiltrated the meetings insisted that attendees also made fascist salutes and defenses of Mussolini and Hitler.[20]

Yet a groundswell of leftist agitation in New York met the rightwing Spaniards' every effort. Labor militants exiled from Spain rallied a majority of the city's twenty-two thousand Spanish residents to the loyalist defense. They organized door-to-door collections, pamphleteered in the streets, boycotted pro-Franco businesses, and picketed in front of Garcia & Diaz's offices. They found allies among the five boroughs' fast-rising Dominican, Cuban, and Puerto Rican populations, once at odds with *peninsulares* over the issue of colonial independence but now united by the shared working-class politics of the *Frente Popular*. Black antifascists, unionists, and leftist entertainers and intellectuals also joined the cause. Local celebrities from the professional wit Dorothy Parker to the stripper Gypsy Rose Lee headlined benefit concerts and staffed Greenwich Village fairs where crowds made small donations to throw darts at "fascist pigs." Rightwing Spaniards grumbled that New York was turning into another "Barcelona."[21]

It was only a matter of time before Manuel and his associates fell under public scrutiny. Someone, maybe a loyalist sympathizer on one of their own ships, had been intercepting their mail. On May 10, 1937, Manuel returned home from one of his trips to Cuba to full-blown scandal, his firm's scheming splashed across the pages of the *Daily Worker* in lurid detail. For five days, the Communist paper luxuriated in a serial exposé about these "fascist pirates" who "infest American ports" and "play ducks and drakes with American neutrality." Alongside its sensational cartoons and editorials, the paper reproduced seven of Manuel's and Marcelino's letters with translations and extended exposition. The stolen correspondence left little doubt that the two shipping agents had thrown in their lot with a network of far-right activists waging a historic and spiritual battle that spanned three continents. In them, Manuel branded Republican leaders "*bandidos*"; English bureaucrats in Bermuda as lazy and worthless as "Zulus"; and American journalists stupid for falling for Communist lies and unwisely belittling "the successes of our glorious army." Manuel had lived in the United States for thirty years but the only hint of domestic American life in the letters came from his contempt for its supposedly mostly "Jewish" press.[22]

The *Daily Worker*'s revelations touched a nerve with more than those on the far left. Breaking only two weeks after Germany's Condor Legion bombed Guernica—Basque protesters had just staged a thousand-person protest outside the office building Garcia & Diaz shared with the Third Reich's consulate—Manuel's and Marcelino's correspondence quickly caught the attention of the newswires and in turn the scrutiny of Congress. Senator Gerald Nye denounced the two shipping agents as leading members of a spy ring "in close touch with strange missions which come from abroad." He demanded that the government investigate and possibly deport Manuel and Marcelino for violating American neutrality policies and threatening the principles of the Monroe Doctrine. Why did the State Department allow such "Spanish Fascists" to remain "on our soil and mock our laws?"

Spanish loyalists protest in front of the building Garcia & Diaz shared with the German consulate. FPG/Hulton Archive/Getty Images.

Representative John T. Bernard echoed in the House. It was not the last time the question would be asked.[23]

In the late thirties, Latin American nations began to outlaw the Falange, deporting its most extreme members and driving the movement underground. But the group's organizing continued unabated in New York. Spanish Nationalists found numerous supporters and crowds for their fundraisers beyond their own community, including many Catholic leaders, who saw the coup as pushback against the increasing persecution of Christians at the hands of godless Communists; conservative businessmen, who likened Franco to George Washington resisting tyranny; and other rightwing New Yorkers inspired by the "Franco way." At one "Americanism and Neutrality" rally, funded in part by Marcelino, some ten thousand attendees cheered on speakers who attacked communism and atheism and applauded references to Europe's dictators. When someone paraded a picture of Father Coughlin through the audience, members of the Christian Front interrupted the proceedings with roughhousing in the aisles.[24]

By late 1938—with its military shredded, its factions turning against each other, and its people starving—the Republic was clearly doomed. Franco's forces won the Battle of Ebro in November and took Barcelona two months later. On the oceans, they had also captured the lion's share of Spain's merchant and navy ships as formerly loyalist crews, sensing an imminent Nationalist victory, defected in droves. Though Manuel and his associates never regained their own expropriated ships while the Republic lasted, they had crippled loyalist attempts to use the vessels for desperately needed imports.[25]

The *Motomar*, for one, never made it to Spain with its supplies. In need of repairs, the ship set sail from Mexico for Bermuda after the US government would not ensure it protection from legal action by Garcia & Diaz if it stopped at Galveston. British officials also refused it permission to drydock, so the ailing vessel slunk back to Veracruz to wait out the war. Losing meant winning for Manuel in New York, too. Hearing the case of the *Navemar* for a final time, the Second Circuit appeals court found ample evidence in the ship's rolls and receipts signed by the captain to suggest that the Spanish Republic had taken legitimate control of the vessel in international waters. A ship was different from the cargo it carried, the court reasoned. Not merely private property, it was a "part of the territory of the sovereign whose flag it flies." Unconvinced by Manuel's and Marcelino's posturing as victims unfairly persecuted by usurpers an ocean away, the court ordered the *Navemar* released to the Spanish Republican consul on March 31, 1939, settling the case the same day that the loyalists capitulated to their enemies across the Atlantic. It was a final, pointless victory for the Republic, won not on the Spanish battlefields but in the American courts. Franco's incoming diplomats took over Spain's New York consulate and promptly returned the ship they inherited to Garcia & Diaz. To celebrate the Republic's demise, Marcelino presided over a dinner dance for hundreds of Casa de España guests. During the toasts, Franco's ambassador, Juan Francisco de Cárdenas, offered special thanks to Germany and Italy, "those countries who have helped us against our common enemy—communism."[26]

Manuel avoided the deportation proceedings his opponents had wanted. Congressmen stirred by Nye's speech despaired to learn that the 1924 immigration reforms included amnesty for those who had already lived in the United States for five years, even for "aliens in the true sense," one expert confirmed. Others forgot or did not care that he had a hand in the downfall of the Spanish Republic, so Manuel went on with his life. He trained his son in the family business and put his daughter through college. He won his neighborhood Rotary Club's trophy for the season's lowest net golf score. The picture of an upstanding citizen, he even testified as a character witness at a murder trial. Manuel and Marcelino made only one important change after their brush with scandal: they filed US naturalization papers. When asked to foreswear allegiance to a foreign prince or state—perhaps with a smirk—they renounced their fidelity to "The Republic of Spain."[27]

By 1939, Manuel was anxious to gather back together the Spanish Line fleet that had been scattered from Veracruz to Istanbul, and to begin transporting mounds of freight for the reconstruction of Spain. He dreamed of repaired commercial ties and soaring tourist traffic. Yet he and Marcelino also worried that taking up US citizenship would lose them the trust of Franco's regime. They made plans to travel to Spain to make their case in person. They explained to the Spanish Ministry of Foreign Affairs that they had not intended to naturalize and only did so after Nye's accusations as a "means to defend their business in this country." They professed uncompromised "*sentimientos españolistas*." Ambassador Cárdenas vouched for them. Manuel and Marcelino, he assured Franco officials, "have been at our side since the beginning."[28]

After vanquishing the Republic, rightwing Spaniards turned their gaze to the increasingly bold actions of Franco's ally Adolf Hitler, who seemed certain to face off with the liberal democracies that had unwisely "made common cause with the people of Israel," as *Arriba España* put it. The liberal world order dreamed up by the League of Nations was a failure, declared José Antonio Primo de Rivera. Instead, he prophesied, the globe would be "ruled by three or four racial units," and Spain should fight to be one of them. When war did come once again in September—this time pitting Germany against France and Britain—the captain of the *Motomar*, back working for Manuel in New York, dispatched a short message to Madrid. Everyone associated with the ship, he relayed, "*sin ninguna excepción*," stood ready for orders.[29]

Interlude

Bermuda to the Azores

13 hours, 10 minutes
1797 nautical miles
Cloudy skies

ON THE EVENING OF FEBRUARY 21, 1943, the *Yankee Clipper*'s inhabitants had only an hour or so left of daylight as they raced away from Bermuda and the setting sun. While the stewards prepared for dinner service in the lounge, passengers sampled hors d'oeuvres and cocktails in their compartments.[1]

What incredibly different passions have brought each of them here. They put their faith in such diverse endeavors—business or law, the stage or the pen—and they rooted for different political parties, futures, empires. They were haunted by different enemies—Cossacks or carpetbaggers, communists or fascists—and by different wars past. Ben could escape his thoughts about the fate of the Confederacy no easier than Spaniards like Manuel found it to accept losing to the Yankees in 1898. The Great War's trenches loomed large for George. For Tamara, the civil war aftermath of the Bolshevik Revolution, and reversals on the Eastern Front, would matter most. And yet, here they were on the same plane, traversing the same planet, hurtling toward the same war and the same disaster. None of them had needed the bombing of Pearl Harbor to wake up to world affairs. Their transnational engagements and crisscrossed movements—Manuel and Tamara making fresh starts in the New World, Harry and George returning to the continent of their forebearers, Frank and Ben seeking adventures in the Pacific—drew attention to the capacity of the twentieth century's accelerating international travel networks to unsettle expectations, identities, peace itself.

Consider the battle unfolding below them as they flew east into the mid-ocean air gap known as the Black Pit. In these waters beyond Bermuda, the Kriegsmarine's "milch cows" waited patiently to reprovision the German seamen stalking surface-going prey in their claustrophobic *Unterseeboots.* Over the horizon to the north, between the ice floes, floated a field of corpses. US Navy patrollers had stumbled upon the scene little more than two weeks earlier near a downed transport: hundreds of life-jacketed dead bobbing alongside rowboats full of men still in their pajamas and frozen to death at the oars. Tonight U-boat wolfpacks were closing in on a westbound convoy of sixty-three ships, slowed to a crawl off the Irish coast by howling winds and towering waves. They will pick fourteen of them off one by one. A straggling merchant vessel, the *Empire Trader*, was now, like the clipper, heaving toward the safety of Azores, but it will never make it. Tomorrow, a British rescue ship, the *Stockport*, will save its survivors, but then it, too, will be torpedoed and all on board will go to watery graves.[2]

Emergency equipment had been stashed away in the *Yankee Clipper*'s various holds in case the plane was shot down at sea: collapsible life rafts and jackets, rations and fresh water, chlorine to drive away sharks, and International Orange calcimine powder to counteract the hull's camouflage paint. Pan Am crews had to drop these supplies down to torpedoed sailors so often that they began carrying an extra kit for such occasions. But it was winter weather, not surface raiders or U-boats, that presented flying boats' greatest enemy on the Atlantic. Subzero temperatures iced their wings and froze their takeoff channels. Storms stretched for miles. The previous February lightning struck Sully's clipper after lift-off from Bermuda, burning a hole through the boat's hydrostabilizer and frying its transmitter. Headwinds for westbound planes proved so punishing in the colder months that the airline now plotted returns to New York via West Africa and Brazil. The *Yankee Clipper* was scheduled for this circuitous southern summer route after its stop at Lisbon.[3]

On the flight deck, Sully and the rest of the crew kept the plane's wing tip and tail running lights off even as it grew dark. With window shades drawn, the aircraft became a moving blackout. The navigator could still estimate its location by spying the stars through a dome-shaped skylight—if and when they peeked through the cloud cover—and radio signals from Pan Am's direction finder in the Azores kept them on course.[4]

Dinnertime. It was customary for Pan Am pilots to join some of the passengers at a captain's table in the lounge. What might Sully have said to his guests? He was not a man of many words, especially when asked about himself. "There is nothing to tell," he insisted to those who tried to pierce through the public persona Pan Am had crafted for their famous flier. On the rare occasions when he agreed to speak to some civic group or school, he did not produce any quotable phrases for the local newspapers. "I am no speaker," he'd claim. "Let the boys ask questions and I'll answer them."[5]

He could have explained to his dinner companions that he had grown up on a rented homestead outside Kearny, Nebraska, just after the turn of the century; that his father, the son of illiterate Irish immigrants, was not one for book learning; and that at school age, he, too, still could not read or write. But their dirt farm had a McCormick binder, a Rock Island lister, and other machinery to tinker with and repair, and such handiness earned him a job as a blacksmith when, like so many other Midwesterners in those years, Sully relocated to Southern California.[6]

If prodded, maybe he related how he joined the navy in 1918 as a chief machinist's mate and became so good at tending the Pacific Fleet's flying boats as they conducted tactical exercises in the coastal waters between Panama and Santa Barbara that he soon set his sights not just on fixing planes but also flying them. Sully was not the ideal candidate navy leaders had in mind for their pilot training courses. They wanted "high caliber" graduates from elite colleges, and at most he had completed basic public schooling and a series of International Correspondence School courses. But postwar demobilization had depleted the military's already modest aviation program, and its proponents were clamoring for new recruits. Navy Air School training earned Sully a spot as a flight instructor and test pilot at San Diego's North Island air station—until 1929 when he skipped off to join Pan American Airways.[7]

Sully's subsequent career highlights, helping Juan Trippe forge an air route across the Pacific, had already been lavishly recounted in magazines, newsreels, and the Warner Bros. film *China Clipper*, starring Humphrey Bogart. So maybe instead he liked to recount for passengers some of his less well-known exploits—about the time he hauled Red Cross supplies to the Dominican Republic in the aftermath of a hurricane, or when he trailed long green streamers from the tail of his plane all the way from Miami to Tampa in honor of St. Patrick's Day. He could have described the first long-range flying boat practice run he and three others had made in March 1935, from Miami to the US Virgin Islands and back without stopping, to simulate the distance from California to Pearl Harbor. Bundled in sweaters and flying suits, and keeping the windows open to dispel a strong fuel vapor, the men had begun the trip cold and uneasy. But just before midnight they reached St. Thomas as planned and turned back, picking up the Bahamas' aquamarine waters at dawn. By the time they finally brought their Sikorsky S-42 down on Florida's Biscayne Bay, they had remained aloft for a record seventeen hours and sixteen minutes.[8]

Probably Sully would not have told his fellow diners about all the close calls he'd had. About the emergency landing he once made near Curaçao after a broken cam gear in his left motor sent his ship plummeting. Or the time he narrowly avoided crashing a B-314 into Baltimore's waterfront freight yard, because the model's early prototypes tended to bounce, skid, and even porpoise in the water. Or about how near disaster he had come when he made the first ever attempt to land a plane at Wake atoll, because no one told him that divers had not finished blasting a path through the lagoon's coral heads. Likely he did not let slip that when the *China Clipper* took off for its celebrated inaugural trip from San Francisco to Manila, the crew did not swoop under the Bay Bridge's cables "for the benefit of watching school children," as the airline claimed, but because the M-130 failed to gain enough altitude to clear them. Nor would it have been right to remind listeners that the other commanding officers on that flight—Fred Noonan, who would leave Pan Am to circumnavigate the globe with Amelia Earhart, and Ed Musick—had since gone missing over the Pacific and were presumed dead. Stories like these hardly would have been suitable dinner conversation thousands of feet above the ocean and hundreds of miles from any kind of solid ground.[9]

Reporters who tracked Sully down during his off hours found that his "chief topics of conversation" were his son, his dog, and his farm, so maybe that's what this "pipe-smoking family man" talked about at the captain's table instead. In San Diego in the early 1920s, he had married another Southern California transplant, Mae Andersen from Davenport, Iowa. They kept a modest house and registered Republican. Sully finished his pilot training, and Mae worked as a bookkeeper—at least until the arrival of their only child, a son, who the couple named Rod, Jr., after his "pop." Setting off from California in a Lockheed Vega in the summer of 1929, Mae and the little "sprout" went with Sully wherever Pan Am assignments took him, first to the Panamanian port Cristóbol, then to the palm-tree-shaded Miami suburb, Coconut Grove, then back west to Oakland. Mae and her son cheered alongside the waterfront crowds who gathered to watch Sully

Sully and his son, Rod, Jr. The Pan Am Historical Foundation.

and his crew begin their Pacific survey flights in 1935. "I think my daddy made the best takeoff I ever saw," Rod, Jr. gushed after watching his father thread a Sikorsky between two orange towers flanking Golden Gate Strait—the beginnings of San Francisco's new suspension bridge. The boy took to wearing his own pilot's uniform and vowed to grow up to be just like his dad.[10]

When Pan Am transferred Sully to its new Atlantic Division in 1937, his family settled on an 800-acre farm in North Carolina where he hoped one day to retire. It was a quiet place, without even a telephone, to spend his down time, raise horses, grow a little tobacco (though the Roosevelt administration's policies thwarted his plans to sell it), and daydream on the sunporch.[11]

Lately, however, wartime operations had been keeping him away from home, not just flying the stepped-up Lisbon schedule but also top-secret missions transporting priority cargoes to and from Africa. After Italy's entrance into the war severed Mediterranean supply lines to Commonwealth forces in the Middle East, the RAF had fortified Imperial Airways' chain of commercial airfields across Africa, so fighter planes and other materiel could be offloaded on the Gold Coast and shuttled east across British and Free French colonial territory rather than sailed all the way around the Cape of Good Hope. But bottlenecks and personnel shortages plagued what quickly became the world's most heavily trafficked air ferry route. Assured full financing from President Roosevelt's personal funds and British reciprocal aid, in mid-1941 Pan Am agreed to expand the RAF's African installations, lengthen runways, and build water towers, guard houses, and high-speed refueling stations, as well as to haul payloads to Sudan and sometimes points beyond—enough tanks, trucks, planes, and other imports, it turned out, to hold Egypt. Sully had spent the past Christmas Eve not with his family but flying the *American Clipper* from Brazil to Liberia, its hold packed to the brim with teletype paper, plane parts, electrical supplies, flying suits, and other items requested from Cairo.[12]

His plane returned from Africa with even more precious contents. All kinds of formerly obscure rocks, metals, and minerals, once bound for experimental labs and collectors' cabinets, had taken on sudden strategic value: rainbow-hued fluorspar for toughening tank steel, shiny chromium for anodizing aircraft frames, shimmery heat-resistant mica for insulating radios and radar units. The Allies would never have met their skyrocketing needs for materials like these had it not been for Africa's mines and laborers. On that holiday run, Sully's ship lugged back thousands of pounds of manifested rubber along with an equally large but undocumented consignment of scheelite and beryllium for the US government's Metals Reserve Corporation. Scheelite contained the rare element tungsten—wolfram to the German agents desperately seeking it—which was used for making gun barrels, artillery shells, and armor-piercing bullets. Beryllium was a vital ingredient for the atomic bomb experiments scientists were conducting. Pan Am's pilots had been secreting it, and uranium, out of the Belgian Congo for the research program that would be known as the Manhattan Project.[13]

It's entirely possible that Sully also smuggled sandbags or unmarked crates of uranium out of the Congo. Special missions took him to the Free Belgian colony at least twice, and though the records were destroyed, his second visit followed a suggestive itinerary. After a scheduled stop at Lagos, Nigeria, he made an unplanned trek to Léopoldville before flying all the way to Fisherman's Lake, Pan Am's seaplane base in Liberia. According to others enlisted in this top-secret program, those carrying the little-understood radioactive element were told to go through in this manner.[14]

Following these trips to Africa, Sully returned to his regular commercial runs to Portugal. Back on the farm Rod, Jr. wrestled with his schoolwork. Mae tended the animals and kept house. They were both there now, awaiting Sully's return.[15]

After dinner, Sully and his crew settled in for the long overnight stretch to Horta on Faial Island in the Azores, the most difficult stop on the route. Horta's port has no protected harbor, so pilots had to set down in the open sea before taxiing behind the breakwater. Hard landings were common, even in surf that was not particularly rough. Three years earlier a rogue wave punched through the hull of the clipper Sully landed there, sending the craft careening toward the docking station. Only Sully's quick-thinking seamanship saved the boat from wiping out the barge. Tonight the harbor's swells were nearing three feet. Any higher and Pan Am's weather watchers advised planes to turn around. But soon Horta's tower received a coded radiogram from the *Yankee Clipper*'s flight deck: "Point of No Return." Sully's crew no longer had enough fuel to reach Bermuda if they turned back now.[16]

On the lower deck, George, Tamara, Manuel, Harry, Frank, Ben, and the other passengers rested. The sofas in their compartments converted into Pullman car style sleeping bunks, fronted by navy blue curtains for privacy. Inside the berths, travelers found coat hangers, a call button, and a reading light. The last time Ben flew this route he had worried at the boldness of undressing and going to bed so far from the earth. The gesture seemed to him "too much like mocking God." Sometime after midnight the plane began to bump and shake, keeping some awake during what for many will be their last night alive.[17]

PART III

1939–1942

London, 1940. Popperfoto via Getty Images.

12

Three-Minute Channel

WHEN WAR BROKE OUT IN Europe on September 1, 1939, Ben Robertson spent the entire day at his father's South Carolina house in front of the radio. Wars, he thought, were such tragic, reckless ventures, started by rich men but fought by the poor. Grandma Bowen had said it best: "Wars cut down the flower of the country's manhood—they leave scalawags and rascals to inherit the earth." This new conflict seemed to Ben little more than a continuation of the last great war. He had no hope for permanent peace among the Europeans. "War is their pattern," he decided, and Americans would "do the world a service by staying out, by saving ourselves." If the United States did enter the conflict, he feared, individual American lives and plans would mean nothing.[1]

Of course he disliked Hitler and wanted the Allies to prevail. As a child he had been taught to love England as the land of the Pilgrim fathers and the mother tongue. He admired how its people had fought valiantly all over the world and built a glorious empire. But, like many Americans, Ben had grown increasingly disenchanted with Britain, especially after a new imperial preference scheme stymied American exports to sterling bloc countries in 1929, and as Whitehall halted its war debt payments in 1934. The few times he took newspaper assignments in London—a dreary place, Ben thought, with too many brussels sprouts and not enough baths— he socialized almost exclusively with Americans while wiring dispatches to his editors about the "errors of Britain" and its schemers. He loathed Conservatives like Neville Chamberlain *and* Labour leaders like Ramsay MacDonald.

He formed "unprintable opinions" about Lord Halifax and Samuel Hoare. Watching those statesmen attempt to appease the continent's fascist regimes led him to decide that Britain was "as crass as Germany or Italy but at least you know where Germany and Italy stand." Ben suspected that "England would turn on us in a minute if it would profit Britain one pound." Much to his surprise as a Southern Democrat, he found himself defending even Herbert Hoover across the Atlantic. "England to me seems so old and so kept," he had complained the month before. "I don't have room to breathe in that little country."[2]

Yet Ben also knew that war meant opportunities for reporters. Soon he scored a position as a foreign correspondent with the newest, most exciting experiment in American journalism, the afternoon daily *PM*. The upstart newspaper's creator, Ralph Ingersoll, wanted to break the hold over the nation's leading print news by the rightwing moguls William Randolph Hearst, Robert McCormick, and his own former employer Henry Luce. Those newspaper owners, he believed, had twisted the modern journalistic ideal of objectivity into a rationale for blunting viewpoints that diverged from their own. Ingersoll asked his assembled staff of mostly left-leaning reporters not for "unbiased journalism" but for "honest journalism," to bring "truth to the people so that they may decide for themselves what to do about it." Free from advertising that might invite corporate influence, the paper hit newsstands in early June 1940. Its high-quality graphics and revelatory exposés quickly earned a following that included several cabinet members and Supreme Court justices as well as the vice president and the first lady.[3] That summer Ingersoll dispatched Ben to London to document Nazi Germany's lightning advance to the shores of France. Before long, Ben found himself caught up in a series of political revelations that would reshape his approach to journalism and propel him, and *PM*, into the vanguard of those advocating for American aid to Britain.

"Do you have a gas mask, sir?"

The Hotel Waldorf's gray-haired chambermaid pulled thick curtains across the windows, blocking a view of Covent Garden, before leaving Ben to inspect his sleeping quarters. The blackout drapes gave the room an oppressive heaviness, but a notice forbade tampering with them after staff drew them for the night. Instructions on the bureau explained that the telephone operator would awaken guests in the event of an air raid. Worried that he might sleep through the warning, Ben sought out the hall porter. "No bloody fear," the attendant told him. The sirens were "loud as destruction itself." Retreating to his room, Ben began his new evening ritual. He stuffed his room key, comb, money, and passport into a bathrobe pocket, arranged his flashlight, gas mask, and slippers near the bed, and lay down, waiting for sleep, or the planes, whichever came first.[4]

The British had been dreading this moment for years. They had watched Hitler remilitarize the Rhineland, annex Austria, and set his sights on Czechoslovakia's Sudetenland. But most nevertheless longed to avoid a conflict, even if it took unsavory bargains. Recent dystopian fiction by H. G. Wells and others had spelled out the next war's possibilities in gruesome detail. Bombardment by zeppelins had killed more than five hundred Londoners during World War I, but advances in aerial warfare since then—most graphically on display in the Spanish Civil War—would leave the Houses of Parliament in ruins, pundits warned. Poison gases that once choked soldiers in the trenches would now seep into family homes, they said; bombs would rain down on hundreds of thousands each week. Thus cheers greeted Prime Minister Neville Chamberlain when he returned from Munich in September 1938, promising peace bought at the bargain price of Czechoslovakia's dismemberment. "What a shave," wrote Virginia Woolf. Yet unease crept back almost immediately, and quietly British strategists hoped merely to stall long enough for rearmament. When German forces marched on Prague less than six months later in violation of the Munich agreement, Chamberlain announced that if the Third Reich also attacked Poland his government would follow that European ally into war.[5]

Hitler's tanks rumbled toward Warsaw on September 1, 1939. In London, sandbags piled against buildings and trenches gutted the parks. Cinemas and theaters closed, hospitals evicted the sick from their beds in anticipation of bombing casualties, corrugated steel shelters mushroomed in back gardens, and barrage balloons sailed over rooftops to deter low-flying airplanes. As reservists mobilized—and armed guards whisked Charles Dickens manuscripts, Shakespeare folios, and other treasures to castles in North Wales and Gloucestershire—BBC broadcasters warned civilians to carry gas masks and affix identifying luggage labels to loved ones. Hundreds of thousands of families euthanized their pets and shipped their sons and daughters off to the countryside. Children without friends or relatives to go to were transported to rural reception areas, where hastily recruited strangers chose them out of a line up and took them home. "This country is at war with Germany," Chamberlain announced on September 3. Hitler would "only be stopped by force . . . may God bless you all." Watching German and soon Soviet forces devour Poland in the coming weeks, Britons reeled between tears, disbelief, anger, and panic.[6]

Then tedium set in. By October, one Londoner recorded in her diary that the "war of nerves" had devolved into a "war of yawns." She fantasized that an uprising in Germany might oust the Nazis and end the nightmare before it fully began. Cinemas and shops reopened. Evacuees trickled home. Commuters forgot to bring their gas masks to work. On November 11, as usual, people pinned poppies to their lapels in honor of the last war's Armistice. Only the island's self-imposed blackout, blamed for a doubling of road fatalities, presented clear danger. In late 1939 it was safer to be a soldier in the British army than a pedestrian on the streets after dark.[7]

But in spring, Europe erupted. Panzer units marched on Denmark and Norway, then the Netherlands, Belgium, Luxembourg, and France. Freighters chugged across the Channel overflowing with refugees, salvaged supplies, and governments-in-exile. Notices seeking missing persons last seen on the continent filled the London classifieds. Commuters carried their gas masks again.[8]

By the time Ben reached England at the end of June, the bungled campaign to stem the Nazi tide had ended with Neville Chamberlain's resignation, a harrowing evacuation of 338,000 Allied troops at Dunkirk, Italy's opportunistic entry into the war, and a shocking truce struck by the French, turning over tremendous territory and resources to be used against their former allies. The Luftwaffe now commanded the coastline from Stavanger to Brest, enabling air attacks against shipping in the Channel and the North Sea as well as probing raids on English ports. Buoyed by so many unexpectedly rapid victories, Hitler ordered Operation Sealion—preparations for a surprise conquest of Great Britain. "The bombing will have to come soon," Ben wrote to his sister.[9]

British authorities met the moment with troubling shortages. More than sixty-eight thousand members of the British Expeditionary Forces had been killed, wounded, or had gone missing in France. Those who escaped Dunkirk returned traumatized and exhausted. To protect four hundred miles of continent-facing English coastline, the army had barely over a dozen divisions, all of them short on personnel, transport, tanks, and ammunition. London Air Staff in turn estimated that five thousand enemy parachutists could bypass coastal defenses, seize key RAF stations, incapacitate Fighter Command, and clear the path for invasion troops in special landing craft. The Germans didn't have the capacity for such a risky amphibious operation, but British officials didn't know that. Reconnaissance photographs and other intelligence painted a picture of formidable forces amassing on the French side of the water.[10]

Invasion fears gripped the islands. Newspapers predicted the date for attack with almanac certainty. Some picked the anniversary of the outbreak of the First World War, given Hitler's "fondness for melodramatic gesture." Others analyzed the moon and the tides. Even out-of-the-way villagers uprooted their road signs and mile markers, dragged old carts and other obstacles into fields to prevent planes from landing, and silenced their church bells, vowing only to ring them again at the sight of the enemy. Government circulars fell through millions of mail slots, instructing residents to be ready to hide their food, maps, and bicycles. Women formed paramilitary groups to practice marksmanship and hand-to-hand combat, while German and Italian nationals along with other potential fascist sympathizers were interned on the Isle of Man. Privately, Ben found, almost everyone agreed that "the assault would be terrific. Thousands and tens of thousands would die."[11]

Ben lost no time getting to work, locating the cable office, seeking out passes for prohibited areas, meeting with the censor, and registering with the police. He interviewed Americans volunteering with the Canadian forces, bought tannic acid jelly, a salve for mustard-gassed skin, and searched fruitlessly for a tin hat. His Southern charm quickly won him many contacts, even though he represented a new publication with an odd name. He was determined to "form a careful, unbiased opinion" about the crisis bearing down on Britain. It should have been easy, given his uncharitable views about England and the British.[12]

But soon he felt himself being "swept away" by London's exhilarating siege mentality. It was like hunkering down in Daniel Boone's stockade, he imagined. Only this time the frontier was located not in the Kentucky prairies but in the English skies. "Resistance was in the air—on the streets, in the papers, everywhere and in everything," Ben wrote. He decided it "would do the people good at home" to know about it.[13]

Few in London after all imagined that Britain could win the war without US assistance. "So much would depend on America, and they knew it," Ben summarized. Yet many Americans, including President Roosevelt, were growing less rather than more willing to intervene that summer. The Blitzkrieg and the fall of France had indeed jolted them. But Britain seemed unlikely to hold out. One of the president's advisors put its odds of survival at no better than one in three. Defeatist talk emanated from Joseph Kennedy's embassy in London, warning that any supplies sent to Britain were likely to fall into Nazi hands. US military planners meanwhile cautioned against selling anything from their already low stocks of armaments needed for hemispheric defense.[14]

British officials beckoned with offers of military secrets and Caribbean bases. They argued that involvement was in Americans' own self-interest. Without the Royal Navy, many reminded, the United States and its one-ocean fleet would face two oceans of threats alone. If unchecked, the Third Reich's influence would seep into the Western Hemisphere. Attempts at backroom diplomacy to make these points hardly seemed sufficient. Many predicted that wresting American intervention would require a multilayered campaign to sway public opinion.[15]

For years, the Germans had been more aggressive in their propaganda efforts in the United States, but by the summer of 1940 British initiatives picked up pace. From a suite of offices in New York's Rockefeller Center, military intelligence officers, BBC representatives, arms procurement specialists, and spies cultivated contacts and lobbied their case with American academics, politicians, and press executives, including Ben's boss at *PM*, Ralph Ingersoll. Circumventing the nation's largely conservative print media, Allied supporters made especially good use of radio broadcasts, news reels, and photographs in mass-circulation magazines, which reached millions of Americans each month—materials often secretly funded by British agencies and designed, as one filmmaker put it, to "scare the pants off the Americans and bring them into the war sooner."[16]

Personal testaments by Americans themselves seemed most likely to arouse US action. Seizing on foreign correspondents in Britain as vital "political instruments," members of the Ministry of Information and the Foreign Office convinced more reticent colleagues at the Ministry of Home Security to grant American visitors an unusual level of access. Journalists posted to London who had been held at arm's length by British high officials before the war suddenly found themselves drawn into "friendly lunch-and-dinner terms with the great," as the reporter Vincent Sheean put it. By August, authorities granted Ben and many of his colleagues permission to enter the restricted southeast coast of England, ground zero in the Battle of Britain.[17]

In Dover, Ben took a room at the Grand Hotel, a seaside destination with uninspired food and a sometimes-working elevator, once full of vacationing clerks, now a magnet for correspondents. At the nearby beach, he watched soldiers uncoil barbed wire in the sand. Piers had been partially dismantled, and civilians had been encouraged to leave, but many stayed. They hauled folding chairs into centuries-old tunnels in the shoreline's cliffs for use during air raids. Some caves had been fitted with lights and hot water. One had been rigged as a makeshift hospital, another a morgue.[18]

Eager for a view of the entire region, Ben hiked up Shakespeare Cliff, one mile west of the city. Sitting on the grassy bluff, amid swarms of butterflies and wild red currant patches, he stared at occupied France on the hazy horizon. It seemed to him like perching at the edge of the world, and beyond lay only chaos. It made him uneasy, knowing how fast a plane could conquer those twenty miles between Kent and Calais. In 1940, the English Channel had become a three-minute body of water. Ben felt the Atlantic Ocean—the whole globe in fact—shrinking.[19]

For much of August, he camped out on that chalky vista to watch the Luftwaffe's campaign to incapacitate British airfields, antiaircraft installations, and other infrastructure. Seagulls announced the impending raids by squawking and flapping their wings before fleeing the incoming sorties. Messerschmitts darted through puffs of ack-ack fire and took aim at Dover's silver barrage balloons, while Spitfires and Hurricanes rose from nearby aerodromes to fend them off. The fighters chased each other across the sky, leaving vapor trails that reminded Ben of ice skaters etching the surface of a frozen pond.[20]

He was joined on the hill by a thickening crowd of seasoned antifascist American journalists: Vincent Sheean for the North American Newspaper Alliance, the broadcaster Edward R. Murrow for CBS radio, Edward Beattie for United Press, Quentin Reynolds for *Collier's*, Virginia Cowles for the *Sunday Times*, Helen Kirkpatrick for *Chicago Daily News*, and the newsreel photographer Arthur Menken for *The March of Time*. Collectively they had witnessed nearly every international conflict since the rise of Hitler, from the Italian invasion of Ethiopia, the Spanish Civil War, and the siege of Nanjing, to the fall of Czechoslovakia, Poland, Finland, Norway, and France. Ben lay in the grass listening to their chatter while skirmishes overhead decided "the fate of the world." In unguarded conversation they began to slip, referring to the planes above not as German and British, but "theirs" and "ours."[21]

In the afternoons, the reporters drifted back down to the Grand Hotel to telephone their reports to London for transmission to New York. Sporadic shelling from across the channel kept them on edge. Sometimes Ben lay in bed listening to bullets rain on the hotel's roof. Other times he leaned out his window in pajamas and a steel helmet to watch British raiders set fire to the French coast. He thought about his childhood, when airplanes had yet to jump over water. That invention of so-called progress, which promised to bring nations closer together, had instead collapsed the boundaries between peace and war. Invasion used to be obvious and ongoing, Ben mused, but now it descended like a bolt of lightning, only to mysteriously disappear.[22]

In the mornings, the reporters repeated their trek to Shakespeare Cliff. As Ben told it, watching those daily dogfights over Dover simplified matters. Any wish to stay detached, all his desires for the United States to remain neutral, and his reservations about the British, evaporated on that summit. Before he had not been able to understand just what had been so wrong "with peace as a nation's thesis." It had seemed like such an admirable doctrine for the United States to adopt— to refuse to join in the killing. But, in peace, he decided, people lived only for themselves. In war, they stood together, for a cause. This war was his war, he decided, even at the risk of death. Americans had enjoyed their fortunes because generations had been willing to die to secure them. At Dover, wrote Ben, "I found it lifted a tremendous weight off your spirit to find yourself willing to give up your life if you have to—I discovered Saint Matthew's meaning about losing a life to find it." He was ready to take his stand "with England."[23]

What crystalized for Ben on that cliff, too, was a new approach to journalism, less beholden to the standards of objectivity. Like witnesses collaborating testimony, he and his colleagues developed tropes and themes they returned to time and again to sell Americans on the British cause. "We want to let the folks at home feel this war as we feel it on the spot," Ben explained in a private letter to Roosevelt. The British were fighting "magnificently," he told the president, and "we want to tell their story for them and tell it in America before the Germans get in their account." The reporters would not focus on questions of British war aims, the problems of mobilization, or the everyday inequalities that the conflict often exacerbated. They portrayed instead a unifying and equalizing war effort, waged by a brave and generous people arrayed upon "the last barricades of Europe," as Ben's friend Hilde Marchant put it. A people suddenly "more human," said Ed Murrow, who talked and shared with strangers on buses and trains. A "single community," rhapsodized Ben, that "had learned that no class and no sex and no city had exclusive possession of any of the qualities which it took to save a nation." One American military attaché posted in London balked at this melodramatic coverage. "The reporters have been feeding the United States a lot of applesauce," he wrote to his wife.[24]

In late August news of raids on the outskirts of the capital drew Ben back to London. Every day that passed without invasion felt like a small victory. In Washington, Roosevelt was becoming more confident of British survival and more willing to chart a risky course that departed from traditional neutrality. But even as he finalized the Destroyers for Bases agreement in early September, the president faced a wide array of domestic antagonists: conservative newspaper barons determined to resist his every move; immigrant voters with complicated loyalties; leftists who feared that mobilization would roll back recent labor gains; their rightwing opponents who worried about the opposite; students and parents who recoiled from the idea of risking lives without clear provocation; and celebrity spokesmen who hoped to rally all these constituencies against intervention by forming the America First Committee on September 4, the day after the Destroyers for Bases deal became public.[25]

Three days later, Londoners found themselves under fierce bombardment. It was Saturday, and Ben had set out with Ed Murrow and Vincent Sheean for a drive to the Thames Estuary. In Murrow's car they unknowingly threaded through the same stretch of London's East End that German planes would target later that day—through Stepney, Poplar, and the Isle of Dogs, where the river's deep bend offered a clear landmark for bombers, and through Silvertown, Beckton, and Barking. In crowded dockside neighborhoods, workers emerged from small, terraced houses to buy potatoes, cabbage, and roasts. Cranes at the water's edge towered over refineries and a handful of passing ships. Much of this would be on fire in a few hours.[26]

At Tilbury, the reporters crossed the Thames on the automobile ferry to Gravesend. Inspecting the countryside for craters and other damage without much success, they reclined at the edge of a turnip field to eat apples and nap in the sun. Shortly after 4 p.m., the hum of far-off motors roused the men to their feet. As the siren wails and gunfire grew louder and closer, a squadron of some thirty German bombers appeared overhead, pursued by British fighters. Falling shrapnel sent Ben and the others to the cover of a roadside ditch. Quickly, they realized, this was "no ordinary raid." A second, larger wave of planes appeared, and then another. Instead of fanning out toward outlying airfields as usual, hundreds of Dornier and Heinkel bombers and their Messerschmitt escorts raced in formation toward the East London docks. Black clouds formed over the oil tanks at Thames Haven, and flames broke out directly across the river. Soon the men spotted smoke billowing to the west over the capital itself. After the sun set they could no longer see the bombers except the occasional wing caught in the crosshairs of a searchlight beam, but for hours they listened to them pass overhead, two at a time, following the fire line along the river started by earlier raids. Soon the entire horizon to the west was alight.[27]

That night the Luftwaffe pummeled East London with 330 tons of high explosives and over a thousand incendiaries. The Royal Victoria Docks, factories in Silvertown, Tate & Lyle's sugar barges, even barrage balloons in the sky caught fire. At the Surrey Docks, 250 acres of Scandinavian pitch pine erupted into a wall of flames so hot it blistered the paint on passing boats. Near the Beckton gasworks, the largest in Europe, leaking sulfurous fumes generated panic about a chemical attack. Firemen struggled to contain the conflagrations. Molten tar from one factory blocked their vehicles. Pepper from a burning warehouse stung their lungs. Caramelized grain from another stuck to their boots. At the Woolwich Arsenal, they battled blazes surrounded by crates of ammunition and nitroglycerine. Water pressure in their hoses gave out under the unprecedented demand.[28]

Four hundred thirty-six people died that night, the first of 15,775 Londoners who would lose their lives during the nine-month blitz to come—cut by flying glass and shrapnel, bludgeoned by falling beams and bricks, suffocated in rubble, burned alive, drowned, or bombed to bits. The shock wave from a blast ripped clothes off backs. "You could actually feel your eyeballs being sucked out," explained one survivor. Bodies were found embedded into walls, hanging from rafters, or never found at all. "During training I had instructed my men to treat the dead with reverence and respect, but I did not think we would have to shovel them up," said one air raid warden.[29]

Ben and the other reporters, who had sought warmth in a haystack as the night air cooled, sat transfixed by the urban inferno. "London is burning. London is burning," Ben said over and over in his South Carolina drawl. It broke his heart, what the Nazis were doing to a city that had taken "thirty generations of men a thousand years to build." It was the Book of Revelation, he said. Biblical apocalypse. It made him frightened and sick.[30]

After the all-clear finally sounded at 4:30 a.m., the reporters caught some sleep at an inn at Gravesend before journeying back toward the still burning East End. Heavy smoke shrouded the morning sun. Vincent Sheean told the others that he had dreamed that the Nazis landed in New Orleans. Ed Murrow wagered that a few more nights like the last one would probably signal invasion. On the northern bank of the Thames, cinders coated crumpled workers' homes and storefronts. Policemen directed traffic around unexploded bombs lodged in the roadways. Repairmen labored over severed water pipes and gas mains, while housewives broke up doors and furniture for kindling to cook breakfast. That first Sunday of the Battle of London felt to Ben like the downfall of civilization.[31]

Ben had barely gotten his bearings back at the Waldorf when the sirens wailed again that evening. He threw open his hotel room curtains to watch as bombers reignited fires and disabled all the rail lines heading south from the capital. This time the raiders reached farther west into The City. The barrage balloons were too low to catch them, and too few antiaircraft guns had been installed. Ben didn't yet know how to judge the distance and direction of bombs by their sound. Several times, when the hotel shook from nearby explosions, he found himself flat on the bathroom floor.[32]

The next night, September 9, brought more of the same. From then on, in fact, not a single night would pass without bombs until November 3, when clouds and fog gave a short respite. Ben lay awake listening. "How mad the world was to destroy so much wealth and work," he thought. What a misuse of the gift of flight. He cabled *PM*: "In the midst of the dark London nights you now know that everybody in the world will be called upon to account for this ruthlessness."[33]

Several factors would ultimately deter an invasion of English shores: Fighter Command's secret radar technology; the ability of the British aircraft industry to outproduce the factories of the Reich; and the fact that, in the end, Kriegsmarine planners could not think their way around the formidable Royal Navy. Following that intense first week of raids on London, which cost the Luftwaffe 298 aircraft, Hitler postponed Operation Sealion again and again. But to keep up the appearance of a possible invasion in hopes of forcing Britain to sue for peace, German bombers expanded their sorties to destroy not only vital infrastructure but also civilian morale. They showered London and other industrial centers with a miscellany of high explosives: time delay devices, splattering oil bombs, clusters of miniature magnesium alloy incendiaries that burned for ten minutes at temperatures that could melt steel, and land mines floated to the earth by parachutes. About 10 percent of the bombs didn't explode on contact. By the end of September, more than 3,700 of these booby traps littered the capital.[34]

Ben never ceased to feel "frightened as a rabbit" under this onslaught, but soon routines set in, steadying his resolve. More antiaircraft installations arrived. Bridges spanned gaping holes in the streets, buses improvised routes, and people greeted each other with talk of raids instead of weather. Newspapers advertised cures for peptic ulcers, hair loss, and other nervous ailments. Shopkeepers held sales "due to enemy action." Thieves learned to run toward burglar alarms. Shelter life also grew more organized, as crowds returned night after night to their chosen cellars, garden pits, church crypts, or other hiding spots. Tiered metal bunks, portable toilets, and a ticketing system were introduced at Tube stations. Vendors sold biscuits and buns. At bedtime, children curled into tight balls on the platforms against their mothers' bellies. When "incidents" occurred—the official innocuous name given to bombings—only the most grievously hurt were carted off to the hospital in commandeered baker's or grocer's vans, their foreheads marked X for internal injury, T for tourniquet, and so on. No one batted an eye at rifles stashed in restaurant cloakrooms or coworkers who turned up for shifts in pajamas. In London it became normal to climb through windows and eat in basements.[35]

The Blitz wrenched Londoners from their comfort zones and into unexpected scenes and relationships. Many confessed to a kind of "ghoulish excitement" in the face of such terror. People slept less, drank more, threw themselves into love affairs, and found or lost sight of God. "The threat of death seems to make people really alive," Quentin Reynolds explained. "Every person you pass has a story that he is living."[36]

To Ben, the experience proved deeply religious. It offered a path to redemption for the British, whose best qualities—courage, faith, duty, and decency, he said—were brought out by the crisis. And for Ben himself, it presented a kind of conversion experience, as he awoke to the cause of Anglo-American alliance. He stalked the city's churches, watching people pray at Westminster Abbey while candles burned at the tomb of the Unknown Soldier and flowers wilted over Neville Chamberlain's newly interred ashes. He lingered before a windowless St. Giles-without-Cripplegate, listening to its organist play Handel, and he returned again and again to the hymn books in the pews of St. Paul's Cathedral. The house of the Lord "was not built of brick and mortar," assured one pamphlet. He "dwellest not in temples made of hands." Ben imagined faith radiating far beyond the city's embattled sites of worship, as though everywhere the capital's people "felt themselves in the sight of God." During the darkest of nights, he decided, London had been "reborn."[37]

For Ben, the redemption brought by the Blitz was not only spiritual but also historical. "Here they were," he reflected about the British, "the

A bomb-damaged St. Paul's Cathedral, where Ben often went to pray. © Imperial War Museum, HU 654.

people who ruled a fourth of the globe," who had built an empire upon which the sun never set. "They had been imperialistic and had exploited, they had subjugated," he admitted, but now "they were demonstrating that they could take the same sort of punishment they had handed out." By bringing them to this terrible moment, Hitler had "saved the British people," Ben believed. Finally, in the blackout darkness the British had remembered their principles. The England of the Magna Carta, the England that stood for freedom, which had been in danger of decline, was "England again."[38]

To Ben's mind, the Blitz not only redeemed Britons' historic mission, it also in bizarre ways validated his own allegiance to the heritage of the Confederacy. Facing those bombs brought to life for him the trials suffered by his Southern ancestors. Their actions more than ever seemed to him noble and justified. In London, he decided, he had come to his very own "Gettysburg." What his grandfather had endured on that Pennsylvania battlefield, he could endure on this one. He would fight for an ideal higher than his own individual life and plans. Just as all previous generations of Americans had done "since the first Virginians stood up against the Indians."[39]

Bombs fell in the duck's pond in St. James's Park, on Covent Garden, and eventually Ben's room at the Waldorf, sending him first to quarters at the front of the hotel and then, when the plumbing failed, to the nearby Savoy. By the fall of 1940, so many foreign correspondents had moved into that storied hotel that British spokesmen took to briefing the press in the American bar off the lobby. Located adjacent to the Thames, the hotel also proved a magnet for raiders. That November, one bomb destroyed the Savoy's Strand entrance parapet, and another pierced through five floors of a corner of the building overlooking the Embankment, killing two. "The old hotel sort of took off like one of the clippers and seemed to sail away," Ben explained. He found himself in his usual position—flat on the bathroom floor with his fingers plugged into his ears. During particularly intense raids, Ben sometimes followed other guests down to a series of subterranean rooms that had been outfitted with pink-curtained bunks tended by first aid nurses. But preferring each other's company to the shelter's stuffy, snore-filled air, the hotel's resident American reporters convinced the management to set aside a windowless room near the Embankment entrance as their own private all-night club, where they could ride out the attacks with chess, poker, and whisky.[40]

Ben confessed to feeling uneasy enjoying such luxury hotel amenities. "The food and the music got on your conscience," he explained, "when hundreds of thousands were in shelters, when people on every side were dying." The question of sheltering, after all, was one of the most contentious issues in wartime London. For those who could afford entrance to the city's nicer clubs, restaurants, and hotels, the price of a meal usually bought a comfortable bunk for the night as well. But the less fortunate lacked adequate facilities. Government preparations for air raids had underestimated how long the overnight attacks would last and how many would be made homeless by the onslaught. The bombardments disproportionately impacted the East End's working classes, who lived closest to targeted docks and industries but whose neighborhoods were underserved by shelters and who did not have savings and social connections to fall back on when bombs upended their lives. The fact that the burdens of the conflict fell so unequally—and not just in terms of sheltering—sometimes erupted into anger. Women decried that, until 1943, men received more compensation for air raid injuries. Hourly wage earners complained that, unlike salaried employees, they lost pay if bombs stopped work during their shifts. Poor families wondered why they had less access to food than the rich, since money rather than ration coupons bought restaurant meals.[41]

It's not that Ben and other reporters didn't know about these and other social problems. East End protesters twice invaded the Savoy, brandishing signs with slogans like "Share the Danger" and "Ration the Rich."[42] And Americans' firsthand inspections of public shelters horrified them. Ben cringed at their rows of people packed together more closely than graveyard corpses, "a sort of hell under earth," he thought, bathed in blue emergency light. Ernie Pyle called the public shelters "little better than underground Hoovervilles." Nevertheless, Ben and most of his colleagues downplayed Britain's domestic conflicts in their reports. "People who live in the West End hotels have it a bit easier than those who sleep in the subway shelters," Quentin Reynolds characteristically downplayed the contrast.[43]

Instead, Ben focused on interviewing cabinet ministers, air raid wardens, and the men who tended the barrage balloons. He shadowed firemen and rode with ambulance drivers. As the Luftwaffe's squadrons widened their target range, he journeyed north to survey the damage in Birmingham, Manchester, Liverpool, Glasgow, and Edinburgh. At Coventry, he discovered, "a thousand years had gone up in a night." After the merciless November 14 raid, only the spire and outer wall of the town's fourteenth-century cathedral stood amid city center streets "flat as pancakes." He poured his heart out in cables to New York and sometimes filled in for Ed Murrow on his CBS radio broadcast, "This is London." He became a household name back in the United States.[44]

As 1940 drew to a close, more than 32,000 London houses had been destroyed and more than 13,000 of the city's residents had been killed. But Ben and other correspondents found cause for hope. No cross-channel invasion had materialized, and the campaign to invest Americans in Britain's plight seemed to be working. Progressive New Dealers, once wary of the volatile, conservative Winston Churchill, had warmed to the prime minster. President Roosevelt made increasingly pro-British statements in public, and a growing parade of special envoys and advisors trekked back and forth across the Atlantic in Pan Am clippers, deepening behind-the-scenes cooperation between the two nation's political and military leaders. Some

60 percent of polled Americans now favored helping Britain even at the risk of war, up from only 35 percent in March.[45]

As hope flickered that winter, Ben and many other American correspondents in London arranged for home leave, to take a break from the bombs but also to speak and write more directly to American audiences. Catching a plane to Lisbon, he waited for a spot on a Pan Am clipper, but two days after Christmas, after being bumped repeatedly by higher priority passengers and mailbags, he and four other reporters set sail on the American Export Lines' SS *Exeter* instead. On December 29, while the journalists floated across a submarine-infested ocean, Nazi planes firebombed London so mercilessly that authorities lifted censorship regulations and allowed reporters to name the historic churches and other landmarks that had been hit. That same night Roosevelt took to the radio to urge Americans to see their nation as "the great arsenal of democracy." Ben and his travel mates greeted the new year of 1941 on overflow bedding in the *Exeter*'s dining room, surrounded by consuls, relief workers, and refugees. One day before the Manhattan skyline appeared, Roosevelt delivered yet another powerful speech before Congress, promising in his State of the Union address a future world "founded upon four essential human freedoms": freedom of speech and worship, and freedom from want and fear. New York, Ben observed upon arrival, felt "nearer than ever to war."[46]

Ben gave speeches up and down the East Coast during January and February, warning audiences that if Americans didn't seize the initiative, "we will have war in our front yard." He pilloried Joseph Kennedy and other opponents of intervention. If the United States did enter the war, the American First spokesman Charles Lindbergh ought to be jailed, he suggested to one South Carolina crowd to roars of approval. His own South had become the nation's most hawkish region. He dashed off a memoir of the Blitz for Knopf, which joined a flood of popular titles about Britain displayed at American bookstores that season. *I Saw England* (1941) would be positively reviewed, and *Reader's Digest* optioned a condensed version for its more than four million subscribers.[47]

But, predicting that the Nazis might still attempt a Channel crossing, Ben was back in London by March. Fears about invasion had indeed come roaring back with the approach of spring, but the novelty and adrenaline of the previous fall was gone. Shipping losses had reached alarming proportions. Food rations had tightened. The nation's dollar reserves were running out. News of the passage of Lend-Lease on March 11—an unprecedented program promising US military equipment and other supplies to countries whose defense was deemed vital to the United States by the president—barely cut through the weariness and doubts that crept into Londoners' diary entries and private conversations. It would take a long time before any benefits of Washington's new legislation materialized, and the two nations' leaders were still squabbling over finances and sites for American bases in the Caribbean.[48]

Ben tried to resurrect the same lofty prose that had seemed so effective in his previous year's reporting. "In the midst of a blazing city I have seen human beings lose all their commonplace littleness and meanness and rush to the greatest heights to which human character can possibly rise," he wrote during a trip to Plymouth, under heavy bombardment. "I have watched them by thousands renouncing property rights and every modern convenience and security for faith and a living cause."[49] But, Ben would find, these rhetorical strategies were running their course.

Maybe Britons could continue to "take it." But alone they could not win this war. Nazi puppet states were spreading across Eastern Europe. Lieutenant General Erwin Rommel's Afrika Korps had reinforced Italian troops in Libya, endangering the fate of North Africa, and a German-supported coup had just succeeded in Iraq, sparking fears of Arab uprisings across the Middle East. The Reich also continued to leverage vital supplies and intelligence through neutral parties to circumvent the British naval blockade. Ben read in the papers that Hitler was touring newly occupied Yugoslavia. No doubt wherever he was, Ben sniffed, the sun was shining, and tonight this "king of kings" would sit down to his boiled cauliflower and spinach and reflect with satisfaction on the state of the world. Ben imagined the Führer reading about Lindbergh's latest speech, about the pro-Axis policies of Spain, and about the mass funeral in Plymouth. Ben felt the temper of the war shifting that April. It had entered a new stage, "more grim, more terrible." The idea of targeting not only Germany's military installations but also its civilians with RAF bombing campaigns had once been controversial, but public support for such reprisals was growing that spring. Ben confessed to his father that he was glad when he heard that Berlin had been hit. "You hope it has been hard hit," he wrote.[50]

Ben's frustrations mounted further after a pair of deadly raids on London that month. On Wednesday the 16th, the heaviest attack so far decimated nineteen churches, started two thousand fires, and yielded unprecedented casualties. One land mine fell outside the Savoy's Embankment entrance, blowing out all the hotel's riverside windows and sending bloodied guests stumbling into the lobby. The incident cost Ben's colleague Don Minifie of the *New York Herald Tribune* sight in one eye. That Saturday brought even more destruction, when German bombers dropped more than a thousand tons of high explosives and nearly 154,000 incendiaries on the capital. Britain's civilian death toll from aerial bombardments approached thirty thousand.[51]

Ben grew angry and impatient in his reports to *PM*. "Churches are burning and hospitals are falling and every night men and women and children are being killed but England is still the world's citadel of freedom." He demanded of American readers: "What would you think if you saw a decent plain working man searching in a pile of rubble for a finger or a foot of his wife and four children?" "Bombs sometimes leave an ear," he noted, "a hand that can be recognized but very often they leave nothing."[52]

Next to what Ben was witnessing in England, the mail that arrived from the States seemed obscene. In one New York newspaper he read about the season's "refreshingly different" dress ribbons, the "four star food and fun" at an advertised nightspot, and a recent high-society barbecue in Palm Beach. Letters from readers responding to Ben's columns proved just as maddening. They rehearsed all the reasons why the British did not deserve Americans' help. Britain was too much ruled by lords and ladies. Englishmen talked down to Americans. All this news was just calculated propaganda. In horror, Ben realized that he had made those very same arguments only a few years before. But no. He wanted to believe that all along on some level he must have known. Manchuria . . . Ethiopia . . . Spain . . . Munich. He must have sensed "that somewhere buried in all these catastrophes there was flowing thread."[53]

Why couldn't other Americans see it? Some, of course, were selfish and fixated on their own comforts, but most wanted to do the right thing, he was sure. They simply remained insufficiently informed about Hitler. In Britain, he decided, he could see things in sharper perspective than his compatriots could at home. He blamed the press. Reporters, just as Ingersoll had warned, had been "so concerned with non-biased reporting, a high ideal," that readers had been gorged on facts while starved of larger meaning. He thought back to the lifeless reports he had written for the Associated Press in Washington. It was so easy to report "strictly factually," he reflected, "you don't have to understand a thing you are writing about."[54] Information was not the same thing as knowledge. And knowing was not understanding.

May brought more setbacks. London newspapers tried to positively spin yet another hasty evacuation of British and Empire forces, this time from Greece. "Risks Boldly Faced," praised one *Times* headline. "Gallant Rearguard Fights," cheered another. But the string of bad news fueled noticeably defeatist sentiments among the masses. Then, on May 10, London suffered its worst attack of the war.[55]

It was a pleasant evening with a full moon, and Ben was at the Savoy as usual. In the hotel's half-empty dining room, Carroll Gibbons's orchestra was playing American tunes when the sirens started. "There's that nasty man," Ed Beattie muttered. The band struck up Irving Berlin as the tableware started to rumble:

The world is hell for you and me
But what a heaven it will be
When that man is dead and gone

The dining room had thick walls strengthened by steel mesh and rods, so customers continued with their meals until one particularly enormous explosion stilled the crowd. Some headed for the hotel's basement shelter, others to the roof or the street to assess the damage. Outside, menacing motors roared overhead. Ben gaped at a blaze engulfing the steeple of St. Clement Danes. A long night loomed ahead.[56]

Settling into the reporters' all-night clubroom, he played chess while wire service correspondents drifted in and out with updates until the telephones started to fail. A nearby blast knocked glasses off the bar. By the time the all-clear sounded at 6:30 a.m., some five thousand houses in London had been destroyed and nearly fifteen hundred people killed. Explosives had fallen on King's Cross, Temple Church, Westminster Abbey, the Commons debating chamber of the Houses of Parliament, and the War Office. They had pierced the tower of Big Ben and destroyed a quarter of a million books at the British Museum. It would take two days to restore gas and water service that had failed across much of the capital. After more than eight months of attacks, one in six Londoners had now been bombed out of their lodging.[57]

In the morning Ben faced that familiar street scene: the acrid soot, the din of burglar alarms, the air raid wardens and policemen pulling bodies from the rubble. It was "criminally negligent," he decided, for Americans not to declare their intentions "one way or other this very hour." The citizens of these "dying British cities," after all, were the same "sort of human beings" as Americans; "they don't like war, they are terrified when bombs fall near them, they grieve as we do and they suffer." They had the same kind of faith and courage, he fancied, that Americans' grandfathers had shown "when they faced Chickamauga and Manassas."[58]

There could be "no half way measures" in this war, he decided. What railroads and automobiles had done to the American continent, airplanes were now doing to bodies of water. Witnesses in England had seen that clearly. They had "lost all faith in the safety of oceans." The world was "closing in," and a United States that hesitated would be lost. If the Germans took control of Dakar or the Azores, it would put them within flying range of Brazil and other New World destinations. If the people of the United States did not act, he thought, the time would come when bombs would whistle down on Times Square, and the war might be fought and lost on the "playing fields of Washington." It was time for "folks at home" to "put up or shut up." The facts were plain. Americans would fight beside Britain or fight alone.[59]

But Ben had already sent so many reports filled with all these plain, sorrowful facts. He had wired "time and again in anguish" that England was burning, that Americans must choose "between fiddling and fighting." But he decided he wouldn't cable it anymore. What good would it do to repeat it?[60]

13

Back to Porridge

ON MAY 10, WHILE FRANK was eating lunch, the radio blurted out a strange code over and over: "BERLIN, B for Bernard, E for Edward . . . L for Ludwig, I for Isaac, N for Niko." He rushed into Batavia, where military trucks choked the streets and guards materialized in front of important public buildings. Dutch officials had hoped that once again their kingdom could survive a world war by remaining neutral, but now German troops were tromping west across their borders. The Netherlands would succumb to the Nazis in less than five days. Fearing that fifth columnists might attempt a coup on Java, officials herded the island's German residents onto sports fields before hauling them off to hidden camps. At the local radio station, where Frank would soon be dispatching emergency news bulletins to San Francisco, employees smashed their substantial German record collection.[1]

By overrunning the Dutch and French metropoles, the Nazis' stunning Blitzkrieg had thrown the future of colonized Asia into sudden jeopardy; the Japanese might see Europe's crisis as an opportunity to mount a southward advance. But on plumeria-scented terraces, over private club reserves of whisky and gin, most colonists batted away such back-of-the-mind fears as preposterous. To Japan's south lay the navies of Western powers determined to keep their grasp on the region's riches. The Japanese wouldn't dare try to breach the fortified ports of Hong Kong, Singapore, or Pearl Harbor. They would stand no match against the British, Dutch, or American crack militias, never mind that these reserves were staffed in part by volunteers who mustered for ceremonial weekend drills. White residents of Southeast

Asia assured themselves that the Japanese were inferior soldiers and poor bombers with terrible eyesight. General Robert Brooke-Popham, commander in chief of the British Far East forces, dismissed them as "sub-human specimens," incapable of forming "an intelligent fighting force." The political situation in the East did "not look too grim," Frank agreed, "so long as Uncle Sam leaves his fleet in the Pacific." And he could not imagine that the United States would jeopardize its rubber and tin supply lines.[2]

By late September the Japanese had moved into bases in northern French Indochina with the consent of France's collaborationist Vichy regime and signed the Tripartite Pact with Germany and Italy. President Roosevelt's decision to extend the US embargo to scrap iron and steel merely redoubled Japanese planners' sense of urgency. Now armed with some of the world's best warships, submarines, and fighter planes, the Emperor's military launched reconnaissance flights over Malaya and the Philippines, drilled soldiers in jungle tactics, and rehearsed the invasion of the East Indies with large-scale map exercises. Japan's War Ministry began designing occupation currencies. "The situation for the South is full of dangers" and Japan might seek further footholds in Indochina and Thailand, reported one of Frank's Chinese contacts in Hong Kong. Frank nevertheless reassured himself with the notion that if the Japanese made a move they would "run into a hornet's nest like nothing they have ever experienced."[3] This fantasy of white supremacy would in many ways prove to be Japan's greatest weapon.

War in Europe scrambled the economy of the East Indies and Frank's business with it. Dutch banks and other companies relocated from Amsterdam to Batavia to escape the Nazis. Exports skyrocketed as American and British purchase orders poured in for rubber, tin, quinine, and kapok, used for aircraft insulation and life jackets. Yet imports to the now self-governing colony were plummeting as former trading partners hoarded strategic materials for themselves. Even the most basic goods—wooden cases, aluminum foil, and gunnysacks, reserved for making sandbags—grew scarce on the islands. Shopkeepers took to wrapping products in leaves.[4]

By late 1940 the "strain of work and war" took such a toll on Frank's health that doctors ordered him to the Peking Union Medical College for treatment, a trip that required permission from Japan's occupying North China Area Army. The break did him good, but upon returning to Java in December, his old stresses and symptoms resurfaced. A nerve specialist diagnosed him with leiodystonia, a form of "neurosis of the tropics" believed to affect White residents after prolonged exposure to the climate and lifestyle of the Far East—"philipinnitis" Americans sometimes called it. Frank's doctor put him on a simple diet of porridge and counseled rest and long swims, which seemed to help. He accepted an invitation to a party at the Batavia Cricket Club (no one dreamed it would be turned into an internment camp for Westerners only a year later), and with friends he organized regular baseball games on a vacant lot. But "those depressed feelings" sometimes crept up on him, especially when he stayed up too late or smoked too many cigarettes. Others thought he didn't look well at all.[5]

The new year brought yet more hassles that left Frank with "hardly a moment to sit down and think." Dodge & Seymour's New York employees were not taking his new business with the Chinese firm Kian Gwan seriously but instead dragged their feet on orders, claimed goods weren't procurable when Frank found them from other suppliers, and charged too much for their buyer's commission. "Dear Larry"—Frank called Mr. Seymour by his first name now—"I don't think that any of you quite realize the potentialities of this working arrangement or the caliber of the executives heading the main concern." Government red tape on Java, too, hindered "practically every step" of Frank's trade operations from ordering to delivery. Wartime censorship meanwhile slowed communications. Dutch tax policies, always frustrating, became more burdensome and byzantine. Still, as the United States surpassed the Netherlands and Japan as the colony's main supplier in 1941, Frank scrambled to procure all and sundry: Campbell soups, dried fruits, and baby bottles; razor blades, bobby pins and scissors; glass tumblers and copper wire; spare parts for boats and lanterns; fountain pen ink and typewriter ribbons; playing cards, roller skates, and carriage bells. His hair was growing gray around the temples.[6]

When he did sit still, nostalgia took hold. Reclining with a chilled mug of beer in the evenings as his houseboy removed his shoes, Frank read letters from home and tried to "roll back the pages of time" to his youth in Cedar Rapids. He wondered: Did high school kids have as much fun today as they had in the early twenties? He inquired about forgotten friends. One of them had died. Another was making a career for himself as a lawyer. Yet another had grown "fat as a balloon." It shocked him to realize that he was nearing forty. He still reminisced about leaping over those 400-meter Olympic

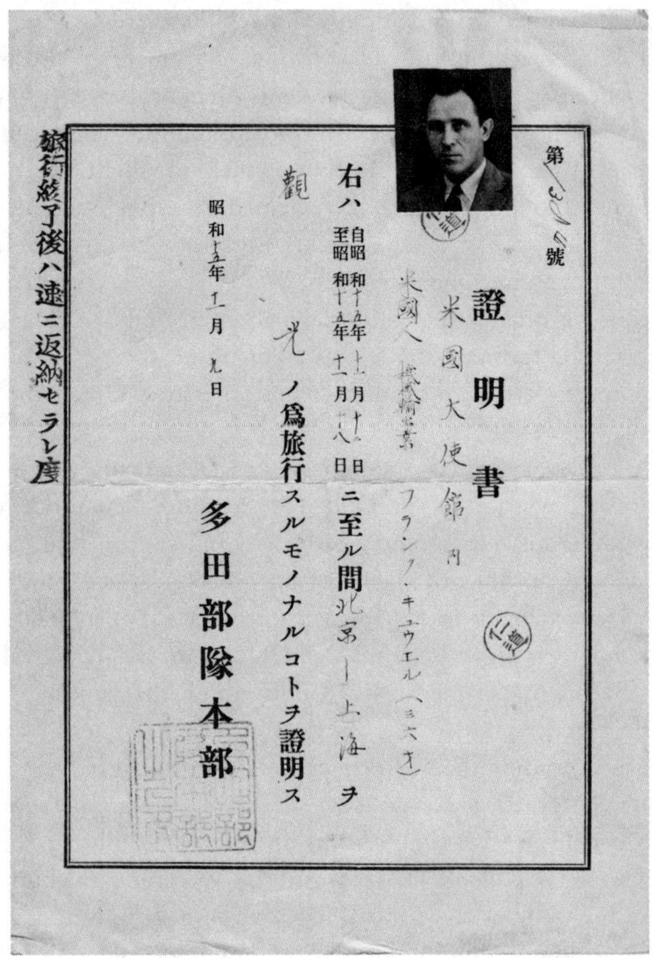

第 [illegible] 號

證明書

米國大使館内

米國人 [illegible] フランク・キウエル（三六才）

右ハ自昭和十五年十一月十二日至昭和十五年十一月十八日ニ至ル間北京―上海ヲ

觀光ノ為旅行スルモノナルコトヲ證明ス

昭和十五年十一月九日

多田部隊本部

旅行終了後ハ速ニ返納セラレ度

A Japanese military pass grants Frank Cuhel permission to travel to Beijing for medical treatment. Courtesy of Michael Safranek/University Archives, The University of Iowa Libraries.

hurdles. "But that, in itself," he admitted, "is the surest kind of sign that I am becoming middle-aged. And the race is so far from being won."[7]

More and more Frank hoped that his years living abroad would soon enter "the home stretch." He imagined "taking it easy" back in Iowa. Perhaps teaching foreign trade at the university, where between classes he could camp out in his favorite soda fountain booth, talking world affairs and football over a double chocolate malted with whipped cream. Maybe he would write a book about his "screwy life." And he decided he should marry. He thought about a red-headed corporate secretary he had met during her Far East tour, Mary Jorzick. She was returning to Java soon. He would discuss it with her. Mary was "beyond girlish ideologies and petty prides," which suited Frank just fine. Companionship was more important than passion, he decided. "I feel pretty sure that the violent forces of love are completely killed in me so I am not looking forward to any rekindling of those fires." He would be happy, he decided, with someone who simply understood him, someone willing to face together life's long-term ups and downs.[8]

Frank thought a lot, too, about years not so long ago, in Manila and Singapore, when it had seemed possible to "belly-up to a bar and settle the world's affairs." Now things were "in a hell of a mess." He wondered if the world could ever "straighten itself out again." Reflecting on the "Japanese problem," he felt sure that conflict with "the little brown boys in the north" was inevitable, and the sooner it was settled the better. He fantasized about a hundred Yankee battleships appearing out of the ocean mist, announcing "Alright you little Japanese bastards, get back to your islands and stay there—or else."[9] Instead, by the end of July, the Emperor's forces had moved without resistance into bases in southern Indochina, putting their planes within range of the East Indies and Malaya.

In response, Roosevelt froze Japanese assets in the United States, effectively halting all purchases including oil and leaving Japan, its naval planners estimated, with only eighteen months of fuel. As a further warning, the president recalled General Douglas MacArthur to active service in the Philippines, putting him in charge of the new US Army Forces in the East, staffed by American and Filipino recruits. MacArthur made the readiness of those under his command sound more impressive than it was, assuring journalists that war would be short and devastating, if not impossible, for the Japanese. But the buildup had been plotted along too long a timeline. By December only a fraction of the general's army would be mobilized. Delays likewise stalled shipments of B-17 bombers and other equipment. Much of the gear that did arrive was obsolete or defective. Enlisted Filipino soldiers, sometimes lacking even shoes, picked over old rifles, dud mortars, and artillery missing sights. MacArthur's confidence nevertheless proved infectious. "When the Japs come down here," bragged one reporter in Manila, "they'll be playing in the big leagues for the first time in their lives."[10]

Complacency blinded colonists to the threats they faced and fueled their collective denial. Across Southeast Asia, evacuation policies for Westerners remained vague, piecemeal, and voluntary. Americans who left had to do so on their own dime and only with the approval of their employers. Many, confident that they could ride the crisis out, remained, and newcomers continued to arrive: agents charged with safeguarding company assets, journalists in search of scoops, nurses and missionaries citing duty, and wives sticking with husbands. As a consequence, more than 130,000 European and American civilians, including more than 40,000 children, would find themselves in the path of the Japanese. Some escaped or were killed. But most, including many of Frank's friends, lived out the war, or died, in internment camps.[11]

By late 1941, military experts on Java had grown increasingly worried. They knew that defending an archipelago, which took five and a half days to traverse by steamship, presented a "baffling problem." The East Indies' security forces had been designed to suppress internal uprisings, not to repel external threats. They were outfitted with only a few Brewster Buffalo planes (disparaged as "flying beer barrels") and other hand-me-downs that had been rejected for military use in Europe and the United States. Batavia boasted only antiquated shore batteries and paltry antiaircraft defenses. Practice flights during blackout tests revealed that, even on moonless nights, the city's wharves and oil stores could be seen under the starry South Pacific sky.[12]

Manpower shortages were even more colonial officials' own making. The Dutch had periodically entertained the idea of instituting compulsory military service on the islands, but conservatives considered the idea of training and arming "the natives" too costly, unnecessary, and dangerous. The colony's 1923 conscription act applied only to Netherlanders. Failure to mobilize more than a tiny fraction of a population of seventy million, or to concede greater political rights to Indonesians, meant that the Dutch would face the Japanese with only some 40,000 army regulars and 60,000 hastily recruited conscripts and poorly armed militia. Repeating platitudes about the political indifference of *kampung* villagers, they misjudged Indonesians' willingness to stand by and watch, or even abet, when the Japanese came to chase the White imperialists from their midst.[13]

Frank grew more tired and ready to go back to the States. He bickered with his bosses and became "fed up" with colleagues. Colonial officials tormented him. Immigration officers detained him and refused to waive a fine, even after the US consul became involved, because Frank would not apologize for his "impolite behavior."[14] He was summoned to court for traffic violations he swore he never committed, billed for a radio license on a set he claimed to no longer own, and menaced by tax authorities who haggled with him over deductions and late fees.[15] And then there was the plumbing. Frank's shower pressure often cut out, leaving him "in a cover of lather to roar blasphemies at the dripping trickle" until someone closer to the pressure pumps turned off their spouts (the Dutch were installing new pipelines, but they would never finish). Determined to return to Iowa by Christmas, he reserved a seat on the Pan Am clipper to San Francisco. Colleagues chastised him for giving up his post. "The world changes, and without question the Dutch Indies will march in the parade, which should mean more business—both export and import," V. A. Dodge urged. Frank paid them no mind. He resigned from his golf club, arranged to sell his furniture, and dismissed the gardener.[16]

In October, a final trip to Sumatra to tally the number of shops carrying Pond's Cold Cream now required a military pass. Visiting the Shell and Standard Oil refineries at Palembang, Frank noticed that they had been rigged for demolition. He and his associates began to speculate about what they might do if war broke out and stranded their shipments while en route. They did not know that the Emperor's military strategists had already settled on an ambitious scheme to conquer all of colonial Southeast Asia, believing their nation's very existence depended on it. Japanese forces planned to move quickly, before a greater buildup of American, British, and Dutch defenses in the region. Under the new, hawkish prime minister, General Tōjō Hideki, a date for the attack was set for early December, the same day Frank was scheduled to fly home.[17]

Diplomatic negotiations dragged on in Washington but continued to falter on American insistence that Japan withdraw from China. Kian Gwan's directors began to write to Frank about *when* the United States joined the war, not *if.* By November 27, Japanese naval and air attack forces were steaming toward Hawai'i and other targets. The Japanese army was now more than eight times the size it had been four years earlier and stood ready with 2.1 million men. Its recruits had been schooled to look on Southeast Asians as "brothers" who had been subjugated for centuries by American and European "armed robbers" and who would welcome them as liberators from the "hated white races." Indeed, many Indonesians would, at least at first.[18]

On December 8, 1941—still December 7 on the other side of the international dateline—Frank headed for Batavia's airport. He traveled light, having shipped most of his belongings two days before. On the way, a friend claimed that Pearl Harbor had just been attacked. Frank told him he was crazy. But at the airport a naval attaché confirmed it.[19] The Imperial Japanese navy had caught the O'ahu base off guard at breakfast time, blasting its planes and ships and killing 2,403 people, only one of a series of coordinated attacks unfolding across the Pacific. In two short months, Japanese fighters would be bombing the very airport where Frank stood and occupying it in less than three.

But that was still inconceivable. News of the attack on Pearl Harbor electrified the White residents of the East Indies. It would be "the salvation of Java," many hoped, the "punch on the nose" that would, if nothing else, stir the United States to protect the precious rubber, oil, and other resources the islands held. "Definitive action" against these "yellow men of small size" was most welcome, voiced one American visitor, to put the matter to rest once and for all. Frank turned back from the airport and telegrammed New York.

> STAYING ON TIME BEING
> PLEASE ADVISE SISTER ALL WELL[20]

14

Ship's Stores

THE SPANISH CIVIL WAR HAD nearly destroyed Manuel's business. Hitler's war would soar it to record heights. Commended for "*patriotismo*" and "praiseworthy work" for Franco's regime, he and his partner Marcelino Garcia regained the Spanish Line account and took over two Brooklyn piers in order to handle the outgoing streams of machine parts, automobiles, and Cuban tobacco as well as incoming tons of paprika, olive oil, canned fish, and assorted wines. Just as they had benefited from the Great War, American dollar diplomacy, and Roosevelt's Good Neighbor policies, the Neutrality Acts played right into their hands. As agents for vessels flying foreign flags, Manuel and Marcelino were exempt from Congress's "cash and carry" provision, which forbade US vessels from sailing into war zones, even to call at neutral ports. While American transatlantic shipping lines barreled toward bankruptcy in the late 1930s, Garcia & Diaz gobbled up more and more of New York harbor's overseas commerce.[1]

The outbreak of conflict in Europe, moreover, rerouted substantial US trade and tourist traffic toward the Latin American routes serviced by Manuel's firm. Garcia & Diaz's southbound passenger loads soon became successful enough to warrant a national magazine ad campaign hawking "ultra-modern" all-expense-paid cruises to Ecuador, Peru, and Chile. By 1940, Manuel and his partner controlled the bulk of merchant shipping between Spain, the United States, and Latin America. They noted in their financial records that their company had been "more active" that year than in the previous ten years combined.[2]

Manuel (*right*) and his partner, Marcelino (*left*), at the height of their company's success. From the periodical *Spain* (published in New York), March 1941. Courtesy of Harvard College Library, Widener Library.

Yet, by that summer, with the swastika flying over Paris, the war had also thrown the fate of Manuel's homeland once again into doubt. The survival of Franco's regime seemed tightly yoked to Axis success, whether or not Spain remained neutral. Spanish Republicans assembled a government-in-exile in Mexico and waited. They assumed, like the Free French, that they would be poised to regain power if the Nazis were defeated. Nationalists like Manuel prayed that wouldn't happen.[3]

As Spain shifted its status from neutral to "non-belligerent," few doubted that Franco would eventually join the fight against the Allies. In recognition of the assistance Germany and Italy had given him during the Spanish Civil War, he signed the Anti-Comintern Pact and a series of confidential accords promising economic and logistical support to the Axis. Franco and his supporters felt a strong "moral solidarity" with German and Italian fascists, as Spain's foreign affairs minister Ramón Serrano Suñer put it, and they hardly kept that enthusiasm a secret. Spanish crowds cheered Nazi victories in the streets. Angry demonstrators decried Americans and the British as the "despoilers" of Cuba and Gibraltar. The nation's press, by all accounts, was rife with Nazi propaganda. "The liberal world is going under," Franco assured his supporters, "victim of the cancer of its own errors."[4]

But Spain lay in ruins. The civil war had claimed over a million dead. Another half million had been cast into exile. Nearly that many languished in Franco's prisons. Farms and factories had barely sputtered back to life. Starvation threatened the poor. The battle-scarred nation and its tattered military did not have the resources or the political leverage to make going to war worthwhile. Negotiations with Hitler stalled over what spoils Franco might expect for his nation's participation.[5]

Spain would in fact prove far more useful to the Axis as a neutral territory than it ever could have been as a belligerent partner. Waging war depended upon frontier zones—regions where spies could prowl, where mail and prisoners could be exchanged and rare commodities traded or smuggled in and out. Spain hosted the world's largest German intelligence operation outside the Reich as well as clandestine Nazi weather and transmission stations, serviced by Luftwaffe planes camouflaged with Spanish insignia. Forty percent of Spain's exports now went to the Third Reich, including substantial amounts of ore, wolfram, hides, citrus, and olive oil. These links extended to North Africa, where Spanish front companies would ship 125,000 tons of supplies to Rommel's forces, and where Spanish consuls worked so vociferously on behalf of German agents that General George S. Patton would later lobby—unsuccessfully—to shut them down.[6]

As Axis victories multiplied, rightwing Spaniards dared to dream not only that Franco's regime would endure and that a new order would triumph in Europe but also that the spirit of *hispanidad* would flourish in the Americas—that the people of Latin America would see through *norteamericanos'* self-interested calls for hemispheric defense and instead turn to Spain for spiritual and political leadership. Serrano Suñer urged Spaniards living overseas to do their part to thwart pan-Americanism—nothing but US imperialism by another name—and help save Western civilization and the Catholic faith from the machinations of Communists, Masons, Jews, and Yankee Protestants.[7] Overseeing the largest shipping network linking the United States, Cuba, South America, and Spain from their perch in New York City, Manuel and Marcelino were better poised than most to contribute to this cause.

Emotions were reaching fever pitch in New York by mid-1940 as the city once again emerged as a gateway to warring Europe, where immigrants and activists of opposing loyalties embroiled themselves in a conflict with as yet deeply uncertain consequences for the United States. Pamphlets pleading the Allied cause rolled off Manhattan's presses alongside pro-Axis diatribes. Midtown hotel suites had become hideouts for British agents, seeking to influence American opinion, and for Vichy secret police, tracking Free French exiles nesting nearby. At the beginning of the war military-age men had flooded the city's Polish, French, and German consulates offering to enlist in their armies. Now partisans argued on the sidewalks. Christian Fronters—nothing more than stormtroopers, their opponents said—held dozens of riotous street meetings each week, even as the group's leaders stood trial in Brooklyn for conspiracy to overthrow the US government.[8] As warnings about sabotage plots clogged the city's switchboards, the police commissioner doubled guard details at piers, consulates, and other locations associated with the war's belligerents. Three bombs rocked New York in the weeks after France fell. One detonated in front of the Union Square headquarters of the *Daily Worker*, the Communist paper that had caused Manuel so much trouble three years before. Another device detectives managed to cart out of the British Pavilion at the World's Fair before it blew up, killing two. The third one exploded in Manuel's office complex at 17 Battery Place, injuring nine.[9]

The Whitehall Building was a target because it hummed with activities benefiting the fascist cause. It housed not only the German consulate and Library of Information, the Reich's main propaganda den in the United States, but also a handful of shipping and purchasing companies under investigation for their trade in Nazi territories.[10] Manuel's proximity to these agencies was fortuitous at the very least. His German connections stretched back to World War I, when Marcelino worked for the Central Powers broker G. Amsinck & Company and when Marcelino's brother-in-law, Cornelius Gundlach, had been identified by Allied authorities as "on the wrong side of the fence." Later, when Gundlach was arrested in Bolivia as a Nazi spy, Marcelino swore that he had never had any personal connection to his brother-in-law, even though on numerous occasions Gundlach had been a guest at his Brooklyn home.[11]

Manuel and his partner moreover had always steered clear of working for enterprises dependent on British investment, serving instead as agents for lines backed by German money, such as Bachi, which used Spanish front men to transport Axis supplies until the British pressured Franco to suspend its operations. Nearly all of Manuel's employees had Spanish backgrounds, but his company's trusted traffic managers were the sons of German-speaking immigrants. By 1940, Manuel also kept exclusively German servants at his house.[12]

As German steamship agencies and other companies found it harder and harder to carry on in the United States, Manuel and Marcelino also began co-opting their accounts. They evacuated Axis nationals from New York on Spanish ships and carried mail bound for the Third Reich. Before long, concerned citizens started walking into FBI field offices warning that Manuel and Marcelino were "pro-Nazi" and working "hand-in-glove with the German consul" over at the Whitehall Building. Investigators who followed up with bank informants found that the company Garcia & Diaz had received numerous payments from German and Japanese officials.[13]

But if Manuel and his partner were "rabid pro-Germans," as one New York exporter called them, they were not alone.[14] A sizable number of Americans had strong affinities for Germany. In 1939 and 1940, Americans sent an avalanche of mail to the Reich, including a "heavy traffic" of cash securities, care packages, and letters from individuals eager to do their "bit" for the Nazis. During the first six months of the war alone, Bermuda's censors rooted out of this correspondence some £4 million. Secret hopes tucked into envelopes alongside these monies hinted at the extent of Axis allegiances in the city where Manuel lived. One Upper West Side woman confided in German to a friend in Cologne that "Roosevelt has had his own way long enough with the damned Jews he's allowed into the country." Germany "must win," she wrote. "Pray for it."[15]

Manuel, too, was hardly the only businessman in the United States with German connections. American holdings in the Reich totaled an estimated $300 million. American markets, moreover, had come to depend on a variety of specialized goods from Germany: optical and surgical instruments, rare horticultural supplies, and certain textile machinery, which could not be procured elsewhere. When British agents surveyed the scope of business between the United States and the Axis, they turned up all kinds of activity across the country: San Francisco's Bank of America, founded by Italians and handling most German finances in the Bay Area; a Firestone subsidiary, sending reclaimed rubber through a secondary company to Switzerland, where it was reportedly turned into large quantities of tires for the German market; even a cousin of Hermann Göring, running some kind of engineering firm out of Chicago.[16]

To thwart the flow of resources to their enemies, British planners reverted to the surveillance system they used during World War I, issuing navicerts, which exempted acceptable cargoes from search, and diverting suspect ships to Trinidad, Gibraltar, and other British weigh stations. Neutral vessels soon jammed the waters off these ports while Royal Navy patrols rifled through their cabins, lavatory cisterns, and pipe-tangled engine rooms, confiscating contraband outright and compensating shippers for other seized cargo, such as oil going to Sweden, which they suspected would end up in Axis hands.[17] Manuel and his Spanish colleagues balked at the imposition. But British authorities threatened to block or delay the Spanish Line's ability to secure bunkers if they did not cooperate.[18]

Yet the navicert system ultimately worked in the Spaniards' favor. Deeply afraid of alienating Americans who they needed on their side, British officials designed their regulations to be as "unprovocative and expeditious" as possible, keeping international waters open to "neighbourly trade" rather than choking off communications and supplies like a traditional blockade. Ships with orderly paperwork escaped detailed searches or detention at inspection points. Navicerts moreover assessed the character of goods rather than the reputation of exporters themselves, and they applied only to consigned cargoes, not to provisions loaded for the use of the crew. Thus shippers conducted their business relatively freely so long as they did not get too greedy padding these "ship's stores," and so long as they had not been blacklisted—and the British Statutory Lists for the United States, fixated on German-run companies, included no Spanish firms at all. Privately, Manuel and his partner alerted Madrid that the British were "interested" in Spanish ships and censoring mail at Bermuda. But publicly, they made a good show of complying with Allied controls, announcing that only properly permitted cargo would be received on their docks. Neutrality was not merely a concept designed to safeguard the weak, or a set of commonsense rules to keep human beings decent even in their worst moments. It also presented an opportunity for brokers and strategists to manipulate to their own advantage.[19]

To many, shippers like Manuel seemed valiant simply for carrying on under the "trade-at-your-own-risk" conditions of wartime. Americans valorized merchant shipping as a lifeline, essential to the survival of the nation's political ideals as much as its security and economic interests. "All freedom," President Roosevelt contended in an oft-repeated theme, "depends on freedom of the seas," what he called an "ancient American doctrine." Yet hazards plagued the Atlantic's open waters. Belligerents warned of their sprawling minefields and forbade neutral ships from travelling by convoy, zigzagging, or other movements without the proper lighting, hull markings, and signaling procedures. Following those guidelines, however, did not guarantee safety. Neutrals were still sunk all the time.[20] Manuel and Marcelino publicized the exploits of their crews, alerting the press if they rescued sailors from torpedoed ships and advertising shipments of medicine, clothing, and other relief supplies they hauled to Spain's typhus-stricken communities. When they announced that they had commissioned Hellenic Lines vessels to run shipments under the Greek flag all the way to Turkey—a route off-limits to US vessels—customers flooded their offices with applications for cargo space. Thanks to Garcia & Diaz, the *Washington Post* cheered, "war-throttled trade routes into the Mediterranean got a new lease on life."[21]

So, Manuel dined at the Waldorf-Astoria's Starlight Room and watched his children come of age. Spanish ships meanwhile steamed east with Axis fugitives as well as precious metals stashed in tobacco bales or cigar boxes, with intelligence tucked into diplomatic pouches and therefore immune to search, and with extra drums of oil, categorized as ship's stores but likely containing either diesel for U-boats, which were secretly refueling in Spanish ports, or lubricating oil, which the Germans were buying up from willing suppliers at "famine prices." They returned west with propaganda to spread, money to launder, and a small number of enemy agents. Perhaps most consequentially, some of the vessels' radio officers signaled information about Allied convoys to German submarines. The head of Spanish espionage in the Western Hemisphere later estimated that this work contributed to the sinking of no fewer than eight hundred Allied ships during the war.[22]

Manuel, of course, faced risks. When containers loaded on the *Magallanes* at New York broke open on the Bilbao docks in late 1940, they revealed not the used clothing listed on the ship's manifest but motors. The supplier for Manuel's firm "pretends to specialize in relief goods," British officials notified American authorities, but this incident gave "absolute proof" that he had been falsifying navicert declarations. British agents resolved to keep a closer eye on the movements of Spanish Line vessels servicing New York and Havana.[23]

Cuban police, who identified "pro-totalitarian Spaniards" as the most dangerous antidemocratic faction on their island, also grew increasingly wary of ships managed by Manuel and his partner. Beefing up Havana's port security in early 1941, they combed over their boats, dug through baggage, censored documents, interviewed disembarking passengers, and tailed crewmembers on shore leave. Over time, the work exposed a small but steady stream of plotters and smugglers, among them a local Falange leader trying to escape with photographs of strategic installations, a suspected Nazi agent with diamonds in a hidden briefcase compartment, a Spanish nun with secret instructions sewn into her robes, and a sailor trafficking in fascist literature.[24] When questioned about the activities of Garcia & Diaz employees in Havana, Marcelino explained that he "knew nothing about their transactions." He had "full confidence" in his overseas agents. They worked independently and chose their own "money making projects."[25]

Some were getting suspicious on the US mainland, too, as diplomatic relays and returning travelers' stories began to build a picture of Spain's logistical importance to the Axis. The disclosure of trade statistics during the Lend-Lease hearings in March 1941 raised the prospect that tinplate, petroleum products, and other strategic materials from the United States ended up in Nazi territory via Spanish suppliers—that Americans might be "arming the Axis when we are supposed to be the arsenal for democracy," as the Democratic representative from Washington John M. Coffee exclaimed.[26] The tightening of oil exports to Spain, expelling of Axis diplomats, and other US government actions that spring seemed calculated to warn of consequences should Spanish collaboration with Germany and Italy become too brazen. In April, federal agents seized two dozen Axis ships docked in American ports on the pretext that they had violated the 1917 Espionage Act. (Manuel and Marcelino arranged the departure of the Italian diplomat ejected from the country for encouraging their crews to sabotage the boats in retaliation.) In June, the Treasury Department froze all accounts in the United States containing Spanish capital, including some of Garcia & Diaz's funds. The following month, President Roosevelt pushed the boundaries of the Western Hemisphere to the shores of Iceland and ordered US troops to the island. The new Economic Defense Board meanwhile began investigating security concerns in Latin America and compiling a Proclaimed List of Certain Blocked Nationals to force the nations to the south to distance themselves from the Axis economy. With covert government funding, Pan American Airways redoubled its efforts to monopolize Latin American air routes and expand its network of bases in the region. These were exactly the kind of moves rightwing Spaniards despised as predatory "Monroeism."[27]

Yet were they not also the desperate moves of a liberal order headed for collapse? The Allies had just been chased out of Yugoslavia and Greece. Rommel commanded more and more of North Africa. Britain's cities were crumbling under Luftwaffe bombs, and U-boat attacks were disintegrating

Allied convoys. After Hitler's forces invaded the Soviet Union that June, the war took on even more moral clarity for rightwing Spaniards. In Madrid mobs hurled rocks at the British embassy and chanted the Führer's name. Volunteers signed up for Spain's Blue Division, which mobilized to fight the Communists on the Eastern Front. Overwhelmed by the glorious turn of events, Franco rhapsodized that "the Allies have lost it." Germany was leading the way in a great battle to redeem "Europe and Christiandom."[28]

Manuel still found plenty of room to maneuver during the second half of 1941. Even after the previous year's Export Control Act, security measures in New York remained piecemeal. Most illicit goods, transported in ounces or handfuls, were easily hidden. And the waters beyond the harbor had many dark reaches, not least around Spain's Canary Islands. Garcia & Diaz specialized in wheat shipments for Switzerland and other cargoes for neutral countries, which its vessels carried to Las Palmas, where loads were transferred to smaller boats and then taken to Genoa. This "shuttle service" had received approval from the British government, but Allied knowledge of shipping and oil refining operations on the Canaries was patchy and kept in check by Spanish authorities. It would not have been difficult to sneak supplies to the Axis at the same time—and, indeed, the Kriegsmarine had made explicit plans to provision their submarines with crude oil brought from the Western Hemisphere to the refinery on Tenerife.[29]

Manuel profited from westward traffic as well. That summer, American Export Lines, sailing from Lisbon to the United States weekly, lost one of its ships to the War Department and stopped selling space to refugees who were not US citizens. To meet the demand, Manuel's ships accelerated their schedules and refitted cargo space for passengers. The odds remained stacked against those attempting to flee the Nazis as governments around the world closed their borders to all but a trickle of newcomers, but without Spanish vessels, including Manuel's, far fewer refugees would have escaped than the hundred thousand estimated to have passed through Portugal's capital.[30]

So into Havana and then New York sailed the *Magallanes*, the *Marqués de Comillas*, the *Navemar*, and the *Motomar*, crowded with the desperate, weary, and stunned. The refugees they carried were survivors of internment camps and prison ships, victims of human smugglers, people who had been stranded in the desert or hiding in the hills, many too scared to be quoted in the newspapers, fearing for relatives still trapped in Europe but ready to riot if refused entry. Spilling off decks piled high with imported cork, they recounted their sorrows to awaiting journalists and port authorities. Among them was a family of German antifascists who bought a fishing smack and planned to sail the English Channel before the boat was destroyed by dive bombers during the Battle of Dunkirk. They only made it to Lisbon after changing their identities. Leapfrogging from precarious haven to haven, many followed what was fast becoming a familiar set of itineraries: Marseille or Nice to Barcelona or Casablanca and eventually Lisbon. One Jewish playwright from Vienna lingered for almost two years in North Africa, where his Catholic wife, unable to take the waiting, killed herself before their renewed exit visas arrived. Still others came by more improbable routes, casting about almost aimlessly through a growing tangle of red tape. One Hungarian composer tried to reach the United States via Bombay but was forced back to Greece and eventually Lisbon because he had been sold the wrong British transit visa. Another man, a decorated World War I veteran of the German infantry, had performed forced labor in a rayon factory after the Nazis liquidated his perfume business in Cologne. He lived "in constant fear" until a Jewish aid society arranged his exit. He had a sister, too, he told immigration agents, but she, her husband, and child had been deported to Poland, and there had been no word from them since. Manuel and Marcelino arranged the sailings that took all these people, and thousands more, to the New World.[31]

But at a price.

Manuel and his colleagues offered Axis nationals passage to Europe for below-market fares of $50–$115.[32] They charged those fleeing the Nazis $500–$1,200 per person, prices that others deemed "entirely out of line, even under the present emergency conditions." American Export Lines, plying the same route, charged only $300–$350. Little of these profits went back into passenger accommodations. On vessels packed three times their normal capacity, refugees braved conditions "below their worst expectations." After nearly a dozen people contracted typhoid and one died en route to New York on the *Magallanes*, passengers sued and port authorities temporarily impounded the boat. Manuel and Marcelino argued that it wasn't their fault. Only one person died, they explained, and who knew if he had caught the disease on board or in port. But the worst was yet to come.[33]

In September, when Manuel's and Marcelino's *Navemar* lurched into New York carrying 769 evacuees, many sick or injured, American newspapers christened it a "hell ship." Survivors, who had paid up to $1,700 for the trip, claimed that the aging cargo vessel's agents promised to sail with only 150 people. Instead, they loaded more than a thousand refugees at Sevilla, separating the men from the women and herding them "like pigs" into barely ventilated holds, some of which lacked even portholes. Passengers who protested said that they were "threatened with concentration camps if they didn't go aboard and forget their complaints."[34]

Two died in the single day it took to travel from Sevilla to its next stop, Lisbon. There the boat lingered for a week while 86 newcomers came aboard before finally setting sail across the Atlantic. During the next thirteen days, travelers endured suffocating air in the vessel's holds or slept in chairs on the deck. One Latvian refugee, kept awake by crying children, nervously eyed the gangrene developing in her diabetic bunkmate's foot. The Spanish crew—rude or indifferent by many accounts—served hastily prepared meals in three sittings, dunking used plates in a bucket of dirty water before passing them to the next round of eaters. Food poisoning ripped through the ship, and four more were buried at sea.[35]

Only after offloading passengers at Bermuda and Cuba, including one who died on shore, did the sailors disinfect the ship's two small washrooms and switch the taps from sea water to fresh water. The *Navemar* dropped anchor at New York's quarantine station forty-eight days after leaving Spain. Inspectors who climbed aboard discovered a garbage-strewn deck with corroded emergency equipment and disheveled lifeboats, one of them smeared with what appeared to be blood. Jerry-rigged stairs led below to compartments lit by generator-powered strands of 25-watt bulbs. In the mess halls they found greasy wooden tables; in the pantry, rotting vegetables and three decomposing chicken heads. One longtime health official admitted he had never seen a ship "so insanitary and so fraught with potential danger not only to the passengers on the vessel in question, but to the country as a whole."[36]

Passengers prepared to sue, but Manuel and Marcelino still refused to refund their fares. These travelers had "pleaded for the conditions they are now complaining about," the agents reasoned. Worried that US officials might start confiscating Spanish vessels if others arrived in similar condition, Franco's regime banned any more Jewish refugees from boarding ships departing Spain for Cuba or the United States.[37]

Manuel was pressing his luck. As winter approached—with US warships escorting Atlantic convoys and tiptoeing into an undeclared naval war—concerns about Spanish ships signaling to U-boats began to pile up in various government offices.[38] In November 1941, a sensational two-week-long exposé by *PM* brought significant public attention to Spaniards' work on behalf of the Axis. Victor Bernstein's investigation of "Spain's local fascists" in New York splashed Manuel's and Marcelino's faces across the page next to a detailed history of their support for Franco. In another article,

I. F. Stone dangled tantalizing evidence that Hitler's Luftwaffe was "being lubricated with American oil" furnished by Spanish agents. Letters from outraged readers inundated federal agencies, pushing the government toward a temporary suspension of oil exports to Spain and a congressional investigation. "WHAT KIND OF SHENANIGANS ARE GOING ON DOWN THERE?" one New Yorker demanded of the State Department. "I have a son in the Army and this revelation of American gasoline and oil going to the Nazis through Franco's Spain certainly makes me boil," wrote another.[39] The mutual suspicion between American officials and Franco's regime deepened still further when Hitler declared war on the United States four days after the Japanese attacks in the Pacific. With the US official entry into Europe's conflict, the future of Manuel's shipping enterprise hung in the balance.

That week, Manuel's firm had been busy preparing for the departure of the *Isla de Tenerife*, a Compañía Trasmediterránea vessel shortly bound for the Canary Islands and Spain. Manuel and Marcelino had been entrusted with a sudden, unusual spate of Trasmediterránea traffic to New York by the company's chief stockholder, Juan March. March, who lobbied Mussolini and Hitler on Franco's behalf during the Spanish Civil War, controlled the oil refinery on Tenerife and had negotiated with the Nazis about the possibility of using Spanish ships to transport German cargos and refuel U-boats. At Brooklyn's State Barge Pier, stevedores carted aboard the *Tenerife* not only wheat and beans consigned to the Swiss and Spanish governments but also a large cache of radio receivers, armored cable, silk, and two hundred drums of lubricating oil, all claimed, obviously falsely, as ship's stores for the use of the crew on the return voyage. The amount of unlicensed oil alone was egregious. The boat's captain admitted privately that the trip required only three to five barrels, hardly two hundred.[40]

It was not the first time Trasmediterránea ships had left Garcia & Diaz's docks in recent months with inexplicably large amounts of oil.[41] But this time, on an informant's tip, federal agents stormed the boat before it escaped to the Lower Bay, discovering the contraband and arresting its captain and chief radio officer. Learning that authorities also intended to charge Manuel and Marcelino for violating the Export Control Act, the two shippers summoned to the Whitehall Building a team of lawyers, including Leo C. Fennelly, who would also defend members of the German American Bund accused of subversive activities. The lawyers advised Manuel and Marcelino that the situation was "extremely serious." To spare them the humiliation of being arrested at their place of business, Fennelly arranged for his clients to surrender themselves at the courthouse. Manuel and Marcelino were "mortified" to be fingerprinted and thrown behind bars "as if we were common criminals." Word of the shipping agents' troubles splashed across New York's papers. These two "had always managed to luck out," Spanish Republicans rejoiced in Brooklyn's *España Libre*, but surely now they would be stopped.[42]

15

Easy Dish

BY JANUARY 1942 STAKES JUTTED out of Batavia's canals to prevent parachutists from landing, and housewives were giving their children pieces of rubber to put between their teeth during the coming bombing raids. Frank admired the businesslike efficiency at one shelter, where relief workers were stocking operating rooms based on emergency procedures used in London. Yet he seemed completely oblivious to other upswelling energies—the huddled crowds of Indonesian shoppers on errands, students in college corridors, and neighbors at civil defense meetings, all daring to imagine independence if the Dutch were forced to leave. For as long as he could, Frank would cling to a set of hopes and illusions—that the war coming to his region of the world was part of the same one consuming Europe, that it would unfold by the same logic, that some territories might fall but that some would be defended with heart like Britain had been, and that the close-knit colonial communities of Southeast Asia in which he had made his home for a decade would somehow be saved. But this would be no reenactment of the Blitz.[1]

The same day that the American naval fleet was crippled at Pearl Harbor—the day Frank Cuhel turned back from the airport and decided to remain in the East Indies—Japanese imperial forces landed in Thailand and Malaya, raided Allied embassies and businesses in Shanghai's International Settlement, and bombed Hong Kong, Guam, Wake, and the Philippines, where they wiped out nearly half the US Far East Air Force on day one of the Pacific War. They stunned again two days later by securing airfields in northern Luzon, sinking the British battleships *Prince of Wales* and *Repulse*, and that night bombarding a still fully lit Singapore, ripping through the shopping arcades of Raffles Place, cratering the Padang sports green, and killing scores in Chinatown. Meanwhile, Yamashita Tomoyuki's 25th Army, which had landed at Kota Bharu hours before the bombs fell on Hawai'i, raced down the Malay Peninsula, its troops bypassing fixed military posts on stolen bicycles. More than a century of British rule collapsed in a blaze of undignified chaos. Officers bickered with each other over defense strategies and disparaged their own Indian troops. Disregarding the welfare of those who would be left behind, officials dumped the rice stores and funneled everything usable toward Singapore, destroying bridges, railways, and power stations as they went. Laden with colonial trappings—rattan chairs, golf clubs, caged canaries—Malaya's White elites filed across the two-lane causeway into the Empire's treasured fortress of the East, which proved no fortress at all.[2]

Japanese landings followed on North Borneo, Mindanao, and Southern Luzon. By December 22, when Homma Masaharu's 14th Army commenced its main assault on the Philippines, the archipelago's US naval and air forces had already retreated south to the East Indies and Australia. Besides the capable but underequipped Philippine Scouts, defense forces on Luzon consisted largely of reservists and draftees fresh from basic training or officer candidate schools. The Japanese soldiers who converged on Manila were veterans of fearsome fighting on mainland China. Evacuating to Corregidor, the Philippine government declared the capital an open city. General Douglas MacArthur and his staff followed to the island in Manila Bay, directing US and Filipino forces to the nearby Bataan Peninsula, where they mustered with what would prove to be an inadequate stock of food, medical supplies, mosquito nets, blankets, and underwear. By the end of the siege in April the majority would be suffering from malaria, dysentery, or beriberi.[3]

Guam fell, and Wake, then Hong Kong on Christmas day. "Help is on the way from the United States," MacArthur assured those on Bataan. "Thousands of troops and hundreds of planes are being dispatched." They weren't. And the Japanese had been so successful that they expedited invasion plans for the East Indies. First, they would take outlying Borneo and Celebes for their airfields, then swoop east and west with synchronized land and sea operations against Sumatra and Bali. The biggest prize would be last: Java.[4]

Europeans and Americans who had fled China, the Philippines, and Malaya nevertheless continued to pour into Batavia. It took one full-time officer and two Chinese clerks at the US consulate just to handle these displaced citizens' cable traffic. At the Hotel des Indes, overflow guests slept on cots in a garden pavilion. It was there that Frank befriended the Columbia Broadcasting System's newly arrived radio commentator Bill Dunn, who mentioned that the Mutual Broadcasting System was in search of a local reporter. Eager for a role to play in the conflict and intrigued by the idea of becoming a war correspondent, Frank contacted Mutual's executives with Dunn's help, and they agreed to give him a trial on the air.[5]

The job presented an enormous opportunity to reach millions of people. By 1942, radio had become a primary medium for the spread of international news, with an estimated 300 million listeners around the globe. Early broadcasting had depended on continuous longwaves that clung to the ground, but shortwave radio, developed in the 1930s, instead beamed transmissions skyward to bounce off the earth's ionosphere and land on far-off continents. Shortwave was beholden to the vagaries of the atmosphere. It whined and sizzled. Sometimes speakers sounded under water, or messages cut out halfway or did not come through at all. But it also fired imaginations. Advertisements featuring antennae soaring into the clouds or shooting lightning bolts across oceans implored customers to "Tune in the World," as one radio set company put it. The East Indies had one of the world's largest radio transmitters and supported nearly two dozen stations through the network Nederlandsch-Indische Radio-Omroep Maatschappij (NIROM) over which Frank delivered his early reports.[6]

In the United States, where Frank's primary audience resided, more than 80 percent of households owned at least one radio set. Before 1938, news had furnished only a sliver of network offerings, but the Munich Crisis that year dramatized the medium's real-time advantages. Current events soon consumed 20 percent of airtime, and by the early 1940s, Americans reported that the radio, rather than newspapers, had become their most trusted source of information. The radio brought foreign affairs to listeners in arresting, live-action format. It deepened their connections to distant places, investing them in obligations far from home. President Roosevelt and others who favored increasing aid to democracies overseas had deliberately embraced the radio; it offered a way to bypass the newspapers, almost entirely in the hands of rightwing moguls, and speak directly to the public. Some worried that instead of uniting Americans in an enlightening marketplace of ideas, this new technology might become the domain of demagogues. But all agreed on its high stakes, which rose only higher as war consumed both Europe and Asia. Next to land, sea, and aerial combat, said one critic, the ether posed a "Fourth Front," a battlefield on which words became "bombs for the mind." It was no accident that invading armies made beelines for enemy transmitters.[7]

Frank's new employer, Mutual, sponsored well-regarded news updates every half hour around the clock. Drawing on stringers stationed across the globe, the network aired more than 1,900 war-related programs in 1942 alone, including its popular Round-Up of World News, on which Frank appeared twice a week. During Frank's first broadcast, atmospherics were so bad that he could not hear his San Francisco contacts, but he did the talk blind in hopes that it might still be picked up. His voice shook at first, and static changed its tone according to listeners who knew him back in the States. But with practice and tips from colleagues his delivery soon strengthened. Frank had a "natural flair for news," Bill Dunn noticed, and emerged as "a formidable competitor almost immediately."[8]

More and more correspondents flocked to Java, which had the region's best intercontinental communication networks not currently controlled by the Japanese. They couldn't believe their luck. "Dreams come true in the strangest fashion, don't they?" mused Frank's friend, the United Press reporter William McDougall, who loved how war had put him "into the thick of things" and allowed him to see more of the world than he had thought possible. Frank, too, sounded "in good spirits and quite optimistic" on the phone to contacts in New York. Gone were those feelings of depression and anxiety that had driven him to seek treatment at the Peking Union Medical College. He was earning four times what he had made as an importer. "From the stipend point of view," he admitted to his sister, "I wish this might go on for the rest of my life!"[9]

Even better, the work was interesting. Radio correspondents had emerged as some of the war's folk heroes. Using the staccato style pioneered by CBS's "Murrow Boys," who early on had put themselves in harm's way in Nazi-threatened Europe, newscasters delivered updates from the world's trouble spots with plainspoken, even-keeled calm. Print journalists had to transmit their reports in cablese, which was then rewritten by others, but radio reporters' stories, Frank rejoiced, went "straight to the listener." Envisioning himself not simply as an announcer of facts but as a "news analyst," Frank spent his days interviewing travelers and decoding information from friendly and enemy transmissions. Alongside scores of other journalists, he worked up stories in a schoolhouse converted into a pressroom, and when broadcasts began to overwhelm NIROM's facilities, he dictated his reports over the post office telephone. In the evenings, he gathered at a bistro with

Bill Dunn and Sydney Albright of NBC to argue war strategy over ham sandwiches and liters of Heineken. On one detail they agreed completely. The only hope for the East Indies rested with massive Allied reinforcement, particularly air power. "On the lips of everyone is the plea for planes, planes and more planes," Frank stressed in one broadcast.[10]

Westerners in Batavia subsisted on rumors that such reinforcements were indeed coming—that ships, piled with supplies, were ready to depart San Francisco, that convoys and fighter squadrons would parade north from Australia in a matter of days. Frank's early reports absorbed this unwarranted hopefulness and passed it on to American listeners. He celebrated the islands' "jungle warriors" who had "many discouraging surprises" for the Japanese. Dutch officials, he assured his followers, were "prepared and able to act as full fledged team-mates with the larger powers with whom they are allied in this struggle." The only outcomes he contemplated were "early success or prolonged campaigning." Lightning-fast defeat had not yet occurred to him. At 1:00 a.m. on January 12, he went on the air to announce the Japanese invasion, no—Frank crossed out invasion—*landing* in the Dutch colony at Tarakan off northeast Borneo and in the Minahasa Peninsula on Celebes: "The Battle of the Indies has begun."[11]

Japanese forces easily overwhelmed the small Dutch garrisons on Tarakan and Celebes, taking their airfields and cutting off the ferry route to the Philippines. During the next few weeks, events accelerated so rapidly that Frank sometimes forgot what month it was. The *Washington Post* praised him for rushing out reports "as fast as the Dutch were popping off Nipponese transports."[12] This cheery statement stood at odds with the actual content of Frank's broadcasts, which told of posts in Malaya and the Indies falling like dominos.

January 19: This is Frank Cuhel speaking from Batavia, Java. . . . There is only silence from the area of Tarakan. The fate of the European civilians has not been learned.

January 22: . . . the Minahasa peninsula of north Celebes is now definitely, and wholly, in the hands of the Japanese.

January 23: Balikpapan is gone. . . . The huge oil reservation whose mammoth refineries extended over a frontage of ten miles along the east coast of Borneo has been completely destroyed by order of the Netherlands High Command. . . .

There are anxious eyes, viewing the Japanese onslaught in Malaya and equally anxious hearts wondering if the help that is needed will arrive in time to save them.

February 1: The siege of Singapore has commenced. The Battle of Malaya is over. . . . Just fifty five days ago, the Japanese started their landing operations at Kota Baru in north Malaya. . . . They have traversed approximately five hundred and fifty miles, or an average of about ten miles a day . . . Penang. . . . Next came Ipoh. . . . Then Kuala Lumpur . . . Port Dickson . . . then Malacca.[13]

The seizure of strategic points on Borneo and Celebes put Japanese planes within range of Java. At the Singosari airfield near Malang, remnants of the 19th Bombardment Group from the Philippines and small numbers of US ground forces assembled to assist in the island's defense. When Captain John Day of the 26th Field Artillery Brigade arrived in mid-January and saw the US Far East Air Force for the first time, he gasped. It was "much less than anyone knows," he wrote in his diary, not over twenty bombers in all. The grassy airstrip had only two machine guns and no antiaircraft weapons. Artillery units had been outfitted with World War I vintage guns and helmets. The GIs reassured themselves that they were merely "the tip of the iceberg" and that there were "quite a few Allied supply convoys on the way." While waiting, they performed maintenance on Flying Fortresses and sought out beer and sex, dubbed *mac-mac*, which could be had for "next to nothing," as one soldier put it, in the local village. Captain Day spent the first two days of February buying a lovely hand-painted tea set and sitting through an army lecture about syphilis. The next day, February 3, bombs rained down on the base, and the onslaught never let up. "I cannot understand why there is no support coming," Day wrote little over a week before his evacuation orders arrived.[14]

Dutch and American pilots at Singosari did their best to hold off the Japanese raids, but language barriers and lack of effective warning systems often caught crews on the ground when attacks began. In the skies seasoned Japanese flyers in nimble Zero fighter planes outnumbered and outmaneuvered their opponents. They were "feeling us out like we were some dame on a sofa," explained Lieutenant Colonel Frank Allen Kurtz, who couldn't help but to be impressed, "from the professional standpoint." Reinforcements barely trickled in. Crated P-40s from the United States arrived in Australia missing parts and manuals, which slowed their assembly. US military leaders had also decided to keep their most experienced pilots on the mainland and in Hawai'i and the Panama Canal Zone, sending those fresh out of training instead. Of the 124 American pursuit pilots ordered to Java, forty-five died in crashes before they even got there. Officials were skittish, too, about transporting reinforcements by sea after the sinking of the *Repulse* and the *Prince of Wales*. Most convoys diverted to Australian ports, and later to India and other zones where commanders were also clamoring for backup. "Too many wars were going on," Kurtz summed it up.[15]

In Batavia, Frank and Bill Dunn first spotted the "red meatball that spelled Hirohito" on February 9, as they stared at the underside of a plane cluster passing the Hotel des Indes terrace. Doubts and fears crept into the rough drafts for Frank's scripts. He squelched them as best he could. He would not tell American listeners of growing frustrations that supplies were not arriving fast enough, or that he found the nighttime air raid alarms terrifying, or that even silent darkness made him wonder if he'd leave the island alive.[16]

Instead, Frank tried to make real the transpacific connections and dependencies Americans often took for granted. He recalled the history of the "romantic spice trade" when swift American clipper ships had anchored off the islands' coral reefs and reminded listeners that East Indies sugar still found its way into their candies, that its Deli-leaf tobacco still wrapped their five-cent cigars. He tried rousing Americans by enumerating the strategic materials that would be lost if help did not arrive soon. Oil, rubber, tin, and bauxite. Kapok to fill lifebelts and quinine to treat malaria. He tried to inspire them by praising the "courage, stubbornness and strength" of the defending forces, and he tried to horrify them by evoking "Japanese hordes," hiking through swamps and streams and unleashing "utterly callous and cruel treatment" upon those in their path. He raised logistical matters. Landings in the Bismarck Archipelago put Japanese planes within eight hundred miles of Australia, he told listeners, the last secure staging ground against the Axis on that side of the world. Burma would be next. China could be lost. And he tried to convince them with comparisons. The Soviets had been sent dramatically more armaments, but they could make tactical retreats when necessary. In the Pacific, Frank explained, the Allies were about to fall into the sea. Other correspondents made similar pleas, but in the end, no matter how sympathetic the stories, no matter how solid the reasoning, the work of reporters, as one Java resident put it, could not "float one warship" to the rescue.[17]

The fate of the region had already been decided in Washington. Military planners estimated that effectively opposing the Japanese would require hundreds of naval vessels and some fifteen hundred aircraft. Even if such supplies could be amassed, they argued, sending them would "constitute an entirely unjustifiable diversion of forces from the principal theater—the Atlantic." Military leaders had long been skeptical about the prospects for Western colonies in the Pacific if war broke out. The proximity of the Philippines to Japan and its distance from the US mainland convinced them that even this largest American colony (never mind Samoa, Guam, Wake, and other outlying islands) could not be effectively guarded. Most were even more loath to expend lives and resources saving the outposts of European empire. They knew how inadequately garrisoned Singapore was, despite its reputation as the Gibraltar of the East. Quietly they had accepted the possibility that the homelands of some 16.4 million Asian and Pacific Islander US nationals, along with military bases and civilian enclaves full of American citizens like Frank, might be overrun. Even now, as the Japanese stormed south, British and American policymakers were privately reaffirming their "Europe First" strategy. Defeating Germany, protecting Britain and the balance of power in Europe, the "decisive theater," took priority. The Allies—now referring to themselves as the United Nations—would divert as little as possible to the Pacific and defend only its most "vital interests," namely Australia, which might serve as a launching pad for eventual counteroffensives. To carry out the unenviable task of overseeing this unwanted theater of war, Roosevelt and Churchill formed the American, British, Dutch, and Australian (ABDA) Command and dispatched the English General Sir Archibald Wavell to lead it.[18]

By the time Frank spotted Japanese planes over Java, the ground assault against Singapore was also under way. Ordinary communications with that colony soon stopped, but informal reports told of dive bombers roaring over the city's defenses and blanketing its insides with explosives. The railroad station and a large part of the waterfront lay in shambles. Residents had taken to sleeping in monsoon drains. British officials promised Singapore's diverse inhabitants that all would fight together, even as they scurried to get Whites off the island and turned others away from departing boats. There was no use evacuating Asians, they said, because they would not be permitted to land in countries that barred their immigration. The Japanese sank as many as ninety ships full of these European and American refugees fleeing Singapore. Anyone who washed back up alive was shot at the shoreline.[19] Those lucky enough to reach the East Indies bought themselves merely days of safety.

Many Asians who watched the Japanese evict White colonizers from the region with such speed and ease saw long-awaited racial reckoning. When Imamura Hitoshi, commander of the 16th Army, reached the shores of Java, locals would greet him bearing bananas, papayas, and coconuts. "It is not the Axis countries but the allied countries—who proclaim themselves heroes of 'democracy'—that have oppressed us all these hundreds of years," reminded the Islamic nationalist Anwar Tjokroaminoto.[20]

But Frank viewed the Japanese campaign instead as the violation of an American and European home front, full of families and communities sustained for generations.

> February 14: Reports from civilian evacuees arriving here from the besieged crossroads of the world reveal the tragedy accompanying their hectic departures: Husbands left behind in the ranks of the volunteers, some of whom will doubtless never see their wives again; Homes abandoned with all cherished possessions gathered from all over the world. Motor cars driven to the dock and left standing for anyone who could make use of them. Businesses, built up over a lifetime, and in some cases many lifetimes, closed up, never to be reopened.[21]

Even more than Singapore, the Dutch island empire was, to Frank, not a stolen place, where those who spoke out against empire were banished to ghastly out-of-the-way prisons, but a "hard earned and conscientiously tended domain," only now threatened by "militaristic mad men." Builders of roads, irrigators of fields, bringers of medicine, the Dutch and other colonial powers were, he claimed, fighting to "continue peaceful pursuits in a decent democratic world in which every man is his own master." The portrait only worked by consigning the region's Indigenous millions to the background scenery. "The fathers, grand fathers and great grand fathers of the men who are now on the parapets, made of this country a tropical treasure house that is the envy of the world. This house will not be surrendered to the thieves who are now battering their way in," Frank promised. "The fight will go on here as long as there are guns to fire, planes to fly and warships to sail." But in fact a white flag flew over Singapore the next evening, and paratroopers were falling on Sumatra.[22]

Sumatra held what *Life* magazine singled out as the "fatal charm" of the East Indies: the Palembang oil complex, which produced some 65 percent of the colony's high-quality fuel, an enormous refining center in one of the world's richest producing fields, surrounded by a collection of Indonesian houseboats and proas, moored to the edge of the Musi River. Planes came in low from the swampy woods behind the refineries and storage tanks, dropping parachutists at the southern side of the river. Some were shot as they flitted toward their targets and crashed to the earth. But others landed and moved quickly to take the Royal Dutch Shell plant. Defenders held them off from Standard Oil's nearby facilities long enough for its employees to evacuate their families and for demolition crews to dynamite the storehouses and other waterfront buildings, producing what Frank called "one of the greatest self imposed fires of all time." Amid the thundering, poisonous flames, Indonesians hustled to save cars and other supplies before Americans and Europeans destroyed them, too. Frank imagined that if oil from shattered storage tanks had drained into the river, those delicate Indonesian homes on stilts and floating platforms, nestled above and below the refineries, must have been consumed. By February 17, Japanese forces had overrun Palembang and were driving toward Sumatra's southern coast. From there, it was only twenty miles of Sunda Strait to Java.[23]

The Dutch in Batavia had been dreaming about fresh-faced Australian soldiers and crack American fighter pilots. But the Allied reinforcements who came instead were the stragglers who had eluded capture in Singapore or Sumatra. They dumped the refuse of their retreat onto the grounds surrounding the US consulate, where the disabled vehicles and machine parts sat, the American consul surmised, until Japanese invaders showed up to put them to use. Frustration boiled over into drunken brawls on the city's streets.[24]

On February 19 and 20, Japanese forces took Bali and Timor, extinguishing the last aviation links with Australia and any real remaining hope. An "ominous hush" settled over Batavia. Merchants stopped accepting letters of credit. Frank noticed that pedestrians moved more briskly during air raid alerts. In between its usual offerings of gramophone music and other scheduled programs, NIROM barked out special codes and announcements. The once-bustling open-air dining room of Hotel des Indes emptied out, leaving only small knots of military men and the usual smattering of tropical birds roosting in the chandeliers.[25]

On the 21st, Frank reported that the enemy was believed to have reached Sumatra's southern coast. Survivors from Singapore were still arriving, but Java had been cut off from the outside world except to the south across the Indian Ocean. "The situation, as I see it here, is grim," Frank admitted. He couldn't help but wonder what could have been: "Five hundred more fighter planes, only a part of the monthly production in the United States, would make such a colossal difference." US consular officials, too, judged the threat "immediate and serious" and evacuated as many Americans as they could, sending the last large cohort off on a forty-year-old cattle boat. The vessel had been loaded so hastily that some of the cows had not been taken off first. They were slaughtered and eaten during the two weeks at sea, and families moved into their stalls.[26]

On the morning of February 25, substantial bombardment of Batavia's port set remaining inhabitants on edge and looking out for attempted landings. Against furious Dutch objections, Wavell ceded his ABDA command and flew with his staff to Ceylon. The bulk of American forces also received permission from Washington to evacuate. By the end of the month only one US army infantry unit, the 2nd Battalion, 131st Field Artillery (formerly of the Texas National Guard), remained to face capture and, from there, POW camps in Japan or forced labor on the Thailand-Burma railroad.[27] Frank made his final broadcast from Batavia.

> February 26: The Japanese are carrying on a steady attack on airports all over the island. . . . We have all heard and read of the gallant fortitude of the British during the terrible raids on their country. That same resolution is being displayed here. . . . News dispatches from Washington lead one to believe that vast quantities of war goods and the men to use them are on their way. I deeply hope so."[28]

But US commanders in Australia had already quietly concluded that it was "all over" on the island. Sending anything more would be "unwarranted wastage." The Battle of the Java Sea on the 27th proved one final costly attempt to turn back the Japanese carriers closing in. It delayed the ground invasion at most by a couple of days. In Batavia, the staff of the US consulate burned their files and shuttered the office. Frank called in his own import office employees for the last time and advised them to act "judiciously" in case of an occupation and to return to their posts as soon as "practicable." Then he drove the mountain passes to Bandung, the hill station where the Dutch government and military intended to wage a last stand and where about a dozen reporters had resolved to follow.[29]

On March 1st sleepers in Bandung were roused from their beds by the news that Japanese forces had landed on Java. Over the course of the day reports arrived of an enemy drive closing in on Batavia from the west, as well as incursions at Indramayu and Rembang. Ambulances appeared with the first casualties Frank had seen. Like in Malaya, he learned, the invaders were coming in light tanks and on bicycles.[30] At midnight he delivered what seems to have been his last broadcast from the island.

> March 2: The Battle of Java is now raging in full force. . . . As I watch the manner in which those here are preparing to turn back the Japanese I can't help but feel that it is a great pity indeed that we in the United States have not been able to send to this country more of what it takes to win wars.[31]

By lunchtime, Frank was watching Zeros pound the local airfield for the fourth time that day from the balcony of his hotel room. Only feeble and ineffectual antiaircraft fire opposed them. It had become obvious to him that "there were not enough allied planes left to keep enemy airmen away." The handful of correspondents still in town considered their options. Japanese ground troops were reportedly twenty-five miles to the north, and the only possible exit point lay southeast at the port of Cilacap. The Reuters correspondent Myron Selby-Walker, who had been run out of Shanghai, Hong Kong, and Singapore, decided he would go no farther. He packed a bag for the hills and was never heard from again. The wire service reporters Witt Hancock and William McDougall decided to stay at least one more day. "I feel I would be letting U.P. and my own conscience down, if I didn't see this through to the end. So I'm sticking," McDougall had written to his mother a few days before. But Frank "didn't think there were enough magicians on our side to pull the situation out of the fire" and resolved to leave for Cilacap that night. Bill Dunn, George Weller of the *Chicago Daily News*, and Winston Turner of the *Sydney Sun* went with him.[32]

The four reporters packed Frank's car with basic gear, said tearful goodbyes to Dutch officials who gave them travel papers, and sped past Bandung's barbed wire barriers and pill boxes at dusk. Frank felt especially "heavy-hearted." Abandoned vehicles littered the road to the coast, and military transports and civilian convoys moved in nonsensical directions. By dark, rumors swirled around their car. The Japanese lurked "just ahead," many told them, and had already taken Cilacap. Others they encountered begged to be taken along. Some of these people Frank had known for years, "but," he agonized, "we couldn't take them because we didn't know where we were going and there was not room in the car."[33]

Around 3:00 a.m., the journalists reached a deserted Cilacap. Four days earlier some twenty thousand evacuating Allied troops had clogged the harbor, boarding ships parked two deep at the pier. Now its rudimentary docks stood vacant except for a lone Javanese sentry. In Malay, the guard directed Frank to the residence of the local Dutch naval commandant who, still awake, assured the reporters of spots on a steamer chartered to take naval personnel to Australia later that day. By evening, the MS *Janssens*, a tubby coastwise vessel, bobbed under the weight of some six hundred people, three times as many as its lifeboats could hold.[34]

Almost no one managed to escape from Cilacap without being bombed from above or torpedoed from below. Among those huddled on the boat with Frank were survivors of ships sunk the day before by Japanese submarines lurking just outside the harbor. But a storm materialized, providing cover for the *Janssens* to slip through. That night Frank slept on the open wooden deck despite the downpour.[35]

The next morning he awoke to the unmistakable "Mitsubishi moan" of Japanese bombers and the clamber of passengers moving toward the lifeboats. Although it had sailed all night, the *Janssens* had crept eastward, still hugging the coast. The passing planes ignored the freighter and continued on to their target, Cilacap, which they set aflame. Frank and his companions were discussing their good luck in the forward cabin two hours later when machine gun fire suddenly ricocheted through the compartment. The men dogpiled under benches and berths as enemy fighters made four passes overhead, their bullets and cannon shot playing the length of the ship "like a xylophone," as George Weller put it. The boat's captain steered the craft into a small bay at Pacitan, not seventy miles from a known Japanese spearhead, to offload the wounded and some three hundred others who chose not to go on. It was March 4, barely lunchtime.[36]

"I must say that it was a difficult decision to make," Frank remembered that moment in the bay as lifeboats shuttled others to the sand. Setting off into the Indian Ocean promised a chance of reaching Australia, but it also held out gruesome possibilities. He had heard many hair-raising stories from survivors of shipwrecks off Singapore. Evacuation would require sneaking past the patrols of Admiral Nagumo Chūichi's First Air Fleet task force.[37] Though Frank would never learn it, his friends Witt Hancock and William McDougall had decided to board a mail boat overloaded with Dutch officers and Shell employees and their families. In three days, Japanese planes would bomb the vessel on its route to Colombo and linger for forty-five minutes, machine-gunning passengers torn between hiding on the sinking craft and jumping into the water. Many went down with the ship, including Hancock—the first but not the last American correspondent killed in the Pacific Theater. Only three lifeboats floated away intact. Stray swimmers, refused spots on the already overpopulated rafts, drifted out to sea. A few Dutch officers carrying pistols shot themselves in the head rather than drown. In the lifeboats, the wounded bled out. Others descended into dehydration and delirium. One of those survivors, William McDougall, vomited salt water and broiled in the "great, glittering frying pan of the sea" for six days until he reached Sumatra—and captivity.[38]

Even if Frank's boat made it all the way to the Australian coast, that would not ensure safety either, since Japanese planes were attacking its northern ports. The day before, nine Zeros had flown nonstop from Timor to Broome, a small pearling town choked with refugees, where fighters destroyed nearly two dozen aircraft and killed around eighty. Lieutenant Colonel Kurtz, who had fallen back with the 19th Bombardment Group, saw the evisceration of civilian-filled flying boats in harbor. He watched a woman standing on the wing of her burning plane with a child in her arms. As she readied herself to jump and swim ashore, cannon shot severed her torso. Both halves of her body fell forward into the water, "but the arms on the top half which held the child never let go of it."[39] The odds of escape were indeed slim. But returning to Java meant certain capture. When the *Janssens* crept away from the cove, Frank and the other reporters were still on board.

Tacking due south and bucking strong headwinds, the boat could do no more than six to eight knots. They'd make "an easy dish" for even a crippled submarine, Frank said. "Easy meat," agreed Winston Turner. That night was deadly clear and moonlit. Frank could not sleep in the fair weather as he had before in the rain. He stayed up, waiting for a torpedo to gut the hull.[40]

Over the next many days, as emergency rations slimmed him "to the figure of a sub-debutante," family and colleagues in the United States puzzled over Frank's disappearance. Calls placed with overseas operators went unanswered. If he had headed for Australia, by all estimates he should have

Japanese troops capture Java. Library of Congress, LC-USZ62-105186.

shown up already. Weeks earlier, he had indicated to Mutual that if the Japanese were driven back, he might follow the retreat to the China coast. "Unfortunately we cannot very well expect to find him there now," one of the network's representatives concluded blandly.[41]

The breeze cooled as the *Janssens* drifted south, but passengers remained fearful. One morning they awoke to the sun on the wrong side of the boat. A rudder had gone out, and the vessel spun in circles for half the day before the steering could be fixed. Another day, Frank spotted the unmistakable conning tower and periscope of a submarine, a couple of miles astern and gaining ground. It kept on their trail for hours before they realized it was friendly. Demoralizing news also sputtered over the radio. Japan's Southern Army was sending out black clandestine programming from Saigon, masquerading as NIROM. Over background Dutch music, they reported inflated numbers of Japanese troops sweeping across Java and fabricated other stories—about fierce attacks on Sydney and Honolulu and labor violence in the United States. On March 8, enemy broadcasts celebrated, this time accurately, the surrender of Bandung. In the end, the Japanese army landed little more than half of the ground troops budgeted for conquering Java. Bill Dunn noticed that Frank, who had left behind so many friends, was "particularly affected."[42]

Eleven days after slipping out of Cilacap, they reached Fremantle. Frank hitched a ride across the outback on a Dutch bomber and headed for Melbourne, headquarters of the fledgling Southwest Pacific Command, and current destination of his former Olympic team leader, Douglas MacArthur.[43] His world was gone, and he would struggle to come to terms with what felt like his own nation's betrayal, but Frank had brushed with death and won.

16

Red Mississippi

WHEN BEN LEFT BOMBED-OUT LONDON, he returned to his father's house to lose himself once again in the Southern past. Sequestered in a back room piled with notes and family papers, maps and pictures pinned to the walls, he churned out page after single-spaced page in lower-case type, a habit learned from writing for the cables. "By the grace of God, my kinfolks and I are Carolinians," he rhapsodized in the opening line of what would become a critically acclaimed tribute to his upcountry roots, *Red Hills and Cotton*. By 1941, as Ben wrote, some Americans, even a few White Southerners, were questioning the romanticized Confederate history they had been taught. But Ben rededicated himself to it. Unapologetically he recounted that his forefathers, after losing a devastating war and languishing under the "unreasoning despotism" of occupying soldiers and Black freedmen, had "ridden at night and terrorized, had not hesitated to vote tombstones in elections," and "nullified an amendment to the Constitution." Ben knew he had a "queer way of translating the Confederacy straight into the present United States." But rehearsing the suffering and courage of his kinfolks steadied him for his own tribulations. It gave him, he thought, special insight into the new war his nation must soon join.[1]

When word of the Japanese attacks in the Pacific arrived on a cold, bright day in early December, Ben cried and wandered into the cotton fields, where his relatives had always gone to contemplate momentous events. Once Congress extended the draft's age limit to thirty-eight, he would have to register for service. Yet volunteering for the military does not seem to have been an option he considered. Perhaps he knew that selection boards rejected men judged too effeminate or suspected of being attracted to other men. Or that enlistees who exhibited such "tendencies" found themselves at risk of being thrown in the military's "queer stockades" followed by undesirable discharge, court martial, or even a spell in a mental institution.[2] He went back to his book writing until a telegram arrived from New York:

> HAVE EXTRAORDINARILY IMPORTANT SPECIAL JOB WHICH ONLY YOU CAN DO FOR PM. MAKES DIRECT CONTRIBUTION TO WINNING THE WAR. HOW SOON CAN YOU COME. . . . MERRY CHRISTMAS AND REGARDS= RALPH INGERSOLL.

Ingersoll wanted to promote the immediate opening of a "second front" against the Nazis in Europe to take pressure off the Soviet forces fighting for their state's very survival. Ben agreed to go to Russia and report for *PM.* After all, a Southerner like himself, he believed, understood better than other Americans what it was like to be invaded.[3]

It took weeks of waiting and a personal intervention from President Roosevelt, but by April Ben secured priority status to fly as far as the Mediterranean Theater along the South Atlantic ferry route forged by Pan American Airways. During the various legs of his journey, from Puerto Rico to Brazil, across the Atlantic and Equatorial Africa, and into the Sahara, he eyed his fellow passengers—technical advisors, oil drillers, mechanics, a deep-sea diver—and marveled at the airport ground personnel who had dropped out of the sky into jungles and sand, with their tools, hot cakes, and pin-up pictures, to build and maintain a string of bases from the Amazon to the Nile. These men were tough and good in "the pioneer way," he thought, a reminder that "the genius of the U.S. is to get things set up quickly." Watching them ditch and drain to improve conditions everywhere they touched, he speculated that their labor was not just on behalf of a temporary wartime supply line but because, when peace came, they wanted "more than yesterday for everyone."[4]

By design a disproportionate number of those striving for "more than yesterday" while ditching and draining the world's newest transportation routes were Black: Caribbean, South American, and African laborers conscripted for backbreaking tasks and Black GIs shunted to the US military's most out-of-the-way hardship postings. President Roosevelt had set a quota of 10 percent Black enlistments for the army, to be deployed roughly evenly across all theaters. But as soon as recruiting began, complaints, fears, and demands poured in from British, Australian, Chinese, and other Allies seeking to keep Black soldiers out of their jurisdictions. Anti-Black racism was not simply an American problem. Already overrepresented in service units earmarked for basic manual labor, Black troops found themselves bound for some of the planet's harshest climes: forcing a highway from Alaska to the forty-eight states through blizzards and ice hills; carving the Ledo Road out of monsoon mud and unsurveyed mountainous hairpin turns between India and China; laying the trans-Iranian railroad in temperatures so hot rings and other metal burned men's skin; and garrisoning Liberia's malaria-ridden Roberts airfield.[5] But as Ben hopscotched across Africa he managed to find fresh excuses for the American racial status quo. "We have lost sight of what was right about our country in our concentration on what was wrong," he cabled home. The United States, he argued, was "nearer social equality" and "our plan of dealing with a minority people has been better than we know."[6]

Stopping in Cairo, Ben caught up with his former journalism school roommate, Edgar Snow, who had been hired by the *Saturday Evening Post* to go to India, Russia, and "then to what was left." Feeling pessimistic about the power of journalism, his old friend hazarded that maybe the only way to make an impact with a pen "was to insert it in a vertical position in the bottom of a Congressman's chair." But Ben had recovered his enthusiasm for reporting since his departure from London. "Ed," he exclaimed, "we're worth as much as a couple of generals." The hot season was just beginning. In the skies above hundreds of white storks were migrating north to Europe. Ben couldn't believe it. Those crazy birds were going to spend the summer with the Nazis.[7]

From Egypt, Ben made his way to Allied-occupied Iran, where a Soviet commercial air service provided one of the last reliable routes into the USSR. Flying north across the barren peaks of the Alborz Mountains seemed to separate Ben from everything he had known before. In the distance he caught sight of a long, green valley sloping toward the Caspian Sea. The Soviet Union. It had always seemed so far away, a "theoretical place" dreamed up by starry-eyed radicals in New York's Union Square. Ben did not share many conservative Americans' intense loathing for "Reds," but neither did he express any interest in Communists' loudly proclaimed antiracist commitments, which inspired many on the left.[8] Just as he had studiously overlooked the parallels between fascist regimes and his own one-party South, so too would he ignore the interracial dimensions of the Soviet experiment he wanted so very much to champion.

Ben's plane touched down at a small city just across the border, where women refueled the craft and checked passengers' passports. As they continued north past vast grain fields and the Volga, swollen with spring waters, Ben reminded himself that this was the second harvest that the Soviets had raised under invasion. To the west the sun began to set over occupied Ukraine. If Hitler's forces pushed further east, they could capture the coal of the Donets Basin and the oil fields of the Caucasus. Ben decided to do some "tall praying" about the Caucasus—and for himself, as the pilot swooped too close for comfort over misty forests and smoking chimneys.[9]

Then he remembered that God had been banished from the Soviet Union. He had never contemplated before what it would be like to be in such a country. He thought about the wooden churches of his South Carolina childhood, where preachers denounced the bankers and prayed for their cotton crops. He thought of his mother reading psalms and the strivings of a million other Americans to find salvation in the bible. Where Ben came from, God had always been nearby. He had stood with his people against the tyrants. But in Russia, he supposed, the church had sided instead with the aristocratic Romanovs—"with property against the human heart." Americans didn't have to approve of Soviet policies, he decided, to understand why a backlash against religion had happened here.[10]

How little Americans and Soviets actually knew about each other, Ben reflected. How separated they had been by politics, religion, and more than twenty years of closed borders. He determined to convince readers back in the States that they actually had much in common with their new, improbable allies. The Russians—Ben liked to call them Russians rather than Soviets—had a big country outlook just like the people of the United States. The Volga flowed like the Mississippi, he reckoned, and Russians, like Americans, drew strength from a rich military past. They felt about their commanders who stood up against Napoleon Bonaparte the same way that Ben felt about George Washington, Stonewall Jackson, and Robert E. Lee.[11]

And besides, the Russians were killing Nazis.

The largest land war in human history had erupted a year before, just after 3:00 a.m. on June 22, 1941, when German batteries opened fire against

Soviet posts along the Bug River. The Wehrmacht's advance units dragged dinghies, submersible tanks, and bridging equipment across the watery frontier while overhead, Luftwaffe squadrons fanned out, strafing and bombing more than a thousand Soviet planes parked at their bases in neat rows. Red Army defenses crumbled against the three million assault troops who stormed the border at sunrise, a force six times larger than Napoleon's Grand Armée had been. Operation Barbarossa's armored spearhead, made up of nineteen panzer units and fifteen motorized infantry divisions, raced ahead of regular troops covering ground by horse and cart into areas the Soviet Union had annexed after Stalin's pact with Hitler—eastern Poland, Lithuania, Latvia, and Estonia—as well as into Soviet Belarus, Ukraine, and the western edges of Russia itself. By June 29, the invaders had reached Minsk, and by July 16, Smolensk, the last major city on the road to Moscow. Soviet workers in the path of the enemy packed up every factory, aircraft assembly plant, steel mill, and blast furnace that could be made portable and shipped them east. Some 16.5 million refugees, along with herds of animals including half the cattle of Ukraine, followed. "If there is any such thing as so-called total war, this is to be it," the CBS broadcaster Erskine Caldwell told American listeners through a shaky connection: "The battle of the Russian steppes will make all previous wars seem like rehearsals." He wasn't wrong.[12]

Millions of individual life-or-death decisions erupted along a vast front from the Baltic to the Black Sea. To hide, to collaborate, to resist, or to flee—no course of action ensured survival. The Germans wanted the vast region not only for its food and fuel but also to fashion for themselves a continental empire rivaling the one conquered by the United States. Existing cities would be leveled. Jews, Slavs, and other presumed inferior natives—like America's Indians, Hitler would point out—would be expelled or annihilated. In their place would arise a bountiful frontier of German farms and villages stretching to the Urals. The Volga, the Führer dreamed, would be the Third Reich's Mississippi. Dispatched with plans to shoot, starve, enslave, or evict millions in their path, the Wehrmacht opened fire on enemy troops trying to surrender, or left them to die in provisionless POW camps. Close on their heels came Einsatzgruppen killing squads charged with executing Jews, Red Army officers, Communist Party members, and others mistaken for them. In frenzied pogroms and meticulously planned ruses alike, Germans and their allies murdered men, women, and children, trapping and burning them alive in barns or shooting them at the edge of ravines.[13]

Nor was life safe in Soviet-held territory, where millions more perished under bombs or succumbed to disease, malnutrition, exhaustion, and exposure. In Leningrad, blockaded by mid-September, roughly two out of five civilians would freeze or starve to death in the siege's first winter. Elsewhere, unknown but clearly staggering numbers of Soviet citizens died as a result of the policies of their own state—during forced evacuations, in labor camps, and at the hands of NKVD secret police, who arrested, tortured, and executed tens of thousands in the first months of the conflict alone. Americans like Ben who visited the Soviet Union, and the US soldiers who later trekked only as far as Berlin, could never fully know this darkest corner of the war.[14]

After capturing Kyiv on September 19, and with Leningrad surrounded, Hitler jubilantly turned his attention to Operation Typhoon: the destruction of Moscow. Some 800,000 troops had stood between his forces and the Soviet capital at the start of September, but by mid-October only 90,000 remained, and they were running out of shells, cartridges, and guns. On October 15, with the Wehrmacht only forty miles away, Stalin moved to evacuate most of his government and the city's embassies east to Kuybyshev while demolition crews mined factories, bridges, and the Bolshoi Theatre. Moscow's rail stations disgorged train convoys filled with commissars, diplomats, foreign correspondents, and, in a special refrigerated car, Lenin's embalmed body. Remaining residents awoke the next day to find the metro closed, the sidewalks unswept, and morning papers missing from the newsstands. Protests and pillage erupted across the capital. To quell the unrest, Stalin announced that he would stay, and Moscow would be defended to the death. Women and children were ordered to dig trenches and tank traps. NKVD units summarily shot looters and other "provocateurs" as examples to the rest. By the end of the month, German forces had penetrated Moscow's outer defenses and stood close enough to see the Kremlin through field glasses.[15]

Two things saved the capital: Soviet grit and *rasputitsa*—mud season. For weeks, it immobilized the invaders in a seemingly bottomless "black pastry," kneaded by thousands of boots and wheels, giving General Georgy Zhukov time to bring up reserves before the mid-November freeze made the roads once again passable. When the battle resumed, a scratch force of some 240,000 troops, their will reinforced by an order to stand fast or face the firing squad, drove the Germans back. Soviet soldiers and journalists seethed at what they found in recaptured villages: gallows with swinging bodies in central squares, ransacked homes with portraits of Hitler tacked up on the

A tank passes through Moscow on its way to the front. Popperfoto via Getty Images.

walls. In Kalinin, the invaders had used the monument to Pushkin for target practice. At Tchaikovsky's country home in Klin, they had set fire to the composer's sheet music and defecated on the floor. "If the Germans want a war of extermination, they shall have it," Stalin bellowed before the Moscow Soviet. By March, Hitler's soldiers backpedaled—tired, overextended, poorly equipped for the cold, and pursued by white-snowsuited troops on skis and all-weather vehicles.[16]

Then once again an eerie silence descended over the battlefields as the spring thaw sent ice floes down the rivers and deep snows melted from the roadsides, revealing a slushy marsh of disabled cars and corpses. Almost four and a half million Soviet soldiers, nearly the equivalent of the entire prewar Red Army, had been killed or captured. The USSR had lost critical farms, coal mines, electric power stations, and rail lines, stretching across territory that had supplied nearly half of the nation's grain harvests and two-thirds of its manufacturing before the war. And the Wehrmacht was planning a new offensive. Ben felt certain—and he was right—that this was the "battlefield on which so much depends." He regarded it as his mission to convince Americans of that urgent fact.[17]

"Stalin's goose is cooked," the *Washington Post* had declared shortly after the invasion began. Few in the United States at first imagined the Soviets could stand up long against the German onslaught, and many did not find this all that worrisome. They questioned the Soviet Union's international ambitions, and some rated atheistic Bolsheviks as a greater menace than Nazis. The only significant difference between Hitler and Stalin, opined the *Wall Street Journal*, was the size of their mustaches. Several public figures expressed hopes that the two regimes would simply destroy each other.[18]

But others argued that the Third Reich posed the greatest threat to US security and world peace and that any help to defeat it had to be embraced. Roosevelt agreed with this position, moving in the summer of 1941 to unfreeze some $40 million in Soviet assets, ruling that the Neutrality Act would not apply to this conflict so that Soviet ports remained open to US ships, and dispatching two envoys to Moscow—Harry Hopkins at the end of July and W. Averell Harriman in September. As the Red Army held the Wehrmacht back from Moscow that fall, American support for aiding the Soviets grew. On November 7, Roosevelt formally extended Lend-Lease support to the USSR. During the next four years, the United States would ship almost 17.5 billion tons of supplies, valued at roughly $10 billion, to Stalin's forces: aluminum, armored steel, and copper; canned food, clothing, and boot leather; trucks, railroad track, and hundreds of thousands of miles of telephone wire.[19]

Yet little arrived as promised at first. Shortages at American factories hampered production. Cargoes piled up for lack of ships at ports assigned to host convoys bound for Murmansk, Arkhangelsk, and Vladivostok. Many of the supplies that did set sail were lost at sea. Others arrived missing parts and manuals. By January 1942, only 85 of 600 promised planes, and 16 of 705 promised tanks, had been received. One Soviet reporter described the sight of such American imports on the Eastern Front as "isolated episodes." Fury about "the absence in Europe of a second front against the German-fascist troops" and veiled threats about a possible separate peace emanated from the Kremlin. The Soviet–American alliance foundered before it had fully begun.[20]

"We've got to go to Europe and fight," Brigadier General Dwight D. Eisenhower confessed to his diary on January 22. "We've got to quit wasting resources all over the world—and still worse—wasting time." Other army commanders echoed this sentiment, advocating for a cross-channel assault by late summer to divert German troops from the Eastern Front. But navy leaders and General MacArthur, on the defensive in the Pacific, clamored instead for an offensive to avenge the losses at Pearl Harbor and to prevent the Japanese, as Admiral Ernest King put it, from overrunning the "white man's countries," Australia and New Zealand. Large segments of the American public agreed with this "Pacific First" outlook, but army strategists persisted, arguing, as Eisenhower did, that beyond maintaining continental and Hawaiian defenses, only three national security objectives stood out as utterly essential, rather than merely desirable: defending the United Kingdom and its sea lanes; preventing German and Japanese troops from converging on India and the Middle East; and keeping the Soviet Union in the war. Concentrating resources on Europe appealed to US planners not only as military strategy but also as a political calculation, to compel trust and gratitude from Stalin's intractable regime. By March, Roosevelt had designated aid to the Soviets as top priority, diverting truck, tank, and plane shipments to them from other recipients. "I find it difficult," he told a frustrated MacArthur, "to get away from the simple fact that the Russian armies are killing more Axis personnel and destroying more Axis materiel than the other twenty-five United Nations put together."[21]

Roosevelt also assured the USSR's minister of foreign affairs Vyacheslav Molotov that Stalin could expect a second front that year. During a series of meetings in Washington, held while Ben was making his way from Egypt to Iran, the president had not elaborated on where or what such a front might entail, nor did he tell the minister that his forces as yet lacked the troops, landing craft, and coordination for a massive cross-channel invasion. The Soviets simply needed encouragement, Roosevelt resolved. On June 11 a public communiqué announced that "full understanding was reached with regard to the urgent tasks of creating a Second Front in Europe in 1942."[22]

Fatefully, in Russia the statement was embraced not as diplomatic flourish but as sacred promise. Molotov heralded it in front of the Moscow Soviet as the "consolidation of fellowship in arms of all freedom-loving nations," as groundwork even for friendly relations and collaboration after the war. Thrilled by the possibility, Ben and two other reporters telegrammed Wendell Willkie from Russia with an idea: the presidential runner-up's goodwill trip to Britain the previous year had been so successful, he should make another one to the Soviet Union. Taking their advice, Willkie began planning for what would subsequently become his famous round-the-world tour.[23]

Ben arrived in Moscow in late June, joining some fifty other Americans posted there during the summer of 1942: embassy officials, clerks, military observers, members of various missions, and a little over a dozen American correspondents, including Larry LeSueur of CBS, Leland Stowe of *Chicago Daily News*, and Henry Cassidy and Eddie Gilmore of the Associated Press. The city center seemed to Ben subdued with purpose. Marching troop detachments and overflowing streetcars rumbled down its wide avenues. Along the sidewalks, propaganda posters—The Motherland Summons!—and piles of sandbags, sewn from colorful cotton scraps, broke up the vista of modern office buildings. At the subway entrances, day and nightshift workers swapped places. Ben thought they had the faces of those who had lived "good hard-working lives," fighting for "their right to live in their own land in their own way."[24]

He reflected on the previous twenty years of history. Only because the Soviets had sacrificed to industrialize their society did they stand any chance against the Wehrmacht, he reasoned. Whereas Americans had lately become obsessed with personal comforts, here people drew upon hardier ideals that reminded him of the conviction of his Confederate grandfather. *PM*'s editors would be sure to excise most of Ben's off-the-wall Lost Cause musings from his dispatches before publishing them, but his other historical analogies they let through. "Russia is as strong now spiritually as America was 200 years ago," Ben told readers in one early report from Russia; it was as much a pioneer country as Massachusetts had been when Cotton Mather preached. Maybe economics drove the Soviets whereas religion had guided the Puritans, he conceded, but "a star can mean as much to a people as a cross."[25]

A softening of Soviet culture since the war began made it easier for Ben and other visitors to draw such rosy portraits. Stalin framed the conflict not only as a test of the USSR and Communism but also as a war to save historic Russia. He heralded the military heroes of the imperial past and eased restrictions on the Orthodox Church. *Pravda* substituted its former call to arms (Proletarians of all lands, unite!) for a new masthead slogan (Death to the German invaders!), and soon a new anthem would play in place of the "Internationale."[26] Coercive aspects of Stalinist rule were carefully hidden from visitors. The fundraising drives that yielded millions in rubles for government war loans, which impressed Ben, were mandatory. The tiny residential garden plots full of strawberries and sweet peas he admired had been declared "of state importance." Because his quest was to invest American audiences in Russia's plight and to portray the Soviets as willing to "sacrifice everything for the idealism of freedom," he had no need to dig below surface propaganda.[27]

Ben and about a dozen other American correspondents lived a stone's throw from the Bolshoi Theatre at the Metropol, a prerevolutionary hotel filled with fin-de-siècle lighting and furniture. Several of them, like Ben, had faced the bombing in London. Others had been in France, Spain, Greece, Norway, and Burma. But here, Ben discovered, they led a decidedly dismal "sort of war life." Only preapproved officials dared to speak with foreigners at any length, and authorities withheld permission for trips outside Moscow, especially near the front. The clerk at the Intourist desk in the Metropol's lobby, poised between decorative busts of Lenin and Stalin, seemed unable to do more for the reporters than secure ballet tickets. One felt constantly watched, explained *Life*'s Walter Graebner, as though the telephones were tapped, and the secret police might arrive at "any moment." "None of the things you want to know are learnable," the *Collier's* correspondent Alice Moats despaired before departing Russia for more promising assignments.[28]

Nurturing a free press had never been a Soviet goal, and since the invasion censors scoured every word and image prepared for publication or broadcast, approving only details acquired from the Soviet Information Bureau or Stalin himself. Sometimes a press conference or a communiqué provided fodder for dispatches, but most of American reporters' source material came from Soviet newspapers. To write their copy, they relied on personal secretaries who arrived at their hotel rooms each morning with the latest editions of *Pravda*, *Izvestiia*, and the Red Army's *Krasnaya Zvezda*. Only Maurice Hindus and Henry Shapiro of the United Press could read Russian. The others took notes while their assistants translated the columns line by laborious line. Their contents reminded Ben more of textbooks than the dailies back home. It proved impossible to wrest from them the kind of human-interest dramas that might move American audiences. Stories about war orphans or hospital heroics designed to pique foreign sympathies had been dismissed by Soviet authorities as no better than begging. Ben pushed at the outer limits of his profession's standards, filling his cables instead with his own crusading pleas.[29]

After work, the reporters spent hours wandering the capital on foot, marveling at the queues for basic goods that snaked along nearly every block—short lines and long lines, sometimes filled with two to three hundred people hoping for scraps of meat, black bread, a tin cup of milk, or $3 eggs. Nearby loudspeakers blared periodic announcements and preapproved programs; private radio sets had been confiscated from all but a select few. Yet forbidden from photographing or writing about these scenes, the correspondents could do little more than return to the Metropol to speculate about the hunger of average families while snacking on their own Diplomatic Store rations. Most of them kept notes or diaries and planned to publish more about this place when they left it. Under a midnight curfew, they played hearts and poker in their hotel rooms while trading stories about the war and home. Ben and Henry Cassidy banged out "old time tunes" on the piano. Eddy Gilmore practiced his Huey Long impression.[30]

Because the Soviet press gave full coverage to German atrocities—the kinds of stories US censors flagged as harmful for morale—the American correspondents at first did not fully grasp how much the newspapers they relied on studiously downplayed Soviet military setbacks and other bad news. "The long-heralded German spring offensive is on the move in only one place—against well-defended Sevastopol," Larry LeSueur wrote with characteristic optimism in his diary in late June. In Ukraine the Red Army seemed to be "holding Hitler's mighty panzer divisions in check," he celebrated, and "America and Britain have 'threatened' a second front in Europe within the year."[31] Everything seemed reasonably under control until suddenly it wasn't.

After sweeping through the eastern end of the Crimean Peninsula, killing or capturing all but a third of the region's Red Army soldiers, Erich von Manstein's 11th Army turned toward Sevastopol. To blast into the heavily fortified Black Sea port, German and Romanian ground forces amassed the world's largest collection of siege artillery, including mortars, howitzers, and the enormous seven-ton-shell-firing railway cannon christened Gustav. By the end of June, dispatches from the battle zone grew increasingly grave, describing how the batteries steadily "blasted to bits" the once beautiful, whitewashed city with a world-class aquarium. The attackers, Ben read, crashed against Soviet defenses "like waves from a living ocean," and corpses piled up higher than they had at Verdun, but still more arrived for the slaughter. On July 4, the Soviet high command admitted that they had lost Crimea. Sevastopol's conquerors held a victory parade through a town that no longer had streets.[32]

Axis forces were also gaining fast ground in North Africa after overrunning Tobruk on June 21. Rommel's divisions were now in Egypt, speeding toward Alexandria and poised for a drive to the Suez Canal, perhaps even Palestine and Syria. More alarming news arrived from the north. Icebergs had forced the Allies' Arctic convoys to hug the Norwegian coast, where in the season's perpetual daylight they suffered catastrophic attacks by bombers and submarines, leading the British Admiralty to suspend further shipments. One member of Moscow's US supply mission returned from a visit to hospitals in Murmansk and Arkhangelsk with news that they were full of armless and legless American merchant seamen. Meanwhile, the stories leaking out of Leningrad, as Leland Stowe admitted, "were too horrible to repeat."[33]

Berlin radio reports simultaneously revealed another startling German drive along the southern Russian front between Kharkiv and Kursk in the direction of the Don River. Reaching Voronezh by July 6, General Fedor von Bock's divisions pivoted south toward Rostov, rapidly flooding into the Donets Basin. Losing the Donbas meant losing thousands of square miles of wheat fields "as important as Nebraska," as Ben put it, as well as coal mines that provided much of Moscow's fuel. The American reporters watched as Soviet authorities ordered the capital's waitresses, stenographers, and other young women into the surrounding forests to chop wood for winter.[34]

"These are anxious times in Moscow," Ben dispatched on July 16, after poring over the latest battle reports. But Red Army soldiers were not beaten, he insisted, "not in the slightest." They were "fighting with their hearts, with their minds and with their souls and bodies." The destiny of the United States was now "one" with the Soviet people, he warned, and until Americans took action they would "automatically become partially responsible for every Russian setback." Opening a second front, he told readers, would "have a magical effect." It would "remove all thought of deceit" and "assure our allies that we, too, are willing to share in the dying in Europe. It will take dying, too. It will take dying by the hundred thousands."[35]

Rostov fell on July 24. In Moscow, the lines to buy newspapers grew longer as their contents grew more ominous. The American correspondents traced Hitler's offensive on their maps as it continued to spread "like wildfire," east into the bend of the Don River and south across the northern Caucasus. German planes taunted Soviet troops abandoning their positions by dropping fliers that read: "And the Second Front?" On July 28, Stalin issued an unusually desperate order to his commanders: "Not a step back!" Those who surrendered or retreated without orders, he warned, would be treated as "traitors to the Motherland."[36]

That night, Ben took a walk in Red Square. Passing the darkened towers of the Kremlin, he thought about how victory once seemed "a final thing." But now he knew that battles had to be fought, ideals had to be defended, time and again. Wars "did not stay won." Before he had not been able to imagine how a powerful nation could collapse in a night. But since the fall of France it had become so terrifyingly clear. He thought about what it would mean to him "if hordes of foreign vandals" attacked St. Louis and Chicago, if Pittsburgh was burned and the mayor of Cleveland hanged in the streets. How must American "tall talk" sound to all those families here who had lost loved ones?[37]

Sure, protests demanding a second front and fundraisers for Russian War Relief had been organized in New York and other American cities. Russian leaders had made the covers of *Time*, and Shostakovich's Seventh Symphony had just received a rapturous ovation after its Radio City Music Hall premiere. But, Ben sighed, it was "going to take much more than attending a concert to halt the tide of this eastern battle." It had been eight months since the bombing of Pearl Harbor. The US Army had mustered more than 3.5 million men in uniform and shipped them to the far corners of the earth. But except for airmen and the few soldiers who escaped the Philippines and Java, American ground troops had yet to face the enemy.[38]

By August, everywhere Americans went in Moscow their hosts pressed them: Why hadn't the British fortified their positions in Libya? If they couldn't even stand their ground there, how would they ever launch a second front? Had the British suspended the northern convoys to keep the supplies for themselves? Some chided that it would be more rational to expect God to send down 150,000 archangels to open a new front than to wait for the Americans and British to do it. Ben began to feel self-conscious going out in his correspondent's uniform.[39]

He escaped to a movie screening at the American Embassy before going for another stroll past St. Basil's domes. He thought about General Sherman who had brazenly marched an army through Georgia. Where was such Yankee daring now? Ben feared that the war could be lost in the next sixty days. If only the Allies landed a thousand commandos in Western Europe, Ben was sure, they could "swing the balance." Returning to his hotel room, he switched on the radio. A German voice reported in English that London authorities agreed that a second front at this time would be premature because of shipping shortages. The words washed over him "like a bucketful of water." Ever since the fall of Singapore, the British government had been afraid to move, he suspected. And there were so many cautious planners in Washington, too. Fear, he decided, was "an endless thing." Looking at the Big Dipper in the Moscow sky, he thought of all the oceans and rivers Americans had to cross to bring help to Russia. The Amazon, the Niger, the Nile, the Tigris and Euphrates, the desert and mountains of Iran. He understood that shipping was limited, but if the Germans took the oil-rich Caucasus, if they marched all the way to the Volga, all hope for a short war would be lost. "Millions and millions of us will die." What cold comfort it would be to explain that the reason was "lack of shipping."[40]

There was no such thing as a safe war, Ben cabled New York on August 6. The Allies had to take risks and expect casualties. "The Russians say that if you would make an omelet, you must break some eggs." But less than a week later, the Wehrmacht captured Krasnodar and the oil installations near Maykop, and Churchill traveled to Moscow via Tehran to inform Stalin that there would be no cross-channel campaign that year. The British and Americans had settled on a North African landing instead.[41]

Soviet press commentary grew increasingly bitter. "My dear friend!" began one open letter to Americans from the novelist Leonid Leonov, "A curtain of solid fire and steel showers hangs today on the main roads of the earth. . . .But we are not strangers. The drops of water in the Volga, the Thames, and the Mississippi are related. They touch in the sky." Lest Americans think that the papers exaggerated German atrocities, he would send them pictures: "You will see children with smashed skulls, women with torn wombs," he told them. "Tell your doubting neighbor that war will rush into his house through a crack, pull his wife and children out by the hair, and kill them before his eyes. . . .There is no limit to the abyss."[42]

Ben and the other correspondents calculated that, in a matter of weeks, the Germans might not only seize the oil centers of Grozny and Baku but also reach the Caspian, launch a campaign for the Middle East, and converge with their Japanese allies on India, where "Gandhi and Nehru have begun their campaign against us," as Ben fumed after learning of renewed protests for independence in the British colony. Finally, on August 19, British, Canadian, and American troops launched a commando raid against the French coast at Dieppe—just the kind of operation Ben had dreamed would save the Allies. It ended in catastrophic defeat. Two days later, German infantry assault boats crashed across the Don. In the Soviet press, mentions of the second front faded away, replaced by a new refrain: Stalingrad.[43]

Once thought a safe war production zone, the great industrial center stood exposed, "no more a fortress than Chicago," as Larry LeSueur despaired, with the waters of the Volga behind it, and in front nothing but easily traversable plains. If the Germans took Stalingrad, they could halt shipping on the river, sever the USSR's main oil supply pipelines, disrupt rail traffic to the Ural factory cities, and threaten Moscow from the southeast. While the

Luftwaffe's 4th Air Fleet carpet-bombed the city and its industrial suburbs, still choked with civilians, panzer units raced across forty miles of steppe and surrounded the city from three sides.[44]

As a distraction, Soviet authorities finally offered foreign correspondents a tour of a small section of the front northwest of Moscow. Ben and the others picked over the remains of a cluster of recently liberated villages near Rzhev, while in nearby fields, peasants rummaged through yellowing grass and rusted debris. Taking back this small, scorched swathe of land came at the cost of some 300,000 Red Army lives, but that detail had been withheld from the reporters. Listening to gunfire in the distance, Ben marveled that modern war had made it possible "to wipe away every sign of man in a single summer." How little, he thought, stood between civilization and a world "covered over with weeds." The Russians would "never forgive us for this Summer," he scolded American readers. Never again could there be "quite the feeling that there would have been had we been ready this August."[45]

From the morning in 1941 when German forces had crashed across the Bug River until June 6, 1944, when Allied troops finally set foot on the beaches of Normandy, the Soviets never faced less than 90 percent of the Wehrmacht's frontline combat strength. Of the fifty to sixty million people who died in the war across the globe, roughly half lost their lives in the Soviet Union. Improved Red Army tactics and leadership, not Allied aid, would ultimately turn the tide at Stalingrad during the last months of 1942, when Americans were still falling short on promised shipments of guns, tanks, and planes.[46] Soviet relations with the United States and Britain, Walter Graebner remarked, "cooled almost as fast and to the same degree as the weather." The gushing tributes to Russian courage written by Ben and other Americans would not be reciprocated in the Soviet press. News of Allied campaigns in North Africa and the Pacific found only small notice on the back pages of Moscow's newspapers. Public acknowledgments of American shipments dwindled. The Soviets would come to understand and remember the Great Patriotic War as one fought and won by themselves alone.[47]

There was nothing left for Ben to do in Moscow. Accepting a new assignment in India, he boarded a transport plane for Tehran on a bright September morning. As his aircraft sped past miles of wheat fields, skimming haystacks and sending cows fleeing in terror, Ben chewed the ends of his fingers. The Soviet airmen laughed and claimed they flew low for security reasons, but Ben suspected that they "liked to hop hedges for the sheer hell of it." By the second day of travel the forests and prairies below gave way to dusty villages and a winding river that led to Baku, where oil wells sprinkled down the sides of brown mountains to the lagoons of the Caspian Sea. This petroleum port seemed to Ben like the most important city in the world. How much depended on holding it. They drank tea and flew on over the Alborz Mountains. Ben felt like he was running away, like he and his nation had once again failed.[48]

17

Hold Your Hats

WHEN DWIGHT D. EISENHOWER ARRIVED in London in late June 1942 to take command of the new European Theater of Operations, he was annoyed at the rising chorus of "homeland strategists" who were crying out for immediate military action. Storming the channel to open a second front, or any other large campaign, he knew, required substantial equipment and reserves, and that summer "there was no such thing as plenty of anything." Slowly it was dawning on him that an assault on French shores might not be possible until 1944. But Roosevelt and Churchill deemed urgent action of some kind necessary to counter the growing despondency among the British and American people. Later that summer they would settle on Operation Torch, an invasion of French North Africa. Given the violent history between British and Vichy forces, only Americans would take part in the initial landings to increase the odds of dissuading the region's French defenders from fighting. George Spiegelberg, already hard at work in London procuring local supplies for arriving US forces, had little more than three months to amass enough materiel for them before they launched the most complex amphibious operation ever attempted. Like his observation balloon service during World War I, the job of procurement may have lacked the drama of frontline combat, but in the end the system of aggressive resource pooling he helped to devise proved to be one of the Allies' greatest long-term advantages over the Axis who, at their own peril, hardly shared at all.[1]

During 1941, it had become "obvious" to George that the United States would have to go to war against Hitler's menacing regime, which, in less than a decade, had swallowed most of Europe and consigned millions to death. By October, as US warships exchanged fire with U-boats in the Atlantic—and torpedo attacks took the lives of 111 servicemen on the USS *Kearny* and the USS *Reuben James*—the days felt so "critical" that he found it difficult to focus on everyday matters. George wanted to go overseas and "do more important work." The idea of working with Roosevelt's administration, which he had actively campaigned against, didn't bother him, even though other Republicans who dared to serve under the president had faced backlash from fellow conservatives for such "party treachery." This would not be the Democrats' war but the nation's war, George reasoned, and good Republicans, such as the lawyer statesman Henry Stimson and the former New York Southern District Court judge Robert P. Patterson who together ran the War Department, were first and foremost loyal to the United States. He contacted Patterson to discuss a possible army commission. The judge invited George to Washington to discuss the matter.[2]

But the army offered George an uninspiring job. He "couldn't see giving up so much"—taking a leave from his law firm, resigning his teaching position at NYU, and moving away from his wife and young son and daughter, now ages four and two. He turned it down and went home.[3] Weeks later the Japanese bombed Pearl Harbor and began their lightning offensive across Southeast Asia.

George stewed over the news, which he feared would get much worse before it got better. He blamed the "Fascist-minded" Americans who had kept the nation unprepared, "America First" men like Charles Lindbergh, Burton K. Wheeler, and Gerald Nye who helped to fuel antisemitic conspiracy theories. "The Lindberghs and Wheelers and the Nyes" of the world, he fumed, owed "a heavy debt to civilization" that "they will probably never be called upon to pay." At the same time, however, he had little faith in the federal government's exploding bureaucratic machinery to meet the urgency of the moment. He sent letters to his congressman about what seemed to him an "inexcusable diversion" of Lend-Lease support to South Africa. He was far from the only Republican skeptical of this unconventional program concocted to "loan" friendly nations defense supplies. Perhaps it didn't matter. With the United States officially in the war, George imagined that the "whole Lease Lend idea" had probably "gone by the boards."[4] Little did he know he would soon be arguing in front of Congress not just to continue Lend-Lease for the duration but also to use Roosevelt's signature foreign policy as the basis for a peacetime international order, a conviction that would take him, at least in terms of world affairs, far away from the philosophies of Herbert Hoover.

No longer able to sit still, George contacted the War Department again in January. This time the military offered him a position as a lieutenant colonel in charge of coordinating procurement for the Signal Corps. Here finally was a job that would keep him "hopping," and who knew "what it may lead to." He made the application and arranged for the final formality, an army medical exam.[5]

In total more than sixteen million Americans would serve in uniform, but the army didn't want just anyone. Its examiners rooted out the epileptic and tubercular, the severe stutterers and bedwetters, the underweight, the addicts, and the insane. They watched closely for recruits so eager to serve their country that they concealed their disqualifying conditions. Lining inductees up in naked rows, they tested their hearts, their urine, their intelligence. They quizzed them about their hobbies, sports, special talents, and interest in women. Their assessments determined the course of each man's life—whether he would be assigned to combat duty and kill and maybe be killed, or shuffle paper far behind the battle lines; whether he would be heralded as a hero or, like the majority of Black selectees, spend the duration making beds, cooking meals, or digging graves; whether he would reap the rewards of an unprecedented bounty of government benefits doled out to veterans at the end of the war, or be branded with the ignominious designation 4F: unfit for any military service. Sometimes "malingerers" feigned deafness or rubbed sand in their eyes to try to escape the draft. But for many men who came of age during the Great Depression, military service promised at least basic subsistence. The army would feed them, fix their teeth, cure their gonorrhea, and teach them to read. In time, it would entitle them to pensions, low-interest mortgages, and college tuition.[6]

George's rejection notice came as a surprise. An irregularity had been spotted on his EKG. The suggestion that he had a "bad heart" he thought preposterous. Except for mild childhood illnesses and a recent, slight case of hypothyroidism he had been healthy all forty-four years of his life. George was not about to let some "fuddy dud medical general" throw him out of the army. He commissioned reports from his family physician and two heart specialists and forwarded them to the Office of the

Surgeon General. But the nation's head doctor was unmoved, explaining that army regulations prohibited accepting anyone with electrocardiographic anomalies. The only way to be waved in would be by Secretary of War Henry Stimson himself. That was hardly a discouragement to a man like George.[7]

Within weeks he received the telephone call that the surgeon general's objections had been overruled. He would serve at the pleasure of the president, although—and this would rankle George a bit—at the rank of major instead of lieutenant colonel. Still, he was anxious to get to work, "the sooner the better." He asked for only ten days, to "finally burn all my bridges," he explained. Relinquishing his faculty position, George said goodbye to his family and hastened to the capital.[8]

In Washington, planners were contemplating Operation Bolero, the monumental goal of transforming the United Kingdom into what Eisenhower described as "one gigantic air base, workshop, storage depot, and mobilization camp." By April 1942, two divisions were training in Northern Ireland and a small bomber command had been ensconced in East Anglia. But a cross-channel assault, they estimated, required thousands of planes and thirty divisions—at least a million GIs on British soil. To manage the buildup, General George C. Marshall commanded the army engineer John C. H. Lee to recruit a team to take with him to London and establish a Services of Supply for the European Theater. Lee in turn appointed the A&P grocery store chain executive Douglas MacKeachie to revive the Office of the General Purchasing Agent, which, under the direction of Charles G. Dawes, had purchased supplies for the American Expeditionary Forces in France during World War I. MacKeachie quickly assembled a staff of his own with backgrounds in law, international affairs, and business. Recognized as an officer who worked in a "superior manner," George was recommended for the unit.[9]

Some "S.O.B." colonel slowed George's transfer, because "tut! tut!—he hadn't been consulted," but by late May George received a gas mask, helmet, and other standard-issue gear, along with orders to report to Major General Lee in London.[10]

"Hold your hats boys, here we go!"

He boarded the MS *Tegelberg*, crowded with British refugees from the Netherlands East Indies. Crossing the Atlantic in a slow eleven days without convoy, the Dutch ocean liner struck an irregular course and weathered "one *hell* of a storm." George would not bother his wife, Helen, with this. He telegrammed upon arrival:

ARRIVED SAFE AFTER FINE TRIP . . . LOVE TO CHILDREN MUCH LOVE TO YOU.[11]

The Blitz had ended more than a year before George set foot in London, but the capital's residents still struggled with rising prices, dwindling comforts, and unrelenting bad news. The empire teetered on the brink of collapse. Hong Kong, Singapore, and Burma had fallen, and British efforts to appease those calling for independence in India had failed. Shortages in the capital struck not only food and petrol but even previously abundant commodities such as coal. To conserve resources, the British government implored citizens to unscrew unnecessary lightbulbs, fill baths with only five inches of water, and stop feeding bread to the birds. The Luftwaffe was pounding England's most historic cities, promising to destroy every building marked three stars in *Baedeker's* tour guide in retaliation for recent Allied raids against German cities. They had just bombed Canterbury's cathedral library, Norwich's sixteenth-century Old Boar's Head pub, and Bath's newly renovated Georgian Assembly Rooms. Toward the end of the month, the Afrika Korps's successful siege of Tobruk, then the Wehrmacht's storming of Sevastopol, portended yet another season of German advances. Graffiti scribbled on London's walls demanded action: Second Front Now.[12]

George joined a vanguard of American officers and planners who headed to Grosvenor Square, where the US Embassy's burgeoning staff spilled over into adjacent hotels and flats.[13] The influx of American personnel set off a frenzied search for start-up equipment. Supply officers scooped up, often at inflated prices, more than a quarter million dollars' worth of desks, filing cabinets, ink, typewriter ribbon, and other office equipment. The Quartermaster Corps meanwhile relieved nearby department stores of five hundred buckets and an "indeterminate number" of flashlights and hurricane lamps. Field service regulations sanctioned such cash purchases, but George knew that further ad hoc scavenging on the open market would unleash competitive procurement, wipe out critical civilian supplies, or otherwise "upset the British war economy." He and his colleagues determined that all acquisitions in the United Kingdom—by every branch of the US military as well as the Office of War Information, the Red Cross, and the nation's newly created intelligence agency, the Office of Strategic Services—had to be centrally coordinated in collaboration with British authorities.[14] Blood typed, identity tagged, and licensed to drive a jeep, George went to work, often eleven hours a day, seven days a week at the Office of Procurement in the Selfridges Annex on Duke Street.[15]

He and his colleagues faced a daunting task. They had to transport, feed, clothe, house, and establish training grounds for shiploads of arriving troops. They needed to commandeer or build barracks, bathrooms, messes, hospital wards, and recreation clubs—and because the US military insisted on strict racial segregation, they needed twice as many of them.[16] At first they drew on British food rations and gear as stop-gap supplies to tide American forces over until their own cargoes arrived in number. But by July it became

George on a London rooftop. Courtesy of Ann S. Brown.

painfully clear that shipping shortages would dramatically limit what could be imported by sea. Local procurement would have to be more sustained and extensive than originally anticipated. During World War I, the Office of the General Purchasing Agent had done just what its name suggested. It bought more than two and a quarter billion dollars' worth of supplies in France for the US Army. But now, given the extensive Lend-Lease assistance the United States had already supplied to Britain, its overwhelming goal would be to avoid purchasing altogether. George took charge of negotiating and formalizing a series of Reverse Lend-Lease agreements with the British and kept track of what was subsequently supplied under their terms.[17]

His position demanded great care. British officials had agreed in principle to mutual aid in February, but they had not anticipated it would ever grow beyond a token level, and many were at first "rather disturbed" at the prospect of not taking dollar payments for articles, services, or facilities. Reciprocal aid, to their minds, would nullify the original purpose of Lend-Lease, which had been devised to continue the flow of supplies from the United States to the United Kingdom on a cashless basis after British gold reserves dwindled. Doubting that Americans would in the end write off Lend-Lease deliveries as simple donations to the war effort rather than loans that would eventually be recalled, British officials sought every way to limit their own indebtedness. "The more generous we are with reverse lend-lease, the more dollars we need," the Foreign Office warned.[18]

The fallout from debts accrued during the First World War weighed heavily on their minds. The peace accords struck at Versailles in 1919 had offered no well-worked plans for Europe's economic reconstruction, no methods to spur the financial recovery that would have been needed for the Allies to settle their astronomical debts to American lenders or for the Central Powers to pay the billions in reparations demanded of them by the victors. Members of the US Congress had found the idea of reducing interest rates, renegotiating, or canceling the loans politically impossible. If Europeans didn't honor their commitments, they reasoned, the bill would fall to American taxpayers. The war's unpaid liabilities set off a cascade of mutual resentments during the 1920s. Germany soon defaulted on its payments. In retaliation, French and Belgian forces occupied the Ruhr. Subsequent hyperinflation of the mark undermined confidence in the new Weimar Republic and drove more disaffected Germans into extremist circles. Disputes about financing and trade meanwhile soured relations between the United States, France, and Great Britain. Unstable currencies and wildly fluctuating exchange rates spooked borrowers, further hobbling the international economy, and when American credit dried up at the end of the decade and the US economy crashed, it dragged much of Europe down with it. Looking back, many saw a direct line between the debt arrangements of the last world war and the road to this one.[19]

Franklin Roosevelt and many of his advisors determined that this time would be different. "It seems to me the thing to do is to get away from a dollar sign," the president mused at the end of 1940 as Britons' desperation for American supplies grew and as their overseas assets dwindled. Americans would open their "arsenal of democracy," he proposed, not for financial compensation but for something priceless: goodwill and a commitment to postwar economic cooperation. The Lend-Lease system that emerged from this thinking inspired Britain's leading economist, John Maynard Keynes, who saw in it the seeds of a novel and durable postwar economic order.[20] But many other British policymakers worried that, despite Roosevelt's public pronouncements, "sooner or later" Americans would present some kind of bill, just as they had after the last war. Maybe they would raise the idea of taking Britain's South American territories as payment, or at least charge for the oil they gave, some suggested. There was "an obvious likelihood," another official wrote, that in the future the Lend-Lease debt would be "used as a club" to force the British government "to do this or that." This was not pure paranoia on their part. Herbert Hoover and other conservatives had campaigned doggedly against the program. Only a minority of Republicans in Congress voted for it when it passed in March 1941.[21]

To fearful British planners, Reverse Lend-Lease seemed to make it even more likely that wartime resource allocation would eventually be converted back into traditional terms of debts and loans. Giving *and* receiving would encourage the Americans to quantify and compare. But as both Lend-Lease aid and American servicemen poured into the United Kingdom, they could see no easy way to ask the US government to pay for supplies from British stores. They resolved instead to make any postwar tallying of costs impossible. To avoid "the idea of a balance sheet which would inevitably show a net credit in favor of the Americans," they instructed recordkeepers that "reciprocal aid should never be catalogued or valued." To the Americans they explained that they simply could not spare the manpower needed to estimate prices for so many goods and services. At first hesitant, the US War Department ultimately agreed. They would measure value not in terms of dollars or pounds or weight in gold but in terms of that most precious wartime currency: shipping tonnage.[22]

By the end of the summer George and his colleagues had worked out the general contours of the reciprocal aid system, and an exchange of notes formalized the two nations' commitments to pool as many goods and services as possible. George's office began to plan for the long term, placing massive orders from the British for coal, blankets, socks, and underwear. They stopped importing their own white flour and switched to Britain's wholemeal National Loaf, which saved on shipping and storage and avoided the possibility of flooding the black market with better-tasting bread. Reverse Lend-Lease quickly extended to housing, transportation, and utilities. His Majesty's government paid the wages of tens of thousands of British civilian contractors, office personnel, and maintenance staff, posted at various US headquarters, warehouses, airfields, and Red Cross hostels, the premises of which had also been provided as mutual aid.[23]

But problems continued to crop up as fast as George could solve them. British terminology for everything from medicine to machine parts befuddled American procurement officers. One group searched the entire island in vain for garbage cans before realizing that they were called dustbins. GIs sometimes grumbled about local replacements for their own familiar provisions. The National Loaf was by all accounts awful. Standard-issue British condoms, many claimed, were too small.[24]

George nevertheless saw tremendous "mutual advantage" in keeping accounting and paperwork of all sorts to a minimum, and he seized every opportunity to stretch the principle of reciprocal aid. He persisted against British counterparts who sometimes rebuffed requests they considered politically problematic or "unduly luxurious," such as American demands for troop provisions that exceeded the allotments they gave to their own forces. The US military insisted that GIs needed their billets heated to 65 degrees Fahrenheit instead of 60 degrees, and that they required 50 percent more meat and twelve more square feet of hospital space than their British counterparts. US sailors expected seven packs of cigarettes per week, not four. And, most provocatively, Americans demanded twenty-two and a half toilet paper squares per man per day, a far cry from the three sheets the Stationery Office had budgeted for UK forces.[25]

British officials ultimately relented on these matters, but George made less headway on his office's even more controversial campaign to extend reciprocal aid to cover damages done by GIs to private property and civilians in the United Kingdom. The question pertained to no small matter. During the subsequent year and a half, American vehicles would figure in almost 29,000 local traffic accidents, 372 of them fatal. In time, as the US military's

Criminal Investigation Branch concluded, American servicemen also committed "every conceivable crime" during their stay. British officials recoiled at the idea of footing the bill for such incidents and even rejected George's request to hire a forensic investigator. US troops ought to "be imbued with a sense of their own responsibility for damage done, lest they do more of it," argued the War Office.[26]

They struck a compromise. Destruction of crops and other private property during training maneuvers would be settled by the British government as reciprocal aid so long as it was not "willful damage to an abnormal extent." Off-duty wrongdoing and traffic accidents due to negligence would be dealt with by a US Claims Commission, which awarded compensation up to $5,000. Larger reparations had to be approved by Congress. But the American claims process moved slowly, and real-world scenarios quickly underscored the difficulty of maintaining even these simple parameters. When a coffee urn exploded at a US military dance and scalded two members of the Women's Land Army, was it gross negligence or an unfortunate accident? When GIs set fire to a haystack during a fireworks display, were they on duty or off? George did not give up. He continued to push for all torts claims to be paid out as Reverse Lend-Lease.[27]

He also determined to force supply officers to heed all his rules to the letter. "This procedure should have been adopted months ago," George winced when he learned that GIs were still erroneously paying for transportation in October. Nothing irritated George more, as he studied the mountains of invoices and requisition forms that crossed his desk, than US forces acquiring goods and services with cash. Only in "extreme emergency" were they supposed to make direct purchases on Form No. 308 (in quintuplicate), and, if they did, they had to immediately report the incident to the General Purchasing Office and justify why they could not go through proper channels. "The military necessity must be real, not fancied," George lectured. What would it take, he wondered, to make reciprocal aid "a fact and not a theory"? Deciding that the Americans and the British both needed to be "brought into line," he began to write a procurement booklet for general distribution. Maybe putting it all down in plain speak would get "this rather difficult problem ironed out" and impress upon everyone the importance of "following instructions."[28]

Despite these difficulties, military victories in North Africa soon confirmed the merits of George's work. When supply chains from the United States broke down, setting off a panic that US forces might not be ready for Operation Torch, George and his colleagues plugged the gaps by turning to British supply officers who donated to the expedition Spitfires, bombs, reconnaissance boats, ambulances, radio equipment stripped from their own vehicles, millions of rounds of ammunition, thousands of tons of artillery, rations, and coal as well as enough warships to convey two-thirds of the invasion force across the seas. Allied equipment in Africa—whether British supplies destined for American beachheads in Morocco and Algeria or Lend-Lease shipments bound for General Bernard Montgomery's forces to the east—became so intermixed that officials found it impossible to break down how much went where and who used what. No matter. At the start of November, the British 8th Army made stunning advances in Egypt followed by successful American landings to the west. In celebration, London's church bells rang for the first time since 1940.[29]

By December, George had order in sight. Months of work had yielded a dictionary that translated between British and American vocabulary. A new directive limited cash purchases by local US armed forces to no more than £5. George finished his self-described "magnum opus," a sixty-nine-page booklet entitled "Principles and Procedures for Local Procurement in the United Kingdom," and sent a copy to every supply officer in the land. That, he hoped, would finally put to rest questions about "correct procedure." For negotiating the contours of reciprocal aid with "unusual efficiency and tact," George received a letter of commendation from Commander Lee. The praise, George noted wryly, "was issued in lieu of promotion."[30]

Since George's arrival in June, reciprocal aid had spared more than three million ships' tons, providing roughly 20 percent of the weight of food consumed by US forces in the United Kingdom as well as more than a third of their supplies and equipment. Commercial purchases by the American military in Britain had amounted to no more than $1 million in cash. US servicemen were now driving British cars, writing memos at British desks, and transmitting their messages via British switchboards and telephone sets. They judged the weather with British meteorological equipment, drilled with British grenades and flame throwers, and landed planes on runways cleared by British snowplows. They watched movies projected by British mobile cinemas, chomped on British candy, washed with British soap, and dried with British towels. At night they curled up under British blankets to read *Yank* and *Stars and Stripes* (printed on British presses) in tents and barracks lit and heated by British fuel. Those who perished in the coming assaults would be embalmed and buried at British expense as well. The program George helped to shape would grow even more dramatically in the next few years as roughly three million US service personnel passed through the United Kingdom. It would equate to twelve million tons of shipping saved by the time of Germany's surrender.[31]

But just as George seemed to have finally whipped the reciprocal aid program into shape, back in the United States the midterm election successes of his own Republican Party, and in particular the resurgent popularity of "America First" sentiments, posed a sudden threat to the whole Lend-Lease system.

Interlude

The Azores to Portugal

7 hours, 4 minutes
914 nautical miles
Hazy, scattered thunderstorms

ON FEBRUARY 22, 1943, THE sun began to rise four hours too early. Or so it seemed to the *Yankee Clipper* passengers roused to wash and dress and wind forward their watches while the stewards restored the seating compartments to their daytime arrangements.[1] That feeling—of time speeding up—had become a familiar one in recent years, and not just for plane travelers racing east. In this war, everything seemed to be happening everywhere all at once.

But of course, that's because this war was in fact many wars. It had been, up to this point, a series of cascading emergencies and wild uncertainties with different origins and inflection points for different people. Americans found themselves, from early on, ensnared in these global crises, because they had longstanding stakes in Europe. They had an empire in the Pacific. But events so far seemed more like the noisy collapse of the nineteenth-century colonial order than the dawn of US superpower. Only over time were the world's troubles beginning to coalesce into a single war. Only later would national narratives and mythologies—ascribing to the conflict clear direction and deeper meaning—congeal and harden.

Eventually the Allies' advantages in this war would become evident. Much more than the Axis they gifted, borrowed, and traded—supplies, ideas, commands. Their leaders would prove far better at taking criticism and learning from mistakes. International cooperation, debate, and decision making, as much as ships and planes, would pull the Allies back from the brink of catastrophe. But so far the Allies' fortunes have been shaped not only by collaborative spirit but also imperial hubris. Time and again, the concept of racial superiority—empire's fuel—has proven for them a strategic liability, a self-inflected wound. Early inaction, even indifference toward the Nazi regime's genocidal intent—against Jews, Slavs, Roma, Sinti, the so-called sexually deviant or disabled, and other commonly discriminated against populations—bought Hitler precious time and opportunity. Underestimating the Japanese, as Frank and many others did, left territories in the Pacific more vulnerable to attack. The US military's choice to build extra cumbersome Jim Crow infrastructure for the armed forces, as George learned, squandered resources and slowed mobilization. And, as Ben would discover in India, Churchill and other imperialists' steadfast refusal to heed colonized peoples' cries for independence undermined the goodwill of Asians, Arabs, and others who might have otherwise rallied to the Allied cause. So insightful, so prescient, so thoughtful in some ways, those committed to defeating the Axis had also been shortsighted, even willfully oblivious.

All night Sully and his crew had flown without any problems. Indeed without any excitement. During these long stretches over the ocean, while their B-314 hummed on autopilot, captains found themselves consumed with little more than paperwork. Every pound and gallon and mile had to be accounted for in a legal-sized logbook, generating thousands of separate entries on a single crossing.[2]

What a far cry this machine management was from the thrill piloting had once been. When Sully and other early aviators first took to the skies, they had done so in rickety biplanes with only the most primitive instruments to keep right side up "in the soup" of clouds or fog. They flew seat-of-the-pants wherever they wanted, eyeballing landmarks on the ground to find their way. Too often they got lost in the desert, crashed in the mountains, or disappeared at sea. Nevertheless, they had been show-offs, banking, spiraling, grazing the treetops. Because they could. They admitted to feeling like gods in their open cockpits, wind and mist and the bake of the sun in their faces, defying gravity and the dull existence of ordinary mortals below. People who met these trailblazers said that their eyes were brighter, their laughter was sharper, and their handshakes were stronger than those who had never left the ground.[3]

But since then, technological advances and an onrush of rules had transformed flying from a freebooting adventure into a regulated industry.

A young Sully (*right*) piloting in goggles. The Pan Am Historical Foundation.

Enclosed flight decks kept pilots away from the elements and advanced dashboards solved their mysteries for them. Governments claimed the airspace above their territories and demanded more supervision over routes. They passed laws mandating pilot licenses, aircraft registration, inspections, and overhaul schedules. And Pan Am embraced its own array of company policies—a uniform code, an alcohol ban, and other guidelines lifted straight out of Lufthansa's employee manual. By the late 1930s, Charles Lindbergh mourned, the pilot had been reduced to a "routine operator" at the mercy of executives and air traffic controllers. "The airplane is no longer anything but a means of transportation," the French aviator poet Antoine de Saint-Exupéry agreed. As boring as a bus.[4]

Sully may have stuck to Pan Am's company line in public, celebrating, like the airline's other spokesmen, flight's transformation into something safe, commonplace, and routine. But in fact he chafed at the rote exercise piloting had become. Long training sessions and repetitive tasks bored and frustrated him. He preferred to "shake a leg." On at least one occasion he got into a shouting match with Pan Am's fastidious operations manager, André Priester. Stay away from my ship, he had told him. To amuse himself during these monotonous trips over the ocean, he liked to prod and prank other crewmembers—sneaking up behind them and shaking their workstations to spill their instruments, pointing under their chins and flicking them on the nose when they looked down, or pulling the height lever on their chairs

An older Sully (*foreground*) piloting with reading glasses. The Pan Am Historical Foundation.

to send them falling to the floor. "If you got anywhere near him, he would punch you jovially on the upper arm," one coworker remembered. "He was always doing some stupid damn thing," recalled another: "Then he'd laugh like that was funny as hell."[5]

Unbeknownst to the passengers below his flight deck, Sully flouted protocol for fun, and occasionally in anger. He preferred to bring his planes in flat and fast, racing the launch to the docks or drenching ground attendants with surf. "He'd land across a river and pull right up to the pier, rather than land down river and taxi for 30 minutes," one crewmember observed. "He knew he could do it, so to him it was not unsafe." Sometimes, when it suited him, he took off without clearance or veered off course. He ferried one clipper overland from Los Angeles to New York rather than stopping at Miami as ordered. He took another across trackless Congolese rain forest canopy instead of following the regular radio beacons. A year before, during a special mission hauling thirty thousand rounds of ammunition to India, the resident RAF commander at Aden had asked him to fly around neutral Arabia to avoid angering its tribesmen. Sully complied at first, but as soon as the clipper passed outside the range of British radar, he ordered his navigator to chart a direct course for Karachi. "Let the British worry about the political consequences!" the assistant radio officer interpreted as his sentiment. "When flying with Sullivan," he explained, "you didn't expect things to be done by the book."[6]

Pan Am's managers considered disciplining their pioneering old timer who acted "as if rules did not exist for him." They had begun hiring and promoting a different breed of pilot, not barnstormers but aeronautical engineers and other studious, detail-oriented types with the skills and temperament to meet an expanding set of professional duties—in customs and immigration control, safety regulations, mail handling, passenger services, and more. But the airline's profits hinged on the prestige of its pilots. How would it look if they grounded this famous "Master of Ocean Flying Boats"? What if the public began to question the safety of Pan Am's operations?

So Sully kept his position. And, because the company made assignments based on a seniority system, he stayed at the top of the Atlantic Division's flight rotation.[7]

Over breakfast more landing papers appeared, and by late morning a seatbelt sign told George, Tamara, Harry, Manuel, Ben, Frank, and the other passengers that the clipper was at last nearing Horta Harbor. The plane pitched sharply to the left just before splashing down, striking some of the travelers as odd. But the groundcrew reassured the disembarking crowd that this was simply Captain Sullivan's signature move. They knew if Sully was steering an incoming plane, they explained, because he "always made a fancy swerve."[8]

While Horta mechanics performed routine servicing on the *Yankee Clipper* and diagnosed the cause of an engine leak, the craft's passengers spent a short layover on shore. George dashed off a quick telegram to his wife:

> EVERYTHING FINE SO FAR LOVE=
> GEORGE SPIEGELBERG.

Then just before noon, with everyone corralled back on board, Sully guided the clipper out between a row of anchored Swedish ships and the breakwater. Three-foot sea swells rammed stubbornly against its hull and shot spray over the windows as it picked up speed. Winter takeoffs from here required full throttle to get up into the skies fast enough to steer clear of Pico Island's volcanic peak. At some point on the way to mainland Portugal the crew documented an enemy sighting. Otherwise, this leg of the journey proceeded without incident all afternoon, as the plane threaded in and out of the clouds seven thousand feet over the Atlantic. Late in the afternoon Sully strolled through the cabin a final time to let his charges know that they'd be in Lisbon by dinnertime.[9]

PART IV

1942–1943

South Pacific, 1943. Photo12/Universal Images Group via Getty Images.

18

Patent Denials

HARRY SEIDEL'S DAUGHTER SUMMED HIM up as a series of sensory impressions. The waft of expensive Cuban cigars. The clack of a cocktail shaker. Caruso on the record player. His peers in the oil industry remarked upon his "broadminded judgment" and "sense of fairplay." *Fortune* magazine crowned him "one of Standard's top diplomats," and indeed skilled international negotiating earned him the Légion d'Honneur and a kiss on both cheeks from a French general. But to prosecutors, by 1942, H. G. Seidel had become a signature, a series of initials, which appeared and reappeared in the piles of corporate documents pried loose by motions for discovery. He was a person of interest in a spiraling series of federal inquiries into Standard Oil of New Jersey's "unlawful restraints and monopolies" and "conspiracy to restrain interstate and foreign commerce." Disembarking from a seaplane at LaGuardia in June, as scandal engulfed his company, Harry came face to face with reporters eager for details about the nature of his visit from London. He declined to comment.[1]

Standard's directors told themselves that Americans were simply looking for someone to blame, to explain away the humiliating defeats of the last six months. They wanted easy answers to account for the shortfalls that had prevented the nation's factories from delivering enough of the planes, guns, and tanks desperately needed on the world's fighting fields. Progressive journalists, fearing that Roosevelt was becoming too deferential to big business as he focused on winning the war, had been happy to oblige with a steady stream of exposés about corporate misdeeds: exporters little inclined to atone for the substantial, war-readying business they had done with Germany and Japan in recent years; manufacturers reluctant to convert their plants to defense production; "dollar-a-year men" coopting the planning boards of Washington and steering fat, no-risk military contracts to their own firms; and still others charging the government inflated prices for zinc, glass, or aluminum. Before long, writers for *PM* and the *New Republic* zeroed in on Jersey Standard's substantial ties to the powerful German chemical conglomerate IG Farben. Their sensational reporting in turn caught the attention of Assistant Attorney General Thurman Arnold, who launched a grand jury investigation into the matter.[2]

Poring over more than forty thousand corporate documents that February, Arnold and other members of the Justice Department's Antitrust Division quickly pieced together a history of Standard's collaboration with IG Farben, which began in the late 1920s, deepened after the rise of Hitler, and persisted in shadowy form well after the outbreak of war in Europe. To Arnold's eye, cartel arrangements between the two firms, and in particular their pooling of patented industrial know-how, was the principal reason for the nation's catastrophic synthetic rubber shortage.[3]

The United States was more dependent on crude rubber than any other imported resource, and virtually all of it had been tapped from the trees of Malaya and the Netherlands East Indies. Yet Americans had made only half-hearted efforts to stockpile reserves or develop alternative sources of supply before the collapse of colonial Southeast Asia. It was a colossal blunder born from a dramatic underestimation of Japanese determination and strength. Not even strict rationing, tire recapping, reclamation campaigns, and hurried efforts to cultivate fields in the Western Hemisphere could make up for the lost import stream. The tacky substance was needed to keep some 140 million tires on the American roads, and it had become a linchpin in the nation's military mobilization, essential to encase walkie-talkie batteries and rifle butts, to line helmets, gas masks, and fuel tanks, to fashion tourniquets, life belts, inflatable mattresses, and barrage balloons. The jeeps and trucks rolling off the production lines contained not only tires but more than two hundred other rubber parts from radiator hoses to fan belts. It took a whopping 826 pounds of the material to build just one medium tank. Unless American factories began mass producing synthetic alternatives in short order, rubber threatened to become the US war effort's Achilles heel. But doing that required wresting cooperation from Jersey Standard, which held patent rights in the United States to IG Farben's superior-grade product, Buna-S. "Any grand jury would vote this one in a jiffy without batting an eye," one reporter snooping around the scandal cabled back to his editor. "Thurman Arnold told me this afternoon NOT FOR USE, that the case stinks so stratospherically that S.O. has agreed to do almost anything to keep the facts off the record."[4]

On March 25, Jersey Standard, six of its subsidiaries, and three of its officers paid small fines and pled no contest to charges of violating antitrust laws. The company's directors agreed to release their synthetic rubber patents royalty-free for the duration, but only after Arnold agreed to drop his accusation that they had impeded American war production. Our "war work is more important than court vindication," Standard's leaders told the press to justify the consent decree and hopefully put the matter to rest.[5]

But the very next day, Arnold hurried to Capitol Hill to parade his mounds of evidence before the Senate's Special Committee Investigating the National Defense Program, chaired by Harry S. Truman. In the crowded Senate Caucus Room, the assistant attorney general declared that Jersey Standard had been engaged in an "illegal conspiracy." Its executives, he charged, had done IG Farben's bidding and rebuffed American and British producers' interest in the development of synthetic rubber by refusing to share samples, offering licensing only on prohibitive terms, and threatening patent infringement litigation. They wanted to keep profitable processes exclusive to their own combine, "to look at the war as a transitory phenomenon and at business as a kind of permanent thing," he explained. Instead, they had placed themselves in a complex, compromising position and been "taken for a ride by the Germans."[6]

Standard's president, William S. Farish, arrived for his testimony prepared to do little more than paint his organization as the victim of government overreach. Without the "brains in industry," he cautioned the senators, "your war effort will fall down." *Your* war effort. Hedging, deflecting, obfuscating, he came off poorly as the committee pummeled him with questions. "Seldom has a U.S. business firm taken such a smearing as Standard Oil Co. of New Jersey got," snickered *Time* magazine. "Thurman Arnold swung the rubber hose while the Truman Committee held the victim." After the hearings, reporters asked an outraged Senator Truman if he thought Standard's actions amounted to treason. "Why, hell, yes. What else is it?" he replied.[7]

Harry Seidel's company was not the only American concern with substantial international ties, including to Axis economies, that had proven difficult to disentangle when war erupted. But it presented an extreme case. By the outbreak of the conflict in Europe in 1939, Jersey Standard's foreign sales and refinery runs, led by state-of-the-art facilities on Aruba and Sumatra, surpassed its refining and marketing operations in the United States itself. Half of its $2 billion in assets, and some 60 percent of its profits, derived from overseas business, accounting for nearly 8 percent of all direct investments by US firms around the world.[8] The exact nature and full extent of Standard's relationship with IG Farben would never be fully revealed. Both corporations destroyed internal records they did not want to become public. But what documents did come to light raised uncomfortable questions about the responsibilities of industries that trafficked in war-essential resources, as well as the obligations of American corporations that had developed astonishing multinational dimensions in the decades after the First World War.

Harry had grown up in the entrepreneurial household of his father, Hermann Seidel, who opened his own bakery in downtown Fitchburg, Massachusetts, only two years after emigrating from Germany. Hermann was progressive and civic minded, a member of the Universalist Church, a trustee at the local library, and a city alderman who championed street lighting and other public services. During World War I, like other liberal German Americans eager to prove their undivided loyalty to the United States, he threw himself into liberty bond sales and, though his business must have suffered, a campaign to ration bread. But Harry, his son, would move into a high church, high society world far removed from these roots.[9]

By early 1919, while the emissaries of nearly three dozen nations converged on Paris to talk peace and postwar borders, Harry made his way back from Romania to New York, where he gathered with other American oil executives for a victory dinner in the flag-bedecked banquet hall of the Biltmore Hotel. "We find ourselves in a new environment," Jersey Standard's chairman Alfred C. Bedford told the tables of tuxedoes before him, "with new conceptions of our responsibility and of our power." During the war, American oil men had sacrificed their own interests to the cause of "country and humanity," he bragged. They had delivered the petroleum needed to vanquish coal-powered Germany. This triumph over the Central Powers, however, paled beside an even more important feat, Bedford intimated. By gaining the trust of the War Fuel Administration, the oil men had forestalled a state takeover of their business, the unlucky fate of the railroads, the radio, and other industries during the crisis. "The petroleum industry, I say it with pride, gentlemen," Bedford effused, remained "free from Government regulation." With the conflict behind them, Harry and his colleagues had much reason for optimism. The United States was burning through petroleum supplies sixteen times faster than anywhere else on the planet. There seemed no bottom to the American appetite for oil.[10]

But Harry's company also had a weakness. The dissolution of Standard Oil's vast empire, ordered by the Supreme Court in 1911, had left the holding company without enough oil fields to keep its refineries and distribution networks running at capacity. Jersey Standard relied too much on purchased crude. Yet acquiring new domestic property seemed likely to invite more litigation and government scrutiny. Geologists, moreover, were predicting that, given the dizzying pace of American consumption, the nation's wells would be sucked dry in less than thirty years. To Jersey Standard's incoming president, Walter C. Teagle, exploration abroad seemed just the answer. Drilling fields on multiple continents would put the company's output closer to emerging foreign markets. It would serve as a check on British and Dutch oil conglomerates' increasingly aggressive prospecting—in Iran, the East Indies, Venezuela, and elsewhere—which seemed poised to capture much of the world's known sources of supply outside the United States. And whereas domestic expansion would be decried by antimonopolists, the recently adopted Webb-Pomerene Act exempted overseas holdings from most antitrust regulations. Indeed, the US government might even back the corporation's foreign ventures since the control of oil had been recognized as of national strategic interest. The future of Jersey Standard "lies outside the United States, rather than in it," declared E. J. Sadler, who Teagle put in charge of the firm's new Foreign Producing Department. Harry—who had been Sadler's assistant in Bucharest—was selected to run the operation's Paris headquarters.[11]

Harry had spent the war in Romania as a bachelor, but now he returned to Europe newly wed to Rosamond Baker Harris, a college-town sweetheart from Providence, Rhode Island. Most American wives traveled on their husband's passports, but business would often take Harry away—for inspection trips, board meetings, industry summits, or diplomatic house calls. Crossed off from Harry's application at last minute, Rosamond acquired a separate passport for herself—and soon the three children who would arrive in quick succession.[12]

Postwar Paris was booming with American enterprise. US bank branches, shops, and other new businesses sprouted up across the capital's fashionable Right Bank, as investors, salesmen, and others angled to break into the continent's markets, once fairly impenetrable to American businessmen but now weakened by war's fallout. Harry's office on the Avenue des Champs-Elysées whirred with activity, as draftsmen, geologists, translators, photographers, and others corralled by the Foreign Producing Department came and went, surveying the continent's every half-promising hill and basin for untapped deposits. Standard's executives were ready to risk millions in the early 1920s. When word arrived that the Nobel Brothers wanted to off-load their production facilities in the Caucasus and what was now eastern Poland, they purchased both in haste. The Bolshevik takeover of the Russian empire would surely be short-lived, they believed, and private property returned to its rightful owners. If they didn't seize these opportunities, they wagered, someone else would. On capitalism's uneven playing fields large corporations could out-spend, out-risk, and out-wait their smaller competitors.[13]

Harry's position bought his family a life of elegance in the French capital: a spacious apartment in the exclusive neighborhood of Passy, a private telephone line, a grand kitchen with oversized copper pots. Their live-in governess managed the children's lessons and buttoned their pea coats for afternoon walks in the Bois de Bologne. The Seidels wintered at exclusive Alpine resorts. Summers they spent at their villa overlooking the English Channel. Only a handful of miles from the drop zones where the British 6th Airborne Division would secure the eastern flank of the Allied invasion of Normandy, Harry's two daughters and son—Rosamond, Mary Frances, and Harry, Jr.— learned to ride horses on the beach.[14]

But in the meantime, the Foreign Producing Department's geologists failed to locate any great new natural reserves on the continent. The Nobel properties in Poland turned out to be badly mismanaged and hobbled by the new state's regulations. Though Harry tried to put them on a firmer footing, they returned only inconsequential yields and deficit after deficit. In the Caucasus, the Communists didn't just confiscate all the oil fields, they were draining them to finance their revolution with international petroleum sales. And by 1926, IG Farben chemists had figured out how to manufacture synthetic gasoline from coal. "I think that this matter is the most important which has ever faced the company since the dissolution," Standard's head of research and development Frank Howard telegrammed Walter Teagle from Farben's pilot plant at Leuna. "This means absolutely the independence of Europe in the matter of gasoline supply." Teagle hastened to Germany to see for himself and begin negotiations to gain access to the technology.[15]

Even where Jersey Standard already had profitable European wells—in Romania—Harry and his colleagues ran into trouble. The postwar kingdom's reigning National Liberal Party, eager to tackle inflation and settle war debts, moved toward a partial nationalization of the country's oil industry, even retroactively claiming subsoil rights for the state on long-term leaseholds. Standard's executives denounced the measures for unfairly targeting foreign investors, not least themselves, who, they argued, had nurtured Romanian prosperity with their own money and expertise for a quarter century. This was, they cried, nothing but "Sovietism" by another name.[16]

Harry traveled to Bucharest to try to convince Liberal leaders to reconsider. Warmly he received them at his office whenever they came to Paris. He dangled before them an additional 4 percent royalty on Româno-Americană's yields and intimated that Standard could extend "its moral support" for the Romanian government in its efforts to secure a large loan in the United States. To drive home the stakes of the matter, Standard's leaders enlisted the heavy-handed charms of the State Department. The kingdom's politicians responded to the multipronged pressure with promises they would not keep.[17]

Losing patience, Walter Teagle fantasized about retribution. He considered launching a price war to steal the kingdom's markets on the upper Danube. Or using Standard's influence to spoil the Romanian government's chances at American financing. If the Liberals failed to receive their much-needed loan, Standard's directors predicted, their government would be toppled by a friendlier one. But by 1928, Harry saw little advantage to waging a vengeful fight. He convinced Teagle to squeeze what profit was left in Româno-Americană's existing installations and cease further investment in Romania—a wise course of action, it turns out, because in little over a decade the kingdom would fall to pro-Axis dictatorship. The Foreign Producing Department needed to look beyond Europe for its next big strike.[18]

The challenge for Harry and his colleagues was geological. Where in the world had just the right subterranean heat and pressure to preserve the ancient life that made internal combustion engines go? But even more so it had become political. What kind of states set just the right conditions for corporate exploitation of fossil fuels? "We are now confronted with nationalistic policies in almost all foreign countries, as well as decidedly socialistic tendencies in many," one Standard executive grumbled. Taxes, tariffs, labor laws, price controls—all ate into profits and set states down the tempting path to expropriation, as had happened in the Soviet Union and would soon also befall Standard's property in Bolivia and Mexico. Far better to invest in places shaped by imperial recent pasts or presents, places governed by biddable leaders or leaders in the thrall of laissez-faire ideology or their own power. Places like Venezuela. That South American country was not only blessed with extensive crude deposits along its Caribbean coastline—which lay closer to the markets of Europe than US Gulf ports—it was also ruled by the dictator General Juan Vicente Gómez, who offered generous terms to foreign investors who promised to make him and his friends rich. After bringing Standard's first commercially viable Venezuelan well online in the late twenties, the company rapidly expanded its holdings in the Maracaibo Basin and purchased a refinery on nearby Aruba.[19]

Still, Standard's executives wanted more. In particular they wanted to break into the jealously guarded reaches of Europe's overseas territories, where colonial officials had reserved most exploration and drilling rights for their own nationals. They had, for example, been trying to gain access to the Netherlands East Indies' high-quality crude, conveniently close to Chinese and Japanese markets, since the 1890s. But Standards' agents, acting under a subsidiary with a Dutch board of directors, only managed to buy a smattering of second-hand concessions already passed over by other prospectors. By the 1910s most of the archipelago's paying fields had been gobbled up by Standard's fiercest international rival, Royal Dutch Shell. Finally, in 1922, one of the Americans' Sumatran wells, dug to a new horizon, struck enough oil to justify commercial production. Hoping that this unexpected find at Talang Akar would give them an entrée into the islands' petroleum industry, Standard ordered laborers to clear a site for a refinery at Sungai Gerong, just east of Palembang on the banks of the Musi River. Harry meanwhile hustled to The Hague to call on the Colonial Minister Simon de Graaff.[20]

De Graaff dissembled. He claimed the Americans had missed important deadlines to be considered for more concessions. He insinuated that his closed bid process was necessary to keep the Japanese out of the colony's oil business. He offered vague assurances of future deals and then in subsequent meetings tried to douse the Americans' interest by claiming that surveys of potential fields had been discouraging. Not for nothing had de Graaff's colleagues given him the moniker "Peter the Liar."[21]

But Harry kept up the campaign, returning to The Hague every few months to press de Graaff for updates. He made small talk about Americans' colonial efforts in the Philippines. He enlisted the support of his local embassy. He showed up on a Saturday. Finally, action by the US Secretary of Interior, who declared the Netherlands a "non-reciprocating" country by the terms of the Mineral Leasing Act of 1920, broke through Dutch resolve. Shell had freely operated a substantial production and marketing business in the United States. Now, unless the Netherlands opened the East Indies to American oil companies, it would be barred from further leases on federal lands. In early 1925, de Graaff invited Harry back to The Hague, this time to work out the details for a concession to enlarge Standard's holdings near Talang Akar. The Americans agreed to hire a majority of Dutch employees and cut the colonial government a share of their profits. It had taken nearly three decades and more than $21.4 million in investments, but Jersey Standard brought its first East Indies products to market in late 1926. From there, American oil installations on the islands multiplied rapidly, soon contributing a quarter of the colony's total petroleum output. Within fifteen years—by the time Dutch demolition squads arrived to blow up what they could before Japanese paratroopers seized Sumatra's oil facilities—the Sungei Gerong refinery would be disgorging some 15.4 million barrels per year of everything from kerosene and tractor fuel to high-octane aviation gasoline.[22]

Harry and his colleagues used the same persistence to muscle their way into the Middle East. The fate of those vast arid lands, stretching from Egypt across the Arabian Peninsula to Iran, had become suddenly up for grabs after the defeat of the German and Ottoman empires in 1918. Arab nationalists, anticolonial intellectuals, and others built formidable mass movements calling for independence in Cairo, Damascus, Baghdad, and elsewhere. But French and British imperialists were determined to divvy up these territorial spoils of war amongst themselves, either as League of Nations mandates, under their own direct control, or else as informal spheres of influence ruled by pliant sheiks and others propped up by European backing. Under the San Remo agreement of 1920, the French traded their claims on Mosul Province for trusteeship over Syria and Lebanon as well as a takeover of German shares in the Turkish Petroleum Company, the multinational firm that held drilling rights on a promising swathe of land east of the Tigris River in the soon-to-be-formed state of Iraq. As oil men set out into the desert with their survey equipment, British and French air forces mobilized to bomb the region's popular uprisings into submission.[23]

Harry and his colleagues in the Foreign Producing Department studied this flurry of European collaboration with growing alarm. They believed that British interests especially, led by Shell and Anglo-Persian Oil, were conspiring to keep Americans, also rightful victors in the late war, out of the Middle East. Britain's bid for commercial dominance around the world, many of them decided, had become a far greater menace to Standard's business than a German victory ever would have been.[24]

In time, with subtle threats, behind-the-scenes maneuvering, and demands for an "Open Door" policy from the State Department, American oil corporations, led by Jersey Standard, wheedled their way into a stake in Iraqi oil exploration. In October 1927, when the group's drilling passed below fifteen hundred feet at Baba Gurgur, their first gusher roared so high above the derrick that it could be seen from the rooftops of Kirkuk five miles away. It took seven hundred hastily recruited Jubur and Al-Obaidi tribesmen nine days to dam the resulting flood rushing toward the surrounding villages.[25]

By the late twenties, Jersey Standard had seized an interest in so many overseas affiliates and subsidiaries that British officials who tried to map the firm's holdings admitted that they could at best guess at a partial list. And it was clear that the geologists had been wrong about impending petroleum shortages. Unexpected discoveries had revived the oil booms of Oklahoma, California, and Texas. Improved cracking techniques were squeezing better and more fuel from each barrel of crude. The Soviets were dumping underpriced surpluses on the international market, and the vast underground lakes of the Middle East had barely been tapped. Just like that, Harry and his colleagues faced a daunting new problem. The race to command the earth's liquid depths had in fact dredged up too much oil.[26]

Oil was the princeliest of international bulk commodities. It was easier to move over long distances than coal. Unlike grain, it did not spoil. But this meant that petroleum from virtually anywhere could come crashing into a market previously thought secure, driving down prices, undermining the revenue projections large corporations relied upon to bankroll their capital-intensive production. Every new gusher threatened to upset the delicate balance between supply and demand. Every upstart producer—"pirates" Harry's company called them—raised the specter of ruinous competition. Jersey Standard's directors did not want to operate in such a free market. They wanted predictable returns, steady market shares. To keep prices stable (and high) in the late 1920s, the oil industry's leaders embarked on an unprecedented effort to cooperate among themselves by striking informal agreements as well as forming official combinations or consortiums. Cartels, critics would call them.[27]

Harry quickly emerged as one of Standard's top go-betweens to facilitate this industry diplomacy. His job was to probe for points of mutual interest and smooth out disputes between erstwhile competitors, to find a path to some kind of quid pro quo. To be closer to Standard's overseas marketing operations, which were coordinated in London, he relocated his family to an English country manor in Surrey. Only a generation before, the bucolic estates just south of Richmond Park had been closed off to all but the titled, landed, or otherwise impeccably well-born. But hard times had forced many of these properties onto the rental market. Professionals, plutocrats, Americans—even a baker's son like Harry—snatched up small mansions styled in what one critic called "stockbroker Tudor." For the Seidels the move meant horse shows, fox hunts, and tennis parties as well as confirmation in the Church of England. For Harry, it led to workday commutes to his London office in a chauffeured Packard followed by thirty-six holes on the weekend at the nearby Coombe Hill Golf Club.[28]

But soon he was mired in endless, tedious negotiations. Despite their pledge to cooperate, suspicion and rivalry persisted between Standard, Shell, and other British producers. Negotiators for France—a heavy importer that lacked its own fields and therefore any incentive to limit output—brought other irreconcilable interests to the table. Standard and other parties to the so-called Red Line agreement, which aimed to operate collectively in the Middle East under the auspices of the Iraq Petroleum Company, found themselves locked in bitter disagreements over when to develop that region's fields, whose port should be the terminus for a proposed pipeline, and how much oil to pump through it. Harry threw his weight behind a plan to build two pipelines, one to French-controlled Tripoli and the other to British-controlled Haifa, but the infighting continued unabated, and before long new companies began to sniff around concessions in Bahrain and Saudi Arabia, threatening to undermine their monopoly altogether. "Whenever a solution seems possible something has always been injected by one party or another preventing a settlement of this problem," Harry despaired to Standard's general counsel after a decade trying to corral the Middle East's oil producers to common cause. Harry feared that only two options remained: to compromise more than Standard wanted or to take the case to court. But the latter course, Harry pointed out, "may open a series of disclosures which, in our business interests, we might wish to avoid." Rather than risk the courts' scrutiny of their affairs, Harry and his colleagues pressed on with the troubled negotiations until the outbreak of war cut them off.[29]

Harry's bosses also tasked him with the impossible job of finding an "orderly" way to accommodate the Soviet surpluses flooding Europe's markets. The industry's major players had at first vowed not to purchase any of this "stolen oil" or deal with such an "irresponsible" government, as E. J. Sadler put it. "The Communists repudiate the civilized code of ethics," Teagle warned; their "basis of operation is deception." But one by one distributors could not resist the cheap product. Standard held out longer than the others on principle, an uneconomical decision, but at last caved. No matter what flattery or bribery Harry tried, subsequent talks with the Soviets, too, proved infuriating.[30]

Doing business with the Germans promised to be far easier. Walter Teagle had struck up a "close and pleasant and personal relationship" with IG Farben's leaders after his 1927 visit to the conglomerate's Leuna factory complex. Two years later they finalized an agreement to form the Standard-IG Farben combine. Standard's researchers would receive the rights to exploit Farben's hydrogenation process outside Germany (they would use it to develop superior-grade fuel), Farben's directors received 2 percent of Standard's stock (they needed the money), and both agreed to stay out of each other's field of expertise. Teagle celebrated that the venture would enable joint research into manufacturing processes, shared management of resulting patents, and other projects of "mutual advantage." Harry became one of the combine's nine directors.[31]

During the following decade, Germany—soon Hitler's Germany—and allies of the Third Reich made ready customers for Jersey Standard. Sales for the firm's subsidiary, the Deutsch-Amerikanische Petroleum Gesellschaft (DAPG), soared from 4.9 million barrels in 1927 to 16 million by 1938. The Nazis' new autobahn superhighway system, which spiked demands for asphalt and gasoline, was a "motorist's dream," gushed Standard's in-house magazine. Harry and his colleagues also recommitted themselves to business with Mussolini's regime even after Roosevelt called for a "moral embargo" on such trade in protest of the Italian invasion of Ethiopia in 1935. "Perhaps there was never a bigger tempest in a smaller teapot," Walter Teagle declared when criticism of the decision appeared in the press. "We started shipping petroleum products to Italy, in tins and barrels, more than threescore years ago," he explained. "We take the bad with the good or quit, just as any business does." Yet short-term profits alone could not explain the firm's decision making during the 1930s. Jersey Standard, for example, took the huge risk of fueling Franco's coup on credit. They, along with the Texas Oil Company, delivered to Nationalist forces, including the Condor Legion bombers that flattened Guernica, more than twice as much petroleum as Spanish Republicans were able to scrounge up for themselves, mostly from the Soviet Union. Anticommunism, as much as old-fashioned entrepreneurship, steered the company's leaders.[32]

Jersey Standard's executives may have wanted to carry on without acknowledging any ethical dimensions to their work—to "take the bad with the good" as Teagle put it—but by 1937, business around the world had become anything but usual, and given their vast international connections Harry and his colleagues were especially well positioned to sense what was brewing. In Europe, Hitler's Four-Year Plan was plainly reorienting the German economy toward single-minded preparations for war, while in Asia, renewed Japanese aggression against Chinese territory brought tensions between the United States and Japan close to a breaking point on December 12, when Japanese aircraft buzzing over the Yangtze River strafed and bombed three Standard Oil tankers and the USS *Panay*, an American gunboat evacuating embassy personnel and oil employees from a besieged Nanjing.[33]

As Roosevelt increasingly sounded the need for all peace-loving peoples to commit themselves to restoring a sense of "international morality" and stand up against aggressive nations' "lawlessness" and "greed for power and supremacy," Standard's directors did not reconsider their investments but instead carefully maneuvered more of their business offshore. They upgraded their refinery on Aruba so it could make aviation gasoline, putting their sales of that vital, specialized resource to Germany outside the purview of any restrictions the president might impose. To contravene Neutrality Law restrictions on the movements of US ships, they transferred a number of Standard's tankers—including the German-built MS *Harry G. Seidel*—to Panamanian registry and staffed them with German crews that could be paid in Reichsmarks with DAPG proceeds, a clever workaround to Hitler's tightening foreign exchange controls. None of this suggested naiveté about the direction of world affairs. That Christmas, while spending the holiday season with his family at the fashionable Austrian mountain town of Kitzbühel, Harry gave his elder daughter a prescient warning. She had been studying art, music, and German outside Munich and planned to go on to Vienna for four months with friends. No, he told her, Hitler was getting "much too aggressive." She needed to return to England instead "while the going was good."[34]

After the Anschluss in March 1938, which Harry had anticipated months before, he and his colleagues assessed the state of their business in Europe. They mulled over the implications of Austrian annexation for DAPG, entertained the idea of a new collaboration with the Italian carmaker Fiat, and brainstormed ways to solve Italy's impending lubricating oil shortage given the "friendly attitude" of Mussolini's government. Frank Howard brought word that German chemists had made important strides with their synthetic rubber program, though, he admitted, "certain difficulties still exist which prevent our I.G. friends from giving us full technical information." Indeed, except for what could be gleaned from published patents, Standard's directors had not received any more information about Buna-S rubber than what they had learned during an IG plant tour in 1931. But "we must be especially careful not to make any move whatever," Howard cautioned, "without the consent of our friends." The German government had refused to allow them to share it "because of military expediency," and until they changed their minds Standard needed to "loyally preserve the restrictions they have placed on us."[35]

IG Farben had been among the earliest and most consequential donors to Hitler's 1933 election campaign and clearly by 1938 no longer made any moves without the full knowledge and approval of the Nazi state. Standard's executives nevertheless continued to pass their technological know-how on to the chemical conglomerate and that fall also acceded to a request to build the Nazi regime a hydrogenation plant capable of producing aviation gasoline from imported oil. Harry and the company's other directors knew that "the economics of the proposal would not justify the expenditure," but they reasoned that if they didn't build the factory someone else would and DAPG would "be dropped out of the Four Year Plan entirely." Agreeing to cooperate with Hitler's campaign to rebuild the German economy "on a basis of maximum internal self sufficiency," the staff at Harry's London office moved to begin negotiations and draft contracts. Frank Howard assured his colleagues that they would receive useful help in the Reich from "our friends in industry and Government circles." Even the narrow avoidance of war that September at Munich, and Hitler's subsequent taking of the Sudetenland, did not lead them to change course. By late October plans for the plant had expanded to include commercial-scale catalytic cracking operations to enable IG Farben's scientists to learn the process "at first hand."[36]

Between its investment in DAPG, which totaled almost $65 million, and its cartel arrangements with IG Farben, Jersey Standard had emerged—by the time Hitler's troops stormed Poland—as the US industrial corporation with the greatest stake in the Third Reich. To Standard's leaders the British were bitter rivals and the Soviets commonplace pirates. The Germans, by contrast, had become valuable customers, collaborators—friends.[37]

Harry's wife, Rosamond, did not want to split up the family in September 1939, but as machine gun nests and other war preparations transformed southern England, she decided that Europe was "no place for any children right now" and hustled her teenaged son and two daughters to a stateroom on the SS *Manhattan* docked at Southampton. While his family headed for the safety of a Park Avenue duplex, Harry turned his attention to emergency arrangements for Standard's European operations. Affiliates in Nazi-controlled or aligned territories, including Romania and Hungary, had abruptly ceased contact, and the Allied blockade put an end to Standard's fuel shipments to the Third Reich. Harry at first nevertheless hoped "if possible" to forestall "more direct Government control" of the oil industry. To join the Allies' transatlantic convoy system and sustain as much of their $500 million annual sales on continental Europe as possible, the company's directors dismissed their Panamanian tankers' German crews, including thirty such men unceremoniously offloaded from the MS *Harry G. Seidel* at Buenos Aires.[38]

Disentangling the intellectual property that the corporation shared with IG Farben would not be so easy, but it was urgent, argued one Standard executive, to ensure that if the United States also entered the war, those patents "should not fall into unfriendly hands"—in other words, seized by the US Alien Property Custodian "who might sell it to an unfriendly interest," that is, to an American competitor. In late September Frank Howard sped to The Hague to meet with German negotiators. "How we are going to make these belligerent parties lie down in the same bed isn't quite clear as yet," he relayed to his colleagues, but, he argued, "technology has to carry on—war or no war." Three days of discussion yielded a new agreement, backdated to September 1, which divided the ownership of some two thousand patents by region of the world rather than by percentages. "We did our best to work out complete plans for a modus vivendi which would operate through the term of the war, whether or not the United States came in," Howard reported. Such realpolitik would come back to haunt Standard's executives.[39]

Stresses and strains bombarded Harry at his London office during the two years before the United States officially joined the war. Convoying slowed shipments to a crawl, and—eager to conserve their dollar reserves—the British and French pivoted to drawing as much crude as they could from the Middle East instead of the Gulf and South America. What oil Harry could import into the United Kingdom was indeed taken over by a new Petroleum Board that consolidated all stocks into a single rationed distribution stream. Across the British countryside, brand-name petrol pumps were painted over dark green and relabeled "POOL."[40] Then the Blitzkrieg and Italy's entrance into the war gobbled up much of what was left of Standard's stockpiles and refineries on the continent. Harry and the other members of his reduced London staff worried about their own physical safety, the fate of their personal assets in Britain, and the future of their careers and company. As Luftwaffe raiders began slicing through the skies overhead, they scrambled to make backup copies of the company books in case the originals were destroyed. One firebomb crashed through their office's elevator shaft. Others nicked Harry's Surrey manor and the fairways at his golf club.[41]

But by other measures Standard's business thrived. Aviation gasoline cost the company only seven cents per gallon to make, but it was selling for twenty. The closing of the Mediterranean to Allied shipping ultimately sent the British government back to the Western Hemisphere for its oil, and the US defense buildup and the beginning of Lend-Lease led to yet more lucrative contracts. The company's refineries were soon breaking records with their crude runs, and the value of its stock soared. Standard's subsidiaries, moreover, continued to supply German and Italian airlines in South America, neutral territories with Axis connections, including the Atlantic island chains of Spain and Portugal, and Japan. "It is not within the province of a private company to constitute itself as judge on the rights and wrongs of international disputes," the company's leaders rationalized to shareholders. Standard's executives had steered their business assets through many wars before and failed to see why they should approach the coming one any differently.[42]

But the Japanese attacks in the Pacific, and subsequently the US entrance into the war, opened Jersey Standard up to a host of new perils. The capture of Southeast Asia consumed the extensive property of Standard's Far East subsidiary Stanvac—storage tanks, deepwater terminals, wells, and other installations that added up to the largest single direct American investment in that part of the world. Nine of the company's American employees died during the retreat from Burma, and hundreds more would be interned. With US ships engaged in open war in the Atlantic, U-boats also began to take a heavy toll on Standard's tankers, in time sinking ninety-three vessels, more than half the company's prewar fleet, including the MS *Harry G. Seidel*, which was torpedoed off the coast of Venezuela. And by spring 1942 another danger stalked the boardrooms of Harry and his colleagues: government oversight.[43]

The Truman committee did not dwell for long on Jersey Standard's collusion with IG Farben—they had other corporate fish to fry—but their findings caught the attention of a group of progressive senators, including Homer T. Bone, the Washington state Democrat who chaired the Senate's Committee on Patents. Vowing to get to the bottom of Standard's apparent manipulation of patent law, Bone opened a new and more extensive round of hearings on April 13. "Total war does not give us time to dicker with totalitarian corporate empires at home," Senator Robert La Follette, Jr., blasted in his opening statement, and "the people are not in a frame of mind to be gentle with industrial treason at home while American boys die on battlefields scattered all over the globe." It almost seemed, he jabbed, like "they regard this war as an annoying interruption to their Fascist economic alliances." Besieged by angry letters from the public, the normally hands-off John D. Rockefeller, Jr., implored Jersey Standard's directors to do something to salvage the company's reputation. Corporate spokesmen denied the charges in mailings and at forums for concerned citizens, but nothing quelled the outrage. In early June so many people showed up to the annual shareholders meeting that it had to be relocated outdoors. Three weeks later, as William Farish prepared for another grueling round of testimony in Washington, Harry arrived from London.[44]

Tempers flared as soon as the Standard Oil executives reached Room 135 of the Senate office building on August 19. "I did not like the tone of your telegrams to me," Senator Bone warned Farish. "I am fed up on big outfits like yours indicating to the public that Congress is trying to ride them. . . . You are one of the biggest corporations in the world."[45]

But Farish pressed forward with his claim that the case against his company was "a jerry-built house." Jersey Standard's executives "have not for one single minute forgotten that the lifelong policy of every American is first, last, and always to put almighty America above any consideration of the almighty dollar."

"Let me stop you right there," Senator Bone interjected. If that was the case, he wondered, then why did it take a consent degree from the courts to force Standard's cooperation with the war effort?[46]

"Others have read into cold legal documents motives which were not there," Farish contended. He tried to explain that this whole matter had started long ago with fears that the oil was running out. He tried bromides: "Since the days of the first Yankee Clippers, Americans have roamed the four corners of the earth, bringing back to this great country of ours new products. . . . We employees of the Standard Oil Co. are proud to be a part of that American tradition." And he pleaded: "We are human beings. In 1927 we could not foresee 1942." But, he added quickly, the company would have done the same thing all over again, because its relationship with Farben had yielded "revolutionary" innovations for making aviation gasoline, TNT ingredients, and Buna-S rubber.[47]

Farish brought forward members of Standard's research and development team to dazzle the committee with technological sideshows. When the senators tried to circle the testimony back to their own concerns, Standard's executives stalled and dodged. They didn't recall some of the things the senators wanted to know. Other things they waved away as too complicated for the senators to understand. At times their sleight of hand appeared effective. No one questioned it when Farish and his vice president, Robert T. Haslam, boasted about how the company selflessly blew up its multimillion-dollar installations on Sumatra to keep them out of the hands of the Japanese but neglected to mention that the destruction had actually been ordered and carried out by Dutch demolition teams. Yet at other times, their claims beggared belief. Asked to explain why, even in November 1938, the company still proceeded with plans to build a hydrogenation and catalytic cracking plant in the Third Reich, Haslam preposterously claimed that at that time—the same month the US ambassador to Germany had been recalled—"the atmosphere was distinctly one of commerce and peace."[48]

What could Standard's directors say? The evidence pointed to only three plausible explanations for the decisions they had made. Either they had been outwitted by savvier competitors, or they had acted unencumbered by moral conscience and patriotic obligation, or they were willing contributors to the Nazi agenda.

Jersey Standard's chairman, Walter Teagle, had enjoyed a cordial relationship with Franklin Roosevelt since the start of Europe's war. As a sign of friendship, the oil man, who was an avid outdoorsman, periodically sent the president pheasants he shot at his hunting lodge in upstate New York. Roosevelt, who had appointed Teagle to the National War Labor Board and brushed away his offer of resignation in March 1942 when Standard's patent troubles began, enjoyed these gifts. He liked to keep the game birds largely to himself, eating them one at a time, sparing only enough for cold leftovers with bacon and bread sauce the next morning. But when another half-dozen Dutchess County specimens arrived at the White House some weeks after the Patents Committee concluded its hearings, Roosevelt did not reply as usual. He still appreciated receiving the pheasants, his personal secretary explained on his behalf, but thought it best if in the future Teagle addressed them to an intermediary rather than the president himself.[49]

That fall, Teagle resigned from the National War Labor Board and stepped down as Jersey Standard's chairman. Harry's mentor, E. J. Sadler, also abruptly retired. Rumors that the departures were related to fallout from the company's collaboration with IG Farben were "without foundation," company spokesmen insisted. Days later, William Farish died suddenly of a heart attack.[50]

After Farish's funeral, Harry made plans to return to London by Pan Am clipper. The Allied invasion of North Africa had sent oil demand skyrocketing. Petroleum products would soon account for two out of every three tons of cargo shipped from the United States. And under new leadership, Jersey Standard would hit upon an effective way to repair its image. US wartime industrial output, which rose to almost four times greater than that of the Third Reich by 1943, had been made possible by massive public funding, the work of the military's technical and planning bureaus, and the coordinating efforts of the War Production Board and other federal agencies. The American government would in fact spend more than double what private companies invested in wartime manufacturing. But Jersey Standard and other corporations hostile to the public sector would bury these details—and their own strained history with the government—by simply taking credit for the nation's production miracle themselves. Standard's international collaborations had led to the wondrous new products proofing the military's gear against fire, ice, water, rust, and rot, the company's spokesmen repeated again and again. They had pioneered the greases and gasolines that made guns aim straighter, tanks and trucks run faster, and planes fly higher and farther. "Enterprising and aggressive American industry laid the foundations for this nation's ultimately surpassing strength in war," championed one publicity pamphlet, echoing the pro-business narrative that would soon become common, unquestioned wisdom, paving the way to a rollback of government regulation and labor gains after the war.[51]

In Europe, IG Farben's directors were keeping close watch on this campaign to rehabilitate Standard's reputation. They worried: what if Hitler came to believe the oil men's claim that they had gained valuable knowledge from Germany's chemists? Farben's scientists had delivered the cutting-edge synthetics that eased the Reich's dependence on foreign oil and rubber and made its wars of conquest possible. And now—as the company's directors were overseeing a new slave labor camp to serve its Buna Works chemical complex within sight and smell of the smokestacks of Birkenau—who could doubt that Farben had fully committed to the Führer's agenda? The guards hired to manage Farben's plant were plucking inmates from nearby Auschwitz and feeding them a starvation diet, figuring they could live off their own fat for three months before dying. "'You . . . you . . . you and you . . .' They pointed a finger, as though choosing cattle or merchandise," Elie Wiesel recalled of his time at the camp. "I was a body. Perhaps less than that even: a starved stomach." When prisoners grew too weak to work or too incapacitated by the guards' frequent beatings, IG Farben provided the poisonous chemicals to murder them, too.[52]

Still, just in case members of the company's staff were approached by Nazi authorities about their relationship with Jersey Standard, August von Knieriem, one of Farben's top contract negotiators, circulated a memo. From the Americans, he explained, they had received "many very valuable contributions for the synthesis and improvement of motor fuels and lubricating oils," including knowledge about a new method of iso-octane production, the benefits of tetraethyl-lead fuel additives, the workings of large-scale polymerization processes, techniques to prevent oxidation, and more. This know-how had enabled them to be "fully prepared" for war. By contrast, they had passed no technical information about Buna-S to Jersey Standard. "Hardly anything was given to the Americans, while we gained a lot," von Knieriem concluded. "With regards and Heil Hitler!"[53]

19

Dangerous Acts

IT'S NOT CLEAR WHAT HAPPENED to the family members Tamara left behind in Ukraine's Poltava Oblast—including her grandmother, who had cowered in that haystack with her while bandits ransacked Sorochyntsi and who Tamara credited as the greatest influence in her life. But by 1942 most traces of Tamara's childhood world, even those that had survived the revolution and civil war, had been stamped out. Collectivization, Terror-Famine, the Great Purge: Stalin's systematic transformation of the region had been so deadly and traumatic that when Hitler's forces stormed the border, some sorely mistaken crowds welcomed the change of power. Little more than ninety days after the invasion began, Romanian forces were battering their way into Tamara's birthplace, Odesa, and the Wehrmacht had crashed across the Dnipro River. "GERMAN ARMIES ENTER KIEV, TAKE POLTAVA," screamed one *New York Times* front page headline above a map with arrows swooping over the village of Tamara's grandmother. A number of Sorochyntsi's inhabitants joined a resistance movement code-named "Victory" and took to the woods with plans to sabotage and ambush enemy installations. But Field Marshal Walter von Reichenau lost no time ordering brutal reprisals against civilians, singling out Jewish inhabitants in Sorochyntsi and other villages to be shot, hung, or burned alive in their homes. Vague, unverified, but bone-chilling reports of systematic slaughter across the region trickled back into New York and began to make the inside pages of local newspapers.[1]

Stalin's pact with Hitler in August 1939 had turned the world upside down for leftist, Russian-speaking New Yorkers like Tamara, but the Nazi invasion of the USSR in June 1941, though heartbreaking and tragic, put the world ideologically right side up again. Once the Soviets joined the Allies Tamara threw herself into singing at benefit concerts and on radio programs for Russian War Relief, a group that raised more than $9.3 million for food, seeds, medicine, and other donations for the Soviet people.[2] Although it had been years since the popular song's release, audiences still knew her as the "'Smoke Gets in Your Eyes' girl." There was something about its composition, ranging from throbbing low notes to trilling high octaves, and the way her voice tripped across its lyrics, that brought tears to eyes and lumps to throats, unleashing upon listeners all at once heartrending sorrow and spine-tingling joy, dragging them across a full scale of emotions Americans were not yet too far removed from Victorian sentimentality to feel. That song "has been haunting me for years," Tamara admitted to one interviewer. "What do people think? That I must coast forever on the singing of one song?"[3]

By late 1942, in fact, she included in her repertoire, set to piano accompaniment or while strumming her own guitar, some 150 Broadway ballads and jazz standards as well as songs in French, Spanish, and Russian. "Please understand I am not a coloratura soprano, or a dramatic soprano . . . nor an opera star of any kind," she explained to one inquiring reporter. "I sing ballads and folk songs, in a very simple way." Such music, by and for the people, leftists like Tamara believed, had extraordinary powers of persuasion. "Songs have been the not-so-secret weapon behind every fight for freedom, every struggle against injustice and bigotry," ventured Tamara's contemporary, the lyricist Yip Harburg. Because "a book, a play, a painting must be sought," he explained, but the song "seeks you."[4]

Audiences would have grasped immediately the antifascist aesthetics at the heart of Tamara's performances. When she sang "The Last Time I Saw Paris," "In an Old Dutch Garden," or "A Nightingale Sang in Berkeley Square," they would have recognized those as nostalgic tributes to places besieged by the Nazis. Tamara did not sing patriotic tunes like "Remember Pearl Harbor." Instead she chose compositions that brought international alliances to life—the melody "As Time Goes By," revived by that year's film *Casablanca*, the Red Army anthem "Song of the Plains." When she slipped between English and other languages, it didn't matter if listeners couldn't understand all the lyrics. Perhaps it was better if they didn't. By feeling out a song's meaning, they would stretch their sympathies beyond linguistic limits. They would discover the universal transcendence of love, loss, hope, and resolve—the leitmotifs in Tamara's sets. In a world ruled by hatred, it took bravery to love freely, to survive separation, and to seek a better day. The songs Tamara chose—"I'll Follow My Secret Heart," "I'll See You Again," "I'm a Dreamer, Aren't We All," "Love Is Love, Anywhere"—asked listeners to search inside for compassion, to consider what it was they had committed to, and what they were willing to lay down their life for.[5]

Tamara would be one of the first Americans to volunteer to travel into the line of fire with the newly created USO-Camp Shows, Inc., which would send entertainers to troop encampments around the world. This war, after all, was hardly the exclusive business of men. Hundreds of thousands of women served in combat roles on all sides and in every theater. Others risked their lives as resistance fighters, frontline nurses, foreign correspondents, and spies. Indeed, in a conflict that would kill more civilians than uniformed personnel, mothers, sisters, and daughters endured more than their usual share of violence, in the path of invading armies, under the onslaught of bombs, even at times at the hands of their own soldiers. This *was* a women's war, and the songs Tamara sang evoked the promise of men and women fighting it together.[6]

Yet cutting against Tamara's message was a powerful, alternative sexual politics that would be seized upon by American wartime administrators. Agencies like the USO and the Office of War Information dismissed "tearjerkers" or "sob songs" like the ones Tamara sang as deflating. Instead, they wanted uplifting music and other entertainment to wow allies, invigorate workers, and rouse the troops. Their vision for the war effort was not of men and women fighting together, but of "boys" fighting *for* "girls." Boys—good, wholesome but virile boys—would risk their lives for rosy cheeks, bright smiles, and shapely legs. Girls—patriotic, dutiful girls—would transform themselves into these objects of desire, these rewards promised.[7] Girl-next-door types were to be rationed out like so many of the nation's other strategic resources. They would distract GIs from taboo pursuits like prostitution and sodomy, or temptations to commit sexual assault. Signing up to boost "morale," one of Americans' central wartime obsessions, and posing as simply "something from home," women like Tamara found themselves enlisted in the ironic work of obscuring their own presence in the war's landscape.[8]

Trouble started as soon as conscripts began to pour into the nation's hastily expanded network of training centers in late 1940. When Congress passed the Selective Training and Service Act that September, conservative members blocked a proposal to include funding for troop entertainment. Only the summer before, after all, they had voted to end the Federal Theatre Project and had no interest in reviving government-sponsored arts, which to them smacked of communism. But with no recreation organized for soldiers after long days marching or scaling barricades, a rising tide of discontent infiltrated the barracks. Unchecked, the souring mood threatened to unleash widespread incidents of insubordination, desertion, even mutiny. Young men would risk their lives for their country, Edgar Snow concluded after touring the unhappy camps, they just "didn't want to be bored to death."[9]

To raise spirits, some base commanders gave their charges license to find their own fun in their off-hours, looking the other way as troops drank, gambled, plastered their bunks with pin-up pictures, hired their own burlesque dancers, and besieged nearby towns in search of any kind of good time. Tamara's midtown neighborhood quickly emerged as one of the nation's most "over-loaded areas," as rowdy soldiers and sailors on leave from New York harbor's receiving ships or training camps on the city's outskirts descended on Manhattan's bars and dance halls. To military authorities—who had made heterosexuality a prerequisite for service—allowing troops the leeway to cut loose and pursue women promised to forge an aggressive, red-blooded fighting force. But the specter of GIs carousing, fighting, and harassing women quickly unleashed its own set of complaints from aggravated civilians and morally outraged chaplains. How long would the public support the draft if the nation's troops earned a reputation as drunkards, misfits, and lotharios?[10]

War Department officials and civic groups scrambled for a solution during 1941. Other armed forces around the world—those defending their homes from invaders or indoctrinated with fascist or communist ideologies—had ready wellsprings to tap for their drive and discipline. But what would motivate the citizens of a liberal democratic state? What the nation needed, Henry Stimson posited, was "a spiritual awakening—what we call a morale—which shall make us impregnable to any threat." Armaments are not enough, he argued, "unless they are backed and inspired by the invincible spirit of the human soul." Seizing on the miracle promise of morale building, war planners set out to find amusements to buck up the troops without resorting to government-run entertainment programs, which conservatives opposed, and all the while simultaneously reassuring GIs' loved ones that military service would not corrupt their sons and husbands. Maybe it was the "business of government in Nazi Germany, Communist Russia, and Fascist Italy," ventured the Republican scion Thomas E. Dewey, but "the private life and the religious guidance of our boys are not a government function in a free country." Thus entered the United Service Organizations (USO), an umbrella agency that combined the resources of the YMCA, Salvation Army, and other civilian welfare groups determined to fortify troops with off-duty recreation and small comforts. With Dewey as chairman—then succeeded by Prescott Bush—the USO established a chain of hundreds of recreation clubs across the Western Hemisphere, offering servicemen "a home away from home" and "wholesome co-ed activities" overseen by carefully vetted hostesses.[11]

In Manhattan, Tamara and many of her colleagues, including her former director Billy Rose and her *Roberta* costar Bob Hope, were also exploring ways to provide professional entertainment to troops with the help of groups like the Friends of New York State Soldiers and Sailors and the American Theatre Wing, which would soon open the Stage Door Canteen. That September, Tamara's husband, Erwin, traveled to Washington for a War Department meeting where the nation's leading advertising executives discussed sponsorships for performances at training camps. The following month the government designated a new organization, USO-Camp Shows, Inc., the sole civilian agency authorized to provide entertainment to the armed forces.[12]

Under the direction of the William Morris talent agency's chairman, Abe Lastfogel, the USO-Camp Shows board got to work organizing programs for stateside camps. Yet what kind of entertainment would strike the right note on this so-called Red, White, and Blue Circuit? Programmers found little to recommend when they surveyed the nation's drama offerings. They deemed Anne Nichols's wildly popular play *Abie's Irish Rose* too "controversial" and Lillian Hellman's award-winning *Watch on the Rhine* too "depressing." Others they judged too "censorable," too "subtle," or too "sophisticated." The possibility of Shakespeare they dismissed outright. The average servicemen, they assumed, did not want to puzzle through complex themes or dialogue. Clifford Odets's boxing drama *Golden Boy* might have worked, but they decided it depended too much on production. German and Italian POWs could be ordered to construct the sets—for this they would be offered better seats at performances than the US military's own Black troops—but only so many props could be hauled from camp to camp.[13]

"It must be a fast show, with plenty of thrills and plenty of girls," the promoter George Hamid proposed at one advisory board meeting. The more than two dozen other committee members, all men, were quickly won over to the idea of some kind of all-weather visual spectacle staffed by magicians, acrobats, torch singers, roller skaters, and minstrel players who would invite audience participation but whose acts could be enjoyed even if a microphone failed. One early troupe dubbed "Happy-Go-Lucky" had the elements they would look for: a master of ceremonies with impeccable timing, three identically dressed sisters—one blonde, one brunette, one redhead—who made "an eye-filling combination," a surefire comedy team, some tap dancers, a foot juggler who had played the Palace in New York and the Palladium in London, and a percussionist in blackface and a baker's costume who did an unusual routine with drumsticks. To launch this vaudeville revival, which would be billed as "the largest circuit of theatres in the history of the world," they would need to budget, the planners reminded themselves. Except of course for the girls, because girls' salaries were "minimum."[14]

Young women would indeed fill the ranks of Camp Shows units, especially as the draft claimed growing numbers of male entertainers. These were showbiz people plucked from combo houses, nightclubs, circuses, and summer stock theaters—eccentrics, exotics, long viewed in more conservative quarters as socially and sexually suspect. But rebranded by the USO as "a delicately fashioned package of goodies," or "an eyeful of prancing cuties," they suddenly became fresh, all-American girls.[15]

This fiction took on even greater power as Abe Lastfogel began sending Camp Shows overseas. A handful of troupes had made short trips to Caribbean defense installations and other Western Hemisphere bases, but in the United Kingdom, the Middle East, and farther afield only Britain's Entertainment National Services Association was staging reliable productions for Allied forces as late as the end of 1942. And these shows, emceed by hosts "as old as Ichabod Crane," observers reported back, just didn't "go over" with American audiences. "The English talking act is dangerous, as far as entertainment value is concerned," one confidant warned. Lastfogel set out to recruit several dozen troupes for the USO's first full winter program on the so-called Foxhole Circuit, which by 1945 would send 5,424 performers to forty-two countries.[16]

Committing to an overseas tour asked so much more of volunteers than playing camps stateside. Recruits had to clear their schedules for months and prepare to depart for parts unknown in exchange for only a fraction of commercial pay. Subject to military rules and the hazards of combat areas, they had no say over routes, schedules, transport, or accommodations.[17] It was an open secret, moreover, that one of the most harrowing aspects of women's service would be managing the constant advances and harassment from the men they had been sent to entertain. Base commanders quickly learned to assign armed MPs to guard female visitors just so they could move around, sleep, and shower in peace. Yet nothing stopped those officers who tried to exploit the rank, or the wolf-whistlers and cat-callers who pushed their way toward the stage. Still that disembodied voice would inevitably rise up to interrupt the show.

"Take it off!"[18]

Abe Lastfogel knew that persuasion would be needed to engage talent for this special task—and that he would have better luck finding it in New York than in Hollywood, because screen actors were beholden to studio contracts and often regarded vaudeville-style variety acts as beneath them. "Entertainment is urgently required at offshore bases," he wrote in a personal appeal to 160 prominent stage actors, singers, and other artists in late 1942. It was "vitally important to the morale of our men," he explained, and "gives you an opportunity to serve your country in a manner second only to the men in uniform." Advertising campaigns in the entertainment industry's premier magazine *Variety* followed. "America Needs an Overseas Army of Soldiers in Greasepaint Now!" one notice screamed. Who was willing to follow "American boys" to the "North African wastes, or the New Guinea jungles, or the bleak Aleutians"?[19]

Tamara volunteered with the first wave of recruits. By the start of 1943 she had been assigned to the USO's Overseas Unit #34, bound for ten weeks in Great Britain, performing for Allied forces and factory workers and with arrangements for a broadcast to BBC listeners around the world, followed by further engagements in North Africa, for a total of up to four months of service in all. Only one troupe so far had completed this demanding itinerary, a group of four women, Carole Landis, Mitzi Mayfair, Kay Francis, and Martha Raye. They had spent a tense night in Bermuda while drunk airmen tried to break into their hotel room, made an emergency landing in England after their plane caught fire, and traveled by blacked-out country roads, performing as many as five shows a day, on makeshift stages or truck beds, in downpours or by torch light. Crossing the Mediterranean by Flying Fortress, gunners at the ready, they repeated their routines in the Sahara Desert, subsisting on Spam sandwiches, washing up out of a helmet, living out of a bag. Junkers attacked one of their transports, and during bombing raids in Algiers an explosion threw Carole Landis—still recovering from an

Martha Raye performing in North Africa for USO-Camp Shows. Margaret Bourke-White/The LIFE Picture Collection/Shutterstock.

emergency appendectomy—clear across the room. "Holy Moses, what did we get ourselves into?" Martha Raye wondered aloud. They made it back safely to the United States. But thirty-seven other entertainers who followed them on the Foxhole Circuit would not.[20]

Tamara knew the risks and hardships she had signed up for. On February 17, 1943, *Variety* published a detailed chronicle of Martha Raye's and her troupe mates' overseas tour. Each had been ordered home by doctors after they " 'cracked up' under the ordeal," they confessed. But they swore they would do it all over again. Four days later Tamara boarded the *Yankee Clipper*.[21]

20

The Charter Offer

"WE CHALLENGE ANY ONE TO produce a shred of evidence to show that we have not always been loyal citizens of the United States," Manuel and Marcelino dared the *New York Herald Tribune*'s readers. Arraigned and released on bail, the two shipping agents moved quickly to "quash the unwarranted rumors" that they had tried to smuggle oil, silk, and other strategic materials aboard the *Isla de Tenerife* only days after the bombing of Pearl Harbor. In open letters to New York newspapers they decried their "unjust arrest" and bewailed that the mishap had cost them the Chilean Line account as well as "untold damage" to their fine reputations, earned, said Marcelino, by "years of hard work and straight living." They demanded that the Justice Department return their fingerprint records and loudly promised to open their files to investigators' scrutiny—"as broad and as deep as you desire." But not before their lawyers first spent days vetting those records. Quietly, they assured Franco's regime that reports on the incident were "totally wrong" and gave up the names of two crew members they believed had informed on them.[1]

It had all been a mistake, they argued. The oil and cable were intended for the use of the company's many other vessels; the silk, they explained, was merely decorative fabric for the shipowner Juan March's Majorcan mansion. When questioned by government agents, the *Tenerife*'s captain professed ignorance about the firm's business dealings: "I don't know just what is aboard," he dissembled. The ship's supplier painted himself as a "babe in the woods" trying to understand the complicated export rules of the port of New York. "When you come down to the facts," the Spaniards' defense counsel argued, the stockpile on the *Tenerife* amounted to only "a small matter," blown up into something sensational by the overactive imaginations of government bureaucrats.[2]

But US prosecutors stood fast, believing that "ample evidence" existed against Manuel and Marcelino. Privately the defendants' lawyers agreed. Given that there was "little doubt" that laws had been violated and the government might demand the forfeiture of the boat, they urged their clients to involve the Spanish ambassador.[3] American officials, after all, wanted desperately to forestall Spain's entry into the war on the side of the Axis due to its location. If Spain went, so too would go Portugal and Gibraltar. If Gibraltar fell, then the British station in Malta would also be doomed and, with it, Allied shipping in the western Mediterranean. Unimpeded Nazi access to Spain as well as its West African colonies would also extend the range of German submarines and bombers. Allied strategists worried most about the Azores, Canaries, and Cape Verde Islands, "outposts of the New World," President Roosevelt called them, less than a dozen hours' flight away and a "springboard for actual attack."[4]

After speaking with Manuel, Ambassador Juan Francisco de Cárdenas cautioned US officials that taking action against Spanish ships and their agents threatened "friendly relations" between the two nations. It was a bluff. Spain depended on American oil and other exports for basic subsistence. But the note piqued Allied fears about the fate of the Iberian Peninsula. British leaders were especially serious about appeasing Franco's regime, which many of them had favored during the Spanish Civil War because it posed less of a threat to British investments in the region, and they had an interest in placating Juan March personally, because they were secretly using him to bribe Spanish military officers. Foreign Office personnel pressed upon their State Department counterparts that they were "anxious to settle" the *Tenerife* case and stop the "personal attacks" against Manuel, Marcelino, and Juan March. American diplomats agreed that seizing the vessel "at this moment would lead to embarrassing questions." Assistant Secretary of State Breckinridge Long convinced the attorney general's office that a "compromise" was "desirable from the point of view of international relations" as well as State Department "interests."[5]

The *Tenerife*'s captain and supplier got off with pleas of *nolo contendere* and nominal fines, which Manuel's firm promptly covered. The Compañía Trasmediterránea paid $20,000 and kept its boat. Manuel and his partner escaped charges completely after a grand jury failed to indict them. Brooklyn's *España Libre* raged about the acquittal of these "two great traitors." Of course the oil was going to Hitler, the newspaper's editors huffed: "The whole world knows that they were guilty." Privately, one of the investigating customs agents remained "sure something was crooked in this set-up" and "firmly convinced" that Manuel's and Marcelino's ships rendezvoused with submarines in the Antilles and Canaries. J. Edgar Hoover reassured Assistant Secretary of State Adolf Berle that an FBI investigation into the two men's business was still "pending."[6]

That January, American authorities remained wholly unprepared for the war about to come crashing down on their shores. As Manuel and Marcelino put behind their brush with the law and set about repairing their reputations, the Kriegsmarine's Admiral Karl Dönitz commenced Operation Drumbeat. Waves of U-boats, weighted with torpedoes, sped from the Bay of Biscay for the Atlantic Seaboard. To their happy surprise, the crews found US coastal waters thick with tankers, freighters, and other cargo vessels, yet with no convoy system or regular air patrols to protect them. Aided by a superior intelligence operation as well as the undimmed lights of seaside communities, they torched hundreds of boats up and down the East Coast even within sight of beachgoers. By mid-1942, when Allied shipping losses surpassed that of any other month during the war, the waters off New York had grown too dangerous even for neutral vessels. Manuel's ships temporarily rerouted to Baltimore.[7]

Warnings about Spanish collaboration with the Axis trickled into Washington. Manuel's South American Line was suspected of trafficking in silk, cocaine, platinum, and other contraband bound for Germany, informed one agent from Montevideo. Spanish sailors signaling to German U-boats was a matter of "gravest import," urged another. By many accounts the Latin American branches of Garcia & Diaz served as meeting points for fascist sympathizers.[8] Along the Brooklyn waterfront, too, Falangist activities were growing "so noticeable" that other seamen wondered why they hadn't been shut down. Not least because of the operations of Manuel's company, the *New Republic* warned, New York had become a "nerve-center" for a Spanish network of consuls, shippers, and others who had "taken over much of the burden of German and Japanese fifth-column work" in the Americas. Nevertheless, the decentralized nature of federal record keeping scattered all this information about Manuel and Marcelino across the files of so many government agencies that it would take another year before anyone attempted to collate it.[9]

That summer, as proof of "undesirable activities" by neutral ships mounted, the State Department finally "put the bee on War and Navy."[10]

Thereafter, the Coast Guard declared New York off-limits to Spanish vessels and escorted them to New Orleans, Philadelphia, or Baltimore, where they were searched as a matter of course and often barred from inner harbors. Teams of FBI agents and military intelligence officers quizzed disembarking passengers and sailors seeking shore leave. They detained not only those who "eloquently defended the Nazi regime" but also the frequent swallowers, the shifty eyed, and the smooth talkers who seemed almost too friendly. Inspectors refused entry to one *Magallanes* seaman simply because he looked like he would "sell out his own mother for a few dollars." They likewise paid particular attention to refugees of "non-Jewish appearance," fearing they might be Abwehr agents in disguise.[11] Censors in Bermuda forwarded copies of Garcia & Diaz's Madrid-bound correspondence to American agents, and, back in New York, authorities began intercepting Manuel's mail and the FBI tapped his phones.[12]

Manuel's boats nevertheless continued to steam past critical installations in the Caribbean and unload people and goods in American ports before tacking back to the edges of the Nazi empire. Again and again, Allied observers singled out Spanish ships for suspicious communications; drifting into strategic areas or failures to follow lane routing; unexplained lingering near submarines on the high seas; unapproved stops in Jamaica, Martinique, or Puerto Rico blamed on "engine trouble"; requests for excessive ship's stores or coal and oil loads that exceeded bunker capacities; and a parade of shadowy figures who came aboard at the docks to confer with crewmembers.[13] Some worried about the fact that Manuel's vessels obtained oil at Jersey Standard's refinery on Aruba, which was not subject to US export licensing. Another FBI agent ventured that, in view of Manuel's and Marcelino's "apparent sympathies," their vessels might be used to attack the Panama Canal.[14]

Still Manuel maintained his innocence. Much of what American officials thought they knew about him and his partner derived from vengeful Spanish Republicans, who were out to get them. The main informants in the *Tenerife* case had been the ship's "red Communist" doctor and an unsavory ex-bootlegging Free Frenchman, hardly reliable witnesses. As for the evidence government agents turned up themselves, it was almost always circumstantial: an envelope mysteriously taped to the bottom of a ship bunk, hidden but empty compartments in a bulkhead, crumpled up cryptic notations in the trash cans of abandoned offices. When spies and smugglers were caught red handed at the docks, the number of middlemen who stood between them and the company owners gave Manuel and Marcelino a ready defense, too. Could the agents back in New York really be held responsible for the rare dubious passenger who slipped in with the faraway embarking crowds? For the few bad apples bound to be among the six or seven dozen crewmembers on board each boat? For the simple sailor wanting to secrete small luxuries for friends and family back in suffering Spain? Unable to prove Manuel's complicity in smuggling or espionage operations, federal officials entertained charging him and his partner for falsifying their foreign agent registration statements or for lying to get citizenship, but neither of those approaches produced a strong enough case either.[15]

Allied officials contented themselves with keeping Manuel and other suspected Spaniards under surveillance, theorizing that maybe it was better to know who was out there, plotting against the Allied war effort, than to scoop them up and have them replaced by unknown quantities. British spy trackers for MI-6 turned a number of would-be Axis operatives into double agents before they even departed the Iberian Peninsula for the Western Hemisphere. By pressuring them into relaying false reports to their handlers, they manipulated Spanish collaboration with the Axis into one of the Allies' greatest intelligence weapons.[16]

Improved interrogation procedures at American ports also transformed the arrival of Manuel's ships from a liability into a source of valuable knowledge for the Allies. Cooperative passengers, who had either snuck out of Nazi-controlled areas or who had been allowed to leave through repatriation agreements, appeared before a "Positive Intelligence Board," where they related what they knew about the effects of bombing campaigns, the existence of underground resistance movements, and the location of transportation facilities, factories, fuel dumps, and antiaircraft installations behind enemy lines. Though fearful of retaliation from Franco's regime, Spanish seamen seeking shore leave could also sometimes be coaxed into revealing information about Mediterranean coastal defenses, the condition of submarines encountered on the high seas, or Spain's collaboration with the Nazis. The captain of the *Tenerife* and a radio operator on the *Motomar* seem to have become two such informants.[17]

By fall 1942 Manuel's position was growing increasingly precarious. Before then, the State Department and Britain's Foreign Office had put the brakes on other agencies more eager to rein in Spanish shipping in hopes of placating Franco. But now, as the Allies geared up for their massive offensive in North Africa, those days were numbered. In October, US authorities arrested the *Motomar*'s captain, handyman, and supplier for conspiracy to export platinum. The following month the wife of a Brooklyn janitor went on trial for posing as a German repatriate on board the *Magallanes* in order to deliver rhodium to a Nazi agent.[18]

These latest arrests set off warning bells about Manuel and Marcelino for the Spanish consul in New York, too. "Presumably these owners knew something," he informed Madrid. Franco's government had encouraged Spanish shipping agents and crews to pass intelligence to Madrid but resented smuggling and other activities that did not benefit the regime directly. Whenever state-owned vessels of the Spanish Line ran afoul of American laws, they risked impound fees and strained already tense relations between Spain and the United States. Outwardly, Spanish officials continued to assail the "malicious," "invented," and "false" accusations about their ships, but secretly they were growing weary of the "lamentably frequent" troubles caused by Manuel's and Marcelino's business. The New York consul recalled all the other scandals Manuel and Marcelino had caused in previous years, not least the "monstrous voyage" endured by refugees on the *Navemar*. These two shipping agents, he concluded, threatened Spain's image and delicate economic negotiations with the Roosevelt administration.[19]

It was at this moment, shortly after the Allied landings in North Africa, and as Franco began to sense that his regime's survival in a postwar world might depend on patching up relations with Britain and the United States, that Manuel approached the War Shipping Administration with an offer. He could charter Spanish vessels himself and then lend them to the US government for transatlantic sailings. The War Shipping Administration found the "Diaz proposal" tempting and requested an opinion from the State Department. Policymakers gingerly debated the idea. "Since we believe most Spanish ships are under German influence I personally doubt the outcome, but I don't want to be put in the position of denying the possibility," one hedged. Even as Manuel made his overture to American officials, more evidence of suspicious activity by his vessels was surfacing. Manuel's lawyers were fighting new customs fines against the captains of the *Marqués de Comillas* and the *Magallanes*. From his Cuban villa, the novelist Ernest Hemingway had just alerted authorities that he saw what he believed to be a Spanish ship consorting with a submarine off the coast.[20]

But the Allies needed boats. Every and all kinds of boats. Maybe even ones that had once aided in sinking Allied vessels. American shipyard construction, which had been at a near standstill before the war, had only just groaned to life. Steel shortages continued to check production. For much of the year heavy losses had depleted the Allied merchant fleet faster than dockworkers could add to it. The invasion of North Africa moreover drew off more cargo vessels than originally anticipated, starving other shipping routes of critical traffic. As British food and fuel stocks dwindled to alarmingly low levels, and as the US military build-up in the United Kingdom stagnated, Allied leaders conceded that the invasion of France would have to be postponed yet again. On January 11, 1943, State Department officials responded to the War Shipping Administration. They registered "no objections" to the proposal. Manuel would fly first to Lisbon, and then to Madrid to broker the deal.[21]

Did American officials let Manuel go in order to track his contacts abroad? Did they think they had turned him into an asset? Would he double cross them? On February 2, Secretary of State Cordell Hull sent a confidential telegram to the Lisbon legation briefing staff about the "activities of Manuel Diaz" and the agent's impending arrival by Pan Am clipper. But its contents remain a mystery. The telegram disappeared, ending the paper trail that had preserved Manuel's story, fragment by fragment, in the desk drawers and file cabinets of over a half dozen government bureaucracies.[22]

21

Small Potatoes

THAT FEELING OF BETRAYAL HAD not abated since Frank's "pretty tight squeeze" getting out of Java. He lay the blame for the fall of the East Indies squarely at the feet of American leaders who had not committed enough resources to the region. "President Roosevelt and Washington in general seemed to feel that the situation in Europe was more acute than that in the Pacific," he charged, "so they diverted war supplies to England on lend-lease rather than sending them to the Dutch for cash." Now, he seethed, "for lack of some planes an empire has been lost, and with it such extremely vital commodities as rubber and tin."[1]

As he settled into Melbourne's Hotel Alexander, war felt to Frank more distant than it had in Bandung or on the bullet-chipped deck of the *Janssens*. But not distant enough. Japanese control of Rabaul and the eastern reaches of the Indian Ocean left Australian coastal cities open to frequent bombing. Air raid alarms and blast protections around Melbourne's port and factories hinted that they might soon become targets.[2]

Other Americans who had fled the Japanese advance were turning up and taking army commissions: Standard Oil employees evacuated from Sumatra, businessmen from China and Malaya who knew the region's transportation routes—men, Frank lamented, who had spent "a great part of their lives in the Far East only to have war consume all that they had built up." Frank considered joining the military, too, figuring it had all sorts of jobs he could handle even at his "old age." But he decided that he could "do more good" by continuing his radio broadcasts. Events in Frank's corner of the world had received only elementary coverage on American airwaves before, but surely now they would get their due.[3]

Radio, after all, was a weapon of war. And the world had become a place where some were tortured and killed simply for listening to it. The need to know was so fundamental to the human condition that people craved news, even bad news, even false news. They risked their lives for any narratives that might piece back together a broken universe. Radio seemed poised to make a difference, especially in the Pacific, given its vast ocean distances and less reliable mail service.[4] Already belligerent powers blanketed the region with round-the-clock programming in a dozen languages. Radio Tokyo lured American and Australian audiences with promises of information about POWs. From Sydney and San Francisco, exiles beamed encouragement to the occupied. To build or undermine consensus, to educate or obfuscate, to boost or bust morale, radio had been tasked with it all. The variety of tactics, the contrast between domestic and overseas messaging, fascinated Frank. His own charge would be to invest listeners on the US mainland in the fate of Southeast Asia and Australia. Renting a furnished flat not far from Douglas MacArthur's new Collins Street headquarters, he applied for war correspondent credentials and wondered if, as a member of the general's 1928 Olympic team, he might win preferential access to the Southwest Pacific Command. Postponing his wedding plans with Mary Jorzick, he telegrammed her in New York:

> PLEASE TRY UNDERSTAND WONT YOU.[5]

In the Allied world, what could be written or said depended on point of origin, not destination. On the US mainland, publishers and broadcasters complied with voluntary restrictions coordinated by the Office of Censorship, but elsewhere accredited journalists were subject to the rules and whims of local civil and military authorities. MacArthur's theater of war kept notoriously tight control of information, and the Australian prime minister John Curtin's government likewise embraced expansive censorship powers. Frank had to pass his dispatches through both of their offices. This meant not only following commonsense bans on disseminating details of use to the enemy, such as base locations or convoy movements, but also avoiding stories about Australia's internal political conflicts, Americans' bruising defeats in the Netherlands East Indies, and—especially—less than flattering portraits of MacArthur. Despite these constraints, from Australia Frank would be able to air outrage and searing critiques that wouldn't have cleared the censors in the United States, where the National Association of Broadcasters issued regulations banning "undue excitement" or "editorializing" in news programs. He would be able to pillory leaders in Washington and London, because it suited the agendas of Curtin and MacArthur. Later, when a complaint about one of Frank's reports arrived at the stateside Office of Censorship, its agents admitted that they could not stop rebroadcast, because it had "originated outside the country" and passed Southwest Pacific Command censorship.[6]

The US Army outfitted Frank and other arriving American correspondents in officers' uniforms, promising access to combat zones, rations, billeting, and compensation in case of capture. Frank stuffed notebooks into the back pocket of his standard-issue trousers, cocked his hat, and surveyed the effect: "we are practically-in-the-army-now." Yet he and the other radio reporters soon realized that they would not make many frontline tours, given their reliance on intercontinental wireless facilities, which were scarce in the Pacific. It was one of the war's great inequalities, Frank's colleague George Weller reflected, that those whose plight would be heard were those who happened to be closest to reliable communication outlets. Frank hunkered down instead in Melbourne with the other broadcasters at a regular restaurant lunch table, dissecting communiqués, studying maps to predict the enemy's next moves, and trying to stick each other with the bill.[7]

Emboldened by their stunning string of victories, Japanese leaders were indeed contemplating a number of possibilities: consolidating their hold on Burma (Rangoon had fallen forty-eight hours after the surrender of Java); joining forces with the Germans to run the British out of India; seizing New Caledonia, Fiji, and Samoa to cut off United States access to the South Pacific; or capturing the Australian territory of Papua as a prelude to an invasion of Australia itself. Repeated bombardments of Papua's capital, Port Moresby, just across the Coral Sea from Queensland, reminded Frank of the "softening up measures" the Japanese had used before landing operations on Java.[8]

Should a southward advance come, Australia was woefully unprepared. The commonwealth's best pilots and army units were tied up in the Middle East or had been captured in Malaya and the East Indies. Only half of its home guard had been called up for duty, and, as Frank correctly assessed, its members lacked the equipment or training "necessary to stand off the Japanese War Machine." Some 25,000 American uniformed personnel had arrived, but no tank or infantry divisions. That March, fewer than one hundred operational planes and 7,000 combat-tested troops could be found on the entire continent. What supplies and forces were available could not be moved quickly across Australia's vast expanses, which were serviced by few all-weather roads and trains that ran on tracks of different gauges.[9]

Some reporters tried to put a positive spin on the situation, taking heart from the arrival of such a high-profile general as MacArthur and celebrating that the Yankees had come to help "boot back to his own land the little yellow man who is trying to move in on a white man's country." But Frank had made that mistake before. He feared he would soon be "reporting the same sad train of events that preceded the fall of Malaya and the Netherlands Indies." When it was his turn to go on the air at the Australian Broadcasting Corporation studio, he splayed his typed and censor-stamped transcripts on the transmission desk, adjusted his earphones, and stood by for the go-ahead signal from San Francisco.[10]

> March 24: The Japanese continue to hammer Port Moresby, in New Guinea. . . . The flow of supplies must be stepped up, for behind the offense, when it starts, must be all that will be required to chase the Japanese back to their own distant islands and that, as the situation now stands, is a long way. A VERY long way.

Few ties had linked the United States and Australia before the war, but now propagandists touted the alliance as a natural one between two "pioneer people," who both believed in sports, hard work, plain facts, and personal freedom. Nevertheless, Frank found the land down under a "strange place" with backwards seasons and curious obsessions. Cars rumbled down the streets with charcoal burners strapped to their backs—a concession to gasoline rationing—and women faced hosiery shortages by flitting down the sidewalks with bare legs. That part, of course, Frank was quick to point out, didn't bother him at all. But there was too much mutton at restaurants, too many Sunday closures, and too many tea breaks when so much work had to be done. "We cannot afford the pleasant democratic pastime of prolonged discussions," he argued. The Allied effort needed "less talking and more clean cut management."[11]

In April, as Allied defenses in Burma crumbled, Frank often went on the air at two or three o'clock in the morning so that his commentary could be heard in the States during waking hours. He worried about supply shortages. Substantial Lend-Lease shipments, coming from thousands of miles away,

Frank broadcasting from Australia. Courtesy of Michael Safranek/University Archives, The University of Iowa Libraries.

would not appear until the second half of 1942, so defense planners scavenged what they could find locally. Nearly a quarter of the stock procured that year by the US military in Australia would come from rerouted "refugee cargoes" auctioned at cost, including boatloads of goods Frank had ordered on behalf of Kian Gwan for shipment to Batavia before war consumed Java. But equipment losses continued to outpace replacements, and planes sat grounded awaiting repairs. "It is going to take a lot more of a lot of things," Frank cautioned listeners. Armies lived and died not by a few publicized convoys but by continuous, dependable streams of materiel. "Not even MacArthur," he told them, could "fashion an airplane out of a wheelbarrow."[12]

By the end of the month, the Yenangyaung oil fields in Burma had been destroyed, Lashio had fallen, and with it, overland access to China. Japanese planes, serviced by a powerful force of warships lingering in the Bay of Bengal, were bombing India's eastern ports and the Royal Navy's Eastern Fleet, which had to retreat to the Kenyan coast. India stood dangerously vulnerable to invasion, but to Frank's horror, the British colony seemed prepared to offer little more than "fly-swatter resistance," as Gandhi and other nationalists made an "untimely" push for independence. Frank conceded the need for "some reform" on the subcontinent but argued that if partisans continued to squabble about India's future rather than unite in its defense, it would be "handed to the Japanese on a silver platter."[13]

Then suddenly the Japanese fleet disappeared from the Bay of Bengal. This "added some big potatoes to the stew," Frank told his audience, predicting it could "mean but one thing": it was steaming into position for an impending assault on Australia. More heavy air raids on Darwin and Port Moresby reinforced his suspicions. As coast watchers and code breakers detected increased Japanese traffic around Rabaul and in the upper Solomons, Australians hastily evacuated their seaplane base on Tulagi, which the enemy took on May 3. The next day Japanese invasion troops departed Rabaul on transports bound for Port Moresby. Told by Washington leaders to make do with what they had, Allied commanders sacrificed half of the Pacific Fleet's carrier strength to turn the Japanese navy back from the Coral Sea.[14]

That early May success, however, little impressed Frank. He was heart-sick over the simultaneous fall of the Philippines. "The American flag that has flown proudly over the rock of Corregidor has been run down, and in its place now waves the symbol of a new and better prepared power," began Frank's May 7 broadcast, his most acerbic yet. The courageous American and Filipino resisters had been "let down." Frank thought it was "exceedingly difficult to see it otherwise." Why, he asked, had they been left to die of malaria, to grub in the dirt and ration mule meat, when a plane-load of quinine and foodstuffs could have sustained them? Americans in the Pacific, he charged, had been "bamboozled" by the Japanese, who had not lived up to their naval treaties, and then soothed by their own government with "cheering assurances" about coming reinforcements when in fact the region had been relegated to the status of a "side-show." With the enemy's ability to redeploy combat troops from the Philippines and Burma, as well as Gandhi's ongoing "diaper defense," Frank speculated that the Japanese might well attempt invasions of both India and Australia.[15]

Moods were noticeably dipping in Melbourne that May and June as troop and cargo arrivals dropped off abruptly. Newspaper readers cursed every report of US forces headed in the opposite direction to Great Britain and Northern Ireland. Once-friendly exchanges between American personnel and waitresses, hotel porters, and taxi drivers turned to bickering over prices. Americans complained about constant labor strikes and what Frank called a " 'let the other fellow do it' attitude." Locals retorted that their new-found allies were straining the city's housing stock, draining its department store inventories, and driving on the wrong side of the road. Fear and anger peaked when one US private assaulted and murdered three women he had accosted on the city's streets. As more Australian soldiers returned from the Middle East, riots erupted between them and their American counterparts. Censors suppressed most of this from international broadcasts, but when a dispatch from New York relayed that Bob Hope and other American entertainers might visit Australia Frank stressed to his listeners that such a trip would be "exceedingly helpful" for morale.[16]

Frank's campaign against "the high councils in Washington and London" continued. What was it going to take, he despaired, to convince Americans "that there IS a war going on in the Pacific"? By the end of the year, an estimated forty million listeners in the United States would tune into Australian news each day. But what kind of broadcasts would rouse them to action? Frank imagined that if he hit on the right mix of content, the right tone, his words might break through. He mixed straight war updates with economic analysis, encyclopedia-worthy South Pacific history lessons, and kangaroo jokes. But Mutual offered little feedback about his dispatches and the letters he received from listeners in the States came mostly from long-lost friends, "ham poets" in search of publishing advice, or "screwy" girls. "Dear Mr. Cuhel," one woman wrote from Seattle, "I was in the bath tub taking a bath and listening to my little radio when your strong, masculine, determined voice came through. I got so excited that I almost drowned." The contents of domestic American newspapers annoyed Frank, too. When their latest editions reached Australia, he bristled at the prominent coverage of the Soviet front and flipped indignantly through them in search of Pacific news he thought ought to have been on the front page.[17]

In fact, the majority of Americans on the mainland did agree with Frank. By more than a two-to-one margin they favored swift retribution against Japan, the power than had actually attacked the United States, over a second front against Germany. This was especially true on the West Coast, where fears of attack spiked after Japanese troops invaded Alaska's Aleutian Islands at the start of June. Nevertheless, no amount of public polling, or behind-the-scenes pleading from the Southwest Pacific Command or the Australian and Chinese governments, and no amount of on-air lobbying by broadcasters like Frank would shake the high-level decision to focus first on defeating the Nazis. The alliance between the United States, Great Britain, and the Soviet Union depended upon it. Chief of Staff George C. Marshall rebuffed MacArthur's repeated requests to launch ambitious offensives, citing grave shipping shortages and "critical situations elsewhere." To Roosevelt the prospect of diverting resources from the cross-channel build-up to the South

Pacific seemed like "taking up your dishes and going away." There would be no great shift in priorities, the president decided, especially not toward "a lot of islands whose military occupation will not affect the world situation."[18]

But these islands were not a strategic abstraction to the millions who lived there, nor to Frank who had called them home for a decade. His friends were missing, and his old haunts had been overrun. Singapore's Raffles Hotel now catered to visiting German and Italian officers. In Manila, a Japanese flag flew over his former residence, the Army and Navy Club. It would be gutted to its concrete frame by fire and days of hand-to-hand combat before the war was over.[19] Individuals who had managed to escape from these conquered territories were showing up in Melbourne with horror stories of roundups, death marches, and torture. Everywhere the Japanese had torn down statues, renamed cities, and forced residents onto Tokyo's clock and calendar. Loudspeakers in public squares barked out compulsory midday exercises. Young men disappeared on forced labor details never to return. As the occupiers geared local economies to their own needs, kitchen gardens were uprooted for mandatory cotton crops that failed to grow. Imports stopped. Wages sank. Inflation soared. News of dire conditions on Java, which he had seen fall firsthand, bothered Frank the most. "The Japs are over-running the country like locusts, taking everything with food value for their own forces and leaving the populace, in at least some sections, on a starvation ration of dry rice, without fish or any meat," Frank broadcast after conferring with one party of refugees. In time, famine and disease would claim an estimated three million lives on that island alone.[20]

At the heart of the occupation lay an optics of racial retribution. Japanese officers humiliated White residents in front of Asian crowds and forced them to use the inferior facilities to which colonists had segregated people of color before the war. President Roosevelt's Executive Order 9066—setting in motion the forced relocation of 120,000 people of Japanese descent on the US West Coast to inland concentration camps—further incensed Tokyo officials, who retaliated by imprisoning over 130,000 American and European residents across occupied Asia.[21] Some of the deadliest sites, run by the notorious Kenpeitai police force, were camps for women on Java, where beatings and sexual sadism became routine. The 29,000 children imprisoned with them ate bugs to supplement their starvation rations, and when boys reached the age of ten or twelve, they were sent, alone, to separate men's facilities. One military officer who arrived after the war found internees living in dog kennels and overcrowded bamboo barracks. It was, he said, like going to "another world and talking to people who had already died."[22]

Yet for the moment Frank still anticipated that Southeast Asia's old order might one day be resurrected. Learning that the Japanese had opened Batavia's Whites-only Harmony Society to Indonesians, he saw it as a move "designed to depreciate the prestige of Europeans" but assured Americans that "the natives" would not take to their "sudden social elevation." The Javanese, he claimed, had been "quite content and happy to squat on their haunches," gambling and gossiping under the coconut trees "in their simple way." Like many Americans, he misunderstood the degree to which the events of 1942 had unleashed long-pent-up anticolonial nationalism. Under Japanese rule, Indonesians were quickly disabusing themselves of the hope that Japan's call for Asian liberation and "co-prosperity" had ever been sincere, but the war's pain and upset only intensified the cry *Indonesia Merdeka*. Free Indonesia.[23]

Frank felt no better even after victory at the Battle of Midway in early June. "Each enemy reverse brings up the question, 'When will the offensive push from Australia start?'" Where were the supplies hinted at in Washington's incredible production figures? What about those armaments American magazines cheerfully pictured rolling off the assembly lines? Given how many planes US factories reportedly churned out, he griped, "there must be a parking problem in the British Isles for aircraft." If just a fraction of those flyers headed for the Pacific, Frank wagered they could kick the Japanese back home as fast as they had advanced. News of the British loss of Tobruk on the 21st sent him to the edge. There was "something deep and fundamentally wrong" with the United Nations' land campaigns, he charged. Lack of inspiring leadership, "bone-head moves," and sorry excuses had left troops as "mentally licked" as a football team on a losing streak. Where, he growled, were the likes of the Great War's Lost Battalion commander Lieutenant Colonel Charles Whittlesey, who though surrounded in the Argonne Forest refused to run up the white flag? Where was Georges Clemenceau, herding taxicabs full of men to the Marne to halt the German advance on Paris? Or British Field Marshal Edmund Allenby, triumphing against overwhelming odds to beat the Ottoman army in Palestine? "Each one of those men had to find the initiative and resourcefulness that would turn defeat into victory," Frank thundered over the airwaves. "And that is what we need an awful lot of Right Now."[24]

Instead, by July, the Japanese were once again, as Frank put it, "busy as beavers." The invasion force that had been turned back from Port Moresby by the Battle of the Coral Sea instead unloaded men and supplies near Buna on the north coast of Papua. Allied bombers failed to stop the landing as troops under the command of Major General Horii Tomitarō took cover in dense foliage beyond the beaches, sending nearby villagers fleeing for their lives. Buna lay less than forty miles on the opposite shore from Port Moresby, but the Kokoda Trail presented the only route between them—a single-file footpath through putrid tropical undergrowth, across rushing rivers and yawning ravines, and over the peaks of the Owen Stanley Mountains, so steep in places that its slimy footholds had to be scaled on hands and feet. It seemed inconceivable to most observers that the Japanese would try to march an army across this terrain. Only two Australian brigades had been garrisoned at Port Moresby. But Frank, remembering how these soldiers had hacked their way through the supposedly impenetrable wilds of Malaya, worried.[25]

By the end of the month some two thousand well-camouflaged Japanese fighters with machetes and state-of-the-art radios had pressed fifty miles inland, overwhelming a small detachment of the Papuan Infantry Battalion and capturing the airfield at Kokoda, the only place to land a plane between Port Moresby and the northeast coast. Ten thousand troops from the Imperial Army's South Seas Detachment and locals conscripted to haul supplies for them climbed into the mountain mists. In their path stood only small numbers of unseasoned Australian militiamen outfitted in desert khaki, dependent on "biscuit tin" air drops, and tasked with holding their ground long enough for a supply line to push through from Port Moresby. American planes searched out enemy positions while Australian ground reinforcements and Papuan carriers (long deemed by White colonists too backward and warlike to rule themselves) rushed into what one reporter described as a "green and sodden hell." Rations went bad in the damp. Insects swarmed. Boots rotted away from toes. And with synchronized frontal assaults and flanking tactics, Horii's forces pushed the defenders back again and again.[26]

To bring army headquarters closer to the fighting, MacArthur relocated his command to Brisbane, but the Queensland capital had no radio facilities capable of sending signals to San Francisco. Frank and Bill Dunn lobbied unsuccessfully to install transmission facilities on Papua New Guinea. They could move no closer to the action than a rented penthouse apartment in Sydney, where they were left contemplating jungle warfare over weekly Sunday brunch pancakes.[27]

To learn as much as he could, Frank huddled with the masses outside of Sydney's newspaper offices, reading the blackboards, chalked with panicked

Indigenous carriers and Australian soldiers climb the "Golden Stairs" to Imita Ridge on the Kokoda Trail. Australian War Memorial.

headlines. By August Japanese troops had seized the Tanimbar Islands, 350 miles due north of Darwin, and the bombing of northern Australia had intensified, reaching all the way east to Townsville. The *Sun* warned that Horii's forces had covered more than half the Kokoda Trail. Prime Minister Curtin declared that Australia was "in deadly peril." Churchill and Roosevelt "Still Blind to Japs," screamed the *Mirror*.[28]

So many assurances had been made, Frank seethed. So many pledges of help that never came. Instead, it had been eight months of defeats and withdrawals, like a never-ending stream of miniature Dunkirks. Frank detested all the excuses, muttered over and over "while our men were being captured by the thousands." Enticing words had "filled the air and congested the cables," newsreels had bragged of American factories breaking all records, of tanks, planes, and guns pouring into every front. But only to England, he charged, had promises been kept.[29]

And what good had that done? Britain had been at war for almost three years and had lost nearly all of Europe. Rommel's forces were marching toward the Suez Canal. The Soviets were backpeddling before the "sledgehammer blows of the Germans," who seemed poised to capture the oil and grain of the Caucasus. India was "in the throes of internal disorder sponsored by the toga garbed trumpeter of immediate autonomy." And the fraction of American troops who had yet to be fully mustered and trained were dispersed all over the world in defensive postures. Predictions from pundits in the United States that the war might end within the year baffled him. How any "rational thinking person" could glance at a world map and think that was "a complete mystery." Frank believed that concentrating forces against the Japanese "would net the greatest quick dividends" by knocking out the weaker Axis flank. "These are days of great decision," he pronounced into his microphone, "and this country is watching anxiously for the leaders of the United States board of strategy to do SOMETHING."[30]

Though Frank had little patience for the matter, the mobilization of US forces faced unmatched difficulties in the Pacific Theater, given its watery stretches and remote bases, thousands of miles from US ports and lacking even basic infrastructure. Supplying and transporting just fifteen thousand ground combat troops to the region required first deploying double that number of service personnel. As a result, far greater numbers of men and resources had been dispatched to the Pacific than military planners initially budgeted. By June, ad hoc boosts to army troop allotments had brought to Australia and the Pacific more than three hundred thousand men, three-quarters of all GIs and nearly all air combat units stationed outside the Western Hemisphere. This build-up enabled the Joint Chiefs to finally approve a hastily assembled amphibious operation in the Solomon Islands. Intelligence officers had learned that the Japanese were building a landing strip on Guadalcanal, which would confer air superiority over the Coral Sea and the eastern approaches to Australia. On August 7, fourteen thousand US Marines waded ashore on that island and nearby Tulagi to stop them. Frank cheered this "first real offensive move of the United Nations in this part of the world."[31] As the Americans solidified the foothold, his excitement erupted into a battery of sports metaphors:

August 24: I think that it is now safe to admit that we were pretty groggy after the opening rounds of the Pacific war, and our side in

> this area had its back against the ropes. But the forces here now have their feet well spaced and set, the guard is up, and the arms are poised and ready to lash out with crushing blows the moment an opening appears.

The Allies scored another victory the following week when they repulsed an elite Imperial Navy landing force at Milne Bay on the eastern tip of Papua. Underestimating the number of Australian troops guarding the location's valuable airstrip, and setting ashore at the wrong location, the Japanese suffered heavy losses and their first clear land defeat.[32] Frank celebrated as the fighting unfolded.

> September 1: Highly touted Jap jungle fighters have been licked at their own game at long last. And for those who have watched with aching hearts all that happened in Malaya and the Indies, this is mighty sweet news.

Fortunes on the Kokoda Trail soon reversed as well. By September 17, Horii's battalions had advanced within sight of the sea, only thirty miles from Port Moresby. But they were exhausted, menaced by air attacks, tropical diseases, and an overstretched supply line. While Australian divisions stood their ground at Imita Ridge, Horii received orders to fall back. "Now the gloves are off," Frank rejoiced.[33]

By November, survivors of the South Seas Detachment were straggling back across the Kokoda Trail to their original beachheads at Gona and Buna— in shredded uniforms or blankets and rice bags, barefoot, starving, limping, or crawling, and without their leader Horii, who had drowned in a river. Frank wanted to believe that the sudden turn of events portended "the awakening of the allied giant." He switched from boxing to football analogies.[34]

> November 7: The goal posts are in Berlin and Tokio. There will be plenty of time to throw our hats into the air and cheer ourselves hoarse when we get to them and tear them down. In the meantime we need a good many more touch-downs . . . before this game is on ice. This is Frank Cuhel speaking from Australia. I return you now to the Mutual Broadcasting System, in the United States.

The next morning, before dawn on the other side of the world, over one hundred ships disgorged 35,000 US troops onto the beaches of Morocco, the opening foray of a massive, surprise campaign to take French North Africa. Sydney newspapers were still piecing together a picture of Operation Torch three days later when the capital's residents gathered to mark the anniversary of the World War I Armistice. Frank followed the crowds to the Cenotaph in Martin Place. During a moment of silence for Australia's 60,000 Great War dead, he imagined he could hear the roar of guns in North Africa and Papua New Guinea, where sons followed in their fathers' footsteps. Walking away from the scene, he wondered where he would like to be at the end of the "most earth shaking event this world will have known for centuries," this "crusade for the right of all people to hereafter live decently." A newsboy's cries at the street corner snapped him out of his reverie: "Paper, sir, the Germans have landed in Tunisia and marched into unoccupied France." Frank realized that he had let his thoughts run too far ahead. American soldiers had yet to engage German troops face-to-face. Men from his home state of Iowa were likely among those forces clawing for beachheads near Casablanca, Oran, and Algiers.[35]

Frank's euphoria about the sudden better odds in the Pacific also proved short-lived as fighting in the region sank into swamps and stalemate. Along the beaches between Gona and Buna Japanese engineers had built an elaborate network of crawl tunnels, machine gun nests, and bunkers insulated by fast growing plants and sand that absorbed heavy mortar fire. The troops who retreated there from the Kokoda Trail had no intentions of surrendering. Casualties mounted as American and Australian soldiers besieged the fortifications, falling prey to leeches and snipers. Impatient and ignorant of the conditions his men faced, MacArthur pressed them to carry to conclusion what would become one of the deadliest, drawn-out Allied victories of the Pacific War. It took more than two months to reclaim the shoreline, and only after Japanese holdouts were dragged one-by-one from their foxholes and defeated in hand-to-hand combat. It was "coldly animal," reported one Australian correspondent. That kind of resistance surprised Frank. What lay ahead, how long would the war last, if the enemy clung this tenaciously to every postage-stamp-sized patch of sand?[36]

Frank grew increasingly restless. He got into a shouting match with Sydney's censors, who were far more difficult to work with than those in Melbourne. Repeatedly they "chopped to pieces" his reports on the fighting in Papua on flimsy pretexts that they would damage morale in the States. What did these "brass hats" know about what was suitable for radio audiences in the United States? Frank was convinced that complacency—for lack of hard truths—posed a greater threat than the possibility of undermining listeners' confidence with unvarnished coverage. Frank thought that Americans wanted, and could handle, "accurate, frank news," that they were "capable of taking the dirtier side of the war in stride."[37]

More rumors also arrived about the Kenpeitai's "gestapo methods" in occupied territories, and about friends locked up or dead. Members of his "old gang" in Singapore and Batavia, he learned, had been killed during the invasions. His Manila roommate, he heard, had been "caught in Cebu." Other acquaintances from the Philippines had been thrown into the dungeons of Fort Santiago. The reporter William McDougall, who had been with him in Bandung, Frank assumed had been shot by the Japanese. In fact, he was imprisoned on Sumatra, engaged in a constant battle against despair, malnutrition, false hopes, and running sores.[38]

Yet, Frank mourned, leaders in Washington continued to treat the crisis in the Pacific as a "secondary issue." Still they sent no great bomber formations to darken Australia's skies. Instead, they announced that Americans would cede their longstanding extraterritorial rights in China, signaling, Frank thought, "the end of occidental domination in the Far East." The colonial order in which he had thrived, he now saw, was gone. He decided he wanted to be "through with tropical countries forever."[39]

As reports of the North African campaign overtook the front pages, journalists who had flocked Down Under at the beginning of the year began to migrate elsewhere. The *Time* correspondent Robert Sherrod pronounced Australia the "lemon of the newsworld." Gazing at the bridge spanning Sydney harbor from the windows of his penthouse, Frank realized how much he wanted to be near the "main action," someplace where he could "follow things right down to the point where the peace will eventually be signed." He wanted to go to North Africa, a battle zone lauded as a "correspondent's paradise," with freer movement, faster action, and lighter censorship. Maybe events in the Pacific, Frank conceded, did only boil down to "pretty small potatoes."[40]

He telegrammed Mutual's directors asking to proceed to North Africa to cover the Allied advance, on a freelance basis if necessary. They agreed. He made arrangements to island hop to California on military transports. From there he would make his way to New York and catch the Pan Am clipper to Lisbon.[41]

On December 3, Frank hitched a ride out of Australia on a Douglas DC-3 crammed with medical supplies, auxiliary gas tanks, corn flakes, and boxed bananas. Its pilot, Captain John Whitaker, was a 200-pound blue-eyed Marine "who put out a paw as big as a Swift's Premium ham," the kind of man, Frank decided, he'd follow anywhere. It took the whole airstrip to get the craft off the ground. Frank pressed his nose to the window as the engines revved. "Toodlee doo," he said silently to Sydney as the city retreated into the distance.[42]

Frank reached California just before Christmas. It had been five years since he had set foot on the mainland. Crossing the country, he marveled at imposing production plants and homesteads where farmers were getting summer quantities of eggs in the winter by waking up their hens extra early. Like other war correspondents passing through the States between assignments, Frank cycled through receptions, lectures, and other appearances to recount his brushes with death and soak up the hero's welcome.[43]

By the time he reached Manhattan, these publicity stunts began to feel "distasteful," and it did not go well when he explained to his fiancée the "impracticableness of marriage under the present circumstances." Otherwise, Frank was "in fine spirits." He talked his way into a regular staff position with Mutual's executives. Maybe they would eventually choose him to head the prestigious London bureau. He saw "an awfully big future in radio," but he also planned to work for magazines, perhaps even for the *Chicago Tribune*. And he wanted to write a book about the fall of Java. He figured he had "the rest of the boys beat" with his firsthand knowledge of the island from the day Germans marched into the Netherlands right up to his own dramatic escape from Cilacap. He signed on with a literary agent and arranged to have his pay sent to his sister. Use it to buy war bonds—or stocks—he told her, "something that will not be too taxable."[44]

Once the war was over, Frank also predicted a "tremendous expansion" in foreign trade, given the enormous stake the United States had acquired in countries around the world through Lend-Lease arrangements. Maybe he would travel the globe again, giving weekly broadcasts about business and economics. He could include advertising plugs, making "clever references" to Parker pens and other name brands and how they were used in different locations. Maybe he would do that during the summers, and the rest of the year teach commerce at some college. Already he had invitations to speak at various universities. He lunched with his former boss Larry Seymour and the president of Pond's to talk possibilities.[45] The future before him seemed boundless.

22

Acid Test

WHEN BEN ROBERTSON ARRIVED AT the edge of the Thar Desert in late September, members of the US Sixth Ferrying Squadron were screening windows, fixing planes, and building latrines at a camp outside Karachi, the first in a string of bare-bones airbases stretching across upper India and over the Himalayan "Hump" to Kunming. This was China's last lifeline. The monsoon winds were still blowing, the sun shone "like a fiery furnace," and India found itself caught between two major wars. To the east, Japanese forces prowled the colony's hilly frontier with Burma, held in check only by the harshness of the wet season and stubborn resistance fighting by the region's Shan, Chin, Kachin, Naga, and other upland peoples. To the west, panzer divisions had pressed perilously close to the Nile and the Suez Canal, forcing Allied officials to draw up evacuation plans not only for Egypt but also for Iran, now the British Empire's primary source of oil and one of the only reliable routes into the Soviet Union. The stakes for holding India—a main supply base for Allied defenses in the Middle East and a necessary launching point for future counteroffensives against the Japanese—could not have been higher.[1]

The architects of Britain's war effort had asked enormous sacrifices of the empire's crown jewel colony, a sprawling, diverse subcontinent comprising more than a dozen British-controlled provinces and more than five hundred indirectly ruled princely states, home to nearly 400 million people. In 1939, the Viceroy Lord Linlithgow had declared war on India's behalf and deployed its troops to the world's four corners without consulting a single Indian leader. Punjabis and Gurkhas, drawn by a long tradition of military service, as well as other Indian volunteers in need of the food and pay, rallied with Commonwealth troops at Dunkirk and flew in the Battle of Britain. They helped to knock out the Italian Tenth Army in East Africa and reinforced Allied occupation forces in Syria, Iraq, and Iran. They battled the Japanese in Malaya and Burma and now faced Rommel's tanks in the Sahara. More than two million men would serve in the Indian Army. Deploying so many of them abroad had left the colony's own defenses shorthanded.[2]

Britain's war effort had squeezed tremendous resources from India's civilian population as well. Allied supply lines gobbled up the subcontinent's jute, cotton, timber, cement, coal, iron, steel, and grain. Indian factories outfitted the empire's armies with armored cars, ammunition, land mines, mosquito nets, sandbags, and barbed wire. Authorities shipped many of the region's best locomotives and freight cars to Iraq and Russia, hobbling India's already rickety transportation infrastructure. In Bengal, the Raj's most populous province, they commandeered bicycles and cars and evicted hundreds of thousands from their homes for land to build aerodromes. Inflationary policy meanwhile kept the rupee in the thrall of London interests, even as it put more and more basic goods out of reach of the poor and reduced millions to bare subsistence. "Voluntary" war fund collections to help British victims of the Blitz coerced yet more money from those with none to spare.[3]

Would these sacrifices be recognized? Would they prove Indians to be worthy of *swaraj*, home rule? Mohandas Gandhi and other anticolonial activists had dared to hope as much during the last great war when their people had contributed 1.5 million troops and £100 million in taxes to the Allied cause. But even after the Armistice the British conceded only token reforms and greeted even peaceful protest with violence. Stagnating conditions for the masses belied imperialists' professed motives to uplift and enlighten. The Raj's administrators continued to encourage the production of cash crops at the expense of local industry and food cultivation, increasing Indians' dependency on imports, most fatefully rice from Burma. Even small shifts in wages or weather had deadly repercussions. Disease came regularly for Indians young and old: cholera, smallpox, malnutrition, dysentery, parasites, plague. Life expectancy hovered just shy of twenty-seven years of age.[4]

Suspicions that the British Empire could not, or would not, safeguard the wellbeing of its colonial subjects intensified with the return of war. Officials in London kept tight limits on shipping to the subcontinent. Much of the medical aid and other supplies that did arrive under Lend-Lease were regifted onward to Chinese forces. Yet the Government of India had not yet instituted price controls to curb runaway living costs or centralized rationing plans to forestall fuel and food shortages. Indian leaders furiously debated whether or not to support the war effort and on what conditions, but so far their efforts had inched the colony no closer to independence. British agents did what they could to inflame tensions between the region's religious and political factions to keep them divided and routinely hustled the Raj's critics off to jail.[5]

By mid-1942, with the fall of Hong Kong, Singapore, Malaya, and Burma, the British Empire's reputation was in tatters. Refugees from the Japanese advance limped into India with tales of colonial officials' bungled defenses, scorched earth policies, and preferential treatment of Westerners during the retreat. Ominous signs hinted that India's people would soon suffer the same misfortune as Southeast Asians. Anticipating an invasion of coastal Bengal, authorities confiscated or destroyed the region's rice stores as well as some 44,000 boats, incapacitating its trade and fishing industries and setting the stage for famine. In Calcutta, air raid preparations clearly catered to the safety of European residents, and only paltry antiaircraft installations lined the shores. Japanese planes showered the city with leaflets calling for Indians to rise up and liberate themselves, and, from Berlin, the radical nationalist Subhas Chandra Bose took to the radio to urge his compatriots to strike an expedient alliance with the Axis. Most anticolonial leaders rejected that idea, but more and more were becoming convinced that only a free India could ensure the subcontinent's defense.[6]

Seizing on the moment's urgency, Gandhi and other members of the Indian National Congress drafted an ultimatum promising civil disobedience if British rule did not definitively end. On August 8, the All India Congress Committee passed this so-called Quit India resolution by an overwhelming majority. Raj officials retaliated by arresting Gandhi, Jawaharlal Nehru, and the rest of the Congress leadership. The hasty move triggered the colony's most serious uprising since 1857. Crowds flooded the streets of Bombay, and spontaneous insurgencies coalesced in Assam, Bihar, and other eastern provinces. Workers walked out of mills and factories. Students picketed schools and courts. Saboteurs derailed dozens of trains and cut thousands of telephone lines. Mobs blocked roads and damaged infrastructure critical to Allied operations. All told rebels destroyed more than two thousand police stations, post offices, and other government buildings. One of the movement's leaders, Aruna Asaf Ali, found the groundswell of action "thrilling." She had heard of underground partisans fighting occupation in Europe and envisioned her struggle the same way.[7]

Yet when Ben reached India amidst this unrest, he was clinging to his view, forged in the crucible of London under the Blitz, that there was a "deep communion of interest and moral faith" between the British and American people, and that one of the reasons chaos now engulfed the globe was because the two had not "stood by each other." Hitler wanted Americans to "tangle with the English," he suspected. He wanted them to argue about "the caste system and about India . . . and poor old Ireland and Oliver Cromwell." But, Ben countered, why squabble about these matters "when the fate of the world is tottering"? India's colonial administrators, he assumed, were "working hard" to win the war and do "what they thought was right."[8]

Indian nationalists, by contrast, confounded him at first. If they hated British rule so much, he wondered, why didn't they "get together" and present unified demands? Maybe, Ben ventured, the Indians were like the Irish: "It is not independence that they want, it is fighting about independence that constitutes their secret pleasure." He combed through reports of chaos in the *Times of India*. A train derailed near Rajkot. Picketing in front of the reserve bank in Karachi. The police "forced to fire" on a large crowd at Eram. The Indian National Congress, Ben decided, was engaged in "sabotage," and sabotage not simply against Britain but against all the Allies, including the United States. "Some force," he concluded, "must be exercised to keep order."[9]

Ben's views dovetailed with increasingly common American sentiments. Press commentators in the United States had long been generally open to the cause of Indian independence, but that support had eroded sharply in recent months as the Anglo-American alliance assumed priority for war strategists, as the colony's security grew increasingly precarious, and as the campaign for self-rule became more militant. Indian nationalists' flat rejection that March of the Labour politician Stafford Cripps's offer to pursue a new constitution and dominion status for India after the war was won struck many American onlookers as brash. The Quit India resolution and subsequent fallout that summer provoked even more dismay. Congress's ultimatum was an attempt to "blackmail the British," decried the once sympathetic *New Republic*, a stab in the back of the United Nations, echoed the *New York Times*. Absorbing British propaganda American editorialists and cartoonists branded Gandhi a stooge and a tool of Japan. Even *PM* criticized the campaign as "untimely." No Americans, charged the *Herald Tribune*, "except Axis sympathizers and professional Anglophobes," could possibly approve of such "promotion of civil disorder in India at this critical hour."[10]

Yet Ben would, moving sharply against his zealous championing of the British and at risk to his own career.

From Karachi Ben flew east on an American transport across the plains of Rajputana to New Delhi, the rear echelon headquarters for the new China-Burma-India Theater. The Raj's oversized, ostentatious capital, purpose-built for the empire's bureaucrats little more than a decade earlier, now bustled with personnel from across the Allied world. Chinese diplomats, South African and Australian trade commissioners, American technical experts, and British air marshals transformed the princely palaces near India Gate into office space for urgent missions. On and around Queensway, arriving GIs pitched tents and temporary barracks before rummaging through nearby shops for Christmas presents. Finding all the rooms taken at the Cecil Hotel, Ben shared a tent on its grounds with *Life* magazine's Jack Belden. He marveled at General Joseph Stilwell's signature on his new accreditation papers, dined on steak and potatoes at Davico's, and joined other correspondents for tours of American air bases in Assam, British defense installations near Dehradun at the foot of the Himalayas, and the new training camp for Chinese soldiers at Ramgarh. He seemed ready to write only the most conventional, celebratory accounts of the Allied war effort in India.[11]

This would have pleased supporters of the Raj. Although doubts about colonialism were growing among Liberal and Labour factions back in Britain, most Conservatives, not least their diehard imperialist leader Winston Churchill, continued to champion the empire as a source of fortune and glory as well as a force for international good. Without the British, they insisted, India would fall apart. With them stood not only British army officers and administrators, for whom postings to the colonies had offered a means to upward mobility, but also many Indians themselves, including police and civil servants who drew their paychecks from the Raj as well as maharajas, nawabs, and other local dignitaries, whose fiefdoms were propped up by the Crown in exchange for loyalty, money, and military recruits. By coopting not only land but even more cunningly the allegiances of local elites, colonial control stole far and wide over the subcontinent's mountains and plains. The British presence was sometimes "unseen," explained one

Indian civil serviceman, but it was never "unfelt." It hovered above like "a cloud over your head all the time."[12]

But the arrival of so many newcomers to wartime India threatened to scramble this established social and political order. Newcomers were strangers who breached decorum and disrupted routine, outsiders who blundered past unspoken rules, interlopers who questioned convention. The presence of Americans—some 150,000 would be stationed in wartime India—seemed especially likely to upend the status quo.[13] Yet, exactly to what ends, no one was sure.

Just maybe the US personnel streaming into India would live up to their long-professed commitment to spreading democracy. Anticolonial sentiments had grown dramatically in recent decades among American scholars, socialists, pacifists, missionaries, civil rights activists, and others. Especially as Japan's victories forced a wide-open future in Asia, more and more Americans were convinced that the age of colonialism was coming to an end. If they threw their weight behind the independence movements in the East, they would affirm that this war was indeed being fought to rid the earth of oppression, and they would ensure friendly relationships with the region's rising nations in the long term. The possibility of such support electrified the world's colonial subjects. "We pray to God to give you strength to remain true to the noble traditions laid down by George Washington," one Indian youth group wrote to President Roosevelt.[14]

Yet again, to many Congress supporters, Chinese allies, and others, the stationing of large numbers of US armed forces on the subcontinent looked prima facie like an endorsement of the Raj's policies. Americans, after all, had a long and deep history of collaboration with Britain's imperialists. Buoyed by a shared sense of Anglo-Saxon destiny, duty, and superiority, they had congregated in far-flung hotel bars together, bought and sold around the world together, spread the gospel together. Some of the most influential American strategists continued to argue that anticolonial nationalism in Asia posed too radical a risk, that alliances with old-hand European administrators offered the surest, swiftest path to global stability and prosperity. "You have made common cause with Great Britain," Gandhi admonished Americans. "You cannot, therefore, disown responsibility for anything that her representatives do in India." In New Delhi, American diplomats contemplated a horrifying possibility: that confrontations on the streets might result in the "shedding of Indian blood by American troops." To counter widespread impressions that American servicemen would become a party to British rule, the State Department announced that Americans would take "scrupulous care" to avoid Indian politics, and that their "sole purpose" was to "prosecute the war of the United Nations against the Axis powers." GIs bound for India were cautioned to sleep with a mosquito net, peel all fruit, and dismiss local affairs as a "purely British and Indian problem."[15]

There was, of course, a third possibility, that Americans would not prop up the Raj or help Indians wrest themselves free but rather act as an imperial force in their own right. British officials watched with alarm as a growing array of American businessmen came calling with "enquiries of a detailed and searching character" about tapping the region's markets. Pan American Airways and American Export Lines had angled for equal access to ports and airfields. The United Press was trying to break Reuters' monopoly on the region's communications network. Such encroachments seemed to forecast American plans to dominate postwar trade.[16] Indians bristled, too, at the impositions Americans made on their communities. The US military's promotion of Jim Crow on and around its bases threatened to expand and deepen racial inequality on the subcontinent, and in ports like Bombay and Calcutta, furloughed GIs were fueling an exploitative sex trade. Despite the precarity of India's food situation, American leaders also insisted on obtaining the bulk of their provisions locally on the terms of reciprocal aid. In Great Britain and Australia, general purchasing boards coordinated such procurement to minimize its impact on the civilian economy. No similar effort took place here. Military buyers scooped goods off the open market and slaughtered cattle, though sacred among Hindus and Jains, for beef rations.[17]

After a few weeks in New Delhi, conditions proved impossible for Ben to ignore. Troops and police had met the capital's massive Quit India demonstrations with lathi charges and gunfire, killing an unknown number of men, women, and children. Authorities banned gatherings of more than five people, instituted a curfew, and shuttered the city's nationalist newspapers. Travelers meanwhile brought word of clashes in other provinces, far more widespread and serious than official communiqués let on. Unshackled from nearly all legal restraints by the Defence of India Act, authorities were flogging and strip-searching suspects, herding them through expedited trials, and throwing them in dingy cells, whatever was deemed necessary for "the maintenance of public order or the efficient prosecution of the war." Security forces tear gassed crowds, or machine-gunned them from the air, and burned villages to the ground. In total, more than 60,000 protesters would be arrested or detained, and police opened fire some 528 times, killing thousands. One official explained colonial riot control technique to Ben. It was simple, he said: "You shoot."[18]

Ben listened with fading tolerance to British administrators as they professed "honest intentions" and begged for pity, claiming that India was "the greatest burden England ever had borne." Freedom would come "after the war," they repeatedly assured. Ben began to distrust their promises. It was so typically smug, he thought, that they called the Viceroy's House in Delhi, that baroque, red sandstone monstrosity, a "lodge" rather than a palace. Whereas Indians always spoke about "freedom and the human spirit," these unimaginative bureaucrats talked only of "law and order." He decided that "they had made up their minds that Indians never could rule themselves." They would shoot, whip, and heap collective fines on village after village to preserve their own power. They would fill the prisons. "We are stronger than they are," one colonial official told Ben revealingly.[19]

Ben began to work to understand Indians' points of view. He studied the various factions in the Indian National Congress, the special concerns of Sikhs, Anglo-Indians, and Dalits, and the dreams of many Muslims for their own separate state. He sought out audiences with prominent figures not currently in prison: Gandhi's son Devdas; the Liberal Party leader Tej Bahadur Sapru; the Madras statesman Chakravarti Rajagopalachari; and the Muslim League spokesman Muhammad Ali Jinnah. He accused them of "being friendly to Japan." They denied it. "We do not want a fresh career of domination under a foreign power," explained the Sikh leader Tara Singh. Ben found himself repeatedly "on the defensive." When he waxed lyrical about the "new spirit in Britain," Indians retorted: What good had that done here? They questioned him not only about British plans but American intensions. India, warned members of the Hindu Mahasabha, was not simply Great Britain's private matter as the Raj's defenders contended; it was "the acid test of the sincerity of purpose of all the Allied Powers."[20]

Ben soon found himself sympathizing even with the subcontinent's radical freedom fighters. Visiting one village where men and women were "being beaten and shot at in the name of the Four Freedoms," and another where "poor, half-starved citizens" had been levied enormous collective fines for someone else's civil disobedience, he was stirred by how protesters had risked all to stay true to their "deepest convictions." He began to feel sheepish about his own ability to move around while so many languished in prison for their beliefs. "Imperialism has failed," he concluded. It had not won cooperation from the masses, and it did not "turn out the maximum number of guns and tanks." All it had yielded was "the alienation of

Oriental people." India, Ben decided, had to be lifted out of the realm of Britain's "domestic problem." The United States had the power to push for open discussion and change, to "smoke hidden things out of hiding."[21]

Ben joined a small vanguard of Americans that fall who, in heartfelt petitions or private pleas, called on Roosevelt to weigh in on the conflict in India, among them the writer Pearl Buck, the ACLU leader Roger Baldwin, and the intellectual W. E. B. Du Bois, as well as Ben's college roommate Edgar Snow and his South Carolinian contemporary Benjamin Mays.[22] For many Americans, grappling with India would lead to deeper reckonings with their own nation's racial inequality. From the editors of the *Chicago Defender*, who called the Raj "Great Britain's Dixieland," to the former Republican presidential nominee Wendell Willkie, now championing the causes of self-determination and civil rights during his round-the-globe goodwill tour—many began to see parallels, to develop theories about the common roots of oppression across the planet, and to call for combatting all forms of injustice together rather than treat them separately. The labor activist A. Philip Randolph, who had adopted Gandhi's nonviolent resistance methods to build a March on Washington movement powerful enough to secure a promise of fair employment practices in American defense industries from Roosevelt the previous year, summed up this emerging perspective bluntly: "Free India—and Free the Negroes."[23]

Ben, by contrast, studiously avoided drawing such connections. In India he would have been questioned relentlessly about the state of American race relations and the spread of Jim Crow to the subcontinent's US military installations. But he made no note of and expressed no interest in these inevitable topics. Though he toured the region's segregated bases, he gave no acknowledgment of Black soldiers' growing discontent with their second-class treatment, and he did not connect their frustrations to those of South Asians. Whereas others increasingly intertwined the fight for civil rights in the United States and the struggle against empire overseas, Ben kept them separate, subtly sidelining the role of racism in the events he was watching unfold and leaving unquestioned the status quo in his own South Carolina.[24] It is often assumed that the bonds of sympathy are proximate, that it's harder to invest in tragedies far afield than it is to see and understand them close at hand. But the opposite has just as often been true. It can be easier to call out injustice halfway around the world than to face it at home.

"Now, this is not the end. It is not even the beginning of the end. But it is, perhaps, the end of the beginning," Winston Churchill exulted at London's Mansion House on November 10. Given the recent successes in North Africa, it was, or at least it was supposed to be, an occasion to celebrate. But the prime minister could not let go of Wendell Willkie's recent anticolonial statements and Roosevelt's follow-up remark that the Atlantic Charter, which listed self-determination as one of the Allies' goals, pertained to "all humanity," not just to nations overrun by the Nazis. "We have not entered this war for profit or expansion," Churchill assured the crowd assembled for the Lord Mayor's dinner. "Let me, however, make this clear. . . . We mean to hold our own. I have not become the King's First Minister to preside over the liquidation of the British Empire." Without "that vast commonwealth and society of nations and communities gathered in and around the ancient British monarchy," he insisted, "the good cause might well have perished from the face of the earth. Here we are and here we stand, a veritable rock of salvation in this drifting world."[25]

Newspaper readers in India followed reports of the Allies' gaining fortunes that month, and they studied the proclamations of Churchill and the world's other leaders. But local conditions had gotten no better. Weeks earlier, a cyclone had swept through Bengal and Orissa, wiping out crops, livestock, and paddy stores already depleted by the Raj's scorched earth policies and the cutoff of rice shipments from Burma. Grain costs had soared and shop shelves had emptied. Desperate people and their crying children were walking long distances chasing rumors of food.[26]

Tensions between visiting American correspondents and Raj officials had also risen sharply. Colonial propagandists had long controlled the Raj's image abroad by flooding overseas airwaves and newspapers with their own arguments while choking off Indian activists' access to international press outlets.[27] But as increased numbers of American reporters came to survey India firsthand, British officials quickly realized that these "well meaning sentimentalists from the U.S.A.," as Viceroy Linlithgow called them, would be "difficult to manage." Invading correspondents, griped one colonial administrator, swallowed whole the Congress point of view even though they had "little or no appreciation of the Asiatic mind."[28] In England, Ben and his colleagues had been encouraged to speak openly about locals' suffering. Here, British leaders wanted no such talk. They kept tight control over journalists' access to accreditation and travel permissions, and at times denied their cables. Furious at the restrictions, some Americans evaded them by sending information by diplomatic pouch or over

US Army channels, or by leaving the region to publish their accounts from theaters with lighter censorship.[29]

By December, much of what Ben wanted to say he would not have been allowed to dispatch from India. On a Sunday morning before daybreak he headed to the airfield and boarded a four-engine bomber overloaded with some kind of metal urgently needed in the United States. While the pilots studied maps and discussed the weather, he worried about the weight of the plane on such a short runway. But it took off "like a wild bird" into a cloudless sunrise. They flew all day without stopping, taking lunch out of tin cans while staring down at the shores of the Arabian Sea. "Getting out of India" felt to Ben "like breaking out of jail."[30]

As they crossed Africa and then the South Atlantic, he listened to the pilots talk about the world's unbroken forests and deserts, the vastness of the war, and their own chances of survival. Reaching Brazil's cloudy tropics, a "lonely humble feeling" took hold of Ben. He wondered about "the law that decides who is to be taken and who to be left." Those who came through this conflict alive, he decided, would have obligations they could never forget. Heavy rain, lightning, and a turbulent landing at Belém made Ben nervous, and when thick fog forced them to circle for over an hour above their next destination, he grew so frightened he shook. But once again they returned safely to the earth to refuel before soaring into the darkening Caribbean skies, aiming for Florida. Ben had travelled twelve thousand miles in seven days.[31]

Back in the States he felt solemn, older. He had experienced so much in the past year but was unsatisfied with all of it. He met up with acquaintances who had been where he had been—Ambassador John Winant, who had arrived at London in the middle of the Blitz; Maurice Hindus, who spent long nights with Ben at the Hotel Metropol in Moscow; Wendell Willkie, who had flown the same global ferry routes. He gave speeches on behalf of Russian War Relief and gathered news of friends imprisoned or dead. In Washington, DC, he traced his old stomping grounds near the Capitol and sent a letter to Franklin Roosevelt about conditions in India. The colony was a prison ruled by policemen who had "lost touch with the people" and whose "imaginations have become brittle," he told the president. "I am a crusader about this India business," he admitted. Ben wished Eleanor Roosevelt and other leading Americans could go to India and see what he had seen.[32]

Even as he made arrangements for a new assignment—a return to London, this time for the *Herald Tribune*—India still weighed on Ben's mind. News of Gandhi's intention to fast for twenty-one days to protest his continued imprisonment made the New York papers on February 11,

Ben and an acquaintance in India. Special Collections and Archives, Clemson University Libraries.

1943. Lord Linlithgow denounced Gandhi's action as "political blackmail" and refused to be moved. A lonely few groups of Americans made appeals on Gandhi's behalf. "England is fighting for freedom for Englishmen; why is it immoral for Indians to fight for theirs?" the NAACP demanded of Churchill. But Roosevelt heeded the Prime Minister's warnings to stay out of the dispute, even as the Mahatma's condition deteriorated. Officials at the State Department prepared a statement to issue in case the seventy-three-year-old died.[33]

Ben wanted to write openly about the fight for freedom in India. He told colleagues at *PM* that he felt more strongly about this story than any other he had ever covered. But speaking out presented serious risks at a moment when the majority of Americans believed that any criticism of the British undermined the war effort. Ben himself had been at the forefront of making that argument. The British might refuse him further travel permissions, and *PM*'s editors warned that if censors opposed the publication of his reporting and they printed it anyway, his war correspondent credentials would surely be revoked.[34]

"But I have to write what I feel about India," Ben decided. Holed up in New York's theater district at the Hotel Piccadilly, waiting for a clipper flight to Lisbon, he prepared his searing indictment of British colonial rule:

> It is a sad and bitter experience to be in India when we are fighting to save the Four Freedoms. India today makes you almost physically ill. . . . Except for certain elements of the community the Indians are doing no more than they have to. Frankly, I don't blame them much any more. . . . The British told me I was a fool to come out to India and spend three months and have the nerve enough to talk to those who had been there for 200 years. I told them . . . it did not take me 200 years to see starvation and suppression, and I could feel hatred when I felt it."[35]

On India, but only about India, Ben found himself arguing the carpetbagger's case.

23

Hot Questions

"WILL YOU SPEAK UP, PLEASE, Major, so that the members of the committee can hear you?"

"My name is George A. Spiegelberg, major, Signal Corps, recorder of the general purchasing board in the office of the general purchasing agent, European theater of our operations. . . . I would like to give you the details of reciprocal aid."[1] At the start of 1943, George found himself back in Washington and unexpectedly thrust into the role of one of the Roosevelt administration's most consequential defenders.

The trouble began the previous November, less than a week before the Allied landings in North Africa, when voters in the US midterm elections registered their mounting frustrations with tax hikes, price controls, proliferating red tape, and, worst of all, lack of progress in the war by retiring thirteen Democratic committee chairmen, many of them staunch allies of the president. Republicans in turn picked up nine seats in the Senate and forty-four in the House, reducing Democrats' control in Congress to its narrowest margin in a decade.[2]

Normally George would have found Republican success at the polls cause for celebration. But these results elevated not only politicians ready to push back against domestic New Deal policies but also those who had resisted US intervention in Europe to begin with and continued to question and criticize the war effort, including its foundational Lend-Lease program. Although a majority of Americans remained committed to beating back aggression in Asia and Europe, a strong undercurrent of opposition to Roosevelt's foreign policies and the United Nations cause had been gaining noticeable strength during 1942. The nation's rightwing tabloids, which reached some fifty million readers, railed against the president for not putting "America First," and instead trying to be "a big shot and a big sap for every foreign country and every alien people in the world," as William Randolph Hearst spluttered. Whereas 28 percent of Americans had described themselves to pollsters as "non-interventionist" before the bombing of Pearl Harbor, an even greater 35 percent identified as such by early 1943.[3]

Dwindling household supplies and new rationing schemes fueled the discontent right as the holiday season approached and Americans aimed to spend their growing paychecks. Firewood disappeared from the lots of New England. Coffee, beef, and butter shortages plagued New York and Chicago. Modest displays and long lines greeted department store shoppers, and there were not enough Thanksgiving turkeys or Christmas trees. In Southern California, straining under the weight of booming populations of war workers, buyers stripped markets of canned goods, soap, and other "hoardable commodities." But, the *Los Angeles Times* helpfully added, delicatessens still had plenty of sausage, because "restrictions are not so great on items used in sausage."[4]

Across the nation, newspapers linked such shortages to Lend-Lease purchasing, which already totaled close to $8.3 billion and in time would reach $50 billion. The average housewife, the *New York Times* explained, "was giving her neighbors across the seas" about one-third of her pork products, one-fifth of her beef and veal, two eggs out of each dozen, and an ounce from each pound of her butter and cheese. In this context, government pronouncements celebrating the year's soaring Lend-Lease expenditures and projected future growth struck many Americans not as a positive sign of an accelerating war effort but as a portent of yet more belt tightening.[5] Rumors spread, especially in publications hostile to Roosevelt's war effort: that bureaucrats were secretly confiscating and shipping American factory equipment to the Soviet Union; that they were using school children as "human guinea pigs" to perfect Lend-Lease soup mixes; that horsemeat had been rejected for export but considered as a solution to the domestic beef shortage. "In other words," scowled one *Chicago Tribune* reader, "if horse meat is to be used for human consumption, let the American civilians and soldiers eat it. Don't send it abroad—they have our good meat."[6]

Thirty countries had signed Lend-Lease agreements so far, but news of food, newsprint, kerosene, and even rayon hosiery going to civilians in Africa elicited the loudest howls of protest. One man decried the idea of donating sweaters to North Africa's "sun-baked natives" or footwear to "people who may never before have worn shoes." For another, learning that the Ethiopians qualified for Lend-Lease proved the last straw. "From reliable sources," he cracked, "I learn that the Patagonians, the Senegambians, the Cameroonians, the Nigerians, the Afghans, the Peruvians, the Zulus, and the Hottentots also feel that they are vital to the defense of the United States, and hope, therefore, to qualify for lend-lease aid." Could Americans also please qualify for Lend-Lease, he snarked, to pay next year's taxes?[7]

Seizing on the bitterness, the president's foes in the Senate demanded investigations. Lend-Lease had been shrouded in too much "mystery," complained the Minnesota Republican Henrik Shipstead. The new Congress must do something about "wasteful spending," New Jersey's William Warren Barbour agreed, and that meant reviewing not only "all depression-created agencies" but also the Lend-Lease budget. "The day of rubber stamp congresses is over," promised the Montana Democrat Burton K. Wheeler. To try to quell opposition to Lend-Lease when it was first introduced in early 1941, the architects of H.R. 1776 had stipulated that the program would be subject to annual reauthorization by Congress. Without renewal, the program would expire in six months. A nervous Lend-Lease director Edward Stettinius considered rushing a funding bill in front of a more friendly lame-duck Congress, but it was too late. When the 78th Congress convened in early January, one Washington reporter concluded, "the Administration appeared certain to face rough sledding."[8]

The escalating controversy over Lend-Lease also set off alarm bells in London. Public opinion analysts at the Ministry of Information pointed out that even members of Congress seemed "largely unaware" that Lend-Lease was not "a one way traffic." The reciprocal aid program needed urgent publicity. But British officials felt they ought to "lay low," that defense for the complex wartime supply system would be more convincing coming from an American.[9] On January 3, George was ordered to proceed by first available transport to Washington to testify before Congress, not simply in hopes of persuading its members to renew Lend-Lease, which a majority of Americans still supported, but to do something that a majority of Americans decidedly opposed—to forgo a postwar accounting of debts. He left five nights later, armed with thousands of pages from his own files as well as those foisted on him by his British counterparts in the Ministry of Supply. On plain white paper he sketched an outline for his public statement. It began: "The last war."[10]

Complaints about Lend-Lease continued to snowball as George arrived in Washington in mid-January. Export traders were grumbling that wartime supply streams threatened their long-term private business opportunities. Wisconsin dairy farmers were demanding a halt of butter shipments to the Soviet Union. Let them eat margarine, suggested their senator, Robert La Follette, Jr. One stubborn claim alleged that the government was giving away powder puffs and beer. When an Associated Press report contended that the United States would soon be spending more on the war than all its allies and enemies combined, it set off cries of disbelief about such "a disproportionately large American contribution."[11]

Lend-Lease officials tried to counter the bad press. They met with corporate leaders, hoping to placate them by agreeing to allow brand names to appear on future shipments. They issued newsreel footage and press releases touting the supply system as one of "intelligent self-interest." Lend-Lease was neither "a loan of money" nor "an act of charity," Edward Stettinius lectured audiences, but rather a program for the "defense of this country." It was "all the same war," he urged. "We cannot measure their lives against our dollars, or their pounds or rubles against our lives." Trying to do so, he thought, would be not just impossible but "a sacrilege."[12]

Still the Hearst newspapers clamored for promises of postwar repayments, and still conservatives griped that Lend-Lease was "all 'free-gratis for nothing'" or worse, a cunning way for Democrats "to extend the New Deal to the whole world at the expense of American taxpayers." Press watchers in Britain's Ministry of Information predicted "hot questions" at the House Foreign Relations Committee's upcoming hearings. "We may be in for a dirty time," Lord Halifax warned.[13]

Stettinius testified first on January 29. He reminded those gathered that Congress had passed the program "in a time of peril," and that it expressed the will of the American people to stand up against Axis attempts "to dominate the free peoples of the world." He demanded, "What would have happened had we not done so?" If Britain had surrendered, would Americans now be fighting Hitler's forces in North Africa or would they be facing battle "on the shores of South America or possibly Maine and Florida?"[14]

Republican skeptics of Roosevelt's foreign policy nevertheless grilled the former US Steel chairman about the myriad stories circulating about Lend-Lease. Did the British turn a profit from American foodstuffs? Were Australians charging Americans rent on warehouses the Americans built? What about those powder puffs? Stettinius tried to dispel the myths. No one was giving anyone powder puffs. Other kinds of civilian supplies were indeed going to North Africa because US forces could not wage an effective offensive in a region undone by famine and unrest. General Eisenhower himself had requested it. The British and Australians were not taking advantage, he insisted; they were giving back. Stettinius hoped that George's upcoming account of reciprocal aid on February 2 would break through: "I should like to say that I have run into nothing in connection with my experience in this war that is more inspiring than the story that Major Spiegelberg will tell."[15]

For the assembled members of Congress, George rattled off the impressive work of Reverse Lend-Lease, the incredible array of goods and services donated to American forces in Britain, how much shipping tonnage they had saved, how little cash the US military had spent, how optimistic he was about avoiding the colossal debts that crippled the international economy after the last war. The British, he declared, had delivered "magnificent assistance" without questions or second guessing. George would not detail for the committee his enormous troubles to make the system work. The stakes were too high.[16]

It took no effort to convince Charles Aubrey Eaton, the committee's ranking Republican from New Jersey. Old Doc Eaton with his white mustache had long pilloried fellow members of Congress who acted as though Americans would be "hornswoggled" if they aligned with the British. Eaton, who would later shepherd the Marshall Plan through the House past his fellow Republicans' suspicions, worried most about feeding, clothing, and housing the world's war victims after the conflict ended. He asked George, "What part in that will the lend-lease program play, in your judgement?" George explained that the collaboration between the US military and the British had impressed him tremendously. He didn't think "that same spirit" would have existed if Americans "had been buying." It was therefore his "profound hope" that the "machinery" of both Lend-Lease and reciprocal aid continue after the war. He knew of no better way to generate a "broad and generous spirit" between nations and thought it offered "the greatest hope of a lasting peace." George's thinking echoed a growing conviction among economists, and others planning for the postwar period, that Lend-Lease, by forgoing the practice of viewing international loans on private business terms and instead embracing cooperative enterprise, had cracked the vicious cycle of debt defaults, retaliatory tariffs, and competing currency depreciations that had been the international economy's undoing before.[17]

But John Vorys, an Ohio Republican who had voted against all of Roosevelt's major foreign policies, refused to be moved. "How is this going to work out," he demanded. It was one thing to delay the accounting—"obviously it would be foolish to stop and take men out of the trenches to put dollar signs on things"—but, he inquired, "Do you think that we can go on indefinitely simply supplying what everybody needs without casting some sort of balance?"

"Well, sir," George replied, "it seems to me that the President was very close to the truth when he suggested that if each nation gave in accordance with its ability to give all would be giving equally."

"Well, who decides 'ability to give'?"

"Well, not I, sir."[18]

"Do you know anything about the formula which is used in determining the respective ability of the countries to contribute?" Karl Mundt, a South Dakota Republican and erstwhile America First member asked, picking up on Vorys's line of questioning. "No, sir; I do not. I do not even know, sir, whether there is such a formula," George replied. This was, he explained, more "what you might well call a new economic theory."[19] George worked closely with officials in the British Treasury, where ideas had been swirling around since the previous winter about a new approach to international finance and exchange, not least the plans of John Maynard Keynes, which, along with parallel proposals by Harry Dexter White in the US Treasury, were paving the way for a groundbreaking postwar economic order that would be sketched out the following year at Bretton Woods, though those designs, too, would draw Republican ire.[20]

Mundt—described by one British observer as "a thorn in the side of the Administration" and "constantly baffled by problems largely outside his mental scope"—believed that the United States should insist on overseas bases and transport facilities or other recompense for its wartime generosity. He had read in *Newsweek* that US war expenditures reached $840 for every American, whereas the British spent only about $440 per citizen, and the idea that the war should cost Americans almost twice per capita as it cost Britons rankled him. George wasn't familiar with the *Newsweek* article, but "as a very amateur student of economics," he speculated that such a discrepancy might simply reflect the far greater purchasing power of the pound.[21]

Herman Eberharter, a Catholic New Dealer from Pittsburgh, proved a less hostile interrogator. He noted how any discussion of continuing "the lend-lease principle" in peacetime always mulishly reverberated back to the question of whether the United States could "afford" it. He wondered if this was the wrong question.

"I can only say this, sir," George agreed. "If, as I hope, we can get a lasting peace we will get something that you cannot measure in terms of dollars."

"In other words, we cannot expect in any future world that the United States could go along by itself and maintain a satisfactory economy by trying to pull itself up by its own bootstraps?"

"I have never known that to succeed, sir." George admitted. His wartime service had led him farther and farther from agreement with Herbert Hoover, an unbending Lend-Lease opponent.

"Your idea as I take it, and I think you have been trying to convey it to the committee, is that the spirit of cooperation and harmony as a result of this lend-lease operation is far greater than we could ever possibly obtain if we attempted to proceed on a cash basis or on a strict financial accountability basis?"

"That is certainly my conclusion, sir."

"That is all." Eberharter ceded the floor.[22]

Bartel Jonkman from Michigan, another Republican opponent of Roosevelt, brought the discussion back to numbers. "I understand that the British annual current expense for war is $20,000,000,000. Ours is $80,000,000,000. That is a ratio of 4 to 1." He suggested that "either the British are better financiers than we are or that we are making a larger contribution." He wanted George to approximate the ratio of Lend-Lease to Reverse Lend-Lease. George stood fast against this line of questioning, explaining that his superior officers had not given him permission to release that information.[23]

The ratio, had George revealed it, would not have impressed Congressman Jonkman—or Mundt and Vorys or anyone else who viewed the world the way a private banker eyed his account ledgers. In total, Americans would advance as much as $30 billion in Lend-Lease to the British and receive maybe $6 billion in return. No nation would build more aircraft, launch more shipping tonnage, or supply more food and oil to the Allied war effort than the United States. By the war's end, the United States would produce two-thirds of all the Allies' supplies, field the world's largest air and naval forces and its second largest army. Americans' gross economic contribution surpassed all others.[24]

But by measures other than money, Americans' sacrifices paled beside those of their major allies as well as their own colonial subjects in US overseas territories. GIs were better fed, better cared for, and in the end less likely to see combat than any other fighting forces. When they did face battle, they were far less likely to die. Civilians in the forty-eight states endured shorter and less severe rationing. They didn't have to watch their children brave sustained bombing or invasion. Their prospects soared while others' finances and cities crumbled to ruins. Roughly 416,000 US citizens gave their lives in this war, or just over 3 percent of those who served in uniform and 0.3 percent of the nation's prewar population. The United Kingdom, with a much smaller population than the United States, counted more than 450,000 deaths, including more than 60,000 civilians. The Ethiopians, Somalis, and Libyans, whose inclusion in Lend-Lease had so angered some Americans, together suffered more than a million military and civilian deaths. The Chinese and the Soviets together lost some forty million people[25]

Of course, much of this would only be realized in retrospect. Americans did not yet know that they would emerge from the conflict to unparalleled prosperity. Many had suffered severe economic hardship during the 1930s and feared that depression would come roaring back again soon. But even if they did not yet understand how blessed they would be, even now, who among them would have traded places with any of the world's Lend-Lease recipients? How many would have preferred the fate of those in Nanjing, Leningrad, or even London? The incommensurability between lives and dollars, the unnerving question of what should—and what should never—be paid for in cash, hung silently over the hearing.

"Are there any further questions?" The committee's chairman Sol Bloom moved to conclude the hearing. "Major, it has been a great pleasure to have you here before us today," he said. "You are a chip off the old block, your father, the Judge." Stettinius rushed forward to thank George for such "excellent" testimony.[26]

The future of Lend-Lease was not yet entirely assured. Republicans still pushed for amendments that would grant Congress the ability to pursue repayment or other compensations for American largesse after the war. Still many balked at plans for long-term international economic coordination and foreign aid initiatives, suspected as attempts to export the New Deal around the world. But onlookers wagered that George had disabused enough skeptics of the idea that the United States "was being played for a sucker," and even Vorys admitted that the major's account had been "quite an eye opener." The BBC correspondent Alistair Cooke championed George as "a modest man to whom Britain owes more than it may ever know."[27] Within weeks the House would vote 178 to 118 to reject an attempt to add new conditions to Lend-Lease renewal, and the Allies' cornerstone policy would subsequently slip through Congress with few dissenters. Back in London, John Maynard Keynes breathed a sigh of relief. Anxious to resume economic negotiations that had been delayed by the crisis, he marveled at how suddenly Lend-Lease had become "among the least controversial of all war measures."[28]

But George had little time to celebrate. Operation Torch had depleted US forces in the United Kingdom to paltry levels. Only one American division remained in England, along with a hollowed-out 8th Air Force drained of all but 25 percent of its supplies. George and his colleagues faced the enormous task of procuring enough local material for an eventual cross-channel invasion. They would need two hundred river barges and a million cabled barrage balloons for the Transportation Corps; nearly fifteen thousand radios, six hundred body armor suits, and more than 160,000 bicycles for the Air Corps; 200,000 telephone poles, two million batteries, and twenty million yards of electric cable for the Signal Corps; 800,000 shrapnel mines for Ordnance and 3.5 million gallons of fog oil for the Chemical Warfare Service; sixty thousand tons of cement and forty million sand bags for the Engineers; two million sheets, ten million bars of soap, and a half million pillows for the Quartermaster Corps; 300,000 x-ray films, nine million cubic feet of oxygen, and fourteen thousand hospital beds for the Medical Corps. And so much more.[29]

Returning to London seemed all the more urgent, because while George completed his business in Washington an army transport plane carrying the head of his unit, Colonel Douglas MacKeachie, disappeared somewhere over the South Atlantic. The only trace of the flight was a life raft that washed up in Brazil with the body of another passenger and MacKeachie's eagle insignia pin, refashioned into a fishing hook. George shuddered to have missed disaster "by an eyelash." Rather than by army transport, he would return to his post on the *Yankee Clipper*.[30]

Conclusion

A Strange and Frightening World

THE PLANE REACHED PORTUGAL AT sunset. Descending to six hundred feet, fifteen minutes ahead of schedule, Sully aimed for the mouth of the Tagus River. Just past the Torre de Belém, the sixteenth-century guard tower announcing the maritime approach to Lisbon, the waterway widened out into an estuary teeming with movement. Sharp, triangular sails carried cutters and smacks across the currents. Fishing trawlers dangled nets in their wake. Some ornately carved vessels with turned-up prows recalled the handiwork of ancient Phoenicians.[1]

On the clipper's passenger deck, those who had made this journey before preoccupied themselves with books or a last highball. One man struggled with painful pressure building in his ears. Others craned their necks to admire the boats and catch a glimpse of Lisbon's terracotta rooftops as they appeared portside. In the middle cabin, just behind the lounge, George and Frank played poker with two other men. Tamara and Jane Froman sat in window seats across the aisle.[2]

As the stewards tidied the galley equipment—the cream pitchers and stemware, the knives, the ice pick—two sharp reports "like ack-ack fire" rang out in the distance, rousing the card players from their game. "Apparently they are shooting at us," George joked. Still, no one moved to close the plane's blackout curtains.[3]

After stowing the cocktail trays, Philip Casprini, one of the stewards who had tended to Franklin Roosevelt during the president's flight to Casablanca the previous month, washed his face and put on his coat. His colleague Craig Robinson climbed the spiral staircase to the crew's quarters to change his shirt.[4]

On the flight deck, Fourth Officer John Burn, who had only recently joined Pan Am, emerged from a sleeping cot drowsy from a nap. Eager for a good view during his first descent into Lisbon, he stood just behind Sully and First Officer Herman Rush, both parked before the windshields in leather chairs. It was dusk and cloudy, Burn noticed, with intermittent rain and thunderstorms in the vicinity, but visibility still extended about seven miles.[5]

Although the *Yankee Clipper* weighed some 4.5 tons and its wingspan stretched 152 feet, the craft was easily controlled by elevators, trim tabs, and other adjustable surfaces on its tail and wings. From the captain's seat of a B-314, it took less force to steer the control wheel or pump the rudder pedals than it took to maneuver the average automobile. But it was difficult to gauge altitude over water, much more difficult than over land, especially if there were no whitecaps, even more so in the dark, and not least because the captain's seat hovered twenty-seven feet above the bottom of the hull. Barometric altimeters were not fast enough to depend on for landing; pilots had to decide when to level off their descent, cut the throttles, and set the plane down. For this reason, just before a clipper's arrival at Cabo Ruivo, airport personnel took a launch out on the Tagus to survey the landing zone and lay out a near-mile-long string of floating lights with a red bulb marking the end. Pilots circled this landing area once at six hundred feet to check for boats or debris—no turns were to be made at lower elevations—before making a final descent parallel to the buoy runway, heading in the direction of its single red light. As the plane inched nearer the river's surface, the lights blurred closer together, providing an important estimate of the water's distance.[6]

At 6:35 p.m., as Sully navigated the seaplane upriver, ground crew radioed instructions to the cockpit. The landing strip had been positioned two miles east of the airport, running south to north. It was now fifteen minutes past sunset. Pilots preferred to land before dark and against a headwind. But Pan Am's precautions would eat up what was left of daylight and require setting down in a slight crosswind.[7]

Ten minutes later the plane reached the light strip. From shore, ground crew could make out the clipper's distinctive silhouette as its cantilevered wings glided toward the liquid runway. On board, passengers saw lightning flash. It was really getting dark now. Stray raindrops grazed the windows as

Lisbon's lights twinkled on and cascaded down to the river's edge. Below, as the plane turned to the left, an inky void loomed closer; no whitecaps disturbed the water's surface.[8]

"Oh, that makes me seasick," Jean Lorraine thought as she watched the tip of the left wing catch the river.

With a prolonged crack, like the sound of splintering ice, the Tagus sheared the wing off, sending the craft spiraling out of control. Heavy beams in the front of the flying boat's hold snapped under the weight of the impact, crushing those below the flight deck. Passengers strapped into their seats toward the tail of the plane flinched as freezing water surged up around them. Unsecured lounge tables barreled through the cabins, pinning survivors as they groped for the exits. Others thrown free in the crash regained consciousness in a sea of debris. Fighting the undertow, they grabbed for nearby seat cushions, which sank like rocks. Engulfed in darkness as the stray landing flares burned out, they could not see around them the blood, the eviscerated contents of overnight bags, or the river rats.[9]

Local fishermen broke into one of the airport's rescue launches and sped toward the capsized fuselage. Airport personnel followed in other boats. Careening past empty life rafts, they trained their search beams in the direction of screams. Survivors with broken bones wailed as they were dragged out of the water by their arms and clothing.[10]

George could not understand why he was swimming deep underwater with his clothes on. Reaching the surface, he heard someone shouting for help. He realized there must have been an accident. Yes, he remembered finishing his whisky and fastening his seatbelt as the plane began to bank left—that same "fancy swerve" it made upon arrival at Horta—then the loudest crash he had ever heard, and an instant later, being knocked out by something "awfully hard." Latching on to a life belt, he treaded water until two men hoisted him into a rescue launch.[11]

What ruthless game of chance ruled moments like this one. The boat George had been pulled into carried twelve people saved from drowning, some gravely injured, others with hardly a scratch. The divine judgment of seating arrangements. Yvette, a former junior lifeguard, had managed to squeeze her way out the window of a fast-sinking compartment and rush to the aid of those who could not swim. She and the diplomat William Walton Butterworth sat there virtually unharmed. But others needed urgent medical attention. The top of Philip Casprini's left femur had been severed. Most of Grace Drysdale's clothes had been torn off in the impact, and she was coughing up blood. Gypsy Markoff had shredded fingers, blood streaming down her face, and an ear dangling from her head.[12]

Another launch collected five more people. John Burn's spine had cracked, and Jane Froman's left leg was nearly taken off below the knee. The two, who had comforted each other in the water awaiting help, would later marry. Their boat also picked up First Officer Herman Rush, dying of internal hemorrhaging, as well as Manuel, barely alive, practically unrecognizable without his glasses, and suffering blunt force trauma to the chest. And it rescued Sully—unconscious but unharmed.[13]

At the shoreline hopeful emergency personnel waiting with too many stretchers enveloped the injured in a torrent of hands and Portuguese. "It was like being born again into a strange and frightening world," Jane Froman marveled. The few passengers strong enough to walk stumbled forward in borrowed coats, their pallid skin encrusted with plane shards. Airport workers scrounged up what brandy they could find for those suffering from shock and exposure, while ambulance drivers tried to resuscitate Manuel on a mattress in the customs shed. When artificial respiration failed to revive him, he was pronounced dead.[14] Over the next few days, clerks at the US legation would take careful notes about the series of suspicious figures with known German connections who came to inquire about the Spanish shipping agent's fate.[15]

The US legation's staff had already been on edge that week, given the latest dire predictions emanating from British intelligence summaries about the city's many enemy plotters. Learning of the accident while attending a ministers' party, the counsellor George F. Kennan rushed to Cabo Ruivo. Pleased to find his friend and former Princeton classmate William Walton Butterworth alive, he and the other officials on the scene began to turn over in their minds possible reasons for the crash. Mechanical failure? Weather? Hostile action?[16] An anonymous caller telephoned to warn that plans were afoot to sabotage another flight. Suspecting that some of the airport's Portuguese staff had Axis sympathies, Pan Am's local manager urged delaying the next plane "preferably on some technical pretext." Urgent orders meanwhile arrived from Washington to suppress the "true identity" of the army officers on board as well as "the plane's relationship to the Navy" since it had gone down in neutral territory.[17]

Salvage work began at dawn. Workers hoisted the clipper's twisted beams, corrugated floor strips, and still-curtained sleeping berths onto the dock at

Santa Apolónia, while guards stood watch over the piles of precious scrap metal. Postal authorities took charge of some thirty-two sacks of mail fished from the Tagus. Letters and packages from New York, Buenos Aires, or Rio de Janeiro and bound for London, Marseille, or Berlin were dried and forwarded for delivery to Ala Littoria, Lufthansa, and other European carriers. Millions of people were killing each other, but they still traded mail.[18] For three weeks, divers combed the riverbed for sensitive information as American legation staff scrambled to account for the diplomatic correspondence, codebooks, and technical equipment that had been on board. Patrols scouring the banks stumbled upon the dead, bloated, half clothed, difficult to identify.[19]

Frank's and Ben's bodies were among those recovered. The two men joined the ranks of more than forty American correspondents and photographers killed abroad while documenting the war, the victims of bombs, torpedoes, tanks, snipers, bandits, and plane crashes. When Frank arrived at the morgue, Lisbon's coroner determined that he had drowned. The river currents meanwhile had carried Ben a considerable distance from the crash site. He was

A large crowd watches a crane lift the *Yankee Clipper*'s wreckage from the Tagus. Navy History and Heritage Command, NH 43451.

found days later missing his coat, shoes, and diamond ring, items perhaps pilfered by a passerby.[20]

Tamara was not found in the Tagus until twelve days after the crash. By then her hair was gone and her hands were just bones, but as the only woman lost in the crash authorities knew it was her. A USO-Camp Shows pin with a white eagle, wings outstretched, still fastened the collar of her petite beige coat.[21]

A month after the accident, four victims were still missing, but twenty others had been discovered and identified, including Harry. Maritime Police confirmed the oil man's identity by the American Express traveler's checks stashed in his pocketbook.[22]

The War Department quietly arranged to inter army officers killed in the crash as ordinary American citizens in Lisbon's cemeteries, and Pan Am sent deceased crewmembers and civilian passengers—including Tamara, Frank, Ben, and Harry—back to the United States on the Portuguese liner SS *San Miguel*.[23] But Manuel received special treatment. Lisbon's Latin American consuls and other leading *hispanos* followed the shipping agent's coffin through the city streets in a funeral procession arranged by the local Spanish ambassador. His remains were then spirited back across the ocean by Garcia & Diaz's *Motomar*—the same ship that had been hijacked from its linseed route and mired in intrigue in Veracruz during the Spanish Civil War, a ship that had evacuated hundreds if not thousands of refugees from Europe, and the ship whose captain had been arrested just four months earlier for smuggling platinum. Conducting routine background checks on the *Motomar*'s passengers, intelligence agents alerted New York port authorities that one Manuel Diaz, suspected of subversive activities dating back to World War I, would be on board the vessel when it arrived. They did not mention, or did not know, that they were reporting on a corpse.[24]

In Lisbon's hospitals and hotels fifteen survivors convalesced.

Suffering severe lung damage, fractured ribs, and eventually complications from an infection to his liver and kidneys, George would spend nearly three months in and out of the Hospital Benfica, by turns drowsy, restless, and delusional. US officials twice wrote to warn his wife, Helen, of the importance of "discretion" in discussing her husband's case. "If the authorities of the neutral country where he is now hospitalized should discover that he is a member of the military forces he might be interned for the duration,"

The remains of civilian passengers and crew arrive at Philadelphia. Courtesy of Michael Safranek/University Archives, The University of Iowa Libraries.

they explained. George tried to preoccupy himself with letter writing, but he was "nuts to get out of this place." From bed he learned that he had been promoted to the rank of lieutenant colonel. "Better late than never," he figured.[25]

Sully initially made a speedy recovery, but when discharged to a room at the Hotel Aviz, a "nervous depression" soon took hold of him. Officials from Pan Am, the US legation, and António Salazar's government were all anxious to uncover the cause of the crash, and Civil Aeronautics Board (CAB) investigators were coming from the United States to undertake their own report. Sully hinted to American diplomats that, "in light of his knowledge," they should not rule out the possibility of sabotage, but otherwise the pilot refused to talk about the accident, even with members of his own crew. He was adamant: he would give his account only once.[26]

"Well, I will tell you. It is going to be very short."

Portuguese authorities, CAB and Pan Am officials, along with George Kennan and a stenographer, had gathered to hear what Sully had to say eleven days after the accident. He told them about reaching the harbor, the distant lightning, the slight crosswind, the string of landing lights. "We had already checked the switches and everything was clear and as we passed to the south end of the lights, we probably had in the neighborhood of seven hundred feet altitude, at which time I felt the plane start to go down, nose down. I thought it might be the automatic pilot still on and grabbed that; it was off. She still went down." Sully described how he had cut the engines and tried to pull back on the control wheel to level the plane, how his first officer also tried to adjust the elevators, but still the plane dove. Once the clipper had plunged to roughly four hundred feet, Sully explained, he had concluded: "Well, we're gone, there is no stopping, but perhaps I might save something." He would try to cushion the blow.[27]

"So I threw the wing down and it went down; I know that," he admitted. "The next thing I was in the water up to here." He gestured to his waist. "I looked over to my First Officer, and I tried to get him out. I realized there was no chance to get him out because he was locked in. The water then was up to here." He gestured to his neck. "I went down and came out somehow, and some distance away. That is all."

"At the moment the accident started to occur, you were circling the landing area?" asked Commander Paulo Viana, Portugal's head investigator.

"Yes," Sully replied.

The commander inquired about the ground staff and the crew. None of them had done anything wrong, Sully averred.

"We are not quite sure, when you explained how the accident occurred—did you say you were circling at the moment or flying straight?" Viana pressed.[28]

"I was just approaching the landing, in straight flight, not to land," Sully contradicted his earlier statement. All the evidence investigators had collected indicated that the plane had turned left and was heading perpendicular to the landing strip at the moment of the crash. In future testimony,

Sully himself would revert to a version of events in which the plane had started to go down "just after we passed at a right angle to the lights."[29]

Viana continued: "You let down your wing, you did that purposely?"

"Yes."

"When you came down, you throttled back the motors, you didn't try to gain altitude by accelerating the motors, you didn't try to put them on again?"

"I don't think it would be a wise thing to try the motors at that altitude," the pilot responded.[30]

Elements of Sully's story didn't sit right with veteran fliers. If the elevators had failed, why didn't he increase engine power or adjust the trim tabs? Either would have been standard troubleshooting measures to gain altitude. And were the elevators really faulty? They had worked fine when the plane first descended for the approach at the mouth of the river, and inspectors found nothing wrong with them after the wreck's recovery. Careful study of salvaged plane parts revealed no other evidence of mechanical failure, no signs of fire or explosion, no indication of malicious tampering. None of the surviving crewmembers recalled anything unusual before the crash, and the copilot Herman Rush could not corroborate Sully's claim that he also grabbed for the controls when the plane began to drop, because he was dead.[31]

Never a talker, Sully grew even more reticent when he and the investigators returned to New York for more hearings. In another B-314, Pan Am test pilots simulated the 45-degree nosedive he described. They found it easy to regain control of the ship without the use of the elevators. "I am afraid I am better off not to try to see what I done; I have no idea," Sully snapped as questions mounted about his judgment.[32]

Separately, the Civil Aeronautics Board and Pan Am's internal review panel would reach the same conclusion. They believed that, given the fading daylight, Sully had decided to land sooner rather than later, and that during a descending turn he misjudged the distance from the river and accidentally clipped it with the left wing. Pan Am's investigators, privy to Sully's history of ignoring protocol and learning of his penchant for making a "fancy swerve" upon descent, were especially confident in their assessment. In top-secret files, they tucked away their verdict: "100% Pilot Error" caused by "undue haste" and careless "exhibitionism."[33]

By the end of May, Pan Am's executives were pushing Sully to resign. But he resisted and asked the Master Pilot Board to review the company's "unfairness." When the Atlantic Division's head pilots assembled to hear both sides of the case, Sully spoke in an uncharacteristically quiet voice. With sunken cheeks and no sparkle in his eyes, he seemed a shell of his former self. Still the board affirmed that the company had been "justified" in asking for his resignation.[34]

Sully was angry. He hopped on a clipper back to Lisbon, where he accused members of the US legation of submitting an unfavorable report about him to Pan Am, saying that he had been drunk from the time of the accident until he returned home, and that his truculence had jeopardized Pan Am's relations with Portuguese authorities. From there he disappeared to Liberia. Rumors indicated he was trying to set up his own African airline. In 1944, when he finally returned to his North Carolina farm, he told his wife and son that an injury to his vertebrae sustained in the crash disqualified him from pilot work but that he had refused Pan Am's offer of a desk job. Still, his life with Mae fell apart. He remarried two years later, opened a business selling wholesale electrical supplies, and never flew professionally again.[35]

Family members of the crash victims first learned of the *Yankee Clipper* disaster over the radio. Then State Department telegrams arrived, often confirming the worst.[36]

The Seidels arranged an Episcopalian memorial service and burial for Harry at the family plot in Swan Point Cemetery in Providence, Rhode Island. He left behind no fewer than five life insurance policies. The London *Times* memorialized him as a leading figure in the clubs and charities of the American colony in Great Britain, praising "his warmhearted concern for others" and "his courage and sense of humour" even in the face of danger. At that year's annual meeting, Jersey Standard's stockholders voted to grant the US government a perpetual, royalty-free license to produce Buna-S synthetic rubber. At Nuremburg's Palace of Justice, thirteen executives from Standard's one-time prized business partner IG Farben would be convicted of war crimes.[37]

Frank was returned to Iowa and buried in the Czech National Cemetery. When Allied forces finally began to island-hop their way toward the Japanese mainland, they would skip past his former home, the Netherlands East Indies. That colony's occupiers would not be ejected until months after the nuclear incineration of Hiroshima and Nagasaki. Even then, Indonesians, like so many other colonized peoples in Asia, faced not peace but a new era of violent upheaval. Frank's boss from the Chinese firm Kian Gwan, who managed to survive the occupation of Java and its aftermath, wrote to Frank's sister about his plans to send his sons to college in the United States. Who knows what will happen, Oei Tjong Hauw told her: "The world nowadays is so small and one day I may find myself in Cedar Rapids."[38]

Ben's family received so many condolence letters from those who knew him or had read his columns that they could not respond to them all. They donated his clothes to Russian War Relief, which shipped them to Soviet troops along with a note explaining that they had belonged to a man who admired the Red Army's courage. British, American, and South Carolina flags draped the rostrum at Clemson College chapel for his funeral. He was laid to rest in the family burial ground looking onto the Blue Ridge Mountains, under the epitaph: "Among my own, in my own country, I sleep."[39]

Federal agents raided the New York offices of Manuel and his partner Marcelino in late 1943. In Marcelino's desk they discovered pictures of Franco's troops storming Madrid and a letter from a friend offering condolences for the derogatory publicity the shipping agents had received in *PM*. Marcelino's reply explained that he had only been "tru[e] to his faith." Investigators scoured the files of Garcia & Diaz but turned up "no definite information on any subversive activities," so the Justice Department closed its case. Other government authorities, however, continued to scrutinize the shipping firm. By the end of the war, claims against it for unpaid taxes and customs duties totaled more than sixty thousand dollars.[40]

At the Frank E. Campbell Chapel on Madison Avenue, the preferred funeral parlor for New York City's brightest stars, some five hundred admirers gathered for a music-filled service to honor Tamara. She had been cremated, breaking with Jewish tradition.[41] The ballad Tamara made famous, "Smoke Gets in Your Eyes," reverberated across the Allied world and stood out in the memories of many of the war's survivors. The song was sung in El Alamein dugouts, Mindanao jungle, and the mountains of France. The Red Cross sent it on phonograph records to POWs in Germany's Stalag II-B, and Moscow's State Symphony Orchestra broadcast it in tribute to their allies. One officer, standing watch on the deck of a troop transport speeding across the Atlantic, stopped to listen to a soldier bang it out on the enlisted men's recreation room piano, and in North Africa, army nurses and airmen danced to it in a house emptied of everything but a Victrola. In Shanghai, the sound of it playing in the distance brought tears to the eyes of captured Doolittle Raiders languishing in basement bamboo cells. Toward the end of the war,

B-29 bomber pilots, speeding toward Japan, even claimed to tune into it on Tokyo radio just before they blanketed that city in flaming napalm.[42]

In war some sacrifices are rewarded and remembered. Others are downplayed and forgotten. Tamara's surviving troupe mates each received $3,600 from the USO as compensation for their injuries and temporary unemployment—the most allowed by the group's sparse accident insurance for overseas performers and far less than they would have received if the USO had been set up as a government organization. Because Tamara had died her family received only a week's back pay, $218.57.[43]

Lawsuits filed against Pan American Airways by victims and their family members did not go far in the courts. Judges ruled again and again that the Warsaw Convention capped the international carrier's liability to just over eight thousand dollars per passenger. To override that limit, the plaintiffs would have had to prove that it was the US government that had provided their transportation or that the disaster was caused by willful misconduct. But the navy's ownership of the clipper had been secret, and during pretrial discovery, judges refused to order Pan Am to turn over its internal records about the crash. When summoned to New York to testify at a final jury trial ten years after the accident, Sully stuck to his story. Sometimes it's hard to know where deceit of others ends and self-deception begins. He died two years later of a heart attack.[44]

Once recovered, George returned to his post in London, where he received the Legion of Merit from General Eisenhower for his work arranging reciprocal aid. In 1944 he followed Allied combat troops into continental Europe as they bombed and blasted their way toward Berlin, bringing hope, salvation, and sometimes justice to the long unfree people in their path, but also more disruption and death. As Chief of the Procurement Control Section, G-4 Division, Supreme Headquarters, American Expeditionary Forces, George set up local supply and claim procedures in liberated and occupied territories and negotiated agreements with the French Committee of National Liberation as well as the governments of Belgium, Luxembourg, the Netherlands, and Norway. In February 1945, he flew back to Washington, this time from Paris, to testify in favor of another Lend-Lease extension.[45]

That August, when Harry Truman unceremoniously terminated the Allies' signature supply program, even before the Japanese surrender had been signed—and Lend-Lease detractors took to the newspapers to praise the president for having "wisely called a halt to this grandiose WPA"—George picked up his pen once again to counter the notion that the United States had unfairly "paid for this war." "I have always assumed that Mr.

Hitler originated this war," he fumed to the *New York Sun*, "and I know that we entered it to save ourselves—and almost too late at that."[46]

George lived until 1979.[47]

The war that George, Tamara, Harry, Manuel, Frank, Ben, and Sully had lived through before boarding the *Yankee Clipper*'s last flight was in many ways not the same one that unfolded after the crash. Whereas the war before February 1943 had been one of stunning Axis gains, the war after would instead be defined by sustained Allied victories. The United Nations would face setbacks of course, as well as individual battles won at too high a price. But once they stood their ground at Stalingrad, Guadalcanal, New Guinea, and in North Africa, Axis forces never regained the upper hand. That March, Rommel left Tunisia to report on his troops' declining fortunes and never returned. Increasingly outgunned and outmanned, Army Group Afrika surrendered in May. The subsequent invasion of Sicily toppled Mussolini's regime and put Allied bombers that much closer to the Reich's factories and cities. By summer the Wehrmacht found itself outnumbered and outsupplied along the vast Soviet front and menaced by resistance fighters nipping at the rear. In November, Admiral Chester Nimitz's Pacific Fleet began its island-hopping campaign toward Japan with victories in the Gilbert Islands. While Axis fuel stocks dwindled, planes and ships poured out of Allied dockyards and depots. No longer would supplying so many combat zones be for the United Nations a zero-sum game. By the end of the year, they had established air and sea superiority in all theaters of war.[48]

It took less than two years after that to sweep the U-boats from the sea lanes and knock the kamikaze fighters from the skies, to storm the beaches and clear the foxholes, to chase the Nazis back to Germany and bomb the Emperor's disciples into submission. While Allied leaders flew off to international summits to debate the planet's future and pose for the cameras, Axis tyrants, the subjects of increasingly serious assassination plots, disappeared underground. It is this chapter of the war, when US industrial, diplomatic, and military might came alive, that generations of Americans would most like to remember. Over time, that focus on the war's final stages has made it harder to reflect on just how close to disaster the world had come and how much Americans' experiences and efforts had been intertwined with, and built upon, the work and resources of other people and places around the globe.

After the war, people did what they often do after wars: clear rubble from the streets and till the fields, paste the schedules back up in train stations and rehang artwork on museum walls. The victors gathered up what documents they could find, to make sense of what had happened, to try the guilty and tally the dead, in some cases with razor-sharp precision, in other instances only through hazarded guesses—and to undertake an extraordinary series of efforts to put the world back together.

Some of the convictions and values the *Yankee Clipper*'s passengers had cherished would endure, even flourish in the postwar world. Ben would have liked to have seen South Asians win their independence. Tamara would have been encouraged by the rising number of married women in the workplace and, in time, their pursuit of all sorts of careers. While other nations turned to more robust forms of welfare state administration, George would have been relieved that in the United States the courts and the common law instead continued to play an outsized role in distributing social justice. The American beauty products, canned food, and other goods that Frank peddled would flood more and more markets overseas, and, in their escalating battles against communism, US officials would increasingly ally with right-wing dictators like Manuel's beloved Francisco Franco. During the second half of the twentieth century, multinational corporations, like Harry's Standard Oil, would stretch ever farther beyond the reach and regulation of single states.

But in other ways, the world these Americans had known before their flight to Lisbon would not survive the war. The privileged White enclaves Frank had joined in Southeast Asia, with their own special hotels, laws, and wages—they would soon be gone, and so would Jim Crow in Ben's South Carolina. As more and more people around the world questioned white supremacy and demanded self-determination, companies like Standard Oil and Pan Am would face renewed negotiations over access rights. Containerization erased the sights, smells, and messy tumult on Manuel's docks—and in any case Franco's postwar autarkical policies drove the Spanish shipping industry into the ground. Red-baiters and blacklisters hounded leftists like Tamara out of the entertainment industry; television killed their styles of live entertainment. During the coming decades, the Republican Party would become less and less welcoming for a liberal like George.

And superpower began to breed insularity and self-assurance even in corners of American society where searching curiosity had existed before. A standing army, a string of military bases ringing the globe, and a proliferating national security state brought new restrictions and burdens to international travel and engagement. The Cold War era would not be designed for party crashers, barnstormers, or stowaways.[49]

Or flying boats. The Second World War had gifted the world an expansive network of airports and runways. Landplanes, soon fitted with jet engines, were faster and easier to load and unload than seaplanes. They were not subject to saltwater corrosion or stalled by rough seas and frozen harbors. After Pan Am inaugurated regular landplane service across the Atlantic in September 1945, it quickly spread to other long-distance routes. The clippers that Sully once splashed down on the Nile, the Congo, the Amazon, and New York's Bowery Bay rusted at their docks. By 1951, every remaining one had been scuttled, scrapped, or sold for parts.[50]

APPENDIX

The *Yankee Clipper*'s Last Passenger Manifest

Crew

R. O. D. Sullivan, Pilot
Herman Stanton Rush, First Officer‡
Merwin Osterhout, Second Officer
Andrew Roy Freeland, Third Officer‡
John Curtis Burn, Fourth Officer
Joseph F. Vaughn, First Engineer‡
William Manning, Second Engineer
David M. Sanders, First Radio Officer
Robert Rowan, Second Radio Officer
Leonard A. Ingles, Supernumerary‡
Philip Casprini, Steward
Craig Robinson, Steward‡
D. Oliva, Radio Officer *(disembarked at Bermuda)*

Passengers

(in order of boarding priority)

James Wright, State Department courier ‡
~~General Hayes A. Kroner~~
~~Lieutenant Colonel Ludwell Montague~~ } *transferred to an earlier flight*
~~Lieutenant Colonel John R. Lovell~~
Lieutenant Colonel Luther D. Wallis ‡
Major James A. Hamlin, US Army ‡
Major George T. Hart, US Army ‡
Major Burton C. Mossman, Jr., US Army ‡
Major George A. Spiegelberg, US Army
Major John N. Poto, US Army ‡
Major Milton H. Weisman, US Army ‡
Captain Joshua Edelman, US Army Corps of Engineers ‡
Captain James E. Pepper, US Army ‡
Major Earl G. Stoy, US Army ‡
Captain Paul Sprout, US Army ‡
Lieutenant Clifford A. Sheldon, US Army
Manuel Diaz, Garcia & Diaz Shipping ‡
William Walton Butterworth, Jr., State Department
Harry G. Seidel, Standard Oil of New Jersey ‡
Theodore W. Lamb, Office of Civilian Defense ‡
Frank J. Cuhel, Mutual Broadcasting System ‡
Ben Robertson, Jr., *New York Herald Tribune* ‡
Arthur A. Lee, Artlee Pictures Corporation ‡
Olga Witkowska [Gypsy Markoff], USO-Camp Shows, Inc.
Roy Rognan, USO-Camp Shows, Inc.‡
Jean N. Rognan [Jean Lorraine], USO-Camp Shows, Inc.
Grace G. Drysdale, USO-Camp Shows, Inc.
Ellen Jane Ross [Jane Froman], USO-Camp Shows, Inc.
Elsa H. Silver [Yvette], USO-Camp Shows, Inc.
Tamara Drasin Swann [Tamara], USO-Camp Shows, Inc. ‡

‡Killed in the crash.

A NOTE ON METHOD, WITH ACKNOWLEDGMENTS

IF YOU WENT BACK IN time and told younger me that I would spend more than a decade researching and writing a book about the Second World War, I would have laughed you out of the room. I came of age in the 1980s and 1990s, during what Emily Rosenberg calls the World War II "memory boom" when signs of the "Good War," fought by the "Greatest Generation," were everywhere. Stephen Ambrose books and Steven Spielberg movies. Fiftieth-anniversary commemorations of the Pearl Harbor bombing and video game reenactments of the D-Day invasion.[1] The conflict—or at least the way Americans had commonly come to recount it—seemed to me exceptionally well-traveled ground.

But over time I began to think more about the particularity of late-twentieth-century American World War II narratives, about how they tended to revolve around two parallel histories of "the men who fought" and the "people at home" and what that framing often obscured: the importance of civilians and uniformed noncombatants to the conflict overseas; the mindboggling global canvas on which this war was waged; the complex and often conflicting political convictions that underwrote Americans' participation; and the degree to which transnational connections, many of them forged long before the bombing of Pearl Harbor, informed and shaped the actions of not just interventionist reporters and politicians but all kinds of Americans. In the 1980s and 1990s Americans understandably turned to nationalistic celebrations of US combat troops' role in the Allied victory—to honor an aging population of veterans, to find a war to be proud of in the wake of Vietnam. But given the challenges of the twenty-first century—globe-wide threats to democracy, environmental perils that will require international cooperation and collective solutions—it's time to revisit Americans' road into, and place among other peoples during this signal conflict.[2]

As I started imagining how I might craft an American World War II story less like *Saving Private Ryan* and more like *Casablanca* (as I sometimes explained the idea for this book), I considered drafting chapters that focused on different kinds of noncombatants abroad: businessmen, correspondents, relief workers, and so on. But such an approach seemed like an invitation to self-fulfilling prophesy. If I structured the book that way, I would be picking categories of people that I deemed important in retrospect and then finding supposedly representative individuals to confirm my assumptions. And I wouldn't be able to capture the remarkable way some participants jumped between different roles during the war.

What if, instead of approaching people as archetypes, I regarded them as modes of inquiry? What if I began with a randomized sampling of individuals caught up in a shared tragedy and let them determine the routes, topics, and chronologies I follow, like in John Hersey's *Hiroshima*? But to recover their lives before the disaster, like in Thornton Wilder's *The Bridge of San Luis Rey*. Weaving together multiple biographies, I thought, might yield up productively dissident accounts in place of master narrative. And a fine-grained analysis of individual lives could offer a way to tell a story with global scope without resorting to an abstract, bird's eye point of view. Historians often turn to microhistory to write evocatively about times and places lacking extensive records. But it can be used to strike a path through otherwise overwhelming terrain and source material, too.[3]

Once I had decided on this method—and began investigating wartime commercial aviation—it did not take long to stumble on the crash of the *Yankee Clipper*. News reports listed only some of the accident's victims, but they offered enough detail to suggest that an interesting mix of people had been on board the plane. (I have since come to believe that any clipper flight would have yielded up an illuminating cross-section of travelers.) I set off for the Pan American Airways archive at the University of Miami to see what documents it might hold about the crash. The trip turned up more than I dared hope for, everything from the flight's manifests and lists of what the stewards stored in the galley to survivor testimony and Sully's employment records. Subsequent digging in the files of the US legation in Lisbon turned up more details about the accident and its victims. In Ireland, Barry O'Kelly gave me access to Irish intelligence records on Pan Am travelers and let me wander around the Foynes Flying Boat Museum's full-size replica of the *Yankee Clipper*. Gerry Gitner put me in touch with the Pan Am Historical Foundation, and Doug Miller found many illuminating photographs of Sully in that group's collections.

As I began preliminary investigations into the other thirty-eight passengers and crewmembers, roughly a dozen seemed possible to trace. Over time, I uncovered much more about some of them than I originally anticipated and began to narrow the cast to those whose biographies bounded off in the most diverse directions. Each of them turned out to be a unique challenge to research.

Finding entry points into the lives of the flight's twelve US Army officers presented a serious puzzle from the start. None of their names, let alone details about their missions, had been released publicly. Military officials were not supposed to fly commercial routes through neutral territories. Handwritten notations on Pan Am's confidential manifests did reveal the men's names and ranks but precious little else. And because all but two of the officers died in the crash, they had no postwar careers to track backwards. Only George—given his political and legal work and earlier enlistment in the navy—left any real threads to pull at.

George's World War I service file survived the 1973 fire at the National Personnel Records Center in St. Louis, and Jordan Pouliot turned up relevant histories of the navy's observation balloon training program. Kathy Peiss told me about fold3.com, which yielded the documents needed to piece together the Great War movements of George's brother, Freddie. Eric Rauchway offered wise advice about interwar Republican politics even though that advice forced me to read more Herbert Hoover. Andrew David, Aaron Hiltner, and Cathal Nolan pointed me to useful sources on the European Theater of Operations. I especially appreciate the assistance of Ann S. Brown, George's daughter. On a bright winter day she invited me to her home to view scrapbooks, military orders, and other documents saved by her father. Details gleaned from these papers enabled me to locate George's Reverse Lend-Lease work in the voluminous World War II–era files of the British and US governments.

I did not expect at first to find Manuel and neutral cargo shipping very interesting. How wrong I was! Newspaper searches quickly turned up evidence of the controversy surrounding Garcia & Diaz during the Spanish Civil War as well as Manuel's arrest in December 1941. But from there the trail went cold. Manuel Diaz was too common a name. I read up on the small Spanish community in early-twentieth-century New York and combed through public records, trying to nail down the timing of Manuel's arrival. When this work turned up other Spanish immigrants working in the shipping industry, I followed them, too. I learned to always page right after locating a microfilmed or digitized document—because sometimes supplementary materials were filed with the standard bureaucratic forms. And one morning, browsing past an ocean liner passenger manifest, there it was: a note Manuel wrote in support of an arriving business associate. His company stationery listed the shipping lines he represented. I suddenly realized, using information gleaned from trade directories and letterhead I could figure out which vessels he regularly serviced. I could follow the ships.

This strategy unlocked information about Garcia & Diaz in the files of more than a dozen different government agencies from the British Admiralty and the Bermuda US consulate to the Foreign Office and the FBI. Brian Desmarais tracked down hard-to-find Spanish Civil War–era court cases, and a FOIA request pried loose important Justice Department case files. The knowledgeable National Archives staff at College Park tipped me off to the fact that the State Department Central Files include a separate run of confidential boxes. Luis Chunga-Celis and David Messenger helped me prepare for a research trip to Madrid, and, given my comically bad conversational Spanish, Pilar Casado at the Archivo del Ministerio de Asuntos Exteriores kindly conversed with me in French. I suspect even more remains to be found—at other archives in Spain, in Latin American port authority records, and at the British National Archives where, at the time of my visits, some files on wartime Spanish shipping remained classified.

Frank—who escaped Java under a hail of Japanese bullets—I knew I wanted to work on right away. But he had no children, no publicly available papers. If he had served as a print journalist during the war, I might have looked up his articles, but the work of a radio broadcaster, I feared, had been lost to the ether. Prospects seemed bleak until I found his great nephew Michael Safranek on ancestry.com. I asked with low expectations: did he by chance know anything about his grandmother's brother? You bet, Michael responded from Chicago. He had all of Frank's things in his closet and offered to send them to me.

Normally historians travel to their archives. In this case the archive came to me: a weather-beaten travel trunk and another oversized container stuffed with diaries, business correspondence, and radio transcripts complete with censors' notations. Michael, I am eternally grateful to you (and Jim) for sharing this treasure trove and so pleased that Frank's papers have found a permanent home at the University of Iowa Libraries. Thanks also to Bob Rothstein at BU's Geddes Language Center, who hauled "legacy" equipment out of deep storage to digitize Frank's 16mm travel movies. Zach Fredman decoded Frank's Japanese military pass and answered my sundry questions about wartime Asia. Andrew Bell did superb research on Papua New Guinea. Jennifer L. Foray and Ethan Mark offered pointed advice on Dutch colonial terminology, and Will Tiemeijer confirmed my interpretation of one particularly important Dutch source.

Running word searches for someone simply called "Tamara" presented another dubious prospect. But because international travel required official identification, Tamara's full name had been recorded. And because the plane crashed, Pan Am communicated with her family members in the aftermath. This turned up her father, Boris Drasin. Boris had played a central role in the establishment of the Jewish cooperative Jersey Homesteads, so his papers, along with other archives from the experimental commune, were preserved by Rutgers University. These files, it turns out, documented not only a labor activist's community organizing but also a proud father's efforts to follow his daughter's blossoming career—with clippings, photographs, set lists, and other memorabilia.

I thank Mark Kukis for locating these Drasin Family Papers and Fernanda Perrone for alerting me to other, unprocessed materials in Rutgers' collections, which proved essential for understanding the Drasins' lives before they immigrated to the United States. Sarah Phillips helped pin down the timing of Tamara's escape from Ukraine by sharing her knowledge about haystacks and plains agriculture, and she interpreted Tamara's sheet music notations. Simon Rabinovich looked up Sorochyntsi in his old Russian encyclopedias, and April French skillfully translated Tamara's handwritten correspondence. Katie Brownell located love letters to Tamara in the miscellaneous folders of Clifford Odets's papers, and Walt Odets gave permission to quote from them. Google Books made it possible to unearth the many references to "Smoke Gets in Your Eyes" in World War II memoirs.

Harry, who sometimes went by H. G., worked for a secretive corporation in a complicated international industry. The archives made available by Standard Oil of New Jersey's successor ExxonMobil contain mostly promotional materials that cast the company in the best possible light. But, in the late 1940s (maybe as part of the effort to rehabilitate their reputation after the patents controversy), Jersey Standard's executives opened their files to a team of business historians who produced a detailed, multivolume account of the company's history. These included scattered but revealing references to Harry's work. Other such traces appeared in the thousands upon thousands of pages of documents gathered during various congressional investigations into the firm's overseas dealings. Because early-twentieth-century colleges, including Brown University, often requested updates from former students about their wartime service and careers, alumni records also helped to establish Harry's business travels and responsibilities at Standard Oil.

David Engerman alerted me to the State Department name index, which turned up more evidence of Harry's diplomacy. Nicole Phelps offered sage advice for finding the records of evacuated legations and consulates, and Nina Martin picked through files that had been spirited from Bucharest during the German occupation. Larry Clark kindly put me in touch with Geraldine Seidel, who shared photographs of Harry as well as his remarkable letters to John D. Rockefeller, Jr. Ann Clark generously donated a copy of the memoir of Harry's daughter, Rosamond Clark. These family keepsakes provided valuable insights into the oil man's life outside the office.

Some leave little trace, others almost too much. Over the course of his career, Ben published hundreds of magazine and newspaper articles. Scores of others were written about his books and speeches, and more than a dozen boxes of his personal papers reside at his alma mater, Clemson University. These contain drafts, revisions, and copies of his cables, which proved especially helpful for tracking the evolution of his ideas over time as well as comparing what he wrote to what his editors ultimately published. As detailed as Ben's story appears here, it could have been two or three times longer.

But his archive has its own curious gaps and silences nevertheless. It is missing the extensive notes he kept while serving as a merchant seaman in 1937 and contains only the barest of clues about his advocacy for White Southern defection to the Republican Party. Outside sources offer more revealing glimpses of his sexual orientation and his racial politics, suggesting that his papers may have been culled and curated before they were donated.

Samuel Zipp shared the telegram Ben and his colleagues sent to Wendell Willkie recommending he take an international goodwill tour. Tony Badger and Bruce Schulman steered me to important works on Southern politics. Paula Austin helped me understand interwar Washington, DC. Joe Crespino, Sarah Phillips, and Bruce Schulman crashed the lobby of the London Savoy with me when I was trying to envision the hotel's layout for

Ben's Blitz chapter, and Megan Black humored me with an outing to the Churchill War Rooms. Alexis Peri offered valuable guidance on the wartime history of the Soviet Union. Ben Siegel did the same for India.

Over the years, I've also accrued debts to so many other historians and archivists—those who commented or questioned at talks, listened to my ideas over dinners and in conference hallways, or answered my email requests for help. A few of these friends and collaborators deserve special mention. Early career mentoring from Mark Bradley, Dan Rodgers, and Mary Dudziak gave me the confidence to undertake this project. Andrew Bacevich put me in touch with John Wright, who helped place this book with Oxford. Sarah Snyder and Danny Fine hosted me during my many research trips to Washington, DC. I may have visited one time more than necessary just for the wonderful company.

I also had morale-sustaining conversations about this project with Beth Bailey, Megan Black, Tim Borstelmann, Dan Bouk, Chris Capozzola, Frank Costigliola, Jeff Engel, David Engerman, Ashley Farmer, Gary Gerstle, Kristin Hoganson, Daniel Immerwahr, Ryan Irwin, Adriane Lentz-Smith, Fred Logevall, David Milne, Kaeten Mistry, Andrew Preston, Bill Rankin, Jennifer Ratner-Rosenhagen, Andrew Robichaud, Jay Sexton, and Jim Sparrow. A buddy system with Brian DeLay kept me going through the darkest days of the pandemic. Dan Margolies fortified me with delicious honey from his beehives, and Nick Guyatt showed mercy and forgiveness when I needed it most.

Funding from Boston University's Peter T. Paul Career Development Professorship and an American Philosophical Society Franklin Research Grant made possible the extensive archival work it took to get this project off the ground. The generosity and resourcefulness of Lou Ferleger, Nazli Kibria, Jon Roberts, Bruce Schulman, Nina Silber, and Cady Steinberg turned up additional aid in the book's later stages. Rhoda Bilansky at the Mugar Interlibrary Loan office worked magic for me more than once.

A Jeffrey Henderson Fellowship from BU's Center for the Humanities and an ACLS Frederick Burkhardt Fellowship, spent in residence at Stanford University's Center for the Advanced Study of the Behavioral Sciences, gave me not only time to write but also the chance to do so in the company of so many talented and engaging scholars. A fellowship from the NEH Public Scholars Program—arriving with wondrous *deus ex machina* timing—got this project over the finish line. Any views, findings, conclusions, or recommendations expressed in this book, of course, do not necessarily represent those of the National Endowment for the Humanities.

Toward the end of the drafting process Mark Bradley, William Hitchcock, Melani McAlister, and Andrew Rotter gathered for an all-day manuscript workshop. They brainstormed inspired solutions to problems I never could have solved on my own. Susan Ferber, who also participated in the workshop, is an editor in a class of her own. I'm so thankful for her patience, unflagging support for this strange experiment, and whip-smart attention to detail.

Cole Parker performed heroic fact checking. Elizabeth Grumer chased down image permissions, and speedy assistance from Tamzen Flanders, Jim Johnson, and Susan Mizruchi, as well as a grant from the BU Center for the Humanities, made possible many of the book's photographs and maps. Thanks also go to Jeremy Toynbee, Joellyn Ausanka, and everyone else who whisked the manuscript through production.

I owe enormous appreciation to my family in California—Teresa, Kirk, Bri, Todd, and Lilah—and in Northern Ireland—Julie, Adele, Iain, Alannah, Aoife, and Emma. You graciously put up with my habit of writing even while on vacation. I can't promise there'll be no more unsolicited history lessons, but I will try.

My biggest thanks go to Jamie—who fed me, read my drafts, and made me laugh—and to my daughter, Ailish. She spent her entire childhood with this project lurking in the background but was too polite to notice. Whenever I told her I was going to work on the book, she responded with the same delightfully unconcerned question:

"What book?"

NOTES

ABBREVIATIONS IN THE NOTES

AJHS	American Jewish Historical Society, New York, New York
AMAE	Archivo del Ministerio de Asuntos Exteriores, Madrid, Spain
BBP	Bruce Barton Papers, Wisconsin Historical Society, Madison, Wisconsin
BFRP	Ben Robertson Papers, Special Collections and Archives, Clemson University Libraries, Clemson, South Carolina
BL	India Office Records and Private Papers, British Library, London, UK
Bonus Files	World War II Bonus Case Files, State Historical Society of Iowa, Des Moines, Iowa
BRTC	Billy Rose Theatre Collection, New York Public Library for the Performing Arts, New York, New York
BUBF	Biographical Files Collection, Brown University Archives, Providence, Rhode Island
BWWI	World War I Correspondence, Brown University Archives, Providence, Rhode Island
CCOH	Columbia Center for Oral History, Columbia University, New York, New York
Census (1850)	*Seventh Census of the United States*, NARA microfilm M432

Census (1860)	*Eighth Census of the United States*, NARA microfilm M653
Census (1870)	*Ninth Census of the United States*, NARA microfilm M593
Census (1880)	*Tenth Census of the United States*, NARA microfilm T9
Census (1900)	*Twelfth Census of the United States*, NARA microfilm T623
Census (1910)	*Thirteenth Census of the United States*, NARA microfilm T624
Census (1920)	*Fourteenth Census of the United States*, NARA microfilm T625
Census (1930)	*Fifteenth Census of the United States*, NARA microfilm T626
Census (1940)	*Sixteenth Census of the United States*, NARA microfilm T627
ConfedRec	*Compiled Service Records of Confederate Soldiers Who Served in Organizations from the State of South Carolina*, NARA microfilm M267
COP	Clifford Odets Papers, Lilly Library, Indiana University, Bloomington, Indiana
DAF	Deceased Alumni Files, Division of Rare Book and Manuscript Collections, Cornell University, Ithaca, New York
DFP	Drasin Family Papers, Special Collections and University Archives, Rutgers University Libraries, New Brunswick, New Jersey
DTMC	Dispatches from *Time* magazine correspondents: first series, 1942–1955, film 00-2345, Houghton Library, Harvard College Library, Cambridge, Massachusetts
EOLP	US Congress, Senate, Committee on the Judiciary and Committee on Interior and Insular Affairs, *Emergency Oil Lift Program and Related Problems*, part 3, appendix A, 85th Congress, 1st session, February 27–March 22, 1957
ExxMo	ExxonMobil Historical Collection, Briscoe Center for American History, University of Texas, Austin, Texas
FBMMA	Foynes Flying Boat & Maritime Museum Archives, County Limerick, Ireland
FDRL	Franklin D. Roosevelt Presidential Library, Hyde Park, New York
FDRPA	*The Public Papers and Addresses of Franklin D. Roosevelt*, 13 volumes, New York, 1938–1950
FFF	Fight for Freedom, Inc. Papers, Mudd Library, Princeton University, Princeton, New Jersey
FJCP	Frank J. Cuhel Papers, Private Collection of Michael Safranek. This collection has since been donated to University Archives, the University of Iowa Libraries, Iowa City, Iowa.

FRUS	US Department of State, *Papers Relating to the Foreign Relations of the United States*
GASP	George A. Spiegelberg Papers, Private Collection of Ann S. Brown
Gorrell's	*Gorrell's History of the American Expeditionary Forces Air Service, 1917–1919*, NARA microfilm M990
HGSP	Harry G. Seidel Papers, Private Collection of Geraldine Seidel
IAR	*Records of the Department of State Relating to Internal Affairs of Romania, 1910–1944*, NARA microfilm M1198
ITVDP	Irita Taylor Van Doren Papers, 1920-1967, Manuscript Division, Library of Congress, Washington, DC
IWP	Ione Wright Papers, Special Collections, Otto G. Richter Library, University of Miami, Miami, Florida
JFP	Jane Froman Papers, The State Historical Society of Missouri, Columbia, Missouri
JJDC	Records of the American Jewish Joint Distribution Committee, Joint Distribution Committee Archives, New York, New York
Lend-Lease	US Congress, House of Representatives, *Extension of Lend-Lease Act: Hearings before the Committee on Foreign Affairs*, 78th Congress, 1st session, January 29–February 23, 1943
MultiCorp	US Congress, Senate, Committee on Foreign Relations, *Hearings before the Subcommittee on Multinational Corporations on Multinational Petroleum Companies and Foreign Policy*, part 8, 93rd Congress, 2nd session, February 20–June 20, 1974
NAA	*Inward passenger manifests for ships and aircraft arriving at Freemantle, Perth Airport and Western Australia outports from 1897–1963*, National Archives of Australia microfilm K269
NARA	National Archives and Records Administration, College Park, Maryland
	RG21 — Records of District Courts of the United States, 1685–2009
	RG24 — Records of the Bureau of Navy Personnel, General Records of the Recreation Services Section, 1943–1946
	RG38 — Records of the Office of Naval Intelligence, Security Classified Administration Correspondence, 1942–1946
	RG59 — General Records of the Department of State, Central Decimal File

	RG60	Department of Justice General Records, Criminal Division, Classified Subject Files, 1930–1987
	RG84	General Records of Foreign Service Posts of the Department of State
	RG85	Records of the Immigration and Naturalization Service, 1787–2004
	RG165	Records of the War Department, Military Intelligence Division Correspondence, 1917–1941
	RG165/G-2	Records of the War Department, Office of the Director of Intelligence
	RG165-R	Records of the War Department, Military Intelligence Division Regional File, 1922–1944
	RG182	Records of the War Trade Board, Digest Record Cards on Firms in New York, 1917–1919
	RG 216	Records of the Office of Censorship
	RG247	Records of the Office of Chief of Chaplains, Management Division, 1920–1945
	RG319	US Army Intelligence Decimal File, 1941-1948
	RG407	Records of the Adjutant General's Office, Special Services Division, Records of Camp Shows, Inc., 1941–1957
	RG498	Records of Headquarters, European Theater of Operations, US Army in World War II

NatDef — US Congress, Senate, Special Committee Investigating the National Defense Program, *Investigation of the National Defense Program Pursuant to S. Res. 71*, part 11, 77th Congress, 1st Session, March 5-April 7, 1942

NavRec — Records of the Bureau of Naval Personnel, 1789–2007, Record Group 24, National Archives at Saint Louis, Missouri

NYAGO — New York State Adjutant General's Office, Abstracts of World War I Military Service, 1917–1919, New York State Archives, Albany, New York

NYCS — State Population Census Schedules, New York State Archives, Albany, New York

NYNav — Headquarters Third Naval District Commandant's Files, 1939–1942, Record Group 181, National Archives at New York, New York

NYPL	Special Collections, New York Public Library for the Performing Arts, New York, New York
OGC	Louis S. Nixdorff 1928 Olympic Games Collection, Archives Center, National Museum of American History, Washington, DC
PA-I	*Passport Applications, 1795–1905*, NARA microfilm M1372
PA-II	*Passport Applications, January 2, 1906 – March 31, 1925*, NARA microfilm M1490
Pan Am	Pan American World Airways, Inc. Records, Special Collections, Otto G. Richter Library, University of Miami, Miami, Florida. Box and folder numbers refer to the collection's original classification system.
Patents	US Congress, Senate, Committee on Patents, *Patents: Hearings on S. 2303, a Bill to Provide for the Use of Patents in the Interest of National Defense or the Prosecution of the War, and for Other Purposes*, 10 parts, 77th Congress, 2nd session, April 13–August 21, 1942
PetrolCartel	US Congress, Senate, Select Committee on Small Business, Subcommittee on Monopoly, *International Petroleum Cartel: Staff Report to the Federal Trade Commission*, 82nd Congress, 2nd Session, August 22, 1952
RPPP	Robert Porter Patterson Papers, Manuscript Division, Library of Congress, Washington, DC
RTP	Roscoe Turner Papers, American Heritage Center, University of Wyoming, Laramie, Wyoming
SCWC	Spanish Civil War Collection, Center for Southwest Research, University Libraries, University of New Mexico, Albuquerque, New Mexico
SIA	*Confidential U.S. State Department Central Files, Spain, Internal Affairs, 1930–1939*, University Publications of America microfilm
SIFA	*Confidential U.S. State Department Central Files, Spain, Internal Affairs and Foreign Affairs, 1940–1944*, University Publications of America microfilm
SSNav	Files on the SS *Navemar*, Saul Sperling Collection, Leo Baeck Institute, New York, New York
TNA	The National Archives, Kew, United Kingdom
	ADM Records of the Admiralty
	AVIA Records of the Ministry of Aviation

	BT	Records of the Board of Trade
	CAB	Records of the Cabinet Office
	DEFE	Records of the Ministry of Defence
	FO	Records of the Foreign Office
	HS	Records of the Special Operations Executive
	MT	Records of Ministries of Transport
	POWE	Records of the Ministry of Power
	T	Records of HM Treasury
	TS	Records of the Treasury Solicitor
	WO	Records of the War Office

Tribunals	Germany (Territory under Allied Occupation: US Zone), *Trials of War Criminals before the Nuernberg Military Tribunals under Control Council Law No. 10*, volumes 7–8, Washington, D.C., 1949–1953
UIA	Alumni and Former Students Vertical Files, University of Iowa Libraries Special Collections, Iowa City, Iowa
VANY	*Passenger and Crew Lists of Vessels Arriving at New York, New York, 1897–1957*, NARA microfilm T715
WSP	Washington Spiegelberg Papers, Fray Angélico Chávez History Library, Santa Fe, New Mexico
WWI Reg	*World War I Selective Service System Draft Registration Cards, 1917–1918*, NARA microfilm M1509
WWII Reg	*Draft Registration Cards, October 16, 1940–March 31, 1947*, Records of the Selective Service System, 1926–1975, Record Group 147, National Archives at St. Louis, Missouri
WWII Reg-NJ	*World War II Draft Cards (Fourth Registration) for the State of New Jersey*, NARA microfilm M1986
WWBP	William Wright Bryan Papers, Clemson University Libraries Special Collections, Clemson, South Carolina
WWP	Wendell Willkie Papers, Lilly Library, Indiana University, Bloomington, Indiana

Introduction

1. Maintenance department monthly summary, February 1943, folder 10, box II:132, Predeparture Movements of the NC18603 and NC18605, March 2, 1943, and passenger manifest, folder 4, box II:145, pamphlet, "Summary of Wartime International Travel Requirements," folder 51, box I:260, Pan Am.
2. Passenger manifest, folder 4, box II:145, Pan Am; Frank Cuhel to Ermengarde Cuhel, February 14, 1943, FJCP.
3. Foreign Service memo, April 26, 1943, 353.113 Swann, Tamara Drasin, box 205, RG59, NARA; Gypsy Markoff to Roscoe Turner, February 19, 1943, folder 18, box 53, RTP. For Tamara's frequent mentions of Ukraine, see for example, clippings, "No Longer Noble," January 24, 1937, and "Bublichki to Roberta," January 2, 1938, both in *Brooklyn Eagle*, TAMARA clipping folder (OF-20a), NYPL.
4. George Spiegelberg draft card, New York, February 15, 1942, *WWII Reg*; Sol Bloom to George Spiegelberg, February 3, 1943, and photograph, scrapbook, volume 1, GASP; Assistant Manager McVitty to Operations Manager, May 26, 1943, and property claims, folder 24, box II:142, Pan Am.
5. Mark Mazower, *Hitler's Empire: How the Nazis Ruled Europe* (New York: Penguin, 2008), 3, 412, 438–41; Richard Evans, *The Third Reich at War* (New York: Penguin, 2009), 380–85, 401–2, 470.
6. Evans, *Third Reich at War*, 407–20; Timothy Snyder, *Bloodlands: Europe between Hitler and Stalin* (New York: Basic, 2010), esp. vii–xiv, 219–20, 236, 241–63, 274, 383.
7. Peter Duus, Ramon Myers, and Mark Peattie, eds., *The Japanese Wartime Empire, 1931–1945* (Princeton, NJ: Princeton University Press, 1996), xii; Van Waterford, *Prisoners of the Japanese in World War II* (Jefferson, NC: McFarland, 1994), 31; Yuki Tanaka, *Hidden Horrors: Japanese War Crimes in World War II* (Boulder, CO: Westview, 1996).
8. Lizzie Collingham, *The Taste of War: World War II and the Battle for Food* (New York: Penguin, 2012), 255–56; Madhusree Mukerjee, *Churchill's Secret War: The British Empire and the Ravaging of India during World War II* (New York: Basic, 2010), 106–18.
9. "Prime Minister in Talk to Commons Declares Aim to Smash Nazis," February 12, 1943, 1, 5, "Roosevelt Promises 'Bad News' for Nazis, Italians and the Japanese," February 13, 1943, 1, 3, and "Goebbels Asks Total Unity Before Red 'Invasion' Threat," February 19, 1943, 1, 8, all in *New York Times*; Goebbels as translated by Evans, *Third Reich at War*, 424; Victor Davis Hanson, *The Second World Wars: How the First Global Conflict Was Fought and Won* (New York: Basic, 2017), 38, 463–99. On naming the conflict, see David Reynolds, "The Origins of the Two 'World Wars': Historical Discourse and International Politics," *Journal of Contemporary History* 38, no. 1 (January 2003): 29–44.
10. Philip Gibbs, "Yankee Clipper from Lisbon Tuesday," *Vogue*, November 1, 1941, 74–77; Joseph March, "Our Amazing Airport," *New York Times*,

November 30, 1941, SM10; confidential memos on security regulations, July 25, 1942, folder 1, box II:434, and August 1, 1942, folder 51, box I:260, report on interned employees, December 1941–September 1945, folder 4, box I:261, all in Pan Am; M. D. Klaäs, *Last of the Flying Clippers: The Boeing B-314 Story* (Atglen, PA: Schiffer, 1997), 217–18.

11. Harry Seidel passport application, February 13, 1914, reel 203, *PA-II*; W. E. Hagerman, confidential memo, March 12, 1943, Lisbon Legation, 1943: vol. 17, box 77, RG84, NARA; ticket transactions summary, folder 24, box II:152, Pan Am.
12. Mary B. R. Longley to M. D. Klaás, April 14, 1966, folder 3, box 1, BFRP; "Yvette, in London, Offers Details on Clipper Crash," *New York Herald Tribune*, March 30, 1943, 15A; M. Parsons to Secretary of State, July 26, 1943, Lisbon Legation, 1943: vol. 17, box 77, RG84, NARA; "War News Summarized" and Bertram Hulen, "Hull and Halifax Confer on India," *New York Times*, February 21, 1943, 1, 21.
13. Passenger manifests, folder 4, box II:145, memo, April 7, 1943, folder 5, and Butterworth statement, February 26, 1943, folder 12, box II:152, Pan Am; "W. Walton Butterworth Dies," *New York Times*, April 2, 1975, 42. On Arthur Lee, see Anthony Slide, *Silent Topics: Essays on Undocumented Areas of Silent Film* (Lanham, MD: Scarecrow Press, 2005), 15–16.
14. Confidential memos, February 27, March 3, and March 12, 1943, box 77, Lisbon Legation, General Records, 1943: vol. 17, RG84, NARA; Jacob Fuller, synopsis report, January 20, 1944, litigation case file 146-7-1883, box 13, RG60, NARA; personal effects inventory, 353.113 Diaz, Manuel, box 1202, RG59, NARA.
15. Passenger manifests, folder 4, box II:145, and folder 14, box II:152, paraphrase of telegram from American minister, Dublin, to Secretary of State, February 10, 1942, folder 28, box II:7, Pan Am; passenger lists and Irish intelligence reports, folders PAA00052, Department of Defence 000025 and 00027, FBMMA; Philadelphia, 47B, reel 2341867, and Roswell, NM, 5A, reel 2341128, both in *Census (1930)*; claims 136608 and 309189, *Bonus Files*; Hanson, *Second World Wars*, 214–15.
16. Ulysses Lee, *The Employment of Negro Troops* (Washington, DC: Office of the Chief of Military History, 1966), 111–15; Thomas A. Guglielmo, *Divisions: A New History of Racism and Resistance in America's World War II Military* (New York: Oxford University Press, 2021), ch. 1; Olga Witkowska statement, March 4, 1943, folder 12, box II:152, Pan Am. Domestic US airlines often refused bookings to customers who sounded Black on the phone, relegated them to segregated seats, or bumped them in transit to accommodate White passengers: Mia Bay, *Traveling Black: A Story of Race and Resistance* (Cambridge, MA: Belknap, 2021), ch. 5. Whether Pan Am's employees resorted to similar tactics is unclear. Pan Am's terminal at its southern hub of Miami was not segregated, but the adjoining airport restaurant was, and the presence of Black travelers on Pan Am clippers was rare enough to warrant comment in the Black press: Lawrence Lamar,

"Jackie Robinson, UCLA Star, Back from Honolulu," December 20, 1941, 5, "Ollie Stewart in Ireland," August 15, 1942, 11, and Deton Brooks, "Jim Crow at America's Air Crossroads Sabotages Latin Good Neighbor Policy," July 3, 1943, 1, all in *Chicago Defender*.

17. Between 1939 and December 1941, the *New York Times* alone contained hundreds of articles detailing the clippers' movements and passengers.
18. Transatlantic Air Service report, January 22, 1942, folder 16, box I:107, Pan Am ad, *Saturday Evening Post*, March 21, 1942, folder 1, box I:25, and War Service of Pan American World Airways, folder 15, box I:259, Pan Am; Klaäs, *Last of the Flying Clippers*, 127, 202.
19. Brief Summary of Trip 9/035, folder 12, box II:152, Pan Am; O.S. Unit reports, box 7, RG407, NARA; photographs, folder 316, JFP. On Gypsy Markoff, see Olga Markoff signed headshot, photographs box, DFP; "Lisbon Clipper Crash Blamed on Air Pocket," *Brooklyn Daily Eagle*, February 24, 1943, 3; *Exochorda* manifest, November 16, 1939, role 6419, *VANY*.
20. "Survivor Depicts Wreck of Clipper," *New York Times*, February 25, 1943, 6; Jean Rognan statement, February 27, 1943, folder 12, box II:152, Pan Am; "Roosevelt's Clipper Here after African Trip with Escort Plane which Met Emergency," February 22, 1943, 7, and "Identifying 19 Dead in Airplane by Teeth," February 2, 1943, 6, both in *New York Times*; James Trautman, *Pan American Clippers: The Golden Age of Flying Boats* (Erin, Ontario: Boston Mills, 2007), 249–52.
21. Wayne Thomis, "Christen Queen of Air for New Atlantic Route," *Chicago Tribune*, March 4, 1939, 1, 5; Civil Aeronautics Board report, September 7, 1943, folder 6, box II:152 [hereafter CAB report], clipping, *New Horizons*, January 1943, folder 107, box I:120a, lists of *Yankee Clipper* firsts and notable passengers, May 20, 1939–January 30, 1942, and transcript of *Herald Tribune* report, "50,000 See Yankee Clipper Open North Beach Trans-Atlantic Base," April 1, 1940, folder 16, box I:107, all in Pan Am; Larry Weirather, *The China Clipper, Pan American Airways and Popular Culture* (Jefferson, NC: McFarland, 2007).
22. CAB report; Aircraft Classified Matter—Security Procedure, November 19, 1942, folder 1, box II:434, list of World War II special missions, folder 52, box I:260, and clipping, "Famous Pilots: R. O. D. Sullivan," *Airmail Magazine*, 1943, folder 23, box I:293, all in Pan Am; Rod Sullivan, Jr., interview, September 24, 1981, folder 14, box 16, and Nell Schactman notes, folder Sullivan, R.O.D. notes and papers, box 9, IWP; John Grover, "Skipper Sullivan to Boss Atlantic Flight," *Chronicle-Herald* (Macon, MO), June 28, 1939, 6; John Chapman, "America Rules the Skyways," *Saturday Evening Post*, March 30, 1940, 18–19, 70–73; "An Atlantic 'Century,'" *New York Times*, January 30, 1943, 14; Paul Rafford, Jr., "Pan Am's Renegade Captain," *Air Classics* 35, no. 4 (May 1999): 10–12, 62–64.
23. Crew list, folder 5, box II:152, and biographical sketches of crew, folder 16, box I:107, both in Pan Am; CAB report; "Flying the China Clippers," *Popular Mechanics*, April 1938, 500–3, 118A–120A; R. H. McGlohn, "I

Fly the Trans-Pacific Clippers," *Popular Aviation*, October 1939, 16–18, 60, 66–70.

24. Brief Summary of Trip 9/035, folder 12, box II:152, and Passenger Deck Plan, folder 11, box I:107, Pan Am; Klaäs, *Last of the Flying Clippers*, 23, 225–26.
25. Thomis, "Christen Queen of Air"; Boeing Clipper Control Room, December 16, 1938, folder 11, box I:107, crew manifest, folder 4, box II:145, and crew command reports, 1942, folder 19, box II:168, Pan Am; Herman Rush draft card, Maryland, June 19, 1941, box 446, *WWII Reg*; *Anzac Clipper* manifest, January 17, 1942, *VANY*; Klaäs, *Last of the Flying Clippers*, 47.
26. Klaäs, *Last of the Flying Clippers*, 47–48; Clare Boothe, "Destiny Crosses the Dateline," *Life*, November 3, 1941, folder 12, box I:261, Pan Am.

Chapter 1

1. Questionnaire and letter, Director of Office of Jewish War Records to Frederick Spiegelberg, Sr., April 8, 1920, folder 2, box 17, *Series II: Questionnaires: Jews*, Record Group H, *Officers, Civilians, Servicemen, Records of the American Jewish Committee—Office of Jewish War Records, 1918–1921; I-9*, AJHS; Frederick Spiegelberg, Jr., *Crimson Days: A Book of War Poetry and Sundry Verse* (New York: Rudge Press, 1919); transfer card, September 30, 1918, and commanding officer memo, October 5, 1918, Official Military Personnel File for George Alfred Spiegelberg, Service Number 001936041, NavRec; Flight 27 commemoration booklet, GASP. On the Goodyear program, see Charles Matthews, *History of U.S. Naval Aviation during the World War: Training in America* (Washington, DC: National Archives and Records Service, 1977), 18, 88–100; W. L. Hamlen, "First Lighter-Than-Air Class at Akron," in Adrian Van Wyen, *Naval Aviation in World War I* (Washington, DC: Chief of Naval Operations, 1969), 38–43.
2. *The Cornellian* (1916), 452–55; (1917), 485; (1918), 164, 519; Frederick Spiegelberg, Jr., '16, 41-2-877, DAF; Frederick Spiegelberg to Solomon Spiegelberg, November 2, December 14, December 21, 1897, and March 8, 1898, folder 8, box 1, WSP.
3. Matthews, *History of U.S. Naval Aviation*, 90; Manhattan Ward 22, 11A, reel 1045, *Census (1910)*; Harry Mack, "Memorial for Frederick Spiegelberg," *Year Book: Association of the Bar of the City of New York* (New York: Association of the Bar of the City of New York, 1938), 418–20. After securing a family passport in early June, George, his brother, and their parents appear to have spent most of August in Munich, where George's uncle Washington lived, and then returned to the United States via Southampton at the start of September: passport application, June 9, 1914, reel 215, *PA-II*; Frederick Spiegelberg Ausweiskarte, München, August 10, 1914, folder 9, box 1, WSP; SS *Lapland* manifest, September 1, 1914, reel 2367, *VANY*.

4. Paul Fussell, *The Great War and Modern Memory* (1975; New York: Oxford University Press, 2000), 36–37, 41–50; Ross J. Wilson, *Landscapes of the Western Front: Materiality during the Great War* (New York: Routledge, 2012), 66–69, 125–40, 164–70; "Britain Rests Serene," in Spiegelberg, *Crimson Days*, 33; A. H. Osman, *Pigeons in the Great War: A Complete History of the Carrier-Pigeon Service during the Great War, 1914 to 1918* (London: "Racing Pigeon" Publishing, 1928), 6.
5. Harold Porter, *Aerial Observation: The Airplane Observer, the Balloon Observer, and the Army Air Corps Pilot* (New York: Harper, 1921), 256–305; Robert Marc Friedman, *Appropriating the Weather: Vilhelm Bjerknes and the Construction of a Modern Meteorology* (Ithaca, NY: Cornell University Press, 1989), 103–5, 161–69.
6. Floyd Fierman, *The Spiegelbergs: Pioneer Merchants and Bankers in the Southwest* (Waltham, MA: American Jewish Historical Society, 1967); Solomon Spiegelberg naturalization certificate, March 27, 1852, clipping, "Solomon J. Spiegelberg," and tribute spoken at grave of S. J. Spiegelberg, April 8, 1898, folder 9, Frederick to Solomon Spiegelberg, October 15 and November 2, 1897, folder 8, all in box 1, WSP; Mack, "Memorial for Frederick Spiegelberg" and "The Great Hebrew Fair," November 10, 1895, 23, and "Alliance Honors William Salomon," April 7, 1913, 9, all in *New York Times*; Stephen Birmingham, *"Our Crowd": The Great Jewish Families of New York* (New York: Harper, 1967), 6, 131–32, 154, 289–96.
7. In memoriam, S. J. Spiegelberg at Temple Emanu-El, April 8, 1898, folder 9, box 1, WSP; Washington Spiegelberg passport application, July 10, 1917, reel 467, *PA-II*.
8. On the range of American opinions about the war between 1914 and 1917, see John A. Thompson, *A Sense of Power: The Roots of America's Global Role* (Ithaca, NY: Cornell University Press, 2015), ch. 2, and Michael S. Neiberg, *The Path to War: How the First World War Created Modern America* (New York: Oxford University Press, 2016).
9. Birmingham, *"Our Crowd,"* 313, 318; "Britain," "The Huns of Paris," "The Aerial Bomber," "The Hun of 1919," in Spiegelberg, *Crimson Days*, 18, 28–30, 47, 98–99.
10. "Louvain in Ashes," *Times* (London), August 29, 1914, 8; "First War Invalid Back in New York," *New York Times*, September 10, 1914, 4; Priscilla Roberts, "The Anglo-American Theme: American Visions of an Atlantic Alliance, 1914–1933," *Diplomatic History* 21, no. 3 (Summer 1997): 333–64; Isabel Hull, *A Scrap of Paper: Breaking and Making International Law during the Great War* (Ithaca, NY: Cornell University Press, 2014). In a sign of his Anglophilia, Frederick, Sr., was an avid collector of English literature first editions: Philip Brooks, "Notes on Rare Books," *New York Times*, October 31, 1937, 34.
11. Ross J. Wilson, *New York and the First World War: Shaping an American City* (Farnham, Surrey, UK: Ashgate Publishing, 2014); "For Freedom and Democracy," *North American Review* 205, no. 737 (April 1917): 481–501.

12. William James, *The Moral Equivalent of War* (New York: American Association for International Conciliation, 1910), 4, 6.
13. "Destruction of British Liner Lusitania with Probable Loss of American Lives," May 8, 1915, 1, and "Enter 18 Orators for Woodford Prize," April 15, 1916, 8, both in *Cornell Daily Sun*; Samuel Hynes, *The Unsubstantial Air: American Fliers in the First World War* (New York: Farrar, Straus and Giroux, 2014), 3–4, 8–9, 22, 30–32, 36, (quote) 95; grade transcript, George Alfred Spiegelberg '18, 41-2-877, DAF; Morris Bishop, *A History of Cornell* (Ithaca, NY: Cornell University Press, 1965), 426–28; Richard Penner, *Cornell University* (Charleston, SC: Arcadia Publishing, 2013), 47.
14. Bishop, *History of Cornell*, 428; "Plattsburg Men Join Aviation Section," *Air Service Journal* 1, no. 7 (August 23, 1917): 219; "Ainsi Soit," in Spiegelberg, *Crimson Days*, 13.
15. Grade transcript, George Alfred Spiegelberg '18, 41-2-877, DAF; George Spiegelberg service card, NYAGO; Charles Whitman, letter of recommendation, May 19, 1918, GASP; enrollment applications, including letters of recommendation, May 14 and 25, 1918, and June 11, 1918, and Navy Bureau of Navigation memo, June 4, 1918, NavRec. On aviation recruiters targeting men at elite East Coast colleges, see "To Start Air Boom in New England," *Boston Globe*, August 6, 1917, 3 and Hynes, *Unsubstantial Air*, 12–13, 18–20, 30–31, 43.
16. Geoffrey Rossano, *Stalking the U-Boat: U.S. Naval Aviation in Europe during World War I* (Gainesville: University Press of Florida, 2010), 261; Matthews, *History of U.S. Naval Aviation*, 88; "Big Camp for Aviators," *New York Times*, April 6, 1917, 13; "Air Defense Stations To Be Made Permanent," *Boston Globe*, November 28, 1918, 6; Hamlen, "First Lighter-Than-Air Class at Akron," 43; Donald A. Yerxa, "The United States Navy in Caribbean Waters during World War I," *Military Affairs* 51, no. 4 (October 1987): 182–87.
17. Frederic Grant to family, June 22, 1917, quoted in Eileen Lebow, *A Grandstand Seat: The American Balloon Service in World War I* (Westport, CT: Praeger, 1998), 24; "Spotting the Hun from a War Balloon Needs Trained Eyes," *Los Angeles Times*, June 30, 1918, II1; "Naval Officer in Derided Kite Balloon at Sea," *Chicago Tribune*, November 17, 1918, A8; Lebow, *Grandstand Seat*, 22–23; Porter, *Aerial Observation*, 272, 281–85, 293–98; general record, ground school report, September 28, 1918, and Akron completing school report, November 29, 1918, NavRec.
18. "U.S. Balloon Runaway," April 8, 1916, 2, and "Soldiers Hurt by Balloon," December 28, 1917, 5, both in *Washington Post*; "Balloon Explosion Kills Two," *Boston Globe*, May 3, 1918, 1; Matthews, *History of U.S. Naval Aviation*, 90, 99–100, 154–61; Lebow, *Grandstand Seat*, 24.
19. "All in a Night's Work," in Spiegelberg, *Crimson Days*, 62; Hunt, "Naval Officer in Derided Kite Balloon at Sea"; Porter, *Aerial Observation*, 256, 289. Quote from Lee Kennett, *The First Air War, 1914-1918* (New York: Free Press, 1991), 29–30.

20. George Spiegelberg service card, NYAGO; Frederick Spiegelberg, Jr., pictured, Series B, 43–44, *Gorrell's*; René Martel, *French Strategic and Tactical Bombardment Forces of World War I*, trans. Allen Suddaby (1939; Lanham, MD: Scarecrow Press, 2007), 250; questionnaire and letter, Director of Office of Jewish War Records to Frederick Spiegelberg, Sr., April 8, 1920, AJHS.
21. "The Call" and "As Always," in Spiegelberg, *Crimson Days*, 20, 53; Squadron Histories, 9th and 10th Aero Squadrons, Series E, Vol. 2, 6–8, *Gorrell's*; Robert H. Ferrell, *America's Deadliest Battle: Meuse-Argonne, 1918* (Lawrence: University Press of Kansas, 2007).
22. "All in a Night's Work," in Spiegelberg, *Crimson Days*, 62; daily squadron reports, October 2 and November 5, 1918, Squadron Histories, 9th and 10th Aero Squadrons, Series E, Vol. 2, n.p., *Gorrell's*. On low work in bad weather, see Hynes, *Unsubstantial Air*, 218–21, 247–49.
23. Hynes, *Unsubstantial Air*, 107; operations orders, October 1918, Marley Perry, Leslie Simpson, and Charles Turner reports, November 21, 1918, and William Leininger, Report on Lights and Flares used in Night Reconnaissance, November 20, 1918, Squadron Histories, 9th and 10th Aero Squadrons, Series E, Vol. 2, 22–57, 141–45, *Gorrell's*.
24. Headquarters, 9th Aero Squadron, Meuse-Argonne Offensive Report for September 24, 1918 to November 11, 1918, Squadron Histories, 9th and 10th Aero Squadrons, Series E, Vol. 2, 138, *Gorrell's*; "Soliloquy," "The Road of Freedom," and "Those Dumb Devils," in Spiegelberg, *Crimson Days*, 24, 82–83, 96–97. On sports metaphors, including quotations, see Hynes, *Unsubstantial Air*, 95, 123, 132, 166, and 173. On the use of timeworn rhetoric and cliché in soldiers' war poetry, see Fussell, *Great War and Modern Memory*, especially 9, 22, 25, 57.
25. Transfer form, December 7, 1918, and War Service Certificate, NavRec; George Spiegelberg service card, NYAGO; Carlo D'Este, *Eisenhower: A Soldier's Life* (New York: Holt, 2015), 136; Jeremy Hughes, October 1918, quoted in Hynes, *Unsubstantial Air*, 260.
26. Information for War Records, DAF; questionnaire and letter from Director of Office of Jewish War Records to Frederick Spiegelberg, Sr., April 8, 1920, folder 2, box 17, AJHS; "Attractive Offices," *Hide and Leather*, January 15, 1921, 49; *Cornell Alumni News*, January 19, 1922, 191; "Sees Princeton Win, Dies in Auto Crash," *New York Times*, November 8, 1925, 2.
27. Robert Gerwarth, *Why the First World War Failed to End, 1917–1923* (New York: Farrar, Straus and Giroux, 2016), 4–8.

Chapter 2

1. Christopher M. Clark, *The Sleepwalkers: How Europe Went to War in 1914* (New York: Harper, 2013), 367–75.
2. Clipping, "No Longer Noble," *Brooklyn Eagle*, January 24, 1937, TAMARA Clipping Folder (OF-20a), NYPL; Peter Warren, "When a Lovely Flame Dies," *Roosevelt Borough Bulletin*, December 1992, 5–6, folder 12, box

1, DFP. Materials gathered in the 1990s for the Drasin Family Papers at Rutgers University list her birth year as 1909, and during the 1930s it appears that she pretended to be two years younger than she was, not uncommon among female performers. Public records, however, show that she was born in 1907.

3. Bel Kaufman, "My Odessa" and Patricia Herlihy, "Odessa Memories," in Nicolas V. Iljine, ed., *Odessa Memories* (Seattle: University of Washington Press, 2003), xlix–lv, 3–37; Robert Rothstein, "How It Was Sung in Odessa: At the Intersection of Russian and Yiddish Folk Culture," *Slavic Review* 60, no. 4 (Winter 2001): 781–801.
4. Robert Weinberg, *The Revolution of 1905 in Odessa: Blood on the Steps* (Bloomington: Indiana University Press, 1993), 9–10, 41; Jarrod Tanny, *City of Rogues and Schnorrers: Russia's Jews and the Myth of Old Odessa* (Bloomington: Indiana University Press, 2011), 17–19, 23, 29.
5. Weinberg, *Revolution of 1905 in Odessa*, 13, 17–21, 31, 33, 40–44, 60–61; Patricia Herlihy, *Odessa: A History, 1794–1914* (Cambridge, MA: Harvard University Press, 1986), 178, 205–22, 295–99; Boris Drasin draft registration, 1942, *WWII Reg-NJ*. Boris had strong socialist convictions, but whether he identified with the Bund or one of Ukraine's other radical factions remains unclear. For a full history of the political world in which he found himself, see Jonathan Frankel, *Prophecy and Politics: Socialism, Nationalism, and the Russian Jews, 1862–1917* (Cambridge: Cambridge University Press, 1981).
6. Charters Wynn, *Workers, Strikes, and Pogroms: The Donbass-Dnepr Bend in Late Imperial Russia, 1870–1905* (Princeton, NJ: Princeton University Press, 1992), 26–28, 69–74, 86–90; Thomas Stevens, *Through Russia on a Mustang* (New York: Cassell, 1891), 182–84; Luigi Villari, *Russia Under the Great Shadow* (London: T. F. Urwin, 1905), 94–96, 103–5, 110–11, 121.
7. Photographs, box 2, photographs, notes, and postcard marking the site of Boris's shop, in Boris's file (unprocessed materials), clipping, Helen Harrison, "Out of Russia's Revolt," *Tower Radio*, September 1934, in Tamara scrapbook, and Lee Drasin to Peter Warren, 1990s, folder 5, and Warren, "When a Lovely Flame Dies," folder 12, both in box 1, DFP; "No Longer Noble."
8. Alfred Meyer, "The Impact of World War I on Russian Women's Lives," in Barbara Evans Clements, Barbara Alpern Engel, and Christine Worobec, eds., *Russia's Women: Accommodation, Resistance, Transformation* (Berkeley: University of California Press, 1991), 208–24; Barbara Alpern Engel, "Not by Bread Alone: Subsistence Riots in Russia during World War I," *Journal of Modern History* 69, no. 4 (December 1997): 696–721; Peter Gatrell, *A Whole Empire Walking: Refugees in Russia during World War I* (Bloomington: Indiana University Press, 1999), 58, 62–63, 115–16, 124–26; Eric Lohr, *Nationalizing the Russian Empire: The Campaign against Enemy Aliens during World War I* (Cambridge, MA: Harvard University Press, 2003), 137–50.

9. Tamara recalled entering school during the war: "Herewith Tamara in Your Eyes," *New York Times*, February 25, 1934, X3. Ekaterinoslav boasted "enlightened" *heders* that took girls as well as boys and which had become an increasingly popular alterative to home tutoring for the daughters of progressive Jewish families. But because Tamara later wrote letters to her family in Russian, rather than Yiddish or Hebrew, she likely attended public school: Salo Baron, *The Russian Jew under Tsars and Soviets* (1964; New York: Macmillan, 1976), 118, 120, 129; Abraham Gannes, *Childhood in a Shtetl* (Cupertino, CA: Ganton, 1993), 100–3.
10. Barbara Evans Clements, "Working-Class and Peasant Women in the Russian Revolution," *Signs* 8, no. 2 (Winter 1982): 215–35; Sheila Fitzpatrick, *The Russian Revolution*, 3rd ed. (Oxford: Oxford University Press, 2008), 44, 53.
11. John Keep, *The Russian Revolution: A Study in Mass Mobilization* (London: Weidenfeld and Nicolson, 1976), 375; Allen Sinel, "Ekaterinoslav in Revolution: Excerpts from the Diary of Princess Urusov," *Russian Review* 29, no. 2 (April 1970): 192–208; Lisa Cooper, *A Forgotten Land: Growing Up in the Jewish Pale* (Jerusalem: Penina, 2013), 125; Henry Abramson, *A Prayer for the Government: Ukrainians and Jews in Revolutionary Times, 1917–1920* (Cambridge, MA: Harvard University Press, 1999), 33–36.
12. Sinel, "Ekaterinoslav in Revolution"; Clements, "Working-Class and Peasant Women in the Russian Revolution." For a concise survey of the complicated politics of revolutionary and civil war Ukraine, see Serhii Plokhy, *The Gates of Europe: A History of Ukraine* (New York: Basic, 2015), 204–27.
13. Esther Markish, *The Long Journey* (New York: Ballantine, 1978), 6–13, (quote) 9; Sinel, "Ekaterinoslav in Revolution."
14. Oleg Budnitskii, *Russian Jews between the Reds and the Whites, 1917–1920*, trans. Timothy Portice (Philadelphia: University of Pennsylvania Press, 2012). In the only clue to the timing of their move, Tamara later mentioned that the family went to the countryside "when Russia withdrew from the conflict": clipping, "Tamara Escaped Russia but Not Its National Anthem," *New York Herald Tribune*, December 3, 1933, TAMARA Clipping Folder (OF-20a), NYPL.
15. Nikolai Gogol, "Sorochintsy Fair," in Nikolai Vasilevich Gogol, *Village Evenings near Dikanka and Mirgorod*, ed. and trans. Christopher English (Oxford: Oxford University Press, 1994), 8–34, here 12. These details loom large in the childhood memories of Jewish refugees Tamara's age who endured similar conditions in neighboring Kyiv Oblast: Gannes, *Childhood in a Shtetl*, 35–36, 43–47, 97, and Lawrence Coben, *Anna's Shtetl* (Tuscaloosa: University of Alabama Press, 2007), 102–5, 118–21, 140.
16. Peter Gatrell, *Russia's First World War: A Social and Economic History* (Harlow: Pearson Longman, 2005), 73–74, 165–69.
17. Lee quoted in clippings, Melanie Eversley, "Actress' Life a Real Life Drama," *Asbury Park Press* (NJ), March 4, 1993, and Ian Fennell, "Former

Roosevelt Resident Inspired Ukrainian Pianist," *Messenger-Press*, January 6, 1994, folder 18, box 1, DFP; clipping, "Song Writer's Prayer Answered by Singer Who's Actress Too," *New York Herald Tribune*, March 26, 1939, TAMARA Clipping Folder (OF-20a), NYPL; Mark Slobin, *Tenement Songs: The Popular Music of Jewish Immigrants* (Urbana: University of Illinois Press, 1982), 2–4, 14, 25–29; Jeffrey Veidlinger, *Jewish Public Culture in the Late Russian Empire* (Bloomington: Indiana University Press, 2009), 219.

18. Gatrell, *Russia's First World War*, 167; Keep, *Russian Revolution*, 173–85; Coben, *Anna's Shtetl*, 2–3, 47–48, 73–76, 102–4, 115–16; photograph, box 2, and clipping, "They Stand Out from the Crowd," *Literary Digest*, May 12, 1934, Tamara scrapbook, DFP; clippings, "No Longer Noble," *Brooklyn Eagle*, January 24, 1937, and "Bublichki to Roberta," *Brooklyn Eagle*, January 2, 1938, TAMARA Clipping Folder (OF-20a), NYPL.
19. "Sorochyntsi," in *Evreiskaia Entsklopediia*, vol. 14 (St. Petersburg: Brokgauz-Efron, 1906–13), 487; "Revolution of 1905," in Ivan Katchanovski, Zenon Kohut, Bohdan Nebesio, and Myroslav Yurkevich, *Historical Dictionary of Ukraine*, 2nd ed. (Lanham, MD: Scarecrow Press, 2013), 505–7; "Report on Mirgorod," August 29, 1923, folder USSR: Localities, Mir-N, JJDC. Even the larger town of Myrhorod had been less than 2 percent Jewish in 1897: "Poltava," in Isidore Singer and Cyrus Adler, eds., *The Jewish Encyclopedia*, vol. 10 (New York: Funk and Wagnalls, 1916), 119–20.
20. Coben, *Anna's Shtetl*, 2–3, 82–90, 94, 96–97, 113–14; Elias Heifetz, *The Slaughter of the Jews in the Ukraine in 1919* (New York: T. Seltzer, 1921), 181; Budnitskii, *Russian Jews between the Reds and the Whites*, 458n36.
21. N. Gergel, "The Pogroms in the Ukraine in 1918–21," *YIVO Annual of Jewish Social Science* 6 (1951): 237–52; Budnitskii, *Russian Jews between the Reds and the Whites,* ch. 6; Coben, *Anna's Shtetl*, 82–88; Barry Fireman, *From the Broken Windows: A Story of Survival* (Bloomington, IN: Xlibris, 2009), 30, 34; *Evidence of Pogroms in Poland and Ukrainia: Documents, accounts of eye-witnesses, proceedings in Polish Parliament, local press reports, etc.* (New York: Information Bureau of the Committee for the Defense of Jews in Poland and Other East European Countries, 1919), 168; Heifetz, *Slaughter of the Jews*, 28–29, 41, 141–45, 148, 168–69, 173, 190–92; Abramson, *Prayer for the Government*, ch. 4.
22. "Bublichki to Roberta"; Weeks, *Russian Revolution*, 186–89; "The Murder of a Race," *Nation*, March 8, 1922, 295–302; Heifetz, *Slaughter of the Jews*, 38, 69, 77–78, 102–3; Harold Williams, "Poltava Rejoices After Red Terror," *New York Times*, August 24, 1919, 3; "Kolchak Retires and Denikin Advances," *Independent*, August 23, 1919, 240–41; Norman Saul, *War and Revolution: The United States and Russia, 1914-1921* (Lawrence: University Press of Kansas, 2001), 410–15, 424–29. American, French, and British strategists as well as Muslim volunteers alike gravitated to the White cause, though each saw different stakes in the conflict: George Stewart, *The White*

Armies of Russia: A Chronicle of Counter-Revolution and Allied Intervention (New York: Macmillan, 1933).

23. Sydney Stahl Weinberg, *The World of Our Mothers: The Lives of Jewish Immigrant Women* (Chapel Hill: University of North Carolina Press, 1988), 58–59; "No Longer Noble"; clipping, "Radio Needed Her," n.d., Tamara scrapbook, DFP; Gergel, "Pogroms in the Ukraine in 1918–21." Awareness of sexual danger by girls Tamara's age or slightly older is ably portrayed in Coben, *Anna's Shtetl*, 6, 87, 131, and Cooper, *Forgotten Land*, 132, 138, 149–50, 156, 160–61, 176, 178, 200.

24. "No Longer Noble"; James Hassell, "Russian Refugees in France and the United States between the World Wars," *Transactions of the American Philosophical Society* 81, no. 7 (1991): 47; Baron, *The Russian Jew under Tsars and Soviets*, 156; Saul, *War and Revolution*, 387.

25. Mark Wischnitzer, *To Dwell in Safety: The Story of Jewish Migration since 1800* (Philadelphia: Jewish Publication Society of America, 1948), 145–53; Andrea Chandler, *Institutions of Isolation: Border Controls in the Soviet Union and Its Successor States, 1917–1993* (Montreal: McGill-Queen's University Press, 1998), 33–40.

26. Gatrell, *Whole Empire Walking*, 31, 189, 213; Budnitskii, *Russian Jews between the Reds and the Whites*, 235; Jerzy Borzęcki, *The Soviet-Polish Peace of 1921 and the Creation of Interwar Europe* (New Haven, CT: Yale University Press, 2008). Of course, it would take a lot more than a treaty to make these borderlands into nation-state territory: Kate Brown, *A Biography of No Place: From Ethnic Borderland to Soviet Heartland* (Cambridge, MA: Harvard University Press, 2005).

27. Warren, "When a Lovely Flame Dies." Possibly they left with at least another mother and pair of sons from Sorochyntsi, who later entered the United States with them: SS *Aquitania* manifest, June 3, 1922, reel 3124, *VANY*. Handwritten notes, Boris's file, DFP, specify only 1920 as their departure time. They might have waited until after the Red Army drove Denikin's forces out of Ukraine and the region's soviet became firmly established at the end of November. In this case, they would have made the journey in winter conditions.

28. Emma Goldman, *My Disillusionment in Russia* (1923; repr., New York: Crowell, 1970), 122–24, 131–33, 153–54; Cooper, *Forgotten Land*, 146, 188, 201, 205; Gannes, *Childhood in a Shtetl*, 162–63; Coben, *Anna's Shtetl*, 147; Henry G. Alsberg, "In the Wake of Denikin," *Nation*, January 10, 1920, 38–40.

29. N. M. Borodin, *One Man in His Time* (New York: Macmillan, 1955), 26–27; Heifetz, *Slaughter of the Jews*, 179–82; Baron, *The Russian Jew under Tsars and Soviets*, 184.

30. Coben, *Anna's Shtetl*, 135; Weinberg, *World of Our Mothers*, 76–79; Gur Alroey, "Bureaucracy, Agents, and Swindlers: The Hardship of Jewish Emigration from the Pale of Settlement in the Early 20th Century," *Studies in Contemporary Jewry* 19 (2003): 214–31; Gannes, *Childhood in a Shtetl*, 48,

130, 133, 139–40, 165–71; Fireman, *From the Broken Windows*, 35–39; Hassell, "Russian Refugees in France and the United States between the World Wars," 9.

31. Gur Alroey, "'And I remained Alone in a Vast Land': Women in the Jewish Migration from Eastern Europe," *Jewish Social Studies* 12, no. 3 (Spring-Summer 2006): 39–72.
32. "No Longer Noble"; "Tamara Escaped Russia but Not Its National Anthem"; Wischnitzer, *To Dwell in Safety*, 332n15. A similar escape is recounted in Fireman, *From the Broken Windows*, 115–30.
33. Handwritten notes, Boris's file, and clipping, "Tamara Arrives and Demands Boulder Dam!" *Rocky Mountain News*, July 14, 1938, Tamara scrapbook, DFP. New York's National Desertion Bureau fielded thousands of cases like Hinda's in the early 1920s from overseas Jewish relief agencies, placing notices in the Gallery of Missing Husbands sections that had become a regular feature of Yiddish newspapers across North America: Reena Sigman Friedman, "'Send Me My Husband Who Is In New York City': Husband Desertion in the American Jewish Immigration Community, 1900–1926," *Jewish Social Studies* 44 (Winter 1982): 1–18.

Chapter 3

1. Passport applications, February 13, 1914, reel 203, March 13, 1919, reel 725, December 8, 1919, reel 1462, *PA-II*; alumni questionnaire, n.d., BUBF.
2. *Liber Brunensis*, vol. 53 (Providence, RI: Brown University, 1911), 139; *Liber Brunensis*, vol. 54 (Providence, RI: Brown University, 1912), 133, 272, 278, 288; Births Registered in the City of Fitchburg, Massachusetts Vital and Town Records, 1841–1925, 1890, 132.
3. *Liber Brunensis*, vol. 54 (Providence, RI: Brown University, 1912), 133; T. J. Kern to Harry Seidel, July 18, 1912, and October 5, 1912, HGSP; Nicolas Andrews, *Ryland B. Andrews in World War I: Military Service in Jassy and Bucharest* (Chevy Chase, MD: Chandos Press, 1997), 5, 8–9; George Sweet Gibb and Evelyn Knowlton, *The Resurgent Years, 1911–1927* (New York: Harper, 1956), 5; Daniel Yergin, *The Prize: The Epic Quest for Oil, Money, and Power* (1991; repr., New York: Free Press, 2009), 27–31, 38–39, 80–82, 88–93.
4. John D. Rockefeller, Jr., to Ryland Andrews, April 22, 1912, reprinted in Andrews, *Ryland B. Andrews in World War I*, 119; John D. Rockefeller, Jr., to Harry Seidel, June 4, 1912, and telegram, John D. Rockefeller, Jr., to Ryland Andrews, June 12, 1912, HGSP. On the rowdiness of production, see Yergin, *The Prize*, 37.
5. Harry Seidel alumni questionnaire, August 23, 1913, BUBF; Harry Seidel to John D. Rockefeller, Jr., June 13, 1913, HGSP; Carl Coke Rister, *Oil! Titan of the Southwest* (Norman: University of Oklahoma Press, 1949), 90–91; Gibb and Knowlton, *Resurgent Years*, 8.
6. Kenny Franks, *The Oklahoma Petroleum Industry* (Norman: University of Oklahoma Press, 1980), 95–98.

7. Kenny Franks, Paul Lambert, and Carl Tyson, *Early Oklahoma Oil: A Photographic History, 1859–1936* (College Station: Texas A&M University Press, 1981), 15–16; Yergin, *The Prize*, 7–9, 34–35, 62–64.
8. Harry Seidel to John D. Rockefeller, Jr., June 13, 1913, HGSP; Rister, *Oil!*, 120–21; Franks, Lambert, and Tyson, *Early Oklahoma Oil*, 84, 135; Franks, *Oklahoma Petroleum Industry*, 91; Gibb and Knowlton, *Resurgent Years*, 137–39.
9. Franks, *Oklahoma Petroleum Industry*, 71–75, 92–93, 142–43; Franks, Lambert, and Tyson, *Early Oklahoma Oil*, 8–9, 39, 48, 80–86; Gibb and Knowlton, *Resurgent Years*, 50–51, 58–59. It was not long before oil companies sought more state control: better law enforcement to sober up workers; labor reforms to keep strike agitators at bay; and conservation measures to stabilize supply and prices. Several such regulations passed shortly after Harry left: Franks, *Oklahoma Petroleum Industry*, 75–77, 97, 139–45.
10. T. J. Kern to Harry Seidel, September 19, 1913, HGSP; telegram, January 4, 1914, quoted in Andrews, *Ryland B. Andrews*, 11. Wages ranged from $6 to $15 per day: Franks, *Oklahoma Petroleum Industry*, 94.
11. Harry Seidel visa request, March 31, 1914, Correspondence American Consulate Bucharest, 1914, vol. 32, RG84, NARA.
12. Gibb and Knowlton, *Resurgent Years*, 32–33, 35, 80–82; Gh. Buzatu, *A History of Romanian Oil*, vol. 1 (Bucharest: Mica Valahie, 2011), 33–36, 39–43; Maurice Pearton, *Oil and the Romanian State* (Oxford: Oxford University Press, 1971), 18–20, 24, 29–33.
13. Harry Seidel to John D. Rockefeller, Jr., March 1, 1915, HGSP; Harry G. Seidel folder, BUBF; Ryland Andrews to Pa, March 25, 1914, reprinted in Andrews, *Ryland B. Andrews*, 120–23; telegrams, Charles Vopicka to Secretary of State, October 10, November 10, and November 24, 1916, 125.0071/7-8, 11, box 1944, excerpts from letter from Anthony Theodoridi, October 8, 1919, 125.0071, and Bucharest Post Report, 1925, 124.71/55, box 1899, RG59, NARA; Bucharest consular report, Petroleum Situation in Rumania, July 10, 1920, 871.6363/60, reel 18, *IAR*.
14. Karl Baedeker, *Austria Hungary, with Excursions to Cetinje, Belgrade, and Bucharest: Handbook for Travellers* (Leipzig: Karl Baedeker, 1911), 564–65; William Bailey and Jean Bates, "Bucharest When the War Came," *Fortnightly Review*, January 1917, 87–99; John Reed, *The War in Eastern Europe* (New York: Scribner's, 1916), 297, 305; alumni questionnaire, January 20, 1920, BUBF.
15. Bailey and Bates, "Bucharest When the War Came"; Winifred Gordon, *Roumania Yesterday and Today* (London: John Lane the Bodley Head, 1918), 23, 110–11, 119; Reed, *War in Eastern Europe*, 295–302.
16. Harry Seidel to John D. Rockefeller, Jr., March 1, 1915, HGSP. Harry belonged to his university's Cercle Français: *Liber Brunensis*, vol. 54 (Providence, RI: Brown University, 1912), 133.
17. Charles Vopicka to Secretary of State, August 19, 1914, *FRUS, Supplement, The World War (1914)*, Part I, 109; Romanian Consolidated Oilfields Limited, "An Account of the Destruction of Its Stocks, Wells, Plant,

Machinery, Etc.," August 1917, TS 27/250, TNA; Gibb and Knowlton, *Resurgent Years*, 82–83; Pearton, *Oil and the Romanian State*, 71–75; Harry Seidel to John D. Rockefeller, Jr., March 1, 1915, HGSP.

18. See, for example, clipping, *Worcester Gazette* (MA), February 24, 1943, Harry G. Seidel folder, BUBF.

19. Ryland Andrews to father, June 2 and 17, 1916, reprinted in Andrews, *Ryland B. Andrews*, 124–28.

20. A. Thomas Devasia, "The United States and the Formation of Greater Romania, 1914–1918: A Study in Diplomacy and Propaganda" (PhD diss., Boston College, 1970), 24–33, 94–95, 100–102; Barbara Jelavich, "Romania in the First World War: The Pre-War Crisis, 1912–1914," *International History Review* 14, no. 3 (August 1992): 441–51. On the centrality of Transylvania to both Romanian and Hungarian nation building, see Holly Case, *Between States: The Transylvania Question and the European Idea during World War II* (Stanford, CA: Stanford University Press, 2009), 9–13, on Romanian angers over Magyarization policies, 20-2.

21. Devasia, "United States and the Formation of Greater Romania," 24–29, 37; Gordon, *Roumania Yesterday and Today*, 133, 135.

22. Gordon, *Roumania Yesterday and Today*, n.p.; Devasia, "United States and the Formation of Greater Romania," 36, 94–95; V. N. Vinogradov, "Romania in the First World War: The Years of Neutrality, 1914–1916," *International History Review* 14, no. 3 (August 1992): 452–61.

23. Charles Vopicka, *Secrets of the Balkans: Seven Years of a Diplomatist's Life in the Storm Center of Europe* (Chicago: Rand, McNally, 1921), 82; Glenn Torrey, "Romania in the First World War: The Years of Engagement, 1916–1918," *International History Review* 14, no. 3 (August 1992): 462–79. Quotes from Gordon, *Roumania Yesterday and Today*, 145.

24. Harry Seidel to John D. Rockefeller, Jr., October 6, 1916, HGSP; Charles Vopicka to Secretary of State, April 14 and September 8, 1916, *FRUS, Supplement, The World War (1916)*, Part 1, 25, 50–53.

25. Torrey, "Romania in the First World War"; Vopicka, *Secrets of the Balkans*, 89; Michael Barrett, *Prelude to Blitzkrieg: The 1916 Austro-German Campaign in Romania* (Bloomington: Indiana University Press, 2013), 67, 274.

26. Harry Seidel to John D. Rockefeller, Jr., October 6, 1916, HGSP; Eftimie Antonesco, *Les Sacrifices Roumains pendant la guerre: Les victimes civiles* (Paris: Imprimerie M. Flinikowski, 1919), 1–2; Nicolae Petrescu-Comnène, *The Great War and the Romanians: Notes and Documents on World War I* (1918; repr., Iaşi: Center for Romanian Studies, 2000), 89–90, 95–96; Comte de Saint-Aulaire, *Confession d'un vieux diplomate* (Paris: Flammarion, 1953), 339; Vopicka, *Secrets of the Balkans*, 89; Grigore Antipa, *L'Occupation ennemie de la Roumanie et ses conséquences économiques et sociales* (Paris: Presses Universitaires de France, 1929), 12–13, 23.

27. Harry Seidel to John D. Rockefeller, Jr., October 6, 1916, HGSP; Alison Fleig Frank, *Oil Empire: Visions of Prosperity in Austrian Galicia*

(Cambridge, MA: Harvard University Press, 2005), 173, 182–85, 189, 199; Yergin, *The Prize*, 160–61, 167; Henry Bérenger, *Le Pétrole et la France* (Paris: Flammarion, 1920), 160.

28. Secret report, December 8, 1916, TS 27/250, and John Norton Griffiths testimony, *Roumanian Consolidated Oilfields, Limited, v. The King*, March 26, 1920, TS 27/250, TNA; Robert Keith Middlemas, *The Master Builders* (London: Hutchinson, 1963), 276–79, 282; Gibb and Knowlton, *Resurgent Years*, 233; Pearton, *Oil and the Romanian State*, 79–80.
29. Secret report, December 8, 1916, TS 27/250, TNA; John Norton Griffiths and Harry Mejor testimony, *Roumanian Consolidated Oilfields, Limited, v. King*; Pearton, *Oil and the Romanian State*, 73–75.
30. Romanian Consolidated Oilfields, Limited, "An Account of the Destruction of its Stocks, Wells, Plant, Machinery, Etc.," August 1917, TS 27/250, TNA.
31. Testimonies of Harry Mejor, John Norton Griffiths, and T. S. Masterson, *Roumanian Consolidated Oilfields, Limited v. The King*; undated report, "Roumanian Oil Damage," TS 27/250, TNA; James Hayes to Green Hackworth, September 28, 1928, *FRUS* 2 (1928): 980–81; Gibb and Knowlton, *Resurgent Years*, 271–73, 321–23.
32. Telegram, Charles Vopicka to Secretary of State, November 29, 1916, 124.71/4, box 1899, RG59, NARA; Petrescu-Comnène, *Great War and the Romanians*, 96–97; Barrett, *Prelude to Blitzkrieg*, 274; Hugh Thomas O'Brien testimony, *Roumanian Consolidated Oilfields, Limited v. The King*; S. B. Hunt's office to Rollin Andrews, January 5, 1917, quoted in Andrews, *Ryland B. Andrews*, 17–18; Gibb and Knowlton, *Resurgent Years*, 234; Vopicka, *Secrets of the Balkans*, 89, 103, 108.
33. "An Account of the Destruction of Its Stocks, Wells, Plant, Machinery, Etc.," August 1917, and C. H. Bateman, "The Destruction of the Romano-Americana Oil Property in 1916," May 17, 1927, TS 27/250, TNA; John Norton Griffiths and John Andrew Sullivan testimony, *Roumanian Consolidated Oilfields, Limited v. The King*; Middlemas, *Master Builders*, 280–81.
34. C. H. Bateman, "The Destruction of the Romano-Americana Oil Property in 1916," May 17, 1927, TS 27/250, TNA; Pearton, *Oil and the Romanian State*, 81; Comte de Saint-Aulaire, *Confession d'un vieux diplomate*, 356; Antipa, *L'Occupation ennemie*, 13; Vopicka, *Secrets of the Balkans*, 106.
35. Antipa, *L'Occupation ennemie*, 13, 19–21, 28–29; Vopicka, *Secrets of the Balkans*, 106–7, 110–12.
36. Antipa, *L'Occupation ennemie*, 24, 28–30, 61.
37. Christopher Endy, "Travel and World Power: Americans in Europe, 1890–1917," *Diplomatic History* 22, no. 4 (Fall 1998): 565–94; Hugh Thomas O'Brien testimony, *Roumanian Consolidated Oilfields, Limited v. The King*; Gibb and Knowlton, *Resurgent Years*, 234–35. American Red Cross personnel arrived in Romania in 1915: Vopicka, *Secrets of the Balkans*, 41–44.

38. Gibb and Knowlton, *Resurgent Years*, 235–36; press clipping from the American Embassy, Paris, January 26, 1917, 124.71/23, note, January 13, 1917, 124.71/13, and telegram from Ryland Andrews, January 14, 1917, 124.71/14, box 1899, RG59, NARA; "Harry Seidel, in Rumania, Is Well, Letters Indicate," *Fitchburg Sentinel*, September 28, 1918, 4; Ryland Andrews to family, December 6, 1918, in Andrews, *Ryland B. Andrews*, 149. After numerous attempts to find their son through State Department channels, word that he was still in Bucharest finally reached Harry's parents via the Spanish Embassy in Vienna in March 1918: Hermann Seidel to Brown War Records, January 18, 1918, folder 44, box 3, BWWI; William Libby to Secretary of State, January 24, 1917, 371.11/159, and correspondence, February–May, 1918, 374.11/99, RG59, NARA.
39. Erwin Rommel, *Attacks* (Vienna, VA: Athena Press, 1979), 122–32; Bailey and Bates, "Bucharest When the War Came"; Antipa, *L'Occupation ennemie*, 29, 32–33, 132, 135.
40. Vopicka, *Secrets of the Balkans*, 313; E. J. Sadler to Rollin Andrews, January 19, 1917, and Ryland Andrews to family, December 6, 1918, in Andrews, *Ryland B. Andrews*, 18, 149. Sadler's statement was made about both of "the boys," Ryland and Harry, though only Harry stayed in occupied Wallachia.
41. Antipa, *L'Occupation ennemie*, 126–27; H. Jacobson testimony, December 5, 1918, TS 27/250, TNA; Buzatu, *History of Romanian Oil*, 56–57; Gibb and Knowlton, *Resurgent Years*, 236; Pearton, *Oil and the Romanian State*, 84–85.
42. Gibb and Knowlton, *Resurgent Years*, 235–36.
43. Vopicka, *Secrets of the Balkans*, 161–62, 167, 178, 203, 311; Gibb and Knowlton, *Resurgent Years*, 236; Pearton, *Oil and the Romanian State*, 86; Glenn Torrey, *The Romanian Battlefront in World War I* (Lawrence: University Press of Kansas, 2011), 303; Harry Seidel to family, March 25, 1918, in Andrews, *Ryland B. Andrews*, 57–58.
44. Ryland Andrews to family, December 6, 1918, in Andrews, *Ryland B. Andrews*, 149; Vopicka, *Secrets of the Balkans*, 201; Gibb and Knowlton, *Resurgent Years*, 237.
45. Torrey, "Romania in the First World War"; Irina Livezeanu, *Cultural Politics in Greater Romania: Regionalism, Nation Building, and Ethnic Struggle, 1918–1930* (Ithaca, NY: Cornell University Press, 1995), 8.
46. Vopicka, *Secrets of the Balkans*, 171; Pearton, *Oil and the Romanian State*, 102; Antipa, *L'Occupation ennemie*, 145–46, 159.
47. "Bucharest," *Living Age*, February 14, 1920, 404–5; Livezeanu, *Cultural Politics in Greater Romania*, 21, 24, 246, 251–55, 272.
48. British Petroleum Commission report re: Romano-Americana Co., Bucharest, April 28, 1919, A. C. Hearn to John Cadman, April 29, 1919, A. C. Hearn to Mr. Rattigan, January 28, 1920, and A. C. Hearn to Mervyn Eager, January 26, 1920, POWE 33/78, TNA; Charles à Court Repington, *After the War: A Diary* (Boston: Houghton Mifflin, 1922), 335, 340–42, 347–49; Bucharest consular report, Petroleum Situation in Rumania, July

10, 1920, 871.6363/60, reel 41, *IAR*; Livezeanu, *Cultural Politics in Greater Romania*, 4, 22.

49. Consular report, The Anti-American Policy of the Liberal Party, September 16, 1920, 8761.6363/62, reel 41, *IAR*; Jay to Secretary of State, August 30, 1921, 124.71/46, box 1899, RG59, NARA; confidential memo, Edwin Kemp to Secretary of State, September 24, 1919, Correspondence American Consulate Bucharest, 1919, vol. 1, RG84, NARA; Buzatu, *History of Romanian Oil*, 78–79.

50. Excerpts from letter from Anthony Theodoridi, October 8, 1919, 125.0071, box 1899, RG59, NARA; Repington, *After the War*, 296, (quote) 309, 324; Bucharest Legation to Secretary of State, June 13, 1919, 125.0071/15, and Wallace to Secretary of State, June 20, 1919, 125.0071/14, box 1944, RG59, NARA.

51. Ryland Andrews to father, October 23, 1918, to family, December 6, 1918, and March 8, 1919, reprinted in *Ryland B. Andrews*, 67, 148–51.

Chapter 4

1. "Spanish Freighter Burns in Bay," *Brooklyn Daily Eagle*, July 14, 1918, 5; "Four Dead in Fire That Sweeps Oil-Laden Steamship," *New York Herald Tribune*, July 14, 1918, 14; "Big Oil Ship Burns in the Lower Bay," July 14, 1918, 12, and "The Weather," July 14, 1918, 21, both in *New York Times*; "4 Die When Ship Blows up and Burns in Bay," *New York Sun*, July 14, 1918, 14.

2. "4 Die When Ship Blows up and Burns in Bay."

3. SS *Amerika* passenger manifest, October 12, 1907, www.ellisisland.org; Jose Moya, *Cousins and Strangers: Spanish Immigrants in Buenos Aires, 1850–1930* (Berkeley: University of California Press, 1998), 26–44, 94, 103, 110; Andres Diego Diestro, ed., *Gijón trasatlántico* (Barcelona: Lunwerg, 2002), 68, 126; Jesús Jerónimo Rodríguez, *Asturias y América* (Madrid: MAPFRE, 1992). On Ellis Island inspections, see Vincent Cannato, *American Passage: The History of Ellis Island* (New York: Harper, 2009), 58–59, 298–99.

4. Moya, *Cousins and Strangers*, 1–2, 19, 62–63, 81, 85, 148–58; Alistair Hennessy, "Cuba," in Mark Falcoff and Fredrick Pike, eds., *The Spanish Civil War, 1936–1939: American Hemispheric Perspectives* (Lincoln: University of Nebraska Press, 1982), 102–8; Ana María Varela-Lago, "Conquerors, Immigrants, Exiles: The Spanish Diaspora in the United States (1848–1948)" (PhD diss., University of California, San Diego, 2008).

5. Caroline Ware, *Greenwich Village, 1920–1930* (1935; repr., Berkeley: University of California Press, 1994), 3, 30, 40, 47–52, 127–28, 140–41, 227–31; Mike Wallace, "New York City and the Spanish-Speaking World from Dutch Days to the Second World War," and James Fernández, "The Discovery of Spain in New York, Circa 1930," both in Edward Sullivan, ed., *Nueva York, 1613–1945* (New York: New-York Historical Society/Scala, 2010), 19–81, 217–33.

6. Victor Alvarez, who became one of Garcia & Diaz's most important employees, was also born in Gijón, and it is possible that this entire migration chain traced back to a set of siblings, cousins, and neighbors: SS *Saratoga* manifest, July 31, 1909, reel 1311, *VANY*; Alvarez passport application, April 9, 1920, reel 1148, *PA-II*. The 1920 census shows Alvarez and a handful of other Spanish export employees, all of whom arrived between 1908 and 1914, living on the same block of Washington Heights, which had begun to attract arrivals well off enough to bypass the *barrios* of lower Manhattan: New York, 13A-14B, reel 1227, *Census (1920)*.
7. Passenger manifest, SS *Amerika*; Marcelino Garcia declaration of intention, November 19, 1926, New York, State and Federal Naturalization Records, 1794–1929, RG21, NARA at New York, NY; American Exporter, *Export Trade Directory, 1919–1920*, B. Olney Hough, ed. (New York: Johnston Export Publishing, 1919), 103; Marcelino Garcia, Jr. (b. February 3, 1908), SS *Primero* manifest, July 21, 1923, reel 148, *Passenger Lists of Vessels Arriving at Philadelphia, Pennsylvania, 1883–1945*, NARA microfilm T840; Frank Reil, "Garcia and Diaz Major Brooklyn Factors in Handling of Spain's Shipments Here," *Brooklyn Daily Eagle*, January 27, 1941, 8.
8. SS *Alfonso XII* manifest, December 10, 1917, reel 2555, SS *Montevideo* manifest, April 28, 1918, role 2572, both in *VANY*. On the 1920 census Manuel claimed, contrary to later documents, to have naturalized in 1913: Kings, New York, 12B, reel 1189, *Census (1920)*. Like Italians, Spanish workers were avid "birds of passage," migrating back and forth across the Atlantic, sometimes several times. Mark Wyman estimates that 40 percent of Spanish entrants to the United States between 1908 and 1923 back-migrated: *Round-trip to America: The Immigrants Return to Europe, 1880–1930* (Ithaca, NY: Cornell University Press, 1993), 11.
9. Frederick Pike, *Hispanismo, 1898–1936: Spanish Conservatives and Liberals and Their Relations with Spanish America* (Notre Dame, IN: University of Notre Dame Press, 1971), 3–6, 48–49, 138—44, 182–83; Isidro Sepúlveda, *El Sueño de la Madre Patria: Hispanoamericanismo y nacionalismo* (Madrid: Marcial Pons Historia, 2005); Sebastian Balfour, *The End of the Spanish Empire, 1898–1923* (Oxford: Clarendon, 1997), 1–2, 64, 232; Eliga Gould, "Entangled Histories, Entangled Worlds: The English-Speaking Atlantic as a Spanish Periphery," *American Historical Review* 112, no. 3 (June 2007): 764–86; Alejandro Quiroga, *Making Spaniards: Primo de Rivera and the Nationalization of the Masses, 1923–30* (New York: Palgrave Macmillan, 2007), 24–25; José Antonio Montero Jiménez, *El Despertar de la Gran Potencia: Las relaciones entre España y los Estados Unidos (1898–1930)* (Madrid: Biblioteca Nueva, 2011).
10. Greg Grandin, *Empire's Workshop: Latin America, The United States, and the Rise of the New Imperialism* (New York: Metropolitan, 2006), 15–27; Alan McPherson, *A Short History of U.S. Intervention in Latin America and the Caribbean* (Malden, MA: Blackwell, 2016); Pike, *Hispanismo*, 186–91, (quote) 142; James Cortada, *Two Nations Over Time: Spain and the*

United States, 1776-1977 (Westport, CT: Greenwood, 1978), 154–60, 182; María DeGuzmán, *Spain's Long Shadow: The Black Legend, Off-Whiteness, and Anglo-American Empire* (Minneapolis: University of Minnesota Press, 2005), xii–xvi, ch. 3; Varela-Lago, "Conquerors, Immigrants, Exiles," 1–2, 7–15, 55; James Fernández, "Entre imperios: Españoles en Nueva York, 1898–1945," in James Fernández, ed., *La colonia: un álbum fotográfico de inmigrantes españoles en Nueva York, 1898-1945* (Piedrasblancas, Castrillón: Valey Centro Cultural de Castrillón, 2012), 13–14, 21–22.

11. Phillips Payson O'Brien, "The American Press, Public, and the Reaction to the Outbreak of the First World War," *Diplomatic History* 37, no. 3 (2013): 446–75, including quote; Donald Yerxa, "The United States Navy in Caribbean Waters during World War I," *Military Affairs* 51, no. 4 (October 1987): 182–87; Friedrich Katz, *The Secret War in Mexico: Europe, the United States and the Mexican Revolution* (Chicago: University of Chicago Press, 1981), ch. 9; Manuel Diaz draft card, reel 1754495, *WWI Reg.*
12. Christopher Capozzola, *Uncle Sam Wants You: World War I and the Making of the Modern American Citizen* (New York: Oxford University Press, 2008), chs.1 and 6; David Kennedy, *Over Here: The First World War and American Society* (New York: Oxford University Press, 1980), 150–58, 165–67.
13. "Box Full of Bombs at Ship Plot Trial," *New York Times*, March 23, 1917, 3; Justus Doenecke, *Nothing Less Than War: A New History of America's Entry into World War I* (Lexington: University Press of Kentucky, 2011), 20–26; Ross J. Wilson, *New York and the First World War: Shaping an American City* (Farnham, Surrey: Ashgate, 2014), 47–49, 111, 115–16, 122; Friedrich Schuler, *Secret Wars and Secret Policies in the Americas, 1842–1929* (Albuquerque: University of New Mexico Press, 2010), 100, 106–7; memo, July 1, 1919, box 15, entry 136, RG182, NARA; American Exporter, *Export Trade Directory*, 103, 333; Robert Matson, *Neutrality and Navicerts: Britain, the United States, and Economic Warfare, 1939–1940* (New York: Garland, 1994), 101–2.
14. Robert Gardiner and Ambrose Greenway, eds., *The Golden Age of Shipping: The Classic Merchant Ship, 1900–1960* (London: Conway Maritime Press, 1994), 7–10, 38–58, 165–71.
15. Jesús Valdaliso, "Growth and Modernization of the Spanish Merchant Marine, 1860–1935" (June 1991): 33-58, and "Spanish Shipping Firms in the Twentieth Century: Between the Internationalisation of the Market and the Nationalism of the State" (December 2007): 21–42, both in *International Journal of Maritime History*; Santiago Roldán, *La formation de la sociedad capitalista en España, 1914–1920*, vol. 2 (Madrid: Confederación Española de Cajas de Ahorro, 1973), 13–89; Robert Forrester, *British Mail Steamers to South America, 1851–1965: A History of the Royal Mail Steam Packet Company and Royal Mail Lines* (Surrey: Ashgate, 2014), 129–41; Michael Miller, "The Business Trip: Maritime Networks in the Twentieth Century," *Business History Review* (Spring 2003): 1–32.

16. Manuel Diaz draft card, *WWI Reg*; Manuel Diaz to Immigration Bureau, July 9, 1918, with *Carasa* manifest, May 30, 1918, reel 2578, *VANY*; Roger Jordan, *The World's Merchant Fleets, 1939: The Particulars and Wartime Fates of 6,000 Ships* (London: Chatham, 1999), 355, 357; Manuel Diaz file, September 5, 1918, box 11, RG182, NARA; Michael Miller, "Ship Agents in the Twentieth Century," in Gordon Boyce and Richard Gorski, eds., *Resources and Infrastructures in Maritime Economy, 1500–2000: Research in Maritime History*, no. 22 (St. John's, Newfoundland: 2002), 5–22; Miller, "The Business Trip."
17. Francisco Romero Salvadó, *Spain 1914–1918: Between War and Revolution* (London: Routledge, 2012), 5, 9–13; Pike, *Hispanismo*, (quote) 294, 4–6, 74–78, 130, (quote) 197, 288.
18. Romero Salvadó, *Spain 1914–1918*, 17, 31, 69, 83–84, 120–22, 130, 150, 153, 165, 182; Javier Ponce, "Spanish Neutrality during the First World War," in Johan Den Hertog and Samuel Kruizinga, eds., *Caught in the Middle: Neutrals, Neutrality, and the First World War* (Amsterdam: Amsterdam University Press, 2011), 53–65.
19. Francisco Romero Salvadó, *The Foundations of Civil War: Revolution, Social Conflict and Reaction in Liberal Spain, 1916–1923* (New York: Routledge, 2008), 52–53, 58; Gerald Meaker, "A Civil War of Words: The Ideological Impact of the First World War on Spain, 1914–18," in Hans Schmitt, ed., *Neutral Europe between War and Revolution, 1917–23* (Charlottesville: University Press of Virginia, 1988), 1–65; Schuler, *Secret Wars*, 142, 144, 225–26, Fernando García Sanz, *España en la Gran Guerra: Espías, diplomáticos y traficantes* (Barcelona: Galaxia Gutenberg, 2014); Hertog and Kruizinga, *Caught in the Middle*.
20. Report on Spanish steamers, September 6, 1918, box 3827, RG165, NARA; Schuler, *Secret Wars*, 140–47, 206; Romero Salvadó, *Foundations of Civil War*, 59; Jamie Bisher, *The Intelligence War in Latin America, 1914–1922* (Jefferson, NC: McFarland, 2016), 144, 152, 198, 214–17, 232. Germany tried to acquire coaling stations and even colonies in the Caribbean Basin before the war, and by 1910 its navy had surveyed all of the Americas' coastlines for clandestine fueling spots. The Reich had also been subverting the US arms embargo of revolutionary Mexico and plans had been drawn up for the destruction of the Panama Canal: Schuler, *Secret Wars*, 33–45, 57, 88–94, 187.
21. Pike, *Hispanismo*, 181–82, 295; Mark Mazower, *Dark Continent: Europe's Twentieth Century* (1998; New York: Vintage, 2000), 3.
22. Gardiner and Greenway, *Golden Age of Shipping*, 9–10, 38–58, 167–68; partnership agreement for Garcia & Diaz, June 2, 1919, case file 149-522, box 42, RG60, NARA; *Exporters' Encyclopædia* (New York: 1921), 134, 1180; American Exporter, ed., *Export Trade Directory, 1921–1922*, (New York: Johnston Export Publishing, 1921), 148–49, 593; F. Larcegui, "Garcia and Diaz," *Spain* (New York), March 1941, 14–15; Manuel

Diaz letter for Victor Alvarez's passport application, April 6, 1920, reel 1148, *PA-II*.

23. Wallace, "New York City and the Spanish-Speaking World"; René De La Pedraja, *Oil and Coffee: Latin America Merchant Shipping from the Imperial Era to the 1950s* (Westport, CT: Greenwood, 1998), 18–35, 75; Paul Drake, "Chile," in Falcoff and Pike, *Spanish Civil War*, 245–90; Grandin, *Empire's Workshop*, 15–27; "South American Trade Attracts Many Lines," September 24, 1927, 24, "South American Shipping Trade Shows Increase," May 5, 1929, L18, and "South American Trade Attracts New Tonnage," July 7, 1929, D8, all in *New York Herald Tribune*; foreign agent registration statements, 1939-1943, and Oscar Lewis to A. Schwartz, June 28, 1943, case file 149-522, box 42, RG60, NARA.
24. "Garcia & Diaz Announce South American Service," November 18, 1924, 32, "Tercero on Way Here for N.Y.-River Plate Trade," January 23, 1926, 22, "New Garcia & Diaz Ships Near Completion," September 27, 1927, 38, "Garcia & Diaz Speeding New Motor Fleet," March 16, 1928, 37, and "Garcia to Sail To Inspect New Motor Liners," August 4, 1928, 20 (incl. quote), all in *New York Herald Tribune*; "World's Fastest Freighter Here on Maiden Trip," *Brooklyn Daily Eagle*, August 10, 1929, 9; "New Spanish Liner Here," November 23, 1928, "Enter Auto Export Trade," November 21, 1929, 55, and "End Passenger Line to South America," July 30, 1930, 43, all in *New York Times*.
25. Pike, *Hispanismo*, 5, 165, 179, (quote) 182, 288–91, (quote) 294, 299; "Spanish Decrees Dissolve Cortes, Suppress Cabinet," *New York Times*, September 17, 1923, 1; Balfour, *End of the Spanish Empire*, 232–33; Quiroga, *Making Spaniards*, 24–26, 35, 70–73; "Sud Africana Arrives from Builders To-day," *New York Herald Tribune*, November 11, 1928, C10.
26. Mazower, *Dark Continent*, 3–5; Pike, *Hispanismo*, 165, 169–72, 227, 292–93, 307–8; Kiran Klaus Patel, *The New Deal: A Global History* (Princeton, NJ: Princeton University Press, 2016), 45.
27. Schuler, *Secret Wars*, 383–84, 439, 423–28, 465–66; Pike, *Hispanismo*, 178, 199, 217, 226, 234–37; Ramón Franco and Julio Ruiz de Alda, *De Palos al Plata* (Madrid: Espasa-Calpe, 1926), 93.
28. Schuler, *Secret Wars*, 382–88, 392–96, 409, 421–24, 434-5, Pike, *Hispanismo*, 191–92, 225, 244, (quote) 245; Varela-Lago, 198–99; "Spanish Envoy Honored Here," *New York Herald Tribune*, March 22, 1932, 17.
29. Manuel Diaz's draft card, reel 1178, p. 9B, *WWI Reg*; SS *Leon XIII* manifest, October 3, 1919, reel 2684, *VANY*; Kings, New York, 12B, reel 1189, *Census (1920)*; Pelham Manor, Westchester, New York, 19A, reel 1664, *Census (1930)*; photo of Manuel Diaz's residence, May 29, 1927, RE2, "Notes of Social Activities in New York and Elsewhere," January 17, 1931, 22, and "Halloween Dances in Westchester," October 30, 1932, 35, all in *New York Times*; F2 society pages, September 8, 1929, November 10, 1929, March 9, 1930, February 22, 1931, and May 17, 1931, all in *New York Herald Tribune*.

Interlude

1. Passenger Accommodations of Boeing 314 Clipper, 1940, folder 11, box I:107, survivor statements, folder 12, and Airplane Rescue Procedure, July 14, 1943, folder 1, box II:152, Pan Am.
2. James Hayes to Cordell Hull, March 5, 1943, 353.113 Seidel, Harry G., box 1202, RG59, NARA; "Notables Die in Disaster of Clipper Plane," *Democrat and Chronicle* (Rochester, NY), February 24, 1943, 12; "Yvette, in London, Offers Details on Clipper Crash," *New York Herald Tribune*, March 30, 1943, 15A.
3. Passenger Accommodations of Boeing 314 Clipper, 1940, folder 11, box I:107, and Steward's Equipment, folder 5, box II:152, both in Pan Am; M. D. Klaäs, *Last of the Flying Clippers: The Boeing B-314 Story* (Atglen, PA: Schiffer, 1997), 35–38, 184, 225–26.
4. Notes on flight from India, 1942, folder 93, box 9, BFRP. On locomotion's transformative effects on human consciousness, see Wolfgang Schivelbusch, *The Railway Journey: The Industrialization of Time and Space in the Nineteenth Century* (1977; Oakland: University of California Press, 2014).
5. Peter Adey, Mark Whitehead, and Alison Williams, eds., *From Above: War, Violence, and Verticality* (New York: Oxford University Press, 2014). Aircraft statistic in Victor Davis Hanson, *The Second World Wars* (New York: Basic, 2017), 67. On the United States specifically, see Michael Sherry, *The Rise of American Air Power: The Creation of Armageddon* (New Haven, CT: Yale University Press, 1987), and Jenifer Van Vleck, *Empire of the Air: Aviation and the American Ascendancy* (Cambridge, MA: Harvard University Press, 2013).
6. Klaäs, *Last of the Flying Clippers*, 49; Betty Stettinius Trippe, *Pan Am's First Lady: The Diary of Betty Stettinius Trippe* (McLean, VA: Paladwr Press, 1996), 130–33; Marius Lodeseen, *Captain Lodi Speaking* (Suttons Bay, MI: Argonaut, 1984), 167.
7. Clipping, "A Who's Who of World Airlines," *Aviation*, March 1939, folder 16, box I:107, Pan Am; T. A. Heppenheimer, *Turbulent Skies: The History of Commercial Aviation* (New York: Wiley, 1995), 6–8, 14, 26–32, 44; Van Vleck, *Empire of the Air*, 69–72; Horace Brock, *Flying the Oceans: A Pilot's Story of Pan Am, 1935–1955* (New York: Jason Aronson, 1978), 43–44; Rod Sullivan, Jr., interview, September 24, 1981, folder 14, box 16, IWP; "Panama Air Mail Completes Year," *Brooklyn Daily Eagle*, February 7, 1930, 13. On Pan Am's often fraught but mutually beneficial relationship with the US government, see Marylin Bender and Selig Altschul, *The Chosen Instrument: Pan Am, Juan Trippe, and the Rise and Fall of an American Entrepreneur* (New York: Simon & Schuster, 1982).
8. Van Vleck, *Empire of the Air*, 92–94. On Aéropostale's South Atlantic route, see Robert Wohl, *The Spectacle of Flight: Aviation and the Western Imagination, 1920–1950* (New Haven, CT: Yale University Press, 2005), ch. 4.

9. S. B. Kauffman, *Pan Am Pioneer: A Manager's Memoir,* ed. George Hopkins (Lubbock: Texas Tech University Press, 1995), 51; William Stephen Grooch, *Skyway to Asia* (New York: Longmans, Green, 1936), 23, 40–45, 50–51, 89–95.
10. "Clipper Prepares for Longest Hop," *Salinas Morning Post* (CA), October 2, 1935, 1; "Clipper Ready to Hopoff on Flight Friday," *Hawaii Tribune-Herald* (Hilo, HI), November 19, 1935, 1; "China Clipper Wings Way over Pacific to Launch Air Mail," *Morning Call* (Paterson, NJ), November 23, 1935, 1-2; Robert Daley, *An American Saga: Juan Trippe and His Pan Am Empire* (New York: Random House, 1980), 169–74; pictures and Victor Wright, "Historic Alameda Flight Recalled," in Stan Cohen, *Wings to the Orient: Pan American Clipper Planes, 1935–1945* (Missoula, MT: Pictorial Histories Publishing, 1985), 166–71, 180–81.
11. Kauffman, *Pan Am Pioneer*, 184; "Husband of Former Davenport Woman Commands Pacific Clipper on Trip Wednesday," *Daily Times* (Davenport, IA), March 17, 1936, 5. Some of Sully's public pronouncements were clearly ghostwritten. "Now the sky above is a canopy dotted with myriad brilliant stars. . . . Inside, capped and coated forms bend over instruments," read one flowery article improbably carrying his byline: "Aboard the China Clipper," *Daily Times* (Davenport, IA), November 23, 1935, 1–2.
12. "Clipper Finishes Wake Island Trip," *Winona Daily News* (MN), August 29, 1935, 5; "Transpacific," *Time*, December 2, 1935, 46; John Grover, "Skipper Sullivan to Boss Atlantic Flight," *Chronicle-Herald* (Macon, MO), June 28, 1939, 6.
13. Klaäs, *Last of the Flying Clippers*, 184; "Old Bermuda," *Life*, August 18, 1941, 61–71; (quote) Alan Jackson, "Machine in the Hibiscus," *Saturday Evening Post*, July 25, 1942, 16–17, 36; Ashley Jackson, *The British Empire and the Second World War* (New York: Hambledon Continuum, 2006), 86.
14. Use of Plane Blackout Curtains, April 21, 1942, folder 1, box I:434, and Brief Summary of Trip 9/035, folder 12, box II:152, both in Pan Am; Klaäs, *Last of the Flying Clippers*, 101, 184.
15. Customs and Defence Clearance certificates and Messages sent or received at North Beach in Connection with Trip Movement NC-18603, folder 5, Summary of Express Shipments—Yankee Clipper, and Baggage recovered from the NC-03 and property claims, folder 4, box II:145, George Wardman, memo, December 19, 1941, folder 17, box II:105, Brief Summary of Trip 9/035, folder 12, box II:152, and clippings on Bermuda controls, folders 50-51, box I:260, all in Pan Am; Milton Bracker, "Bermuda Censors Fill Two Hotels," May 27, 1941, 14, and "Bermuda Censors at Nazi Spy Trial," February 18, 1942, 13, both in *New York Times*; British Postal Censorship Extracts on Enemy Sympathizers in America, 1940–1943, Bermuda, Hamilton Consulate General, RG84, NARA; Bermuda contraband control reports, 1940–1941, DEFE 1/145, TNA; intercepts of lawyers' bills and Garcia & Diaz correspondence, folder 560 Isla de Tenerife, box 1165, RG319, NARA.

Chapter 5

1. Frank Cuhel's passport, July 15, 1933, Frank Cuhel, "The Log" and "Notes on the Singapore Mess," *Singapore Lyre*, December 25, 1936, Frank Cuhel to V. A. Dodge, December 27, 1933, Straits Settlements Driver's License, May 16, 1935, all in FJCP. He also drove in the Netherlands East Indies: Nederlands-Indië Internationaal Rijbewijs, October 19, 1938, FJCP.
2. Frank caught his first whiff of beer the following year on a train to London: "An 'Oil Tanker' to the Olympic Games by Bab Cuhel," July 12, 1924, FJCP.
3. Frank Cuhel record, June 9, 1924, and State and War Department questionnaire for correspondent accreditation, February 18, 1942, FJCP; Cedar, Linn, Iowa, 7B, reel 410, *Census (1910)*. Frank's father, Ludvik, a trained cabinetmaker, died when Frank was a toddler. Before that he had struggled to support the family with woodworking and spent much of his time clerking in Cedar Rapids, first at a grocery store, then at the meat market of his younger brother, Godfrey, who had followed him to Iowa: Frank Cuhel, memoir drafting, "The Start," FJCP; Ludvik R. Cuhel passport application, April 14, 1898, reel 504, No. 3954, *PA-I*; Godfrey Cuhel, naturalization petition, June 28, 1907, Iowa, Federal Naturalization Records, RG21, NARA at Kansas City, Missouri; *The* Evening Gazette*'s Cedar Rapids City and Business Directory* (Keokuk, IA: McCoy, 1906), 102; *The* Evening Gazette*'s Cedar Rapids City and Business Directory* (Rockford, IL: McCoy, 1907–8), 91; photograph of Cuhel gravestone in Czech National Cemetery, Iowa Gravestone Photo Project, iowagravestones.org.
4. Cuhel, "The Start."
5. The Federal Writers' Project of the Works Progress Administration, *Guide to Cedar Rapids and Northeast Iowa* (Cedar Rapids, IA: Laurance Press, 1937), 16, 22; Martha Griffith, *The History of Czechs in Cedar Rapids*, vol. 1: 1850–1942 (1944; repr., Cedar Rapids, IA: Czech Heritage Foundation, 1982). For the Midwest's longstanding world connections, see Kristin L. Hoganson, *The Heartland: An American History* (New York: Penguin, 2019).
6. *Cedar Rapids, Iowa: A Wonderful Place to Live* (Cedar Rapids: Tru-Art Corp. for the Chamber of Commerce, ca. 1928), (quote) 3, 14; Federal Writers' Project, *Guide to Cedar Rapids*, 15, 22; William Shirer, *20th Century Journey: The Start, 1904–1930* (New York: Simon and Schuster, 1976), 17, 173, 186; Frank Cuhel to Ermengarde Cuhel, November 15, 1932, FJCP.
7. Cedar Rapids Ward 3, Linn, Iowa, 12A, reel 500, *Census (1920)*; Frank Cuhel, memoir drafting, "The Start" and "1921," and Iowa address book and diary, 1921, FJCP.
8. Frank Cuhel, Iowa address book and diary, 1921, clipping, Frank Cuhel, "Dr. Anderson, Leader of Crusade Gives Interview to Reporter!" *Spark Plug*, January 22, 1922, 1, Frank Cuhel, "The Start" and "1922," and clipping, "Another Schoolboy Phenom Reports for Olympic Trial," sports scrapbook, all in FJCP.

9. Steven Pope, *Patriotic Games: Sporting Traditions in the American Imagination, 1876–1926* (New York: Oxford University Press, 1997); Clifford Putney, *Muscular Christianity: Manhood and Sports in Protestant America, 1880–1920* (Cambridge, MA: Harvard University Press, 2001), 1–3, 6, (quote) 35, 36, 46–67, 73–75, 99–101; Mark Dyreson, *Making the American Team: Sport, Culture, and the Olympic Experience* (Urbana: University of Illinois Press, 1998), ch. 1; Theodore Roosevelt, "The Strenuous Life," speech before the Hamilton Club, Chicago, April 10, 1899, in *The Works of Theodore Roosevelt*, vol. 12 (New York: Collier, 1900), 3–22; Robert Pruter, *The Rise of American High School Sports and the Search for Control, 1880–1930* (Syracuse, NY: Syracuse University Press, 2013), 67–83.
10. Griffith, *History of Czechs in Cedar Rapids*, vol. 1: 1850–1942, 39–44; "Why America Wins Championships," *Literary Digest*, August 13, 1921, 48–50; Georges Lechartier, "Americans and Sport," *Living Age*, September 10, 1921, 648–64; Lawson Robertson, Report of Head Coach Track and Field Team, in *Report of the American Olympic Committee: Ninth Olympic Games, Amsterdam, 1928* (New York: American Olympic Committee, 1928), 95–96; Dyreson, *Making the American Team*.
11. Frank Cuhel, "1923," FJCP.
12. Sports scrapbook clippings and transcript for Hall of Fame ceremony, n.d., FJCP; "Cedar Rapids Grabs Glory," *Los Angeles Times*, June 1, 1924, 10. On Stagg's meet, see Pruter, *Rise of American High School Sports*, 196–97.
13. Sports scrapbook clippings and letter to Frank Cuhel from Cedar Rapids, July 9, 1924, FJCP.
14. "Oil Tanker" journal entries, June 26–30, July 2, and July 6, 1924, FJCP.
15. "Oil Tanker" journal entries, June 30–July 9, 1924, FJCP.
16. "Oil Tanker" journal entries, July 8–31, 1924, and Frank Cuhel passport, June 24, 1924, FJCP; David Goldblatt, *The Games: A Global History of the Olympics* (New York: Norton, 2016), 116–25. On the Olympic Village, see *Les Jeux de la VIIIe Olympiade: Rapport Officiel* (Paris: Comité Olympique Français, 1924), 60–61.
17. Barbara J. Keys, *Globalizing Sport: National Rivalry and International Community in the 1930s* (Cambridge, MA: Harvard University Press, 2006), 2, 31–38; Dyreson, *Making the American Team*, 5, 32; interview with Jackson Volney Scholz, in Don Holst and Marcia Popp, *American Men of Olympic Track and Field* (Jefferson, NC: McFarland, 2005), 119–27, here 126; Frank Cuhel, broadcast transcript, ca. 1942, FJCP.
18. Elwood Brown, "Teaching the World to Play," *Outlook*, December 28, 1921, 689–93; Allen Guttmann, *Games and Empires: Modern Sports and Cultural Imperialism* (New York: Columbia University Press, 1994); Gerald R. Gems, *The Athletic Crusade: Sport and American Cultural Imperialism* (Lincoln: University of Nebraska Press, 2006); Steven Pope, "An Army of Athletes: Playing Fields, Battlefields, and the American Military

Sporting Experience, 1890-1920," *Journal of Military History* 59, no. 3 (July 1995): 435–56; Putney, *Muscular Christianity*, 4, 132–37.

19. Pope, "An Army of Athletes"; Keys, *Globalizing Sport*; Douglas MacArthur report, in *Report of the American Olympic Committee: Ninth Olympic Games, Amsterdam, 1928* (New York: American Olympic Committee, 1928), 1–7, (quote) 7; Douglas MacArthur, *Reminiscences* (New York: McGraw-Hill, 1964), 81–82.
20. Frank Cuhel, MBS broadcast, ca. late 1942, FJCP.
21. "Olympic Games Doomed," *Times* (London), July 22, 1924, 14; Ida Treat, "Another War Victim," *Nation*, June 25, 1924, 738–39; Pierre de Coubertin, *Olympic Memoirs* (1979; repr., Madison: University of Wisconsin Library, 1989), 122; *Jeux de la VIIIe Olympiade*, 79; David Goldblatt, *The Games: A Global History of the Olympics* (New York: Norton, 2016), 98, 101, 116–20.
22. "Oil Tanker" journal entries, July 13–17 and July 23–26, 1924, FJCP.
23. "Oil Tanker" journal entries, July 18–20, 1924, photographs from 1924 trip, and Frank Cuhel, MBS broadcast, September 29, 1942, FJCP.
24. "Oil Tanker" journal entries, July 28, 1924, FJCP. Seven stowed away on the SS *America*, three immigrants and four American boys, including Frank: stowaway manifest, August 6, 1924, reel 3520, *VANY*.
25. "Oil Tanker" journal entries, July 28–August 4, 1924, FJCP.
26. "Oil Tanker" journal entries, August 5–10, 1924, FJCP. On the souvenirs he "hooked," see also "Oil Tanker" journal entries, July 13–14, and 18, 1924; stowaway manifest, August 6, 1924, reel 3520, *VANY*.
27. Leo Novak to Frank, February 23, 1926, untitled clipping, sports scrapbook, and Leo Novak to Frank Cuhel, n.d, all in JFCP.
28. Otto Sikora to Frank Cuhel, December 18, 1924, Robert Riesnow to Frank Cuhel, January 22, 1925, Morton Mumma to Frank Cuhel, February 23, 1925, Chuck Harrison to Frank Cuhel, May 16, 1926, E. Ruth Whiteside to Frank Cuhel, December 15, 1926, and University of Iowa transcript, all in FJCP. After ROTC officers threatened to report him to the War Department, Frank threw himself into military training. Senior year he was elected the university's cadet-colonel and chairman of the military ball committee: clipping, "'Bab' Cuhel Named IA. Cadet Colonel," sports scrapbook, FJCP.
29. Ermengarde Cuhel to Frank Cuhel, November 11, November 19, and October 1, 1924, January 10, and October 2, 1925, and [undated] 1926, Lillian to Frank Cuhel, October 4, 1926, and war correspondent accreditation questionnaire, February 18, 1942, all in FJCP.
30. Clippings, Ralph Cannon, "The Campus Canopy," ca. mid-1930s, Robert Waples, "Psi Psi Olympic Star, Bab Cuhel, Out to Nip-off Nip-on in Far East," *Shield of Phi Kappa Psi*, May 1942, "Bab Cuhel Circles Globe Twice as Old Gold's Ambassador of Athletics," and "Famous Hurdler Enters Oxford University in the Autumn," sports scrapbook, Frank Cuhel passport, July 15, 1933, Ermengarde Cuhel to Frank Cuhel, July 14, 1925, clippings on Bab Cuhel's travels, June–August 1926, and Hall of Fame

ceremony transcript, n.d, all in FJCP; "Iowa Coach Hunts for New Brookins," *Cedar Rapids Republican*, January 10, 1926, 7; *Report of the American Olympic Committee*, 110.

31. J. P. Abramson, "Olympic Team Off," *New York Herald Tribune*, July 12, 1928, 22; MacArthur, *Reminiscences*, 86.
32. MacArthur, *Reminiscences*, 86; D. Clayton James, *The Years of MacArthur*, Vol. 1: 1880–1941 (Boston: Houghton Mifflin, 1970), 325–31; interviews with Anne Vrana O'Brien, October 1987, Lemuel Clarence "Bud" Houser, May 1988, and Herman Brix, April 1988, all in *Olympians Oral History Project* (Los Angeles: Amateur Athletic Foundation of Los Angeles, 1988), 7, 13, 24; Louis Nixdorff diary entries, July 30, August 5, and August 7, 1928, folder 1, box 1, OGC.
33. *Report of the American Olympic Committee: Ninth Olympic Games, Amsterdam, 1928*, 128, 152, 458, 462; Abramson, "Olympic Team Off"; "U.S. Is Beaten In 3 Events," *New York Herald Tribune*, July 31, 1928, 1. Abramson reported that Frank knocked down his ninth hurdle and placed five feet back from Burghley at the tape, but footage shows no knocked hurdles and a much closer finish: www.youtube.com/watch?v=9dk5JvLbT9g.
34. *Report of the American Olympic Committee: Ninth Olympic Games, Amsterdam, 1928*, 2–3, (quote) 6, 29; James, *Years of MacArthur*, vol. 1, 329; Guttmann, *Games and Empires*, 180–84.
35. Frank Cuhel to Ermengarde Cuhel, July 23, July 24, August 7, and August 10, 1928, letter to Frank Cuhel from Cedar Rapids, July 9, 1924, C. B. Robbins to Frank Cuhel, April 16, 1928, reference letters from Governor John Hammill, June 8, 1928, and President of University of Iowa, June 22, 1928, memoir drafting, "1928," all in FJCP. On Dodge & Seymour, see Mira Wilkins and Frank Ernest Hill, *American Business Abroad: Ford on Six Continents* (1964; 2nd ed., New York: Cambridge University Press, 2011), 44–45, 78, 129; "Dodge Makes Longest Tour of Career," *Singapore Lyre*, December 25, 1936, and Dodge & Seymour letterhead, 1932, both in FJCP.
36. "1928," and Frank Cuhel broadcast, ca. late 1942, both in FJCP.

Chapter 6

1. Handwritten notes, Boris's file (unprocessed materials), and Peter Warren, "When a Lovely Flame Dies," *Roosevelt Borough Bulletin*, December 1992, 5–6, folder 12, box 1, DFP; Norman Saul, *War and Revolution: The United States and Russia, 1914–1921* (Lawrence: University Press of Kansas, 2001), 432–33. Permanent quota legislation in 1924 would include no such exemption: John Higham, *Strangers in the Land: Patterns of American Nativism, 1860–1925* (1955; 2nd ed., New Brunswick, NJ: Rutgers University Press, 1994), 309, 324.
2. SS *Aquitania* manifest, June 3, 1922, reel 3124, *VANY*; Kathie Friedman-Kasaba, *Memories of Migration: Gender, Ethnicity, and Work in the Lives of*

Jewish and Italian Women in New York, 1870–1924 (Albany: State University of New York Press, 1996), 102–3, 139, 143, 145; Susan Glenn, *Daughters of the Shtetl: Life and Labor in the Immigrant Generation* (Ithaca, NY: Cornell University Press, 1990), 51–53; photo, Boris and Hinda in New York, box 2, and photo of Drasins on Catskills farm, summer 1923, Boris's file, DFP.

3. Bronx Assembly District 4, 10B, reel 1136, *Census (1920)*; Resettlement Administration Personal Data for Boris Drasin, September 30, 1935, folder 3, Boris Drasin statement, 1938, folder 8, and Boris Drasin to David Dubinsky, December 26, 1933, folder 4, all in box 1, DFP; Russell Maloney, "Hattie Carnegie," *Life*, November 12, 1945, 62–70. Boris consistently gave 1916 as his year of entry into the United States, but it remains unclear if he had been sent abroad on a wartime mission, escaped from a POW camp, or deserted and posed as a civilian to receive permission to emigrate from the German authorities who controlled most of the Pale by late 1915: Salo Baron, *The Russian Jew Under Tsars and Soviets* (1964; 2nd ed., New York: Macmillan, 1976), 160–61.
4. Tony Michels, *A Fire in Their Hearts: Yiddish Socialists in New York* (Cambridge, MA: Harvard University Press, 2005), 5–6, 11, 23–27, 72; Charles Leinenweber, "Socialists in the Streets: The New York City Socialist Party in Working Class Neighborhoods, 1908–1918," *Science & Society* 41, no. 2 (Summer 1977): 152–71; Leon Trotsky, *My Life* (1930; New York: repr., Dover, 2007), 271–78; Robert Fogelson, *The Great Rent Wars: New York, 1917–1929* (New Haven, CT: Yale University Press, 2013), 6, 9; Dana Frank, "Housewives, Socialists, and the Politics of Food: The 1917 New York Cost-of-Living Protests," *Feminist Studies* 11, no. 2 (Summer 1985): 255–85; Deborah Dash Moore, *At Home in America: Second Generation New York Jews* (New York: Columbia University Press, 1981), 74–78.
5. Michels, *Fire in Their Hearts*, 217–19; Trotsky, *My Life*, 276–77; Benjamin Stolberg, *Tailor's Progress: The Story of a Famous Union and the Men Who Made It* (Garden City, NY: Doubleday, Doran, 1944), 94, 96; 23–24, 70–71; Julian Jaffe, *Crusade Against Radicalism: New York During the Red Scare, 1914–1924* (Port Washington, NY: Kennikat, 1972), 77; greetings from B. Drasin, *Report of Proceedings of the Seventeenth Convention of the International Ladies' Garment Workers' Union* (New York: May 1924), 10.
6. "Second Day Nets Few Slackers Here," *New York Times*, September 5, 1918, 3; Christopher Capozzola, *Uncle Sam Wants You: World War I and the Making of the Modern American Citizen* (New York: Oxford University Press, 2008), 30–31, 45–49; Jerome Davis, *The Russian Immigrant* (New York: Macmillan, 1922), 174, 184; Jaffe, *Crusade Against Radicalism*, 80–87, 90–92, 96, 173–74, 179–84, 189, 228–30, 238–39. As a 33-year-old alien, Boris was not obligated to serve with the American Expeditionary Forces, but he was supposed to come forward during the September 1918 registration drive. The refugee from the tsar's army does not appear to have done so.

7. Steven Cassedy, *To the Other Shore: The Russian Jewish Intellectuals Who Came to America* (Princeton, NJ: Princeton University Press, 1997), xi, xix, xxii–xxiii, 8–10, 35, 63–64, 104; Michels, *Fire in Their Hearts*, 5, 10, 42, 64–65, 111.
8. Daniel Soyer, "Transnationalism and Mutual Influence: American and European Jewries in the 1920s and 1930s," in Jeremy Cohen and Moshe Rosman, eds., *Rethinking European Jewish History* (Oxford: Littman Library of Jewish Civilization, 2009), 201–20; Stolberg, *Tailor's Progress*, 98; "Starving Russians Killing Americans," *New York Times*, April 14, 1922, 18.
9. Theodore Komisarjevsky, *Myself and the Theatre* (New York: Dutton, 1930), 100–102; M. K. Argus, *Moscow-on-the-Hudson* (New York: Harper, 1948), 19–20, 56; Vladimir Mayakovsky, "My Discovery of America" (1925–1926), reprinted in Olga Peters Hasty and Susanne Fusso, trans. and eds., *America Through Russian Eyes, 1874—1926* (New Haven, CT: Yale University Press, 1988), 159–220; Ruth Gay, *Unfinished People: Eastern European Jews Encounter America* (New York: Norton, 1996), 56–58, 61; Jeffrey Gurock, *Jews in Gotham: New York Jews in a Changing City, 1920–2010* (New York: New York University Press, 2012), 18–20; Henry Feingold, *A Time for Searching: Entering the Mainstream, 1920–1945* (Baltimore: Johns Hopkins University Press, 1995), ch. 1. Population statistics in *The Jewish Communal Register of New York City, 1917–1918* (New York: Jewish Community of New York City, 1918), 82.
10. SS *Aquitania* manifest, June 3, 1922, reel 3124, *VANY*; Gurock, *Jews in Gotham*, 15; Evelyn Diaz Gonzalez, *The Bronx: A History* (New York: Columbia University Press, 2004), 62, 65–71; Federal Writers' Project, *New York City Guide* (New York: Random House, 1939), 113, 514–15; Gay, *Unfinished People*, 89–92; Kate Simon, *Bronx Primitive: Portraits in a Childhood* (New York: Viking, 1982), 6–7, 61–64. Tamara alluded to the family's cold, fourth-floor apartment in Tamara to family, ca. December 1928, folder 6, box 1, DFP.
11. Gay, *Unfinished People*, 5, 46, 67. For her Russian see, for example, Tamara to Mama, ca. October 1928, folder 6, box 1, DFP. For her accented English see the film *Sweet Surrender* (1935) and clipping, "Tamara, Sloe-Eyed Songster, Arrives," *Denver Post*, July 14, 1938, Tamara scrapbook, DFP.
12. Clipping, "Herewith Tamara in Your Eyes," *New York Times*, February 25, 1934, TAMARA clipping folder (OF-20a), NYPL; clipping, Mildred Palmer, "Meet Your Neighbor," *The Midtowner*, January 7, 1932, Tamara scrapbook, and rooftop pictures, 1920s, Boris's file, DFP; Simon, *Bronx Primitive*, 38, 44–45, 65, 87–88, 111–12, 123–26, 139–45, 159–67, 172–79.
13. Tamara to Mama, ca. October 1928, Tamara to family, ca. December 1928, folder 6, box 1, and photograph of Drasins on a Catskills farm, 1923, Boris's file, DFP; *Report of Proceedings of the 17th Convention of the ILGWU*, 10, 160.
14. *Report of the General Executive Board to the 17th Convention of the ILGWU* (New York: May 5, 1924), 14–15, and *Report of Proceedings*

(New York: May 5, 1924), 197, 222; *Report of the General Executive Board to the 18th Convention of the ILGWU* (New York: November 30, 1925), 24–27, 126–29, and *Report of Proceedings* (New York: November 30, 1925), 187–88; *Report and Proceedings of the Nineteenth Convention of the ILGWU* (Philadelphia: May 1928), 242–45; Stolberg, *Tailor's Progress*, 95, 106, 109, 113–17, 130, 135–42, 148–51; Gus Tyler, *Look for the Union Label: A History of the International Ladies' Garment Workers' Union* (Armonk, NY: Sharpe, 1995), 148–51, 154, 158; Annelise Orleck, *Common Sense and a Little Fire: Women and Working-Class Politics in the United States, 1900–1965* (Chapel Hill: University of North Carolina Press, 1995), 172, 182–83; "Left Wing Garment Workers Lose," *New York Times*, February 20, 1927, 12; Jenna Weissman, *Our Gang: Jewish Crime and the New York Jewish Community, 1900–1940* (Bloomington: Indiana University Press, 1983), 118–28.

15. Sidney Stahl Weinberg, *The World of Our Mothers: The Lives of Jewish Immigrant Women* (Chapel Hill: University of North Carolina Press, 1988), 196–99; Riv-Ellen Prell, *Fighting to Become Americans: Jews, Gender, and the Anxiety of Assimilation* (Boston: Beacon Press, 1999), 107, 109, 114, 281n56; Dash Moore, *At Home In America*, 95–102; Daniel Bender, "'Too Much of Distasteful Masculinity': Historicizing Sexual Harassment in the Garment Sweatshop and Factory," *Journal of Women's History* 15, no. 4 (Winter 2004): 91–116.
16. Prell, *Fighting to Become Americans*, 59–60, 62, 85, 104–5; Weinberg, *World of Our Mothers*, 119, 208–11, 218–22; Friedman-Kasaba, *Memories of Migration*, 61, 125, 136–37, 173.
17. Clippings, "Radio Needed Her," Helen Harrison, "Out of Russia's Revolt," *Tower Radio*, September 1934, and "Tamara Arrives and Demands Boulder Dam!" *Rocky Mountain News*, July 14, 1938, all in Tamara scrapbook, DFP; clippings, "Herewith Tamara in Your Eyes," *New York Times*, February 25, 1934, and "Song Writer's Prayer Answered by Singer Who's Actress, Too," *New York Herald Tribune*, March 26, 1939, TAMARA clipping folder (OF-20a), NYPL; Anzia Yezierska, *Bread Givers* (1925; repr., New York: Persea Books, 2003), 75, 220, 237.
18. Nina Warnke, "Going East: The Impact of American Yiddish Plays and Players on the Yiddish Stage in Czarist Russia, 1890–1914," *American Jewish History* 92, no. 1 (March 2004): 1–29; Jeffrey Veidlinger, *Jewish Public Culture in the Late Russian Empire* (Bloomington: Indiana University Press, 2009), 172, 186–219.
19. Valleri Hohman, *Russian Culture and Theatrical Performance in America, 1891–1933* (New York: Palgrave Macmillan, 2011); David Lifson, *The Yiddish Theatre in America* (New York: Thomas Yoseloff, 1965), 281–86, 291–93; Feingold, *Time for Searching*, 64–66.
20. Lifson, *Yiddish Theatre in America*, 96, 358, 487–89, 490–92, 413, 496, 501–2, 531, 600n45; Felix Mayrowitz, "The Yiddish Theater in Transition," *The Menorah Journal*, May 1929, 448–55; Frank Rich with Lisa Aronson,

The Theatre Art of Boris Aronson (New York: Knopf, 1987), 10–15, 31–37; Kenneth MacGowan, "Stagecraft Shows Its Newest Heresies," February 14, 1926, SM9, "Theatrical Notes," February 22, 1927, 23, and J. Brooks Atkinson, "The Play," March 11, 1927, 24, all in *New York Times*; clipping, "Bublichki to Roberta," *Brooklyn Eagle*, January 2, 1938, TAMARA clipping folder (OF-20a), NYPL.

21. Atkinson, "The Play."
22. Clipping, "Tamara, She's Singing Hit Song Again in 'Leave It to Me!'," *Brooklyn Daily Eagle*, January 29, 1939, TAMARA clipping folder (OF-20a), NYPL; clipping, "Radio Needed Her"; Nils Granlund, *Blondes, Brunettes, and Bullets* (New York: David McKay, 1957), 72; Robert Snyder, *The Voice of the City: Vaudeville and Popular Culture in New York* (New York: Oxford University Press, 1989), 94–95, 99–100; Arthur Frank Wertheim, *Vaudeville Wars: How the Keith-Albee and Orpheum Circuits Controlled the Big-Time and Its Performers* (New York: Palgrave Macmillan, 2006), 158.
23. Jimmy Durante and Jack Kofoed, *Nightclubs* (New York: Knopf, 1931), (quote) 57, 56–58, 64; Granlund, *Blondes, Brunettes, and Bullets*, (quote) 5, 6; Snyder, *Voice of the City*, 54–55; Burton W. Peretti, *Nightclub City: Politics and Amusement in Manhattan* (Philadelphia: University of Pennsylvania Press, 2007), 202, 212–14.
24. Alfred Bernheim, *The Business of the Theatre: An Economic History of the American Theatre, 1750–1932* (1932; repr., New York: Benjamin Blom, 1964); Granlund, *Blondes, Brunettes, and Bullets*, (quotes) 67 and 97; Wertheim, *Vaudeville Wars*, 98, 103–5, 162–63, 167, 172–73, 175, 189, 213, 218–20, 229–36; Paul Gemmil, "Types of Actors' Trade Unions," *Journal of Political Economy* 35, no. 2 (April 1927): 299–303.
25. Tamara to family, August 30, 1928, and Tamara to Bertha and children, ca. October 1928, folder 6, box 1, DFP; "At the Theaters," *Amarillo Globe-Times* (TX), October 8, 1928, 9, and October 9, 1928, 11; "College Cut-Ups Open New Hipp Offering Today," November 8, 1928, 7, and advertisement, November 9, 1928, 14, both in *Waco News-Tribune* (TX); Snyder, *Voice of the City*, 48–57, 111–12, 119; Wertheim, *Vaudeville Wars*, 230.
26. Tamara to Bertha and children, Tamara to Mama, and Tamara to Las, ca. October 1928, folder 6, box 1, DFP.
27. Tamara to Bertha and children, ca. October 1928, and Tamara to family, November 1928, and ca. November-December 1928, folder 6, box 1, Tamara to family, ca. September 1928, Boris's file, clipping, "Here Are Misses Who Will Sell Tribunes for Relief Fund Thursday," *Tulsa Tribune*, September 26, [1928], Tamara scrapbook, all in DFP; advertisement, *Waco News-Tribune* (TX), November 9, 1928, 14; Herbert Lloyd, *Vaudeville Trails Thru the West* (Philadelphia: Herbert Lloyd, 1919), 211; Wertheim, *Vaudeville Wars*, 173–75, 239, 241, 249–50; Snyder, *Voice of the City*, 61, 158–59.
28. Tamara to family, November 1928 and ca. November–December 1928, folder 6, box 1, DFP; Lloyd, *Vaudeville Trails Thru the West*, 27, 50, 54, 211;

Granlund, *Blondes, Brunettes, and Bullets*, 72; Wertheim, *Vaudeville Wars*, 170, 174.

29. Weinberg, *World of Our Mothers*, 152–66, 173–77, 187–92, 205–8; Melissa R. Klapper, *Jewish Girls Coming of Age in America, 1860–1920* (New York: New York University Press, 2005), 56, 219–23; Glenn, *Daughters of the Shtetl*, 63–72, 79, 83–89; Friedman-Kasaba, *Memories of Migration*, 135, 137, 171–72; Tamara to family, ca. September 1928, Boris's file, Tamara to Mama, ca. October 1928, and Tamara to family, ca. early October–November 1928, folder 6, box 1, DFP. The expectation that children would sustain mothers and fathers was so strong that parents often sued their offspring in cases of nonsupport before New York's Jewish Conciliation Court, a legal arbitration body—and won: Beth Wenger, *New York Jews and the Great Depression* (New Haven, CT: Yale University Press, 1996), 49–50.
30. Tamara to Mama, ca. October 1928, and Tamara to family, ca. December 1928, folder 6, box 1, DFP.
31. Tamara to family, November 1928 and ca. December 1928, folder 6, box 1, DFP; Prell, *Fighting to Become Americans*, 37–39; Weinberg, *World of Our Mothers*, 118, 128, 205; Wenger, *New York Jews*, 60–62. *Shmendrik* was a Yiddish epithet on the softer side of *schmuk*.
32. Tamara to family, ca. December 1928, folder 6, box 1, DFP; Prell, *Fighting to Become Americans*, 37, 62–65, 86–87, 101; Weinberg, *World of Our Mothers*, 51, 95–96, 110; Wenger, *New York Jews*, 50–52.
33. Nancy Green, *Ready-to-Wear and Ready-to-Work: A Century of Industry and Immigrants in Paris and New York* (Durham, NC: Duke University Press, 1997), 23, 46–48, 56–57, 62–63; Stolberg, *Tailor's Progress*, 148–53; Orleck, *Common Sense and a Little Fire*, 193–94.
34. *Report and Proceedings of the Twentieth Convention of the ILGWU*, (Cleveland: December 2, 1929), 113–14; "Union Authorizes Dress Strike Here," August 9, 1929, 21, "Plan to Unionize 5,000 Dressmakers," September 19, 1929, 34, "Seize 10 Students Aiding Union Drive," November 13, 1929, 29, "Whalen's Removal Urged in Petition," March 17, 1930, 3, "300 Fifth Av. Shops Face Strike Today," September 25, 1930, 29, "27 Arrested in Melee in 5th Av. Dress Strike," September 30, 1930, 15, "Mrs. Roosevelt Backs Fifth Av. Dress Strike," October 4, 1930, 38, "Dress Shops Spurn Strike Peace Move," November 7, 1930, 18, "Arbitration Fails in Garment Strike," November 26, 1930, 16, all in *New York Times*; Marilyn Johnson, *Street Justice: A History of Police Violence in New York City* (Boston: Beacon Press, 2003), 153–64, for "Tammany Cossacks," 161. Eleanor Roosevelt did not forget the garment workers of Local 38; in 1933 she hired them to make her presidential inaugural ball gown: "Mrs. Roosevelt Picks Ball Gown," *New York Times*, March 2, 1933, 3.
35. Wenger, *New York Jews*, 10–14.
36. Tamara to family, ca. December 1928, folder 6, box 1, DFP.

37. Bernheim, *Business of the Theatre*, 75–84; Wertheim, *Vaudeville Wars*, 252–54, 266–70, 276.

Chapter 7

1. "Sees Princeton Win, Dies in Auto Crash," November 8, 1925, 2, "Prior Convictions against Leopold," November 13, 1926, 19, and "Leopold Confesses He Sped into Crash," November 20, 1926, 19, all in *New York Times*.
2. "Sees Princeton Win, Dies in Auto Crash"; "Prior Convictions against Leopold"; "Leopold Confesses He Sped into Crash"; "Wants J. M. Leopold Barred as a Driver," *New York Times*, October 31, 1926, 23.
3. "Wants J. M. Leopold Barred as a Driver"; "Leopold Auto Case Set for Rehearing," *New York Times*, November 2, 1926, 10.
4. Harvard University, *Quinquennial Catalogue of the Officers and Graduates, 1636–1930* (Cambridge, MA: The University, 1930), 1421; Cornell alumni questionnaire, March 3, 1937, George Alfred Spiegelberg '18, 41-2-877, DAF; Stephen Birmingham, *"Our Crowd": The Great Jewish Families of New York* (New York: Harper, 1967), 5–6, 180–82, 258. For examples of George's letters to the editor, see clippings, *New York Herald Tribune*, November 9, 1929, and December 24, 1930, GASP. Frederick, Sr., had been rooting for Tammany to be "crushed" since at least the 1890s: Frederick Spiegelberg to Solomon Spiegelberg, October 15, 1897, November 2, 1897, and March 8, 1898, folder 8, box 1, WSP. Frederick served twenty years on the bench as a Municipal Court justice, arbitrating labor disputes, helping to revise the Municipal Court Code, and drafting rent laws with better protections for tenants: "Wise Visits Dinner Although in Grief," *New York Times*, May 13, 1913, 4; "Spiegelberg, 74, City Rent Law Champion, Dies," *New York Herald Tribune*, July 11, 1937, 20A.
5. "Prior Convictions against Leopold"; "Leopold Confesses He Sped into Crash"; "Leopold Auto Case Set for Rehearing"; "Leopold Loses Motor License," *New York Times*, December 11, 1926, 19.
6. George Spiegelberg, "The New York Statute of Limitations Applicable to Actions in Equity Based on Legal Rights," *New York University Quarterly Review* 18 (1940–1941): 182–200; New York Bar Association, *Proceedings of the Sixtieth Annual Meeting* (Albany: Argus, 1937), 87–88, 93–94; Alexis de Tocqueville, *Democracy in America*, trans., ed., with introduction by Harvey C. Mansfield and Delba Winthrop (1835; Chicago: University of Chicago Press, 2002), 251–58, (quote) 252; "Want College Men in Bar," December 31, 1926, 12, "Hears Plea June 5 on Bar Standards," June 1, 1931, 14, "Stricter Rule Urged in Bar Qualifications," December 16, 1933, 8, "Favor Probation for Young Lawyers," June 24, 1934, 25, and "Harnett Arrested by Dewey as Taker of $67,000 Bribes," November 17, 1938, 1, 3, all in *New York Times*; "City Bar Urges Change in U.S. Bankruptcy Act," May 26, 1932, 21, and "Probation Period Urged for All Young Lawyers," June 24, 1934, 16, both in *New York Herald Tribune*. On the worldview of trial lawyers like George, see also Robert

Gordon, "'The Ideal and the Actual in the Law': Fantasies and Practices of New York City Lawyers, 1870–1910," in *The New High Priests: Lawyers in Post-Civil War America*, ed. Gerard Gawalt (Westport, CT: Greenwood Press, 1984), 51–74; Kenneth de Ville, "New York City Attorneys and Ambulance Chasing in the 1920s," *The Historian* 59, no. 2 (October 2007): 291–310; Robert Gordon, "The American Legal Profession, 1870–2000," in *The Cambridge History of Law in America*, ed. Michael Grossberg and Christopher Tomlins, vol. 3 (New York: Cambridge University Press, 2008), 73–126; and Daniel Ernst, "The Politics of Administrative Law: New York's Anti-Bureaucracy Clause and the O'Brien-Wagner Campaign of 1938," *Law and History Review* 27, no. 2 (Summer 2009): 331–71.

7. Calvin Coolidge address to the American Society of Newspaper Editors, January 17, 1925, Online by Gerhard Peters and John Woolley, The American Presidency Project, https://www.presidency.ucsb.edu/node/269410; Judith Stein, "The Birth of Liberal Republicanism in New York State, 1932–1938" (PhD diss., Yale University Press, 1968), 11–14, 32–33, 38, 64, 69; Heather Cox Richardson, *To Make Men Free: A History of the Republican Party* (New York: Basic, 2014), xvii, 182–83, 188–89.
8. Terry Golway, *Machine Made: Tammany Hall and the Creation of Modern American Politics* (New York: Liveright, 2014), 237–41, 245, 250, 266, 270–71. See also Robert Chiles, *The Revolution of '28: Al Smith, American Progressivism, and the Coming of the New Deal* (Ithaca, NY: Cornell University Press, 2018).
9. "Koenig Exonerated of Costuma Charge at Stormy Meeting," February 19, 1926, 1, "New Move in Koenig Fight," May 10, 1926, 21, "New County Club Denounces Koenig," June 25, 1926, 23, "Up-State Drys Win Primary Victories," September 15, 1926, 1, "Hoover Men Force Bronx Leader Out," February 17, 1930, 1, "Mack Leads Fight to Depose Koenig," December 29, 1932, 7, "Is He Irremovable?" January 2, 1933, 22, and "Mills and Stimson Lead Party Chiefs in Fight on Koenig," May 28, 1933, 1, all in *New York Times*; George Spiegelberg and Harry Mack, "The Cry 'Koenig Must Go'," November 11, 1929, 16, and "G. A. Spiegelberg Slated to Make Congress Race," July 21, 1934, 7, both in *New York Herald Tribune*; The Reminiscences of Samuel S. Koenig, CCOH; Stein, "Birth of Liberal Republicanism, 8, 39–49; Golway, *Machine Made*, xx–xxi. Other law men leading the charge against Koenig included Elihu Root, Charles S. Whitman, Ogden Mills, and Henry Stimson.
10. Mason B. Williams, *City of Ambition: FDR, La Guardia, and the Making of Modern New York* (New York: Norton, 2013), 87–88, 112–16; Burton W. Peretti, *Nightclub City: Politics and Amusement in Manhattan* (Philadelphia: University of Pennsylvania Press, 2011), 122–45; "Koenig Refuses to Admit Defeat," *New York Times*, September 21, 1933, 16.
11. Herbert Hoover speech transcript, "The Consequences of the Proposed New Deal," October 21, 1932, https://millercenter.org/the-presidency/presidential-speeches/october-21-1932-campaign-speech-madison-square-gar

den; Herbert Hoover, *The Challenge to Liberty* (1934; repr., Rockford, IL: The Herbert Hoover Presidential Library Association, 1971), 4, 160, 166; William E. Leuchtenburg, *Herbert Hoover* (New York: Holt, 2009), (public trough) 151; Elliot A. Rosen, *The Republican Party in the Age of Roosevelt: Sources of Anti-Government Conservatism in the United States* (Charlottesville: University of Virginia Press, 2014), 10, 13, 17, 19; Eric Rauchway, *Winter War: Hoover, Roosevelt, and the First Clash over the New Deal* (New York: Basic Books, 2018), 10, 23, 41, 45.

12. "Hoover Men Unite to Restore Party for Victory in '34," April 24, 1933, 1, "Mills Urges Party to Replace Koenig," July 12, 1933, 2, and "Spiegelberg Is Approved," July 21, 1934, 26, all in *New York Times*; "Mrs. Lorenz Named Vice-President of Republican Group," *New York Herald Tribune*, July 24, 1934, 15; Dick Lee, "Hyland Vows to Undertake Write-In War," *New York Daily News*, October 27, 1934, 6; Republican campaign brochure, 1934, GASP.
13. "17th District Voters Turn Out in House Fight," *New York Herald Tribune*, November 4, 1936, A6; Richard Fried, *The Man Everybody Knew: Bruce Barton and the Making of Modern America* (Chicago: Ivan R. Dee, 2005), 159.
14. "Republicans Open Fight on New Deal," *New York Times*, July 24, 1934, 13; "A Candidate for Congress," *New York Herald Tribune*, October 29, 1934, 5; Spiegelberg election brochure, 1934, GASP; Barry Cushman, "The Great Depression and the New Deal," in Grossberg and Tomlins, *Cambridge History of Law in America*, 268–318; Ernst, "The Politics of Administrative Law."
15. "Lawyers Back Spiegelberg," *New York Times*, October 30, 1934, 10; campaign headquarters stationary, Frederick Warburg to Bruce Barton, October 1, 1934, George Spiegelberg to Bruce Barton, September 12, 1934, and Bruce Barton to George Spiegelberg, September 14, 1934, all in folder 4, box 65, BBP.
16. Bruce Barton to Helen Reid, October 25, 1934, folder 4, box 65, BBP; Spiegelberg election brochure, 1934, GASP; "Lehman Bowed to Tammany, Baldwin Says," October 4, 1934, 7, "Women Voters Attend Political Cocktail Party," October 25, 1934, 22, and "A Candidate for Congress," October 29, 1934, 5, all in *New York Herald Tribune*; "Miss Couch Scores the Recovery Act," October 31, 1934, 12, "Tammany 'Kick-Back' Is Linked to Peyser," November 2, 1934, 17, and Arthur Krock, "Tide Sweeps Nation," November 7, 1934, 1, 3, all in *New York Times*; Dick Lee, "First Lady and Lehman Speakers at O'Day Dinner," *New York Daily News*, November 2, 1934, 8.
17. "17th District Voters Turn Out in House Fight," *New York Herald Tribune*, November 4, 1936, A6; Arthur Krock, "Tide Sweeps Nation," *New York Times*, November 7, 1934, 1, 3.
18. Franklin Roosevelt, Address at Madison Square Garden, October 31, 1936, vol. 5, *FDRPA*, 566–73.

19. New York Bar Association, *Proceedings of the Sixtieth Annual Meeting*, 87–88; "Helen Pisek Married to G. A. Spiegelberg," December 14, 1935, 15, and "Corner in Old Textile Zone Sold by Bank, May 13, 1939, 28, both in *New York Herald Tribune*; Cornell alumni questionnaire; NYU appointment letter, October 22, 1934, scrapbook, volume 3, GASP; New York, New York, 2A, reel 2655, *Census (1940)*; conversation between the author and Ann S. Brown, January 7, 2012. George and Dorothy Borg married in March 1924, honeymooned in Europe, and then leased an apartment at 157 East 72nd Street: "Miss Dorothy Borg Is Wed," *New York Times*, March 19, 1924, 21; "Apartment Seekers Keep Brokers Busy in Many Sections," *New York Herald Tribune*, June 15, 1924, B13. Two years later they seem to have secured a Paris divorce, a common practice among New York elites seeking to circumvent their own state's strict divorce laws and avoid publicity in the local papers. A ship manifest, showing the couple returned from Europe in August 1926, first recorded Dorothy's surname as Spiegelberg, but this was crossed off and replaced with her maiden name. Little more than a week later, George leased for himself a new apartment on Fifth Avenue: *Orbita* manifest, August 23, 1926, reel 3909, *VANY*; "Apartments Renting Fast in Houses on East Side," *New York Herald Tribune*, September 3, 1926, 26. The two remained on good terms. George served as an usher at Dorothy's sister's wedding, and George's father officiated: "Miss M. Borg Weds Richard Loengard," *New York Times*, September 9, 1927, 29. On Borg, see "Dorothy Borg, 91, East Asia Scholar at Columbia, Dies," *New York Times*, October 28, 1993, D27. On Paris divorces, see Brooke L. Blower, *Becoming Americans in Paris: Transatlantic Politics and Culture between the World Wars* (New York: Oxford University Press, 2011), 150.
20. "Property Rights Explained to 100," *Brooklyn Daily Eagle*, October 4, 1935, 6; conversation between the author and Ann S. Brown, January 7, 2012; Lewis L. Gould, *Grand Old Party: A History of the Republicans* (New York: Random House, 2003), 277–79; Rosen, *Republican Party in the Age of Roosevelt*, 80–81.
21. Stein, "The Birth of Liberal Republicanism, 213–14; Golway, *Machine Made*, 290–95; Williams, *City of Ambition*, 300–301. On George's continued support for La Guardia, see "La Guardia Backed by Lawyers' Group," *New York Times*, October 24, 1937, 2N.
22. Richard J. Evans, *The Third Reich in Power* (New York: Penguin, 2005), 10–14, 16, 27, 44–45, 54, 67, 73–76, 79, 118, 443.
23. Cornell alumni questionnaire. Their daughter, Ann, married in New York's Brick Presbyterian Church: The Brick Church register, June 17, 1964, VAULT FOLIO BX 9211.N70028 B72 v.10, *United States, Presbyterian Church Records, 1701-1907,* Presbyterian Historical Society, Philadelphia, Pennsylvania; Evans, *Third Reich in Power*, 14–15, 537, 545, 550, 575, 577.
24. Evans, *Third Reich in Power*, 580–90, 657–61.

25. Evans, *Third Reich in Power*, 564, 574–77, 594–97.
26. Rosen, *The Republican Party in the Age of Roosevelt*, 77, 116; Kathryn S. Olmsted, *The Newspaper Axis: Six Press Barons Who Enabled Hitler* (New Haven, CT: Yale University Press, 2022), 176–78, 181–82.
27. "Republican Club's Dance Show Will Present Elephant," January 31, 1940, 19, and "2,500 Pounds of Debutante at Republican Ball," February 6, 1940, 3A, both in *New York Herald Tribune*; "Minnie the Elephant at Republican Fete," *New York Times*, February 6, 1940, 4.
28. "Big Armed Forces Urged for Defense," February 7, 1940, 6, "Plattsburg Groups Asks Conscription," May 23, 1940, 1, and "Plattsburg Group Asks to Aid Allies," May 24, 1940, 17, all in *New York Times*; Olmsted, *Newspaper Axis*, 176. On Barton, see Susan Dunn, *1940: FDR, Willkie, Lindbergh, Hitler—the Election amid the Storm* (New Haven, CT: Yale University Press, 2013), 65, 216, 277.
29. Rosen, *Republican Party in the Age of Roosevelt*, 71, 73, 109–10, 120; Dunn, *1940*, 100; Beth Wenger, *New York Jews and the Great Depression* (New Haven, CT: Yale University Press, 1996), 133–34; George Spiegelberg to Robert Patterson, June 22, 1949, folder "S" Miscellany, 1947–52, box 45, RPPP. On Willkie's growing internationalism after the 1940 election, see Nicholas Wapshott, *The Sphinx: Franklin Roosevelt, the Isolationists, and the Road to World War II* (New York: Norton, 2015), 265–66.

Chapter 8

1. Journal entry, February 1, 1935, folder 33, box 3, BFRP; Ben Robertson, "King George Strives to Please," *Saturday Evening Post*, February 4, 1939, 5–7, 66-9.
2. Journal entries, February 1 and February 7 or 8, 1935, folder 33, box 3, BFRP; David Brinkley, *Washington Goes to War* (New York: Knopf, 1988), 84, 184. Other mentions of Roosevelt's ship collection include journal entries, March 2, 1936, folder 33, April 12, 1936, folder 31, box 3, and March 30, 1936, folder 35, box 4, BFRP.
3. Journal entries, February 1 and February 7 or 8, 1935, folder 33, box 3, BFRP. On the excitement of Roosevelt's early press conferences, see Delbert Clark, *Washington Dateline* (New York: Stokes, 1941), 80–82; Leo Roster, *The Washington Correspondent* (New York: Harcourt, 1937), 49–53; Graham White, *FDR and the Press* (Chicago: University of Chicago Press 1979), ch. 1.
4. Ben Robertson to Edgar Snow, January 3, 1937, folder 15, box 2, BFRP; Donald Richie, *Reporting from Washington: The History of the Washington Press Corps* (New York: Oxford University Press, 2005), 2–3; Flecher Knebel, "The Placid Twenties," in Cabell Phillips, ed., *Dateline: Washington* (Garden City, NY: Doubleday, 1949), 61–74; Oliver McKee, "Washington as a Boom Town," *North American Review* 239, no. 2 (February 1, 1935): 177–83; Roster, *Washington Correspondent*, 3, 116.

5. Ben Robertson to Edgar Snow, January 3, 1937, folder 15, box 2, and journal entry, March 16, 1936, folder 35, box 4, both in BFRP.
6. "Ben Robertson, Jr.," *New York Herald Tribune*, February 24, 1943, 22; Ed Murrow broadcast transcript, February 28, 1943, folder 21, box 2, BFRP. See also Jean Nicol, *Meet Me at the Savoy* (Bath: Cedric Chivers, 1952), 61; Mary Longley to M. D. Klaás, April 14, 1966, and M. D. Klaás, "Lest We Forget," folder 3, box, 1, BFRP; Helen Kirkpatrick Milbank interview, April 4, 1990 (Washington, DC: Washington Press Club Foundation, 1997); Bess Furman, *Washington By-Line: The Personal History of a Newspaperwoman* (New York: Knopf, 1949), 290. On Ben's approach toward women, see also his commentary about Frances Perkins, Hattie Caraway, and Eleanor Roosevelt in drafts for May 5–15, 1936, folder 31, and journal entry, February 5, 1935, folder 33, box 3, BFRP.
7. Ben Robertson to Alan Villiers, January 14, 1937, folder 15, box 2, and Ben Robertson to Dorothy Spalding, January 31, 1937, folder 37, box 4, BFRP; John Howard, *Men Like That: A Southern Queer History* (Chicago: University of Chicago Press, 1999), xi, xvii.
8. See Ben Robertson, "Dry Agents Raid 20 Alcohol Dives on the Bowery," October 26, 1930, 1, 6, and coverage of college student protest ride to Kentucky, March 25–April 3, 1932, all in *New York Herald Tribune*; Ben Robertson to B. O. Williams, December 6, 1937, folder 15, box 2, BFRP; and Lacy K. Ford, "The Affable Journalist as Social Critic: Ben Robertson and the Early Twentieth-Century South," *Southern Cultures* 2 (1996): 353–73. Kirkpatrick quoted in William Walker, Jr., "Ben Robertson, War Correspondent (master's thesis, University of South Carolina, 1971).
9. J. P. Richards to Ben Robertson, June 29, 1939, B. Greenwood to Ben Robertson, August 11, 1939, Ben Robertson to Millard Tydings, July 28, 1940, and Ben Robertson to Henry Cabot Lodge, July 28, 1940, folder 16, box 2, BFRP.
10. For Ben's religious sensibilities, see, for example, journal entries, March 21, 1936, folder 37, box 4, April 12, 1936, folder 31, box 3, and Ben Robertson to John Whitaker, January 3, 1937, folder 15, box 2, BFRP; Ben Robertson, *Red Hills and Cotton: An Upcountry Memory* (1942; repr., with a new introduction by Lacy K. Ford, Jr., Columbia: University of South Carolina Press, 1991), 9–10, 13, 32, 86–87, 203–7. See also Paul Harvey, *Redeeming the South: Religious Cultures and Racial Identities among Southern Baptists, 1865–1925* (Chapel Hill: University of North Carolina Press, 1997).
11. Robertson, *Red Hills and Cotton*, 25, 32, 75, 79, 101, 251, 258, 260, 263; Anderson Kiwanis Club speech, November 1937, folder 38, box 4, BFRP; John Kneebone, *Southern Liberal Journalists and the Issue of Race, 1920–1944* (Chapel Hill: University of North Carolina Press, 1985). For stereotypical profiles of Black Americans in Ben's writing, see clipping, B. F. Robertson, "The Old Stone Church," *Clemson College Chronicle*, February 1922, folder 47, box 5, BFRP; Ben Robertson, "Last of Slaves Owned by Battles Dies in

Leap from Bronx Home," *New York Herald Tribune*, December 24, 1931, 1, 12; Ben Robertson, *Traveler's Rest* (Clemson, SC: Cottonfield, 1938), 123–25, 136; Robertson, *Red Hills and Cotton*, 251. On these tropes, see David W. Blight, *Race and Reunion: The Civil War in American Memory* (Cambridge, MA: Belknap of Harvard University Press, 2003), 284–91; Nina Silber, *This War Ain't Over: Fighting the Civil War in New Deal America* (Chapel Hill: University of North Carolina Press, 2018), 15–16, 30, 68.

12. Robertson, *Red Hills and Cotton*, 6–7. Other scholars have downplayed Ben's commitments to white supremacist democracy, assuming that his opposition to lynching could be equated with across-the-board support for racial equality and civil rights: Ford, "The Affable Journalist as Social Critic" and Jodie Peeler, *Ben Robertson: South Carolina Journalist and Author* (Columbia: University of South Carolina Press, 2019), 16, 73.
13. Robertson, *Red Hills and Cotton*, 3, 5, 7, 9, 21.
14. Robertson, *Red Hills and Cotton*, 56–59, 62, 64, 75, 80, 98, 113–14.
15. Robertson, *Red Hills and Cotton*, 26–29, 43, 89–93, 105, 108; Anderson Kiwanis Club speech, November 1937, folder 38, box 4, BFRP; William T. Bowen, service record, reel 184, *ConfedRec*; Slave Schedules for Pickens, South Carolina, *Census (1860)*. Bowen had registered eleven enslaved people on his property in 1850: Eastern Division, Pickens, South Carolina, 459B, reel 857, *Census (1850)*; Matthew Karp, *This Vast Southern Empire: Slaveholders at the Helm of American Foreign Policy* (Cambridge, MA: Harvard University Press, 2016), 1–4; Blight, *Race and Reunion*, 282–83.
16. Robertson, *Red Hills and Cotton*, 26, 28–29, 91–92, 259.
17. Robertson, *Red Hills and Cotton*, 113, 258–62; Allen Trelease, *White Terror: The Ku Klux Klan Conspiracy and Southern Reconstruction* (New York: Harper, 1971), 72–73; Bruce E. Baker, *What Reconstruction Meant: Historical Memory in the American South* (Charlottesville: University of Virginia Press, 2007), 10–11, ch. 3.
18. Robertson, *Red Hills and Cotton*, 113, 259, 262–63; J. C. A. Stagg, "The Problem of Klan Violence: The South Carolina Up-Country, 1868–1871," *Journal of American Studies* 8, no. 3 (December 1974): 303–18; Wilma A. Dunaway, *The African-American Family in Slavery and Emancipation* (New York: Cambridge University Press, 2003), (quote) 246; Trelease, *White Terror*, 72–73, 114–17, 351–80; Eric Foner, *Reconstruction: America's Unfinished Revolution, 1863–1877* (New York: Harper, 1988), 569–75. On white victimization narratives, see also Silber, *This War Ain't Over*, 66–69.
19. Robert Smalls, "Election Methods in the South," *North American Review* 151, no. 408 (November 1890): 593–600 as reprinted in Rhondda Robinson Thomas and Susanna Ashton, eds., *The South Carolina Roots of African American Thought: A Reader* (Columbia: University of South Carolina Press 2014), 70–76; George Tindall, "The Campaign for the Disenfranchisement of Negroes in South Carolina," *Journal of Southern History* 15, no. 2 (May 1949): 212–34; Edward Ayers, *The Promise of the New South: Life After*

Reconstruction (New York: Oxford University Press, 1992), 225–28, 285–89; J. Morgan Kousser, *The Shaping of Southern Politics: Suffrage Restriction and the Establishment of the One-Party South, 1880–1910* (New Haven, CT: Yale University Press, 1974). Unlike most other Southern states, South Carolina's Jim Crow regime did not disenfranchise poor Whites: Bryant Simon, *A Fabric of Defeat: The Politics of South Carolina Millhands, 1910–1948* (Chapel Hill: University of North Carolina Press, 1998), 4, 16–17. On Ben's family members' part in this history, see Robertson, *Red Hills and Cotton*, 75, 79–80, 113, 262–63.

20. Robertson, *Red Hills and Cotton*, 202, 231–34, 251–52, 257–58, 263. See also Jennifer Ritterhouse, *Growing Up Jim Crow: How Black and White Southern Children Learned Race* (Chapel Hill: University of North Carolina Press, 2006).
21. Robertson, "Old Stone Church"; Robertson, *Red Hills and Cotton*, 218; Benjamin E. Mays, *Born to Rebel: An Autobiography* (1971; repr., Athens: University of Georgia Press, 2003), 7–9, 17, 22–25, 33–34; Joseph Crespino, *Strom Thurmond's America* (New York: Hill and Wang, 2012), 16–17; "South Carolina Uses Taxes—None For Us," *Chicago Defender*, December 8, 1923, A1. South Carolina would lose 8.2 percent of its Black population during the 1920s: "Decrease in South Carolina Population," *Chicago Defender*, April 11, 1931, 13.
22. Mays, *Born to Rebel*, 43; Robertson, *Red Hills and Cotton*, 138, 234.
23. *Taps*, vol. 16 (Clemson, SC: Clemson A&M College, 1923), 74, 83; *Constitution of the State of South Carolina* (Abbeville, SC: Hugh Wilson, 1900), 11; Howard, *Men Like That*, xi, xiv, 18–19, 43, 59–63. On how young Ben regarded Tillman with "awe and wonder," see Ben Robertson, "Clemson Twice a Week," June 14 and 17, 1938, folder 64, box 6, BFRP.
24. Lecture notes, September 1923, folder 23, box 2, and speech draft, folder 37, box 4, both in BFRP; Ben Robertson, "He Never Went to College," *New York Herald Tribune*, November 23, 1930, SM10. See also Michael Schudson, "The Objectivity Norm in American Journalism," *Journalism* 2, no. 2 (August 2002): 149–70.
25. Clipping, "All Southerners Become Gentlemen," *Atlanta Journal*, June 11, 1939, folder 65, box 6, Notes on an American and Britain, folder 43, and Adelaide notes, 1929, folder 49, box 5, BFRP; Robertson, *Traveler's Rest*, vii; "American Likes Us," *News* (Adelaide), July 21, 1937, 3. It's not clear if Ben actually received a degree from Missouri. The school's 1926 yearbook lists his graduation year as 1927, but he does not appear in the 1927 edition: *Savitar* (1926), 77.
26. Ben Robertson to R. N. Brackett, January 30, 1929, folder 13, box 1, BFRP; Richard Kluger, *The Paper: The Life and Death of the* New York Herald Tribune (New York: Knopf, 1986), 8–9, 232, 241–45, 273–74; Stanley Walker, *City Editor* (New York: Stokes, 1934), 23, 34, 38–39, (quote) 158; New York journal entries, 1929–1932, folder 29, box 3, BFRP. See also Ben's

many by-lined articles in the *New York Herald Tribune* between October 6, 1929 and November 9, 1931.

27. "Walton Gets No By-Line in N.Y. Herald Tribune," April 18, 1931, 4, and "Lester Walton Quits N.Y. Herald-Tribune," April 25, 1931, 2, both in *Pittsburgh Courier*; Ben Robertson to father, January 24, 1930, folder 14, box 1, BFRP; Robertson, *Red Hills and Cotton*, 11, 28.
28. Journal for 1935, folder 33, and typed draft, ca. 1936, folder 31, both in box 3, Ben Robertson to Edgar Snow, January 3, 1937, folder 37, box 4, all in BFRP; Roster, *Washington Correspondent*, 116–23; Richie, *Reporting from Washington*, 113–18.
29. Robertson, *Red Hills and Cotton*, 153, 162, 167, 272–73, 287, 289; Ira Katznelson, *Fear Itself: The New Deal and the Origins of Our Time* (New York: Liveright, 2013), 15–17, 21, 144-63.
30. Journal entries, March 22 and April 1, 1936, folder 35, box 4, journal entry April 26, 1936, and typed notes, folder 31, box 3, BFRP; Federal Writers' Project, *Washington: City and Capital* (Washington, DC: Works Progress Administration, 1937), 545–46. On Southern Agrarian outlooks, see Twelve Southerners, *I'll Take My Stand: The South and the Agrarian Tradition* (New York: Harper, 1930).
31. Journal entries, February 15, 1935, folder 33, box 3, and March 16 and 17, 1936, folder 35, box 4, BFRP.
32. Journal entries, March 7–9, 12, and 24, 1936, folder 35, box 4, April 13 and 17, 1936, folder 31, box 3, and Ben Robertson to Edgar Snow, January 3, 1937, folder 15, box 2, all in BFRP.
33. Journal entries, February 7 and 11, 1935, folder 33, April 12, 25, and 26, 1936, folder 31, box 3, and March 22, 1936, folder 35, box 4, handwritten notes for memoir, folder 97, box 10, all in BFRP; Robertson, *Traveler's Rest*, viii, 161–62.
34. Carl Abbott, *Political Terrain: Washington, D.C. from Tidewater Town to Global Metropolis* (Chapel Hill: University of North Carolina Press, 1999), 87–88; Eric S. Yellin, *Racism in the Nation's Service: Government Workers and the Color Line in Woodrow Wilson's America* (Chapel Hill: University of North Carolina Press, 2013), 162–63, 181–87.
35. Rosskam, *Washington*, 23; Constance McLaughlin Green, *The Secret City: A History of Race Relations in the Nation's Capital* (Princeton, NJ: Princeton University Press, 1967), 227–37; Brinkley, *Washington Goes to War*, 18–19; Chris Myers Asch and George Derek Musgrove, *Chocolate City: A History of Race and Democracy in the Nation's Capital* (Chapel Hill: University of North Carolina Press, 2017), 250–57; Paula C. Austin, *Coming of Age in Jim Crow DC: Navigating the Politics of Everyday Life* (New York: New York University Press, 2019), 42–45, 50–51, 76; Eric Marsden, "Washington: City of Pandemonium," *American Mercury* 37, no. 145 (January 1936): 22–29; Alden Stevens, "Washington: Blight on Democracy," *Harper's*, December 1, 1941, 50–58.

36. Richie, *Reporting from Washington*, xiii, 28–36, 93–4, 98, (Waters quote) 28; Yellin, *Racism in the Nation's Service*, 196; Asch and Musgrove, *Chocolate City*, 258–59; Stevens, "Washington: Blight on Democracy."
37. Richard Wright, "The Ethics of Living Jim Crow," in *Uncle Tom's Children* (1938; repr., New York: Harper Perennial Modern Classics, 2008), 1–15; journal entries, March 11 and 20, 1936, folder 35, box 4, BFRP.
38. Journal entry, March 17, 1936, folder 35, box 4, BFRP; Austin, *Coming of Age in Jim Crow DC*, 78.
39. Ben Robertson to Jean Muir, January 18, 1937, folder 15, box 2, and journal entry, March 24, 1936, folder 35, box 4, BFRP; Richie, *Reporting from Washington*, 98–99.
40. James Q. Whitman, *Hitler's American Model: The United States and the Making of Nazi Race Law* (Princeton, NJ: Princeton University Press, 2017); Johnpeter Horst Grill and Robert Jenkins, "The Nazis and the American South in the 1930s: A Mirror Image?" *Journal of Southern History* 58, no. 4 (November 1992): 667–94.
41. Grill and Jenkins, "Nazis and the American South"; Glenda Gilmore, *Defying Dixie: The Radical Roots of Civil Rights, 1919–1950* (New York: Norton, 2008), 158–59, (quote) 168, 169, 199; journal entry, March 17, 1936, folder 35, box 4, BFRP.
42. Robertson, *Red Hills and Cotton*, 15; Thomas Sheridan to Ben Robertson, October 26, 1935, folder 14, box 1, Thomas Sheridan to Ben Robertson, April 29, 1936, folder 15, box 2, and notes on Honolulu's King Street, ca. 1929, folder 48, box 5, BFRP; Robertson, *Traveler's Rest*, vii, 161.
43. Ben Robertson to John Whitaker, Jan. 3, 1937, folder 15, box 2, BFRP; Bruce Schulman, *From Cotton Belt to Sunbelt: Federal Policy, Economic Development, and the Transformation of the South, 1938-1980* (1991; rev. ed., Durham, NC: Duke University Press, 1994), 14–15, 39–52; Gilmore, *Defying Dixie*, 202–4, 227–28, 234–35, 280–81, 299, 383; Jason Morgan Ward, *Defending White Democracy: The Making of a Segregationist Movement and the Remaking of Racial Politics, 1936–1965* (Chapel Hill: University of North Carolina Press, 2011), 2, 18–23; Simon, *Fabric of Defeat*, 188–89; Franklin Roosevelt, Message to the Conference on Economic Conditions of the South, July 4, 1938, *FDRPA*, 421-2.
44. Clippings, Ben Robertson, "Maybank Under Fire as Candidates Move into Piedmont Region," August 3, 1938, and "Sins of Charleston Painted as Issue in Gubernatorial Race," August 4, 1938, both in *Anderson Independent*, folder 63, box 6, BFRP.
45. Simon, *Fabric of Defeat*, 206; "8,000 Race Voters Banned," *Pittsburgh Courier*, September 24, 1938, 3.
46. Simon, *Fabric of Defeat*, 204–6, 210.
47. Clippings, Ben Robertson, "Clemson Twice a Week," June 10 and 24, 1938, folder 64, box 6, BFRP. Ben reprised this courthouse scene in a lightly revised fashion and transposed it onto the 1936 presidential primary for *Red Hills and Cotton*, 207–9. For a full accounting of the

1938 Senate campaign in South Carolina, see Simon, *Fabric of Defeat*, ch. 11.

48. Susan Dunn, *Roosevelt's Purge: How FDR Fought to Change the Democratic Party* (Cambridge, MA: Harvard University Press, 2010), (*Atlanta Constitution* quote) 188; Ben Robertson to Turner, March 1, 1938, folder 15, box 2, BFRP; "Forget Gettysburg, Clemson Writer Says," *The News and Courier* (Charleston, SC), July 1, 1939, 12. If Ben indeed voted for Smith as he intimated, his political trajectory tracked closely to that of his college classmate Strom Thurmond, who idolized Tillman as a child, at first supported the New Deal, but broke from Roosevelt to vote for Smith in 1938, and became an early defector from the Democratic Party: Crespino, *Strom Thurmond's America*, 18, 24, 29, 35–39.
49. Clippings, "Central Women Hear Robertson," ca. February 18, 1939, "Why the South Needs 2 Parties," ca. June 1939, and "An Upcountry Voice," *News and Courier*, ca. June 8, 1939, folder 43, box 5, BFRP. On voting Republican, see also handwritten notes for memoir, folder 97, box 10, and Ben Robertson to father, July 28, 1940, folder 16, box 2, BFRP; Mark Sullivan, op-ed, *Washington Post*, July 2, 1939, B6.
50. Eric Schickler, *Racial Realignment: The Transformation of American Liberalism, 1932–1965* (Princeton, NJ: Princeton University Press, 2016); Kari Frederickson, *The Dixiecrat Revolt and the End of the Solid South, 1932–1968* (Chapel Hill: University of North Carolina Press, 2001).
51. Harvard Sitkoff, "Racial Militancy and Interracial Violence in the Second World War," *Journal of American History* 58, no.3 (December 1971): 661–81; Gilmore, *Defying Dixie*, ch. 8; Pete Daniel, "Going among Strangers: Southern Reactions to World War II," *Journal of American History* 77, no. 3 (December 1990): 886–911; Ward, *Defending White Democracy*, 38–44, 57–61; Simon, *Fabric of Defeat*, 219–20, 225.

Chapter 9

1. "Different Causes Are Given for Club Abbey Mix-up by Bad Men," *Variety*, January 28, 1931, 63; Lilian Brandt, *An Impressionistic View of the Winter of 1930–31 in New York City* (New York: Welfare Council of New York City, 1932), 7–8, 22.
2. Burton W. Peretti, *Nightclub City: Politics and Amusement in Manhattan* (Philadelphia: University of Pennsylvania Press, 2007), 73, 102–7; Helen Krich Chinoy, *The Group Theatre: Passion, Politics, and Performance in the Depression Era* (New York: Palgrave Macmillan, 2013), 15–16; Krystyn Moon, "On a Temporary Basis: Immigration, Labor Unions, and the American Entertainment Industry, 1880s–1930s," *Journal of American History* 99, no. 3 (Dec. 2012): 771–92; "To Aid Jobless Musicians," December 12, 1930, 38, and "4,000 at Concert to Aid Musicians," January 21, 1931, 24, both in *New York Times*.
3. "Tables for Two," June 7, 1930, 70–72, and "Goings On About Town,' July 12, 1930, 4, both in *New Yorker*; Julian Jerome, "Floor-Show," *Vanity Fair*,

February 1931, 68, 86; "Came the Dawn," *Vogue*, February 15, 1931, 43–44, 120; Jimmy Durante and Jack Kofoed, *Nightclubs* (New York: Knopf, 1931), 211–12.

4. Billy Rose, *Wine, Women and Words* (New York: Simon and Schuster, 1946), (quote) 83, 84–97; Durante and Kofoed, *Nightclubs*, (quote) 58; Nils Granlund, *Blondes, Brunettes, and Bullets* (New York: David McKay, 1957), 137–46, 162–69; Peretti, *Nightclub City*, 25, 30, 39–40, 124––39; Marilyn Johnson, *Street Justice: A History of Police Violence in New York City* (Boston: Beacon, 2003), 115–21.
5. Granlund, *Blondes, Brunettes, and Bullets*, 223, 241–42; Durante and Kofoed, *Nightclubs*, 39, 211–12; Marc Mappen, *Prohibition Gangsters: The Rise and Fall of a Bad Generation* (New Brunswick, NJ: Rutgers University Press, 2013), 172–74.
6. "'Dutch' Schultz Eludes Search in Abbey Shooting," *New York Herald Tribune*, January 27, 1931, 4; "Gambler Is Stabbed in Night Club Fight," January 25, 1931, 3, "Racketeer Hunted in Club Abbey Fight," January 26, 1931, 12, "Larry Fay Queried on Club Stabbing," January 27, 1931, 12, "1 A.M. Curfew Asked as Mulrooney Wars on Night Club Gangs," January 28, 1931, 1, "Says He Left Club before Gang Fight," February 27, 1931, 14, and "Walsh Seen at Club Only Before Fight," February 14, 1931, 6, all in *New York Times*; Lloyd Morris, *Incredible New York: High Life and Low Life of the Last Hundred Years* (New York: Random House, 1951), 330, 348–49. The Abbey employees remained uncooperative three months later when Schultz resurfaced and they were again brought in to view a line up: "Schultz Gives Up in Club Abbey Case," *New York Times*, April 13, 1931, 2. On the third degree, see Johnson, *Street Justice*, 122–32.
7. Columbia Broadcasting Station script, May 15, 1931, and clipping, Irene Thirer, "S. Eilers Adorns Trite Roxie Talkie," January 14, 1933, Tamara scrapbook, DFP; "Goings On About Town," *New Yorker*, November 12, 1932, 4; "Today on the Radio," *New York Times*, December 22, 1932, 22; clippings "A Singer of Sad Songs," *New York Sun*, December 16, 1933, and "Tomorrow Night . . ." *New York World Telegram*, December 16, 1936, TAMARA clipping folder (OF-20a), NYPL; clippings, Whitney Bolton, "Tunes, Gags Fair," *Morning Telegraph*, May 21, 1931, and Edwin Stein, "Stooge's Holiday," n.d., Tamara scrapbook, MWEZ XXX n.c. 25,505, BRTC. On *Crazy Quilt*, see also Peretti, *Nightclub City*, 194–97.
8. "Goings On About Town," April 19, 1930, (quote) 4–6, October 15, 1932, 4, October 22, 1932, 6, February 25, 1933, 6, March 11, 1933, 6, May 20, 1933, 4, June 3, 10, and 24, 1933, 2, all in *New Yorker*; James Hassell, "Russian Refugees in France and the United States between the World Wars," *Transactions of the American Philosophical Society* 81, no.7 (1991): 11; John Hope Simpson, *The Refugee Problem: Report of a Survey* (London: Oxford University Press, 1939), 469–70; Boris Raymond and David Jones, *The Russian Diaspora, 1917–1941* (Lanham, MD: Scarecrow, 2000), 53–54; Federal Writers' Project, *New York City Guide* (New York: Random House, 1939), 30, 111, 122–23.

9. "Tables for Two," *New Yorker*, December 17, 1932, 32–34; M. K. Argus, *Moscow-on-the-Hudson* (New York: Harper, 1948), 5, 58–59, 69; Marc Raeff, *Russia Abroad: A Cultural History of the Russian Emigration, 1919–1939* (New York: Oxford University Press, 1990), 99; Alice Hughes, "A Woman's New York," *Washington Post*, July 1, 1939, 13.
10. Martha Leavitt, "Dressing Room Chats Before the Play," *New York Herald Tribune*, December 24, 1933, TAMARA clipping folder (OF-20a), NYPL; clipping, untitled, n.d., Tamara scrapbook, DFP; "Tamara," *Radio Mirror*, April 1934, 18, 55.
11. Clippings, Burns Mantle, "'They All Come to Moscow'—Why?" n.d., Richard Lockridge, "The New Play," *New York Sun*, May 12, 1933, and Percy Hammond, "The Theaters," *New York Herald Tribune*, May 12, 1933, Tamara scrapbook, DFP.
12. Christopher Herr, *Clifford Odets and American Political Theatre* (Westport, CT: Praeger, 2003), 5, 13, 20; Edward Murray, *Clifford Odets: The Thirties and After* (New York: Frederick Ungar, 1968), 9–11, 33; Clifford Odets diary, July 5, 1933, folder 9, box 8, COP. In early 1933, Clifford lived in the backroom of a rundown Group Theatre flat the troupe christened Groupstroy after the new Soviet dam Dniprostroy in Ukraine: Chinoy, *Group Theatre*, 81, 172–73.
13. Clifford Odets to Tamara Drasin, June 3 and 4, 1933, box 1, COP.
14. Clifford Odets to Tamara Drasin, June 8, 1933, box 1, COP; clippings, "Herewith Tamara in Your Eyes," *New York Times*, February 25, 1934, and "Tamara Escaped Russia but Not Its National Anthem," *New York Herald Tribune*, December 3, 1933, TAMARA clipping folder (OF-20a), NYPL; clippings, Mildred Palmer, "Meet Your Neighbor," *The Midtowner*, January 7, 1932, and "Tamara, Sloe-Eyed Songster, Arrives," *Denver Post*, July 13, 1938, Tamara scrapbook, DFP; sheet music collection, boxes 5 and 6, DFP.
15. Clifford Odets to Tamara Drasin, June 11, 1933, box 1, COP.
16. Clifford Odets to Tamara Drasin, June 13, 1933, box 1, COP.
17. Clifford Odets to Tamara Drasin, June 14, 1933, box 1, COP.
18. Herr, *Clifford Odets and American Political Theatre*, 1–2, 6; Clifford Odets to Tamara Drasin, June 20, 1933, box 1, and Clifford Odets diary, June 30, 1933, folder 9, box 8, COP.
19. Elia Kazan in Helen Krich Chinoy, *Reunion: A Self-Portrait of the Group Theatre* (Washington, DC: American Theatre Association, 1976), 532–36; Clifford Odets to Tamara Drasin, July 19, 1933, box 1, COP; Wendy Smith, *Real Life Drama: The Group Theatre and America, 1931–1940* (New York: Knopf, 1990), 136, 139–42; Chinoy, *Group Theatre*, 81–91, 176. On Green Mansions and other adult summer camps, see Joey Adams, *The Borscht Belt* (New York: Bobbs-Merrill, 1959).
20. Morgan Himelstein, *Drama Was a Weapon: The Left-Wing Theatre in New York, 1929–1941* (Westport, CT: Greenwood, 1963); Smith, *Real Life Drama*, 125–27, 155–57; Chinoy, *Group Theatre*, 4–8, 167, 170–71; Michael

Denning, *The Cultural Front: The Laboring of American Culture in the Twentieth Century* (London: Verso, 1997), esp. 9, 12, and 125. Traces of Tamara's benefit work around this time appear in "Peacock Ball Gives World Panorama," November 5, 1932, 19, and "'A Russian Night' Is Held," May 10, 1933, 14, both in *New York Times.*

21. Resettlement Administration Personal Data for Boris Drasin, September 30, 1935, folder 3, and Boris Drasin to David Dubinsky, n.d., and December 26, 1933, folder 4, box 1, DFP.
22. Studs Terkel, *Hard Times: An Oral History of the Great Depression* (New York: Pantheon, 1970), 413–19, 433–35; Clifford Odets to Tamara Drasin, June 27, 1933, box 1, COP. For these themes, see also Christine Stansell, *American Moderns: Bohemian New York and the Creation of a New Century* (New York: Metropolitan Books), ch. 7.
23. Clifford Odets diary, July 5, 1933, folder 9, box 8, COP; "Tables for Two," July 8, 1933, 47, and "Goings On About Town," August 12, 1933, 2–3, both in *New Yorker*; clippings, "Loew's State, New York," July 8, 1933, Alice Hart, "Tamara Swears by Natural Makeup," *Times-Star* (Bridgeport, CT) and other regional papers, July 24, 1939, and untitled, n.d., Tamara scrapbook, DFP. On glamour as labor, see Sherrie Tucker, *Swing Shift: "All-Girl" Bands of the 1940s* (Durham, NC: Duke University Press, 2000), 59–63.
24. "Herewith Tamara in Your Eyes"; clipping, "Tamara to Sing in Musical Show," *New York American*, July 24, 1933, Tamara scrapbook, DFP; David Lee Joyner, *American Popular Music* (Madison, WI: Brown & Benchmark, 1993), 28–29. On the romance and foreign affairs genre, see Emily Rosenberg, "'Foreign Affairs' After World War II: Connecting Sexual and International Politics," *Diplomatic History* 18, no. 1 (January 1994): 59–70.
25. Bob Hope, *Have Tux, Will Travel: Bob Hope's Own Story* (1954; repr., New York: Simon and Schuster, 2003), 106–8; clipping, "'Roberta,' 150 Showings Old," *New York World-Telegram*, March 28, 1934, Tamara scrapbook, DFP; Ethan Mordden, *Sing for Your Supper: The Broadway Musical in the 1930s* (New York: Palgrave Macmillan, 2005), 53–55.
26. "Herewith Tamara in Your Eyes"; newspaper sketches and photographs in New York newspapers, TAMARA clipping folder (OF-20a), NYPL; Marshall Field's ad, Tamara scrapbook, DFP; David Ewen, *Great Men of Popular Song* (Englewood Cliffs, NJ: Prentice-Hall, 1972), 137–8l; John Irwin, *F. Scott Fitzgerald's Fiction: An Almost Theatrical Innocence* (Baltimore: Johns Hopkins University Press, 2014), 39; Carlo Bohlander, "The Evolution of Jazz Culture in Frankfurt," in Michael Budds, ed., *Jazz and the Germans* (Hillsdale, NY: Pendragon, 2002), 167–78, here 168; Leavitt, "Dressing Room Chats Before the Play."
27. Clifford Odets to Tamara Drasin, July 5 and 6, 1933, box 1, COP.
28. Clifford Odets to Tamara Drasin, June 25, June 27, July 10, and August 4, 1933, box 1, Clifford Odets diary, June 30, July 5, July 8, and July 15, 1933, folder 9, box 8, COP. On Clifford's affair with Tamara, see also Margaret

Brenman-Gibson, *Clifford Odets: American Playwright: The Years from 1906 to 1940* (New York: Applause Theatre & Cinema Books, 1981), 261–72.

29. Clifford Odets to Tamara Drasin, July 26, 1933, box 1, COP; Stella Adler and Phoebe Brand in Chinoy, *Reunion*, 506–19; Chinoy, *Group Theatre*, 203–16; Mari Jo Buhle, *Women and American Socialism, 1870–1920* (Urbana: University of Illinois Press, 1981), 180–84, 198, 268, 281–83, 300, 321; Constance Coiner, *Better Red: The Writing and Resistance of Tillie Olsen and Meridel LeSueur* (New York: Oxford University Press, 1995), esp. intro, chs. 1–2.
30. Clifford Odets to Tamara Drasin, August 9, 1933, box 1, COP.
31. Clipping, Helen Harrison, "Out of Russia's Revolt," *Tower Radio*, September 1934, Tamara scrapbook, DFP; Andrea Chandler, *Institutions of Isolation: Border Controls in the Soviet Union and Its Successor States, 1917–1993* (Montreal: McGill-Queen's University Press, 1998), 34. Tamara claimed to have US citizenship through her father, but unlike her younger brother, she was not a minor child when Boris naturalized in 1927. Likely she had no citizenship status until marriage: Resettlement Administration Personal Data for Boris Drasin, September 30, 1935, folder 3, box 1, DFP; flight manifest, February 13, 1932, *Passenger Manifests of Airplanes Arriving at Miami, Florida*, RG85, NARA; entry card, June 28, 1935, reel 3, *Soundex Card Manifests of Alien and Citizen Arrivals at Hogansburg, Malone . . . and Waddington, New York*, NARA microfilm M1482.
32. Harrison, "Out of Russia's Revolt"; Peretti, *Nightclub City*, 39.
33. Leavitt, "Dressing Room Chats Before the Play."
34. *Roberta* playbill, 1934, Lee Drasin's files (unprocessed), DFP. On Tamara's obfuscation, see, for example, Palmer, "Meet Your Neighbor," Lyceum Theatre playbill, "Couldn't Be Done; They Did It," *Cincinnati Enquirer*, June 13, 1939, and Jack Stinnett, "A Candid Talk with Tamara," *Evening Post* (Bridgeport, CT), July 17, 1939, Tamara scrapbook, DFP; clippings, "Herewith Tamara in Your Eyes," and "No Longer Noble," *Brooklyn Daily Eagle*, January 24, 1937, TAMARA clipping folder (OF-20a), NYPL. Tamara kept an extensive sheet music collection in Yiddish along with the other languages she knew: boxes 5 and 6, DFP.
35. Mary Antin, *The Promised Land* (New York: Houghton Mifflin, 1912), 132; Prell, *Fighting to Become Americans*, 52–53; Henry Feingold, *A Time For Searching: Entering the Mainstream, 1920–1945* (Baltimore: Johns Hopkins University Press, 1992), 87–88, 90–97, 150; Beth Wenger, *New York Jews and the Great Depression* (New Haven, CT: Yale University Press, 1996), 184; Susan Glenn, "'Funny, You Don't Look Jewish': Visual Stereotypes and the Making of Modern Jewish Identity," in Susan Glenn and Naomi Sokoloff, eds., *Boundaries of Jewish Identity* (Seattle: University of Washington Press, 2011), 64–90; Kirsten Fermaglich, *A Rosenberg by Any Other Name: A History of Jewish Name Changing in America* (New York: New York University Press, 2018), ch. 1.

36. Clipping, "Tomorrow Night . . ." *New York World Telegram*, December 16, 1936, TAMARA clipping folder (OF-20a), NYPL; clippings, Palmer, "Meet Your Neighbor," Barbara Steele, "Tamara, French Siren Tells of State Life," *Shortridge Daily Echo*, March 24, 1935, Irene Thirer, "Long Island's Film Folk Enjoy Shooting Scenes Despite Heat," *Sunday News*, [1935], and "Tamara, Sloe-Eyed Songster, Arrives," Tamara scrapbook, DFP; Leavitt, "Dressing Room Chats Before the Play"; Riv-Ellen Prell, *Fighting to Become Americans: Jews, Gender, and the Anxiety of Assimilation* (Boston: Beacon, 1999), 25, 29, 32, 34, 47–48, 50. On antisemitism in New York, see Ronald Bayor, *Neighbors in Conflict: The Irish, Germans, Jews, and Italians of New York City, 1929–1941* (Urbana: University of Illinois Press, 1988), 57–104; Leonard Dinnerstein, *Antisemitism in America* (New York: Oxford University Press, 1994), chs. 5–7.

37. Melissa R. Klapper, *Jewish Girls Coming of Age in America, 1860–1920* (New York: New York University Press, 2005), 36–45; Steven Belluscio, *To Be Suddenly White: Literary Realism and Racial Passing* (Columbia: University of Missouri Press, 2006), 176–78, 197–98; Sydney Stahl Weinberg, *The World of Our Mothers: The Lives of Jewish Immigrant Women* (Chapel Hill: University of North Carolina Press, 1988), (Yezierska quote) 121; Susan Glenn, "The Vogue of Jewish Self-Hatred in Post-World War II America," *Jewish Social Studies* 12, no. 3 (2006): 95–136; Melissa R. Klapper, *Ballots, Babies, and Banners of Peace: American Jewish Women's Activism, 1890—1940* (New York: New York University Press, 2013), 177, 189–90, 204, 209.

38. Harley Erdman, *Staging the Jew: The Performance of an American Ethnicity, 1860–1920* (New Brunswick, NJ: Rutgers University Press, 1997), 51–57; Julia Foulkes, "Angels 'Rewolt!': Jewish Women in Modern Dance in the 1930s," *American Jewish History* 88, no. 2 (June 2000): 233–52; Andrea Most, *Making Americans: Jews and the Broadway Musical* (Cambridge, MA: Harvard University Press, 2004); Ted Merwin, *In Their Own Image: New York Jews in Jazz Age Popular Culture* (New Brunswick, NJ: Rutgers University Press, 2006). Even Bara, however, never denied and was widely known to be Jewish: Ronald Ginini, *Theda Bara: A Biography of the Silent Screen Vamp* (Jefferson, NC: McFarland, 1996), 16–19, 50. Sarah Bernhardt's stage strategies also come to mind: Susan Glenn, *Female Spectacle: The Theatrical Roots of Modern Feminism* (Cambridge, MA: Harvard University Press, 2000), 31–34. On images of Russian Whites, see Oksana Bulgakowa, "The 'Russian Vogue' in Europe and Hollywood: The Transformation of Russian Stereotypes through the 1920s" and Beth Holmgren, "Cossack Cowboys, Mad Russians: The Émigré Actor in Studio-Era Hollywood," both in *Russian Review* 64, no. 2 (April 2005): 211–50.

39. Boris Drasin to Mr. Brown, n.d., folder 4, Resettlement Administration notice, October 1, 1935, folder 3, and handwritten note by Lee to Peter Warren, folder 5, box 1, DFP; Hickman Powell, "New Deal Town, Now

30 Months Abuilding," *New York Herald Tribune*, May 7, 1936, 1; Perdita Buchan, *Utopia, New Jersey: Travels in the Nearest Eden* (New Brunswick, NJ: Rivergate, 2007), 173–201. On Odesa's artels, Robert Weinberg, *The Revolution of 1905 in Odessa: Blood on the Steps* (Bloomington: Indiana University Press, 1993), 58–62. On colonies similar to Jersey Homesteads in the Soviet Union, see Jonathan Dekel-Chen, *Farming the Red Land: Jewish Agricultural Colonization and Local Soviet Power, 1924–1941* (New Haven, CT: Yale University Press, 2005).

40. Ralph Armstrong, "Four-Million-Dollar Village," *Saturday Evening Post*, February 5, 1938, 5–7, 34–39; George Weller, "The Promised Land," in *New Letters in America*, ed. Horace Gregory (New York: Norton, 1937), 210–19; "Hightstown Project Will Be Speeded Up," January 27, 1936, 26, "Seek Homesteads' Facts," August 30, 1936, 15, "Garment Workers Soon to Occupy Jersey Homesteads," June 14, 1936, RE1, "Pioneers Dedicate RA Factory-Farm," August 3, 1936, 17, all in *New York Times*; "Tugwell Hands Out $1,800,000 for 'Commune' in New Jersey," *Evening Sun* (Hanover, PA), May 15, 1936, 3; Tamara Drasin to family, ca. June 1938, folder 6, and S.C. Kohs to Boris Drasin, September 22, 1938, folder 3, box 1, DFP.

41. "Couldn't Be Done; They Did It"; Frank Mittauer, "Operetta at Its Best," *Evening News*, June 7, 1938, Tamara scrapbook, DFP.

42. "Goings On About Town," *New Yorker*, March 24, 1934, 6; clippings and advertisements, 1935, in Tamara scrapbook, DFP.

43. Robert Francis, "Candid Close-Ups," *Brooklyn Daily Eagle*, September 10, 1939, TAMARA clipping folder (OF-20a), NYPL; Palmer, "Meet Your Neighbor," Steele, "Tamara, French Siren Tells of State Life," and untitled clipping, n.d., Tamara scrapbook, DFP.

44. "Relief Fund Show March 4," February 26, 1934, 21, and " 'Tide Rising' To Aid Nursery Tonight," January 21, 1937, 20, both in *New York Times*; ad, *New Yorker*, April 27, 1940, 90; clippings, "Tamara to Head Judson Benefit," *New York Journal and American*, May 9, 1939, Kelcey Allen, "Amusements," *News Record* (NY), June 8, 1939, "Notables to Share Frolic of Village Fair," *Women's Wear*, June 6, 1939, "Broadway Comes to FTP Rescue," n.d., "Cabaret to Stage Birthday Frolic," *New York Mirror*, May 3, 1939, and "Cabaret TAC Birthday," *New York Herald-Tribune*, May 1, 1939, Tamara scrapbook, DFP; "Needy Gets Cash-Patrons a Hot Show at Apollo," *Chicago Defender*, June 8, 1940, 20. On TAC, see Denning, *Cultural Front*, 326–27.

45. Tamara Drasin to family, 1932, Boris Drasin to Lana, October 25, ca. mid. 1930s, and Tamara Drasin to family, ca. June 1938, folder 6, box 1; Tamara Drasin to Hinda Drasin, ca. 1935, Boris's file (unprocessed materials), Harrison, "Out of Russia's Revolt," and Ian Fennell, "Former Roosevelt Resident Inspired Ukrainian Pianist," *Messenger-Press*, January 6, 1994, folder 18, box 1, DFP.

46. *Who's Who in America*, vol. 21 (Chicago: Marquis, 1940), 243; Daniel Pope and William Toll, "We Tried Harder: Jews in American

Advertising," *American Jewish History* 72 (September 1982): 26–51; "Tamara, Sloe-Eyed Songster, Arrives"; Tamara Drasin to family, ca. June 1938, folder 6, box 1, DFP. Tamara and Erwin appeared mismatched enough that he has been mistaken for her father: photograph of Tamara and Boris [*sic*], box 2, DFP.

47. Conflicting accounts are given in *Who's Who* (1940) and *Who's Who in America*, 38th edition, vol. 2 (Chicago: Marquis, 1974–75), 3013. The Erwin D. Swann papers at the Library of Congress contain no documentation on his life before 1949.
48. New York, New York, 19A, reel 2656, *Census (1940)*; clippings, "Song Writer's Prayer Answered by Singer Who's Actress, Too," *New York Herald Tribune*, March 26, 1939, and Francis, "Candid Close-Ups," TAMARA clipping folder (OF-20a), NYPL; clippings, George Tucker, "Man About Manhattan," *News-Times* (Danbury, CT) April 18, 1939, "Couldn't Be Done; They Did It" (including quotes), and Hughes, "A Woman's New York." No marriage record or announcement could be found, but one source gives a date of September 28, 1935: *Who's Who* (1974–75).
49. Ella and Samuel Spewack, script for *Leave It to Me*, 1938, BRTC; clipping, "Tamara, She's Singing Hit Song Again in 'Leave It to Me!'," *Brooklyn Daily Eagle*, January 29, 1939, TAMARA clipping folder (OF-20a), NYPL.
50. Ruth McKenney, "Anti-Fascist Comedy," *New Masses*, November 22, 1938, 30; John Cambridge, "Democracy Boosted in New Musical Comedy," *Daily Worker*, November 14, 1938, 7. See also clippings in TAMARA clipping folder (OF-20a), NYPL, and Tamara scrapbook, DFP.
51. Clippings, "Great Neck Theater Dark Next Week," and "Leave It to Us," *New York Post*, July 19, 1939, "Tamara Sailing Today for New Gypsy Songs," *New York World-Telegram*, July 19, 1939, Frank Reil, "Line on Liners," *Brooklyn Eagle*, July 20, 1939, "Sailings," *Variety*, July 19, 1939, and "Singer Won't Sing," July 1939, Tamara scrapbook, DFP.
52. Francis, "Candid Close-Ups"; clippings, *Daily Mirror*, August 15, 1939, and "'Leave It to Me!' Reopens at the Imperial Theatre," *News Record* (New York), September 6, 1939, Tamara scrapbook, DFP; "'Leave It to Me!' Closes Tonight," *New York Times*, September 16, 1939, 24.

Chapter 10

1. Frank Cuhel, "The Log," *Singapore Lyre*, December 25, 1936, FJCP.
2. Frank Cuhel to Ermengarde Cuhel, November 20, 1931, Frank Cuhel to G. R. Hamer, January 12, 1933, Frank Cuhel to Kirk Yerkes, January 31, 1933, Frank Cuhel to James Stowell, January 21, 1933, and "Personals," *Singapore Lyre*, all in FJCP; Lewis Gleeck, *The Army and Navy Club of Manila* (Manila: Carmelo & Bauermann, 1976), ch. 4 and 43–44; Lewis Gleeck, *The Manila Americans (1901–1964)* (Manila: Carmelo & Bauermann, 1977), 64–72, 124, 176, 207.
3. Frank Cuhel, Manila office annual report, 1930, Frank Cuhel to James Stowell, January 21, 1933, Frank Cuhel to James Greene, April 24, 1933,

Adjutant General to Frank Cuhel, March 6, 1933, and Frank Cuhel broadcasts, February 14 and May 7, 1942, FJCP; American Express, *Manila and the Philippines* (Manila: American Express Travel Department, ca. 1932), 12.

4. Stanley Karnow, *In Our Image: America's Empire in the Philippines* (New York: Random House, 1989), 194; Lewis Gleeck, *American Business and Philippine Economic Development* (Manila: Carmelo & Bauermann, 1975), 1–3.
5. Mark Twain, "To the Person Sitting in Darkness," *North American Review* 172, no. 2 (February 1901): 161–76.
6. Eric T. L. Love, *Race over Empire: Racism and U.S. Imperialism, 1865–1900* (Chapel Hill: University of North Carolina Press, 2004), ch. 5, quotes 182.
7. Albert J. Beveridge, "In Support of an American Empire," *Congressional Record*, 56 Cong., I Sess. (January 9, 1900): 704–12. On American racial thought and imperial rationales, see also Paul Kramer, *The Blood of Government: Race, Empire, the United States, and the Philippines* (Chapel Hill: University of North Carolina Press, 2006).
8. Gleeck, *Manila Americans*, 80, 92, 103, 134; Karnow, *In Our Image*, 210–18, 224–25, 243–50. The Payne-Aldrich Act (1909) provided for free, unlimited imports from the US to the Philippines and lifted duties but not quotas on exports to the mainland. The Underwood-Simmons Act (1913) removed those quotas: M. C. Ricklefs et al., *A New History of Southeast Asia* (New York: Palgrave Macmillan, 2010), 253–54.
9. Ricklefs, *New History of Southeast Asia*, 253–54; Theodore Friend, *Between Two Empires: The Ordeal of the Philippines* (New Haven, CT: Yale University Press, 1965), 6; Karnow, *In Our Image*, 225–26.
10. American Express, *Manila and the Philippines*, 37, 42, 45. See also Norma Alarcón, *The Imperial Tapestry and American Colonial Architecture in the Philippines* (Manila: University of Santo Tomas, 2008), 151–53.
11. Henry L. Stimson, "Future Philippine Policy under the Jones Act," *Foreign Affairs* 5, no. 3 (April 1927): 459–71; Frank Cuhel draft memoir on Netherlands East Indies, September 1939–December 1941, FJCP.
12. Frank Cuhel, Manila office annual report, 1930, and Frank Cuhel to Ermengarde Cuhel, November 15, 1932, FJCP; Daniel Doeppers, "Metropolitan Manila in the Great Depression: Crisis for Whom?" *Journal of Asian Studies* 50, no.3 (August 1991): 511–35.
13. John Kunau to Frank Cuhel, January 7, 1933, Frank Cuhel to Kirk Yerkes, January 31, 1933, Frank Cuhel to V. A. Dodge, March 14 and April 20, 1933, Frank Cuhel to H. W. Whalan, March 22, 1933, Dodge to Frank Cuhel, May 11, 1933, and Frank Cuhel to G. R. Hamer, June 28, 1933, all in FJCP.
14. Karnow, *In Our Image*, 252–54, 263–64, 272; Theodore Friend, *The Blue-Eyed Enemy: Japan against the West in Java and Luzon, 1942–1945* (Princeton, NJ: Princeton University Press, 1988), 14–19.

15. Frank Cuhel to Ermengarde Cuhel, November 15, 1932, Frank Cuhel to Kirk Yerkes, January 31, 1933, Frank Cuhel to Samuel Fitzpatrick, June 1, 1933, and Frank Cuhel to V. A. Dodge, June 30, 1933, all in FJCP.
16. T. Ingles Moore, "The Philippines: Japanese and American Policy," *Sydney Morning Herald*, March 19, 1932, 18; Friend, *Between Two Empires*, 72, 169–70.
17. Frank Cuhel to Ermengarde Cuhel, November 15, 1932, Frank Cuhel to Kirk Yerkes, January 31, 1933, and Frank Cuhel to V. A. Dodge, March 15, 1933, all in FJCP; Gary Hess, "The Emergence of U.S. Influence in Southeast Asia," in Akira Iriye and Warren Cohen, eds., *American, Chinese, and Japanese Perspectives on Wartime Asia, 1931–1949* (Wilmington, DE: Scholarly Resources Books, 1990), 179–221. On the legislative road to the commonwealth and independence, see Friend, *Between Two Empires*, chs. 9–11 and Frank Hindman Golay, *Face of Empire: United States-Philippine Relations, 1898–1946* (Madison: University of Wisconsin-Madison Center for Southeast Asian Studies, 1998). On envisioning the region as Southeast Asia, see Hajime Shimizu, "Southeast Asia as a Regional Concept in Modern Japan: An Analysis of Geography Textbooks," in Saya Shiraishi and Takashi Shiraishi, eds., *The Japanese in Colonial Southeast Asia* (Ithaca, NY: Cornell Southeast Asia Program, 1993), 21–61.
18. Brooke L. Blower, "Nation of Outposts: Forts, Factories, Bases, and the Making of American Power," *Diplomatic History* 41, no. 3 (June 2017): 439–59; Mira Wilkins, *The Emergence of Multinational Enterprise: American Business Abroad from the Colonial Era to 1914* (Cambridge, MA: Harvard University Press, 1970). On extraterritorial rights, see Eileen P. Scully, *Bargaining with the State from Afar: American Citizenship in Treaty Port China, 1844–1942* (New York: Columbia University Press, 2001) and Teemu Ruskola, *Legal Orientalism: China, the United States, and Modern Law* (Cambridge, MA: Harvard University Press, 2013).
19. American and Japanese scholars continue to disagree about how exactly to apportion blame for the origins of the Pacific War, as more nuanced understandings of Japanese perspectives have developed over time, but the cast of characters and contours of the road to war narrative have nevertheless remained remarkably constant since Herbert Feis, *The Road to Pearl Harbor: The Coming of the War Between the United States and Japan* (Princeton, NJ: Princeton University Press, 1950). See, for example, Gordon W. Prange, *At Dawn We Slept: The Untold Story of Pearl Harbor* (New York: McGraw-Hill, 1981); Akira Iriye, *The Origins of the Second World War in Asia and the Pacific* (London: Longman, 1987); Michael A. Barnhart, *Japan Prepares for Total War: The Search for Economic Security, 1919–1941* (Ithaca, NY: Cornell University Press, 1987); Eri Hotta, *Japan 1941: Countdown to Infamy* (New York: Vintage, 2013). For notable exceptions—all by British historians—that firmly situate the coming conflict in the longer history of boots-on-the-ground Western imperialism and racism, see Christopher Thorne, *Allies of a Kind: The United*

States, Britain and the War against Japan, 1941–1945 (New York: Oxford University Press, 1978); John Costello, *The Pacific War, 1941–1945* (1981; repr., New York: Harper Perennial, 2009); H. P. Willmott, *Empires in the Balance: Japanese and Allied Pacific Strategies to April 1942* (Annapolis, MD: Naval Institute Press, 1982).

20. Christopher Bayly and Tim Harper, *Forgotten Armies: The Fall of British Asia, 1941–1945* (London: Allen Lane, 2004), 30–35, 45–47, 59–62; John Gunther, *Inside Asia* (1938; repr., New York: Harper, 1939), (better Gibraltar) 305, 311, 315, (swagger stick) 316.
21. Bayly and Harper, *Forgotten Armies*, 30–35, 45–47, 59–62; Jim Baker, *The Eagle in the Lion City: America, Americans and Singapore* (Singapore: Landmark Books, 2005), 95, 125, 146–57. See also Ann Laura Stoler, *Carnal Knowledge and Imperial Power: Race and the Intimate in Colonial Rule* (Berkeley: University of California Press, 2002).
22. Frank Cuhel home movies, clippings, "Bab Cuhel Comes All The Way From Borneo," *Cedar Rapids Gazette*, November 7, 1937, Robert Waples, "Psi Psi Olympic Star, Bab Cuhel, Out to Nip-off Nip-on in Far East," *Shield of Phi Kappa Psi*, May 1942, 267, and "Society in Singapore," *Singapore Lyre*, all in FJCP. On American businessmen's typical lack of concern for imperialism, so long as it provided stable markets, see Anne L. Foster, *Projections of Power: The United States and Europe in Colonial Southeast Asia, 1919–1941* (Durham, NC: Duke University Press, 2010), x, 44–49. On the importance of pleasing the senses and bodily practice in imperial culture, see Andrew J. Rotter, *Empires of the Senses: Bodily Encounters in Imperial India and the Philippines* (New York: Oxford University Pres, 2019).
23. "Notes on the American Mess," "Phantom Robbers of the American Mess," and "Personals," in *Singapore Lyre*, "Notes on the American Mess in Singapore," and "'Monkey Mint,' Or Who Stole Walker's Julep Makings," in *The Yankee Doodler*, December 25, 1937, 2, and clipping, "Bab Cuhel Comes All The Way From Borneo," FJCP.
24. Baker, *Eagle in the Lion City*, 136–37; Shakila Yacob, *The United States and the Malaysian Economy* (London: Routledge, 2008), 41, 129; advertisements, June 2, 1934, 14, February 9, 1935, 14, January 7, 1937, 2, and November 12, 1940, 14, all in *Straits Times*.
25. Notes on Persia and Palestine, n.d., "The Log" and "Another New Office for Dodge & Seymour Ltd.," in *Jerusalem Jester*, December 25, 1934, "The Log," "Did You Know That," and "The Elephants' Last Stand," in *Singapore Lyre*, clipping, James Hanlon, "Frank Cuhel Relates Experiences as Radio Correspondent in the South Pacific," ca. January 1943, Frank Cuhel to Ermengarde Cuhel, February 4 and 14, 1934, Frank Cuhel to V. A. Dodge, December 27, 1933 and February 14, 1934, and President Dodge & Seymour to Frank Cuhel, November 28, 1932, FJCP. On American "long-distance" capitalists' confidence, see Victoria deGrazia, "Globalizing Commercial Revolutions," in Oliver Janz, Sebastian Conrad,

and Gunella Budde, eds., *Transnationale Geschichte: Themen, Tendenzenund, Theorien* (Göttingen: Vandenhoeck & Ruprecht, 2006), 238–53 and Foster, *Projections of Power*, x, 46–47, 89.

26. "The Log" and book list, in *Jerusalem Jester*, Frank Cuhel to Ermengarde Cuhel, February 4, 1934, Frank Cuhel to V. A. Dodge, November 19, 1938, draft memoir on Netherlands East Indies, September 1939–December 1941, "Co-ordination of American Shipping," *Jerusalem Jester*, and "Editorial," *Singapore Lyre*, all in FJCP. See also Philip D. Curtin, *Cross-Cultural Trade in World History* (Cambridge: Cambridge University Press, 1984) and Mira Wilkins, *The Maturing of Multinational Enterprise: American Business Abroad from 1914 to 1970* (Cambridge, MA: Harvard University Press, 1974).

27. "Trade Mark Prosecution," *Straits Times*, June 23, 1935, 12; "False Trade Mark," *Singapore Free Press*, June 24, 1935, 3; President of Dodge & Seymour to Frank Cuhel, November 1, 1932 and January 4, 1933, Frank Cuhel to A. A. Undt, December 29, 1932, Frank Cuhel to F. F. Fairman, January 14, 1933, Frank Cuhel to V. A. Dodge, January 2 and 27, 1933 and February 17, 1933, V. A. Dodge to Frank Cuhel, February 17 and April 19, 1933, Frank Cuhel to Ermengarde Cuhel, February 4, 1934, and "Editorial," *Singapore Lyre*, FJCP.

28. "The Log," *Jerusalem Jester*, "I 'Did' America," *Singapore Lyre*, Frank Cuhel to James Stowell, January 21, 1933, Frank Cuhel to V. A. Dodge, January 28, 1933, and Frank Cuhel to A. Douglas, September 22, 1941, FJCP. On the parallel culture of Europeans working for overseas trading firms in this era, see Michael Miller, *Europe and the Maritime World: A Twentieth-Century History* (New York: Cambridge University Press, 2012), ch. 3.

29. L. D. Seymour to Frank Cuhel, December 21, 1932, Frank Cuhel to L. D. Seymour, March 10, 1933, and "Personals," *Singapore Lyre*, FJCP. See also Doeppers, "Metropolitan Manila in the Great Depression" and Foster, *Projections of Power*.

30. "The Log," *Singapore Lyre*; Sugiyama Shinya and Milagros Guerrero, eds., *International Commercial Rivalry in Southeast Asia in the Interwar Period* (New Haven, CT: Yale Southeast Asian Studies, 1994); Shiraishi and Shiraishi, *Japanese in Colonial Southeast Asia*; Thomas Steep, "White Failure in the East Indies," *Current History* 38, no. 6 (September 1933): 683–87; W. G. Huff, "Entitlements, Destitution, and Emigration in the 1930s Singapore Great Depression," *Economic History Review* 54, no. 2 (May 2001): 290–323.

31. Edgar Snow, "The Decline of Western Prestige," *Saturday Evening Post*, August 26, 1933, 12–13, 67–69; W. G. Beasley, *Japanese Imperialism, 1894–1945* (Oxford: Clarendon Press, 1987); Herbert P. Bix, *Hirohito and the Making of Modern Japan* (New York: HarperCollins, 2000), 10–11, 195–96, 200, 264–69.

32. Larry Seymour to Frank Cuhel, September 23, 1938, and Frank Cuhel memos, April 22, 1938, and May 30, 1939, FJCP. Dodge & Seymour's previous Batavia office, staffed by a Dutchman, had closed in 1933: Frank Cuhel to Ermengarde Cuhel, February 4, 1934, FJCP.

33. Frances Gouda and Thijs Brocades Zaalberg, *American Visions of the Netherlands East Indies/Indonesia: US Foreign Policy and Indonesian Nationalism, 1920–1949* (Amsterdam: Amsterdam University Press, 2002), 68–77; Friend, *Blue-Eyed Enemy*, 14; Shigeru Sato, "Indonesia 1939–1942: Prelude to the Japanese Occupation," *Journal of Southeast Asian Studies* 37, no. 2 (June 2006): 225–48; Gerlof Homan, "The United States and the Netherlands East Indies: The Evolution of American Anticolonialism," *Pacific Historical Review* 53, no. 4 (November 1984): 423–46; Walter Foote, Future of the Netherlands Indies, June 27, 1942, Classified Records, Batavia Consul General in Melbourne, Australia, 1941–1945, RG84, NARA. On belated American efforts to stockpile strategic imports from Southeast Asia, see Jonathan Marshall, *To Have and Have Not: Southeast Asian Raw Materials and the Origins of the Pacific War* (Berkeley: University of California Press, 1995), 36–47.
34. Homan, "The United States and the Netherlands East Indies"; "Dutch East Indies: Its Vast Riches Tempt Japan," *Life*, January 22, 1940, 54–65. Consular officials estimated that some eight hundred Americans lived in the Netherlands East Indies on the eve of war with Japan: Paul Paddoc and V. Lansing Collins, Jr., Work of the Consulate General, Batavia, December 8, 1941–February 28, 1942, May 5, 1942, Classified Records, Batavia Consul General in Melbourne, Australia, 1941–1945, RG84, NARA.
35. E. Alexander Powell, "The Emeralds of Wilhelmina," *Scribner's Magazine* 69, no. 5 (May 1921): 514–31; Adele de Leeuw, "The Dutch in the East Indies," *Current History* 34, no. 2 (May 1931): 231–33; "Banquet at Batavia," *Rotarian*, March 1942, 20–24; Gouda and Zaalberg, *American Visions of the Netherlands East Indies/Indonesia*, 17, 66–67, 73–76, 102–3.
36. A. Vandenbosch, "The Effect of Dutch Rule on the Civilization of the East Indies," *American Journal of Sociology* 48, no. 4 (January 1943): 498–502; Frances Gouda, *Dutch Culture Overseas: Colonial Practice in the Netherlands Indies, 1900–1942* (1995; repr., Singapore: Equinox, 2008), 23–24; M. C. Ricklefs, *A History of Modern Indonesia since c. 1200* (1981; repr., Stanford, CA: Stanford University Press, 2008), 183–84; Imamura Hitoshi, "Java in 1942," in Anthony Reid and Oki Akira, eds., *The Japanese Experience in Indonesia: Selected Memoirs of 1942–1945* (Athens: Ohio University Center for International Studies, 1986), 31–77, here 34.
37. A. Vandenbosch, "The People Speak in the Dutch East Indies," *Asia*, March 1941, 166–68; Frank Clune, *Isles of Spice* (New York: E. P. Dutton, 1942), 141; Ricklefs, *History of Modern Indonesia*, 189–93; Gouda, *Dutch Culture Overseas*, 20–23; Walter Foote, Future of the Netherlands Indies, June 27, 1942, Classified Records, Batavia Consul General in Melbourne, Australia, 1941–1945, RG84, NARA.
38. Ricklefs, *History of Modern Indonesia*, 201–13, 220–21, 269–71; Foster, *Projections of Power*, 19, 27–29; Carlos Romulo, *I Saw the Fall of the Philippines* (Garden City, NY: Doubleday, Doran, 1943), 17–24, quotes on 17 and 20. On Indonesian views about the Japanese, see also Ethan Mark,

Japan's Occupation of Java in the Second World War (London: Bloomsbury, 2018), ch. 2.

39. Arthur Müller Lehning, "Indonesian Students in the Dutch Courts," *Nation*, June 27, 1928, 728; Gouda, *Dutch Culture Overseas*, 26–28, 84, 87–88, 90–91; Ricklefs, *History of Modern Indonesia*, 214, 224, 230–31.
40. Powell, "The Emeralds of Wilhelmina"; W. Robert Moore, "Through Java in Pursuit of Color," *National Geographic*, September 1929, 333–62; Clune, *Isles of Spice*, 97, (quote) 162, 186; Cuhel broadcast, February 23, 1942, FJCP.
41. "Dutch East Indies: Its Vast Riches Tempt Japan"; Clune, *Isles of Spice*, 101; Rosalie Warner to Frank Cuhel, August 9, 1942, and Frank Cuhel to Lew and Rosalie Warner, October 15, 1942, FJCP.
42. "Far East: Hints of Superships Disturbs East Indies Burghers," April 3, 1937, 20, and "US Keeps Wary Eye on Japan Amid Mounting Pacific Tension," April 29, 1940, 29, both in *Newsweek*; Clune, *Isles of Spice*, 214; Jan van Apeldoorn, *Departure Delayed* (Melbourne: Robertson & Mullens, 1943), 174; George Gordon to Secretary of State, February 4, 1938, and Erle Dickover to Secretary of State, August 8, 1936, and November 17, 1939, box 2631, RG165-R (Netherlands East Indies), NARA; Nicholas Tarling, *A Sudden Rampage: The Japanese Occupation of Southeast Asia, 1941–1945* (London: Hurst, 2001), 47.
43. Erle Dickover, strictly confidential memo, February 9, 1939, box 2631, RG165-R (Netherlands East Indies), NARA; Edward S. Miller, *Bankrupting the Enemy: The U.S. Financial Siege of Japan before Pearl Harbor* (Annapolis, MD: Naval Institute Press, 2007).
44. Frank Cuhel to V. A. Dodge, February 6, 1939, FJCP.
45. Frank Cuhel to V. A. Dodge, February 6, 1939, Frank Cuhel to Ermengarde Cuhel, December 2 and 12, 1939, and V. A. Dodge to Frank Cuhel, March 20, 1940, FJCP.
46. J. Panglaykim and I. Palmer, "Study of Entrepreneurialship in Developing Countries: The Development of One Chinese Concern in Indonesia," *Journal of Southeast Asian Studies* 1, no. 1 (March 1970): 85–95; Charles Coppel, "Liem Thian Joe's Unpublished History of Kian Gwan," *Southeast Asian Studies* 27, no. 2 (September 1989): 177–87; Yoshihara Kunio, *Oei Tiong Ham Concern: The First Business Empire of Southeast Asia* (Kyoto: Center for Southeast Asian Studies, 1989), 74–94; Frank Cuhel to Ermengarde Cuhel, December 2, 1939, FJCP.
47. Frank Cuhel to Ermengarde Cuhel, December 2 and 12, 1939, Larry Seymour to Frank Cuhel, December 29, 1939, and May 2, 1940, V.A. Dodge to Frank Cuhel, March 20, 1940, and Frank Cuhel to Larry Seymour, May 1, 1941, FJCP.
48. Clipping, "Power of Both Britain and U.S. Needed for Japs, Says Cuhel." On similar views among American traders and investors in China and Japan, see Mira Wilkins, "The Role of U.S. Business," in Dorothy Borg and

Shumpei Okamoto, eds., *Pearl Harbor as History* (New York: Columbia University Press, 1973), 341–76.

Chapter 11

1. Federal Writers' Project, *New York Panorama: A Companion to the WPA Guide to New York City* (1938; repr., New York: Pantheon, 1984), ch. 17.
2. "Spanish Line Revives Sailings to Mexico," January 10, 1935, 41, "Events of Interest in Shipping World," December 1, 1935, S10, travel page ad, April 12, 1936, XX5, "Events of Interest in Shipping World," November 12, 1939, 51, all in *New York Times*; "Garcia and Diaz Named Agents for Spanish Line," *New York Herald Tribune*, September 27, 1935, 26; foreign agent registration statements, 1939–1943, case file 149-522, box 42, RG60, NARA; Jesús Valdaliso, "Management, Profitability and Finance in Twentieth-Century Spanish Merchant Shipping," *Research in Maritime History* 6 (June 1994): 67–90. American cruise passengers to Latin America rose from just over 2,500 in 1929 to more than 64,000 by 1937: Mike Wallace, "New York City and the Spanish-Speaking World from Dutch Days to the Second World War," in Edward Sullivan, ed., *Nueva York, 1613–1945* (New York: New-York Historical Society/Scala, 2010), 19–81.
3. "Notes of Social Activities in New York and Elsewhere," January 17, 1931, 22, "Honors New Ambassador," March 22, 1932, 23, "Spaniards to Give Charity Ball Here," January 22, 1933, N5, "The Spanish Ball a Colorful Event," February 4, 1933, 12, "Trade with Spain is Aim of Bowers," May 9, 1933, 15, and "40 Ship Lines Band to Act under NRA," December 8, 1933, 47, all in *New York Times*. Garcia & Diaz's connections to Falangist politics are briefly discussed in Javier Juárez Camacho, *Madrid Londres Berlín: Espías de Franco al Servicio de Hitler* (Madrid: Temas de Hoy, 2005), 161–64, 178; Marta Rey García, *Stars for Spain: La Guerra civil española en los estados unidos* (Sade, A. Coruña: Castro, 1997), 154–55, 159; and Allan Chase, *Falange: The Axis Secret Army in the Americas* (New York: Putnam, 1943), 211–19, 237–38, though the latter should be used with care.
4. *Fé*, February 1937, and Falange's 26 points, quoted in Stephen Naft, "Falangism and Hispanidad in Latin America," and *Voz de España*, December 8, 1938, quoted in Willard Espy and H. R. Southworth, "The Spanish Phalanx in the Western Hemisphere," both in Latin American Branch, Security Classified General Correspondence, 1941–1946, box 1003, RG165/G-2; *El Correo Español*, March 1, 1939, quoted in "Spain and Neutrality," *Voices of Spain* (London), August 12, 1939, 76; Chase, *Falange*, 6. See also Julian Maria Rubio, "Nationalist Spain and the South American Countries," *Spain*, March 1, 1939, 18–19; María Escudero, "Hispanist Democratic Thought versus Hispanist Thought of the Franco Era," in Marina Pérez de Mendiola, ed., *Bridging the Atlantic: Toward a Reassessment of Iberian and Latin American Cultural Ties* (Albany: State University of New York Press, 1996), 169–86.

5. Mike Wallace, "New York and the World: The Global Context," in Peter Carroll and James Fernández, eds., *Facing Fascism: New York and the Spanish Civil War* (New York: Museum of the City of New York and New York University Press, 2007), 21–29; Ronald Bayor, *Neighbors in Conflict: The Irish, Germans, Jews, and Italians of New York City, 1929–1941* (Urbana: University of Illinois Press, 1988), 57—104; Theodore Irwin, "Inside the 'Christian Front,'" *Forum*, March 1940, 102–8.
6. Paul Preston, *The Spanish Civil War* (1986; repr., New York: Norton, 2006), 78–80, 102–3; Hugh Thomas, *The Spanish Civil War* (1961; repr., New York: Modern Library, 2001), 129–36.
7. Manuel Diaz and Marcelino Garcia to Juan Claudio Güel, March 5, 1937, and Manuel Diaz to unnamed friend, March 4, 1937, both in the *Daily Worker*, May 10, 1937, 4–5, and full translations in "Espionage in the United States," *Congressional Record*, May 10, 1937, 4269–73; "Spanish Ship Here Was Hit by Firing," August 2, 1936, 31, and "Ex-Envoy Assails Spanish Loyalists," May 12, 1938, 8, both in *New York Times*; Preston, *Spanish Civil War*, 190, 304; Thomas, *Spanish Civil War*, 371, 523, 707–12.
8. Mark Falcoff and Fredrick Pike, eds., *The Spanish Civil War, 1936–1939: American Hemispheric Perspectives* (Lincoln: University of Nebraska Press, 1982); T. G. Powell, *Mexico and the Spanish Civil War* (Albuquerque: University of New Mexico, 1981), ch. 1; Allen Guttmann, *The Wound in the Heart: America and the Spanish Civil War* (New York: Free Press, 1962); Rey García, *Stars for Spain*; Carroll and Fernández, *Facing Fascism*.
9. Norman J. Padelford "Foreign Shipping during the Spanish Civil War," *American Journal of International Law* 32, no. 2 (April 1938): 264–79; Jay Allen, "Spain's Revolt Leaders Find Help in Lisbon," *Chicago Tribune*, August 29, 1936, 1; Thomas, *Spanish Civil War*, 194, 276, 339–40, 805–6; Willard Frank, "Naval Operations in the Spanish Civil War, 1936–1939," *Naval War College Review* 37, no. 1 (January–February 1984): 24–55; Michael Alpert, *A New International History of the Spanish Civil War* (New York: St. Martin's, 1994), 113–24; Gerald Howson, *Arms for Spain: The Untold Story of the Spanish Civil War* (London: John Murray, 1998). On Anglo-American policy, see Richard Traina, *American Diplomacy and the Spanish Civil War* (Bloomington: Indiana University Press, 1968); Douglas Little, *Malevolent Neutrality: The United States, Great Britain, and the Origins of the Spanish Civil War* (Ithaca, NJ: Cornell University Press, 1985); and Dominic Tierney, *FDR and the Spanish Civil War: Neutrality and Commitment in the Struggle that Divided America* (Durham, NC: Duke University Press, 2007).
10. Congress Against War and Fascism resolution, May 30, 1937, 852.01B11/10, reel 44, *SIA*; Roy Hudson, "Shipowners Plot Against Spanish Democracy," pamphlet (New York: Workers Library Publishers, c. 1937), box 1c, SCWC; "Spanish Rebels Gun for Cargo of Mexican Arms," *Chicago Tribune*,

September 12, 1936, 4; "Majorca Gripped by the Spy Fever," *New York Times*, November 3, 1937, 2; Michael Alpert, *La guerra civil española en el mar* (Madrid: Siglo XXI, 1987).

11. Decree trans. in *The* Navemar, *Compañía Española de Navegación Maritima, S.A., v. Crespo et al.*, 102 F. 2d 444 (U.S. Court of Appeals, 2d C., March 6, 1939); "Spanish Ships Seized," *Washington Post*, December 4, 1936, X5; "Spain's Consul Strips Chamber Here of Power," *New York Herald Tribune*, January 13, 1937, 10; Manuel Diaz and Marcelino Garcia to Juan Claudio Güel, March 5, 1937, reproduced in *Daily Worker*, May 10, 1937, 4; "Portugal and the War in Spain," *Voice of Spain* (London), June 24, 1939, 45-6; K.D. Abbot memo, May 2, 1942, litigation case file 146-7-1883, box 13, RG60, NARA.

12. *The* Navemar, *Cia. Española de Navegacion Maritima, S.A., v. Crespo et al.*, 17 F. Supp. 495 (E.D.N.Y December 22, 1936), 18 F. Supp. 153 (E.D.N.Y. January 28, 1937), 102 F. 2d 444 (U.S.C.A., 2d C., March 6, 1939), and 103 F. 2d 783 (U.S.C.A., 2d C., April 18, 1939); statements reprinted in *American Maritime Cases*, 1937, 13–35; *The* Navemar, 90 F. 2d 673 (C.C.A., 2d C., June 7 and 24, 1937) and 24 F. Supp. 495 (E.D.N.Y. July 26, 1938); *Compañía Española de Navegación Maritima, S.A., v. The* Navemar, 303 U.S. 68; 58 S. Ct. 432; 82 L. Ed, 667 (U.S. Supreme Court January 7, 10, and 31, 1938); "Spanish Ships Seized," December 4, 1936, X5, and "Spain Owns Ship, U.S. Court Rules," June 9, 1937, 2, both in *Washington Post*; "Spanish Ship Seized While in Harbor Here," December 10, 1936, 22, and "Spanish Ship Free," April 23, 1939, 22, both in *New York Times*; Manuel Diaz and Marcelino Garcia to J. C. Güel, March 5, 1937, reproduced in *Daily Worker*, May 10, 1937, 4; Charles Hyde, "Concerning the *Navemar*," July 1939, 530–34, and "State Immunity and the Requisition of Ships during the Spanish Civil War: II. Before the Courts of the United States," January 1942, 37–55, both in *American Journal of International Law*.

13. Manuel Diaz to Federico Varela, February 8, 1937, and Manuel Diaz and Marcelino Garcia to Juan Claudio Güel, March 5, 1937, both reproduced in *Daily Worker*, May 10, 1937, 4; *The* Motomar, *Linea Sud-Americana, Inc., v. 7,295.40 Tons of Linseed and Archer-Daniels-Midland Co.* (U.S. District Court, S.D.N.Y. May 10, 1939), 757–76, and *The* Motomar, *Linea Sud-Americana, Inc., v. Archer-Daniels-Midland Co.* (U.S. C.C.A., Second Circuit, January 8, 1940), 130–34, both in *American Maritime Cases*; "Motomar's Crew Figures in Rioting at Veracruz," May 11, 1937, 18, and "Loyalist Freighter Is Armed in Mexico," March 28, 1937, 25, both in *New York Times*; *Excelsior*, July 21, 1937, trans. in Pierre de L. Boal, confidential memo, July 23, 1937, 852.3300 Motomar/19, reel 66, *SIA*. On Mexican assistance for the Spanish Republic, see Powell, *Mexico and the Spanish Civil War*, ch. 3.

14. Manuel Diaz and Marcelino Garcia to Frederico Varela, February 8, 1937, and Manuel Diaz to unnamed friend, April 8, 1937, in the *Daily Worker*, May 10, 1937, 4–5; Preston, *Spanish Civil War*, 193–95.

15. Manuel Diaz to Federico Varela, February 8, 15, and 20, 1937, Manuel Diaz to an unnamed friend, April 8, 1937, and Manuel Diaz and Marcelino Garcia to Don Juan Claudio Güel, March 5, 1937, reproduced in *Daily Worker*, May 10, 1937; Josephus Daniels, "Espionage Ring in the United States Sponsored by General Franco," May 21, 1937, and *Solidaridad Obrera* (Barcelona), June 6, 1937, 852.01B11/5-17, reel 44, *SIA*; "Ship with War Cargo from U.S. Sunk Off Spain," *Chicago Tribune*, March 9, 1937, 4; "Neutrality War," *Time*, January 18, 1937, 15; "Loyalists Copy Rebel Letters in Coup Here," *New York Herald Tribune*, May 11, 1937, 8; "Bilbao (batalla naval)," "Mar Cantábrico," and "Marqués de Comillas" in Manuel Rubio Cabeza, *Diccionario de la guerra civil española* (Barcelona: Planeta, 1987), 125, 508, 515; "Exportation of Arms and Munitions to Spain," *Congressional Record*, January 6, 1937, 73–75. Mexican officials took steps to deport Federico Varela, the customs house official who had reported on loyalist ships but were unsuccessful. Marcelino and Manuel rewarded him by making him their local representative after the civil war: Powell, *Mexico and the Spanish Civil War*, 74; US Coast Guard memo, December 31, 1941, FW852.8592/1, reel 33, *SIA*.
16. From their correspondence, it is clear that Marcelino and Manuel were also involved in the legal battles over the Compañía Naviera Vascongada's *Cristina*, confiscated by loyalists at Cardiff: Lawrence Preuss, "State Immunity and the Requisition of Ships during the Spanish Civil War: I. Before the British Courts," *American Journal of International Law* 35, no. 2 (April 1941): 263–81; Manuel Diaz to unnamed friend, April 8, 1937, and Victor Alvarez to Manuel Diaz, March 20, 1937, in "Espionage in the United States," *Congressional Record* and exposition in Harry Raymond, "Conspires for Gunboat to Shell Ships," *Daily Worker*, May 10, 1937, 1, 4–5.
17. Press reports, confidential memos, and undercover intelligence, 852.3300 Motomar/1-54, reel 66, *SIA*; James Fogarty, editorial, May 14, 1937, 22, "More Arms Bought in Mexico by Spain," March 21, 1937, 28, "To Aid Valencia Vessel," August 27, 1937, 4, and "Munitions Reach Mexico," November 5, 1937, 4, all in *New York Times*; cross reference file (1940-1944), 711.00111/655, box 2102, RG59, NARA; Powell, *Mexico and the Spanish Civil War*, 71–75.
18. E. W. Timberlake, G-2 report, March 1938, 852.3300 Manuel Arnus/6 and Havana embassy dispatch, April 1, 1938, 852.33/1, reel 66, R. Ackerman, memo on SS *Manuel Arnús*, June 17, 1942, 852.852/17, reel 32, all in *SIA*; Alistair Hennessy, "Cuba," in Falcoff and Pike, *Spanish Civil War*, 123–27; Rafael Gonzalez Echegaray, *La Marina Mercante y el Trafico Maritimo* (Madrid: San Martín, ca. 1977), 87–88, 239.
19. Juan Francisco de Cárdenas report on the Casa de España, October 18, 1938, R-1004/3, AMAE; FBI memo, December 31, 1941, 800.01B11 Registration Garcia and Diaz/16, box 3101, and statement of Miguel Erbmahced (aka DeChambre), 711.00111 Unlawful Shipments/591-720.5, box 2010, both in RG59, NARA; G-2 report, November 5, 1941, George

Hinman, "First Report on Political Aspects of Falangist Activity in the United States and Canada," February 25, 1942, confidential report on Spanish Falange, September 18, 1942, and FBI New York Field Division report, April 13, 1943, all in box 2, and FBI survey of Spanish Activities in the New York Field Division, September 1, 1942, folder 291.2 Spanish August 1, 1942–October 20, 1942, box 396, RG319, NARA; O. Lewis to A. Schwartiz, June 28, 1943, case file 149-522, RG60, NARA. Marcelino's cable was published in *Diario de la Marina*, March 13, 1937, and reprinted in *Daily Worker*, May 12, 1937, 5. On the Falange, see Stanley G. Payne, *Falange: A History of Spanish Fascism* (Palo Alto, CA: Stanford University Press, 1961); Ricardo Chueca, *El fascismo en los comienzos del régimen de Franco: Un estudio sobre FET-JONS* (Madrid: Centro de Investigaciones Sociológicas, 1983); Rosa María Pardo Sanz, *Con Franco hacia el Imperio! La política exterior española en América latina, 1939–1945* (Madrid: Universidad Nacional de Educación a Distancia, 1995); and Joan Maria Thomàs, *La Falange de Franco: Fascismo y fascistización en el régimen franquista, 1937–1945* (Barcelona: Plaza Janés, 2001).

20. Herbert Matthews, "Franco Gives Interview," *New York Times*, December 5, 1938, 11; "El Día de la Raza en Nueva York," October 18, 1941, 2, photo insert, "Actividades de la Casa de España," May 10 and 15, 1941, 6, and ads, March 1, April 26, and September 27, 1941, 6-7, all in *Cara al Sol*; S. R. Herbert, "Franco's Phalanx Invades U.S.A.," *Protestant Digest*, April–May 1941, 9–19; Espy and Southworth, "Spanish Phalanx in the Western Hemisphere"; Jacob Fuller synopsis report, January 20, 1944, litigation case file 146-7-1883, box 13, RG60, NARA; Rey García, *Stars for Spain*, 158–62.

21. Federal Writers' Project, *New York Panorama*, 121–25; Gabriel Haslip-Viera, "The Evolution of the Latino Community in New York City," in *Hispanic New York: A Sourcebook*, ed. Claudio Iván Remeseira (New York: Columbia University Press, 2010), 33–55; César Andréu Iglesias, *Memoirs of Bernardo Vega*, trans. Juan Flores (New York: Monthly Review, 1984); Carroll and Fernández, *Facing Fascism*; "20 Are Seized Here in Fight over Spain," *New York Times*, June 7, 1938, 12; S. R. Herbert, "The Franco Front in America," *Protestant Digest*, March 1940, 24–41.

22. "Congress Must Act," May 10, 1937, 1, "Foster Urges Seamen Aid in Baring Spies," May 12, 1937, 5, and photostat of Garcia & Diaz letters, May 10, 1937, 4–5, all in *Daily Worker*; SS *Virginia* manifest, May 10, 1937, reel 5976, *VANY*.

23. "Nazi Consulate Picketed," May 9, 1937, 35, and "Nye Sees 'Spy Ring' Aiding Franco Here," May 11, 1937, 18, both in *New York Times*; "Espionage in the United States" and "Abuse of Diplomatic Passports," *Congressional Record*, May 10, 1937, 4269–73, 4303–4; Liam Lenihan, "Group Said to Be in Touch with Agent at Valladolid," *Washington Post*, May 10, 1937, 1, 4; *Solidaridad Obrera* (Barcelona), June 6 and 9, 1937, 852.01B11/9, pt. 1, reel 44, *SIA*. On international reactions to the bombing of Guernica, see Ian

Patterson, *Guernica and Total War* (Cambridge, MA: Harvard University Press, 2007), 16–23, 30–48.

24. Confidential report on Spanish Falange, September 18, 1942, and J. Edgar Hoover to Adolf Berle, November 16, 1942, folder 000.24 Falange, box 2, RG319, NARA; "10,000 Rally Here for Franco Cause," *New York Times*, February 20, 1939, 8; "Enemies at Home," *New Republic*, July 27, 1942, 117; Rey García, *Stars for Spain*, 162–68, 253–64; Herbert, "Franco Front in America"; Patrick McNamara, "Pro-Franco Sentiment and Activity in New York City," in Carroll and Fernández, eds., *Facing Fascism*, 95–101; J. David Valaik, "Catholics, Neutrality, and the Spanish Embargo, 1937-1939," *Journal of American History* 54, no. 1 (June 1967): 73–85.
25. Telegram from Tunis, March 7, 1939, 852.33/1, pt. 1, reel 66, *SIA*; "The Nationalist Fleet," *Spain*, September 1, 1939, 15–17.
26. Press reports, confidential memos, and undercover intelligence, 852.3300 Motomar/1-54, reel 66, *SIA*; *The* Navemar, *Compañía Española de Navegación Maritima, S.A., v. Crespo et al.*, 102 F. 2d 444 (U.S.C.A., 2d C., March 6, 1939), and 103 F. 2d 783 (U.S.C.A., 2d C., April 18, 1939); "U.S. Delivers Spanish Ship to Agents Here," *New York Herald Tribune*, April 23, 1939, B10; "Spanish Ship Free," April 23, 1939, 22, and "New Envoy Thanks Friends of Franco," April 16, 1939, 27, both in *New York Times*.
27. Royal Copeland (D-NY) in "Espionage in the United States," *Congressional Record*; "Rotary Club Honors 10," January 28, 1938, 6, "Diaz-Eads," October 20, 1941, 12, and "Sabbatino Gets Five to Ten Years," December 11, 1941, 29, all in *New York Times*. Something prompted Manuel and Marcelino to declare their intent to become citizens in 1926, but they let these "first papers" expire and only went through with it in 1937: Manuel Diaz and Marcelino Garcia declarations of intention, November 19, 1926, Manuel Diaz naturalization petition, October 4, 1937, and Marcelino Garcia naturalization petition, October 15, 1937, New York, State and Federal Naturalization Records, 1794–1929, RG21, NARA at New York, NY. They were granted citizenship despite formal protests from antifascist activists: "2 Spy Suspects Seek Citizenship," *New York Post*, October 4, 1937, 12.
28. Frank Reil, "Line on Liners," *Brooklyn Daily Eagle*, March 3, 1939, 24; "Spain Recognition to Spur Sea Trade," *New York Times*, April 2, 1939, 64; "Shipping Lines See Service to Spain Starting," April 2, 1939, B10, and "Spanish Ship Line Agent to Confer on U.S. Service," April 23, 1939, 6, both in *New York Herald Tribune*; Juan Francisco de Cárdenas to Ministerio de Asuntos Exteriores, October 21, 1938, R-1004/3, Juan Francisco de Cárdenas to Francisco Gómez Jordana y Sousa, April 17 and 20, 1939, R-1083/16, AMAE.
29. *Arriba España*, November 20, 1938, as quoted in "Spain and Neutrality"; José Antonio quoted in Naft, "Falangism and Hispanidad in Latin America"; signed statement, September 29, 1939, R-1655/57, AMAE.

Interlude

1. M. D. Klaäs, *Last of the Flying Clippers: The Boeing B-314 Story* (Atglen, PA: Schiffer, 1997), 185.
2. Ashley Jackson, *The British Empire and the Second World War* (New York: Hambledon Contiuum, 2006), 81; "Rescue Crewman's Story," *Washington Post*, February 24, 1943, 1; Bernard Edwards, *The Twilight of the U-boats* (Barnsley, UK: Leo Cooper, 2004), 62–73.
3. Emergency Procedure, November 17, 1942, and confidential route instructions, February 8, 1943, folder 5, box II:145, and E. McVitty, confidential memo, September 18, 1942, folder 17, box II:105, Pan Am; Klaäs, *Last of the Flying Clippers*, 149, 163.
4. Klaäs, *Last of the Flying Clippers*, 51–53, 226.
5. Klaäs, *Last of the Flying Clippers*, 185; "Noted Flier Speaker to Sanford Kiwanians," January 8, 1940, 5, and Sadie Root Robards, "An Interview with Captain R. O. D. Sullivan," December 28, 1941, 30, both in *News and Observer* (Raleigh, NC); John Chapman, "America Rules the Skyways," *Saturday Evening Post*, March 30, 1940, 18–19, 70–73.
6. Frederika, Bremer, Iowa, 218A, reel 378, *Census (1870)*; Frederika, Bremer, Iowa, 262D, reel 328, *Census (1880)*; Odessa, Buffalo, Nebraska, 144A, reel 917, *Census (1900)*; Phillip Sullivan, "Public Sale," February 14, 1908, 3, and "Riverview and Vicinity," February 28, 1908, 8, both in *Elmcreek Beacon* (Nebraska); *San Diego City and County Directory* (San Diego, CA: San Diego Directory Co., 1912), 724.
7. US Army WWI Transport Service, Passenger Lists, 1919, p. 66, NARA; USS *Aroostook*, San Diego, California, 4A, reel 2041 *Census (1920)*; *San Diego City and County Directory* (San Diego, CA: San Diego Directory Co., 1920), 863; "Clipper Service," *New York Times*, July 2, 1939, E2; James Mooney, ed., *Dictionary of American Naval Fighting Ships*, vol. 1A (Washington, DC: Navy Department, 1959–1981), 400–422; Wayne Heiser, *U.S. Naval and Marine Corps Reserve Aviation*, vol. 1 (McHenry, IL: Dihedral Press, 2006), 8–10; Rod Sullivan, Jr, interview, September 24, 1981, folder 14, box 16, and Nell Schactman notes, folder Sullivan, R.O.D. notes and papers, box 9, IWP; "City Briefs," October 15, 1923, 5, and "Come by Airplane from California," June 8, 1929, 6, both in *Daily Times* (Davenport, IA); personnel record and "Famous Pilots: R. O. D. Sullivan," *Airmail Magazine*, 1943, folder 23, box I:293, Pan Am.
8. "2 Pan-American Planes Reach Santo Domingo," *Miami Herald*, September 5, 1930, 4; "Honors St. Patrick," *Tampa Tribune*, March 18, 1934, 9; Robert Daley, *An American Saga: Juan Trippe and His Pan Am Empire* (New York: Random House, 1980), 145–48.
9. Memo, December 13, 1929, folder 5, box I:120A, Pan Am; "China Clipper Wings Way over Pacific to Launch Air Mail," *Morning Call* (Paterson, NJ), November 23, 1935, 1–2; Victor Wright, "Historic Alameda Flight Recalled," in Stan Cohen, *Wings to the Orient: Pan American Clipper Planes, 1935–1945* (Missoula, MT: Pictorial Histories Publishing, 1985), 180–81; Horace Brock,

Flying the Oceans: A Pilot's Story of Pan Am, 1935–1955 (New York: Jason Aronson, 1978), 129–30; Daley, *American Saga*, 162–63, 169–74, 248; Klaäs, *Last of the Flying Clippers*, 142.

10. John Grover, "Skipper Sullivan to Boss Atlantic Flight," *Chronicle-Herald* (Macon, MO), June 28, 1939, 6; San Diego County voter registration index, 1926, reel 10, Great Registrar of Voters, 1900–1968, California State Library, Sacramento, CA; Rod Sullivan, Jr., interview; "Come by Airplane from California," June 8, 1929, 6, and "Farewell Parties Honoring Mrs. Sullivan," September 18, 1929, 8, both in *Daily Times* (Davenport, IA); "Pony," February 9, 1934, 1, and photograph caption, May 20, 1934, 20, both in *Miami Herald*; "Family Greets Trail Blazer," *Los Angeles Daily News*, March 30, 1935, 2; "Take Off of Big Radio Guided Ship," *Pottsville Republican* (PA), April 17, 1935, 1; Deep River, Lee, North Carolina, 6B, reel 2935, *Census (1940)*; photograph in *Oakland Tribune* (CA), April 17, 1935, 17.
11. Chronology of Bermuda services, folder 2, box I:315, and accredited flight time records, folder 10, box II:168, Pan Am; "R.O.D. Sullivan," *Chatham Record* (Pittsboro, NC), February 21, 1935, 4; Sadie Root Robards, "An Interview with Captain R. O. D. Sullivan," December 28, 1941, 30, and "Mrs. Sullivan Hears News of Air Accident," February 24, 1943, 3, both in *News and Observer* (Raleigh, NC).
12. Clipping, "British-Built Airports: Expansion of Pre-War Bases," IOR/L/E/9/147, BL; Deborah Ray, "Pan American Airways and the Trans-African Air Base Program of World War II" (PhD diss., New York University, 1973), vii, 3–4, 6–7, 11, 35, 98, 102–6, 164, 171–78; Nancy Ellen Lawler, *Soldiers, Airmen, Spies, and Whisperers: The Gold Coast in World War II* (Athens: Ohio University Press, 2002), 39–56; statistical data, special mission no. 64, folder 11, box I:261, Pan Am. For an overview of Pan Am's worldwide, wartime operations, see Mark Cotta Vaz and John Hill, *Pan Am at War: How the Airline Secretly Helped America Fight World War II* (New York: Skyhorse, 2019).
13. Raymond Dumett, "Africa's Strategic Minerals during the Second World War," *Journal of African History* 26, no. 4 (1985): 381–408; Ray, "Pan American Airways and the Trans-African Air Base Program," 152, 179; statistical data, special mission no. 64, folder 11, box I:261, Pan Am; Susan Williams, *Spies in the Congo: America's Atomic Mission in World War II* (New York: Public Affairs, 2016), 7, 207. On the critical role of beryllium in early atomic bomb experiments, see Richard Rhodes, *The Making of the Atomic Bomb* (1986; repr., New York: Simon & Schuster, 2012).
14. World War II special missions, folder 52, box I:260, board inquiry notes, folder 5, box II:152, Pan Am; Marius Lodeesen, *Captain Lodi Speaking* (Suttons Bay, MI: Argonaut, 1984), 158; William Stanley, "Trans-South Atlantic Air Link in World War II," *GeoJournal* 33, no. 4 (August 1994): 459–63.

15. "Man Hopes Pilot is Never Forgotten," *Sanford Herald* (NC), December 13, 2009, 1, 8A; Robards, "An Interview with Captain R. O. D. Sullivan"; "Mrs. Sullivan Hears News."
16. S. B. Kauffman, *Pan Am Pioneer: A Manager's Memoir*, ed. George Hopkins (Lubbock: Texas Tech University Press, 1995), 70; Klaäs, *Last of the Flying Clippers*, 144, 147–48; Scott Flower, The Bottom Damage Story of the B-314, NC-18604 at Horta Azores, folder 168, box I:120B, and Pan Am Flight Watch and Notification Messages Sent, folder 5, box II:145, Pan Am.
17. Passenger accommodations of Boeing 314 Clipper, 1940, folder 11, box I:107, and Jean Rognan statement, February 26, 1943, folder 12, box II:152, Pan Am; Klaäs, *Last of the Flying Clippers*, 33–34, 39; Ben Robertson, *I Saw England* (New York: Knopf, 1941), 3.

Chapter 12

1. Ben Robertson to Dorothy Spalding, September 1, 1939, folder 16, box 2, notes on September 1939, folder 45, and clipping, "Ben Robertson Heard at Meet," *Anderson Independent*, folder 43, box 5, BFRP; Ben Robertson, *Red Hills and Cotton: An Upcountry Memory* (1942; repr., with new introduction by Lacy K. Ford, Jr., Columbia: University of South Carolina Press, 1991), 112.
2. Ben Robertson to Edgar Snow, January 3, 1937, and Ben Robertson to Jean Muir, January 18, 1937, folder 15, Ben Robertson to Louis Adamic, August 1, 1939, folder 16, box 2, notes on September 1939, folder 45, clipping, "Ben Robertson Heard at Meet," *Anderson Independent*, and draft, "An American and Britain," ca. 1941, folder 43, box 5, BFRP; Ben Robertson, "King George Strives to Please," *Saturday Evening Post*, February 4, 1939, 5–7, 66–69; Ben Robertson, *I Saw England* (New York: Knopf, 1941), 17. On Americans' shifting relations with the British, see Nicholas John Cull, *Selling War: The British Propaganda Campaign against American "Neutrality" in World War II* (New York: Oxford University Press, 1995), 6–10; David Reynolds, *The Creation of the Anglo-American Alliance, 1937–41: A Study in Competitive Co-operation* (Chapel Hill: University of North Carolina Press, 1982), 13–15, 23–25. On White Southerners' particular views about Britain, see Tennent S. McWilliams, *New South Faces the World: Foreign Affairs and the Southern Sense of Self, 1877–1950* (1988; repr., Tuscaloosa: University of Alabama Press, 2008), 90–92.
3. Hodding Carter, *Where Main Street Meets the River* (New York: Rinehart, 1953), 112; Ralph Ingersoll, memo to staff, April 1, 1940, PPF 6646, FDRL; Paul Milkman, *PM: A New Deal in Journalism, 1940–1948* (New Brunswick, NJ: Rutgers University Press, 1997), 1–3, 39–42. On rightwing moguls' grip on the nation's print media, see Kathryn Olmsted, *The Newspaper Axis: Six Press Barons Who Enabled Hitler* (New Haven, CT: Yale University Press, 2022).
4. Robertson, *I Saw England*, 10–12, 124.

5. Juliet Gardiner, *Wartime: Britain, 1939–1945* (London: Headline, 2004), xv, (quote) xvi, xvii, 9, 13, 18; Richard Overy, *The Twilight Years: The Paradox of Britain between the Wars* (New York: Penguin, 2009), ch. 8. On halting rearmament, see Daniel Todman, *Britain's War: Into Battle, 1937–1941* (New York: Oxford University Press, 2016), pt. II.
6. Neville Chamberlain's radio address, September 3, 1939, https://avalon.law.yale.edu/wwii/gb3.asp; Norman Longmate, *How We Lived Then: A History of Everyday Life during the Second World War* (1971; repr., London: Pimlico, 2002), 16–18, 25–33, 216; Richard Overy, *The Battle of Britain: The Myth and the Reality* (New York: Norton, 2000), 50; Gardiner, *Wartime*, xvi, 6–8, 20, 22, 28–30, 48–49, 66, 382, 463–67; Todman, *Britain's War*, 247–49.
7. Mollie Panter-Downes, *London War Notes, 1939–1945* (1939; repr., New York: Farrar, Straus, and Giroux, 1971), 15, 21, 23; Longmate, *How We Lived Then*, 76, 90; Gardiner, *Wartime*, 61; Todman, *Britain's War*, 255–56, 259, 262.
8. Hilde Marchant, *Women and Children Last: A Woman Reporter's Account of the Battle of Britain* (London: Victor Gollancz, 1941), 35; Panter-Downes, *London War Notes*, 54, 75–76.
9. Panter-Downes, *London War Notes*, 72; Virginia Cowles, *Looking for Trouble* (New York: Harper, 1941), 397; Gardiner, *Wartime*, 191–92, 198, 218–21; Overy, *Battle of Britain*, 18, 21, 51; Ben Robertson to sister, July 28, 1940, folder 16, box 2, BFRP. On the timing of Ben's arrival, see "Bermuda Visit Makes Skeptics of 18 on Clipper," *New York Herald Tribune*, June 21, 1940, 9; Ben Robertson, "War Has Ended Britons' Reserve," *Boston Globe*, January 28, 1941, 6.
10. Edward Beattie, *Passport to War* (London: Peter Davies, 1943), 263–66; Overy, *Battle of Britain*, 102; Gardiner, *Wartime*, 203, 209, 218, 224, 236, 304.
11. Ernie Pyle, *Ernie Pyle in England* (New York: Robert M. McBride, 1941), 198; Edward Murrow, *This Is London* (1941; repr., New York: Schocken, 1989), 131; Panter-Downes, *London War Notes*, 71, 83–84; Longmate, *How We Lived Then*, 105–7; Gardiner, *Wartime*, 221–22, 233–34, 241, 246; Todman, *Britain's War*, 374–76, 377, 380, 388–90; Robertson, *I Saw England*, 55; Ben Robertson to Wildon, August 5, 1940, folder 16, box 2, BFRP.
12. Ben Robertson to Wildon, August 5, 1940, and Robertson to Bob Unseld, August 5, 1940, folder 16, box 2, BFRP; Robertson, *I Saw England*, 15, 17, 85. One Ben's affable nature and social connections, see Ernie Pyle, "60 American Newsmen Here," *Boston Globe*, January 14, 1941, 7; Vincent Sheean, *Between the Thunder and the Sun* (New York: Random House, 1943), 214; Pyle, *Ernie Pyle in England*, 23; Jean Nicol, *Meet Me at the Savoy* (Bath: Cedric Chivers, 1952), 61.
13. Ben Robertson to Earl, George, and Harry, August 2, 1940, folder 16, box 2, BFRP; Robertson, *I Saw England*, 17.

14. Robertson, *I Saw England*, 13; Reynolds, *Creation of the Anglo-American Alliance*, 112–14.
15. Reynolds, *Creation of the Anglo-American Alliance*, 117; Cull, *Selling War*, 3, 76–77, 86, 170–73; Anthony J. Cumming, *The Royal Navy and the Battle of Britain* (Annapolis, MD: Naval Institute Press, 2010), 123–24, 131.
16. Cull, *Selling War*, 12, 18, 36, 66–67, 75, 82, (quote) 84, 85–88, 106–8, 128–29.
17. Cull, *Selling War*, 24–25, 88, (quote) 89, 90–91, 101, 103, 105; Cumming, *Royal Navy and the Battle of Britain*, 138–39; Reynolds, *Creation of the Anglo-American Alliance*, 50; Sheean, *Between the Thunder and the Sun*, 214–17; Robertson, *I Saw England*, 86–87.
18. Ben Robertson to Earl, George, and Harry, August 2, 1940, folder 16, box 2, BFRP; Robertson, *I Saw England*, 50, 88, 99, 101–2; Gardiner, *Wartime*, 237.
19. Press tract for *PM*, ca. June 23, 1941, folder 44, box 5, and Ben Robertson to Earl, George, and Harry, August 2, 1940, folder 16, box 2, BFRP; Robertson, *I Saw England*, 50, 88, 105.
20. Ben Robertson, "Ancient Cinque Port Awaits Invasion and Looks at Guns Across Channel," August 2, 1940, 6, Ben Robertson, "'A Fine Summer Day in England'," August 16, 1940, 14, and Ben Robertson, "I Saw 5 Planes Crash," August 29, 1940, 5, all in *PM*; Robertson, *I Saw England*, 89–91; Overy, *Battle of Britain*, 67–68; Juliet Gardiner, *The Blitz: The British Under Attack* (London: Harper Press, 2010), 5.
21. *PM* press tract, ca. June 23, 1941, folder 44, box 5, BFRP; Robertson, *I Saw England*, 92–93, 95–96; Cowles, *Looking for Trouble*, 403–5; Sheean, *Between the Thunder and the Sun*, 194–96, 204; Beattie, *Passport to War*, 271–78, 280–85, 292; See also Vincent Sheean, "So Many Owe So Much to So Few," *Saturday Evening Post*, December 21, 1940, 9–11, 70–72, and *Between the Thunder and the Sun*, 197–99, 204. The globe-girdling itineraries of these and other American correspondents are compiled in Robert Desmond, *Crisis and Conflict: World News Reporting between Two Wars, 1920–1940* (Iowa City: University of Iowa Press, 1982) and *Tides of War: World News Reporting*, 1940–1945 (Iowa City: University of Iowa Press, 1984).
22. Robertson, "'A Fine Summer Day in England'"; Robertson, *I Saw England*, 34, 93–94, 100, 104–5; England notes, 1940, folder 41, box 5, BFRP.
23. Robertson, *I Saw England*, 36, 93; Ben Robertson, "Robertson Watched the RAF Give Germans Perfect Hell," *PM*, August 22, 1941, 7; Ben Robertson to Lady and Lord Astor, July 28, 1940, folder 16, box 2, BFRP.
24. Ben Robertson to Franklin Roosevelt, September 4, 1940, PPF 6870, FDRL; Marchant, *Women and Children Last*, 45; Murrow, *This Is London*, 152; Robertson, *I Saw England*, 206–7; Raymond Lee to Jeanette Lee, August 29, 1940, in James Leutze, ed., *The London Observer: The Journal of General Raymond E. Lee, 1940–1941* (London: Hutchinson, 1972), 40.

25. Reynolds, *Creation of the Anglo-American Alliance*, 30–31, 113. For a recent narrative of this stand-off between the president and his foreign policy foes, see Nicholas Wapshott, *The Sphinx: Franklin Roosevelt, the Isolationists, and the Road to World War II* (New York: Norton, 2015).
26. Murrow, *This Is London*, 157–58; Robertson, *I Saw England*, 119–20; Sheean, *Between the Thunder and the Sun*, 210.
27. Sheean, *Between the Thunder and the Sun*, 219–25; Robertson, *I Saw England*, 120–22; Murrow, *This Is London*, 157–58; Vincent Sheean, "London Raid Havoc Awes Witnesses," *New York Times*, September 9, 1940, 3; Gardiner, *Wartime*, 332–33; Overy, *Battle of Britain*, 92–93.
28. Gardiner, *Wartime*, 334–36; Drew Middleton, *The Sky Suspended* (New York: Longmans, Green, 1960), 159–61; Howard Block, ed., *Black Saturday: The First Day of the Blitz, East London Memories of September 7th 1940* (London: T.H.A.P., 1984).
29. Gardiner, *The Blitz*, (quote) 13, 23, (quote) 112, 274. Statistics on Londoners killed between September 7, 1940, and May 11, 1941, from Amy Helen Bell, *London Was Ours: Diaries and Memoirs of the London Blitz* (London: Tauris, 2008), 4.
30. Sheean, *Between the Thunder and the Sun*, 225; Murrow, *This Is London*, 157–59; Robertson, *I Saw England*, 121–22.
31. Sheean, *Between the Thunder and the Sun*, 226–28; Robertson, *I Saw England*, 122–23; Murrow, *This Is London*, 157–61; Gardiner, *Wartime*, 336–37; Gardiner, *The Blitz*, 11; Marchant *Women and Children Last*, 58, 69, 74–75.
32. Gardiner, *The Blitz*, 30, 34; Robertson, *I Saw England*, 124–25; Ben Robertson, "Hail of Nazi Bombs Turns London into Hell on Earth," *PM*, September 9, 1940, 4.
33. Gardiner, *The Blitz*, 36; Robertson, *I Saw England*, 129–30; Ben Robertson, "London, Ready for Sacrifice, Says Proudly: 'We Can Take It!'" *PM*, September 10, 1940, 4.
34. Overy, *Battle of Britain*, xii, 17–18, 43–46, 94–99, 108–9, 119–23; Todman, *Britain's War*, 444–48; Cumming, *Royal Navy and the Battle of Britain*, ch. 3; Gardiner, *The Blitz*, 103–5.
35. Ben Robertson, "I Lived Through 500 Bombings," January 27, 1941, 3, and "Business as Usual London's Motto," January 30, 1941, 3, both in *Boston Globe*; Robertson, *I Saw England*, 130–31, 137; Marchant, *Women and Children Last*, 90, 96; Pyle, *Ernie Pyle in England*, 40–41; Amy Bell, "Landscapes of Fear: Wartime London, 1939–1945," *Journal of British Studies* 48, no. 1 (January 2009): 153–75; Gardiner, *The Blitz*, 79–84, 88–92, 107, 324–30, 347; Murrow, *This Is London*, 150–52.
36. Gardiner, *The Blitz*, 23, 184, 192, (quote) 241, 264–65, 367; entry for October 10, 1940, in Quentin Reynolds, *A London Diary* (New York: Random House, 1941), 65. See also Bell, "Landscapes of Fear," and Frank Costigliola, "Pamela Churchill, Wartime London, and

the Making of the Special Relationship," *Diplomatic History* 36, no. 4 (September 2012): 753–62.

37. Handout from St. Paul's Cathedral, England journal, 1941, and draft, "An American and Britain," ca. 1941, folder 43, box 5, BFRP; Ben Robertson, "Bombs Have Given Britons a New Sense of Values," *PM*, October 17, 1940, 4; Robertson, *I Saw England*, 114–19, 147, 174.

38. Robertson, *I Saw England*, 154; Ben Robertson, "Nazi Bombs Have Destroyed British Social Barriers," *PM*, August 17, 1941, 5; *PM* press tract, spring 1941, folder 44, box 5, BFRP.

39. Robertson, "Nazi Bombs Have Destroyed British Social Barriers"; Robertson, *Red Hills and Cotton*, 29; Robertson, *I Saw England*, 139; clipping, press release for the Committee to Defend America, for release Nov. 9, Robertson, "The Sands are Slipping," folder 43, draft, "An American and Britain," ca. 1941, folder 45, all in box 5, BFRP.

40. Robertson, "I Lived Through 500 Bombings"; Robertson, *I Saw England*, 140, 146–47, 181, 199; Raymond Daniell, "Nazi Bombs Strike the London Savoy," *New York Times*, November 29, 1940, 4; Pyle, *Ernie Pyle in England*, 22–23, 125–27; Charles Graves, *Off the Record* (London: Hutchinson, ca. 1942), v; Hector Bolitho, *War in the Strand* (London: Eyre and Spottiswoode, 1942), 72–73; Nicol, *Meet Me at the Savoy*, 30–31, 36–40, 50, 68–69, 76–77; Stanley Jackson, *The Savoy: The Romance of a Great Hotel* (New York: Dutton, 1964), 41–46, 58–59, 63–64, 72–76, 161–62, 169–73, 181, 184–85, 188–90, 193.

41. Robertson, *I Saw England*, 137; Gardiner, *Wartime*, 177, 391, 393, 397; Gardiner, *The Blitz*, 368; Todman, *Britain's War*, 477–79, 489–95, 505–6; Sonya Rose, *Which People's War? National Identity and Citizenship in Wartime Britain, 1939–1945* (Oxford: Oxford University Press, 2003), 34–35, 38–44, 107–22; Bell, *London Was Ours*, 47–48, 62–71, 77–78.

42. Phil Piratin, *Our Flag Stays Red* (London: Thames, 1948), 73–74; "Poor Demand Refuge in Rich London Hotel," *New York Times*, September 15, 1940, 40; "London's Poor to Get Better Raid Shelters," *PM*, September 17, 1940, 4; Larry Rue, "Give Workers More Food, Cry London Women," *Chicago Tribune*, January 30, 1941, 5. Larry Rue, who wrote for Robert McCormick's fiercely anti-interventionist newspaper, gave some of the only critical portraits of the war effort in Britain. On the politics of the *Chicago Tribune*, see Olmsted, *Newspaper Axis*.

43. Robertson, *I Saw England*, 153–54; Pyle, *Ernie Pyle in England*, 110–15, 127, (quote) 128; Quentin Reynolds, "London, City of Caves," *Collier's*, November 16, 1940, 15, 68.

44. Robertson, *I Saw England*, 133, 136, 138, 141, 181, 190, 194; Ben Robertson, "Germans Failed in Coventry," *Boston Globe*, January 26, 1941, 1–2; telegram, September 24, 1940, folder 16, box 2, BFRP; "London Spotlight," *Vogue*, December 1, 1941, 149; "Thrilling Stories Done by Foreign Correspondents," *Chicago Tribune*, December 7, 1941, E24.

45. Longmate, *How We Lived Then*, 133; Todman, *Britain's War*, 479; Reynolds, *Creation of the Anglo-American Alliance*, 143, 183–84; Cumming, *Royal Navy and the Battle of Britain*, 126–27.
46. Beattie, *Passport to War*, 328–29; Robertson, *I Saw England*, 207, 211. His reporter companions were Quentin Reynolds, Edward Beattie, Merrill Mueller of INS, and Victor Bienstock of the Jewish Telegraphic Agency: Robertson, journal entry, England 1941, folder 43, box 5, BFRP; SS *Exeter* manifest, January 7, 1941, reel 6519, *VANY*; On the December 29 firebombing of London, see Robert Post, "Havoc in 'The City'," *New York Times*, December 31, 1940, 1–2; Cecil Beaton, *History Under Fire* (London: Batsford, 1941); and Gardiner, *The Blitz*, 231–42.
47. "Socialism Seen as Aftermath of Europe's War," *Atlanta Constitution*, January 31, 1941, 9; Bess Furman, *Washington By-Line: The Personal History of a Newspaperwoman* (New York: Knopf, 1949), 292; "Ben Robertson Cheered," *Index-Journal* (Greenwood, SC), January 29, 1941, 8; clippings of reviews of *I Saw England*, folder 11, box 1, BFRP; Cull, *Selling War*, 109–11, 176–78. On the emergence of strong interventionism in the American South, see Joseph Fry, *Dixie Looks Abroad: The South and U.S. Foreign Relations, 1783–1973* (Baton Rouge: Louisiana State University Press, 2002), 199–206, and McWilliams, *New South Faces the World*, 129, 132, 138.
48. Pyle, "60 Newsmen Here"; "Hitler to Move After March 1, Reporters Aver," *Washington Post*, February 20, 1941, 16; Sheean, *Between the Thunder and the Sun*, 295–96; Leutze, *London Observer*, 243; Panter-Downes, *London War Notes*, 129, 133–35, 137, 142–44; Sandra Koa Wing, ed., *Our Longest Days: A People's History of the Second World War* (London: Profile, 2008), 78, 83, 87; Gardiner, *The Blitz*, 268; Reynolds, *Creation of the Anglo-American Alliance*, 160–68. The desertion rate in the British army also peaked at this moment. For this and early 1941 shipping woes and dollar reserves, see Todman, *Britain's War*, 526–27, 555–62.
49. Ben Robertson, "Plymouth Ablaze," *Boston Globe*, March 27, 1941, 1. See also England notes, 194[1], folder 41, and cable to *PM*, spring 1941, folder 43, both in box 5, BFRP; Gardiner, *The Blitz*, 304–9.
50. Reynolds, *Creation of the Anglo-American Alliance*, 196–97; Todman, *Britain's War*, 562–65; England journal, June–December 194[1], folder 42, box 5, and Ben Robertson to father, April 13, 1941, folder 17, box 2, BFRP; Robertson, "Holy Week in England," *Boston Globe*, April 13, 1941, B1, 16; Overy, *Battle of Britain*, 70, 90–91; Todman, *Britain's War*, 520–21.
51. Gardiner, *Wartime*, 429–30; Gardiner, *The Blitz*, 342, 348–49, 285. For the Savoy incident on April 16, see Bolitho, *War in the Strand*, 77, 79–80, 84, 104; Nicol, *Meet Me at the Savoy*, 78–81; Compton Mackenzie, *The Savoy of London* (London: Harrap, 1953), 97–98; Jackson, *The Savoy*, 199–200.
52. Copy, April 20, 1941, folder 43, box 5, BFRP.
53. Journal entry, ca. March-April 1941, folder 43, and *PM* press tracts, May 1941, folder 44, both in box 5, BFRP. See also Robertson, *I Saw England*, 78.

54. Speech draft, England journal, May–June, 1941, and ("sharper perspective") press tract, ca. May 3, 1941, folder 44B, box 5, BFRP.
55. "80% of Empire Troops Out of Greece," May 1, 1941, 4, "How the British Forces Left Greece," May 2, 1941, 4, and "End of Evacuation from Greece," May 3, 1941, 4, all in *Times* (London); Graves, *Off the Record*, 136, 139–40, 142–43; Reynolds, *Creation of the Anglo-American Alliance*, 196–99.
56. Press tract, ca. May 11, 1941, folder 44B, box 5, BFRP; Larry Rue, "London: Scene during Bomb Raid and After," *Chicago Tribune*, May 12, 1941, 3; Quentin Reynolds, "Full Moon Over London," *Collier's*, June 28, 1941, 14, 73; Ben Robertson, "Tears and Trouble: Another 'Blitz' Tries London's Courage," May 12, 1941, 3, and "Ben Robertson Says the Germans Can't Destroy London from the Air," August 15, 1941, 8–9, both in *PM*; Quentin Reynolds, *Only the Stars Are Neutral* (New York: Random House, 1942), 32–36; Nicol, *Meet Me at the Savoy*, 68–69.
57. Reynolds, *Only the Stars Are Neutral*, 36–37; Gardiner, *Wartime*, 432–34; Longmate, *How We Lived Then*, 134; Gardiner, *The Blitz*, 116.
58. Press tract, ca. May 11, 1941, folder 44B, box 5, BFRP; Ben Robertson, "Let's Tell Britain Now Whether We Intend to Help," *PM*, May 20, 1941, 2; journal entry, May 26, 194[1], folder 41, box 5, BFRP.
59. Robertson, "Let's Tell Britain Now Whether We Intend to Help"; press tract, ca. May 3, 1941, folder 44B, and press tracts for *PM*, spring 1941, and Ben Robertson to Ralph Ingersoll, ca. May 19, 1941, folder 44, box 5, BFRP.
60. Press tract, ca. May 11, 1941, folder 44B, box 5, BFRP.

Chapter 13

1. W. L. Burn, "Precarious Neutrality: The Netherlands in Europe and Asia," *Contemporary Review*, April 1939, 432–40; Suppression of "Fifth Column" Activities in the Netherlands Indies, confidential memo, June 7, 1940, box 2631, RG165-R (Netherlands East Indies), NARA; Frank Cuhel, draft memoir on Netherlands East Indies, September 1939–December 1941, FJCP; Rudolf Mrázek, *Engineers of Happy Land: Technology and Nationalism in a Colony* (Princeton, NJ: Princeton University Press, 2002), 179.
2. H. C. Zentgraaff, "Defense of the East Indies," *Asia*, November 1938, 699–700; "Dutch East Indies: Its Vast Riches Tempt Japan," *Life*, January 22, 1940, 54–65; Frank Clune, *Isles of Spice* (New York: Dutton, 1942), 214–19; John Lardner, *Southwest Passage: The Yanks in the Pacific* (Philadelphia: Lippincott, 1943), 106; Christopher Bayly and Tim Harper, *Forgotten Armies: The Fall of British Asia, 1941–1945* (London: Allen Lane, 2004), 66; John Dower, *War Without Mercy: Race and Power in the Pacific War* (New York: Pantheon, 1986), 98–112, (Brooke-Popham quotes), 99; Christopher Thorne, *Allies of a Kind: The United States, Britain, and the War against Japan, 1941–1945* (New York: Oxford University Press, 1978), 3–5, 55–56; Frank Cuhel to Ermengarde Cuhel, July 14, 1940, FJCP.

3. Ronald Spector, *Eagle Against the Sun: The American War with Japan* (New York: Free Press, 1985), 45–47, 76; Stanley Karnow, *In Our Image: America's Empire in the Philippines* (New York: Random House, 1989), 281; Gerlof Homan, "The United States and the Netherlands East Indies: The Evolution of American Anticolonialism," *Pacific Historical Review* 53, no. 4 (November 1984): 423–46; [K. C.] Oei Tjong to Frank Cuhel, March 2, 1941, and Frank Cuhel to Raymie and Phil Barnes, February 17, 1941, FJCP.
4. Walter Foote, "The Netherlands Indies: Foreign Trade," February 22, 1944, Classified Records, Batavia Consul General in Melbourne, Australia, 1941–1945, RG84, NARA; Rupert Emerson, "The Dutch East Indies Adrift," *Foreign Affairs* 18, no. 4 (July 1940): 735–41; "Dutch East Indies' Value to U.S. Is Explained," *Chicago Tribune*, December 15, 1941, 32; Frank Cuhel, draft memoir on Netherlands East Indies, September 1939–December 1941, FJCP; Herman Theodore Bussemaker, "Paradise in Peril: The Netherlands, Great Britain, and the Defence of the Netherlands East Indies, 1940–41," *Journal of Southeast Asian Studies* 31, no. 1 (March 2000): 115–36; Shigeru Sato, "Indonesia 1939–1942: Prelude to the Japanese Occupation," *Journal of Southeast Asian Studies* 37, no. 2 (June 2006): 225–48.
5. Frank Cuhel to Ermengarde Cuhel, July 14, 1940, Oei Tjong Tjiat to Frank Cuhel, December 30, 1940, Frank Cuhel to Het Hoofd van de Afdeling Immigratiedienst, January 7, 1941, Frank Cuhel to Oei Tjong Tjiat, January 9, 1941, Frank Cuhel to M. C. Parsons, Jr, February 20, 1941, Frank Cuhel to Batavia Cricket Club, April 1, 1941, Frank Cuhel to Theron Hill, July 1, 1941, all in FJCP; P. M. Van Wulfften Palthe, "Leiodystonia, an Endocrine-Autonomic Neurosis of the Tropics," *Brain* 56, no. 4 (December 1933): 479–90; Warwick Anderson, *Colonial Pathologies: American Tropical Medicine, Race, and Hygiene in the Philippines* (Durham, NC: Duke University Press, 2006), 74–87, 130–42. On the Cricket Club's transformation into "The Box," see John McCutcheon Raleigh, *Pacific Blackout* (New York: Dodd, Mead, 1943), 120–21.
6. Orders to Dodge & Seymour, February–November 1941, Frank Cuhel to Tan Tek Peng, December 4, 1941, Frank Cuhel to Raymie and Phil Barnes, February 17, 1941, Frank Cuhel to George, March 7, 1941, Frank Cuhel to Theron Hill, July 1, 1941, Frank Cuhel to Basil Dahl, February 12, 1941, Frank Cuhel to V. A. Dodge, February 13, 1941, Frank Cuhel to Larry Seymour, May 1, 1941, and draft memoir on Netherlands East Indies, all in FJCP. Trade statistics in Gary Hess, "The Emergence of U.S. Influence in Southeast Asia," in Akira Iriye and Warren Cohen, eds., *American, Chinese, and Japanese Perspectives on Wartime Asia, 1931–1949* (Wilmington, DE: Scholarly Resources Books, 1990), 179–221.
7. Frank Cuhel to George, March 7, 1941, Frank Cuhel to Robert O'Boyle, March 10, 1941, and Frank Cuhel to Raymie and Phil Barnes, February 17, 1941, FJCP.

8. Frank Cuhel to George, March 7, 1941, and Frank Cuhel to Ermengarde Cuhel, July 14, 1940, FJCP. On Mary Jorzick, see "Hoosiers Who Helped Build and Operate the New York World's Fair," *Edinburg Daily Courier* (IN), August 11, 1939, 2; Ruth Millett, "We, the Women," *Times Recorder* (Zanesville, OH), November 22, 1937, 7.
9. Frank Cuhel to Edward Adler, February 27, 1941, Frank Cuhel to Robert O'Boyle, March 10, 1941, Frank Cuhel to Raymie and Phil Barnes, February 17, 1941, and Frank Cuhel to George, March 7, 1941, FJCP.
10. Spector, *Eagle Against the Sun*, 74–75; Karnow, *In Our Image*, 282–84, (quote) 283.
11. Frank Martin, "Many Americans Who Foresaw Jap War Stranded in Orient," *Los Angeles Times*, December 15, 1941, 4; Frank Hindman Golay, *Face of Empire: United States–Philippine Relations, 1898–1946* (Madison: University of Wisconsin-Madison Center for Southeast Asian Studies, 1998), 395; Lewis Gleeck, *The Manila Americans (1901–1964)* (Manila: Carmelo & Bauermann, 1977), 226, 236–38; Bernie Archer, *The Internment of Western Civilians under the Japanese, 1941–1945* (London: Routledge Curzon, 2004), 5, 33–55.
12. Amry Vandenbosch, *The Dutch East Indies: Its Government, Problems, and Politics* (1933; repr., Berkeley: University of California Press, 1944), (quote) 343, 346–47; Erle Dickover, confidential memo to Sec. of State, April 11, 1940, box 2631, RG165-R (Netherlands East Indies), NARA; William Dunn, *Pacific Microphone* (College Station: Texas A&M University Press, 1988); Raleigh, *Pacific Blackout*, 16, 64–70; Bayly and Harper, *Forgotten Armies*, (flying beer barrels) 107; A. C. Tjepkema, "Strategic Dilemmas of a Small Power with a Colonial Empire: The Netherlands East Indies, 1936–1941," in Wim Klinkert and Herman Amersfoort, eds., *Small Powers in the Age of Total War, 1900–1940* (Boston: Brill, 2011), 321–49.
13. Vandenbosch, *Dutch East Indies*, 348–49, 421; Tjepkema, "Strategic Dilemmas"; L. De Jong, *The Collapse of a Colonial Society: The Dutch in Indonesia during the Second World War* (Leiden: KITLV Press, 2002), 32–33; Jan van Apeldoorn, *Departure Delayed* (Melbourne: Robertson & Mullens, 1943), 196–97. A similar dilemma bedeviled US military officials in the Philippines who waited too long to build up a colonial army: Brian McAllister Linn, "Cerberus' Dilemma: The US Army and Internal Security in the Pacific, 1902–1940," in David Killingray and David Omissi, eds., *Guardians of Empire: The Armed Forces of the Colonial Powers, c. 1700–1964* (Manchester: Manchester University Press, 2000), 114–36.
14. Frank Cuhel to Larry Seymour, May 1, 1941, Frank Cuhel to A. Douglas, September 22, 1941, Oei Tjong Hauw to Frank Cuhel, October 6, 1941, Frank Cuhel to Oei Tjong Hauw, October 18, 1941, Kian Gwan to Dodge & Seymour, November 8, 1941, Frank Cuhel to Het Hoofd van de Afdeling Immigratiedienst, January 7, 1941, Frank Cuhel to the American Consul General, February 5, 1941, and Het Hoofd van den Immigratiedienst to Frank Cuhel, February 17, 1941, all in FJCP.

15. Frank Cuhel's secretary to Frank Cuhel, September 14, 1940, correspondence between Frank Cuhel and Dutch officials, December 1940–October 1941, and F. J. Cuhel income tax files, 1939–1941, FJCP.
16. Frank Cuhel broadcast, May 26, 1942, Frank Cuhel to Ermengarde Cuhel, September 26, 1941, Kian Gwan to Dodge & Seymour, November 8, 1941, V. A. Dodge to Frank Cuhel, November 12, 1941, Michael's Travel Bureau to Frank Cuhel, September 30, 1941, Frank Cuhel to Secretary of Buitenzorg Golf Club, September 9, 1941, and Frank Cuhel to M. S. Wartman-Taylor, October 29, 1941, FJCP.
17. Frank Cuhel to Het Departement van Oorlog, September 24, 1941, Hein ter Poorten to Frank Cuhel, September 27, 1941, Het Kantoor der Divisiecommandant memo, September 30, 1941, Frank Cuhel to Liem Djing Lioe, June 6, 1941, Frank Cuhel to Tong Sian Hok, August 15, 1941, Frank Cuhel memo, October 20, 1941, Frank Cuhel to Larry Seymour, October 28, 1941, Frank Cuhel broadcast, February 19, 1942, Batavia Kian Gwan import division memo, October 15, 1941, and American Foreign Insurance Association manager, Singapore branch office, to Frank Cuhel, October 23, 1941, FJCP; Herbert Bix, *Hirohito and the Making of Modern Japan* (New York, 2000), 397–415.
18. Tan Tek Peng to Frank Cuhel, November 26, 1941, FJCP; Bix, *Hirohito*, 396; Nicholas Tarling, *A Sudden Rampage: The Japanese Occupation of Southeast Asia, 1941-1945* (London: Hurst, 2001), 128–36; Ethan Mark, *Japan's Occupation of Java in the Second World War* (London: Bloomsbury, 2018), 2, 30, 70–71, 75–77, 82. On the development and varieties of pan-Asianism, see also Eri Hotta, *Pan-Asianism and Japan's War, 1931–1945* (New York: Palgrave Macmillan, 2007).
19. Freight receipt, December 6, 1941, and clipping, "Power of Both Britain and U.S. Needed for Japs, Says Cuhel," FJCP.
20. Van Apeldoorn, *Departure Delayed*, 178–79; Chandler Gardiner to Johnson Automatics Incorporated, December 11, 1941, box 2631, MID-NEI; R. E. Selfridge to Ermengarde Cuhel, December 10, 1941, FJCP.

Chapter 14

1. Juan Francisco de Cárdenas to Madrid, April 17 and 20, 1939, R-1083/16, AMAE; "Spanish Line Resumes Atlantic Run This Week," November 12, 1939, C4, and "Garcia & Diaz Reports Big Traffic Gain," December 3, 1939, B10, both in *New York Herald Tribune*; "Spanish Liner Arrives," *New York Times*, November 16, 1939, 47; New York City WPA Writers' Project, *A Maritime History of New York* (1941; repr., New York: Going Coastal, 2004), 5, 16, 235–39, 262; Charles H. C. Pearsall, "Transportation Problems," *Annals of the Academy of Political and Social Science* 204 (July 1939): 155–63; Robert Divine, *The Illusion of Neutrality* (Chicago: Quadrangle, 1962), 314–24, 331–35.

2. "Chilean Line Soon to Inaugurate 2 New Cruises to Latin America," November 5, 1939, 27, and Frank Reil, "Brooklyn Waterfront," January 27, 1941, 8, both in *Brooklyn Daily Eagle*; "Chilean Line Plans," December 20, 1939, 37, and "Chilean Liners to Re-enter N.Y. Service Oct. 19," October 3, 1939, 30, both in *New York Herald Tribune*; ads in *Time*, February 12, 1940, 52, and *Atlantic Monthly*, February 1940, 294; J. Edgar Hoover to Adolf Berle, February 27, 1942, Confidential 852.20200 March, Juan/30, box C185, RG59, NARA. Charter rates for South American trade shot up from 80 cents per ton before the war to $5.50 to $7.00 in 1940, and New York handled close to 70 percent of US trade with South America: WPA Writers' Project, *Maritime History of New York*, 226, 240.
3. T. G. Powell, *Mexico and the Spanish Civil War* (Albuquerque: University of New Mexico Press, 1981), 159–62.
4. Christian Leitz, *Sympathy for the Devil: Neutral Europe and Nazi Germany in World War II* (New York: New York University Press, 2001), 114, 121–22; Stanley Payne, *Franco and Hitler: Spain, Germany, and World War II* (New Haven, CT: Yale University Press, 2008), 26–31, 44–45, 62–65, 71–75, 87, (quote) 186–87; Javier Tusell, *Franco, España y la II Guerra Mundial: Entre el Eje y la Neutralidad* (Madrid: Temas de Hoy, 1995); Carlton Hayes, *Wartime Mission in Spain, 1942–1945* (New York: Macmillan, 1946), 69–70.
5. Leitz, *Sympathy for the Devil*, 118; Payne, *Franco and Hitler*, 101–4.
6. Brooke L. Blower, "New York City's Spanish Shipping Agents and the Practice of State Power in the Atlantic Borderlands of World War II," *American Historical Review* 119, no. 1 (February 2014): 111–41; Manuel Ros Agudo, *La Guerra Secreta de Franco (1939–1945)* (Barcelona: Critica, 2002); Christian Leitz, *Economic Relations between Nazi Germany and Franco's Spain, 1936–1945* (Oxford: Clarendon, 1996); Payne, *Franco and Hitler*, 115–27. On Patton, see airgram to Secretary of State, July 30, 1943, box 901, Visa and Passport Control Branch, RG165/G-2, NARA.
7. Ros Agudo, *Guerra Secreta*, 303–7; Confidential Office of Naval Intelligence report on the Spanish Falange, October 28, 1941, FW 852.202/7, reel 10, *SIFA*; George Hinman summary report on Falangist propaganda, April 2, 1942, folder 000.24 Falange, August 1, 1939–March 31, 1942, box 2, RG319, NARA; reports on the Falange, box 1003, Latin American Branch, Security Classified General Correspondence, 1941–1946, RG165/G-2, NARA.
8. Nicholas Cull, *Selling War: The British Propaganda Campaign against American "Neutrality" in World War II* (New York: Oxford University Press, 1996); reports and press releases from New York City, 1939–1941, folders 4 and 7, box 21 and folders 8 and 15, box 27, FFF; "Consulates Here Put in Busy Day," September 2, 1939, 3, and "Consulates Here Keep Late Hours," September 10, 1939, 45, both in *New York Times*; Theodore Irwin, *Inside the "Christian Front"* (Washington, DC: American Council on Public Affairs, 1940); Steven Jaffe, *New York at War: Four Centuries of Combat, Fear, and Intrigue in Gotham* (New York: Basic, 2012), 222–35.

9. "Ten Hurt by Bombs Here Near Red, Nazi Agencies," June 21, 1940, 1, 5, "Police Act to Foil Further Bombings," June 22, 1940, 17, "Police Die in Blast," July 5, 1940, 1–2, "Mayor at Scene, Reassures Public," July 5, 1940, 2, and "Bombing Is Third within Two Weeks in City," July 5, 1940, 2, all in *New York Times*.
10. "Nazi Library Aided by Consulate Here," *New York Times*, September 14, 1940, 5; statutory lists reprinted in Robert Matson, *Neutrality and Navicerts: Britain, the United States, and Economic Warfare, 1939–1940* (New York: Garland, 1994), 87–179; Hamilton Consulate General records, Bermuda, British Postal Censorship Extracts on Enemy Sympathizers in America, 1940–1943, RG84, NARA; reports on Falangism and fascism in New York City, 1939–1942, folder 000.24 Falange, box 2, RG319, NARA.
11. New York FBI report, July 23, 1942, case file 100-13382, Confidential 852.20200 March, Juan/43, box C185, RG59, NARA; Jacob Fuller, synopsis report, January 20, 1944, litigation case file 146-7-1883, box 13, RG60, NARA. On Gundlach's visits, see passenger manifests, which list Marcelino's Brooklyn address as his destination, for June 16, 1924, reel 3500, May 10, 1927, reel 4053, and January 24, 1933, reel 5285, *VANY*.
12. Oscar Lewis to A. Schwartz, June 28, 1943, and supplemental registration statements, case 149-522, box 42, RG60, NARA; J. Edgar Hoover to Adolf Berle, February 27, 1942, and FBI report, July 23, 1942, Confidential 852.20200 March, Juan/30 and 43, box C185, RG59, NARA. On Amsinck and Bachi, see British Embassy, Washington, DC, to Ministry of Economic Warfare, March 19, 1940, FO 837/1074, and Ministry of War Transport files, 1942–1944, MT 59/1455, TNA. On Spanish firms dependent on British capital, none of them represented by Garcia & Diaz, see Jesús Valdaliso, "The Rise of Specialist Firms in Spanish Shipping and Their Strategies of Growth, 1860 to 1930," *Business History Review* (Summer 2000): 267–300. James Gurge, who worked with Garcia & Diaz from the beginning and served as a sworn witness for Manuel's naturalization petition, had German-speaking parents from the Austro-Hungarian empire. Paul Boise, appointed to traffic manager upon Gurge's death in 1938, was the son of German immigrants: Bergen, New Jersey, 17A, reel 1019, and Kings, New York, 4B, reel 1157, *Census (1920)*; "James V. Gurge," *New York Times*, July 9, 1938, 13; *Traffic World* 62 (1938): 172; Bergen, New Jersey, 1B-2A, reel 2812, *Census* (1940).
13. "Streams of Germans Leave for Homeland," *New York Times*, March 28, 1941, 13; "Liner Leaves U.S. with 191 on Their Way to Germany," *Chicago Tribune*, March 27, 1941, 7; H. G. Foster report, February 2, 1942, litigation case file, 146-7-1883, box 13, RG60, NARA.
14. FBI report, November 1, 1940, quoted in H. G. Foster report, February 2, 1942, litigation case file, 146-7-1883, box 13, RG60, NARA.
15. "Europe's Late Mail off on Two Liners," *New York Times*, July 12, 1940, 33; clipping, Robert Waithman, "£4,000,000 for Nazis Found in Letters," *News Chronicle*, February 24, 1940, folder 9, box II:417, Pan Am; ads

for Fortra gift packages to Germany, folder 15, box 27, FFF; Hamilton Consulate General records, Bermuda, British Postal Censorship Extracts on Enemy Sympathizers in America, 1940–1943, RG84, NARA; Bermuda contraband control reports, January–March 1940, DEFE 1/145, TNA. See also Bradley Hart, *Hitler's American Friends: The Third Reich's Supporters in the United States* (New York: St. Martin's, 2018).

16. Matson, *Neutrality and Navicerts*, 28, 87–179; Gabriel Kolko, "American Business and Germany, 1930–1941," *Western Political Quarterly* 15, no. 4 (December 1962): 713–28; Hart, *Hitler's American Friends*, 131.

17. "Cargo Seizures by British Stir No U.S. Protest," *Chicago Tribune*, October 28, 1939, 3; Matson, *Neutrality and Navicerts*; Kenneth Benton, "The ISOS Years: Madrid, 1941–3," *Journal of Contemporary History* 30, no. 3 (July 1995): 359–410.

18. "All Spanish Ships Ordered Off Seas," *New York Times*, August 6, 1940, 12; secret report, "Economic Warfare Through Shipping Control," early 1941, BT 271/616, TNA.

19. Memorandum on Economic Pressure through Control of Shipping, July 11, 1940, report on ship warrant scheme, August 16, 1940, and secret note, August 29, 1940, MT 59/285, memo, January 7, 1941, FO 71/28738, Instructions to Governors of West Indian islands, January 13, 1941, and decypher, February 10, 1941, FO 371/28759, C. N. Stirling to Captain Hallifax, July 23, 1941, ADM 1/26874, all in TNA; Juan Francisco de Cárdenas to Ministerio de Asuntos Exteriores, August 4, 1940, R-1655/33, AMAE; "Events of Interest in Shipping World," *New York Times*, August 4, 1940, S8; Blower, "New York City's Spanish Shipping Agents."

20. Franklin Roosevelt, "'We Choose Human Freedom,'" May 27, 1941, 181–95, vol. 10, *FDRPA*; North Atlantic pilot chart, December 1939, and special warnings, ca. 1939, folder 32, box II: 7, Pan Am. By October 1942, thirteen Spanish ships would be sunk without warning and more would follow: Foreign Office memo, October 13, 1942, FO 371/31217, TNA.

21. Everett Nash, "American Aid for Spanish Needy," *Spain*, July 1, 1940; "Ship with American Cargo of Food Arrives in Spain," *Chicago Tribune*, June 11, 1940, 5; "Two Ships with Fully Navicerted Cargoes Get British Approval," *New York Times*, August 8, 1940, 34; "Greek Line Starts Regular Sailings to Mediterranean," *Washington Post*, September 18, 1940, 25. Manuel and Marcelino made much of the relief supplies they shipped, but their vessels were noticeably absent from the list of neutral ships chartered by the Red Cross during the war: David Miller, *Mercy Ships* (London: Continuum, 2008), 81.

22. "Francis Pershings Honored at Dinner," *New York Times*, September 6, 1940, 18; engagement notice, *Brooklyn Eagle*, October 20, 1941, 6; Oscar Lewis to Asher Schwartz, June 28, 1943, case 149-522, RG60, NARA; A. Roberts, undated report, folder Marques de Comillas, box 1169, RG319, NARA; "Undesirable Activities of Spanish and Portuguese Ships in the Atlantic," July 1, 1942, and J. Edgar Hoover to State Department,

September 14, 1943, 852.85/181 and 241, reel 31, *SIFA*; J. Edgar Hoover to Adolf Berle, February 4, 1944, 852.20210/2-444, box 5235A, RG59, NARA; W. N. Medlicott, *The Economic Blockade,* vol. I (London: Longmans, Green, 1952), (quote) 131, 453–57; Robert Wilcox, *Japan's Secret War* (New York: Morrow, 1985), esp. 21–34, 69–73, 80–85, 124–28; Javier Juárez Camacho, *Madrid Londres Berlín: Espías de Franco al Servicio de Hitler* (Madrid: Temas de Hoy, 2005), ch. 7. On refueling U-boats in Spanish waters, see Charles B. Burdick, "'Moro': The Resupply of German Submarines in Spain, 1939–1942," *Central European History* 3, no. 3 (September 1970): 256–84 and Ros Agudo, *Guerra Secreta*, ch. 3.

23. British Embassy memo, December 9, 1940, 711.0011 Unlawful Shipments/648, box 2101, RG59, NARA; C. N. Stirling to Captain Hallifax, July 23, 1941, ADM 1/26874, TNA.

24. "Cuba Holds Two as Spies," September 6, 1941, 5, "Cuban Falangist Hides," October 10, 1941, 10, "Guests of Franco Barred by British," October 14, 1941, 13, and "Held in Smuggling of Metal to Nazis," November 7, 1942, 17, all in *New York Times*; "Spanish Fascist Will Yield to Cuba," *Washington Post*, November 9, 1941, 10; G. Gordon to Hoover, April 15, 1941, 852.20211/4, reel 10; State Department and navy correspondence and intelligence, June–August 1942, 852.85/181-2, 189, and June–August 1943, 852.85/231, 240, reel 31, Carl Breuer memo, October 4, 1941, and State Department memo, December 11, 1942, 852.8591/114, 522, and J. Edgar Hoover to Adolf Berle, May 11 and July 28, 1942, 852.85/165, 175, reel 32, all in *SIFA*; New Orleans District intelligence report, April 1, 1943, folder Marques de Comillas, box 1169, RG319, NARA. Descriptions of Cuban security measures are given in folders Magallanes, box 1168, RG319, NARA, and Hoover to Berle, July 24, 1943, and accompanying report on *Marqués de Comillas*, 852.85/227, reel 32, *SIFA*. On Spanish extremism in Cuba, see Hoover to Berle, December 4, 1941, with report from Havana, October 9, 1941, 852.20237/67, reel 10, *SIFA*.

25. Jacob Fuller, synopsis report, January 20, 1944, litigation case file 146-7-1883, box 13, RG60, NARA.

26. Selwyn James, "'Appeasement' Faces Fresh Defeat in Franco's Spain," *PM*, March 7, 1941, 6–7; S. S., "Nazis Soft Pedal in Latin America," *Living Age*, April 1941, 139–42; "Trade with Axis Powers in Essential War Materials" and H. Con. Res. 30 by Mr. Coffee, May 5, 1941, 3550, 3602, H. Res. 225 by Mr. Coffee and "Investigation of Aid from the United States to the Axis Powers," June 5, 1941, 4723, 4735, "Is America Arming the Axis?" radio address, June 20, 1941, Appendix 1941–1942, A2989-91, all in *Congressional Record*; "Probe of U.S. Sales to Axis Sought," *Washington Post*, May 6, 1941, 4; I. F. Stone, "Snub-and-Sell Diplomacy," *Nation*, June 14, 1941, 687–88; Coffee, radio address, June 20, 1941, reprinted in "Is America Arming the Axis?" Appendix to *Congressional Record*, A2989-91.

27. "Naval Attaché of Italy Ousted by U.S. Departs," April 26, 1941, 7, and "Recalled Italian Diplomat Put on Ship at Bermuda," May 14, 1941, 6,

both in *Chicago Tribune*; L. H. Woolsey, "The Taking of Foreign Ships in American Ports," *American Journal of International Law* 35, no. 3 (July 1941): 497–506; Denis Smyth, *Diplomacy and Strategy of Survival: British Policy and Franco's Spain, 1940–41* (Cambridge: Cambridge University Press, 1986), 182–87; J. Sharp to J. Edgar Hoover, October 15, 1943, case 149-522, RG60, NARA; FBI New York Field Division survey of Spanish activities, September 1, 1942, folder 291.2 Spanish, box 396, RG319, NARA. On reimaging the boundaries of the Western Hemisphere, see Alan K. Henrikson, "The Map as an 'Idea': The Role of Cartographic Imagery during the Second World War," *American Cartographer* 2, no. 1 (1975): 19–53. On the Proclaimed List, see Max Paul Friedman, *Nazis and Good Neighbors: The United States Campaign against the Germans of Latin America in World War II* (New York: Cambridge University Press, 2003), 88–94. On Pan Am's covert Airport Development Program, see Stetson Conn and Byron Fairchild, *The Framework of Hemispheric Defense* (Washington, DC: Center of Military History, 1989), ch. 10.

28. Payne, *Franco and Hitler*, 133, 137–39, (quote) 140.
29. "Spanish Ship to Take Cargo for the Swiss," *New York Times*, September 6, 1941, 31; J. Cárdenas to State Department, December 23, 1941, 852.85/132; Swiss legation memo, December 23, 1941, 852.85/133, reel 31, *SIFA*; secret report, "Economic Warfare Through Shipping Control," early 1941, BT 271/616, TNA. On spotty intelligence on the Canaries, see memo to Welles, November 10, 1941, 852.6363/236, reel 13, naval intelligence report, February 10, 1942, 852.85/150, reel 25, and Max Thornburg memo, February 19, 1942, 852.24/1018, reel 31, all in *SIFA*; meeting notes, August 21, 1940, and list of Atlantic bunkering stations, August 25, 1940, MT 59/285, notes on Canaries, May 29, 1941, HS 6/912, TNA; British Embassy in Madrid to Ministerio de Asuntos Exteriores, February 19, 1940, R-1190/25, AMAE; Spanish security reports on "actividades anglófilas" in the Canaries, January–May 1942, *Documentos Inéditos para la Historia del Generalísimo Franco*, vol. III (Madrid: Fundación Nacional Ferancisco Franco, 1992), 210–14, 496–97, 532–45. On German plans for the Canaries, see Robert Whealey, *Hitler and Spain: The Nazi Role in the Spanish Civil War, 1936–1939* (Lexington: University of Kentucky Press, 1989), 121–24.
30. "Women Make Up Half of Travel Lists," *Chicago Tribune*, May 13, 1941, 7; "N.Y.-Lisbon Run Continues with Only 3 Vessels," *New York Herald Tribune*, June 8, 1941, B12; Ronald Weber, *The Lisbon Route: Entry and Escape in Nazi Europe* (Lanham, MD: Ivan R. Dee, 2011), 78–82; David S. Wyman, *Paper Walls: America and the Refugee Crisis* (Amherst: University of Massachusetts Press, 1968), 142, 150–54.
31. "Belgians Get Here with Gem Fortune," September 26, 1940, 25, "Spanish Ship Here after Mishap at Sea," December 7, 1940, 7, "4 Liners Bringing 1,000 Here in Next 3 Days," January 5, 1941, S8, "German Refugee Here After Flight," January 9, 1941, 11, "Composer's Scion Yields to Jazz," March 13, 1941, 11, "Viennese Author a Saddened Exile," March 25, 1941, 26, and

"Report Refugees Detained in Cuba," August 25, 1941, 16, all in *New York Times*; interrogations of passengers arriving on Spanish ships, boxes 1168-70, RG319, NARA.

32. "Cunard Line Lifts Eastbound Fares," *New York Times*, October 3, 1939, 48; Hoover to Berle and FBI memo, December 31, 1941, 800.01B11 Registration Garcia and Diaz/16, box 3101, RG59, NARA; H. G. Foster report, February 2, 1942, litigation case file 146-7-1883, box 13, RG60, NARA. For further comparison, Garcia & Diaz advertised $170 fares from New York to Spain in the mid-thirties: *New York Times* ad, April 12, 1936, XX5.

33. "Angry Refugees on Crowded Ship," August 21, 1941, 19, "555 Refugees," August 24, 1941, E2, and "Liner Will Charge $1,300 Third Class," July 14, 1942, 5, all in *New York Times*; Hoover to Berle and FBI memo, December 31, 1941, 800.01B11 Registration Garcia and Diaz/16, box 3101, RG59, NARA; Serrano Suñer to Compañía Trasatlántica, July 6, 1942, Compañía Trasatlántica to Ministerio de Asuntos Exteriores, July 7, 1942, Serrano Suñer to Cárdenas, July 8, 1942; Serrano Suñer telegram, October 15, 1941, and José Contreras to Compañía Trasatlántica, October 15, 1941, R-2246/57, AMAE; "Typhoid Found in Passengers Deboarded Here by Spanish Ship," *New York Herald Tribune*, June 3, 1941, 21.

34. H. F. White to the Surgeon General, September 15, 1941, folder 1, box 1, clippings, "Refugee Claims upon Navemar Total 3 Million," *New York Herald Tribune*, January 28, 1942, "30 on 'Hell Ship' Sue for $676,000," [unknown newspaper], September 18, 1941, and "Refugees Sue 'Hell Ship' For $725,000," *New York Post*, September 19, 1941, all in folder 3, box 1, SSNav.

35. H. F. White to the Surgeon General, September 15, 1941, folder 1, box 1, SSNav; Raissa Gutman, "Illness Hits at the Crowded 'Hell Ship,'" September 17, 1941, 28, and "Havana Stop Only Bright Day in 'Hell Ship's' Voyage," September 18, 1941, 27, both in *Los Angeles Daily News*.

36. H. F. White to Surgeon General, September 15, 1941, Theo DeMars to Saul Sperling, November 5, 1941, folder 1, and clipping, "Passengers Ask For $676,500 in Navemar Suits," *New York Herald Tribune*, September 19, 1941, folder 3, box 1, SSNav; "Ship, Packed Like a Cattle Boat with 769 Exiles," *New York Times*, September 13, 1941, 19.

37. "Refugee Claims Upon Navemar Total 3 Million"; "Refugees Sue 'Hell Ship' for $725,000"; Ministerio de Industria y Comercio prohibición, October 23, 1941, R-1190/83, AMAE.

38. Telegram, November 12, 1941, reel 9, *SIFA*; J. Edgar Hoover to Office of Naval Intelligence, December 2, 1941, and Military Intelligence Division report, December 17, 1941, folder Marques de Comillas, 1941–July 10, 1943, Third Naval district report, November 5, 1941, folder Marques de Comillas 1941–July 10, 1943, box 1169, G-2 report, November 5, 1941, folder Falange, August 1, 1939–March 31, 1942, box 2, all in RG319, NARA.

39. Victor Bernstein, "Franco Official Admits a Phalanx Exists Here," November 6, 1941, 10, Victor Bernstein, "Local Shipping Men, Once

Labeled in Senate as Spies, Greet Ship," November 7, 1941, 13, I. F. Stone, "Confidential Figures on Recent Shipments Arouse Washington Insiders," November 14, 1941, 3, I. F. Stone, "Huge Oil Leak to Axis Assailed in Congress," November 16, 1941, 2, and I. F. Stone, "Defense Board Halts U.S. Oil Shipments to Franco," November 23, 1941, 6, all in *PM*; R. B. Rogers to State Department, December 4, 1941, Fred Wright to Scott Lewis, November 15, 1941, and other protests to congressmen, Eleanor Roosevelt, etc., 852.24/957-92, 852.01/958, 852.6363/237-84, RG59, NARA. On the periodic withholding of oil to force Spanish cooperation, see Leonard Caruana and Hugh Rockoff, "An Elephant in the Garden: The Allies, Spain, and Oil in World War II," *European Review of Economic History* 11 (2007): 159–87.

40. Memos and notes, December 23, 1941–January 15, 1942, 852.85/132, 134A, 136, 140–1, reel 31, *SIFA*; Justice Department hearing, January 8, 1942, photostat of intercepted letter, Hunt, Hill and Betts to Marcelino Garcia and Manuel Diaz, August 6,1942, and other documents in folder 560 Isla de Tenerife, box 1165, RG319, NARA; statement of Fernand DeChambre and Customs Agents Pike and Dougherty reports, January 15, 1942, folder 711.00111 Unlawful Shipments/591–720.5, box 2101, RG59, NARA; Garcia & Diaz communication, January 9, 1942, R-1330/59, AMAE. On March, see Hugh Thomas, *The Spanish Civil War* (New York: Harper, 1986), 194, 276, 339–40; Ros Agudo, *Guerra Secreta*, 74–75, 85–88; 852.20200 March, Juan, reel 10, *SIFA*; Instituto de Moneda Extranjera to Don Juan March, September 17, 1942, and March's undated response, *Documentos Inéditos para la Historia del Generalísimo Franco*, vol. III, 587–607.

41. E. H. Kellogg had delivered between 150 and 230 drums of oil to Trasmediterránea ships on at least four prior occasions since July: Garcia & Diaz to Cía. Trasmediterránea, March 2, 1943, R-1330/59, AMAE.

42. Lawyers' logs, June 8, 1942, and August 7, 1942, and Hunt, Hill & Betts to Manual Diaz and Marcelino Garcia, August 6, 1942, Confidential 852.20200 March, Juan/42, box C185, RG59, NARA; Marcelino Garcia to Francis Biddle, December 31, 1941, box 3, RG60, NARA; "Spanish Ship Held," December 16, 1941, 22, and "Spanish Ship Seized under Enemy Law," December 17, 1941, 18, both in *New York Times*; "Seizure Bares Vast Spanish Smuggle Ring," *New York Daily News*, December 17, 1941, 4; "GARCIA y DIAZ, Agentes de Franco, Detenidos," *España Libre*, December 19, 1941, 1. On Fennelly, see "Leo Fennelly Dies at 81," *New York Times*, April 3, 1979, C18. The *New York Herald Tribune* claimed that even by 1941, Manuel and Marcelino spoke "little or no English" and relied upon an interpreter at their arraignment: "Garcia and Diaz Face Neutrality Violation Case," *New York Herald Tribune*, December 16, 1941, 23.

Chapter 15

1. John McCutcheon Raleigh, *Pacific Blackout* (New York: Dodd, Mead, 1943), 67, 73, 82, 87, 102–3; Satyawati Suleiman, "The Last Days of

Batavia," *Indonesia* 28 (October 1979): 55–64; Dorothy Read and Ilse Evelijn Veere Smit, *End the Silence* (Greenbank, WA: Double-Isle, 2011), 20–22; Elly Touwen-Bouwsma, "The Indonesian Nationalists and the Japanese 'Liberation' of Indonesia: Visions and Reactions," *Journal of Southeast Asian Studies* 27, no. 1 (March 1996): 1–18; Frank Cuhel broadcast, January 8, 1942, FJCP.

2. Ronald Spector, *Eagle Against the Sun: The American War with Japan* (New York: Free Press, 1985), 105–8; Christopher Bayly and Tim Harper, *Forgotten Armies: The Fall of British Asia, 1941–1945* (London: Allen Lane, 2004), 110–17, 123–37.
3. Spector, *Eagle Against the Sun*, 106–13, 135; Stanley Karnow, *In Our Image: America's Empire in the Philippines* (New York: Random House, 1989), 288–95.
4. Spector, *Eagle Against the Sun*, 113, 129; William H. Bartsch, *Every Day a Nightmare: American Pursuit Pilots in the Defense of Java, 1941–1942* (College Station: Texas A&M University Press, 2010), 16.
5. Frank Cuhel to *News-Week* magazine, January 6, 1942, in reference to a cable he sent offering his services on December 10, 1941, FJCP; Raleigh, *Pacific Blackout*, 124; William J. Dunn, *Pacific Microphone* (College Station: Texas A&M University Press, 1988), 98–99; US consular officials estimated that their Batavia office assisted 1,100–1,200 Americans: Paul Paddoc and V. Lansing Collins, Jr., Work of the Consulate General, Batavia, December 8, 1941–February 28, 1942, May 5, 1942, Batavia Consul General in Melbourne, Australia, Classified General Records, 1941–1945, RG84, NARA.
6. Charles Rolo, *Radio Goes to War* (New York: Putnam, 1942), 13; David Holbrook Culbert, *News for Everyman: Radio and Foreign Affairs in Thirties America* (Westport, CT: Greenwood Press, 1976), 15; Daniel Headrick, *The Invisible Weapon: Telecommunications and International Politics, 1851–1945* (New York: Oxford University Press, 1991), 122, 180, 202–6; Susan Douglas, *Listening In: Radio and the American Imagination* (New York: Random House, 1999), 177; Jerome Berg, *On the Short Waves, 1923–1945: Broadcast Listening in the Pioneer Days of Radio* (Jefferson, NC: McFarland, 1999), 87, 108, 115, 152; Rudolf Mrázek, *Engineers of Happy Land: Technology and Nationalism in a Colony* (Princeton, NJ: Princeton University Press, 2002), 163–70, 182.
7. Culbert, *News for Everyman*, 5, 15, 24; Douglas, *Listening In*, 7, 23–24, 162–63, 166, 175–76, 189; Gerd Horten, *Radio Goes to War: The Cultural Politics of Propaganda during World War II* (Berkeley: University of California Press, 2002), 2, 13–14, 26–29, 32; David Hosley, *As Good As Any: Foreign Correspondence on American Radio, 1930–1940* (Westport, CT: Greenwood Press, 1984), 6, 19, 22, 24; Barbara Dianne Savage, *Broadcasting Freedom: Radio, War, and the Politics of Race, 1938–1948* (Chapel Hill: University of North Carolina Press, 1999); Douglas Craig, *Fireside Politics: Radio and Political Culture in the United States, 1920–1940*

(Baltimore: Johns Hopkins University Press, 2000), 164, 205–11, 228–33; Bruce Lenthall, *Radio's America: The Great Depression and the Rise of Modern Mass Culture* (Chicago: University of Chicago Press, 2007); Rolo, *Radio Goes to War*, 3, 12, 209.

8. Frank Cuhel to Ermengarde Cuhel, January 19, 1942, R. E. Selfridge to Ermengarde Cuhel, January 12, 1942, and clipping, Dora Jane Hamblin, "Power of Both Britain and U.S. Needed for Japs, Says Cuhel," *Cedar Rapids Gazette*, January 3, 1943, FJCP; Dunn, *Pacific Microphone*, 99, 104. Mutual, established in 1934, was a cooperative for networks unaligned with NBC and CBS: Larry Wolters, "Mutual Gears All Operations to War Effort," *Chicago Tribune*, December 27, 1942, S4; Culbert, *News for Everyman*, 15; L. D. Seymour to Ermengarde Cuhel, January 15, 1942, FJCP.
9. William McDougall to family, February 13, 1942, in William McDougall, Jr., *If I Get Out Alive: World War II Letters & Diaries of William H. McDougall Jr.* ed., Gary Topping (Salt Lake City: University of Utah Press, 2007), 47–48; Dunn, *Pacific Microphone*, 28, 92, 110, 122; L. D. Seymour to Ermengarde Cuhel, January 15, 1942, and Frank Cuhel to Ermengarde Cuhel, January 19, 1942, FJCP.
10. Douglas, *Listening In*, 180–82, 188–89, 194–95; Frank Cuhel to Larry Seymour, August 3, 1942, Frank Cuhel to Mr. Clapp, January 5 and 8, 1942, clipping, "Power of Both Britain and U.S. Needed for Japs, Says Cuhel," and Frank Cuhel broadcast, January 19, 1942, FJCP; Dunn, *Pacific Microphone*, 104.
11. Raleigh, *Pacific Blackout*, 50, 105, 109; Dunn, *Pacific Microphone*, 105; Frank Cuhel broadcasts, January 7, 8, and 12, 1942, FJCP. Frank was far from alone in overestimating early on the superior "dash" of fighters in the Indies. See, for example, "Indomitable Dutch," *New York Times*, January 18, 1942, SM8; "Borneo Head-hunters Ready to Round Up Jap Trophies," January 20, 1942, 3, and "U.S. and Dutch Deal Heaviest Blow to Japs," January 26, 1942, A, both in *Los Angeles Times*.
12. "Bartsch, *Every Day a Nightmare*, 54, 56; "Frank Cuhel, Once Iowa Hurdler Now Mutual's Voice in Batavia," *Washington Post*, February 22, 1942, L5. Frank misdated his broadcasts between January 8 and 19, thinking that it was still December.
13. Frank Cuhel broadcasts, January 19, 22, 23, and February 1, 1942, FJCP.
14. Frank Cuhel broadcasts, February 4 and 5, 1942, FJCP; Bartsch, *Every Day a Nightmare*, 57, 100; diary entries, January 12–29 and February 2–4, 16, and 23, 1942, in John Day, *An Officer in MacArthur's Court: A 39-month wartime odyssey through the Southwest Pacific Area from San Francisco through Java, Australia, New Guinea, and the Philippines* (Los Gatos, CA: Robertson Publishing, 2014), 84–95, 98–102, 112–13, 121–24; Frank Fujita, *Foo, A Japanese-American Prisoner of the Rising Sun: The Secret Prison Diary of Frank "Foo" Fujita* (Denton: University of North Texas Press, 1993), 57–59, 62–66.

15. W. L. White, *Queens Die Proudly* (New York: Harcourt, Brace, 1943), 10–11, 95, 144, 166, 172–79, 192, 198, 206–7; Bartsch, *Every Day a Nightmare*, 2–14, 56, 198, 338–39; George Weller, *Weller's War: A Legendary Foreign Correspondent's Saga of World War II on Five Continents*, ed. Anthony Weller (New York: Crown, 2009), 265, 316; Maurice Matloff and Edwin Snell, *Strategic Planning for Coalition Warfare, 1941–1942* (Washington, DC: Center of Military History United States Army, 1990), 131–36.
16. Crossed-out passages in Frank Cuhel broadcasts, January 19 and February 11, 1942, FJCP; Dunn, *Pacific Microphone*, 111.
17. Frank Cuhel broadcasts, January 8, 12, 15, 19, 22, 26, 29 and February 1 and 5, 1942, FJCP; unnamed importer quoted in Jan van Apeldoorn, *Departure Delayed* (Melbourne: Robertson & Mullens, 1943), 194.
18. Spector, *Eagle Against the Sun*, 56-59, 66, 114, 123, 127–28; Bartsch, *Every Day a Nightmare*, 14–16; Mark Stoler, "George C. Marshall and the 'Europe-First' Strategy, 1939-1951: A Study in Diplomatic as well as Military History" *Journal of Military History* 79, no. 2 (April 2015): 293–316; Matloff and Snell, *Strategic Planning for Coalition Warfare*, 120–24. On population totals for US nationals in the Philippines, Guam, and American Samoa, see Daniel Immerwahr, *How to Hide an Empire: A History of the Greater United States* (New York: Farrar, Straus, and Giroux, 2019), 11.
19. Frank Cuhel broadcasts, February 1, 9, 11, 14, 16, and 19, 1942 and Frank Cuhel to V. A. Dodge, May 18, 1942, FJCP; Harold Guard, *The Pacific War Uncensored: A War Correspondent's Unvarnished Account of the Fight Against Japan* (Philadelphia: Casemate, 2011), 58, 67, 86–89; Helen Colijn, *Song of Survival: Women Interned* (Ashland, OR: White Cloud Press, 1995), 75–77; Bayly and Harper, *Forgotten Armies*, 120–21, 137–39, 148; Bernice Archer, *The Internment of Western Civilians under the Japanese, 1941–1945* (London: Routledge Curzon, 2004), 42–49.
20. Imamura Hitoshi, "Java in 1942," in Anthony Reid and Oki Akira, eds., *The Japanese Experience in Indonesia: Selected Memoirs of 1942–1945* (Athens: Ohio University Center for International Studies, 1986), 31–77; Ethan Mark, *Japan's Occupation of Java in the Second World War* (London: Bloomsbury, 2018), 28–29.
21. Frank Cuhel broadcast, February 14, 1942, FJCP.
22. Frank Cuhel broadcast, February 14, 1942, FJCP; Bayly and Harper, *Forgotten Armies*, 144.
23. Frank Cuhel broadcasts, February 2, 16, and 19, 1942; "Dutch East Indies: Its Vast Riches Tempt Japan," *Life*, January 22, 1940, 54–65; Johan Fabricius, *East Indies Episode: An Account of the Demolitions Carried Out and Some Experiences of the Staff in the East Indies Oil Areas of the Royal Dutch Shell Group during 1941 and 1942* (London: Shell Petroleum, 1949), 86, 91–93, 102, 116; Bergen Herod, report on petroleum in Sumatra, February 16, 1942, confidential interview with Jefferson Davis, May 4, 1942, Naval Attaché Intelligence report, summary letter from E. J.

Sadler to Walace Phillips, June 18, 1942, and transcript of interview with evacuated Standard Vacuum employees, May 25, 1942, box 2631, RG165-R (Netherlands East Indies), NARA.

24. Raleigh, *Pacific Blackout*, 48-9; Walter Foote, confidential memo, "The Fall of the Netherlands Indies," May 29, 1942, and suppressed *Sydney Morning Herald* article from March 6, 1942, Batavia Consul General in Melbourne, Australia, Classified General Records, 1941–1945, RG84, NARA.

25. Foote, "The Fall of the Netherlands Indies"; Frank Cuhel broadcasts, February 16 and 19, 1942, FJCP; W. L. White, "Queens Die Proudly: Part II," *Reader's Digest* 42 (May 1943): 111–44; Mrázek, *Engineers of Happy Land*, 171, 189.

26. Frank Cuhel broadcast, February 21, 1942, FJCP; Paul Paddoc and V. Lansing Collins, Jr., Work of the Consulate General, Batavia, December 8, 1941–February 28, 1942, May 5, 1942, Batavia Consul General in Melbourne, Australia, Classified General Records, 1941–1945, RG84, NARA.

27. Frank Cuhel broadcast, February 28, 1942, FJCP; Bartsch, *Every Day a Nightmare*, 198–202, 284–7; diary entry, February 23, 1942, in Day, *An Officer in MacArthur's Court*, 121–24; Ronald Marcello, "Lone Star POWs: Texas National Guardsmen and the Building of the Burma-Thailand Railroad, 1942–1944," *Southwestern Historical Quarterly* 95, no. 3 (January 1992): 293–321; Kelly Crager, "'God Knows What's Going to Happen to Us': The Lost Battery of Texas's 'Lost Battalion' during World War II," *Southwestern Historical Quarterly* 112, no. 1 (July 2008): viii–32.

28. Frank Cuhel broadcast, February 26, 1942, FJCP.

29. Bartsch, *Every Day a Nightmare*, 203, 283, 285; Paul Paddoc and V. Lansing Collins, Work of the Consulate General, Batavia, December 8, 1941–February 28, 1942, May 5, 1942, Batavia Consul General in Melbourne, Australia, Classified General Records, 1941–1945, RG84, NARA; Frank Cuhel to Oei Tjong Hauw, May 4, 1942, and Frank Cuhel to V. A. Dodge, May 18, 1942, FJCP; Dunn, *Pacific Microphone*, 113–15.

30. Frank Cuhel broadcasts, March 1 and 2, 1942, FJCP. For a comprehensive military history, see P. C. Boer, *The Loss of Java: The Final Battles for the Possession of Java Fought by Allied Air, Naval and Land Forces in the Period of 18 February–7 March 1942* (Singapore: National University of Singapore Press, 2011).

31. Frank Cuhel broadcast, March 2, 1942, FJCP.

32. Frank Cuhel broadcasts, ca. March 22 and June 1, 1942, Frank Cuhel to V. A. Dodge, May 18, 1942, Frank Cuhel draft, "Java to Australia," and clipping, "Power of Both Britain and U.S. Needed for Japs, Says Cuhel," FJCP; William McDougall to mother, February 28, 1942, in McDougall, *If I Get Out Alive*, 48–49; Dunn, *Pacific Microphone*, 122–25.

33. Frank Cuhel broadcast, ca. March 22, 1942, Frank Cuhel to Oei Tjong Hauw, May 4, 1942, Frank Cuhel to V. A. Dodge, May 18, 1942, and clipping, "Power of Both Britain and U.S. Needed for Japs, Says Cuhel,"

FJCP; Dunn, *Pacific Microphone*, 122–25; Chandler Gardiner to Johnson Automatics Incorporated, December 11, 1941, box 2631, RG165-R (Netherlands East Indies), NARA.

34. Diary entry, February 27, 1942, in Day, *An Officer in MacArthur's Court*, 125–27; Foote, "The Fall of the Netherlands Indies"; Dunn, *Pacific Microphone*, 122–25; Frank Cuhel broadcast, ca. March 22, 1942, and Frank Cuhel to V. A. Dodge, May 18, 1942, FJCP. Besides the four journalists and Dutch naval personnel, the *Janssens* carried a group of wounded US servicemen evacuated from the USS *Marblehead* and left under the care of Dr. C. M. Wassell. Two years later, Cecil B. DeMille would embellish on the servicemen's escape on board the *Janssens* in the Technicolor film, *The Story of Dr. Wassell*, starring Gary Cooper: Weller, *Weller's War*, 232, 241.
35. Frank Cuhel broadcast, ca. March 22, 1942, FJCP. Japanese forces picked off seventeen unarmed freighters departing Cilacap and captured three more. By March 5, seventeen more lay scuttled, many by the Dutch, in the harbor itself: Jeffrey Cox, *Rising Sun, Falling Skies: The Disastrous Java Sea Campaign of World War II* (Oxford: Osprey, 2014), 395–400.
36. Quotes from Dunn, *Pacific Microphone*, 128, and clipping, George Weller, "Bullets Play Tattoo on Ship," *Seattle Times*, March 16, 1942, FJCP. See also Frank Cuhel broadcast, ca. March 22, 1942, and clipping, Winston Turner, "Perilous Escape," *The West Australian*, March 17, 1942, 6, FJCP; George Weller dispatch, May 5, 1942, in Weller, *Weller's War*, 332–33.
37. Frank Cuhel broadcasts, February 9, 11, 14, 16, and 19, 1942, and Frank Cuhel to V. A. Dodge, May 18, 1942, FJCP; Bartsch, *Every Day a Nightmare*, 286. The Japanese sank an estimated forty Dutch vessels fleeing Java, with the loss of some three thousand lives: Ralph Ockerse and Evelijn Blaney, *Our Childhood in the Former Colonial Dutch East Indies: Recollections before and during Our Wartime Internment by the Japanese* (Xlibris, 2011), 203.
38. William McDougall, Jr., *Six Bells Off Java: A Narrative of One Man's Private Miracle* (New York: Scribner, 1948), chs. 6–8, (quote) 133; diary entries, March 5, 7, 12, and 13, 1942, in McDougall, *If I Get Out Alive*, 53–62; Fabricius, *East Indies Episode*, 123–35; Colijn, *Song of Survival*, 8–36, 53–55.
39. White, *Queens Die Proudly*, 239; Bartsch, *Every Day a Nightmare*, 287, 327–31.
40. Frank Cuhel broadcast, ca. March 22, 1942, Frank Cuhel to V. A. Dodge, May 18, 1942, and clipping, Winston Turner, "Perilous Escape," *The West Australian*, March 17, 1942, 6, FJCP.
41. Frank Cuhel broadcast, ca. March 22, 1942, Frank Cuhel to Mr. Clapp, January 5 and 8, 1942, and Harold Wagner to Ermengarde Cuhel, March 11, 1942, FJCP. Word that Frank had survived only reached the United States on March 17: R. E. Selfridge and L. R. Hodgson to Ermengarde Cuhel, March 17, 1942, FJCP.
42. Frank Cuhel broadcast, ca. March 22, 1942, FJCP; Dunn, *Pacific Microphone*, 131–33, 139. For other escapes from Cilacap and the messages

heard over the radio that week, see Day, *An Officer in MacArthur's Court*, 132–38, and van Apeldoorn, *Departure Delayed*, 220. Japanese officials judged their radio operation a factor in their quick subjugation of Java: report, "Conclusion of the Java Invasion Operation and the Operations of the Allied Forces," and report, "The Black Clandestine Broadcasts by the Southern Army," in Willem Remmelink, ed. and trans., *The Invasion of the Dutch East Indies, Compiled by the War History Office of the National Defense College of Japan* (Leiden: Leiden University Press, 2015), 574–85.

43. *Janssens* manifest, March 13, 1942, reel 91, NAA; Frank Cuhel to V. A. Dodge, May 18, 1942, FJCP.

Chapter 16

1. Ben Robertson to Lewis Gannett, August 8, 1941, folder 17, and Jeanne Gadsden to T. R. Waring, February 26, 1943, folder 21, box 2, BFRP; Ben Robertson, *Red Hills and Cotton: An Upcountry Memory* (1942; repr., with a new introduction by Lacy K. Ford, Jr., Columbia: University of South Carolina Press, 1991), xii, xxx–xxxi, 3, 29, 113. On reception, see review clippings, folder 12, box 1, BFRP; Katherine Woods, "In South Carolina's Upcountry," *New York Times*, August 23, 1942, BR5; Tony Stanley Cook, "Remembering the South Carolina Upcountry: Ben Robertson's *Red Hills and Cotton*," *Southern Studies* 26 (Fall 1987): 217–38. On growing pushback against the Lost Cause narrative, see Nina Silber, *This War Ain't Over: Fighting the Civil War in New Deal America* (Chapel Hill: University of North Carolina Press, 2018), 68, 135–36.
2. Robertson, *Red Hills and Cotton*, 294–95; Ben Robertson draft card, South Carolina, February 15, 1942, box 162, *WWII Reg;* Allan Bérubé, *Coming Out Under Fire: The History of Gay Men and Women in World War Two* (New York: Free Press, 1990), ch. 5; Margot Canaday, *The Straight State: Sexuality and Citizenship in Twentieth-Century America* (Princeton, NJ: Princeton University Press, 2009), ch. 2.
3. Telegram, Ralph Ingersoll to Ben Robertson, December 23, 1941, folder 17, box 2, clipping, Frances Smythe, "Says Southerners Can Appreciate Conditions Prevailing in Russia," folder 105, box 11, BFRP; Paul Milkman, *PM: A New Deal in Journalism, 1940–1948* (New Brunswick, NJ: Rutgers University Press, 1997), 99–103.
4. Ralph Ingersoll memo, March 15, 1942, PPF 6870, Ralph Ingersoll to General Watson, March 15, 1942, and memo for General Watson, April 2, 1942, PPF 6646, FDRL; entry declaration #2945867, April 4, 1942, *Passenger and Crew Manifests of Airplanes Arriving at San Juan, Puerto Rico*, RG85, NARA; draft, "With the Ferry Pilots," folder 93, press relay, May 24, 1942, folder 90, box 9, and clipping, Ben Robertson, "Yanks Inspired by Corregidor," *PM*, ca. May 10, 1942, folder 12, box 1, BFRP; Edgar Snow, *People on Our Side* (New York: Random House, 1944), 6–7; Ben Robertson, "Passengers Come Last," *PM*, April 29, 1942, 18.

5. Ulysses Lee, *The Employment of Negro Troops* (Washington, DC: Office of the Chief of Military History, 1966), 609–22; John Stevens, "Black Correspondents of World War II cover the Supply Routes," *Journal of Negro History* 57, no. 4 (October 1972): 395–406; Daniel Hutchinson, "Defending the Lands of their Ancestors: The African American Military Experience in Africa during World War II," in Judith Byfield, Carolyn Brown, Timothy Parsons, and Ahmad Alawad Sikainga, eds., *Africa and World War II* (Cambridge: Cambridge University Press, 2015), 401–19; David Reynolds, *Rich Relations: The American Occupation of Britain, 1942–1945* (London: Phoenix Press, 1995), 216–17; Kate Darian-Smith, *On the Home Front: Melbourne in Wartime, 1939–1945* (Melbourne: Melbourne University Press, 1990), 216.
6. Ben Robertson press collect, May 8, 1942, folder 90, box 9, BFRP. For this tendency, see also John Kneebone, *Southern Liberal Journalists and the Issue of Race, 1920–1944* (Chapel Hill: University of North Carolina Press, 1985), 176, 183–86. On others whose racial politics instead shifted left during the war, see Glenda Gilmore, *Defying Dixie: The Radical Roots of Civil Rights, 1919–1950* (New York: Norton, 2008), 203–4, 234–35, 383.
7. Snow, *People on Our Side*, 5–6; Robertson, "Cairo's Beer From Jersey," *PM*, May 4, 1942, 19; press relay, May 24, 1942, folder 90, box 9, BFRP.
8. Draft, July 25, 1942, folder 96A, box 10, BFRP; Gilmore, *Defying Dixie*.
9. Press collect, June 23, 1942, folder 96, and draft, July 25, 1942, folder 96A, both in box 10, BFRP; Ben Robertson, "Journey Into Russia One Year After," *PM*, June 25, 1942, 15; Ben Robertson, "Second Front Would Boom Soviet Morale," *PM*, July 15, 1942, 18. On the alternative, increasingly treacherous Arctic route into the Soviet Union, see Eddy Gilmore, *Me and My Russian Wife* (New York: Greenwood Press, 1968), 19–22, 52; Larry LeSueur, *Twelve Months That Changed the World* (New York: Knopf, 1943), 3–19, 27–52; Jay E. Caldwell, *Erskine Caldwell, Margaret Bourke-White, and the Popular Front: Photojournalism in Russia* (Athens: University of Georgia Press, 2016), 205–12.
10. Draft, July 25, 1942, folder 96A, box 10, BFRP.
11. Ben Robertson, "How Russia's Capital Looks After a Hard Year of War," *PM*, July 20, 1942, 14; undated draft, folder 96, and draft, July 30, 1942, folder 96A, both in box 10, BFRP.
12. John Erickson, *The Road to Stalingrad: Stalin's War with Germany*, vol. 1 (London: Weidenfeld and Nicolson, 1975), 104–5, 113–16, 233, 235; Richard Overy, *Russia's War: Blood Upon the Snow* (New York: Penguin Putnam, 1997), 102–3, 109, 112–13, 121; Evan Mawdsley, *Thunder in the East: The Nazi-Soviet War, 1941–1945* (2005; repr., London: Bloomsbury, 2016), 54–55; Rodric Braithwaite, *Moscow 1941: A City and Its People at War* (London: Profile Books, 2006), 66; Rebecca Manley, *To Tashkent Station: Evacuation and Survival in the Soviet Union at War* (Ithaca, NY: Cornell University Press, 2009), 1, 7–8. Caldwell quoted in Ralph

Levering, *American Opinion and the Russian Alliance, 1939–1945* (Chapel Hill: University of North Carolina Press, 1976), 54.

13. Timothy Snyder, *Bloodlands: Europe between Hitler and Stalin* (New York: Basic, 2010), esp. 160–66, 173–84, 194–96, 219–22. See also Carroll P. Kakel, *The American West and the Nazi East: A Comparative and Interpretive Perspective* (New York: Palgrave Macmillan, 2011).

14. Memo, October 1941, in Alexander Hill, *The Great Patriotic War of the Soviet Union, 1941–1945: A Documentary Reader* (London: Routledge, 2009), 68–69; John Barber and Mark Harrison, *The Soviet Home Front, 1941–1945* (London: Longman, 1991), 66–67, 118; Overy, *Russia's War*, 106–9, 200; Snyder, *Bloodlands*, xiv. On Leningrad, see Alexis Peri, *The War Within: Diaries from the Siege of Leningrad* (Cambridge, MA: Harvard University Press, 2017), 24.

15. Overy, *Russia's War*, 124–31, 146; Catherine Merridale, *Ivan's War: Life and Death in the Red Army, 1939–1945* (New York: Metropolitan Books, 2006), 120; evacuation order, October 15, 1941, and decree, October 19, 1941, in Hill, *Great Patriotic War*, 70–71; Erickson, *Road to Stalingrad*, 220, 250; Manley, *To Tashkent Station*, 58–63, 107–17, 120–21; Henry Cassidy, *Moscow Dateline, 1941–1943* (Boston: Houghton Mifflin, 1943), 150–54.

16. "Russian Mud and Blood Stall German Army," *Life*, November 17, 1941, 33–36; Vasily Grossman, *A Writer at War: A Soviet Journalist with the Red Army, 1941–1945*, ed. and trans. Antony Beevor and Luba Vinogradova (New York: Vintage, 2005), 36–38, (quote) 38; Overy, *Russia's War*, 146–47, 150–58; Merridale, *Ivan's War*, 117–19; dispatches from Yevgeny Petrov, December 16, 1941, Boris Polevoy, December 17, 1941, and Ilya Ehrenburg, December 30, 1941, reprinted in S. Krasilshchik, ed., *World War II: Dispatches from the Soviet Front*, trans. Nina Bouis (New York: Sphinx Press, 1985), 46–48, 52–57; Stalin speech, November 6, 1941, in Hill, *Great Patriotic War*, 75–76.

17. Ilya Ehrenburg dispatch, April 20, 1942, in Krasilshchik, *World War II: Dispatches*, 97; Erickson, *Road to Stalingrad*, 232–33, 236; Barber and Harrison, *Soviet Home Front*, 127; Merridale, *Ivan's War*, 3; Robertson, "Journey into Russia One Year After."

18. Raymond Dawson, *The Decision to Aid Russia, 1941* (Chapel Hill: University of North Carolina Press, 1959), 71–72, (quote) 73, 80–86, 102–3, 108, 139–40, 218–20; Levering, *American Opinion and the Russian Alliance*, 43, 46, 49.

19. Dawson, *Decision to Aid Russia, 1941*, xi-xii, 70–1, 122, 261; Levering, *American Opinion and the Russian Alliance*, 48–9; George C. Herring, *Aid to Russia, 1941-1946* (New York: Columbia University Press, 1973), xiii, 10–12, 15–22.

20. Herring, *Aid to Russia*, 12–13, 34, 39–46, 55–57, 66, 72–73; Ilya Ehrenburg dispatch, April 20, 1942, reprinted Krasilshchik, *World War II: Dispatches*, 99; Mark A. Stoler, *The Politics of the Second*

Front: American Military Planning and Diplomacy in Coalition Warfare, 1941–1943 (Westport, CT: Greenwood, 1977), 28, 30; Stalin speech, November 6, 1941, in Hill, *Great Patriotic War of the Soviet Union*, 75–76.

21. Levering, *American Opinion and the Russian Alliance*, 68, (DDE quote) 78; Stoler, *Politics of the Second Front*, 3, 28–33; Herring, *Aid to Russia*, xiv, 58–61, (FDR quote) 61.
22. Stoler, *Politics of the Second Front*, 46–49.
23. "The Text of Molotoff's Statement to Supreme Soviet on Allied Accords," *New York Times*, June 20, 1942, 4; press collect, summer 1942, folder 94, box 9, draft, June 24, 1942, and undated draft, folder 96A, box 10, BFRP; LeSueur, *Twelve Months*, 249; Erickson, *Road to Stalingrad*, 397–98; telegram, Maurice Hindus, Ben Robertson, and Eddy Gilmore to Wendell Willkie, June 24, 1942, folder Trip to Russia and Mideast, box 114, WWP. For Willkie's subsequent trip, see Samuel Zipp, *The Idealist: Wendell Willkie's Wartime Quest to Build One World* (Cambridge, MA: Belknap, 2020).
24. Draft, June 24, 1942, folder 96A, undated draft, June 1942, and press collects, July 15 and 19, 1942, folder 96, all in box 10, BFRP; Robertson, "How Russia's Capital Looks After a Hard Year of War"; Ben Robertson, "Russians Now Look to Urals," *PM*, July 22, 1942, 14; LeSueur, *Twelve Months*, 101; Walter Graebner, *Round Trip to Russia* (Philadelphia: Lippincott, 1943), 61–62; Philip Jordan, *Russian Glory* (London: Cresset, 1942), 162; Barber and Harrison, *Soviet Home Front*, 69. Ben arrived at Kuybyshev on June 18: Walter Thurston to Secretary of State, June 19, 1942, 811.Robertson, Ben, box 26, Moscow Embassy, Records of the Consular Section, RG84, NARA.
25. Ben Robertson, "It's Total War in Kuibyshev," June 28, 1942, 14, and "Ben Robertson Finds the July 4th Spirit," July 5, 1942, 18, both in *PM*. For an example of editors taking out Ben's Confederate musings, compare press wire, July 13, 1942, folder 96, box 10, BFRP and Ben Robertson, "Second Front Would Boom Soviet Morale," *PM*, July 15, 1942, 18.
26. Overy, *Russia's War*, 202-3; Merridale, *Ivan's War*, 132.
27. Press collect, July 15, 1942, folder 96, undated draft and draft, July 30, 1942, folder 96A, box 10, BFRP; Karel C. Berkhoff, *Motherland in Danger: Soviet Propaganda during World War II* (Cambridge, MA: Harvard University Press, 2012), 74, 99–100. Ben was far from the only American visitor to give idealized accounts of the wartime Soviet Union. See, for example, Wendell Willkie, *One World* (New York: Simon & Schuster, 1943), 50–54.
28. Wire report draft, ca. July 1942, folder 96A, box 10, BFRP; Jordan, *Russian Glory*, 143; Alexander Werth, *Moscow War Diary* (New York: Knopf, 1942), 27; Quentin Reynolds, *Only the Stars Are Neutral* (New York: Random House, 1942), 64–65, 71, 82, 86–87, 107, 136, 159, 207; Graebner, *Round Trip to Russia*, 54, 58–59, (quote) 182–83; LeSueur, *Twelve Months*, 79, 235, 243, 256; Cassidy, *Moscow Dateline*, 80; Robert W. Desmond, *Tides of*

War: World News Reporting, 1940–1945 (Iowa City: University of Iowa Press, 1984), 165, 170, 173–77; Alice Leone Moats, "Russia Uncensored," *Collier's*, April 25, 1942, 40–44.

29. Berkhoff, *Motherland in Danger*, 3–5, 12–13, 21, 30–4; Phillip Knightley, *The First Casualty: The War Correspondent as Hero and Myth-Maker from the Crimea to Kosovo* (1975; repr., Baltimore: Johns Hopkins University Press, 2000) ch. 11; press collect, July 21, 1942, folder 96, and draft, July 30, 1942, folder 96A, box 10, BFRP; Gilmore, *Me and My Russian Wife*, 9, 59, 81; Leland Stowe, *They Shall Not Sleep* (New York: Alfred A. Knopf, 1944), 214; Graebner, *Round Trip to Russia*, 67–69, 71–72; Fred Myers to Joseph Barnes, August 24, 1942, folder Wendell Willkie World Tour, 1942, Russia, box 15, ITVDP. Such editorializing was sometimes question by other reporters. See, for example, James Brown, *Russia Fights* (New York: Scribner, 1943), 124–25.

30. Erskine Caldwell, "Behind Russian Lines," *Life*, July 28, 1941, 21; Moats, "Russia Uncensored"; Graebner, *Round Trip to Russia*, 60, 74–75, 166–67; Stowe, *They Shall Not Sleep*, 220–23; Jordan, *Russian Glory*, 162; LeSueur, *Twelve Months*, 84, 214–16; press collects, July 15 and 19, 1942, folder 96, and wire report draft, ca. July 1942, folder 96A, box 10, BFRP; Robertson, "How Russia's Capital Looks After a Hard Year of War"; Robertson, "Russians Now Look to Urals." On wartime Soviet food policies and widespread hunger, see Wendy Z. Goldman and Donald Filtzer, *Fortress Dark and Stern: The Soviet Home Front during World War II* (New York: Oxford University Press, 2021), chs. 3–4.

31. Berkhoff, *Motherland in Danger*, 30–34, 46–47, 74, 96–97, 122–33; LeSueur, *Twelve Months*, 223–24. See also, Stowe, *They Shall Not Sleep*, 212–13; Brown, *Russia Fights*, 44, 85.

32. Draft, summer 1942, folder 96A, press collect, July 2, 1942, folder 96, box 10, BFRP; Cassidy, *Moscow Dateline*, 236; LeSueur, *Twelve Months*, 225, 232–33; Stowe, *They Shall Not Sleep*, 226–28; dispatches from Yevgeny Petrov, June 25, 1942, and Boris Voitekhov, June 26, 1942, in Krasilshchik, *World War II: Dispatches*, 113–17, 122–26; Merridale, *Ivan's War*, 148–50; Mawdsley, *Thunder in the East*, 135–36. On German summer offensive strategy, see Gerhard L. Weinberg, *A World at Arms: A Global History of World War II* (1994; repr., Cambridge: Cambridge University Press, 2005), 409–16.

33. Brown, *Russia Fights*, 20–26; LeSueur, *Twelve Months*, 223; Stowe, *They Shall Not Sleep*, 226–27, (quote) 236; Herring, *Aid to Russia*, 62–65.

34. Press collect, July 21, 1942, folder 96, box 10, BFRP; Cassidy, *Moscow Dateline*, 237; Graebner, *Round Trip to Russia*, 47–48, 169; LeSueur, *Twelve Months*, 238, 245, 302; Stowe, *They Shall Not Sleep*, 220, 228–30.

35. Press collects, July 21, 1942, folder 96, draft, July 27, 1942, folder 96A, box 10, undated draft, folder 94, box 9, BFRP; Robertson, "Second Front Would Boom Soviet Morale"; Ben Robertson, "Russia Fears Another 'Too Little, Too Late,'" *PM*, July 16, 1942, 15; Ben Robertson, "Until Second

Front Is Opened, U.S. Shares Blame for Defeats," *Boston Globe*, July 17, 1942, 4; Robertson, "Russians Now Look to Urals."

36. LeSueur, *Twelve Months*, 265–67; Cassidy, *Moscow Dateline*, 238–39, (quote) 238; Stowe, *They Shall Not Sleep*, 231–32; Grossman, *Writer at War*, 116–17; Stalin's Order No. 227, July 28, 1942, in Hill, *Great Patriotic War*, 100–2.
37. Press collect, summer 1942, folder 94, box 9, undated draft, folder 96, and draft, Moscow, July 29, 1942, folder 96A, box 10, BFRP.
38. Draft, July 27, 1942, folder 96A, box 10, BFRP; Levering, *American Opinion and the Russian Alliance*, 73–74, 77, 81–86; "Second Front?" *Life*, July 27, 1942, 21–27.
39. Robertson, "Russia Fears Another 'Too Little, Too Late' "; Ralph Parker, "Russians Make War with Hate in their Hearts," *New York Times*, July 26, 1942, E3; LeSueur, *Twelve Months*, 229, 268–69; Leland Stowe, *They Shall Not Sleep*, 228–32; Graebner, *Round Trip to Russia*, 114; Maurice Hindus, *Mother Russia* (Garden City, NY: Doubleday, Doran, 1942), 372; press collect, summer 1942, folder 94, box 9, BFRP.
40. Ben Robertson, "Moscow Fears 'Explanations,'" *PM*, August 7, 1942, 18; drafts, July 25, 1942, August 3, 1942, and undated, folder 96A, undated draft, folder 96, all in box 10, BFRP; Robertson, "Moscow Fears 'Explanations'." See also Ben Robertson, "Russia Loses Hope of Aid," August 14, 1942, 15, and "We'll Fight Beside Soviets," August 20, 1942, 19, both in *PM*.
41. Robertson, "Moscow Fears 'Explanations' "; Erickson, *Road to Stalingrad*, 400–1; Stoler, *Politics of the Second Front*, 59–62.
42. Herring, *Aid to Russia*, 66–68; Leonid Leonov, "To an Unknown American Friend," August 1942, reprinted in Krasilshchik, *World War II: Dispatches*, 127–34.
43. Undated draft, ca. August 1942, folder 96A, box 10, BFRP; Cassidy, *Moscow Dateline*, 238–39; LeSueur, *Twelve Months*, 266, 287–88; Stowe, *They Shall Not Sleep*, 231–32; Graebner, *Round Trip to Russia*, 130.
44. Grossman, *Writer at War*, 118–19; LeSueur, *Twelve Months*, 295; Stowe, *They Shall Not Sleep*, 236–37; Overy, *Russia's War*, 205–6; Weinberg, *World at Arms*, 422; Mawdsley, *Thunder in the East*, 152, 155.
45. Draft, August 31, 1942, folder 96A, box 10, BFRP; LeSueur, *Twelve Months*, 284–87; Graebner, *Round Trip to Russia*, 150–52; Brown, *Russia Fights*, 97–111; Berkhoff, *Motherland in Danger*, 48; Weinberg, *World at Arms*, 427; Ben Robertson, "Nazis Strive to Cut Russia In Two Before Snowfall," *PM*, August 26, 1942, 18.
46. Barber and Harrison, *Soviet Home Front*, 39–40; Merridale, *Ivan's War*, 159–65; David M. Glantz, *Colossus Reborn: The Red Army at War, 1941–1943* (Lawrence: University Press of Kansas, 2005), 4 and passim.
47. Graebner, *Round Trip to Russia*, 114; Herring, *Aid to Russia*, 69, 80–81, 89; Berkhoff, *Motherland in Danger*, 251–55, 261–68.
48. Ben Robertson, "'A Humiliating Summer for Americans in Russia,'" *PM*, September 28, 1942, 19. Ben exited the Soviet Union on September 4: Ben

Robertson to Llewellyn Thompson, September 11, 1942, and US Embassy, Kuybyshev, to People's Commissariat for Foreign Affairs, October 5, 1942, file 350-Robertson, Ben, box 25, Moscow Embassy, Records of the Consular Section, RG84, NARA. For the Moscow-Kuybyshev-Tehran air route, see also Reynolds, *Only the Stars Are Neutral*, 216–28; Jordan, *Russian Glory*, 175–80; Cassidy, *Moscow Dateline*, 204–6; LeSueur, *Twelve Months*, 339–41; Brown, *Russia Fights*, 244–49.

Chapter 17

1. Robert H. Ferrell, ed., *The Eisenhower Diaries* (New York: Norton, 1981), 64; Dwight D. Eisenhower, *Crusade in Europe* (Garden City, NY: Doubleday, 1948), 52–54, 68–71, 77; Victor Davis Hanson, *The Second World Wars: How the First Global Conflict Was Fought and Won* (New York: Basic, 2017), 449–52.
2. George Spiegelberg to Joseph Millbourn, November 5, 1941, and George Spiegelberg to Alastair Fraser, January 15, 1942, GASP; oral history, June 7, 1960, Robert P. Patterson Project, CCOH; James Hagerty, "Stimson and Knox Disowned by Party," *New York Times*, June 21, 1940, 1, 4.
3. George Spiegelberg to J. R. Millbourn, January 31, 1942, GASP.
4. George Spiegelberg to Alastair Fraser, January 15, 1942, George Spiegelberg to J. R. Millbourn, January 31, 1942, and George Spiegelberg to Joseph Clark Baldwin, December 27, 1941, GASP.
5. George Spiegelberg to J. R. Millbourn, January 31, 1942, GASP.
6. War Department, "Standards of Physical Examination during Mobilization," *Selective Service Regulations, September 23, 1940, to February 1, 1942* (Washington, DC: US Government Printing Office, 1944), 339–76; Lee Kennett, *G.I.: The American Soldier in World War II* (Norman: University of Oklahoma Press, 1987), chs. 1–2; James Sparrow, *Warfare State: World War II Americans and the Age of Big Government* (New York: Oxford University Press, 2011), 203–8.
7. George to Helen Spiegelberg, March 2, 1943, scrapbook, vol. 1, and statement, army board proceedings, October 19, 1945, scrapbook, vol. 3, GASP. Though George likely knew Henry Stimson—both belonged to New York's Republican elite and had sat on the same Fusion Lawyers' Committee to reelect Mayor La Guardia—Robert Patterson, the War Department's main advocate for more flexible and aggressive recruitment options for skilled professionals, was likely the champion of George's case: "La Guardia Backed by Lawyers' Group," *New York Times*, October 24, 1937, N4; Keith Eiler, *Mobilizing America: Robert P. Patterson and the War Effort, 1940–1945* (Ithaca, NY: Cornell University Press, 1997), 250–55.
8. War Department temporary appointment letter, March 10, 1942, and War Department pay and allowance memo, scrapbook, vol. 1, George Spiegelberg to Conrad Snow, March 4, 1942, George Spiegelberg to Frank H. Sommer, March 12, 1942, and Frank Sommer to George Spiegelberg, March 30, 1942, GASP.

9. Eisenhower, *Crusade in Europe*, 55; brochure, "We Bought the Eiffel Tower," folder History, May 1942–September 1945, box 3589, and General Purchasing Board interim report, November 1, 1943, folder Report to Washington, 1943, box 6416, RG498, NARA; Edward Stettinius testimony, January 29, 1943, *Lend-Lease*, 4; Ronald Ruppenthal, *Logistical Support of the Armies* vol. 1 (1953; Washington, DC: Center of Military History, 1995), 32–35; David Reynolds, *Rich Relations: The American Occupation of Britain, 1942–1945* (1995; repr., London: Phoenix Press, 2000), 92–93, 108; efficiency report for George Spiegelberg, June 18, 1942, scrapbook, vol. 1, and Edward Greenbaum to Samuel Turnbull, September 9, 1943, scrapbook, vol. 2, GASP.
10. Rear Echelon, Services of Supply memo, May 26, 1942, secret War Department memos, May 18 and 26, 1942, and notes, scrapbook, vol. 1, GASP.
11. Telegram, George Spiegelberg to Helen Spiegelberg, June 17, 1942, and notes, scrapbook, vol. 1, GASP.
12. Mollie Panter-Downes, *London War Notes, 1939–1945* (1939; repr., New York: Farrar, Straus, and Giroux, 1971), 210–42; Juliet Gardiner, *Wartime: Britain, 1939–1945* (London: Headline, 2004), 611–13; Norman Longmate, *How We Lived Then: A History of Everyday Life during the Second World War* (1971; repr., London: Pimlico, 2002), 222, 260, 275, 321–32, 355, 485–87.
13. Eisenhower, *Crusade in Europe*, 54; Geoffrey Williamson, *Star-Spangled Square: The Saga of "Little America" in London* (London: Geoffrey Bles, 1956), 152–53; Ruppenthal, *Logistical Support of the Armies*, 76.
14. George Spiegelberg to Mr. Batch, December 2, 1942, folder Correspondence with Ministry of Works, E. C. Betts to George Spiegelberg, June 29, 1942, George Spiegelberg to Douglas MacKeachie, July 16, 1942, A. E. Sutherland to Wayne Allen, August 5, 1942, Spiegelberg memo, August 11, 1942, and Douglas MacKeachie memo, November 19, 1942, folder Correspondence—February 1942–December 1942—Purchase Procedure, meeting notes, November 3, 1942, and E. W. Playfair to George Spiegelberg, November 26, 1942, folder Correspondence with H.M. Treasury, General Purchasing Board interim report, November 1, 1943, folder Report to Washington, 1943, all in box 6416, and correspondence in folder Correspondence—Bills with HMSO, 1942, box 6414, RG498, NARA; "We Bought the Eiffel Tower."
15. Instructions for officers reporting for duty, June 16, 1942, secret memo, motor vehicle operator's permit, and handwritten notes, scrapbook, vol. 1, GASP. On the annex headquarters, see also "We Bought the Eiffel Tower"; Ruppenthal, *Logistical Support of the Armies*, 77; Reynolds, *Rich Relations*, 114.
16. Graham Smith, *When Jim Crow Met John Bull: Black American Soldiers in World War II Britain* (New York: St. Martin's, 1987), 83–84, 102; Reynolds, *Rich Relations*, 83–84, 217–18.

17. Stettinius testimony, *Lend-Lease*, 4; George Spiegelberg testimony, February 2, 1943, *Lend-Lease*, 49; "We Bought the Eiffel Tower"; Reynolds, *Rich Relations*, 92–93, 148–49. George's title was Recorder for the General Purchasing Board and the Board of Contracts and Adjustments.
18. "Agreement between the Governments of the United Kingdom and the United States of America on the Principles applying to Mutual Aid in the Prosecution of the War against Aggression" (London: His Majesty's Stationery Office, 1942), Acting British Consul General, New York, to Foreign Office, July 19, 1941, Halifax to Foreign Office, April 2, 1942, F. G. Lee to King, July 21, 1942, and other correspondence in WO/32/9621, and Foreign Office to Halifax, February 18, 1942, BT 11/2051, TNA.
19. Melvyn Leffler, "The Origins of the Republican War Debt Policy, 1921–1923," *Journal of American History* 59, no. 3 (December 1972): 585–601; Eric Rauchway, *The Money Makers: How Roosevelt and Keynes Ended the Depression, Defeated Fascism, and Secured a Prosperous Peace* (New York: Basic, 2015), 7–9, 14–15.
20. Rauchway, *Money Makers*, 138–58, (quote) 139. For the full legislative genesis of Lend-Lease, see Warren Kimball, *The Most Unsordid Act: Lend-Lease, 1939–1941* (Baltimore: Johns Hopkins University Press, 1969).
21. Maurice Bridgeman to E. W. Playfair, March 5, 1942, and meeting notes, April 27, 1942, WO/32/9621, Kennet Bewley to E. W. Playfair, May 26, 1942, BT 11/2051, Foreign Office memo, February 6, 1942, FO 371/32450, and general correspondence in T 160/1241, all in TNA. On Republican opposition, see Nicholas Wapshott, *The Sphinx: Franklin Roosevelt, the Isolationists, and the Road to World War II* (New York: Norton, 2015), 260–62, 266–71, 285.
22. Memo, July 20, 1942, CAB 115/670, TNA. See also Wilcox to Hobbs, March 24, 1941, and D.O. to Australian, New Zealand, and South African Governments, May 7, 1942, WO/32/9621, TNA.
23. General Purchasing Board interim report, November 1, 1943, folder Report to Washington, 1943, and memo, October 12, 1942, folder Correspondence with H. M. Treasury, box 6416, RG498, NARA; "We Bought the Eiffel Tower"; Spiegelberg testimony, *Lend-Lease*, 57–61.
24. "We Bought the Eiffel Tower"; Reynolds, *Rich Relations*, 207. On the National Loaf, see also Longmate, *How We Lived Then*, 154.
25. George Spiegelberg to A. Ross, July 17, 1942, folder Correspondence—February 1942–December 1942—Purchase Procedure, George Spiegelberg to H. H. Hobbs, December 3, 1942, folder Correspondence with War Office, 1942–1944, General Purchasing Board interim report, November 1, 1943, folder Report to Washington, 1943, and War Office memo, December 16, 1942, folder War Office Memo—Engineer, box 6416, US Navy Forces memo, March 2, 1943, folder UK, box 3611, RG498, NARA; Spiegelberg testimony, *Lend-Lease*, 56; Reynolds, *Rich Relations*, 117, 149; "We Bought the Eiffel Tower."

26. Secret Semi-Annual Report, Criminal Investigation Branch Office of the Theater Provost Marshal, European Theater of Operations, June 6, 1944–December 31, 1944, box 1172, Provost Marshal General, Military Police Division, ETO Activities to Criminal Investigations, RG389, NARA; H. H. Hobbs to George Spiegelberg, January 5, 1943, folder Correspondence with War Office, 1942–1944, box 6416, RG498, NARA; E. W. Playfair to George Spiegelberg, July 15, 1942, E. W. Playfair to H. H. Hobbs, July 18, 1942, and E. W. Playfair to Thomas Barnes, September 16, 1942, T 160/1412, TNA. On car accidents, see Reynolds, *Rich Relations*, 112.
27. G. D. Roseway to SOS ETOUSA, September 16, 1942, E. W. Playfair to H. H. Hobbs, October 16, 1942, Cabinet paper, Civil Claims against Members of the United States Forces, and other correspondence in T 160/1412, TNA.
28. George Spiegelberg to H. H. Hobbs, October 15, 1942, folder Correspondence with War Office, 1942–1944, MacKreachie memo, October 13, 1942, and George Spiegelberg to Deputy Chief, Transportation, October 30, 1942, folder Correspondence—Transportation Charges, August 1942–January 1946, George Spiegelberg to J. A. Drew, November 12, 1942, D. A. Drew to George Spiegelberg, November 14, 1942, George Spiegelberg to H. H. Hobbs, November 15, 1942, and George Spiegelberg meeting notes, November 19, 1942, folder Correspondence—February 1942–December 1942—Purchase Procedure, E. W. Playfair to George Spiegelberg, November 26, 1942, folder Correspondence with H.M. Treasury, box 6416, RG498, NARA.
29. Supply Committee memo, January 6, 1943, AVIA 38/1096, TNA; Stettinius testimony, *Lend-Lease*, 7–8; "We Bought the Eiffel Tower"; General Purchasing Board interim report, November 1, 1943, folder Report to Washington, 1943, box 6416, RG498, NARA; Ruppenthal, *Logistical Support of the Armies*, 90–99; Eisenhower, *Crusade in Europe*, 72; Rick Atkinson, *Army at Dawn: The War in North Africa* (New York: Holt, 2002), 17, 26–27, 31, 50; Panter-Downes, *London War Notes, 1939–1945*, 250.
30. Procurement procedures pamphlet, December 31, 1942, John Lee to George Spiegelberg, December 7, 1942, and scrapbook notes, vol. 1, GASP; George Spiegelberg to Commanding General, Eastern Base Section, December 23, 1943, folder Correspondence—February 1942–December 1942—Purchase Procedure, box 6416, RG498, NARA; "We Bought the Eiffel Tower."
31. Reynolds, *Rich Relations*, xxiv; Ministry of Information American Division confidential report, c. late 1942, CAB 115/670, TNA; Spiegelberg testimony, *Lend-Lease*, 52–61; H. H. Hobbs to C. H. Gurney, February 18, 1943, folder Correspondence with War Office, 1942–1944, and General Purchasing Board interim report, November 1, 1943, folder Report to Washington, 1943, box 6416, RG498, NARA; HM Treasury, "Second Report on Mutual Aid (Reverse Lend-Lease)" (New York: British Information Services, 1944); "We Bought the Eiffel Tower."

Interlude

1. M. D. Klaäs, *Last of the Flying Clippers: The Boeing B-314 Story* (Atglen, PA: Schiffer, 1997), 186.
2. John Chapman, "America Rules the Skyways," *Saturday Evening Post*, March 30, 1940, 18–19, 70–73.
3. Robert Wohl, *The Spectacle of Flight: Aviation and the Western Imagination, 1920–1950* (New Haven, CT: Yale University Press, 2005), 4, 199–200, 289–90, 293–94, 305–8, 312; S. B. Kauffman, *Pan Am Pioneer: A Manager's Memoir*, ed. George Hopkins (Lubbock: Texas Tech University Press, 1995), 198; T. A. Heppenheimer, *Turbulent Skies: The History of Commercial Aviation* (New York: Wiley, 1995), 1, 9.
4. Heppenheimer, *Turbulent Skies*, 10, 14, 123, 143–44; Stuart Banner, *Who Owns the Sky?: The Struggle to Control Airspace from the Wright Brothers On* (Cambridge, MA: Harvard University Press, 2008), chs. 2 and 5; Kauffman, *Pan Am Pioneer*, 10; Wohl, *Spectacle of Flight*, 292–94, (Saint-Exupéry quote) 309, (Lindbergh quote) 319.
5. William Masland, *Through the Backdoors of the World in a Ship that Had Wings* (New York: Vintage, 1984), 196–97; William Stephen Grooch, *Skyway to Asia* (New York: Longmans, Green, 1936), 176–78; Scott Flower, "The Bottom Damage Story of the B-314, NC-18604 at Horta Azores," May 26, 1989, folder 168, box I:120B, Pan Am; Horace Brock, *Flying the Oceans: A Pilot's Story of Pan Am, 1935–1955* (New York: Jason Aronson, 1978), 143; M. D. Klaas, "Clipper Flight 9035," *Air Classics* 29, no. 2 (February 1993): 14–32; Paul Rafford, Jr., "Pan Am's Renegade Captain," *Air Classics* 35, no. 4 (May 1999): 10–12, 62–64; Marius Lodeesen, *Captain Lodi Speaking* (Suttons Bay, MI: Argonaut, 1984), 168; Cornelius K. Dunbar oral history transcript, SFO Museum, San Francisco, California.
6. Board inquiry notes, folder 5, box II:152, Pan Am; "First Clipper in Non-Stop Hop across U.S.," *New York Daily News*, September 21, 1941, 46; W. B. Nash and George Jordan oral histories in Eugene J. Dunning, ed., *Voices of My Peers: Clipper Memories* (Nevada City, CA: Clipper Press, 1996), (quote) 20, 22–23; Rafford, "Pan Am's Renegade Captain"; Robert Daley, *An American Saga: Juan Trippe and His Pan Am Empire* (New York: Random House, 1980), 163, 248, 492.
7. Lodeesen, *Captain Lodi Speaking*, 167–70; Daley, *American Saga*, 249–51; Kauffman, *Pan Am Pioneer*, 182, 184.
8. Klaäs, *Last of the Flying Clippers*, 186; memo, February 7, 1944, folder 1, survivor testimonies, folder 12, box II:152, Pan Am.
9. Civil Aeronautics Board report, September 7, 1943, folder 1, survivor testimonies and accident report, folder 12, radiogram to North Beach, April 1943, folder 13, and E. T. Peck to Security Control Officer, April 20, 1943, folder 5, box II:152, Pan Am; Klaäs, *Last of the Flying Clippers*, 101–2; telegram, February 22, 1943, and clipping, "Eyewitness Report on the Clipper Crash," scrapbook, vol. 1, GASP.

Chapter 18

1. Rosamond Harris Seidel Clark, *My Life in Three-Quarter Time: A Memoir* (Private Printing, 2007), 19, 27, 40; *London Times* transcript, March 4, 1943, and clipping, "France Honors Harry Seidel for Good Work," *Fitchburg Sentinel* (MA), November 17, 1931, Harry G. Seidel folder, BUBF; Standard Oil *Fortune* portrait, 1940, folder Fortune Series, box 2.207/G221, ExxMo; complaint and motions for discovery, April 21, 1953, *EOLP*, 1593–1638; "Flying Ace Brings 17 from Europe," *New York Times*, June 24, 1942, 13; "Export Airline Craft Ends First Atlantic Flight," *New York Herald Tribune*, June 24, 1942, 4. Harry's multifaceted leadership roles in Standard's European and Middle Eastern subsidiaries and advisory boards are documented in Harry G. Seidel folder, BUBF; personnel lists, *World Petroleum Directory*, 1932, 415–16, 435, 455; personnel lists, *World Petroleum Directory*, 1937, 605, 623, 953, 1098; "Two New Directors," *The Lamp*, April 1929, 7, box 2.207/D78, and "Board Reduced to Ten," *The Lamp*, June 1934, 4, box 2.207/D79, ExxMo; and Henrietta Larson, Evelyn Knowlton, and Charles Popple, *New Horizons, 1927–1950* (New York: Harper, 1971), 9, 17–19, 25.
2. Paul Milkman, *PM: A New Deal in Journalism, 1940–1948* (New Brunswick, NJ: Rutgers University Press, 1997), 70–75; Mark Wilson, *Destructive Creation: American Business and the Winning of World War II* (Philadelphia: University of Pennsylvania Press, 2016), 60–61, 82–83, 89, 112–16; Larson, Knowlton, and Popple, *New Horizons*, 441–43.
3. Thurman Arnold testimony, March 26, 1942, *NatDef*, 4308, 4314; Robert Hunter testimony, May 20, 1942, *Patents*, 2622.
4. Stanley Johnston, "Our Rubber, Tin, Silver Supplies," *Chicago Tribune*, January 18, 1942, G8; William Tuttle, "The Birth of an Industry: The Synthetic Rubber 'Mess' in World War II," *Technology and Culture* 22, no. 1 (January 1981): 35–67; John Tully, *The Devil's Milk: A Social History of Rubber* (New York: Monthly Review Press, 2011), 18, 25, 319–20, 328–29; John Crider to James McConaughy, February 21, 1942, and to David Hulburd, February 1942, reel 1, DTMC. On efforts to grow rubber, see Mark Finlay, *Growing American Rubber: Strategic Plants and the Politics of National Security* (New Brunswick, NJ: Rutgers University Press, 2009).
5. Larson, Knowlton, and Popple, *New Horizons*, 431–33; Tuttle, "Birth of an Industry"; Alfred Friendly, "Standard Oil Will Release Nazi Patents," *Washington Post*, March 26, 1942, 1, 4; William Farish testimony, August 21, 1942, *Patents*, 5236.
6. Thurman Arnold testimony, March 26, 1942, *NatDef*, 4308–9, 4312–16, 4327, 4340, 4347; clipping, Nathan Robertson, "Standard Oil Deal Called 'Treason,'" *PM*, March 27, 1942, 2, folder Research: Synthetic Rubber, 1918–1978, box 2.207/G237, ExxMo.
7. William Farish testimony, March 31, 1942, *NatDef*, 4371; Larson, Knowlton, and Popple, *New Horizons*, 436–37; "Dinner-Table Treason,"

Time, April 6, 1942, 15–16; Robertson, "Standard Oil Deal Called 'Treason.'"

8. Standard Oil *Fortune* portrait; Larson, Knowlton, and Popple, *New Horizons*, 199, 204, 342. On the perils of multinational business in this period more broadly, see Christopher Kobrak and Per H. Hansen, eds., *European Business, Dictatorship, and Political Risk, 1920–1945* (New York: Berghahn, 2004) and Volker Berghahn, *American Big Business in Britain and Germany: A Comparative History of Two "Special Relationships" in the 20th Century* (Princeton, NJ: Princeton University Press, 2014). Uncorroborated, speculative studies of Standard's relationship with IG Farben also abound. See, for example, Charles Higham, *Trading with the Enemy: An Exposé of the Nazi-American Money Plot, 1933–1949* (New York: Delacorte, 1983).
9. Fitchburg Ward 4, 2B, reel 1240691, *Census (1900)*; ad, "Save the Flour They Need," May 11, 1918, 5, and "Hermann Seidel, Long Prominent, Dies Today, 75," July 15, 1937, 1, 6, both in *Fitchburg Sentinel.*
10. "The American Petroleum Institute," and A. C. Bedford, "The Panorama of War," *Oildom* 10, no. 4 (April 1919): 20–22, 26–30; Daniel Yergin, *The Prize: The Epic Quest for Oil, Money, and Power* (1991; repr., New York: Free Press, 2009), 160–62; George Gibb and Evelyn Knowlton, *The Resurgent Years, 1911–1927* (New York: Harper, 1956), 239–43, 247; Wilson, *Destructive Creation*, 7–8, 11, 13, 22–23, 47.
11. E. J. Sadler, "Producing Oil," *The Lamp*, February 1922, 18–21, box 2.207/D78, ExxMo; John DeNovo, "The Movement for an Aggressive American Oil Policy," *American Historical Review* 61, no. 4 (July 1956): 854–76; Gibb and Knowlton, *Resurgent Years*, 106, (quote) 107, 260–68, 274–76; Larson, Knowlton, and Popple, *New Horizons*, 4, 37–39; Yergin, *The Prize*, 178–80.
12. Engagement notice, *Fitchburg Sentinel*, June 21, 1919, 2; alumni questionnaires, September 17, 1923, and March 24, 1943, and biographical sketch, March 10, 1942, BUBF; passport applications for Harry and Rosamond Seidel, July 23, 1919, reel 846, and August 21, 1922, reel 2090, *PA-II*; Clark, *My Life*, 5–6.
13. Brooke L. Blower, *Becoming Americans in Paris: Transatlantic Politics and Culture between the World Wars* (New York: Oxford University Press, 2011), 25–29; Gibb and Knowlton, *Resurgent Years*, 275–77, 318; Larson, Knowlton, and Popple, *New Horizons*, 58; Bennett Wall and George Gibb, *Teagle of Jersey Standard* (New Orleans: Tulane University Press, 1974), 221–24, 227, 235–36.
14. Alfred Brace, ed., *Americans in France: A Directory* (Paris: American Chamber of Commerce in France, 1926), 214; Harry Seidel, Jr., passport, September 6, 1932, HGSP; Clark, *My Life*, 13, 15, 17–28. According to Harry's daughter, their villa was in Cabourg, which lay just past the paratroopers' initial objectives, the Caen Canal and the bridges on the Orne River.

15. "Standard Nobel Co. in Poland Ltd.," *World Petroleum Directory*, 1937, 590; Robert T. Haslam testimony, August 19, 1942, *Patents*, 5040–44; Gibb and Knowlton, *Resurgent Years*, 319, 323–26; Larson, Knowlton, and Popple, *New Horizons*, 145–46, 154; Gregory Nowell, *Mercantile States and the World Oil Cartel, 1900–1939* (Ithaca, NY: Cornell University Press, 1994), 151–52; Yergin, *The Prize*, (Howard quote) 313.
16. J. P. Hughes to Harry Seidel, August 8, 1928, 871.631/6, reel 18, *IAR*; "An Experiment in Sovietism," *The Lamp*, October 1924, 4–5, box 2.207/D78, ExxMo.
17. James Harp to Secretary of State, June 23, 1925, 800.51W89 Romania/72, RG59, NARA; W. S. Culbertson to Secretary of State, February 19, 1926, 871.63/33, reel 18, W. S. Culbertson to Secretary of State, October 13, 1927, 871.6363/296, and Charles Wilson to Secretary of State, January 28, 1929, 871.6363/310, reel 19, *IAR*; W. S. Culbertson to Secretary of State, March 31, 1928, Robert Patterson to Secretary of State, July 5, 1928, and Harry Seidel to Chester Swain, September 26, 1928, *FRUS* 3 (1928): 7, 811–13; Harry Seidel to Walter Teagle, March 19, 1928, cited in Gibb and Knowlton, *Resurgent Years*, 711n6.
18. W. S. Culbertson to Secretary of State, February 19, 1926, 871.63/33, reel 18, *IAR*; J. P. Hughes to Harry Seidel, August 8, 1928, 871.631/6, reel 18, *IAR*; Robert Patterson to Secretary of State, June 22, 1928, *FRUS* 3 (1928): 810–11; Harry Seidel to Walter Teagle, March 19, 1928, cited in Gibb and Knowlton, *Resurgent Years*, 321.
19. Marketing memo, January 19, 1935, in *Patents*, 3683–6; Yergin, *The Prize*, 251–52; Timothy Mitchell, *Carbon Democracy: Political Power in the Age of Oil* (London: Verso, 2011), 114–15; Larson, Knowlton, and Popple, *New Horizons*, 42–43, 47–50, 117–23, 127–38.
20. Peter Mellish Reed, "Standard Oil in Indonesia, 1898–1928," *Business History Review* 32, no. 3 (Autumn 1958): 311–37; James Gould, *Americans in Sumatra* (The Hague: Martinus Nijhoff, 1961), 48–54, 59–60.
21. Harry Seidel memo, January 11, 1923, and Louis Sussdorff to Secretary of State, January 18, 1923, 856d.6363/218, RG59, NARA; Reed, "Standard Oil in Indonesia."
22. Harry Seidel memo, January 11, 1923, and Louis Sussdorff to Secretary of State, January 18, 1923, 856d.6363/218, H. G. Seidel memo, June 2, 1923, and F. D. Asche to Secretary of State, June 21, 1923, 856d.6363/264, RG59, NARA; Reed, "Standard Oil in Indonesia; Gould, *Americans in Sumatra*, 60–63; Charles Popple, *Standard Oil Company (New Jersey) in World War II* (New York: Standard Oil Company, 1952), 259–61; Bergen Herod, Petroleum in Sumatra, February 16, 1942, Regional File for Netherlands East Indies, box 2631, RG165, NARA.
23. Mitchell, *Carbon Democracy*, 47–48, 87, 94; Yergin, *The Prize*, 173, 184–85.
24. Gibb and Knowlton, *Resurgent Years*, 283–85, 286, 707n6.
25. Documents relating to Iraq and the Iraq Petroleum Company in *MultiCorp*, 495–529; Edward Peter Fitzgerald, "Business Diplomacy: Walter

Teagle, Jersey Standard, and the Anglo-French Pipeline Conflict in the Middle East, 1930–1931," *Business History Review* 67 (Summer 1993): 207–45; Mitchell, *Carbon Democracy*, 95–97; Yergin, *The Prize*, 187–88; Michael Quentin Morton, *In the Heart of the Desert: The Story of an Exploration Geologist and the Search for Oil in the Middle East* (Aylesford, UK: Green Mountain Press, 2006), 8–14.

26. J. J. Wills memo, September 14, 1928, POWE 33/319, TNA; Gibb and Knowlton, *Resurgent Years*, 299, 304–5; Larson, Knowlton, and Popple, *New Horizons*, 5, 59–60; Yergin, *The Prize*, 206, 229–33.
27. Larson, Knowlton, and Popple, *New Horizons*, 60; Yergin, *The Prize*, 244–47, 248–50; Mitchell, *Carbon Democracy*, 39–40. "Pirates" in *PetrolCartel*, 320.
28. Address sheet, Harry G. Seidel folder, BUBF; correspondence in folder History of Standard Oil (NJ) vols. 1–3: Secretary records, affiliates, foreign marketing, 1934, box 2.207/K100B, ExxMo; Clark, *My Life*, 33–35, 40–41; Larson, Knowlton, and Popple, *New Horizons*, 320–22; David Cannadine, *The Decline and Fall of the British Aristocracy* (New Haven, CT: Yale University Press, 1990), 342, 353–67.
29. Harry Seidel to Walter Teagle, July 10, 1934, and February 10, 1936, Harry Seidel to Stuart Morgan, July 10, 1934, and April 13, 1939, Harry Seidel to Guy Wellman, July 19, 1935, February 17, 1938, and February 25, 1938, and Harry Seidel to William Farish, March–April 1939, in *PetroCartel*, 76–82; Larson, Knowlton, and Popple, *New Horizons*, 51–57, 310-11; Fitzgerald, "Business Diplomacy"; Edward Peter Fitzgerald, "Compagnie Française des Pétroles and the Defense of the Red Line Regime in Middle Eastern Oil, 1933–36," *Business and Economic History* 20 (1991): 117–26; Walter Adams, James Brock, and John Blair, "Retarding the Development of Iraq's Oil Resources: An Episode in Oleaginous Diplomacy, 1927–1939," *Journal of Economic Issues* 27, no. 2 (March 1993): 69–93.
30. "Bahrein Oil Deal Is Believed Near," *New York Times*, October 18, 1935, 19; Control of Russian Oil, New York conference, May 1932, *PetrolCartel*, 240; Gibb and Knowlton, *Resurgent Years*, 341–58, (Sadler quote) 348; Wall and Gibb, *Teagle of Jersey Standard*, 223, (Teagle quote) 225; Larson, Knowlton, and Popple, *New Horizons*, 305–7; Nowell, *Mercantile States and the World Oil Cartel*, 161-3; Yergin, *The Prize*, 223, 226, 247–49.
31. "Teagle Explains Part in Chemical Company," April 28, 1929, (quotes) N9; "Standard Oil Makes New Dye Trust Deal," November 24, 1929, N9, N12, and "Plan Wider Rights for Oil Conversion," December 2, 1929, 48, all in *New York Times*; Yergin, *The Prize*, 313–14; Kathryn Steen, *The American Synthetic Organic Chemicals Industry: War and Politics, 1910–1930* (Chapel Hill: University of North Carolina Press, 2014), 243, 250. Harry also became a director of the spin-off International Hydrogenation Patents Company: "International Hydrogenation Patents Co. Ltd.," *World Petroleum Directory*, 1937, 605.

32. "Willkommen in Deutschland," *The Lamp*, April 1937, 10–16, box 2.207/D79, ExxMo; Larson, Knowlton, and Popple, *New Horizons*, 334, 336; Walter Teagle, "Oil and War," *Collier's*, April 25, 1936, 7–8, 72–76; Hugh Thomas, *The Spanish Civil War* (1961; repr., New York: Modern Library, 2001), 916; Robert Whealey, *Hitler and Spain: The Nazi Role in the Spanish Civil War, 1936–1939* (Lexington: University of Kentucky Press, 1989), 122. For press criticism, see, for example, "Oil on Troubled Waters," *Nation*, December 18, 1935, 700.
33. Irvine Anderson, *The Standard-Vacuum Oil Company and United States East Asian Policy, 1933–1941* (Princeton, NJ: Princeton University Press, 1975), 105–8.
34. Franklin D. Roosevelt, "Quarantine Speech," October 5, 1937, *FDRPA*, vol. 6, 406–11; Larson, Knowlton, and Popple, *New Horizons*, 215–16, 383; Register of Tank Vessels, *World Petroleum Directory*, 1937, 438. In 1938 DAPG in Germany bought more refined products from Jersey affiliates than any other foreign company except Anglo-American, mostly from Aruba: Standard Oil *Fortune* portrait; Clark, *My Life*, 38–39.
35. Frank Howard to R. P. Russell, March 15, 1938, and executive committee meeting minutes, May 17, 1938, in *Patents*, 2906, 3196–7; executive committee meeting minutes, April 4, 1938, Frank Howard to F. H. Bedford, April 20, 1938, and M. B. H. to Frank Howard, October 20, 1938, in *NatDef*, 4598–99, 4623–24.
36. Adam Tooze, *The Wages of Destruction: The Making and Breaking of the Nazi Economy* (New York: Penguin, 2006), 99–103, 116, 227–30; executive committee minutes, May 6, 1938, and Frank Howard to E. J. Sadler, November 16, 1938, in *Patents*, 3194, 5243–44; Frank Howard to Orville Harden, September 20, 1938, and executive committee meeting minutes, September 29 and October 28, 1938, in *NatDef*, 4664–68; Frank Howard, Notes on European Trip: Germany, in *Patents*, 2899–2902. On this history from IG Farben's point of view, see Joseph Borkin, *The Crime and Punishment of I.G. Farben* (New York: Free Press, 1978), ch. 4.
37. Tooze, *Wages of Destruction*, 132–33.
38. Clipping, "Mrs. Seidel, Three Children Flee London Home for U.S.," *Providence Journal*, September 8, 1939, folder Harry G. Seidel, BUBF; Clark, *My Life*, 51–52; Rosamond Seidel to Mr. Worthington, March 6, 1943, Harry G. Seidel folder, BUBF; Standard Oil *Fortune* portrait; Harry Seidel to Orville Harden, October 2, 1939, in *MultiCorp*, 70–71; Guy Wellman to C. M. Davison and Harry Seidel, January 25, 1940, in *EOLP*, 1606; Larson, Knowlton, and Popple, *New Horizons*, 323, 384–85, 387, 393; "30 German Sailors on Japanese Liner," *New York Times*, February 19, 1940, 6.
39. Frank Howard to A. C. Minton, October 16, 1939, and extract from executive committee memo, October 18, 1939, folder Standard Oil Development Correspondence: IG Farben/JASCO, 1939–1965, box 2.207/G42, ExxMo; W. Schaefer to F. H. Bedford, September 8, 1939, Frank

Howard memo, October 12, 1939, R. C. Wilson to H. W. Fisher, November 14, 1939, and Frank Howard testimony, August 19, 1942, in *Patents*, 1857–59, 2639, 4135, 5069–70.

40. Frank Howard to William Farish, October 12, 1939, in *NatDef*, 4584–87; Standard Oil *Fortune* portrait; Larson, Knowlton, and Popple, *New Horizons*, 386, 388, 397.
41. Popple, *Standard Oil in World War II*, 77; Joseph Mantsch, "Business as Usual in London Town," *The Lamp*, April 1941, 8–12, box2.207/D80, ExxMo; "Sketches of Some on Clipper," *New York Herald Tribune*, February 24, 1943, 14. Harry's London office had been moved from Thames House, Millbank, to 36 Queen Anne's Gate in August 1940: change of address notice, August 29, 1940, Harry G. Seidel folder, BUBF.
42. Executive committee meeting minutes, October 4, 1939, in *Patents*, 3222; annual report, 1940, folder Standard Oil Company (NJ) Annual Reports, 1932–1940, box 2.207/D92, ExxMo; Larson, Knowlton, and Popple, *New Horizons*, 396; Popple, *Standard Oil in World War II*, 78. On Allied authorities' growing concern about Standard's business with Condor and Lati in Brazil and on neutral Atlantic islands, see meeting notes, August 21, 1940, and draft telegram, August 23, 1940, MT 59/285, TNA; Adolf Berle to Mr. Collado, October 22, 1941, folder Board of Economic Operations, October–December 1941, box 56, Adolf Berle Papers, FDRL; William Farish testimony, August 19, 1942, *Patents*, 5063–65. On the participation of Standard's subsidiary Stanvac in US policy to continue a carefully controlled flow of oil to Japan, see Anderson, *Standard-Vacuum Oil Company*, 13, 140–43, 166–67.
43. Anderson, *Standard-Vacuum Oil Company*, 4; Popple, *Standard Oil in World War II*, 204, 275, 311; "Land 48 at Venezuela Port," *Chicago Tribune*, May 5, 1942, 5.
44. "Senators to Study All Patent Rights," *New York Times*, March 29, 1942, 9; Robert La Follette opening statement, April 13, 1942, *Patents*, 10–14; clipping, Nathan Robertson, "On Oil and Patents," *PM*, May 24, 1942, 9, folder Research: Synthetic Rubber, 1918–1978, box 2.207/G237, ExxMo; Wall and Gibb, *Teagle of Jersey Standard*, 315–16; Larson, Knowlton, and Popple, *New Horizons*, 441–50.
45. Homer Bone, August 19, 1942, *Patents*, 5036.
46. William Farish testimony, August 19, 1942, *Patents*, 5084.
47. William Farish testimony, August 19 and 21, 1942, *Patents*, 5036, 5087, 5236.
48. William Farish and Robert Haslam testimony, August 20, 1942, *Patents*, 5122, 5131–32. On the Dutch Army's demolition of Stanvac's East Indies installations, see Popple, *Standard Oil in World War II*, 259–61.
49. Memo on correspondence, March 23, 1942, Franklin Roosevelt to Walter Teagle, November 16, 1939, November 25, 1941, January 23, 1942, Teagle to Roosevelt, October 5, 1942, and Grace Tully to Teagle, October 21, 1942, folder Teagle, Walter Clark, PPF 5316, FDRL.

50. "Age Retires Standard Oil Men," November 23, 1942, 31, 33, and "Wm. S. Farish Dies," November 30, 1942, 23, both in *New York Times*.
51. "Many Oil Leaders at Farish Funeral," *New York Times*, December 1, 1942, 25; Michael Stoff, "The Anglo-American Oil Agreement and the Wartime Search for Foreign Oil Policy," *Business History Review* 55, no.1 (Spring 1981): 59–74; Standard Oil pamphlet, "Victory in the Making," folder Corporate Public Affairs: Publications, 1942–1943, box 2.207/L12C, ExxMo; "Secrets Turned into Mighty War Weapons," *Petroleum Times*, December 25, 1943, reprinted in *Tribunals*, vol. 7, 1297–1303; Tooze, *Wages of Destruction*, xxiii; Wilson, *Destructive Creation*, 2–3, 5, 62–63, 92–93, 99–100, 112–16.
52. Testimony of August von Knieriem, *Tribunals*, vol. 7, 1312–19; Yergin, *The Prize*, 314–16, 327–29; Elie Weisel, *Night*, trans. Stella Rodway (1958; repr., New York: Bantam, 1982), 47, 50; Tully, *Devil's Milk*, chs. 18–19.
53. Translation of August von Knieriem memo, June 6, 1944, *Tribunals*, vol. 7, *Tribunals*, 1303–11.

Chapter 19

1. "Tamara," *Radio Mirror*, April 1934, 18, 55; C. Brooks Peters, "Nazis Slash Ahead," *New York Times*, September 20, 1941, 1, 3; Truman Anderson, "Incident at Baranivka: German Reprisals and the Soviet Partisan Movement in Ukraine, October-December 1941," *Journal of Modern History* 71, no. 3 (September 1999): 585–623; Karel Berkhoff, *Harvest of Despair: Life and Death in Ukraine under Nazi Rule* (Cambridge, MA: Harvard University Press, 2004); David Wyman, *Abandonment of the Jews: America and the Holocaust, 1941–1945* (1984; repr., New York: New Press, 2007), 4, 19–20.
2. "Aid Russia in the Common Fight!" December 12, 1941, 27, and Janet Jones, "10,000 Attend Russian Benefit," December 15, 1941, 1, both in *Boston Globe*; "Programs of the Week," January 25, 1942, X8, "Russian War Relief Concert," February 2, 1942, 11, "Exhibition of Art to Aid 3 Nations," March 20, 1942, 22, "Radio Today," June 10, 1942, 41, and "Rally in Garden to Hear Litvinoff," June 21, 1942, 22, all in *New York Times*; clippings, 1942, folder 18, box 1, DFP; Greater New York Campaign of Russian War Relief, Inc. report, 1942, folder Russian War Relief, box 59, John Golden Papers, BRTC.
3. Undated clipping, ca. June 1947, and Jack Stinnett, "A Candid Talk with Tamara," *Evening Post* (Bridgeport, CT), July 17, 1939, Tamara scrapbook, DFP; recording, Leo Reisman and His Orchestra, with vocals by Tamara, Brunswick Record Corporation, 1933. On Victorian versus modern expressions of feeling, see Peter Stearns, *American Cool: Constructing a Twentieth-Century Emotional Style* (New York: New York University Press, 1994).
4. Set lists, folder 11, box 2, "Tamara, Sloe-Eyed Songster, Arrives," *Denver Post*, July 13, 1938, (for quote), and other clippings in Tamara scrapbook,

DFP; Yip Harburg quoted in Harold Meyerson and Ernest Harburg, *Who Put the Rainbow in the Wizard of Oz?: Yip Harburg, Lyricist* (Ann Arbor: University of Michigan Press, 1993), 3; Robbie Lieberman, *"My Song Is My Weapon": People's Songs, American Communism, and the Politics of Culture, 1930–1950* (Urbana: University of Illinois Press, 1989), chs. 2–3.

5. Set lists, folder 11, box 2, and notes about segues in Sheet Music boxes, DFP; "Music in the Air," *New York Times*, January 25, 1942, X10; John Bush Jones, *The Songs that Fought the War: Popular Music and the Home Front, 1939–1945* (Waltham, MA: Brandeis University Press, 2006), 6, 9, 19, 75, 84. Tamara notably did not sing boop-oop-a-doop flapper tunes like "I Wanna Be Loved by You," which portrayed women as needy and dependent, and she did not sing bluesy torch laments about cruel men such as "Moanin' Low" or "My Man." For these alternative love song genres, see John Moore, "'The Hieroglyphics of Love': The Torch Singers and Interpretation," *Popular Music* 8, no. 1 (January 1989): 31–58 and Stacy Holman Jones, *Torch Singing: Performing Resistance and Desire from Billy Holiday to Edith Piaf* (Lanham, MD: Atla Mira, 2007), 1–2, 41.

6. D'Ann Campbell, "Women in Combat: The World War II Experience in the United States, Great Britain, Germany, and the Soviet Union," *Journal of Military History* 57 (April 1993): 301–23; Sandra Trudgen Dawson, ed., "Special Issue: Women and the Second World War," *International Journal of Military History and Historiography* 39, no. 2 (October 2019).

7. Isabel Morse Jones, "Place of Music in Global War Conditions Defined," *Los Angeles Times*, October 3, 1943, C1; Jones, *Songs that Fought the War*, 10–13; Annegret Fauser, *Sounds of War: Music in the United States during World War II* (New York: Oxford University Press, 2013), 85, 94–97, 107–7, 127. On female wartime obligation, see Robert Westbrook, "'I Want a Girl, Just Like the Girl That Married Harry James': American Women and the Problem of Political Obligation in World War II," *American Quarterly* 42, no. 4 (December 1990): 587–614; Marilyn Hegarty, *Victory Girls, Khaki-Wackies, and Patriotutes: The Regulation of Female Sexuality during World War II* (New York: New York University Press, 2008); Melissa McEuen, *Making War, Making Women: Femininity and Duty on the American Home Front, 1941–1945* (Athens: University of Georgia Press, 2010).

8. Abe Lastfogel to Board of Directors, January 16, 1943, box 2, RG407, NARA; Sherrie Tucker, *Swing Shift: "All-Girl" Bands of the 1940s* (Durham, NC: Duke University Press, 2000), 122–23, 237–38, 268–69; Kara Dixon Vuic, *The Girls Next Door: Bringing the Home Front to the Front Lines* (Cambridge, MA: Harvard University Press, 2019), 61–70.

9. Lynn O'Neal Heberling, "Soldiers in Greasepaint: USO-Camp Shows, Inc. during World War II" (PhD diss., Kent State University, 1989), 7, 27–28, 33–36; Jane DeHart, *Federal Theatre, 1935–1939: Plays, Relief, and Politics* (1967; repr., Princeton, NJ: Princeton University Press, 2015), ch. 6; Edgar Snow, "They Don't Want to Play Soldier," *Saturday Evening Post*, October

25, 1941, 14–15, 61–66; Lee Kennett, *The American Soldier in World War II* (Norman: University of Oklahoma Press, 1997), 66–80.

10. Pamphlet, "What Everyone Wants to Know about the U.S.O.: A Handbook for Committee Members," 1942; civilian complaints and shore patrol reports, folder P13-2 Conduct—Offenses, box 280, NYNav; correspondence and complaints, November 1940–January 1941, in folder 250.1 Morals and Conduct, Entertainment, box 193, RG247, NARA; Brooke L. Blower, "VJ-Day, 1945, Times Square," in *The Familiar Made Strange: American Icons and Artifacts after the Transnational Turn*, ed. Brooke L. Blower and Mark Philip Bradley (Ithaca, NY: Cornell University Press, 2015), 70–87; Aaron Hiltner, *Taking Leave, Taking Liberties: American Troops on the World War II Home Front* (Chicago: University of Chicago Press, 2020) chs. 1–2.

11. Henry Stimson, "Arming Our National Spirit," *Defense Morale: A Transcript of the Proceedings of the Defense Morale Conference of United Service Organizations for National Defense* (Washington, DC, 1941), 11; confidential report, Maintaining the Will to Win: A Key Statement for the National USO Campaign, box 76, and memo, Basic Standards for USO Hostess Groups in Military Areas, January 7, 1943, box 26, RG24, NARA. On the conservative ideology underpinning the USO, see also Sam Lebovic, "'A Breath from Home': Soldier Entertainment and the Nationalist Politics of Pop Culture during World War II," *Journal of Social History* 47, no. 2 (Winter 2013): 263–96.

12. Maxene Andrews and Bill Gilbert, *Over Here Over There: The Andrews Sisters and the USO Stars in World War II* (New York: Zebra Books, 1993), x, 30–31; "Advertising News and Notes," *New York Times*, September 11, 1941, 37; Citizens Committee for the Army and Navy report, folder USO Camp Shows—Organizational Chart and History, box 1, USO Camp Shows Publicity Records, Series 1—History of the USO, BRTC; "What Everyone Wants to Know about the USO," 8; *The USO Bulletin*, October 1942, box 76, RG24, NARA; Lowell Matson, "Theatre for the Armed Forces in World War II," *Educational Theatre Journal* 6, no. 1 (March 1954): 1–11; Frank Coffey, *Always Home: 50 Years of the USO* (Washington, DC: Brassey's, 1991), 25. Tamara was entertaining sailors in New York as early as 1939, participated in American Theatre Wing benefits, and appeared at the Stagedoor Canteen: clippings, "Gobs an' Gals—an' Wot Gals!" and "Cast of Show Stages Performance Afloat," May 1939, Tamara scrapbook, DFP; "Rally in Garden to Hear Litvinoff"; "American Theatre Wing," *Billboard*, February 19, 1944, 5.

13. Talent Advisory Committee and Band Committee meeting minutes, March 17, 1942, and Legitimate Committee Meeting minutes, October 20, 1942, box 2, RG407, NARA; Personnel for Entertainment Section meeting notes, August 17, 1942, Production Committee Meeting minutes, September 1942, box 72, and Norvelle Sharpe memo, August 19, 1942, box 63, RG24, NARA. On seats for POWs and Black troops, see Larry Bolton

to Emil Friedlander, July 12, 1945, box 74, RG24, NARA, and Tucker, *Swing Shift*, 232, 240.

14. Talent Advisory Committee and Band Committee meeting minutes, March 17, 1942, box 2, RG407, NARA; lists of early Red-White-and-Blue Circuit units, box 63, and Abe Lastfogel to board of directors, November 23, 1942, box 72, RG24, NARA.
15. Lawrence Phillips, Winter Program Proposal, September 21, 1942, box 72, and reprint of Jean Block, "Entertaining Soldiers: The USO Camp Shows Try to Find What the Military Enjoys," *New York Times*, March 1, 1942, box 76, RG24, NARA; Tucker, *Swing Shift*, 22–23, 227; Maurice Zolstow, "Uncle Sam Brings Vaudeville Back," *Saturday Evening Post*, September 12, 1942, 21, 69–70. For complaints when shows did not live up to girl-next-door fantasies, see folders 250.1 Morals and Conduct, Entertainment, boxes 193–94, RG247, NARA.
16. USO Camp Shows history, box 1, memo, ENSA Overseas Entertainment, n.d., Dwight D. Eisenhower to Chester Barnard, October 9, 1942, Harry Foster to Abe Lastfogel, November 24, 1942, Justin Doyle to Lawrence Phillips, November 26, 1942, Walter Currie, ETO memo, December 4, 1942, and Abe Lastfogel to board of directors, January 16, 1943, box 2, Abe Lastfogel to USO-Camp Shows Board of Directors, August 1, 1943, box 3, RG407, NARA; Lawrence Phillips report on 1942-1943 Winter Program, box 72, USO-Camp Shows, Inc. Report on Year of 1945, box 74, RG24, NARA. By one estimate, USO-Camp Shows would entertain 72 million people around the world in 1945 alone: Julia Carson, *Home Away from Home: The Story of the U.S.O.* (New York: Harper, 1946), 130.
17. Abe Lastfogel to board of directors, November 23, 1942, box 2, RG407, NARA; Abe Lastfogel, Second Winter Program report, and memo regarding overseas salaries, box 72, RG24, NARA; USO Standard Contract, Lawrence Phillips to all USO-Camp Shows Entertainers, July 7, 1943, and Lawrence Phillips to James Norris, November 6, 1943, folder 250.1 Morals and Conduct, Entertainment, box 193, RG247, NARA; Zolstow, "Uncle Sam Brings Vaudeville Back"; John Desmond, "The Troupers Go to the Troops," *New York Times*, April 2, 1944, SM16–17, 46. Photographs showing the circuit's rudimentary conditions can be found in folder USO Camp Shows World War II (Miscellaneous), box 1, USO Camp Shows Publicity Records, Series I—History of the USO, BRTC.
18. Carole Landis, *Four Jills in a Jeep* (New York: Random House, 1942), 45–46, 68, 74; BBC overseas transmission script, November 28, 1942, box 2, RG407, NARA; Andrews and Gilbert, *Over Here Over There*, 94–95, 101, 240–41; Louise Buckley report, n.d., box 3, RG407, NARA; Bob Hope, *I Never Left Home* (New York: Simon and Schuster, 1944), 154, 157, 172; Tucker, *Swing Shift*, 59, 246, 260–61, 265, 275–78, 304–5; Vuic, *Girls Next Door*, 91–98, 118–21.

19. Norvelle Sharpe memo, August 19, 1942, box 63, Abe Lastfogel, Letter Addressed to 160 Well-Known Artists, September 24, 1942, and *Variety* notice, June 16, [1943], box 72, RG24, NARA; Abe Lastfogel to board of directors, November 23, 1942, box 2, RG407, NARA.
20. Overseas Unit reports, box 7, and Abe Lastfogel to board of directors, January 16, 1943, box 2, RG407, NARA; Landis, *Four Jills in a Jeep*, 19–20, 42–43, 73, 92–98, 138–50, 164–73, (quote) 150; Coffey, *Always Home*, 26.
21. "Kay, Mitzi Describe Bomb Ducking in Charting CSI Route into Africa," *Variety*, February 17, 1943, 2, 47.

Chapter 20

1. "Garcia and Diaz Are Exonerated in Ship Inquiry," *New York Herald Tribune*, December 30, 1941, 11; "Garcia, Diaz Cleared in Smuggling Case," *New York Times*, December 30, 1941, 11; intercepts of lawyers' bills and records, folder 560 Isla de Tenerife, box 1165, RG319, NARA; Marcelino Garcia to Francis Biddle, December 31, 1941, box 3, Jacob Fuller, synopsis report, January 20, 1944, litigation case file 146-7-1883, box 13, and Reese Alsop to Francis Biddle, January 13, 1942, case 149-522, box 42, RG60, NARA; note to Excmo. Sr. Subsecretario de Asuntos Exteriores, n.d., Hunt, Hill & Betts to Cía. Trasmediterránea, c/o Garcia & Diaz, January 27, 1942, and Juan Francisco de Cárdenas to Ministerio de Asuntos Económicos, January 31, 1942, R-1330/59, AMAE.
2. Department of Justice informal hearing, January 8, 1942, folder 560 Isla de Tenerife, box 1165, RG319, NARA.
3. Mathias Correa to Attorney General, December 20, 1941, box 3, RG60, NARA; Hunt, Hill & Betts to Manual Diaz and Marcelino Garcia, August 6, 1942, Confidential 852.20200 March, Juan/42, box C185, RG59, NARA. On the subsequent flurry of correspondence between Manuel, Marcelino, the Spanish embassy in Washington, and Trasmediterránea and Franco officials in Spain, see Garcia & Diaz to Cía. Trasmediterránea, January 7, 1942, telegram to Washington, February 9, 1942, Cía. Trasmediterránea to Ministerio de Asuntos Exteriores, January 14, 1942, and Serrano Suñer to Director General Comunicaciones Marítima, January 17, 1942, R-1330/59, as well as correspondence in R-1655/28, AMAE.
4. Carlton Hayes, *Wartime Mission in Spain, 1942–1945* (New York: Macmillan, 1946), 5–16, 54; Roosevelt, "We Choose Human Freedom," May 27, 1941, 181–95, vol. 10, *FDRPA*; W. E. Lucas, "Hitler Eyes Portugal," *Nation*, April 26, 1941, 495–96; Stanley Payne, *Franco and Hitler: Spain, Germany, and World War II* (New Haven. CT: Yale University Press, 2008), 77–78. Allied strategists also worried that if Spain's neutrality ended, its more than 200 deep water ships would fall into Axis hands: naval intelligence report, February 10, 1942, 852.85/150, reel 31, *SIFA*.
5. H. G. Foster report, February 2, 1942, litigation case file 146-7-1883, box 13, RG60, NARA; Samuel Hoare to Foreign Office, December 24, 1941, FO 954/27A, TNA; Juan de Cárdenas note, February 5, 1942, 852.6363/276, reel

25, Juan de Cárdenas note, December 23, 1941, E. Saugstad to Breckinridge Long, January 2, 1942, and Long to Francis Biddle, January 9, 1942, and reply, January 14, 1942, Juan de Cárdenas to Cordell Hull, January 19, 1942, 852.85/132, 134A, 138, 140, reel 31, Cárdenas to Sumner Welles, July 27, 1942, 711.522/90, reel 36, all in *SIFA*; Payne, *Franco and Hitler*, 54–55, 68–71, 105, 126–40; Denis Smyth, *Diplomacy and Strategy of Survival: British Policy and Franco's Spain, 1940–41* (Cambridge: Cambridge University Press, 1986); Manuel Ros Agudo, *La Guerra Secreta de Franco (1939–1945)* (Barcelona: Critica, 2002), 88–96, 111–12, 122; Andrew Buchanan, "Washington's 'Silent Ally' in WWII? United States Policy Towards Spain, 1939–1945," *Journal of Transatlantic Studies* 7, no. 2 (June 2009): 93–117.

6. Summary of charges and plea agreements, file 146-12-11, box 3, RG60, NARA; Pike and Dougherty to Customs Commissioner, January 15, 1942, 852.85/145.5 and 852.85/136-41, reel 31, *SIFA*; FBI report, July 23, 1942, Confidential 852.20200 March, Juan/43, box C185, RG59, NARA; USA, *v.* Steamer *Isla de Tenerife* (SDNY 12 January 1942) in *American Maritime Cases* (1942), 334; "Spanish Ship Freed," *New York Times*, January 13, 1942, 3; "El Caso de García y Díaz," *España Libre*, January 1, 1942, 1; J. Edgar Hoover to Adolf Berle, December 31, 1941, 800.01B11 Registration Garcia and Diaz/16, box 3101, RG59, NARA.

7. David Fairbank White, *Bitter Ocean: The Battle of the Atlantic, 1939–1945* (New York: Simon & Schuster, 2006), 146–50; Evan Mawdsley, *The War for the Seas: A Maritime History of World War II* (New Haven, CT: Yale University Press, 2019), 253–58; New York FBI report, July 23, 1942, for case file 100-13382, Confidential 852.20200 March/Juan/43, box C185, RG59, NARA.

8. H. G. Foster report, February 2, 1942, and D. E. Balch memo, March 5, 1942, litigation case file 146-7-1883, box 13, RG60, NARA; Panama Embassy to Secretary of State, April 28, 1942, 800.01B11 Registration Garcia and Diaz/34, box 3101, RG59, NARA; Military Intelligence Division memo on Falangist Activity, April 18, 1942, folder 000.24 Falange April 1–May 31, 1942, box 2, Navy official, March 1942, quoted in W. Christ report, November 28, 1942, folder Marques de Comillas, 1941–July 10, 1943, box 1169, RG319, NARA; April 29, 1942 report cited in Undesirable Activities of Spanish and Portuguese Ships in the Atlantic, July 1, 1942, 852.85/181, reel 31, *SIFA*.

9. F. S. Doll report, June 26, 1942, folder 000.24 Falange June 1–August 31, 1942, box 2, RG319, NARA; "Enemies at Home," *New Republic*, July 27, 1942. 117; Oscar Lewis to Asher Schwartz, July 17, 1943, case 149-522, box 42, RG60, NARA.

10. Undesirable Activities of Spanish and Portuguese Ships in the Atlantic, July 1, 1942, 852.85/181, (quote) Laurence Duggan to S. Chapin, June 26, 1942, 852.85/189, reel 31, *SIFA*. The Allies suspected all kinds of neutral ships of suspicious activities but none more than the Spanish. By 1943, British

statutory lists included 37 Spanish ships versus 15 Argentine, 5 Portuguese, 2 Turkish, 2 Swedish, and 1 Panamanian: British statutory list, MT59/1455, TNA.

11. Since World War I, passports had become indispensable travel documents, yet they remained imperfect guides to who people were or what they were up to. Vichy France, the Iberian Peninsula, and Cuba all supported thriving black markets in forged papers: Alexander Powell, "The Passport and Visa Racket," April 28, 1942, and other correspondence in folder Nov. 1941–May 1942, box 901, Visa and Passport Control Branch, RG165/G-2, NARA; Navy correspondence and intelligence reports, June–August 1942, 852.85/181-2, and June–August 1943, 852.85/231, 240, reel 31, Department of State memo, December 11, 1942, 852.8591/522, and Hoover to Berle, May 11 and July 28, 1942, 852.85/165, 175, reel 32, Sumner Welles memo of conversation with Juan Francisco de Cárdenas, July 17, 1942, 852.86/4, reel 33, all in *SIFA*; New Orleans District intelligence report, April 1, 1943, folder Marques de Comillas, box 1169, Military Intelligence Division report, New Orleans, July 14, 1943, and panel interrogations, folders 560 S.S. Magallanes, box 1168, passenger list report, October 27, 1942, and questionnaires of crew and passengers arriving New Orleans, March 1, 1943, folder 560 M. V. Imperial, box 1165, RG319, NARA.
12. Intercepts of Garcia & Diaz correspondence, folder 560 Isla de Tenerife, box 1165, RG319, NARA; New York FBI report, July 23, 1942, for case file 100-13382, Confidential 852.20200 March/Juan/43, box C185, RG59, NARA.
13. Undesirable Activities of Spanish and Portuguese Ships in the Atlantic, July 1, 1942, 852.85/181, reel 31, J. Edgar Hoover to Adolf Berle, October 8, 1942, 852.8591/466, reel 33, both in *SIFA*; reports in folder 560 S.S. *Magallanes*, 1941–September 19, 1942, box 1168, and folder Marques de Comillas, 1941–July 10, 1943, box 1169, F. S. Doll report, June 26, 1942, and G-2 report, February 5, 1942, folder 000.24 Falange, box 2, all in RG319, NARA; naval operations reports in map room files, folder Location of Spanish ships, 1942-1943, box 127, FDRL; memos and reports, February–July 1942, Confidential 852.20200 March, Juan, box C185, reports and correspondence for 1942, 852.85 and 852.8591, RG59, NARA; J. Sharp memo, June 24, 1942, and J. Edgar Hoover request, August 1942, case 149-522, box 42, RG60, NARA; Bryce Oliver, "Franco Invades Latin America," *American Mercury*, May 1942, 543–51; "Spain Is Suspected of Aiding U-Boats," *New York Times*, June 14, 1942, 21; William Shirer, "The Propaganda Front," *Washington Post*, July 5, 1942, B7; "British Delay Spanish Ship on Belief One Aided U-Boat," *Chicago Tribune*, July 19, 1942, 2.
14. Military Intelligence Division memo, October 15, 1942, folder 560 S.S. *Magallanes* (September 21–December 31, 1942), box 1168, RG319, NARA; New York FBI report, July 23, 1942, for case file 100-13382, Confidential 852.20200 March/Juan/43, box C185, RG59, NARA.
15. Wendell Berge to Immigration and Naturalization Service, May 2, 1942, Fred Searls, Jr., to Oscar Cox, December 1, 1943, and Jacob Fuller, synopsis

report, January 20, 1944, litigation case file 146-7-1883, box 13, J. Sharp to J. Edgar Hoover, October 15, 1943, case 149-522, and Tenerife charges, summary, and plea agreement, February 18, 1942, file 146-12-11, all in RG60, NARA; FBI New York Field Division report, April 13, 1943, folder 000.24 Falange, box 2, and Chet Wadsworth, March 15, 1944, folder Marques de Comillas, 1941–July 10, 1943, box 1169, RG319, NARA; Pike and Dougherty to Commissioner of Customs, January 15, 1942, 711.00111 Unlawful Shipments/817, box 2101, and State Department inquiries into fraudulent naturalization, February 1942, 800.01B11 Registration Garcia and Diaz/16, box 3101, RG59, NARA; Robert Wilcox, *Japan's Secret War* (New York: Morrow, 1985), 24, 124–27, 130; confidential memo, Bert Fish to Secretary of State, December 3, 1941, folder A7-2/LOCI #1, box 92, RG38, NARA; J. Edgar Hoover to Adolf Berle, May 22, 1944, 852.8591/5-2244, reel 33, *SIFA*.

16. Kenneth Benton, "The SOS Years: Madrid, 1941–3," *Journal of Contemporary History* 30, no. 3 (July 1995): 359-410; Wilcox, *Japan's Secret War*, 127–33; J. C. Masterman, *The Double-Cross System: The Incredible True Story of How Nazi Spies Were Turned into Double Agents* (New Haven, CT: Yale University Press, 1972). Most famously, the British washed a corpse onto Spanish shores disguised as a Royal Marine carrying fictitious top-secret plans, to suggest the Allies intended to invade Greece or Sardinia rather than Sicily in spring 1943. As expected, local Spanish authorities offered the information to Abwehr agents, who took the bait: Ben Macintyre, *Operation Mincemeat* (New York: Harmony, 2010).

17. Panel interrogations, boxes 1168-70, RG319, NARA; cross-reference file on Captain Jose Alberti, June 16, 1942, 852.20200 March, Juan, reel 10, *SIFA*; navy communiqué, August 8, 1942, folder 560 S.S. *Motomar*, box 1170, RG319, NARA.

18. "Spanish Ship Captain Seized in Plot to Export Platinum," *Los Angeles Times*, October 9, 1942, 1; "Held in Smuggling of Metal to Nazis," *New York Times*, November 7, 1942, 17. On British pushback, see, for example, Buenos Aires cypher to Foreign Office, April 17, 1942, FO 837/1112, and correspondence and notes in FO 371/31217 and 371/37431, TNA. Only after the Allies gained the upper hand in 1943 would British officials really crack down on Spanish ships. See, for example, telegram draft, Ministry of Economic Warfare to Foreign Office, July 17, 1943, FO 371/34732, TNA.

19. "Spain Again Denies Giving Aid to Nazi Submarines," *Chicago Tribune*, October 25, 1942, 19; "Spain Denies U.S. Charges That Nazis Use Canary Islands," *Washington Post*, October 26, 1942, 9; reports in R-1655, Pleitos del vapor "Magallanes," R-2246/57, and consul report quoted in Juan Francisco de Cárdenas, November 3, 1942, R-1655/19, AMAE.

20. David Scoll to Jesse Saugstad, January 7, 1943, State Department memo, January 9, 1943, 852.852/28, reel 32, naval intelligence memo, February 18, 1943, 852.8591/687, reel 31, Philip Bonsal to L. Duggan, February 4, 1943,

852.8591/647, reel 33, both in *SIFA*; Cía. Trasatlántica to Ministerio de Asuntos Exteriores, January 30, 1943 and March 9, 1943, and Ministerio de Asuntos Exteriores memo, March 11, 1943, R-2247/4, AMAE; Jacob Fuller, synopsis report, January 20, 1944, litigation case file 146-7-1883, box 13, RG60. Hemingway likely sighted the *Marqués de Comillas*: J. Edgar Hoover to Adolf Berle, January 4, 1943, folder Marques de Comillas 1941–July 10, 1943, box 1169, RG319, NARA.

21. Pearsall, "Transportation Problems"; Paul Maxwell Zeis, "Ships and New Fronts," *Nation*, July 11, 1942, 26–28; Richard Leighton, "Merchant Shipping and the British Import Crisis," in *Command Decisions*, ed. Kent Roberts Greenfield (New York: Harcourt, Brace, 1959), 199–223; Mark Milner, "The Atlantic War, 1939–1945," in *The Cambridge History of the Second World War*, ed. John Ferris and Evan Mawdsley, vol. 1 (Cambridge: Cambridge University Press, 2015) 455–84, here 474; Jesse Saugstad to David Scoll, January 11, 1943, 852.852/28, reel 32, *SIFA*.
22. Only a reference record for telegram no. 169 remains in 820.02 DIAZ, Manuel, vol. 15, box 75, Lisbon (Portugal) Legation General Records, 1943, RG84, NARA.

Chapter 21

1. Frank Cuhel to Ermengarde Cuhel, March 24, 1942, clipping, "Power of Both Britain and U.S. Needed for Japs, Says Cuhel," MBS broadcast from Honolulu, December 1943, and Frank Cuhel broadcast, March 30, 1942, FJCP.
2. Frank Cuhel to Ermengarde Cuhel, March 24, 1942, FJCP; Kate Darian-Smith, *On the Home Front: Melbourne in Wartime, 1939–1945* (1990; repr., Melbourne: Melbourne University Press, 1990), 17, 21–23.
3. Frank Cuhel to Ermengarde Cuhel, March 24, 1942, Cuhel broadcast, April 30, 1942, and Frank Cuhel to V. A. Dodge, May 19, 1942, FJCP; Charles Rolo, *Radio Goes to War* (New York: Putnam, 1942), 209; David Holbrook Culbert, *News for Everyman: Radio and Foreign Affairs in Thirties America* (Westport, CT: Greenwood Press, 1976), 6, 201–2; Larry Wolter, "War News Puts Radio Stations on 24 Hour Basis," *Chicago Tribune*, December 14, 1941, C6.
4. Cuhel broadcast, June 30, 1942, and Netherlands Indies Government Information Service release, May 13, 1942, FJCP; Paul Fussell, *Wartime: Understanding and Behavior in the Second World War* (New York: Oxford University Press, 1989), 36, 47. Radio's early development owed to its military applications: Daniel Headrick, *The Invisible Weapon: Telecommunications and International Politics, 1851–1945* (New York: Oxford University Press, 1991), 116, 118, 124–27, 144. On taking risks to listen in the occupied East Indies and the Philippines, see Bernice Archer, *The Internment of Western Civilians under the Japanese, 1941–1945* (London: Routledge Curzon, 2004), 78–79; Ralph Ockerse and Evelijn Blaney, *Our Childhood in the Former Colonial Dutch East*

Indies: Recollections before and during Our Wartime Internment by the Japanese (Xlibris, 2011), 76–77; Frank Ephraim, *Escape to Manila: From Nazi Tyranny to Japanese Terror* (Urbana: University of Illinois Press, 2003), 107. On "surprisingly robust" mail service between North America and Europe and less reliable connections in the Far East, see David Miller, *Mercy Ships* (London: Continuum, 2008), 144.

5. Cuhel broadcasts, April 1 and 7, June 1, 4, and 30, 1942, Frank Cuhel to Ermengarde Cuhel, March 24, 1942, and Frank Cuhel to Mary Jorzick, May 4, 1942, FJCP; Walter A. Foote, reports on Japanese radio propaganda, October 26, 1942, box 1, Batavia Consul General in Melbourne, Australia, General Records, 1941–45, RG84, NARA; L. D. Meo, *Japan's Radio War on Australia, 1941–1945* (Melbourne: Melbourne University Press, 1968), 161–65; Roger Purdy, "Nationalism and News: 'Information Imperialism' and Japan, 1910–1936," *American-East Asian Relations* 1, no. 3 (Fall 1992): 295–325; Michael A. Krysko, "Homeward Bound: Shortwave Broadcasting and American Mass Media in East Asia on the Eve of the Pacific War," *Pacific Historical Review* 74, no. 4 (November 2005): 511–44; John Hilvert, *Blue Pencil Warriors: Censorship and Propaganda in World War II* (St. Lucia: University of Queensland Press, 1984), 134; Jerome Berg, *On the Short Waves, 1923–1945: Broadcast Listening in the Pioneer Days of Radio* (Jefferson, NC: McFarland, 1999), 205, 214, 219–23, 229–33, 246–27; William J. Dunn, *Pacific Microphone* (College Station: Texas A&M University Press, 1988), 147–51, 156.
6. Advice to Accredited War Correspondents, May 29, 1942, FJCP; Phillip Knightley, *The First Casualty: The War Correspondent as Hero and Myth-Maker from the Crimea to Kosovo* (1975; repr., Baltimore: Johns Hopkins University Press, 2000), 306–7; E. Daniel Potts and Annette Potts, "American Newsmen and Australian Wartime Propaganda and Censorship, 1940–1942," *Historical Studies* 21, no. 85 (October 1985): 565–75; Michael S. Sweeney, *Secrets of Victory: The Office of Censorship and the American Press and Radio in World War II* (Chapel Hill: University of North Carolina Press, 2001), 21, 37, 41, 44, 48, 51, 66–67, 70, 73, 95–96; Hilvert, *Blue Pencil Warriors*, 142–49; William H. Bartsch, *Every Day a Nightmare: American Pursuit Pilots in the Defense of Java, 1941–1942* (College Station: Texas A&M University Press, 2010), 334–37; Robert W. Desmond, *Tides of War: World News Reporting, 1940–1945* (Iowa City: University of Iowa Press, 1984), 90; J. H. Ryan to Charter Heslep, August 12, 1942, foreign origin broadcasts, folder Australian, box 385, RG216, NARA.
7. Cuhel broadcast, March 30, 1942, Standing Orders for Accredited War Correspondents and for Field Press Censors, 1942, William Dunn broadcast script, February 23, 1943, and Christopher Cross to Ermengarde Cuhel, March 10, 1943, FJCP; Dunn, *Pacific Microphone*, 149–51, 158; George Weller, *Weller's War: A Legendary Foreign Correspondent's Saga of World War II on Five Continents*, ed. Anthony Weller (New York: Crown, 2009), 261.

8. John Costello, *The Pacific War, 1941–1945* (1981; repr., New York: Harper Perennial, 2009), 218–19; John Robertson, *Australia at War, 1939–1945* (Melbourne: William Heinemann, 1981), 104, 130; Steven Bullard, "Japanese Strategy and Intensions towards Australia," in Peter J. Dean, ed., *Australia 1942: In the Shadow of War* (Cambridge: Cambridge University Press, 2013), 124–39; James P. Duffy, *War at the End of the World: Douglas MacArthur and the Forgotten Fight for New Guinea, 1942–1945* (New York: NAL Caliber, 2016), 72; Cuhel broadcast, March 24, 1942, FJCP.
9. MBS broadcast from Honolulu, December 1943, FJCP; Lardner, *Southwest Passage: The Yanks in the Pacific* (Philadelphia: Lippincott, 1943), 60–61, 243; Dunn, *Pacific Microphone*, 154; Robertson, *Australia at War*, 22, 99–100; John Hammond Moore, *Over-Sexed, Over-Paid, and Over Here: Americans in Australia, 1941–1945* (St. Lucia: University of Queensland Press, 1981), 21–22, 52, 70; Duffy, *War at the End of the World*, 5, 66, 80.
10. *Brisbane Telegraph* quoted in Moore, *Over-Sexed, Over-Paid, and Over Here*, 96; MBS broadcast, December 1943, and undated clippings, 1942, FJCP. See also Potts and Potts, "American Newsmen"; Duffy, *War at the End of the World*, 67–69.
11. "Australia: Imperiled Continent Resembles United States," February 9, 1942, 76–85, and Cecil Brown, "The Australians," June 8, 1942, 82–91, both in *Life*; *Instructions for American Servicemen in Australia* (Washington, DC: U.S. Army, 1942), 3, 5; Frank Cuhel to Ermengarde Cuhel, March 24, 1942, Frank Cuhel draft, March 31, 1942, and Cuhel broadcasts, March 26, September 5, 1942, FJCP.
12. Frank Cuhel to Ermengarde Cuhel, October 12, 1942, Frank Cuhel to Oei Tjong Hauw, May 4, 1942, Frank Cuhel to V. A. Dodge, May 18, 1942, and Frank Cuhel broadcasts, April 6, 23, 28, and 30, 1942, FJCP; Walter Foote memos, December 19, 1942, and March 19, 1944, Batavia Consul General in Melbourne, Australia, General Records, 1941–45, RG84, NARA; Moore, *Over-Sexed, Over-Paid, and Over Here*, 57, 119, 289–90.
13. Cuhel broadcast, April 2, 6, 9, and 23, and May 4 and 5, 1942, FJCP; Robertson, *Australia at War*, 131; Costello, *Pacific War*, 228–31.
14. Cuhel broadcasts, April 23, 27, 28, and 30, and May 4, 1942, FJCP; Costello, *Pacific War*, 245–47, 250–52, 273.
15. Cuhel broadcast, May 7, 1942, FJCP. Frank was not alone in underestimating the significance of the Battle of the Coral Sea: Lardner, *Southwest Passage*, 213–21. On rage and resentment about the Allies' Europe first policy inside the Philippines, see Daniel Immerwahr, *How to Hide an Empire: A History of the Greater United States* (New York: Farrar, Straus, and Giroux, 2019), 191–93.
16. Cuhel broadcasts, May 7, 12, and 21, June 18, 25, and 29, 1942, FJCP; Richard Leighton and Robert Coakley, *Global Logistics and Strategy, 1940–1943* (Washington, DC: Department of the Army, 1955), 176–77; Lardner, *Southwest Passage*, 222, 242; John McCutcheon Raleigh, *Pacific Blackout*

(New York: Dodd, Mead, 1943), 189–93; Dunn, *Pacific Microphone*, 170–71; Darian-Smith, *On the Home Front*, 32–49, 149, 161, 172, 210–25; Moore, *Over-Sexed, Over-Paid, and Over Here*, ix, 1–4, 91–93, 108, 147–49, 190–98, 207–23, 289–90; E. Daniel Potts and Annette Potts, *Yanks Down Under, 1941–45: The American Impact on Australia* (Melbourne: Oxford University Press, 1985), 98–100, 133–38, 169, 228–37, 281–96, 302–14; Lardner, *Southwest Passage*, 153–55; Potts and Potts, "American Newsmen"; Hilvert, *Blue Pencil Warriors*, 147–49.

17. Cuhel broadcasts, May 19, May 21, and July 27, 1942, Frank Cuhel to Larry Seymour, August 3, 1942, and clipping, "Australia Calling U.S.A.," *Pix*, November 21, 1942, FJCP.
18. Duffy, *War at the End of the World*, 69, 71, (Marshall quote) 80, 81; Mark A. Stoler, "The 'Pacific-First' Alternative in American World War II Strategy," *International History Review* 2, no. 3 (July 1980): 432–52, (Roosevelt quotes) 442; Roger Bell, *Unequal Allies: Australian-American Relations and the Pacific War* (Melbourne: Melbourne University Press, 1997), ch. 3. According to polls, 65 percent of Americans favored early action against the Japanese, versus 25 percent who favored a Second Front in Europe: Costello, *Pacific War*, 222.
19. Cuhel broadcasts, May 25 and 26, 1942, FJCP; Christopher Bayly and Tim Harper, *Forgotten Armies: The Fall of British Asia, 1941–1945* (London: Allen Lane, 2004), 230; Lewis Gleeck, *The Army and Navy Club of Manila* (Manila: Carmelo & Bauermann, 1976), 46–47.
20. Cuhel broadcast, May 12, 1942, FJCP; escapee interviews and reports on conditions in the East Indies, Batavia Consul General in Melbourne, Australia, General Records, 1941–45, RG84, NARA; Weller, *Weller's War*, 254–55; Ephraim, *Escape to Manila*, 100–2; M. C. Ricklefs, *A History of Modern Indonesia since c. 1200* (1981; repr., Stanford, CA: Stanford University Press, 2008), 235–38; Costello, *Pacific War*, 215–17; Van Waterford, *Prisoners of the Japanese in World War II* (Jefferson, NC: McFarland, 1994); Bayly and Harper, *Forgotten Armies*, 208–14, 226–27; Ethan Mark, *Japan's Occupation of Java in the Second World War* (London: Bloomsbury, 2018), 2.
21. Karl Hack and Kevin Blackburn, "Japanese-Occupied Asia from 1941 to 1945," in Hack and Blackburn, eds., *Forgotten Captives in Japanese-Occupied Asia* (London: Routledge, 2008), 1–20; Doetje Van Velden, *De Japanse Interneringskampen voor Burgers Gedurende de Tweede Wereldoorlog* (1963; repr., Franeker Wever, 1977), 43–46; Sarah Kovner, "A War of Words: Allied Captivity and Swiss Neutrality in the Pacific, 1941–1945," *Diplomatic History* 41, no. 4 (2017): 719–46; Archer, *Internment of Western Civilians under the Japanese*, 5; Waterford, *Prisoners of the Japanese*, 25–27. Among the Americans caught on Java were Pan Am employees, oil men, journalists, nurses, missionaries, students, clerks, and engineers: Red Cross list of American civilians now interned, September 23, 1943, Batavia Consul General in Melbourne, Australia, General Records, 1941–45, RG84, NARA.

Some 30,000 people of Japanese ancestry had also been interned in the Philippines upon the outbreak of hostilities: Immerwahr, *How to Hide an Empire*, 181–82.

22. Archer, *Internment of Western Civilians under the Japanese*, 138–39, 142–50, 175, 200–6; Dorothy Read and Ilse Evelijn Veere Smit, *End the Silence* (Greenbank, WA: Double-Isle Publishing, 2011), xi, 67–76, 79, 111, 114; Ockerse and Blaney, *Our Childhood in the Former Colonial Dutch East Indies*, 17, 107–8, 206–7; Michael van Reijsen, "How I Remember World War Two in the Dutch East Indies," in Sheri Tromp, ed., *Four Years Till Tomorrow: Despair and Hope in Wartime Dutch East Indies* (Altona, Canada: Friesen Printers, 1999), 1–5. Quote in Waterford, *Prisoners of the Japanese*, 47.
23. Cuhel broadcast, May 26, 1942, FJCP; Anthony Reid, "Indonesia: From Briefcase to Samurai Sword," in Alfred W. McCoy, ed., *Southeast Asia under Japanese Occupation* (New Haven, CT: Yale University Southeast Asia Studies, 1980), 16–32; Mark, *Japan's Occupation of Java*.
24. Cuhel broadcasts, June 11 and 23, 1942, FJCP. That spring the National Association of Manufacturers and other business groups were indeed flooding American media, including Frank's network MBS, with propaganda touting the miraculous accomplishments of private industry: Mark Wilson, *Destructive Creation: American Business and the Winning of World War II* (Philadelphia: University of Pennsylvania Press, 2016), 100–6.
25. Cuhel broadcasts, July 28 and ca. early August, 1942, FJCP; Daera Ganiga, memoir of the invasion, in Neville K. Robinson, *Villagers at War: Some Papua New Guinea Experiences in World War II* (1979; repr., Canberra: Australian National University, 1981), 198–203; Neil McDonald, *Chester Wilmot Reports: Broadcasts that Shaped World War II* (Sydney: ABC Books, 2004), 318, 276–77; George Johnston *The Toughest Fighting in the World: The Australian and American Campaign for New Guinea in World War II* (1943; repr., Yardley, PA: Westholme Publishing, 2011), 107; Omar White, *Green Armour* (Sydney: Angus and Robertson, 1945), 43, 102–6, 151; Robertson, *Australia at War*, 139–41.
26. Johnston *Toughest Fighting in the World*, 112–14, 137, (quote) 139, 162; McDonald, *Chester Wilmot Reports*, 305–16, 326, 330–36; White, *Green Armour*, 106–19, 140, 154, 164–65; Costello, *Pacific War*, 317, 375; Duffy, *War at the End of the World*, 127–28; Kokoda Initiative, *Voices from the War: Papua New Guinean Stories of the Kokoda Campaign, World War Two* (Canberra: Governments of Papua New Guinea and Australia, 2015). For typical colonial rationales in Papua New Guinea, see J. R. Halligan, "Administration of Native Races," *Oceania* 9, no. 3 (March 1939): 276–85.
27. Dunn, *Pacific Microphone*, 162–66, 174; Robertson, *Australia at War*, 135. Reporters broadcasting to Australian audiences, by contrast, got much closer to the fighting in Papua New Guinea and transmitted accounts from Townsville: McDonald, *Chester Wilmot Reports*, 275. But print journalists also struggled for access to this campaign: White, *Green Armour*, 66–67,

152; Steven Casey, *The War Beat, Pacific: The American Media at War against Japan* (New York: Oxford University Press, 2021), ch. 4.

28. Cuhel broadcasts, July 27, 28 (incl. Curtin quote), July 30, August 3, 4, 6, and n.d. (early August), 1942, and Frank Cuhel telegram to MBS, August 7, 1942, FJCP; "Curtin Warns Japan Thrust Holds," *Sydney Sun*, July 28, 1942, 1. "No Reactions in England! 'Trickle-of-Aid' Charge," *Truth* (Brisbane), August 9, 1942, 9.
29. Cuhel broadcast, July 30, 1942, and Frank Cuhel telegram to MBS, August 7, 1942, FJCP.
30. Cuhel broadcast, July 11, July 14, and August 6, 1942, FJCP.
31. Maurice Matloff and Edwin Snell, *Strategic Planning for Coalition Warfare, 1941–1942*, vol. 1 (Washington, DC: Center of Military History, 1953), 357–59; Cuhel broadcasts, August 10 and 11, 1942, FJCP; Costello, *Pacific War*, 314–15, 320–23; Robertson, *Australia at War*, 137–38.
32. Duffy, *War at the End of the World*, 153–66.
33. Robertson, *Australia at War*, 143; Costello, *Pacific War*, 336; Cuhel broadcast, October 15, 1942, FJCP.
34. Cuhel broadcast, November 7, 1942, FJCP; Costello, *Pacific War*, 376; Duffy, *War at the End of the World*, 152.
35. Cuhel broadcast, November 12, 1942, FJCP. On Australian coverage of Operation Torch, see, for example, the *Sydney Morning Herald*, November 9–11, 1942.
36. Cuhel broadcasts, November 26 and 28, 1942, FJCP; Johnston *Toughest Fighting in the World*, 192, 206–9, (quote 207), 229; Robertson, *Australia at War*, 142–44; Costello, *Pacific War*, 377–81.
37. Diary, Java to Australia (memoir), Cuhel broadcast draft, October 29, 1942, radio broadcast transcript, San Francisco, ca. January 1943, Frank Cuhel formal complaint, November 20, 1942, and clipping, "Sidelights, Highlights," *Shipping News*, (San Francisco), January 7, 1943, FJCP; Stanley Woodward, "An Old Hurdler Gets Around," *New York Herald Tribune*, January 16, 1943, 14. Sydney's censors were notorious: Raleigh, *Pacific Blackout*, 225–33. On censors' efforts to cultivate morale and trust while avoiding public complacency, see Sweeney, *Secrets of Victory*, 66–67, 73, 95–96. and John McCallum, "U.S. Censorship, Violence, and Moral Judgement in a Wartime Democracy, 1941–1945," *Diplomatic History* 41, no. 3 (2017): 543–66.
38. Cuhel broadcast, October 29, 1942, Sam Wagner to Frank Cuhel, August 9, 1942, Frank Cuhel to the Warners, October 15, 1942, and clipping, "Power of Both Britain and U.S. Needed for Japs, Says Cuhel," FJCP; Dunn, *Pacific Microphone*, 158–59; William H. McDougall, Jr., *By Eastern Windows: The Story of a Battle of Souls and Minds in the Prison Camps of Sumatra* (New York: Scribner, 1949).
39. Cuhel broadcast, October 13, 1942, FJCP.
40. Cuhel broadcasts, November 10 and 14, 1942, diary, Java to Australia (memoir), Frank Cuhel to Mr. Opfinger and Mr. Clapp, September 28,

1942, and Frank Cuhel to Ermengarde Cuhel, October 12, 1942, FJCP; Potts and Potts, *Yanks Down Under*, (Sherrod quote) 170. On North Africa as a "correspondents' paradise," see Quentin Reynolds, *Only the Stars Are Neutral* (New York: Random House, 1942), 247; and Knightley, *First Casualty*, 332–33, 336. Twenty-six correspondents had landed with the Allied invasion; during the next several months their numbers swelled to somewhere between one and two hundred: Desmond, *Tides of War*, 300–1.

41. Frank Cuhel to W. MacMahon Ball, November 16, 1942, Frank Cuhel telegrams to MBS, November 14 and 17, 1942, MBS telegram to Frank Cuhel, November 19, 1942, Lester Gottlieb, publicity release, Frank Cuhel to US Press Relations Officer, Sydney Area, November 30, 1942, and J. W. Smith to Frank Cuhel, December 9, 1942, FJCP.
42. Frank Cuhel to US Press Relations Officer, Sydney Area, November 30, 1942, and diary, Java to Australia (memoir), FJCP.
43. Army plane manifest, December 21, 1942, *Passenger Lists of Vessels Arriving at San Francisco, California*, RG85, NARA; clipping, "Sidelights, Highlights," *Shipping News* (San Francisco), January 7, 1943, Frank Cuhel WOR broadcast, January 29, 1943, script and recording for Double or Nothing appearance, January 15, 1943, radio broadcast transcript, San Francisco, ca. January 1943, and clipping, James Hanlon, "Frank Cuhel Relates Experiences as Radio Correspondent in the South Pacific," ca. January 1943, FJCP.
44. Frank Cuhel to Larry Seymour, August 3, 1942, Frank Cuhel to Ermengarde Cuhel, February 14, 1943, and Seymour to Ermengarde Cuhel, February 24, 1943, FJCP.
45. Frank Cuhel to Larry Seymour, August 3, 1942, Frank Cuhel to Ermengarde Cuhel, October 12, 1942, Frank Cuhel to the Warners, October 15, 142, Larry Seymour to Ermengarde Cuhel, March 16, 1943, Frank Cuhel to Mr. Opfinger and Mr. Clapp, September 28, 1942, Dean of Columbia School of Business to Frank Cuhel, February 16, 1942, Joseph L. McDonald to Frank Cuhel, February 19, 1942, and Ermengarde Cuhel to Joseph L. McDonald, March 5, 1942, FJCP.

Chapter 22

1. Draft, "With the Ferry Pilots," folder 93, and article draft, folder 94, box 9, BFRP; Richard Leighton and Robert Coakley, *Global Logistics and Strategy: 1940–1943* (Washington, DC: Office of the Chief of Military History, 1955), 527–30; Christopher Bayly and Tim Harper, *Forgotten Armies: The Fall of British Asia, 1941–1945* (Cambridge, MA: Harvard University Press, 2005), 83–84, 197–206; Ashley Jackson, *Persian Gulf Command: A History of the Second World War in Iran and Iraq* (New Haven, CT: Yale University Press, 2018), 5, 260, 277–80.
2. Secret Board of Economic Warfare report, "India's Economy in the Present War," March 1942, folder Roger Mission, box 1, Commission of the United States to India, New Delhi, Supplemental Confidential Records,

RG84, NARA; Bayly and Harper, *Forgotten Armies*, 73, 78, 206–7; Srinath Raghavan, *India's War: World War II and the Making of Modern South Asia* (New York: Basic, 2016), 68; Jonathan Fennell, *Fighting the People's War: The British and Commonwealth Armies and the Second World War* (Cambridge: Cambridge University Press, 2019), 66–69, 119–22, 142–43, 183–84, 209.

3. Secret Board of Economic Warfare report, "India's Economy in the Present War"; Charles Romanus and Riley Sunderland, *Stillwell's Mission to China: China-Burma-India Theater* (Washington, DC: Center of Military History, United States Army, 1987), 208; Raghavan, *India's War*, 1–2; Yasmin Khan, *India at War: The Subcontinent and the Second World War* (Oxford: Oxford University Press, 2015), 51–54, 162–67; Madhusree Mukerjee, *Churchill's Secret War: The British Empire and the Ravaging of India during World War II* (New York: Basic Books, 2010), 4–5; Jon Wilson, *India Conquered: Britain's Raj and the Chaos of Empire* (London: Simon & Schuster, 2016), 457–58.
4. Secret Board of Economic Warfare report, "India's Economy in the Present War"; Wilson, *India Conquered*, 390–91, 398–99, 402–7; Mukerjee, *Churchill's Secret War*, 49, 107; Khan, *India at War*, 56–57; Raghavan, *India's War*, 8, 33–34, 86–87.
5. Report of the American Technical Mission to India, August 1942, E&O 11613/42-Visit to India of the American Technical Survey Mission, IOR/L/E/8/2540, BL; Romanus and Sunderland, *Stillwell's Mission to China*, 205, 209; Raghavan, *India's War*, 63, 209–10. The Government of India did not ration or take centralized control of food distribution until 1943: Benjamin Robert Siegel, *Hungry Nation: Food, Famine, and the Making of Modern India* (Cambridge: Cambridge University Press, 2018), 121–24. Churchill explicitly favored a divide-and-rule approach to Indian politics: Mukerjee, *Churchill's Secret War*, 9–10, 13.
6. Zareer Masani, *Indian Tales of the Raj* (Berkeley: University of California Press, 1987), 30–31; Bayly and Harper, *Forgotten Armies*, 186–88, 193, 206–7; Khan, *India at War*, 96–99, 101–4, 110–11, 119–21, 132–33, 163–66, 176; Raghavan, *India's War*, 258–69; Wilson, *India Conquered*, 448–50; Indivar Kamtekar, "The Shiver of 1942," in Kaushik Roy, ed., *War and Society in Colonial India, 1807–1945* (New Delhi: Oxford University Press, 2006), 330–57; Mukerjee, *Churchill's Secret War*, 63–67.
7. Arun Chandra Bhuyan, *The Quit India Movement: The Second World War and Indian Nationalism* (New Delhi: MANAS, 1975), ch. 3; Khan, *India at War*, 178–86; Raghavan, *India's War*, 270–72; Masani, *Indian Tales of the Raj*, (quote) 116–17.
8. Journal entries, March 17, 194[1], folder 41, and summer 1941, folder 43, box 5, draft, "Yanks, Know Your Britain!" 1942, folder 86, box 8, drafts, October 15, 1942, folder 93, and ca. September 1942, folder 94, box 9, BFRP.

9. Draft, October 15, 1942, and press collect, ca. early October 1942, folder 93, notes on India, folder 94, box 9, BFRP.
10. Gary Hess, *America Encounters India, 1941–1947* (Baltimore: Johns Hopkins University Press, 1971), 14–15, 18–21, 44, 67, 70–71, 78; Bhuyan, *Quit India Movement*, 196–99, 213; M. S. Venkataramani and B. R. Shrivastava, *Quit India: The American Response to the 1942 Struggle* (New Delhi: Vikas, 1979), 132–33, 152–54, 174–75, 185–86, (quotes) 187–88, 189, 205, 213, 226–28, 232, 263–64, 278; Susan Brewer, *To Win the Peace: British Propaganda in the United States during World War II* (Ithaca, NY: Cornell University Press, 1997), 139–40, 153–54.
11. Nayantara Pothen, *Glittering Decades: New Delhi in Love and War* (New Delhi: Viking, 2012), 3, 5–8, 24–27, 32–35, 40, 64–76, 84; Leland Stowe, *They Shall Not Sleep* (New York: Knopf, 1944), 190–91; Khan, *India at War*, 155; Romanus and Sunderland, *Stillwell's Mission to China*, 193–204; draft, folder 93, notes on India and dispatches, c. September and early October 1942, folder 94, box 9, BFRP; Ben Robertson, "India Looks to U.S. for Help in the Future," *PM*, February 25, 1943, 5–6.
12. Khan, *India at War*, 7–8; Daniel Todman, *Britain's War: Into Battle, 1937–1941* (New York: Oxford University Press, 2016), 51; Masani, *Indian Tales of the Raj*, (quote) 7.
13. Pothen, *Glittering Decades*, 4, 79–86; Khan, *India at War*, 267.
14. Christopher Thorne, *Allies of a Kind: The United States, Britain, and the War against Japan, 1941–1945* (New York: Oxford University Press, 1978), 12, 16, 209, 241; Erez Manela, "Global Anti-Imperialism in the Age of Wilson," in Ian Tyrrell and Jay Sexton, eds., *Empire's Twin: U.S. Anti-Imperialism from the Founding Era to the Age of Terrorism* (Ithaca, NY: Cornell University Press, 2015), 137–52; David Hollinger, *Protestants Abroad: How Missionaries Tried to Change the World but Changed America* (Princeton, NJ: Princeton University Press, 2017); The Youth of India to Franklin Roosevelt, August 12, 1942, folder India, PSF, FDRL.
15. Paul Kramer, "Empires, Exceptions, and Anglo-Saxons: Race and Rule between the British and United States Empires, 1880–1910," *Journal of American History* 88, no. 4 (March 2002): 1315–53; Kristin Hoganson and Jay Sexton, *Crossing Empires: Taking U.S. History into Transimperial Terrain* (Durham, NC: Duke University Press, 2020); memo to State Department, August 11, 1942, folder 127.8, box 1, US Embassy, New Delhi, India, Classified General Records, RG84, NARA; H. Freeman Matthews to Anthony Eden, August 14, 1942, File 6751/1942, IOR/L/PJ/7/5539, and pamphlet, "Useful Hints for Soldiers Arriving in India," ca. October 1942, IOR/MIL/17/5/2328, BL.
16. Report on commercial relations between India and the United States, United Press request for special facilities, India Office confidential reports on shipping, November 13, 1943, aviation, October 7, 1943, telegraphic communications, September 26, 1943, and American interest in India's oil and mineral resources, September 26, 1943, all in Coll

47/1 Indian-American relations, IOR/L/PS/12/4624, and memos and correspondence, American Technical Mission to India, 1942, File 462/32F, IOR/L/I/1/806, BL; Raghavan, *India's War*, 212, 219–20.

17. Romanus and Sunderland, *Stillwell's Mission to China*, 204–5, 208–9; Leighton and Coakley, *Global Logistics and Strategy*, 173, 547–48; Khan, *India at War*, 144, 149–52, 178.
18. Memos on New Delhi conditions, August 10–October 14, 1942, folder 800-Political Telegrams (1942) Confidential, US Embassy, New Delhi, India, Classified General Records, RG84, NARA; Bhuyan, *Quit India Movement*, ch. 3; Venkataramani and Shrivastava, *Quit India*, 266, 334; Khan, *India at War*, 11–12, 192–93; article draft, folder 94, box 9, BFRP.
19. Article draft, folder 94, box 9, BFRP; Ben Robertson articles in *PM:* "India Leaders Seek to Break Deadlock," October 12, 1942, 13, "British Colonial Imperialism and Four Freedoms Clash in India," February 22, 1943, 8–9, and "How Britain's 'Practical' Men Rule Over India," February 23, 1943, 4.
20. Article drafts and notes on India, folder 94, box 9, transcript of statement, October 1942, folder 100, box 10, BFRP; Ben Robertson, "British Colonial Imperialism and Four Freedoms Clash in India" and "Gandhi—Alive or Dead—Holds Key to India," *PM*, February 24, 1943, 7.
21. Draft for cable to *Chicago Sun*, October 15, 1942, folder 93, and notes and drafts on India, 1942, folder 94, box 9, BFRP; Ben Robertson, "India Leaders Seek to Break Deadlock" and "British Colonial Imperialism and Four Freedoms Clash in India."
22. File 462/32 American interest in the Indian situation, IOR/L/I/1/799, BL; Hess, *America Encounters India*, 84–85, 90; William Roger Louis, *Imperialism at Bay: The United States and the Decolonization of the British Empire, 1941–1945* (Oxford: Oxford University Press, 1978), 9, 11, 225–27.
23. Nico Slate, *Colored Cosmopolitanism: The Shared Struggle for Freedom in the United States and India* (Cambridge, MA: Harvard University Press, 2016), (*Defender* quote) 43, 143–50; Gerald Horne, *The End of Empires: African Americans and India* (Philadelphia: Temple University Press, 2008), 101–3; Venkataramani and Shrivastava, *Quit India*, (Randolph quote) 295; Penny von Eschen, *Race Against Empire: Black Americans and Anticolonialism, 1937–1957* (Ithaca, NY: Cornell University Press, 1997), ch. 2. On Mays and Randolph, see Sudarshan Kapur, *Raising Up a Prophet: The African-American Encounter with Gandhi* (Boston: Beacon Press, 1992). On Willkie, see Samuel Zipp, *The Idealist: Wendell Willkie's Wartime Quest to Build One World* (Cambridge, MA: Harvard University Press, 2020).
24. Slate, *Colored Cosmopolitanism*, 158; Khan, *India at War*, 267–69. Lacy K. Ford, Jr., a leading academic biographer for Ben Robertson, assumes that the South Carolinian's "close contact with the caste system seemed to nudge Robertson toward sharper and more outspoken criticism of racial segregation in the American South." But no evidence could be found to support this claim: introduction to Ben Robertson, *Red Hills and Cotton: An Upcountry Memory* (1942; rev. ed., with new introduction

by Lacy K. Ford, Jr., Columbia: University of South Carolina Press, 1991), xxxix.

25. Louis, *Imperialism at Bay*, 9, 11; "Prime Minister Churchill's Speech," *New York Times*, November 11, 1942, 4.
26. Memos to the State Department, August 18 and October 7, 1942, folder 800-Political Telegrams (1942) Confidential, US Embassy, New Delhi, India, Classified General Records, and clippings from *The Hindu* and *Madras Mail*, October 27–29, 1942, Correspondence, American Mission, New Delhi, 1942, volume 9, 711.2 to 800, box 10, New Delhi Mission, India, General Records, RG84, NARA; article draft, folder 94, box 9, BFRP; Bayly and Harper, *Forgotten Armies*, 253, 284–86; Khan, *India at War*, 205.
27. Venkataramani and Shrivastava, *Quit India*, 163–64, 214, 265–66, 278–79; Brewer, *To Win the Peace*, 141, 144–45, 155, 157; Raghavan, *India's War*, 240–44. See also Auriol Weigold, *Churchill, Roosevelt and India: Propaganda during World War II* (New York: Routledge, 2008).
28. Venkataramani and Shrivastava, *Quit India*, 262, 319; memo, Relations between United States officials in India and the population, (Asiatic mind quotes) summary of Indian censorship report, March 15, 1943, and Roger Lumley, confidential report, May 24, 1943, Coll 47/1 Indian-American relations, IOR/L/PS/12/4624, memo to Mr. Clauson, October 24, 1941, File 462/32D American journalists and photographers in India, IOR/L/I/1/803, BL.
29. Howard Donovan, memo, December 5, 1942, folder 880-891, box 5, US Embassy, New Delhi, India, Classified General Records, RG84, NARA; "Our News from India Is Inadequate," *Nation*, September 26, 1942, 251; Ben Robertson, press collect draft via Imperial to *Toronto Star*, 1942, folder 94, box 9, BFRP; file 155 American press, IOR/L/I/1/388, file 3687/1941 Grant of transit visas for India to accredited American war correspondents, July 1941-November 1942, IOR/L/PJ/7/4675, file 131/4 Press correspondents accredited to the Government of India, IOR/L/I/1/334, file 462/32D American journalists and photographers in India, IOR/L/I/1/803, and summary of Indian censorship report, March 15, 1943, Coll 47/1 Indian-American relations, IOR/L/PS/12/4624, BL.
30. Notes on flight from India, 1942, and article draft, folder 93, box 9, BFRP.
31. "With the Ferry Pilots"; notes for a third article on the flight from India, 1942, folder 90, and article drafting, folder 93, box 9, BFRP.
32. Journal notes, January–February 1943, folder 46, box 5, Stephen Early to Ben Robertson, December 29, 1942, and Russian War Relief press release January 3, 1943, folder 18, box 2, BFRP; cover letter, Ben Robertson to Stephen Early, and Ben Robertson to Franklin Roosevelt, December 15, 1942, Official File, folder India 1942, August-December, Official File 48h, FDRL.
33. Journal notes, February 1943, folder 46, box 5, BFRP; "Gandhi Starts Fast to Protest Arrest," February 11, 1943, 4, "Hull and Halifax Confer on

India" and "Gandhi's Condition Grows Worse as British Put End of Fast Up to Him," February 21, 1943, 21, all in *New York Times*; Hess, *America Encounters India, 1941–1947*, 102.

34. Victor Bernstein, "Ben Robertson, Jr." and John Lewis, "On a Newspaperman," *PM*, February 24, 1943, 17.
35. Bernstein, "Ben Robertson, Jr." and Lewis, "On a Newspaperman"; Robertson, "British Colonial Imperialism and Four Freedoms Clash in India"; hotel information from passenger manifest, folder 4, box II:145, Pan Am.

Chapter 23

1. George Spiegelberg testimony, February 2, 1943, *Lend-Lease*, 49.
2. Arthur Krock, "The Election Message Was Not in Code," *New York Times*, November 5, 1942, 24; "Our New Cornucopia Congress," *Los Angeles Times*, January 6, 1943, B4; William Klingaman, *The Darkest Year: The American Home Front, 1941–1942* (New York: St. Martin's, 2019), 285–90; Lewis Gould, *Grand Old Party: A History of the Republicans* (New York: Random House, 2003), 292–93.
3. Kathryn S. Olmsted, *The Newspaper Axis: Six Press Barons Who Enabled Hitler* (New Haven, CT: Yale University Press, 2022), 211, (quote) 214, 228.
4. "Rationing Halts Sale of Coffee Today for Week," November 22, 1942, 17, "Meat Shortage Forces 500 Shops to Close Doors," December 3, 1942, 11, and "Packers Assure Chicagoans of Christmas Meat," December 11, 1942, 25, all in *Chicago Tribune*; "Coffee Sales Halt after Wild Buying; A Rush for Butter," November 22, 1942, 1, "Many Areas Report Shortages in Food," November 25, 1942, 20, and "Severe Shortage of Meat Imminent," December 2, 1942, 27, all in *New York Times*; "Housewives Make More Runs on Food," December 16, 1942, 1, 12, and "End of Butter Supply Seen," December 17, 1942, 13, both in *Los Angeles Times*; Klingaman, *Darkest Year*, 284, 296, 299.
5. "Food Shipments Abroad in 1942 Cut Heavily into Home Supplies," *New York Times*, December 27, 1942, 30. See also "Lend-Lease: Seventh Stage," *New York Times*, December 12, 1942, 16; "Lend-Lease and Military Food Needs to Rise 50%," *Washington Post*, November 2, 1942, 1; "Lend-Lease Rises to 643 Million Record in Month," October 25, 1942, 10, and "Lend-Lease Aid Rises to Nearly Billion in Months," November 16, 1942, 8, both in *Chicago Tribune*. On Lend-Lease totals, see Edward Stettinius testimony, January 29, 1943, *Lend-Lease*, 4; David Reynolds, *Rich Relations: The American Occupation of Britain, 1942-1945* (1995; repr., London: Phoenix Press, 2000), 47.
6. "Charges Secret Lend-Lease Grab of U.S. Machines," December 16, 1942, 14, "U.S. Concocts Exotic Foods for Lend-Lease," December 15, 1942, 1, "Horsemeat Sale Rises as Meat Shortage Grows," November 17, 1942, 3, and B.E.W., "Horse Meat," November 25, 1942, 12, all in *Chicago Tribune*.

7. "Sweaters for Tropics," December 1, 1942, 1, and J. M. Newcomb, "Lend-Lease, It's Wonderful," December 23, 1942, 10, both in *Chicago Tribune*. See also William Scott, "Feeding the World," *Los Angeles Times*, December 16, 1942, B4.
8. "Asks Full Data on Lend-Lease Sent to Britain," December 8, 1942, 2, and "Calls for Stronger Congress," December 31, 1942, 3, both in *Chicago Tribune*; "Senator Asks End to Waste," *Los Angeles Times*, December 22, 1942, 6; Robert De Vore, "Lend-Lease Probe Likely in Senate," January 1, 1943, 3, and Arthur Hachten, "Other New Deal Issues to Meet with Hard Sledding," January 4, 1943, 8, both in *Washington Post*; Halifax to Foreign Office, December 10, 1942, T 160/1241, TNA; Nicholas Wapshott, *The Sphinx: Franklin Roosevelt, the Isolationists, and the Road to World War II* (New York: Norton, 2015), 267–71, 284–85.
9. F. T. to Jock Henderson, December 17, 1942, T 160/1241, Ministry of Information American Division confidential report, ca. late 1942, CAB 115/670, Supply Committee, London, to B.S.C. in North America, January 1, 1943, AVIA 38/1096, and Halifax to Foreign Office, January 16, 1943, T 160/1153, TNA.
10. Supply Committee, London, to B.S.C. in North America, January 6, 1943, AVIA 38/1096, and Foreign Office to Halifax, January 8, 1943, T 160/1241, TNA; secret orders, ETO HQ, January 4, 1943, outline for testimony, S. A. Dismore to George Spiegelberg, January 6, 1943, and A. J. McCrystal to George Spiegelberg, January 6, 1943, scrapbook, vol. 1, restricted US Army pamphlet, March 29, 1944, scrapbook, vol. 2, GASP. According to Gallup polling in early 1943, 82 percent of Americans favored Lend-Lease, but 71 percent also believed that it should be repaid after the war: Gallup Polls # 1943-0287: Question 4, USGALLUP.012743.RK07B, and # 1943-0291, Question 24, USGALLUP.43-291.QKT09B, Gallup Organization (Cornell University, Ithaca, NY: Roper Center for Public Opinion Research, 1943).
11. "Fear New Inroads in Foreign Trade," January 7, 1943, 29, "Wants Butter Kept in U.S.," January 12, 1943, 25, "Fight U.S. Inroads on Private Cargo," January 20, 1943, 32, and "Lend-Lease Anxious to Assist Traders," February 5, 1943, 27, all in *New York Times*; "The American Share," January 16, 1943, 10, and "Alien Raiding of U.S. Butter Upheld by CIO," February 5, 1943, 11, both in *Chicago Tribune*; "House Informed Powder Puffs Sent Abroad by Lend-Lease," *Los Angeles Times*, January 29, 1943, A; Ministry of Information American Division report on press reaction to Stettinius report, January 30, 1943, T 160/1153, TNA.
12. "Lend-Lease Anxious to Assist Traders," *New York Times*, February 5, 1943, 27; Robert De Vore, "8 Billions Aid Given Allies in 21 Months," *Washington Post*, January 26, 1943, 1, 4; Halifax to Foreign Office, February 6, 1943, T 160/1153, TNA; Army talks pamphlet, GASP.
13. W. S. Stowell, "Lend-Lease to Africa," *Boston Globe*, January 23, 1943, 8; Arthur Sears Henning, "F. D. R. Submits All-Time High Budget Today," *Chicago Tribune*, January 11, 1943, 1. See also "New Congress Plans a Bigger

Part for Itself," *New York Times*, January 10, 1943, E3; weekly summary of American press items, Interdepartmental Committee on Lend Lease Publicity, January 6, 1943, FO 371/32450, Halifax to Foreign Office, January 16, 1943, Comment on Lend-Lease, Ministry of Information American Division, January 19, 1943, and Ministry of Information American Division survey of comment on Lend-Lease, January 21, 1943, T 160/1153, TNA.

14. Stettinius testimony, *Lend-Lease*, 2.
15. Stettinius testimony, *Lend-Lease*, 1–48, (quote) 5.
16. George Spiegelberg testimony, February 2, 1943, *Lend-Lease*, 49–61.
17. Intelligence on Americans who will review Lend-Lease, T 160/1153, TNA; "A Close Division," November 13, 1941, 1, 22, and "C. A. Eaton Is Dead," January 24, 1953, 15, both in *New York Times*; Spiegelberg testimony, *Lend-Lease*, 61–62, 64; Elizabeth Borgwardt, *A New Deal for the World: America's Vision for Human Rights* (Cambridge, MA: Belknap, 2005), 93–96, 101; Mark Mazower, *Governing the World: The History of an Idea* (New York: Penguin, 2012), 192–211.
18. Spiegelberg testimony, *Lend-Lease*, 64–65.
19. Spiegelberg testimony, *Lend-Lease*, 70. On Mundt, see also Elliot A. Rosen, *The Republican Party in the Age of Roosevelt: Sources of Anti-Government Conservatism in the United States* (Charlottesville: University of Virginia Press, 2014), 129.
20. Rosen, *The Republican Party in the Age of Roosevelt*, 161–62; Borgwardt, *New Deal for the World*, 107–9, 255. Just how enlightened the postwar economic order was, both in terms of the power struggles between its British and American architects, and in terms of its motives towards less prosperous nations, remains a source of debate. See Benn Stell, *The Battle of Bretton Woods: John Maynard Keynes, Harry Dexter White, and the Making of a New World Order* (Princeton, NJ: Princeton University Press, 2013) and Eric Helleiner, *Forgotten Foundations of Bretton Woods: International Development and the Making of the Postwar Order* (Ithaca, NY: Cornell University Press, 2014).
21. Thomas Hachey "American Profiles on Capitol Hill: A Confidential Study for the British Foreign Office in 1943," *Wisconsin Magazine of History* 57, no. 2 (Winter 1973–1974): 141–53; Spiegelberg testimony, *Lend-Lease*, 70–71.
22. Spiegelberg testimony, *Lend-Lease*, 75. On Hoover's opposition to Lend-Lease, see Wapshott, *Sphinx*, 260–62.
23. Spiegelberg testimony, *Lend-Lease*, 75–76.
24. Alan Dobson, *US Wartime Aid to Britain, 1940–1946* (New York: St. Martin's Press, 1986), 1; Richard Overy, "Economies in Total War," in *Oxford Illustrated History of World War II*, ed. Richard Overy (Oxford: Oxford University Press, 2015), 232–57; Victor Davis Hanson, *The Second World Wars: How the First Global Conflict Was Fought and Won* (New York: Basic, 2017), 62–63, 454, 460, 495.

25. Reynolds, *Rich Relations*, 50–54; Dobson, *US Wartime Aid to Britain*, 11; Overy, "Economies in Total War"; Hanson, *Second World Wars*, 62, 214–17, 468–69, 494–99, 520.
26. Spiegelberg testimony, *Lend-Lease*, 78–79; Edward Stettinius to George Spiegelberg, February 2, 1943, scrapbook, vol. 1, GASP.
27. Oscar Cox to Robert Patterson, February 2, 1943, Andrew to George Spiegelberg, February 3, 1943, Sol Bloom to George Spiegelberg, February 3, 1943, E. S. Greenbaum to George Spiegelberg, February 5, 1943, and clippings, "Allied Pool," n.d., and Alistair Cooke, "Your Debt to Mr. Spiegelberg," n.d., scrapbook, vol. 1, GASP; Halifax to Foreign Office, February 3 and 6, 1943, T 160/1153, and Ministry of Information American Division, March 1, 1943, T 160/1153, TNA; brochure, "We Bought the Eiffel Tower," folder History, May 1942–September 1945, box 3589, RG498, NARA. Vorys in Dean Acheson testimony, February 3, 1943, *Lend-Lease*, 103.
28. Clipping, Alistair Cooke, "Your Debt to Mr. Spiegelberg," scrapbook, vol. 1, GASP; Alex Singleton, "House Votes Lend-Lease Extension," *Washington Post*, March 11, 1943, 1–2; Keynes memo, March 17, 1943, T 160/1153, TNA.
29. "We Bought the Eiffel Tower"; Ronald Ruppenthal, *Logistical Support of the Armies*, vol. 1 (1953; Washington, DC: Center of Military History, 1995), 99–102.
30. "Mackeachie, Brunner Are Missing in Action," *New York Times*, February 3, 1943, 13; "Officer Dead, 25 Missing in Plane Crash," *Los Angeles Times*, February 23, 1943, 4; "We Bought the Eiffel Tower"; clipping, "Purchasing Agent for European Troops, Air Officer Missing," *Washington Post*, February 3, 1943, 1 and scrapbook notes, vol. 1, GASP.

Conclusion

1. Civil Aeronautics Board report, September 7, 1943, folder 1 [hereafter CAB report], survivor statements and flight path map, folder 12, box II:152, Pan Am; Clifford Albion Tinker, "Lisbon, the City of the Friendly Bay," *National Geographic*, November 1922, 505–17, 533–52.
2. Survivor statements, folder 12, and Casprini statement, March 11, 1943, folder 13, box II:152, passenger deck diagram, folder 11, box I:107, Pan Am.
3. Survivor statements, folder 12, and list of stewards' equipment, folder 5, box II:152, A. E. LaPorte confidential memo, March 30, 1942, folder 1, box II:434, Pan Am.
4. Casprini statement, March 11, 1943, folder 13, box II:152, Pan Am; clipper crew to Franklin Roosevelt, January 30, 1943, PPE 4393, FDRL.
5. CAB report and notes of Burn interview, folder 1, questionnaire on crew experiences, folder 5, and Burn testimony, May 3, 1943, folder 6, box II:152, Pan Am.

6. Wayne Thomis, "Christen Queen of Air for New Atlantic Route," *Chicago Tribune*, March 4, 1939, 1, 5; CAB report; Harold Hansfield, Boeing Clipper control room report, ca. 1938, folder 11, box I:107, and R. O. D. Sullivan testimony, March 5, 1943, folder 13, box II:152, Pan Am; Stuart Speiser, *Lawyers and the American Dream* (New York: Evans, 1993), 60–63.
7. CAB report.
8. NC-03 accident causes summary, folder 6, instrument and control readings, March 1, 1943, and survivor testimonies, folder 12, statements by ground crew, March 2–4, 1943, folder 13, box II:152, Pan Am.
9. John Burn interview notes and John Leslie, "Airplane Rescue Procedure," folder 1, pilot board testimony, May 3, 1943, folder 6, survivor testimonies, folder 12, surviving crew testimonies, folder 13, box II:152, Pan Am; letter to Helen Spiegelberg, April 10, 1943, scrapbook, vol. 1, GASP.
10. Medical aid furnished survivors, March 25, 1943, and W. G. Eldridge report, April 10, 1943, folder 12, ground crew statements, March 2–4, 1943, folder 13, box II:152, Pan Am.
11. George Spiegelberg testimony, March 1, 1943, folder 12, box II:152, Pan Am; George Spiegelberg to Helen Spiegelberg, March 2, 1943, scrapbook, vol. 1, GASP.
12. Yvette (Elsa Harris Silver) and William Walton Butterworth statements, February 26, 1943, folder 12, notes on statements by doctors and W. G. Eldridge memo, April 10, 1943, folder 12, box II:152, Pan Am; Grace Drysdale to her mother, n.d., box 72, RG24, NARA; clipping, "First Hand Details of the Lisbon Crash," scrapbook, vol. 1, GASP. Jane Froman later claimed that she and Tamara switched seats, but no evidence from the time of the crash could be found to corroborate this claim.
13. Notes on survivors, February 25, 1943, W. G. Eldridge memo, April 10, 1943, and notes on statements of doctors, folder 12, box II:152, Pan Am; Jane Froman, "I Lived It!" *American Weekly*, March 30, 1952, 13, 27; American Foreign Service report of the death of an American citizen, March 13, 1943, 353.113 Rush, H. Stanton, and República Portuguesa Certidão de Óbito, March 23, 1943, 353.113 Diaz, Manuel, box 1201, RG59, NARA; W. E. Hagerman confidential reports, February 23 and 26, 1943, Lisbon legation, vol. 17, box 77, RG84, NARA.
14. Olga Witkowska statement, March 4, 1943, doctors' reports, February 25, 1943, medical aid furnished survivors, March 25, 1943, A. W. Anderson report, n.d., and W. G. Eldridge report, April 10, 1943, folder 12, ground crew statements, March 2–4, 1943, folder 13, status reports on wounded, folder 1, box II:152, Pan Am; Isabella Taves, "Jane Froman: Courage Unlimited," *McCall's*, May 1952, 30–31, 56, 61, 66.
15. Confidential memos and lists of persons inquiring about Manuel Diaz, February 23–March 3, 1943, Lisbon Legation General Records, 1943: vol. 17, box 77, RG84, NARA.
16. Confidential correspondence, vol. 1, 1943, box 5, Legation Lisbon Classified, RG84, NARA; George Kennan, *Memoirs, 1925–1950*

(Boston: Little, Brown, 1967), 143, 145; Report on Accident to Yankee Clipper, folder 12, box II:152, Pan Am.

17. Howard Railey to American Embassy, February 22, 1943, 811.7965/60, box 4046, Bert Fish to Secretary of State, February 24, 1943, Confidential 811.7965/69, and Henry Stimson to Secretary of State, May 3, 1943, Confidential 811.7965/136, box C92, RG59, NARA.
18. Report on mail handling procedure, March 31, 1943, folder 12, and J. Whitney to Harold Bixby, March 26, 1943, folder 24, box II:152, Pan Am; Pinto Basto to Edward Crocker, March 11, 1943, Courier-avion récupéré après l'accident survenu le 22 février, and Bert Fish to Secretary of State, May 31, 1943, Lisbon Legation, 1943: vol. 17, box 77, RG84, NARA; Bert Fish confidential telegrams to Secretary of State, February 1943, 811.7965/82 and 811.7965/84, box C92, RG59, NARA.
19. Bert Fish to Secretary of State, May 31, 1943, Lisbon Legation, 1943: vol. 17, box 77, RG84, NARA; list of material in classified briefcase of NC03, and E. T. Peck, April 20, 1943, folder 24, box II:152, Pan Am.
20. Tribute to "Soldiers of the Press," December 15, 1946, and clipping, "War Memorial," September 26, 1948, FJCP; República Portuguesa Certidão de Óbito, March 23, 1943, 353.113 Cuhel, Frank J., box 1729, RG59, NARA; M. Parsons to Secretary of State, July 26, 1943, Lisbon Legation, 1943: vol. 17, box 77, RG84, NARA. Ben's sister later claimed that Ben was on a secret mission for the OSS at the time of his death, but no evidence could be found to support this claim.
21. Confidential report, March 6, 1943, Lisbon Legation, 1943: vol. 17, box 77, RG84, NARA; "Tagus Surrenders 2 Clipper Victims," *New York Times*, March 7, 1943, 15.
22. Still missing were crewmembers Leonard Ingles and Craig Robinson and passengers Major James Hamlin and Theodore Lamb: status of passengers and crew reports, March 14, 1943, folder 12, box II:152, Pan Am; American Foreign Service report of the death of an American citizen, March 13, 1943, 353.133 Seidel, Harry G., box 1202, RG59, NARA; W. E. Hagerman, confidential memo, March 12, 1943, Lisbon Legation, 1943: vol. 17, box 77, RG84, NARA.
23. Luther Wallis, George Hart, John Poto, Milton Weisman, Burton Mossman, Jr., Earl Stoy, James Pepper, and Paul Sprout were interred at the British Cemetery. Captain Joshua Edelman of the U.S. Army Corps of Engineers was laid to rest at the Jewish cemetery. Others transported on the SS *Miguel* were the State Department courier James Wright, the film distributor Arthur Lee, USO volunteer Roy Rognan, and three Pan Am crewmembers—Herman Rush, Andrew Freeland, and Joseph Vaughn: status of passengers and crew reports, March 14, 1943, and report on medical aid, March 25, 1943, folder 12, box II:152, Pan Am; Robert Solborg memo, April 5, 1943, 330.00, box 4, US Consulate General Classified, RG84, NARA; Henry Stimson to Secretary of State, May 3, 1943, Confidential File 811.7965/136, box C92, RG59, NARA; "Ship Brings

Dead in Clipper Crash," *New York Times*, April 12, 1943, 12; "Liner Arrives with 10 Dead in Clipper Crash," *New York Herald Tribune*, April 12, 1943, 3A; "Cargo of Pathos," *New York Daily News*, April 13, 1943, 25.

24. "Manuel Diaz: Special Rites in Lisbon," *New York Daily News*, March 23, 1943, 24; "Diaz Is Honored in Lisbon," *New York Times*, March 23, 1943, 10; military intelligence memo, March 5, 1943, folder 560 SS *Motomar*, box 1170, RG 319, NARA.
25. Notes on survivors, February 25, 1943, folder 12, box II:152, Pan Am; medical reports, March 10–12, 1943, Lisbon Legation, 1943, vol. 17, box 77, RG84, NARA; Graham to Clifton, February 27, 1943, telegrams, March–April 1943, A. Ulio to Helen Spiegelberg, February 23, 1943, H. B. Lewis to Helen Spiegelberg, May 18, 1943, George Spiegelberg to Helen Spiegelberg, April 10 and 16, 1943, scrapbook, vol. 1, GASP.
26. Notes on survivors, February 25, 1943, folder 12, and Lisbon Legation to Secretary of State, February 27, 1943, folder 24, box II:152, Pan Am.
27. Brief Summary of Trip 9/035, folder 12, and R. O. D. Sullivan testimony, March 5, 1943, folder 13, box II:152, Pan Am
28. Sullivan testimony, March 5, 1943, folder 13, box II:152, Pan Am.
29. Sullivan testimony, March 5, 1943, folder 13, and Sullivan board testimony, May 4, 1943, folder 6, box II:152, Pan Am.
30. Sullivan testimony, March 5, 1943, folder 13, box II:152, Pan Am.
31. CAB report; pilot board testimony, May 3, 1943, and NC-03 Accident Cases, Exhibit D, folder 6, survivor testimonies, folder 12, surviving crew testimonies, folder 13, box II:152, Pan Am; Speiser, *Lawyers and the American Dream*, 70–71, 103, 106, 152–53.
32. CAB report; pilot board testimony, May 4, 1943, folder 6, box II:152, Pan Am.
33. CAB report; note and accident report sheet, folder 1, and NC-03 Accident Cases, Exhibit D, folder 6, box II:152, Pan Am.
34. Andre Priester confidential memo, May 29, 1943, F. S. K. Lewis and A. E. LaPorte memos, July 14, 1943, and correspondence about resignation, July 1943, folder 5, box II:152, Pan Am; Marius Lodeesen, *Captain Lodi Speaking* (Suttons Bay, MI: Argonaut, 1984), 172.
35. Record of conversation by Mr. Cootes, July 28, 1943, Lisbon legation, vol. 17, box 77, RG84, NARA; confidential radio telegrams, October 1, 9, 13, 1943, December 24, 1943, February 18, 1944, and March 18, 1944, folder 30, box II:483, personnel record, folder 23, box I:293, Pan Am; marriage record, July 19, 1946, North Carolina County Registers of Deeds, Record Group 48, North Carolina State Archives, Raleigh, NC; Rod Sullivan, Jr., interview, September 24, 1981, folder 14, box 16, IWP.
36. Mary Lee to Franklin Roosevelt, March 1, 1943, 811.7965/100, RG59, NARA.
37. News clipping, ca. March 1943, and London *Times* transcript, March 4, 1943, Harry G. Seidel folder, BUBF; Rosamond Harris Seidel Clark, *My Life in Three-Quarter Time: A Memoir* (Private Printing, 2007), 59–60;

James Hayes to Cordell Hull, March 5, 1943, 353.113 Seidel, Harry G., box 1202, RG59, NARA; annual report, 1943, folder Standard Oil Company (NJ) Annual Reports, 1932–1940, box 2.207/D92, ExxMo.

38. Clipping, "Bab Cuhel Rites Set Friday," and Oei Tjong Hauw to Ermengarde Cuhel, June 11, 1946, FJCP; Christopher Bayly and Tim Harper, *Forgotten Wars: Freedom and Revolution in Southeast Asia* (Cambridge, MA: Belknap, 2007).

39. Note by Ben Robertson's sister, folder 19, Francine Bradley to Julian Langley, April 27, 1943, folder 21, box 2, BFRP; Ben Robertson Tribute Paid, in Clemson Rites," *New York Herald Tribune*, April 19, 1943, 10A.

40. Jacob Fuller, synopsis report, January 20, 1944, litigation case file 146-7-1883, box 13, RG60, and file 54-62-29 reference card, box 638, General Index, 1928-51, RG60, NARA.

41. "500 Attend Service for Tamara Swann," *New York Times*, April 17, 1943, 13; burial rites, cremation form, and funeral services program in Lee Drasin—Personal Documents, DFP.

42. Angelo Spinelli, *Life Behind Barbed Wire: The Secret World War II Photographs of Prisoner of War Angelo M. Spinelli* (New York: Fordham University Press, 2004), 198–99; Annegret Fauser, *Sounds of War: Music in the United States during World War II* (New York: Oxford University Press, 2013), 105; Craig Nelson, *The First Heroes: The Extraordinary Story of the Doolittle Raid—America's First World War II Victory* (New York: Penguin, 2003), 265–66; Byrd Stuart Leavell, *The 8th Evac.: a History of the University of Virginia Hospital Unit in World War II* (Richmond: Dietz, 1970), 34; Mildred MacGregor, *World War II Front Line Nurse* (Ann Arbor: University of Michigan Press, 2006), 139; John Gordon, ed., *A Job to Do: New Zealand Soldiers of 'The Div' Write about their World War Two* (Auckland: Exisle, 2014), 179; Craig Smith, *Counting the Days: POWs, Internees, and Stragglers of World War II in the Pacific* (Washington, DC: Smithsonian, 2012), 104; Minoru Masuda, *Letters from the 442nd: The World War II Correspondence of a Japanese American Medic* (Seattle: University of Washington Press, 2008), 154–55; Andrew J. Rotter, *Hiroshima: The World's Bomb* (New York: Oxford University Press, 2008), 143. Another song, "I'll Be Seeing You," which Tamara helped Sammy Fain and Irving Kahal develop for the short-lived Broadway musical *Right This Way*, also became a sudden wartime hit, topping the charts in 1944: Michael Whorf, ed., *American Popular Song Composers: Oral Histories, 1920s–1950s* (Jefferson, NC: McFarland, 2012), 78; John Bush Jones, *The Songs That Fought the War: Popular Music and the Home Front, 1939–1945* (Waltham, MA: Brandeis University Press, 2006), 247.

43. Lawrence Phillips, memo on victims' expenses, August 6, 1943, and Weil, Gotshal & Manges to Lawrence Phillips, August 17, 1943, box 4, RG407, NARA; "USI Pays 3 Crash Victims," *Billboard*, September 18, 1943, 4. Years later, Congress also awarded three of the crash's surviving entertainers, Jane Froman, Gypsy Markoff, and Jean Rognan

(subsequently Rosen), a little more than $23,000 each: "Froman Bill Gains," August 23, 1957, 9, and "Damage Awards Given," August 29, 1958, 13, both in *New York Times*.

44. "Asks $110,000 in Tamara's Death," March 4, 1944, 10, "Asks $225,750 of Airline," June 20, 1944, 21, "$100,000 Suit in Clipper Crash," February 20, 1944, 9, "$777,745 Suit Dismissed," September 9, 1944, 17, "Jane Froman Can Collect $8,291 at Most for Lisbon Crash," April 15, 1949, 16, "Court Sets $9,050 as Froman Award," March 19, 1953, 36, and "Air Crash Defense Rests," March 17, 1953, 31, all in *New York Times*; Speiser, *Lawyers and the American Dream*, 86, 89; "Capt. Sullivan, Veteran Pilot, Dies in Office," *Sanford Herald* (NC), July 11, 1955, 1.
45. Clipping, "Legion of Merit Awarded to Spiegelberg, Shearer," vol. 2, and travel orders, February 16, September 13, and October 18, 1944, air transport tickets, February 19 and March 2–5, 1944, confidential memo on George's service, R. W. Crawford, February 14, 1945, certificate of service and service record, and photograph, February 16, 1945, vol. 3, scrapbook, GASP; William I. Hitchcock, *The Bitter Road to Freedom: A New History of the Liberation of Europe* (New York: Free Press, 2008).
46. *New York Sun* clippings, George Sokolsky, "The End of Lend-Lease," August 29, 1945, and George Spiegelberg to the editor, n.d., scrapbook, vol. 3, GASP.
47. "George A. Spiegelberg Dies at 82," *New York Times*, November 10, 1979, 28. On his postwar legal career, see also George Spiegelberg resume, folder "S" Miscellany, 1947–52, box 45, RPPP, and George Spiegelberg oral history, June 7, 1960, Robert Patterson Project, CCOH.
48. Victor Davis Hanson, *The Second World Wars* (New York: Basic, 2017), 107, 130, 143, 194, 206, 214, 230, 232, 260, 280–83, 300–3, 452–53, 509.
49. On the one-sidedness of American international engagements after the war, see Sam Lebovic, *A Righteous Smokescreen: Postwar America and the Politics of Cultural Globalization* (Chicago: University of Chicago Press, 2022).
50. A. W. French to David Greenbaum, May 15, 1959, folder 8, box I:288, Pan Am; M. D. Klaäs, *Last of the Flying Clippers: The Boeing B-314 Story* (Atglen, PA: Schiffer, 1997), 263–64, 269. On American aviation and international relations during the Cold War, see Jeffrey Engel, *Cold War at 30,000 Feet: The Anglo-American Fight for Aviation Supremacy* (Cambridge, MA: Harvard University Press, 2007) and Jenifer Van Vleck, *Empire of the Air: Aviation and the American Ascendancy* (Cambridge, MA: Harvard University Press, 2013). On the broader problem of war surplus disposal, see Lebovic, *Righteous Smokescreen*, ch. 2.

A Note on Method, with Acknowledgments

1. Emily S. Rosenberg, *A Date Which Will Live: Pearl Harbor in American Memory* (Durham, NC: Duke University Press, 2003), 1. On

late-twentieth-century World War II memory and mythology, see also John Bodnar, *The "Good War" in American Memory* (Baltimore: Johns Hopkins University Press, 2010); Patrick Finney, *Remembering the Road to World War Two: International History, National Identity, and Collective Memory* (London: Routledge, 2011); and Elizabeth D. Samet, *Looking for the Good War: American Amnesia and the Violent Pursuits of Happiness* (New York: Farrar, Straus and Giroux, 2021). Beth L. Bailey and David Farber's *The First Strange Place: Race and Sex in World War II Hawaii* (New York: Free Press, 1992) offered a notable exception to this increasingly popular home front/war front framing.

2. For recent illuminating histories of filmmakers, missionaries, reporters, and other specific groups of noncombatants abroad, see Mark Harris, *Five Came Back: A Story of Hollywood and the Second World War* (New York: Penguin, 2015); Matthew Avery Sutton, *Double Crossed: The Missionaries Who Spied for the United States during the Second World War* (New York: Basic, 2019); Samuel Zipp, *The Idealist: Wendell Willkie's Wartime Quest to Build One World (*Cambridge, MA: Harvard University Press, 2020); Kathy Peiss, *Information Hunters: When Librarians, Soldiers, and Spies Banded Together in World War II Europe* (New York: Oxford University Press, 2020); Deborah Cohen, *Last Call at the Hotel Imperial: The Reporters Who Took on a World at War* (New York: Random House, 2022); and Matthew F. Delmont, *Half American: The Epic Story of African Americans Fighting World War II at Home and Abroad* (New York: Viking, 2022). For new and revealing histories of the impact of US troops engaged in noncombat work in overseas staging grounds, see Zach Fredman, *The Tormented Alliance: American Servicemen and the Occupation of China, 1941–1949* (Chapel Hill: University of North Carolina Press, 2022) and Rebecca Herman, *Cooperating with the Colossus: A Social and Political History of US Military Bases in World War II Latin America* (New York: Oxford University Press, 2022).

3. On these methodological choices, see also Carlo Ginzburg, John Tedeschi, and Anne Tedeschi, "Microhistory," *Critical Inquiry* 20, no. 1 (1993): 10–35; Matti Peltonen, "The Micro-Macro Link in Historical Research," *History & Theory* 40, no. 3 (2001): 347–59; Gunilla Budde, Sebastian Conrad, and Oliver Janz, eds., *Transnationale Geschichte: Themen, Tendenzen un Theorien* (Göttingen: Vandenhoeck & Ruprecht, 2006); Roundtable, "Historians and Biography," *American Historical Review*, 114, no. 3 (June 2009): 576–661; Bernhard Struck, Kate Ferris, and Jacques Revel, "Introduction: Space and Scale in Transnational History," *International History Review* 33, no. 4 (December 2011): 573–84; and Julia Laite, "The Emmet's Inch: Small History in a Digital Age," *Journal of Social History* 53, no. 4 (Summer 2020): 963–89.

INDEX

Figures are indicated by an italic *f* following the page number